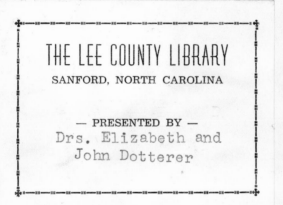

THE COLLECTED WORKS OF
ABRAHAM LINCOLN

THE COLLECTED WORKS OF

ABRAHAM LINCOLN

THE ABRAHAM LINCOLN ASSOCIATION
SPRINGFIELD, ILLINOIS

I

ROY P. BASLER, *EDITOR*

MARION DOLORES PRATT AND LLOYD A. DUNLAP
ASSISTANT EDITORS

RUTGERS UNIVERSITY PRESS
NEW BRUNSWICK, NEW JERSEY

TO THE MEMBERS
OF THE ABRAHAM LINCOLN ASSOCIATION
WHOSE INTEREST AND SUPPORT
THROUGHOUT THE YEARS HAVE MADE POSSIBLE
THE WORK ACCOMPLISHED

FOREWORD

From 1924, when the Lincoln Centennial Association became a research organization, later renamed The Abraham Lincoln Association, Logan Hay, who served so long and ably as its president, had in mind the publication of *The Collected Works of Abraham Lincoln* as an ultimate objective. To this end the collecting of Lincoln's unpublished writings and speeches became a constant effort on the part of successive Executive Secretaries—Paul M. Angle, Benjamin P. Thomas, Harry E. Pratt, and William E. Baringer. But not until 1945, three years after Mr. Hay's death, was the Association prepared to consummate this project.

Meanwhile the resources of the Association were devoted primarily to the collection and publication of other historical materials which have greatly increased our knowledge of the character and development of Lincoln, especially during the years prior to 1861. The numerous books published by the Association are known to historians everywhere, and the editors of the present work hope that our efforts have maintained the tradition of scholarship established by our predecessors.

As revitalized and renamed in 1929, The Abraham Lincoln Association was composed largely of citizens of Springfield, Illinois, who believed that knowledge of Abraham Lincoln was one of the most important contributions that the city where he made his home could give to the world. Although membership in the Association has expanded to include residents of all but three states in the Union and several foreign countries, the core of its spiritual as well as its financial being has remained as it began, in Springfield. To the people of Lincoln's home town, the preservation of his works and the memory of his deeds, not in idolatry but in honest fact, is an enduring monument, better perhaps than marble or bronze.

The intensive effort of the editorial staff has been devoted to the *Collected Works* for more than five years. During that time, the task of collecting, cataloging, reducing to typescript, and annotating each discoverable writing or speech of Abraham Lincoln, has occupied the time of two, and for most of the period three, full-time editors. In addition, part-time help has been employed as needed in special research. Although the project was recognized from the beginning as one of magnitude, it is scarcely amiss to note that its present size was hardly envisioned.

It was not anticipated that additions to previous compilations would approximate a total number of items close to twice as many as had appeared in the so-called *Complete Works of Abraham Lincoln* edited by John G. Nicolay and John Hay (1894, 1905) or *The Writings of Abraham Lincoln* edited by Arthur Brooks Lapsley (1905), plus those in the several compilations by Ida M. Tarbell (1900), Gilbert Tracy (1917), Brown University (1927), Paul M. Angle (1930), and Emanuel Hertz (1931), which from time to time had gathered up pieces previously uncollected. Nor was it anticipated that so many previously unknown items would prove to add a considerable contribution to the understanding of Lincoln both in his private and public capacity.

Although we could not discover an equivalent of the Gettysburg Address, a close student of these volumes will be gratified to find in them a surprisingly large number of new and important items. The early letters to William Butler, January 26 and 31, and February 1 and 23, 1839, which averted a duel between two of Lincoln's close friends; the letter to William S. Wait, March 2, 1839, containing one of Lincoln's few statements on taxation; the fragmentary report of Lincoln's speech at Carthage, October 22, 1858, containing his direct answer to Douglas' charge that as attorney for the Illinois Central Railroad Lincoln was lobbying to help the railroad escape its tax obligations; the letter to John Hill, September, 1860, which Lincoln never sent, containing his reply to an old friend who was misrepresenting him; the several revisions of the First Inaugural Address and the Message to Congress of July 4, 1861, which illustrate the care with which these addresses were prepared; and the reprimand to Captain James Madison Cutts, October 26, 1863, which Nicolay and Hay referred to only anonymously in a footnote in the *Complete Works* (I, 151-52), revealing the workings of Lincoln's sense of justice and human sympathy in the midst of a burdened executive schedule—these are but representative of the many additions which contribute to a larger understanding of the man.

Our effort has been to collect all extant writings or public utterances that come within the scope defined by the editors and editorial advisers. In order that our procedure may be properly understood, some definition of our scope should be given. Manuscripts in Lincoln's handwriting are included with two exceptions: (1) copies made by Lincoln of the compositions of others for transmittal or preservation in his own file, and (2) law cases and documents appertaining thereto (such as receipts for fees, affidavits, declarations, praecipes, etc.). Lincoln's law cases have been arbitrarily relegated to separate volumes which the Association proposes to publish at a future date, but in rare instances where a document pertaining to a law case is part of a letter, or in a few cases where the question involved concerns Lincoln's personal appearance as plaintiff or defendant, the documents have been included.

Manuscripts and documents not in Lincoln's handwriting but bearing his signature, or signed for him by his authority, have been included with certain exceptions. The following have not been included unless particular significance of content or circumstances seems to demand their presence: acts of congress, treaties, commissions, authorizations, appointments, pardons, land grants, checks, ships' papers, certificates of service, credences, discharge papers, military orders (except those personally drafted or primarily Lincoln's), draft orders, routine letters and endorsements of transmittal, routine pardon and clemency endorsements (such as "Let this man take the oath of December 8, 1863, and be discharged"), approvals, letters written and signed by his secretaries, form replies to requests for an autograph, and nominations to office submitted to the United States Senate. Concerning the last category, nominations, it was decided that such routine and repetitive communications should be excluded on two grounds: first, that they are in print in the *Executive Journal* of the United States Senate, and second, that they would swell the proportions and cost of the *Collected Works* by an additional volume. With the exception of nominations, land grants, discharge papers, ships' papers, routine pardon and clemency endorsements, draft orders, approvals, appointments, authorizations, and commissions, however, an effort has been made to list in Appendix II all known documents which have not been included.

Public utterances not available in manuscript have been included from contemporary newspaper sources in so far as even fragmentary reports have been found. In instances where more than one report is available, completeness and reliability have been the criteria for choosing one over another. Two sources have been employed occasionally when neither is complete in itself. When the manuscript of a speech is extant, it has been followed in preference to the printed report, but when notable variations occur in the printed version, they have been incorporated in footnotes or within brackets as explained in footnotes. Utterances recorded only in memoirs, diaries, and reminiscences have been excluded for obvious reasons.

In reproducing the text of a printed source we have made a minimum of alterations in style of printing to bring about consistency with the style adopted for the present edition. Typographical errors have been corrected without use of brackets, but other editorial emendations of a printed source have been bracketed.

In editing the text of a manuscript, we have endeavored to reproduce the original in so far as reasonably possible. Normalization of heading and close of letters has been adopted in so far as spacing and arrangement are concerned. Editorial emendations, whether of punctuation, spelling, or diction, have been bracketed. Incorrect and variant spellings have been reproduced as they appear, without benefit of *sic*, except in instances which would seem likely to confuse the reader. In thus reducing the incidence of *sic* the editors believe they have acted in the interest not merely of appearance but also of readability. Habitual misspelling or casual error is to be expected and becomes obvious without the employment of *sic*, and the appearance of this device many times on a printed page scarcely guarantees the accuracy of editing.

Lincoln's chirography is, in comparison with that of his contemporaries, unusually clear as well as highly individual. And yet certain peculiarities of penmanship make it occasionally difficult to decide on appearance alone, for example, whether a character should be printed as a capital or lower case letter, or whether "a" or "o," "a" or "e," or "e" or "i," should be printed in a particular instance. Although a long and constant familiarity with Lincoln manuscripts has imparted a degree of assurance in these matters, the editors admit that in some instances there is room for divergence of opinion as to what Lincoln wrote, particularly when a photostat reproduces mere spots as periods or commas. The text as we have printed it represents our collective best judgment in such cases, at the time we go to press, and often represents sessions of debate and revision of decision out of all proportion to the importance, as it would impress the casual reader, of the question involved. In brief, the text is as faithful to the original as we have been able to make it.

Certain peculiarities of Lincoln's punctuation have been normalized throughout in the interest of appearance and modern styling. The habitual dash at the end of a sentence or following an abbreviation has been printed as a period. Double periods as Lincoln often employed them, particularly following the initial in his signature and beneath the superposed character terminating an abbreviation (as in "Gen!." or "15.ᵗʰ") have been normalized, and all superposed characters have been lowered to their normal position. The position of the apostrophe, when it appears at all, has ordinarily been made to conform according to usage, even though Lincoln in common with most of literate humanity was not always particular about where the point of his pen made contact with paper. Punctuation marks which he failed to make and which are absolutely necessary for clarity have been inserted in brackets.

The policy pursued in these matters for the text of Lincoln's manuscripts has also been followed in the quotations from other manuscript sources which appear in the annotation.

For ready reference, we have assigned a date line at the beginning of each item in the position customary for dating letters. When a document is dated by Lincoln at the end rather than the beginning, however, we have retained the end date regardless of duplication, in order that the circumstance may be recorded.

While our project has been under way, *The Collected Works of Abraham Lincoln* has sometimes been referred to as the definitive edition. To this expectation the editors wish to enter a *caveat*. Although our effort has been to achieve definitiveness, we recognize that our wish has been approximated only to the degree that possibility would permit. Even as we go to press, five new and hitherto unknown Lincoln letters have come to light under circumstances wholly unsuspected, and they remind us that in spite of a search continuously pursued for many years and with great intensity since 1945, there are other documents at present unknown and unsuspected. Real disappointment, however, lies in our failure to obtain access to certain minor collections of papers which are known to contain Lincoln material. The extent to which this failure affects the completeness of the *Collected Works* is a matter of uncertainty, since we do not accurately know the holdings of those who have refused their co-operation. It is hoped, however, that the preservation of copies of important items in other sources, such as The Robert Todd Lincoln Collection of the Papers of Abraham Lincoln, the Herndon-Weik Manuscripts, and the John G. Nicolay Papers, has prevented omission of all but a few items of consequence.

Although we have tried to work entirely from original manuscripts or photostatic copies of originals, necessity has dictated in some instances the use of typescript and longhand copies. In not a few cases facsimiles have been relied upon in the absence of the original. Photographic facsimiles made in recent years are as a rule very good, but early facsimiles (and not a few later ones) made by etching processes which require tracing by hand are no better than the workmanship that produced them. We have verified the fact that words have been changed or omitted in numerous facsimiles which have been widely distributed in past years, and in at least one instance—the Bixby letter—the facsimiles are known to be forgeries, although there can be no question of the genuineness of the letter's composition. For each item included in the *Collected Works* we have used what seems to be the best available source.

Concerning forgeries, it should be said that great care has been exercised in determining the inclusion or exclusion of documents which have not a clear provenance or which are for other reasons of suspicious nature. When access to the original or a photostat has been possible, we have some confidence in our judgment, but when circumstances have prevented this essential knowledge, we can only present our source for what it is worth. The number of Lincoln forgeries is increasing every year, accelerated by the large demand for Lincoln autographs and the high prices which the market brings. To say that Lincoln forgeries are sometimes the work of a master is no exaggeration, as collectors and dealers have repeatedly learned to their sorrow. While the editors make no pretense to omniscience in the matter of forgeries, we have concluded that a legitimate function of our project should be to designate in the chronological index (Appendix II) all forgeries which have come to our attention as documents which presumably would belong in the *Collected Works* if they were genuine. This listing does not include forgeries of legal papers, which will be dealt with in the volumes of Lincoln's law cases when published. In thus listing forgeries we believe that we are acting in the interest of everyone concerned, but we recognize that where monetary value is involved in a document, the present owner may feel that his property has been damaged by our opinion of it. In most instances, owners have been glad to receive our opinion, but inevitably there have been and will be repercussions. If, in spite of our effort to the contrary, we have failed to detect a forgery, we hope that its appearance in the *Collected Works* will be promptly brought to our attention.

Appendix I contains a few items which have come to our hands too late for inclusion in their proper sequence and all undated items for which we have not been able to supply a date with reasonable accuracy. Each undated item which could be supplied with a date has been incorporated in its proper place in the text.

Appendix II is a chronological index of items not printed in the body of the *Collected Works*, as explained in the headnote to this appendix.

The general index, prepared by James N. Adams of the Illinois State Historical Library, lists a wide range of topical headings as well as the customary proper names, and every effort has been made to increase its usefulness to the general reader as well as the specialist.

It has been also a major concern to provide in the footnotes, upon the first appearance of a proper name, an identification of each person mentioned in Lincoln's writings, and to furnish so far as available as much information as is necessary to an understanding of the text. Contemporary records of all kinds have been utilized in this process, and when an answer was not forthcoming, a note to that effect has been given. The editors are aware, however, that even so extensive a search as has been undertaken must sometimes miss the object sought, and to a further pursuit we commend him who will achieve where we have failed.

II

A work which has been accomplished over a period of years and has enlisted the co-operation of hundreds of individuals, distributed throughout a majority of the states and even a few foreign countries, presents a problem to the editor who wishes to observe the usual amenities of book publication. From the beginning, our project has been not merely one of scholarship in the usual channels, but has enlisted the assistance of persons in all walks of life. In more than one sense *The Collected Works of Abraham Lincoln* is representative of our democracy, for it is no exaggeration to say that it has been made possible by the people themselves.

Well-known collections of Lincoln manuscripts preserved in public institutions have contributed great numbers of documents, but private citizens, whose autograph treasures may be numbered on the fingers or listed on several pages of typescript, have contributed almost as many. The single autograph letter which reposes in a village library or in the album of a collector has often proved to be an important document. The appeal of Lincoln's fame has made his autographs the most sought for and the most widely scattered of those of our national heroes, and among family heirlooms of grandchildren of Lincoln's contemporaries are often treasured letters of the martyred president.

When the fact could be verified, the institution or the individual owning the original manuscript has been acknowledged in the first footnote to each item in the text. For identifying the document and the institution holding it, a set of established symbols has been employed, as listed with explanations in the front pages of each volume. Beyond this acknowledgment, the editors could not go without being caught on one horn or the other of a dilemma—whether to acknowledge in the Foreword only a few big collectors and collections and to slight the lesser contributor whose co-operation has often been most valuable and most welcome because it came from an unsuspected source, or to list alphabetically the hundreds of names which are to be found in the files of our correspondence.

Similarly, the problem of acknowledging the assistance of hundreds of librarians, research assistants, scholars in their private capacity, both professional and amateur, and of friends and well-wishers everywhere who have contributed information to the annotation of these volumes, is beyond possibility without burying the identity of the individual in an alphabetical list of names that would require many pages. The staffs of such great repositories of Lincolniana as The Library of Congress, Illinois State Historical Library, The Henry E. Huntington Library, Brown University Library, and The National Archives have necessarily been called upon most heavily, but their splendid co-operation exceeds that of institutions holding fewer Lincoln documents only in proportion to their greatness. From each we have received, as a general rule, all that he could lend, and to all we extend the same appreciation.

Under the general chairmanship of the president of The Abraham Lincoln Association, George W. Bunn, Jr., editorial advisers Paul M. Angle, J. G. Randall, and Benjamin P. Thomas have directed both the planning and the execution of our work. By reason of his residence in Springfield, Dr. Thomas has been able, in addition, to review all of the manuscript as it has been prepared. Back of these men stands the vivid and inspiring character of Logan Hay, whose death in 1942 deprived us all of his participation in the completion of the work which he so long envisaged.

For directly contributing to the financing of the editorial preparation of these volumes, the following members of The Abraham Lincoln Association are due thanks: Paul M. Angle, Mr. and Mrs. George W. Bunn, Jr., Mrs. Logan Hay, and Mr. and Mrs. Pascal E. Hatch. But without the timely aid of The Rockefeller Foundation, through Mr. David H. Stevens, the financial backing of The Abraham Lincoln Association would have been inadequate to our task, and to the Foundation the Association and the editors express their sincere thanks.

In a class by themselves are the dealers in autographs who supplied photostats of manuscripts held by them. The fact that some dealers refused co-operation makes the generosity of others the more noteworthy because it entailed sacrifice of time and trouble without financial reward. To the following our thanks: Ralph G. Newman of The Abraham Lincoln Book Shop, Chicago; Edwin Wolf, 2nd., John Fleming, and William H. McCarthy, Jr., of the Rosenbach Company, Philadelphia and New York; Gordon Banks of Goodspeed's Book Shop, Boston; and King V. Hostick, Springfield.

Thanks are also due Frederick Hill Meserve for the photographs used in frontispieces.

Invaluable assistance was rendered by Mrs. Helen Bullock, who was employed by The Association through The Library of Congress for more than a year in searching manuscript sources in Washington, D. C., and by James N. Adams and Miss Corinda Baliva, who typed the manuscript.

To his assistant editors, Mrs. Marion Pratt and Lloyd Dunlap, the editor pays especial tribute for constant devotion to our common objective.

III

What editor who has undergone the drudgery of collecting, the disappointment of many a day's quest for illumination that would provide only a footnote, and the wearisome repetition of marking and remarking manuscript and proof sheets, has not asked himself the question: to what purpose this exact and exacting toil—the weighing of minutiae in a mountain? The insouciance with which journalists, politicians, and everyman in his sphere will misquote and misrepresent history will scarcely be altered permanently toward perfection by our work. Myth, both as lie and as poetry, will continue to accumulate around the symbolic figure of a great man. Even our zealous cudgeling of brains and harassing of attics must miss that which we do not know, or mistake that which we misunderstand.

To our question, two answers must suffice. First, the labor was its own reward. If the prophets of doom should be right and the destruction of civilization should be accomplished by the evil forces never wholly absent from the world, ours would have been a large privilege, to survey more completely than any of our contemporaries, the slow and constant development of a great mind and personality oriented to the light in the midst of much darkness. Although the second answer is not of equal certainty, it embodies more of hope. It is that the record of past human effort, in failure and in success, in error and in truth, is the chief source from which mankind can draw an understanding of the meaning of the present and the hope of the future. To have helped in preserving an accurate record of a great man's work is a privilege of the present which the future can properly assess only by pledging itself in some degree to those principles of honesty, justice, and human brotherhood which will distinguish the writings of Lincoln as long as they are read.

Springfield, Illinois   ROY P. BASLER

SOURCES
AND LOCATION SYMBOLS

DESCRIPTION OF SOURCES

THE following symbols provide a description of sources as cited at the beginning of the first footnote to each item. In addition to the customary symbols for describing manuscripts, the editors have employed symbols or single words to identify other sources which have been cited repeatedly in the first footnote.

AD	Autograph Document
ADS	Autograph Document Signed
ADf	Autograph Draft
ADfS	Autograph Draft Signed
AE	Autograph Endorsement
AES	Autograph Endorsement Signed
AL	Autograph Letter
ALS	Autograph Letter Signed
ALS copy	Autograph Letter Signed, copied by Lincoln and preserved in his papers
Copy	Copy not by Lincoln
D	Document
DS	Document Signed
Df	Draft
DfS	Draft Signed
ES	Endorsement Signed
F	Facsimile—following any of the preceding symbols
LS	Letter Signed
P	Photostat—following any of the preceding symbols

Angle	*New Letters and Papers of Lincoln.* Compiled by Paul M. Angle. Boston and New York: Houghton Mifflin Company, 1930.
Herndon	*Herndon's Lincoln: The True Story of a Great Life.* By William H. Herndon and Jesse W. Weik. 3 volumes. Chicago, New York, and San Francisco: Belford, Clarke & Company, [1889].
Hertz	*Abraham Lincoln: A New Portrait.* By Emanuel Hertz. 2 volumes. New York: Horace Liveright, Inc., 1931.
Lapsley	*The Writings of Abraham Lincoln.* Edited by Arthur Brooks Lapsley. 8 volumes. New York: P. F. Collier and Son, 1905.

NH   *Complete Works of Abraham Lincoln.* Edited by John G. Nicolay and John Hay. 12 volumes. New York: Francis D. Tandy Company, 1905.

OR   *The War of the Rebellion: A Compilation of the Official Records of the Union and Confederate Armies.* 4 series; 70 "volumes"; 128 books. Washington: Government Printing Office, 1880-1901. Roman numerals are used for Series, Volume, and Part (if any); pages are in arabic.

Tarbell   *The Life of Abraham Lincoln.* . . . By Ida M. Tarbell. 2 volumes. New York: The Doubleday & McClure Company, 1900.

Tracy   *Uncollected Letters of Abraham Lincoln.* Edited by Gilbert A. Tracy. Boston and New York: Houghton Mifflin Company, 1917.

Wilson   *Uncollected Works of Abraham Lincoln.* Edited by Rufus Rockwell Wilson. 2 volumes. Elmira, New York: Primavera Press, 1947-1948.

LOCATION SYMBOLS

CCamStJ   St. John's Seminary Library, Camarillo, Calif.

CLCM   Los Angeles County Museum Library, Los Angeles, Calif.

CSmH   Henry E. Huntington Library, San Marino, Calif.

CoHi   State Historical Society of Colorado, Denver, Colo.

CoU   University of Colorado Library, Boulder, Colo.

Ct   Connecticut State Library, Hartford, Conn.

CtHi   Connecticut Historical Society, Hartford, Conn.

CtLHi   Litchfield Historical Society, Litchfield, Conn.

CtSoP   Pequot Library, Southport, Conn.

CtWat   Watertown Library Association, Watertown, Conn.

CtY   Yale University Library, New Haven, Conn.

DLC   Library of Congress, Washington, D. C.

DLC-HW   Herndon-Weik Collection, Library of Congress

DLC-RTL   The Robert Todd Lincoln Collection of the Papers of Abraham Lincoln, Library of Congress

DLM   Lincoln Museum, Ford's Theatre, National Park Service, Washington, D. C.

DNA   National Archives, Washington, D. C. All additional abbreviations and numbers given with this symbol are those employed by the National Archives at the time the manuscript was located.

DNM   National Museum Library, Washington, D. C.

DeHi	Historical Society of Delaware Library, Wilmington, Del.
DeWI	Wilmington Institute Free Library, Wilmington, Del.
I-Ar	Archives Division, Illinois State Library, Springfield, Ill.
IBloHi	McLean County Historical Society, Bloomington, Ill.
ICHi	Chicago Historical Society, Chicago, Ill.
ICU	University of Chicago Library, Chicago, Ill.
IDecJ	James Millikin University Library, Decatur, Ill.
IFre	Freeport Public Library, Freeport, Ill.
IHi	Illinois State Historical Library, Springfield, Ill.
IJI	Illinois College Library, Jacksonville, Ill.
ISLA	The Abraham Lincoln Association, Springfield, Ill.
IU	University of Illinois Library, Urbana, Ill.
IaCrM	Iowa Masonic Library, Cedar Rapids, Iowa
IaDaM	Davenport Public Museum, Davenport, Iowa
IaHA	Iowa State Department of History and Archives, Des Moines, Iowa
In	Indiana State Library, Indianapolis, Ind.
InFtwL	Lincoln National Life Foundation, Fort Wayne, Ind.
InHi	Indiana Historical Society, Indianapolis, Ind.
InLTHi	Tippecanoe County Historical Association, Lafayette, Ind.
InU	Indiana University Library, Bloomington, Ind.
KyBC	Berea College Library, Berea, Ky.
KyU	University of Kentucky Library, Lexington, Ky.
LU	Louisiana State University Library, Baton Rouge, La.
MB	Boston Public Library, Boston, Mass.
MCon	Free Public Library, Concord, Mass.
MFai	Millicent Library, Fairhaven, Mass.
MH	Harvard University Library, Cambridge, Mass.
MHi	Massachusetts Historical Society, Boston, Mass.
MS	Springfield Library Association, Springfield, Mass.
MSHi	Connecticut Valley Historical Society, Springfield, Mass.
MdAA	Hall of Records, State of Maryland, Annapolis, Md.
MdHi	Maryland Historical Society, Baltimore, Md.
MeHi	Maine Historical Society, Portland, Me.
MiD	Detroit Public Library, Detroit, Mich.
MiK-M	Kalamazoo Public Library Museum, Kalamazoo, Mich.
MiU-C	William L. Clements Library, University of Michigan, Ann Arbor, Mich.

MiU-Hi	Michigan Historical Collection, University of Michigan, Ann Arbor, Mich.
MnHi	Minnesota Historical Society, St. Paul, Minn.
MnSM	Macalester College Library, St. Paul, Minn.
MoHi	State Historical Society of Missouri, Columbia, Mo.
MoSHi	Missouri Historical Society, St. Louis, Mo.
N	New York State Library, Albany, N. Y.
NAuE	Fred L. Emerson Foundation, Auburn, N. Y.
NBLiHi	Long Island Historical Society, Brooklyn, N. Y.
NBuG	Grosvenor Library, Buffalo, New York
NBuHi	Buffalo Historical Society, Buffalo, N. Y.
NDry	Southworth Library, Dryden, N. Y.
NHi	New-York Historical Society, New York City
NIC	Cornell University Library, Ithaca, N. Y.
NN	New York Public Library, New York City
NNC	Columbia University Library, New York City
NNP	Pierpont Morgan Library, New York City
NRU	University of Rochester Library, Rochester, N. Y.
NSh	John Jermain Memorial Library, Sag Harbor, N. Y.
NSk	Skaneateles Library Association, Skaneateles, N. Y.
NWM	U. S. Military Academy Library, West Point, N. Y.
NbO	Omaha Public Library, Omaha, Nebr.
NcGu	Guilford College Library, Guilford, N. C.
NhExP	Phillips Exeter Academy, Exeter, N. H.
NjP	Princeton University Library, Princeton, N. J.
OCHP	Historical and Philosophical Society of Ohio, Cincinnati, Ohio
OClCS	Case Institute of Technology, Cleveland, Ohio
OClWHi	Western Reserve Historical Society, Cleveland, Ohio
OFH	Hayes Memorial Library, Fremont, Ohio
OMC	Marietta College Library, Marietta, Ohio
ORB	Oliver R. Barrett Collection, Chicago, Ill.*
OSHi	Clark County Historical Society, Springfield, Ohio
OrHi	Oregon Historical Society, Portland, Ore.
PHC	Haverford College Library, Haverford, Pa.
PHi	Historical Society of Pennsylvania, Philadelphia, Pa.

* After the *Collected Works* was in press, the collection of the late Oliver R. Barrett was sold at auction by Parke-Bernet Galleries (Catalog 1315) on February 19-20, 1952. It has been impossible to trace all new owners of the more than two hundred items, and impracticable to change the source citations for those which are known, but many of the more important items went to such well-known collections as those in the Library of Congress (Debates Scrapbook, purchased for the Alfred Whital Stern Collection) and Illinois State Historical Library (letters to Joshua F. Speed, etc.).

PMA	Allegheny College Library, Meadville, Pa.
PP	Free Library of Philadelphia, Philadelphia, Pa.
PPDrop	Dropsie College Library, Philadelphia, Pa.
PSt	Pennsylvania State College Library, State College, Pa.
PU	University of Pennsylvania Library, Philadelphia, Pa.
RPAB	Annmary Brown Memorial Library, Providence, R. I.
RPB	Brown University Library, Providence, R. I.
THaroL	Lincoln Memorial University, Harrogate, Tenn.
THi	Tennessee Historical Society, Nashville, Tenn.
ViU	University of Virginia Library, Charlottesville, Va.
VtU	University of Vermont Library, Burlington, Vt.
WBeloHi	Beloit Historical Society, Beloit, Wis.
WHi	State Historical Society of Wisconsin, Madison, Wis.
WvU	West Virginia University Library, Morgantown, W. Va.

Courtesy of Frederick Hill Meserve

1846 (c.)
By N. H. Shepherd

THE COLLECTED WORKS OF
ABRAHAM LINCOLN

PAGES FROM
LINCOLN'S SUM BOOK
1824 · 1826

Justin G. Turner

Justin G. Turner

Compound Multiplication

Q What is Compound Multiplication

A When several numbers of divers Denomination
are given to be multiplied by one common multiplier
this is called Compound multiplication

£	s	d			lb	℔	dwt	gr
17	3	4½			11	5	12	16
		2						3
2)34	6	2¼		3)32	4	18	0	
17	3	1¼		17	5	12	16

567 at 7 cents   4367 at 9 cents
3969   9

                     4T 1/03   6543 lb at 89 lb 2 Barrel
                                      89
                                    58887

Bought 26 yards at 6 4 6¾

    6   4   6   4
                26
    38 - 7 - 8 - 4
   129 - 2 - 8
   168 - 0 - 6 - 4

An army of a 10000 men having plundered a
City took so much money, that when it was
shared among them each man had 27 £ I dem
how much money was taken in all

              10000
                27
              70000
             20000
          2)27000 10000
            27 0000

To Exercise Multiplication

There were 40 men concerned in payment a sum of money and each man paid 12-71£ how much was paid in all ——

12 71
40

0 50840
1271

If 1 foot contain 12 inches I demand how there *many* are in 126 feet ——

126
12

252
126

12)1512
126

# of Compound Division

Q What is compound Division

A When several numbers of Divers Denomination are given to be divided by 1 common divisor this called Compound Division —

£	S	D
2)8	12	6½
4	6	3¼
		2
8	12	6½

lb	oz	dr
5)16	12	10
9	5	13
		5
16	12	10

Abraham Lincoln His Book

950564247964324
342 3449 6124 3096
564 153 2072 1224
950 564 2479 64324

12 381
avilion 64767
another name

517652400

Said mall

7947912
2449303
443401

The Single Rule of Three

If 2oz of silver cost 17/8 what
will 48 oz cost

$$
\begin{array}{r}
48 \\
17 \\
\hline
336 \\
48 \\
\hline
3|8|16|13 \\
2|2|12|13 \\
\hline
72 \\
60 \\
\hline
12
\end{array}
$$

If 1 gallon of ale cost 8d
what cost 36 gallons answer
£ 1 - 4 - b

$$
\begin{array}{r}
36 \\
8 \\
\hline
12)28\,8 \\
20)2\,4 \quad 1-4
\end{array}
$$

If 1 lb sugar cost 4½ what cost
48 lb answer 18 shillings

$$
\begin{array}{r}
48 \\
4½ \\
\hline
d \\
1 \quad 7 \\
18
\end{array}
$$

① What do you observe concerning the 1st & 3rd terms

Ⓐ they must be of the same nameere kind

① What do you observe concerning the 4th term

ⓐ it must be of the same nameare but...

① What do you observe of three given terms taken together

Ⓐ that the two first are supposition the last is a demande

Ⓐ how is the third term known

Ⓐ it is known by these or like the words what last known

how much

① how many sorts of proportion are there

Ⓐ two direct one inverse

Of Direct Proportion

Multiply 46723
By 2
2) 93446
46723

Multiply 673427
By 3
3) 2020241
673427

Multiply 5764327
By 5
5) 24442605
5764327

M 34567
B 500
500) 17243500
34567

Multiply 345674
By 324
1342772
691356
1037034
324) 111999672 345674
972
1479
1296
1439
1620
2196
1944
2527
2264
2592
2592
0000

Multiply 3456743
By 23425
13703302
6913664
10370302
6913664
90969
23425) 80969423757832 34567434
90269
96945
93692
183903
137116
124451
140538
142495
163567
199347
147544
119434
70269
93692
93692
00000

M 3245000
500
5000) 1022500000000
3245000

5 X 5
7 7

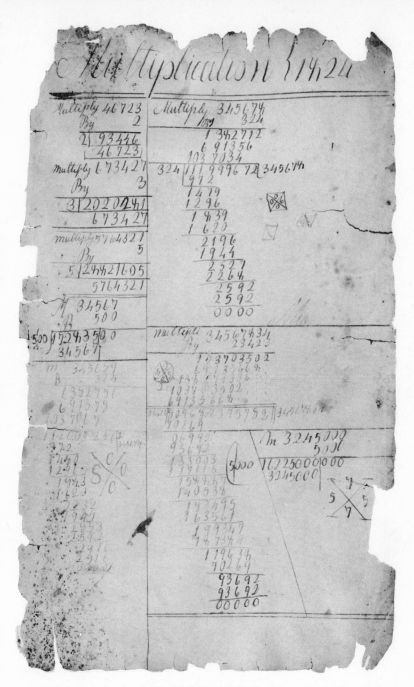

Examples

multiply 342435
By 342

```
M  345674 2              674870
B    304 3 8           1369740
   2 0 7 40 692       1027305
 138 27 128 0
1037 5 4 2 0 8      342 171. 1277 0 342435
105 069 1 3 4 92 3456742    1026
97 21 4                     1451
138 449                     1368
27 6 2                       932
172 521       8  5  4        684
152 030           5         1447
20 6 713                    1368
74 2436                     1197
2377 7                      1026
13 442                      1710
249 329                     1710
243 244
60412                 171  345 679
60412                 B     334
3 5000               1352 112
                     1037 34
                     1729 39 0
M  3 6000    9  3    1945.9205 2 345679
B   3000    3  3      1.602
                9         2439
90000        534      2136
                          3032
multiply                  2670
By                        3620
 1369366 9                3264
10279401                  4165
1369966                   3739
546936
                          4272
                          4272
                          5000
2 7 0 2
145 4 7     5
1369 3 6   2   7
099 345        5
               Abraham Lincoln
102702            Book
106 071 8
136936
239367
19 546 4
329 638
329 638
0 00000
```

Simple interest

what is the amount of a
bond for 387 dollars 50 cent
for 1 year at 6 percent
per annum

$$
\begin{array}{c}
38750 \mid 38750 \\
3225 \\
23\mid2\,5\,9\,9\quad 41975 \\
38750 \\
2225 \\
41\,0\,75
\end{array}
$$

Case 2

when there is a fraction
as ¼ ½ ¾ &c in the
percent

Rule

multiply the principal
by the rate percent
to the product add
¼ ½ or ¾ of said fraction
and divide by 100 for
the interest required

Examples

what is the interest of
£ 526–10² for 1 year at
5½ percent per annum

$$
\begin{array}{c}
526-10 \\
5\frac{1}{2} \qquad 1/80 \\
2632-10 \qquad 4 \\
263\cdot\,5 \qquad 3/2\,8 \\
2895-15 \\
20 \\
19\,15 \qquad £ \\
12 \qquad 28-19-
\end{array}
$$

what is the interest of 428 do
for one year at 6¾ percent
annum

$$
\begin{array}{c}
428 \\
6\frac{1}{4} \\
2568 \\
214 \\
107 \\
\$ \ 28\mid59 \ cents
\end{array}
$$

what is the interest of
£ 216–5⁵ for one year at
5½ percent per annum

$$
\begin{array}{c}
216-5 \\
5\frac{1}{2} \\
1081-5 \\
108-2 \\
1189-7 \\
90 \\
1789 \\
12 \\
180 \\
87 \\
1050 \\
7 \qquad £ \ s \ d \\
2\mid0\,0 \ \ 11-17-10\frac{1}{2}
\end{array}
$$

what is the interest
£400 for one year
cent per annum

$$
\begin{array}{c}
400 \\
6\frac{1}{4} \\
2400 \\
100 \\
25\mid0.0
\end{array}
$$

Foreman M. Lebold

Simple Interest

what is the interest of
£855–17–6 for one year at
5¾ percent per annum

855–17–6
1   5¾

727–7–6
427–13–6
213–16–3
4920–17–3
20
517
12
57

2|07
4   £ s d
|25   49–4–2

what is the interest of
for one year at 6¼
cent per annum

300
6¼
1800
75
1875

what is the interest of £426–18
one year at 4½ percent
per annum   426 18
4½

17092
309
19|1781| 19–17–8

Case 3

when the interest of a sum
given for several years is
required

Rule

Multiply the interest
of the given for one
year by the number of
years

Examples

what is the interest of £246–18
for 5 years at 4¼ percent
per annum

246–18   £   s   d
4¼   10–9–9¾
987–12   5
6¼ 7
10|48–19   52–8–10¼
20
9|79
12
9|48
4
1|9 2

Simple Interest

Examples

(Genuine
H H Bauman)

What principal at interest
for 5 year at 6 per cent
per anum will amount to

£ 650

$$\begin{array}{c} 5 \\ 6 \\ 30 \\ 130 \end{array} \quad 130 \mid 650\,00 \mid 500$$
$$\underline{650}$$
$$1000$$

What principle at interest
for 10 years at 6 percent
per anum will amount to

£ 1300 —

$$\begin{array}{c} 10 \\ 6 \\ 60 \\ 100 \\ 160 \end{array} \quad 160 \mid 1300\,00 \mid 512\,£$$
$$1250$$
$$200$$
$$160$$
$$400$$
$$320$$
$$84$$
$$20$$
$$1\,600\,0 \mid 10\,\delta$$
$$160$$
$$0$$

What principal at interest
for 4 year at 7 percent
per anum will amount to £64

$$\begin{array}{c} 4 \\ 7 \\ 28 \\ 100 \\ 128 \end{array} \quad 128 \mid 5700 \mid 44 - 53 - 1 \cdot$$
$$512$$
$$580$$
$$512$$
$$6\,800$$
$$6\,40 \qquad 160$$
$$400 \qquad 128$$

Case the Second

to find the rate per cent when
amount time and principal
are given

Rule

As the product of the time
principal is to the interest for
the whole time So is 100 pounds
or dollars to the rate percent

Examples

at what rate per cent £ per
annum will £ 500 amount
to £ 650 in 5 years

$$\begin{array}{c} 500 \\ 5 \\ 2500 \end{array} \quad \begin{array}{c} 650 \\ 500 \\ 150 \end{array} \mid 25\,00 \mid 150\,0 \mid 6$$
$$150 - 100$$
$$100$$

at what rate percent per annum will £ 500 amount to
£ 725 in 9 years

$$\begin{array}{c} 500 \\ 9 \\ 4500 \end{array} \quad \begin{array}{c} 725 \\ 500 \\ 225 \end{array} \mid 45\,00 \mid 22\,500 \mid 5\,\text{per}$$
$$225 - 100$$
$$100$$
$$2\,25,00$$
$$225$$
$$0$$

Simple Interest

At what rate percent per annum
will $600 amount to $856
60 cts. in 9 years and 6 months

600
9½
540 856 50
228 600
285 256 50
285
0

Case 7

To point the time when
the principal amount
and rate percent are
given

Rule

as the interest of the principle
for one year is to one year
so is the whole interest
to the time required

Examples

In what time will $500
amount to $725 at 6 percent

500
5
25)00 725
500
25)225(9 years

In what time will $540 amount
to £734 8s at 4 percent per annum

540 734 8
4 540
21)60 194 8
20 20
12)00 432)3888(9
3888

21
20
432

At what time will £800
amount to £1020 51 cts at
6½ percent per annum

800
5½
4785 1020 51
418 ½ 800
209 ¼ 135)73404(4 years
931 ½ 77404
9251

A testator left his son beside
providing for his education
$1500 to receive the amount
thereof at 6 percent per annum
when he should arrive at the
age of 21 years which his
guardian then found to be
£2332 50 cents how old was
the Boy at his fathers decease

1500 2332 50
1500
9)00 8250(4
81
2250

Discount 1826

Bought goods to the value of
£104-10-5 to be paid at 9 months
what present money will dischar
the same if I am allowed
6 percent per annum discount

12 - 9 6   104 10 14   109-10
    6   20
12 594 - 2090   219000/104
  73   2090
                       10000
                        8360
                        1640
                       2820 15
                       2090
                       1900
                      10450
                       1450
       £   d   12
104-15-8/4   17460/8
                      16720
                        680
                          4
                       2720/1
                       2090
                        630

what is the present worth of
£161-10⁵ for 19 months discount
at 5 percent per annum

12 - 14 5   107-18-4   161-10 .
     5   20
12 937 215 8   8230
  84   12   12
 11 2585 2   3756000/14
 20   25852
229/18   117088   not room
 11   103408
100   136720
 96

           £ 149-13-0½

What is the present
worth of $ 430 = 17/6/10
for 19 months Discount
at 8 percent.

12 - 14 5   as 107-91-6   43067
     5
18/15/7   107916   9306 7000 504
 84   323748
1100/91   1069220
103   971234
 20   979860
 12   971184
 50/6   862400
  8   755412
                          1025 50
                           371 2
                          10064

What is the Rebate of
£ 112 - 12/3 for 20 months
at 7 percent per annum

12 40 7   111 13-4   112-12
    7   20   20
12/140/11   233   2252
 12   12   12
 20   26800   2702900/100
 11   26800
  8   224 00
 20   20
160/13   448000/16
 12   26800
 40   180000
 36   160800
  4   19200
                       12
112-12-0-0   23040 /8
100-16-8-2   21440 0
11 - 15 3 2   16000
                  4
               64000/2
               59600

Discount march 1st 1820

Discount is an allowance made for the payment of a sum of money before it becomes due, according to a certain rate percent agreed on between the parties concerned. the preasant worth of any sum or debt due some time hence is such a sum as if put to interest for that time at a certain rate percent would amount to the sum or debt {See Case 5 Simple interest}

Rule

As the ammount of 100 pounds or dollars at the rate and time given is to 100 pounds or dollars so is the whole debt to the preasant worth

Proof

Find the amount of the preasant worth for the time and rate proposed which must equal the sum or debt

Examples

what is the preasant worth and what the discount of £ 500 payable in 10 months at 5 percent perannum

```
      m  £                                          Ans { persen £ 480
as 12-5- 10        1043-4  100   500                    { Discount  20
      10             20           20
   12/50/4.         2083        10000
      48              12          12              £
       2          25000     |12000000| 480 ans
      20                     100000
   12/40/3                  200000
      36                    200000
       4                        00
```

L M & P

71 - 1 - 3 - 10
44 - 2 - 5 - 16
26 - 1 - 5 - 34
71 - 1 - 3 - 10

Subr

Y f J B

48 - 0 - 1 - 2
12 - 0 - 3 - 1
36 - 0 - 10 - 1
48 - 0 - 1 - 2

# of Land Measure

A R P
4 40

12 - 1 - 10
5 - 3 - 17
6 - 1 - 33
12 - 1 - 10

A R P
4 40

17 - 3 - 17
12 - 3 - 23
4 - 3 - 34
17 - 3 - 17

a y h
4 40

28 - 1 - 7
19 - 1 - 28
8 - 3 - 19
28 - 1 - 7

# of Dry Measure

Ch - B P
36 4

17 - 2 - 1
10 - 1 - 3
7 - 0 - 2
17 - 2 - 1

C C h
36 4

42 - 1 - 2
16 - 5 - 1
23 - 32 - 1
40 - 1 - 2

q B P
8 4

19 - 1 - 1
12 - 7 - 2
6 - 1 - 3
19 - 1 - 1

Abraham Lincoln
his hand and pen
he will be good but
god knows When

Long Measure

Peter H. Brandt

Peter H. Brandt

THE COLLECTED WORKS OF

ABRAHAM LINCOLN

———◄◆►———

Copybook Verses[1]
[1824-1826]

Abraham Lincoln
his hand and pen
he will be good but
god knows When[2]

Abraham Lincoln his hand and pen he will be good
but god knows When Time What an emty vaper
Meter   tis and days how swift they are swift as an indian arr[ow]
fly on like a shooting star the presant moment Just [is here]
then slides away in h[as]te that we [can] never say they['re ours]
                      but [only say] th[ey]'re past[3]

Abraham Lincoln is my nam[e]
And with my pen I wrote the same
I wrote in both hast and speed
and left it here for fools to read

[1] AD, DLC-HW; AD, ORB; AD, owned by Justin Turner, Los Angeles, California. The original text of these verses appears on pages of Lincoln's self-made arithmetic book, which was given to William H. Herndon by Lincoln's step-mother Sarah Bush Johnston Lincoln. The sheets have been dispersed, and some of the original sheets have not been accounted for. Those which are known are reproduced in facsimile on the preceding pages.

Whether any of the verses were original with the boy Lincoln, has been questioned. His propensity for verse-making at this period is attested, however, by the tradition among the Spencer County, Indiana, citizens from whom Herndon gathered information. Mrs. Josiah Crawford provided from memory the so-called "Chronicles of Reuben," composed in parody of Biblical narrative and satirizing a neighborhood wedding, and a few satirical verses which were purported to have been made and circulated by Lincoln as a youth. Although Herndon speaks of the "Chronicles of Reuben" as having come to light in a manuscript in "Lincoln's handwriting," the only version Herndon seems to have had was the one written down by S. A. Crawford, as recited from memory by his mother, forty years after Lincoln was said to have composed them. Such a text has not seemed to the

[1]

editors to afford sufficient authenticity for inclusion in the writings of Lincoln. The pages of the arithmetic book seem to be the only extant manuscripts of this early period.

² Albert J. Beveridge notes that this "same inscription is in the Mordecai Lincoln copy of Bailey's *Dictionary*, 'Mordecai' being in place of 'Abraham' and 'you' in place of 'God' " (*Abraham Lincoln, 1809-1858*, I, 64, n.3). The suggestion is that the verse was traditional among the older generation of Lincoln's family.

³ Bracketed words are supplied from Herndon's text of the verse, taken down before the original manuscript became badly frayed and foxed.

Petition to Macon County Commissioners' Court[1]

May 26, 1830

To the Hon County Comrs. Court for the County of Macon

We the undersigned qualified voters in Decatur Precinct earnestly request your honors to change the present place of holding Elections in said Precinct from Permenius Smallwoods to the Court house in Decatur

26th May 1830

David Miller	M. C. Shaw
Thomas Law	Charles Lewis
Saml. B Dewees	S. Sennitt
D. H. Stewart	Robert Stewart
S R Sheppard	John Dickey
John Miller	William Dickey
William Hall	Thomas Cowan
J. B. Brown	I. C. Pugh
Squire Hall	James Miller
William Hanks	Philip D. Williams
Thomas Cole	Buel Stevens
John Biglow	David Florey
Landy Harell	Moses Hand
Alfred Hall	David Owen
William Foren	Randolph Rose
John Pettyjohn	Isaac Miller
Reuben Brown	Jas. Johnson
James Martin	John Ballard
H. J. Armstrong	Phillip Ballard
Henry Ewing	John Hankes
Joseph Stevens	John D. Johnston
John Grimsley	A Lincoln
Andrew W Smith	

¹ DS, Macon County Clerk's office, Decatur, Illinois. Perhaps the earliest document signed by Lincoln after his arrival in Illinois in March, 1830. He was not technically a qualified voter at the time, six months' residence being required.

Appraisal of an Estray[1]

December 16, 1830

We the under signers having been called on to apprais an Estray Mare Taken up by Jonathan B. Brown on Monday the 12th. day of Decr. 1830: Do find her to be four years old next Spring a bright bay 14 hands high—a Small blaze and a Snip in her face—right hind foot white—right fore foot with a white Stripe down the hough and white hairs around the edge of the hough no brands perceiveable black mane and tail appraised to 30 Dollars[.] Given under hands this 16th. day of December 1830

A LINCOLN
JOHN. W. REED

[1] AD, Macon County Clerk's office, Decatur, Illinois. The document is in Lincoln's hand, except for Reed's signature and the notarization at the bottom of the page by Philip D. Williams. Jonathan B. Brown and John W. Reed were Macon County farmers.

Petition to Sangamon County Commissioners' Court for Appointment of a Constable[1]

March [11] 1831

The Hone. the county commissioners court of Sangamon county at the March term for 1831.

We the undersignd. petitioners would represent to your Hone. body that whereas it [is] represented to us that there is a vacancy in the office of constable in the Springfield district, and whereas the Statute in such cases made and provided, authorises your Hone. Court to fill such vacancy upon petition.

We therefore request you to fill sd. vacancy with some suitable person.

[1] DS, IHi. The document carries twenty-nine names, including those of Lincoln, John Hanks, and John D. Johnston, all three signed by Lincoln.

Document Drawn for James Eastep[1]

November 12, 1831

Know all men by these presents that I James Eastep am held and firmly bound in the penal Sum of twenty Dollars unto Solomon Teter for the conveyance of a certain tract or parcel of land it being the part of a certain tract (situated in St. Clair County and State of Illinois) which falls to my wife as an heir of Abraham Teter deceased.

[3]

The condition of the above obligation is such. If the said James Eastep shall make a good and lawful patent to said Teter for the afforesaid parcel of land by the twelfth day of November in the year of our Lord one thousand eight hundred-and thirty six the above obligation is to be null void and of no effect. Otherwise to Remain in full force and Virtue at law.

In testimony whereof the said James Eastep has hereunto set his hand and seal this twelfth day of November in the year of our Lord one thousand eight hundred and thirty one.

Attest   JAMES EASTEP (SEAL)

A LINCOLN

[1] ADS, owned by Mrs. Dillard Estep Samuel, Chicago, Illinois. The document is entirely in Lincoln's hand, including the signature of James Eastep, who was a farmer and operator of a "horse mill" near the location of the present town of Petersburg. His wife was Abigail Teter, daughter of the Abraham Teter named in the document.

Bill of Sale Drawn for John Ferguson[1]

January 25, 1832

Know all men by these presents that I John Ferguson for and in considderation of the sum of thirty five dollars have given granted bargained and sold all my right and title in and to the New Salem ferry in Sangamon County unto Alexander Trent

In testimony where of I have hereunto set my hand this 25th. January 1832   JOHN FERGUSON

[1] AD, IHi.

Draft Drawn on James Rutledge[1]

March 8, 1832

Mr. James Rutledge please to pay the bearer David P Nelson[2] thirty dollars and this shall be your receipt for the same

March 8th. 1832.   A LINCOLN

                         for D Offutt[3]

[1] ADS, DLC. James Rutledge, mill owner and tavern keeper, was co-founder of New Salem.

[2] Dr. David P. Nelson resided not far from New Salem; on moving to Texas he employed Lincoln to raft his goods and family down the Sangamon River to Beardstown.

[3] Denton Offutt was a merchant who employed Lincoln in March, 1831, to take a flatboat of produce to New Orleans. Upon returning Lincoln clerked in Offutt's store at New Salem.

Communication to the People of
Sangamo County[1]

To the People of Sangamo County   March 9, 1832

FELLOW-CITIZENS: Having become a candidate for the honorable office of one of your representatives in the next General Assembly of this state, in accordance with an established custom, and the principles of true republicanism, it becomes my duty to make known to you—the people whom I propose to represent—my sentiments with regard to local affairs.

Time and experience have verified to a demonstration, the public utility of internal improvements. That the poorest and most thinly populated countries would be greatly benefitted by the opening of good roads, and in the clearing of navigable streams within their limits, is what no person will deny. But yet it is folly to undertake works of this or any other kind, without first knowing that we are able to finish them—as half finished work generally proves to be labor lost. There cannot justly be any objection to having rail roads and canals, any more than to other good things, provided they cost nothing. The only objection is to paying for them; and the objection to paying arises from the want of ability to pay.

With respect to the county of Sangamo, some more easy means of communication than we now possess, for the purpose of facilitating the task of exporting the surplus products of its fertile soil, and importing necessary articles from abroad, are indispensably necessary. A meeting has been held of the citizens of Jacksonville,[2] and the adjacent country, for the purpose of deliberating and enquiring into the expediency of constructing a rail road from some eligible point on the Illinois river, through the town of Jacksonville, in Morgan county, to the town of Springfield, in Sangamo county. This is, indeed, a very desirable object. No other improvement that reason will justify us in hoping for, can equal in utility the rail road. It is a never failing source of communication, between places of business remotely situated from each other. Upon

[1] *Sangamo Journal*, March 15, 1832. Nicolay and Hay state that this communication was distributed as a handbill. If so, no copies seem to have survived. Lincoln had been a resident of New Salem a little more than six months, and was to enlist in the Black Hawk War on April 21. Returning late in July, he had time to make a brief campaign before election day, August 6. He was defeated, running eighth in a field of thirteen candidates, but he received a heavy majority in New Salem precinct—277 of the 300 votes cast.

[2] On December 28, 1831; reported from *Illinois Patriot* (Jacksonville) in *Sangamo Journal*, January 5, 1832.

the rail road the regular progress of commercial intercourse is not interrupted by either high or low water, or freezing weather, which are the principal difficulties that render our future hopes of water communication precarious and uncertain. Yet, however desirable an object the construction of a rail road through our country may be; however high our imaginations may be heated at thoughts of it—there is always a heart appalling shock accompanying the account of its cost, which forces us to shrink from our pleasing anticipations. The probable cost of this contemplated rail road is estimated at $290,000;—the bare statement of which, in my opinion, is sufficient to justify the belief, that the improvement of Sangamo river is an object much better suited to our infant resources.

Respecting this view, I think I may say, without the fear of being contradicted, that its navigation may be rendered completely practicable, as high as the mouth of the South Fork, or probably higher, to vessels of from 25 to 30 tons burthen, for at least one half of all common years, and to vessels of much greater burthen a part of that time. From my peculiar circumstances, it is probable that for the last twelve months I have given as particular attention to the stage of the water in this river, as any other person in the country. In the month of March, 1831, in company with others, I commenced the building of a flat boat on the Sangamo, and finished and took her out in the course of the spring. Since that time, I have been concerned in the mill at New Salem. These circumstances are sufficient evidence, that I have not been very inattentive to the stages of the water. The time at which we crossed the mill dam, being in the last days of April, the water was lower than it had been since the breaking of winter in February, or than it was for several weeks after. The principal difficulties we encountered in descending the river, were from the drifted timber, which obstructions all know is not difficult to be removed. Knowing almost precisely the height of water at that time, I believe I am safe in saying that it has as often been higher as lower since.

From this view of the subject, it appears that my calculations with regard to the navigation of the Sangamo, cannot be unfounded in reason; but whatever may be its natural advantages, certain it is, that it never can be practically useful to any great extent, without being greatly improved by art. The drifted timber, as I have before mentioned, is the most formidable barrier to this object. Of all parts of this river, none will require so much labor in proportion, to make it navigable, as the last thirty or thirty-five miles; and going with the meanderings of the channel, when we are this distance above its mouth, we are only between twelve and eighteen miles above Beardstown, in something near a straight direction; and this route is upon such low ground as to retain water in many places during the season, and in all parts such as to draw two-thirds or three-fourths of the river water at all high stages.

This route is upon prairie land the whole distance;—so that it appears to me, by removing the turf, a sufficient width and damming up the old channel, the whole river in a short time would wash its way through, thereby curtailing the distance, and increasing the velocity of the current very considerably, while there would be no timber upon the banks to obstruct its navigation in future; and being nearly straight, the timber which might float in at the head, would be apt to go clear through. There are also many places above this where the river, in its zig zag course, forms such complete peninsulas, as to be easier cut through at the necks than to remove the obstructions from the bends—which if done, would also lessen the distance.

What the cost of this work would be, I am unable to say. It is probable, however, it would not be greater than is common to streams of the same length. Finally, I believe the improvement of the Sangamo river, to be vastly important and highly desirable to the people of this county; and if elected, any measure in the legislature having this for its object, which may appear judicious, will meet my approbation, and shall receive my support.

It appears that the practice of loaning money at exorbitant rates of interest, has already been opened as a field for discussion;[3] so I suppose I may enter upon it without claiming the honor, or risking the danger, which may await its first explorer. It seems as though we are never to have an end to this baneful and corroding system, acting almost as prejudicial to the general interests of the community as a direct tax of several thousand dollars annually laid on each county, for the benefit of a few individuals only, unless there be a law made setting a limit to the rates of usury. A law for this purpose, I am of opinion, may be made, without materially injuring any class of people. In cases of extreme necessity there could always be means found to cheat the law, while in all other cases it

[3] Lincoln very probably is referring to a local issue, but no contemporary speeches on the subject have been located. However, it may be noted that the relationship between debtors and creditors was an issue of some contemporary importance, and that President Jackson's Message to Congress of December 30, 1831, had attacked the cruelty and avarice of creditors in general and had recommended the abolition of laws effecting imprisonment for debt. The latter part of Lincoln's paragraph on usury suggests sarcastic humor leveled at local circumstances which are now lost in obscurity.

[7]

would have its intended effect. I would not favor the passage of a law upon this subject, which might be very easily evaded. Let it be such that the labor and difficulty of evading it, could only be justified in cases of the greatest necessity.

Upon the subject of education, not presuming to dictate any plan or system respecting it, I can only say that I view it as the most important subject which we as a people can be engaged in. That every man may receive at least, a moderate education, and thereby be enabled to read the histories of his own and other countries, by which he may duly appreciate the value of our free institutions, appears to be an object of vital importance, even on this account alone, to say nothing of the advantages and satisfaction to be derived from all being able to read the scriptures and other works, both of a religious and moral nature, for themselves. For my part, I desire to see the time when education, and by its means, morality, sobriety, enterprise and industry, shall become much more general than at present, and should be gratified to have it in my power to contribute something to the advancement of any measure which might have a tendency to accelerate the happy period.

With regard to existing laws, some alterations are thought to be necessary. Many respectable men have suggested that our estray laws—the law respecting the issuing of executions, the road law, and some others, are deficient in their present form, and require alterations. But considering the great probability that the framers of those laws were wiser than myself, I should prefer [not?] meddling with them, unless they were first attacked by others, in which case I should feel it both a privilege and a duty to take that stand, which in my view, might tend most to the advancement of justice.

But, Fellow-Citizens, I shall conclude. Considering the great degree of modesty which should always attend youth, it is probable I have already been more presuming than becomes me. However, upon the subjects of which I have treated, I have spoken as I thought. I may be wrong in regard to any or all of them; but holding it a sound maxim, that it is better to be only sometimes right, than at all times wrong, so soon as I discover my opinions to be erroneous, I shall be ready to renounce them.

Every man is said to have his peculiar ambition. Whether it be true or not, I can say for one that I have no other so great as that of being truly esteemed of my fellow men, by rendering myself worthy of their esteem. How far I shall succeed in gratifying this ambition, is yet to be developed. I am young and unknown to many of you. I was born and have ever remained in the most humble walks of life. I have no wealthy or popular relations to recommend me. My case is thrown exclusively upon the independent voters of this county, and if elected they will have conferred a favor upon me, for which I shall be unremitting in my labors to compensate. But if the good people in their wisdom shall see fit to keep me in the background, I have been too familiar with disappointments to be very much chagrined. Your friend and fellow-citizen,

New Salem, March 9, 1832. A. LINCOLN.

Receipt to William Barnett[1]

March 26, 1832

Received of Wm. Barnett in full of all due debts and demands up to this date A LINCOLN
    March 26. 1832. for D Offutt

[1] ADS, owned by Foreman Lebold, Chicago, Illinois.

Receipt to William Sampson[1]

April 21, 1832

Received of William Sampson in full of all demands up to this day April 21. 1832 A LINCOLN
for D Offutt

[1] ADS, owned by James W. Bollinger, Davenport, Iowa. William Sampson was a farmer living near New Salem.

Receipt for Arms[1]

April 28, 1832

Received, April 28, 1832, for the use of the Sangamon County Company, under my command, thirty muskets, bayonets, screws and wipers, which I oblige myself to return upon demand.

A. LINCOLN, Capt.

[Guns.	Bayonets.	Screws.	Wipers.
19	15	9	21
3	2	1	1
1	1	4	1
1	1	. .	. .
1	1	. .	. .
1	. .	. .	. .
—	—	—	—]
26	20	14	23

[1] *Illinois State Journal*, April 9, 1869; NH, I, 9-10. The original document from which the *Journal* printed this item has not been located. The Nicolay and Hay version differs from the *Journal* version in a few details which are indicated by brackets in the tabulation of arms and in Hardin's special order as printed below. Lincoln's receipt was presumably written on this special order which he presented to the quartermaster and on which were tabulated the arms as issued:

Special Order No. 7.   BEARDSTOWN, April 28, 1832.

The Brigade Inspector having inspected Capt. Abram Lincoln's company, and mustered them into the service, reports that thirty guns are wanting to arm the company completely. Quartermaster General Edwards will furnish the Captain with that number of arms, if to be had in this [his] department[.]

By order of   JOHN J. HARDIN, Brig. Major.
    Brig. Gen. SAMUEL WHIT[E]SIDE.
    Com'dg. B.M.V. Ill.

Governor John Reynolds called on April 16 for the militia to meet at Beardstown on April 22. Lincoln enrolled on April 21, at Richland, nine miles from New Salem; he was elected captain of the local company. When his thirty-day enlistment ended, he re-enlisted on May 27 as a private in Captain Elijah Iles' company of Independent Rangers. On June 16, he re-enlisted for thirty days in the Independent Spy Corps under Captain Jacob M. Early, a Methodist preacher and physician from Springfield who had been a private in the companies of Lincoln and Iles.

The persons whose names appear in the document were as follows: Cyrus Edwards, acting quartermaster general, a leading Madison County Whig; John J. Hardin, inspector general and mustering officer who enrolled Lincoln's company into state service, a Morgan County attorney whose law office was in Jacksonville, and who appears often in Lincoln's subsequent writings; and Samuel Whiteside, brigadier general in charge of volunteers, a Democrat of Madison County whose experience in Indian fighting went back to 1811, when he was captain of one of the ten companies of mounted rangers organized to protect the West from Indians.

Muster Roll of Lincoln's Company[1]

May 27, 1832

Muster Roll of Captain Abraham Lincolns Company of the [4th Rgt. of the] Brigade of Mounted Volunteers commanded by Brig. Genl. Samuel Whiteside [mustered out of service at the mouth of Fox River May 27th 1832]

[1] ADS, owned by Mrs. Gordon Hicks, Chicago, Illinois. Bracketed passages were written in by Nathaniel B. Buckmaster, Inspector and Muster Officer, and the same hand also wrote crosswise between numbers 45 and 52, "Capt. Lincoln 4th Rgt." Lack of space dictates the omission of a column headed "Where enrolled," between "When enrolled" and "Where discharged." All men were listed as enrolled in Sangamon County. A second copy of the Muster Roll, printed in facsimile in Thomas P. Reep, *Lincoln at New Salem* (1927), includes two additional names between numbers 67 and 68—Thomas Long and William Green. This copy also designates the place of enrollment as Richland, except for number 63, which is Beardstown, and number 68, which is Dixon's Ferry; and the column "Where discharged" is omitted. There are no "Remarks" for numbers 3 and 7, and remarks "absent on furlough" are given for numbers 37 and 56.

No.	Names	Rank	When enrolled	Where discharged	Remarks
1	Abraham Lincoln	Captain	21st. Apl	Mouth of Fox River Ills	
2	Samuel M Thompson	1st Lieut.	"	"	Resigned the 30 day of April
3	John Brannen	2 "	"	"	Absent on extra duty
4	John Armstrong	1 Serg.	"	"	
5	Tavner B Anderson	2 "	"	"	
6	George W. Foster	3 "	"	"	Transferred to a foot company April 29
7	Obadiah Morgan	4 "	"	"	Absent on furlough
8	Thomas Combs	1 Corp.	"	"	
9	John Plaster	2 "	"	"	Resigned 20 day of May & served as a private since
10	William F Berry	3 "	"	"	
11	Alexander Trent	4 "	"	"	
12	John Erwin	private	"	"	Promoted to 3rd Sergeant in room of G W Foster Apl 29
13	John H. Houghton	" .	"	"	
14	Thomas Pierce	"	"	"	
15	Samuel Tibbs	"	"	"	
16	Henry Hadley	"	"	"	
17	Samuel Dutton	"	"	"	
18	Calvin Pierce	"	"	"	
19	Joseph Tibbs	"	"	"	
20	William Kirkpatrick	"	"	"	Promoted from the Ranks April 30th
21	Cyrus Elmore	"	"	"	
22	Elijah Pierce	"	"	"	
23	Lewis W Farmer	"	"	"	
24	Bordry Matthews	"	"	"	
25	Ep. Sulivan	"	"	"	
26	Valentine Crete	"	"	"	
27	Charles Sulivan	"	"	"	
28	James Simmons	"	"	"	
29	Hugh Armstrong	"	"	"	Promoted to 1st Lieutenant April 30th
30	Allen King	"	"	"	
31	Joseph Dobson	"	"	"	
32	David Rankin	"	"	"	Transferred to a foot company May 19th.

No.	Names	Rank	When enrolled	Where discharged	Remarks
33	Urbin Alexander	"	"	"	
34	Henry Cox	"	"	"	
35	Merrit M. Carman	"	"	"	
36	Royal Potter	"	"	"	
37	David M Pantier	"	"	"	
38	Joseph Hohimer	"	"	"	
39	George Warburton	"	"	"	
40	Evan T. Lamb	"	"	"	
41	Clardey Barnette	"	"	"	
42	John M Rutledge	"	"	"	
43	William Cox	"	"	"	
44	Usil Meeker	"	"	"	
45	Richard Jones	"	"	"	Promoted from the Ranks May 2nd.
46	Charles Pierce	"	"	"	
47	James Clemment	"	"	"	
48	John Y Lane	"	"	"	
49	Richard Lane	"	"	"	
50	Royal Clary	"	"	"	
51	Pleasant Armstrong	"	"	"	
52	James Yardley	"	"	"	
53	David Rutledge	"	"	"	
54	Michael Plaster	"	"	"	absent without leave
55	John Mounce	"	"	"	absent without leave
56	William Hohimer	"	"	"	
57	Isaac Anderson	"	"	"	
58	William Marshall	"	"	"	
59	William Cummins	"	"	"	
60	John Jones	"	"	"	absent without leave
61	Travice Elmore	"	"	"	
62	William Foster	"	"	"	Transfered to a foot company April 29
63	Nathan Drake	"	29 April	"	
64	Robert S. Plunkett	"	"	"	
65	William T. Sprouce	"	"	"	Promoted from the Ranks May 2nd
66	William Clary	"	"	"	
67	Jacob Heaverer	"	"	"	
68	Isaac Guliher	"	May 19th.	"	

I certify on honour that this Muster Roll exhibits a true Statement of Captain A Lincolns company of Mounted Volunteers of

Illinois Militia on this day and that the remarks set opposite the names are accurate and Just. ABRAHAM LINCOLN Capt.

Election Return[1]

September 20, 1832

At an election held at the house of John McNeil in the New Salem precinct in the County of Sangamon and State of Illinois on the 20th. day of September in the year of our Lord one thousand eight hundred and thirty two the following named persons received the number of votes annexed to their respective names—for Constable—

John Clary had Forty one	Votes for Constable
John R. Herndon had Twenty two	votes for constable
William McNeely had Thirteen	votes for constable
Baxter B. Berry had Nine—	votes for constable
Edmund Greer had Four—	votes for constable

JAMES RUTLEDGE
HUGH ARMSTRONG } Judges of the election
JAMES WHITE

Attest

A. LINCOLN
WILLIAM GREEN } Clerks of the election

I certify that the above Judges and clerks were qualified according to law

September 20. 1832 BOWLING GREEN J P

[1] ADS, IHi. In Lincoln's hand except for other signatures. Voters' names and tally of individual votes have not been printed for reasons of difficulty and inconsequence of data.

Promissory Note to James D. Henry[1]

$104.87½ No 13 October 30, 1832

SIX MONTHS after date we or either of us, promise to pay to J. D. HENRY Sheriff of Sangamon County, or order, (for the benefit of the creditors of V. A. Bogue)[2] the sum of one hundred & four dollars Eighty Seven ½ cents, value received this 30th Oct., 1832. NELSON ALLEY

A LINCOLN

[1] Printed form, DS, ICU.

[2] Vincent A. Bogue was the Sangamon County entrepreneur who promoted navigation of the Sangamon River by the steamboat *Talisman,* which Lincoln and J. Rowan Herndon piloted to Bogue's mill in March, 1832. Lincoln and Alley, proprietor of the tavern at New Salem, were among his backers, and when Bogue went bankrupt they were levied upon.

Election Return[1]

November 5, 1832

At an election held at the house of Samuel Hill in the New Salem precinct in the County of Sangamon and State of Illinois on the fifth day of November in the year of our Lord one thousand eight hundred and thirty two the following named persons received the number of votes annexed to their respective names for the following described offices (to Wit)

Daniel Stookey had one hundred & eighty five votes for elector of President & Vice President

Abner Flack had one hundred & eighty five votes for elector of President & Vice President

James Evans had one hundred & eighty five votes for elector of President & Vice President

Adam Dunlap had one hundred & eighty five votes for elector of President & Vice President

John C Alexander had one hundred & eighty five votes for elector of President & Vice President

William B. Archer had Seventy votes for elector of President & Vice President

Leonard White had Seventy votes for elector of President & Vice President

James B. Moore had Seventy votes for elector of President & Vice President

Elijah Iles had Seventy votes for elector of President & Vice President

Pierre Menard had Seventy votes for elector of President & Vice President

A LINCOLN ⎱ Clerks of
WILLIAM GREEN ⎰ the election

JAMES RUTLEDGE ⎱
BOWLING GREEN ⎰ Judges of
HUGH ARMSTRONG ⎰ the election

[1] ADS, IHi. Tabulation of voters has not been reproduced here. The first group of electors were Jackson electors, the second group, Clay electors. The document is certified by Bowling Green, Justice of the Peace.

Bill for Surveying[1]

[1833?]

I herewith enclose my bill for surveying . . . this County
Sangamon. . . .

> To . . . . as Surveyor $12.00
> To making map   .50
>
> $12.50
>
> A. LINCOLN

[1] Sale catalog, Anderson Auction Company, April 16, 1914. This is the only
record of this document from which even a fragmentary text can be taken.

Statement of James Eastep's Account with Henry Onstot[1]

[1833]

James Eastep to Henry Onstot   Dr

To		
	Sack Salt	$4 90½
	tobacco paid Summers[2]	25
	articles paid E. Eastep	75
	articles paid self	1 50
		$7.40½

[1] AD-P, ISLA. Henry Onstot operated a cooper shop at New Salem.
[2] Levi Summers (?).

Mortgage Drawn for William Green, Jr. to Reuben Radford[1]

January 15, 1833

William Green, Jr. to Reuben Radford

Know all men by these presents that I William Green Jr. of the
County of Sangamon and State of Illinois, for and in consideration
of the sum of Two hundred dollars to me in hand paid the receipt
whereof I do hereby acknowledge have given granted, bargained
and sold and by these presents do give grant bargain and sell, all
my right title interest and estate in and to

The West half of lot number five, North of Main Street, in the
1st survey in the town of New Salem in the county and State afore-

[15]

said together with all and singular the appurtenances thereunto belonging or in anywise appertaining thereunto—Reuben Radford, his heirs, and assigns forever. In testimony whereof I have hereunto set my hand and seal this fifteenth day of January in the year of Our Lord, One Thousand Eight Hundred and Thirty Three.
Attest: A. LINCOLN   WILLIAM GREEN JR. (SEAL)

The condition of the above obligation is such, if the said William Green Jr. shall comply with the requisites of two promissory notes made and executed on this day for the sum of one hundred and eighty-eight dollars and fifty cents each payable to the said Reuben Radford the above Deed of bargain to be null and void and of no effect. But if the said William Green Jr. shall prove insolvent, and utterly unable to comply with the demands of said notes the above deed of bargain is to remain in full force and virtue at law.

In testimony whereof the said William Green Jr. and Reuben Radford have hereunto set their hands this 15th of January 1833.

WILLIAM GREEN JR.

REUBEN RADFORD

1 ADS, Sangamon County Recorder's office (Book F, p. 471). Lincoln's document is notarized under date of July 10, 1833, and recorded as of August 1, by Robert Conover, J.P. The document records the purchase of Radford's store by Green. Later on the same day, Lincoln and his new partner William F. Berry bought the same from Green for approximately $750, paying $265 cash, and assuming the payment of the two notes of $188.50 each given by Green to Radford. Berry gave Green a horse, saddle, and bridle for the remainder.

Bond of David Rutledge[1]

January 31, 1833

Know all men by these presents that we David Rutledge. William Green Jr. and A. Lincoln are held and firmly bound unto Alexander Trent— and Martin S. Trent in the penal sum of one hundred and fifty dollars well and truly to be paid unto them—as witness our hands and seals this 31st. of Jany. 1833—

DAVID RUTLEDGE (SEAL)
WILLIAM GREEN (SEAL)
A. LINCOLN (SEAL)

The condition of the above obligation is such If the above bounden David Rutledge shall make a good and lawful deed of conveyance to the said Alexander Trent and Martin S. Trent for the East half of Lot Number five South of Main street in the first survey in the town of New-Salem—on or before the first day of July next the above obligation is to be null void and of no effect—otherwise to remain in full force and virtue at law.

In testimony where of the said David Rutledge Alexander Trent and Martin S. Trent have here unto set their hands and seals this 31st. day of January. 1833   DAVID RUTLEDGE   (SEAL)

                                         M. S. TRENT   (SEAL)

                                         A. TRENT   (SEAL)

[1] ADS, ORB. The Trents, New Salem businessmen, sued Rutledge, Green, and Lincoln on this bond on August 26, 1833, to secure conveyance of the land described therein. The case was dismissed on September 16, each party paying one-half of the costs. David Rutledge was the son of James Rutledge, co-founder of New Salem.

Petition to the County Commissioners' Court
Concerning a Road
from Petersburg to Beardstown[1]

February 4, 1833

To the Honorable the County Commissioners Court of Sangamon County the undersigned Citizens of Petersburg and its Vicinity Respectfully Requests your Honors to grant a Review of a Road to commence at Petersburg and Run in a direction to beardstown to Morgan County Line and appoint th[r]ee suitable persons to Lay out and Mark said Road and your petitioners as in Duty bound will Ever Pray &c—

February 4 1833.

[1] DS, IHi. The petition was drawn by Bowling Green and carries fifty-eight signatures, including Lincoln's.

Petition to County Commissioners
Concerning Benjamin Elmore[1]

February 9, 1833

To the County Commissioners Court for the County of Sangamon when met at their March term for the year 1833

We the undersigned citizens of Sangamon County being personally acquainted with Benj. Elmore (who also is resident in said County—) and knowing him to be insane and wholly unable to earn a livelihood either by labour or any other employment—and

[17]

to have no relatives who can be lawfully made chargeable for his maintenance Therefore we respectfully request that his case be taken into considderation by your honorable body—

New Salem   Feb. 9, 1833

Bowling Green	James Clemment	Joseph Cogdall
Robert Cownover[2]	Henry Trent	Royal Clary
Levi Summers	David Hart	Jason Duncan
Julius Elmore	Jeremiah Graham	Robert Loyed
Hugh Armstrong	John Potter	James Rutledge
J R Herndon	William Cox	David Whray
P S Harvel	John C. Nance	A. Lincoln
Jacob Bale	Williamson Trent	M. S. Trent
Josiah Crawford	Henry Clark	Martin Waddel

[1] ADS, IHi. Not only the petition but all but six of the names are in Lincoln's hand.
[2] Probably Robert Conover, justice of the peace. Spellings of names are given as they appear in original document.

Deed Drawn for Jesse and Christiana Baker[1]

July 26, 1833

This Indenture made this twentysixth day of July in the year of our Lord one thousand eight hundred and thirtythree between Jesse Baker and Christiana his wife of the county of Sangamon and State of Illinois of the one part—and James Eastep of the county and State aforesaid—of the other part Witnesseth—That the said Jesse Baker and Christiana his wife for and in consideration of the sum of the sum of [*sic*] Five hundred dollars to them in hand pa[id] the receipt whereof is hereby acknowledged have given granted bargained and sold and by these presents do give grant bargain and sell all their right title interest and estate in and to the West half of the South east quarter of Section two Township Eighteen north of Range Seven West—containing Eighty acres—also the North East fourth of the South East quarter of Section two in Township Eighteen North of Range Seven West containing Forty acres, both in the district of lands offered for sale at Springfield Illinois—To have and to hold unto the said James Eastep his heirs and assigns for ever the above described tracts of land together with all and singular the previleges and appurtenances thereunto belonging[.] And the said Jesse Baker and Christiana his wife do covenant to and with the said James Eastep to Warrant and forever defend the title of said land against any and all claim or claims of any and all person or persons whomsoever—

In testimony whereof the said Jesse Baker and Christiana his

[18]

wife have here unto set their hands and seals the day and year above written.

B. GREEN ⎫   JESSE BAKER

HUGH ARMSTRONG ⎭   CHRISTINIA BAKER

[1] AD-P, ISLA. In Lincoln's hand excepting signatures. Verso of document contains Bowling Green's notarization dated July 27, 1833, and certificate of Edward Mitchell, Recorder of Sangamon County, dated September 9, 1833.

To Eli C. Blankenship[1]

E. C. Blankenship: New Salem, Aug. 10, 1833.

Dear Sir: In regard to the time David Rankin served the enclosed discharge shows correctly—as well as I can recollect—having no writing to refer. The transfer of Rankin from my company occurred as follows—Rankin having lost his horse at Dixon's ferry and having acquaintance in one of the foot companies who were going down the river was desirous to go with them, and one Galishen[2] being an acquaintance of mine and belonging to the company in which Rankin wished to go wished to leave it and join mine, this being the case it was agreed that they should exchange places and answer to each others names—as it was expected we all *would* be discharged in *very* few days. As to a blanket—I have no knowledge of Rankin ever getting any. The above embraces all the facts now in my recollection which are pertinent to the case.

I shall take pleasure in giving any further information in my power should you call on me. Your friend,   A. LINCOLN.

[1] Tarbell (Appendix), 265. Blankenship was a merchant in Springfield, Illinois.

[2] Probably a misreading for "Guliher." The muster roll of Lincoln's company shows that David Rankin transferred to the foot company of Captain Seth Pratt on May 19, and on this same day Isaac Guliher transferred to Lincoln's company from Pratt's company. The name appears as "Guliher" on the muster roll, but appears in other sources as "Gulihur," "Golliher," or "Gollihur."

Letter Written for James Eastep to Edward Mitchell[1]

Mr. Mitchell   September 28, 1833

I have resold the land to Jesse Baker for which a Deed was left in your office to be recorded.[2] If you have not recorded it—it is my request that you should not, but deliver it up to the bearer Jesse Baker.   Sept. 28—1833   JAMES EASTEP

[1] AD-P, ISLA.

[2] *Vide supra*, July 26, 1833. The deed was recorded on September 9, 1833.

Promissory Note to Reuben Radford[1]

October 19, 1833

One day after date we or either of us promise to pay Reuben Radford Three hundred and Seventy nine dollars and eighty two cents for value Received as witness our hands and seals this 19th day of October 1833

W F BERRY (SEAL)

A LINCOLN (SEAL)

WM GREEN (SEAL)

[1] Legal document owned by William H. Townsend, Lexington, Kentucky. The praecipe filed by Stuart and Dummer on April 7, 1834, in Peter Van Bergen *v.* Berry, Lincoln, and Green, contains a copy of the note. The original has not been identified. Radford having collected part of the note made a partial assignment to Van Bergen, who got judgment on November 19, 1834, in the amount of $154. Lincoln and Berry being unable to pay, the sheriff levied on their personal possessions, and Lincoln's horse, saddle, bridle, and surveying instruments were sold on execution. James Short bid them in and returned them to Lincoln.

Appraisal of New Salem Lots Owned by Henry Sinco[1]

October 25, 1833

Illinois Viz—We the Subscribers being Summoned & Sworn by D. Dickinson Deputy Sheriff of Sangamon County to Value Lot No. 5 North of Main Street, in first Survey and Lot No. one in Second Survey of the Town of Salem, Levied on as the property of Henry Sinco to satisfy an Execution in favour of Nelson Alley, do Value Lot No. 5 to $100—& Lot No. one to $50. Given under our hands and Seals this 25th. day of October 1833.

Test—

A. LINCOLN (SEAL)

H. ARMSTRONG (SEAL)

J. CLEMMENT (SEAL)

[1] DS-P, ISLA. The document was written by Dickinson and signed by the appraisers.

Certificate of Survey for Russell Godbey[1]

1834 }
Jany. 14 } Surveyed for Russel Godby[2]—the West half of the North East quarter of Section 30 in Township 19 North of Range 6 West. Begining at a White oak 12 inches in diameter bearing N 34 E 84 Links a White oak 10 inches S 58 W. 98 Links. Thence

Survey for Reason Shipley, January 6, 1834. John Calhoun was surveyor of Sangamon County; chainmen Richard Soward and Alexander Latimer were neighbors of Shipley.

Mrs. Herman G. Wilms

South 40 chains to a White oak 12 inches. N 73 E. 20 Links. Thence East 20 chains to a Black oak 12 inches S 54 W. 16 Links. Thence North 40 chains to a Post & mound. Thence West 20 chains to the begining

| Chainmen | J. Calhoun, s s c |
| Hercules Demming | BY A. LINCOLN |

[1] ADS, DLC-HW.
[2] A farmer living six miles north of New Salem.

Petition to County Commissioners[1]

February 25, 1834

To the county commissioners court for the county of Sangamon at its March term 1834—

We the undersigned respectfully request your honorable body to appoint viewers to view and locate a road from Musick's ferry on Salt creek via New Salem to the county line in the direction of Jacksonville

Feb. 25th. 1834

[1] ADS, IHi. This petition drawn by Lincoln contains eighty-eight names, including Lincoln's; the last twelve names are also in his handwriting.

Report of a Political Meeting[1]

March 1, 1834

PUBLIC MEETING.

At a respectable meeting of the citizens of New Salem, held pursuant to public notice, on Saturday, 1st March, 1834, for the purpose of nominating a suitable person to fill the office of Governor of this State: *Bowling Green,* Esq, was called to the chair, and *A. Lincoln* appointed Secretary. The object of the meeting being explained by the chair, Dr. John Allen and Messrs. Nelson Alley and Samuel Hill were appointed a committee, to draft a preamble and resolutions expressive of the sense of the meeting; who, after an absence of a few minutes, presented the following, which were unanimously adopted:—

Whereas the election of our executive officer is always interesting to the people, and should at all times demand their deliberate and serious consideration: and, whereas, the financial and infantile situation of this State is such as to demand more than ever the deliberate attention and united efforts of its inhabitants, for the election of a Chief Magistrate, who is free from and above party

[21]

and sectarian influence; who respects the rights of his fellow citizens, and who has wisdom to devise, and energy to execute such laws as are conducive to the political happiness of the people, and to the development of the great resources of our State: and, whereas, there is at this time no candidate for that high and responsible office before the people, to whom we can, or to whom, in our opinion, the people in this section of country will give a cordial and hearty support: and whereas we have the most implicit confidence in the honor, integrity and firmness of our fellow citizen, Gen. JAMES D. HENRY[2]—therefore

Resolved, That the patriotic services, discreet and unaspiring character of Gen. *James D. Henry,* are such as to merit the confidence of the people of this State; and to place his title to the gubernatorial chair paramount to that of any of the candidates now before the people.

Resolved, That we will use every laudable effort to promote the election of General *Henry* to the first office in the gift of the people of this State, at the next August election; and we recommend him to our fellow citizens, as a suitable person for the office, believing that by choosing him they will confer due honor on an individual, and advance the paramount welfare of the State.

Resolved, That the proceedings of this meeting be signed by the Chairman and Secretary, and forwarded to the editors of the Sangamo Journal for publication. And,

On motion, the meeting adjourned.

A. LINCOLN, Secretary.   BOWLING GREEN, Chairman.

---

[1] *Sangamo Journal,* March 15, 1834. Of the leading citizens of New Salem taking part in the meeting, Bowling Green was an influential Democrat and close friend of Lincoln's; Dr. John Allen, graduate of Dartmouth, was a leading physician and religious leader in the community; Nelson Alley operated a tavern; Samuel Hill was the principal merchant.

[2] Formerly sheriff of Sangamon County and Black Hawk War hero, General Henry died in New Orleans on March 5, following this meeting.

Survey for Jesse Gum[1]

1834 ⎫
March 3rd. ⎬ Surveyed for Jesse Gum the following tracts of land
—(viz) 1st. Composed of the North half of Section 32—and the South East quarter of Section 29—the East half and South West fourth of the North East quarter of Section 29 and the South West fourth of North West quarter of Section 28—in Township 18 North of Range 7 West. Begining at the South East corner of said tract at a rock. Thence North 80 chains to a rock. Thence East 20 chains to

a rock. Thence North 20 chains to a rock. Thence West 20 chains
to a rock. Thence North 20 chains to a rock. Thence West 20 chains
to a rock. Thence South 20 chains to a rock[.] Thence West 20
chains to a rock. Thence South 60 chains to a Sugar tree 16 inches
in diameter bearing N 62 E. 7 Links—another Sugar tree 10 inches
S 35 W. 38 Links. Thence West 40 chains to a Hickory 12 inches
S 61 W. 68 Links White Walnut 17 inches N 39 E. 45 Links. Thence
South 40 chains to an Elm 10 inches N 24 W. 32 Links—Black
Walnut 12 inches S 38 E. 48 Links. Thence East 80 chains to the
begining. 2nd. The East half of the South West quarter of Section
28 in the above Township—begining at the South East corner of
said quarter at a rock. Thence North 40 chains to a rock. Thence
West 20 chains to a rock. Thence South 40 chains to a rock[.] Thence
East 20 chains to the begining. 3rd. The South East fourth of the
North West quarter of Section 33 in the above Township. Begining
at the South East corner of of [sic] said quarter at a stake[.] Thence
North 20 chains to a stake. Thence West 20 chains to a stake.
Thence South 20 chains to a stake. Thence East 20 chains to the
begining[.] 4th. The West half of the South East quarter of Section
30 in the above Township. Begining at the South West corner of
said quarter at a Mulberry 4 inches S 47 E. 24 Links. Thence North
40 chains to an Overcup[2] 10 inches—S 42 E. 92 Links[.] Thence
East—20 chains to an Elm—20 inches. S 57 W. 90 Links. Thence
South 40 chains to a Black Oak 18 inches—N 39 E. 7 Links.
Thence West 20 chains to the begining.

Chainmen[3]—   J. Calhoun s. sc
Jeremiah Davis   BY A LINCOLN
Thomas Gum—

[1] ADS, owned by Harry E. Beekman, Petersburg, Illinois. Jesse Gum was a
farmer whose land, as surveyed by Lincoln, lay between Petersburg and Tal-
lula, now in Menard County.
[2] *Quercus lyrata*, a variety of oak.
[3] Thomas was Jesse Gum's son, and Jeremiah Davis was Jesse Gum's son-
in-law.

Election Return[1]

May 5, 1834

At an election held at the house of William F. Berry the New
Salem precinct in the county of Sangamon and State of Illinois on
the fifth day of May in the year of our Lord one thousand eight
hundred and thirty four the following named persons received the
number of votes annexed to their respective names for the following described office to wit

Garrett Elkin had eighty four votes for Sheriff
David Dickinson had seventy seven votes for Sheriff
Zechariah Peter had four votes for Sheriff

Certified by us

BOWLING GREEN ⎱
HUGH ARMSTRONG ⎰ Judges of
Attest   DAVID WHRAY   the election

A. Lincoln ⎱
Mentor Graham ⎰ Clerks of the election

I certify that Hugh Armstrong   David Whray   Mentor Graham and A. Lincoln were qualified by me according to law as Judges and Clerks of the election   BOWLING GREEN J. P.[2]

I certify that Bowling Green was qualified by me according to law as Judge of the election   MENTOR GRAHAM[3]

[1] ADS, IHi. Tabulations of voters and votes are omitted.
[2] Green's signature.
[3] Graham's signature.

To the County Commissioners' Court[1]

June [2], 1834

To the county commissioners court for the county of Sangamon at its June term 1834.

We the undersigned being appointed to view and locate a road. Begining at Musick's ferry on Salt Creek. (Via) New Salem to the county line in the direction to Jacksonville—respectfully report— that we have performed the duties of said view and location as required by law and that we have made the location on good ground and believe the establishment of the same to be necessary and proper.

The enclosed Map[2] gives the courses and distances as required by law[3]   MICHAEL KILLION

HUGH ARMSTRONG

A. LINCOLN

[1] ADS, DLC-RTL.
[2] See facsimile on facing page, which shows the portion of the road in the area near New Salem. Lincoln notes the "Whole length of the road" as being "26 miles & 70 chains."
[3] Endorsement in pencil on the report, not in Lincoln's hand:

A. Lincoln 5 dys at $3.00	$15.00
John A. Kelsoe chain bearer for 5 dys at 75 cts	$3.75
Robert Loyed " "	$3.75
Hugh Armstrong for services as axeman 5 dys at 75 cts.	3.75
A. Lincoln for making plat & report	$2.50

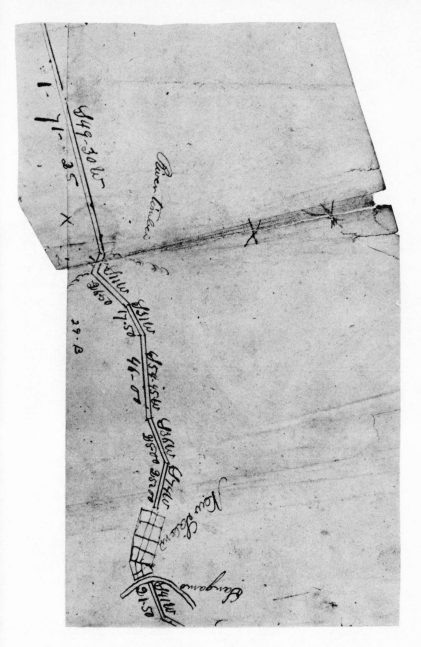

Portion of a Map of the Road from Musick's Ferry, June 2, 1834
Robert Todd Lincoln Collection, Library of Congress

Map of South Boundary Line of Section 24—Township 17, November 4, 1834
Illinois State Historical Library

Receipt to Charles R. Matheny[1]

June 3, 1834

Recd of C. R. Matheny Clerk $10.00 depositted by me at the last Term of com. court on application for a road

June 3rd 1834   A. LINCOLN

[1] DS, IHi. In Matheny's hand, signed by Lincoln.

To George C. Spears[1]

Mr. Spears   [July 1, 1834]

At your request I send you a receipt for the postage on your paper. I am some what surprised at your request. I will however comply with it. The law requires News paper postage to be paid in advance and now that I have waited a full year you choose to wound my feelings by insinuating that unless you get a receipt I will probably make you pay it again. Respectfully

A. LINCOLN

Received of George Spears in full for postage on the Sangamo Journal up to the first of July 1834.   A. LINCOLN, PM

[1] ALS, owned by J. Colby Beekman, Petersburg, Illinois, great-grandson of George C. Spears, one of the early settlers of Clary's Grove and an influential citizen of New Salem. Lincoln was appointed postmaster of New Salem on May 7, 1833, and held the appointment until its discontinuance on May 30, 1836.

Election Return[1]

October 27, 1834

At an election held at the house of William F Berry in the New Salem precinct in the county of Sangamon and state of Illinois on the twenty seventh day of October in the year of our Lord one thousand eight hundred and thirty four the following named persons received the number of votes annexed to their respective names for the following described office (to wit)

William L. May had Seventy two votes for Representative to congress

James Turney had one vote for Representative to congress

Benjamin Mills had three votes for Representative to congress

certified by us

Attest   } clerks of   JAMES PANTIER   } Judges of
A. LINCOLN   } the election   POLLARD SIMMONS   } the election
MENTOR GRAHAM   }   WILLIAM JONES   }

[25]

I certify that the Judges and Clerks of this Election was Sworn according to Law

New Salem, October 27, 1834 BOWLING GREEN J.P.
and John Clary
Served as Constable

[1] ADS, IHi. In Lincoln's hand except for other signatures and the notarization by Bowling Green. Tabulation of voters and votes has been omitted.

To the County Commissioners' Court[1]

November 4, 1834

To the county commissioner's court for the county of Sangamon—

We the undersigned being appointed to view and relocate a part of the road between Sangamontown and the town of Athens—respectfully report that we have performed the duty of said appointment according to law—and that we have made the said relocation on good ground—and believe the same to be necessary and proper.

Athens Nov. 4. 1834. JAMES STRAWBRIDGE—
LEVI CANTRALL—
A. LINCOLN—

Herewith is the map.[2] The court may allow me the following charges if they think proper—

1 day's labour as surveyor—	$3.00
Making map—	50
	$3.50.

A. LINCOLN

[1] ADS, IHi.
[2] See facsimile of map facing page 25.

Notice to Illinois Legislature of a Bill to Limit Jurisdiction of Justices of Peace[1]

Mr. Speaker. [December 5, 1834]

I now give notice that on monday next or some day thereafter I shall ask leave to introduce a bill entitled an act to limit the jurisdiction of Justices of the Peace.[2]

[1] AD, I-Ar.
[2] *Infra*, December 9, 1834.

Portion of a Bill Introduced in Illinois
Legislature Concerning Estrays[1]

December 6, 1834

. . . . And every person taking up an estray horse, mare or colt, shall within two months after the same is appraised provided the owner shall not have claimed his property during that time deposit with clerk of County Comr. court who shall transmit to the nearest editor of a public newspaper a particular description of such estray or estrays, and the valuation thereof, together with the name of the county and place of residence, certified by the clerk of the county commissioners court, or justice of the peace before whom such estray or estrays was appraised, to be advertised three weeks in said newspaper.[2]

SEC 3 And if no owner appears and proves his property within two years, after such publication, the property shall be vested in the taker up; nevertheless the former owner may at any time thereafter, by proveing his property, recover the valuation money.

SEC 4 And if any person shall trade, sell, or take away any such estray or estrays out of the state, for any purpose whatever, before the expiration of said two years, he or she so offending, shall forfeit and pay the sum of, one hundred and fifty dollars to be recovered by any person suing for the same in any court of record within this state having[3] cognizance thereof—the one Half to the informer and the other half to the County Treasury: and where the owner of any Estray head of neat cattle sheep hog or goat does not prove his property within twelve months after the same has been published at the door of the Court house as aforesaid, and where the valuation does not exceed Five Dollars, the property shall be vested in the taker-up but when the valuation shall exceed Five Dollars, and no owner appears within the time aforesaid, the property shall also be vested in the taker up. Nevertheless the former owner may at any time by proving his property recover the valuation thereof.[4] And it shall not be lawful for any person to take up any estray (except such as shall be herein after excepted) unless he shall be a free holder or a housekeeper. Any person finding an estray horse, mare, or colt runing at large without any of the settlements of this state may take up the same, and shall immediately take such estray or estrays before the nearest justice of the peace and make oath that he has not altered the marks or brands of such estray or estrays, since taking up; and if such taker up shall be a free holder or housekeeper, within that county it may and shall be lawful for him to post such estray or estrays as herein before directed in this act; as if the same had been taken up on his plantation or place of residence. And when the taker up shall not be qualified as aforesaid he. . . .[5]

[1] AD, I-Ar. This was probably Lincoln's first chore at lawmaking. John T. Stuart introduced the bill on December 6, 1834. The first one and one-half pages of the manuscript appear to be in Stuart's hand. Then come the portions which are in Lincoln's hand, except for an occasional insertion by Stuart, as given here. A third amanuensis carries on for the remainder of the manuscript, which is incomplete. The entire law as finally approved may be found in *Laws of Illinois*, 1835, pp. 229-35.
[2] This paragraph is crossed out.
[3] The rest of this sentence and the next are not in Lincoln's hand.
[4] Lincoln's hand begins again at this point.
[5] Remainder is not in Lincoln's hand.

Bill Introduced in Illinois Legislature
to Limit Jurisdiction of Justices of Peace[1]

[December 9, 1834]

An act to limit the jurisdiction of Justices of the Peace.

Be it enacted by the people of the State of Illinois represented in the General Assembly—That hereafter Justices of the Peace shall not e[n]tertain jurisdiction of any civil case whatever—unless it be in the precinct in which the defende[nt] resides or [*sic*]—or in which the contract on which suit is brought was made and entered into, or made payable—any thing in former laws to the contrary notwithstanding.

This act to be in force from and after the first day of June next.

[1] AD, I-Ar. This was Lincoln's first bill. Much revised and amended in committee, it passed the House, but was tabled by the Senate.

Notice to Illinois Legislature
of a Bill to Authorize Samuel Musick
to Build a Toll Bridge[1]

Mr. Speaker   [December 9, 1834]

I now give notice that Thursday next,[2] or some day thereafter I shall ask leave to introduce a bill entitled an act to authorize Samuel Musick[3] to build a toll bridge across Salt creek in Sangamon county.

[1] AD, I-Ar.
[2] Lincoln introduced the bill on December 15. *Vide infra*.
[3] Musick operated a ferry on Salt Creek northeast of New Salem, Illinois.

Amendment to House Rules[1]

[December 11, 1834]

47. It shall not be in order, to offer amendments to any bill after[2] its third reading

[1] AD, I-Ar. Lincoln's amendment was voted down.
[2] Lincoln had written "upon"; this was deleted and "after" substituted in another hand.

Bill Introduced in Illinois Legislature
to Authorize Samuel Musick to Build a Toll Bridge[1]

[December 15, 1834]

An act to authorize Samuel Musick to build a toll bridge across Salt Creek in Sangamon county—

SEC 1. Be it enacted by the people of the State of Illinois represented in the General Assembly. That Samuel Musick his heirs and assigns be and they are hereby authorized to erect a toll bridge across Salt creek in Sangamon county at or near the place where the said Musick is now authorized to keep a ferry. At either end of said bridge the said Musick, his heirs and assigns, are hereby authorized to place a toll gate, where he or they may ask and demand of all and every person passing, the rates of toll which may from time to time be fixed by the county commissioners court of the county of Sangamon.

SEC 2. The said Samuel Musick his heirs and assigns, shall commence the building of said bridge within nine months and have it so far completed within eighteen months from and after the passage of this act as to admit the safe passing of persons, waggons, teams, cattle &c. over it.

SEC 3. The said Samuel Musick his heirs and assigns, shall at all times after the completion thereof, keep said bridge in good repair, and allow a speedy passage to all persons and their property over it, upon the receipt of the toll, in such cases allowed as herein before provided—and if at any time the said bridge be left out of repair, so that the same be impassable, for the space of twelve months at any one time, the said bridge shall accrue and belong to the county of Sangamon: Provided however, That the destruction of said bridge by fire, high water or other casualty, shall not work a forfeiture of the previlege hereby granted, but the said Samuel Musick heirs or assigns shall proceed immediately to repair the same.

SEC 4. No person shall within ten years hereafter build a bridge, or establish a ferry accross said creek within the distance of one mile above or below the said bridge—provided the said Samuel Musick his heirs or assigns shall erect and keep up said bridge for that space of time as by this act authorized.

SEC 5. Whenever the county commissioners of the said county of Sangamon shall deem it expedient to purchase said bridge, they shall have the right so to do by paying the said Samuel Musick his heirs or assigns the original cost of said bridge. And for the purpose of enabling the county commissioners to make said purchase, it shall be the duty of said Samuel Musick his heirs or assigns, to file with the clerk of the county commissioners court of said county such vouchers as shall be deemed sufficient by the commissioners to ascertain the cost of said bridge.

SEC 6. If the said Samuel Musick his heirs or assigns shall at any time obstruct the ford in said creek at or near the said bridge, in any manner—he or they so offending—shall forfeit and pay the sum of one hundred dollars, for every such offence to be recovered by action of debt in any court having competent jurisdiction thereof, one half of which shall go to the use of the person informing and the other to the use of the county.[2]

SEC 7th. That the county commissioners of said county have full power to levy a tax on said bridge, as is provided in an act to provide for the establishment of ferries, toll bridges, and turn pike roads: approved February 12th. 1827.

[1] AD, I-Ar. Introduced on December 15, the bill was passed on December 26, and appears in *Laws of the State of Illinois*, 1835, pp. 84-85.

[2] The original bill contains only the first six sections. The seventh appears in the official engrossed copy, as added later by Lincoln's own hand.

Report of Committee
on Public Accounts and Expenditures Concerning Relief of Purchasers of Vandalia Lots[1]

Mr. Speaker   [December 16, 1834]

The committee on public accounts and expenditures, to whom was refered the resolution, requiring said committee to inquire into the expediency of granting further relief to certain purchasers of Vandalia lots,[2] have directed me to report, that they have had said resolution under consideration and that they are of opinion no further relief ought to be extended to said purchasers—and that they ask to be discharged from the further consideration of said resolution.

1 AD, I-Ar. Lincoln wrote the report, but it was delivered to the House by another member of the committee, John D. Hughes, representative from St. Clair County.

2 The resolution asked relief for those "who have relinquished their lots and paid one tenth of the purchase money; so as to provide for refunding to purchasers the several amounts by them so paid. . . ." (*House Journal*, Ninth General Assembly, First Session, p. 107).

Report of Committee
on Public Accounts and Expenditures
Concerning the Contingent Fund[1]

Mr Speaker   [December 16, 1834]

The committee on public accounts and expenditures to which was refered the report of the Auditor of public accounts relative to the contingent fund have had the same under consideration, and have directed me to report—That in their opinion, the principal part of said fund has not been misapplied. The committee however, are of opinion that some charges which have been allowed are exorbitant—and have resulted in a useless expenditure of the public money. The committee ask to be discharged from the further consideration of this subject.

1 AD, I-Ar. The report was written by Lincoln but delivered to the House by John D. Hughes.

Speech in Illinois Legislature Concerning
the Surveyor of Schuyler County[1]

January 6, 1835

Mr. Lincoln said, That if, as appeared to be the opinion of legal gentlemen, there was no danger of the new surveyor's ousting the old one so long as he persisted not to die—he would suggest the propriety of letting matters remain as they were, so that if the old surveyor should hereafter conclude to die, there would be a new one ready made without troubling the legislature.

1 *Sangamo Journal*, January 17, 1835. The occasion for Lincoln's humorous remarks was the resolution proposed by Jacob Vandeventer of Schuyler County, as follows: "That the nomination of Samuel McHatton, for County Surveyor of Schuyler county . . . be vacated for the reason that said office was not vacant at the time said nomination was made" (*House Journal*, Ninth General Assembly, First Session, p. 233). The resolution was tabled, in effect following Lincoln's suggestion.

Resolution Introduced in Illinois Legislature
Concerning Revenue from the Sale of Public Lands[1]

January 10, 1835

Resolved by the General Assembly of the State of Illinois, That our Senators be instructed, and our Representatives requested to use their whole influence in the Congress, of the United States, to procure the passage of any law relative to the public lands, by the operation of which, the State of Illinois, would be entitled to receive annually, a sum of money not less in amount than 20 per cent upon the amount annually paid into the Treasury of the United States, for public lands lying within the limits of the said State of Illinois.

Resolved, That the Governor of this State be requested to forthwith transmit a copy of these resolutions to each of our Senators and Representatives in Congress.

[1] *House Journal,* Ninth General Assembly, First Session, p. 269. The resolution was tabled.

An Act of the Illinois Legislature
to Lay Out a State Road from the Wabash to the Yellow Banks of the Mississippi River[1]

[January 12, 1835]

SEC 1   Be it enacted by the People of the State of Illinois represented in the General Assembly. That [Parnick Owens of Knox Co. Samuel Allen of Peoria Co. and Robert Bird of Putnam County] be and they are hereby appointed commissioners to view, mark and locate a road from a point on the eastern bound'ry line of this State —where a line runing due West from Logansport in the State of Indiana would cross said State line. Thence Westward the nearest and best rout to Allenton at the head of Lake Peoria on the Illinois river. Thence to the seat of justice of Knox county. Thence to the seat of justice of Warren county. Thence to the Lower Yellow Banks on the Mississippi river.

SEC 2nd.   The said commissioners or a majority of them shall meet at [Knoxville] on or before the [first] day of [June] next and after being duly sworn by some Justice of the Peace—faithfully to view and locate said road without partiality favour or affection, shall immediately thereafter proceed to discharge the duties required of them by this act, placing in the prairy, through which the same shall pass stakes of a reasonable size of durable timber

[32]

Sec 3. As soon as practicable, after said road is located, said commissioners or a majority of them shall make out a report accompanied by a map or plat of said road denoting the courses and distances from point to point—with such other remarks as they or a majority of them may deem necessary and proper; and transmit the same to the Secretary of state. And they or a majority of them shall make a map or plat of so much of said road as lies within the respective counties, and transmit it to the clerk of the county commissioners court of the respective counties through which the same may pass which shall be filed and preserved in the office of said court.

Sec 4. When said road shall be located it shall be to all intents and purposes a state road, four poles wide, and shall be opened and kept in repair as other roads are in this state.

Sec 5. The county commissioners court of each county through which the said road may pass are hereby authorized [if they shall think proper] [2] to allow to said commissioners one dollar and fifty cents per day for the time necessarily employed in locating the said road in each of their respective counties: Provided that nothing herein contained shall be so construed as to create any liability on the part of this state to pay said commissioners for their services, rendered under the authority of this act.

This act to be in force from and after its passage.

[1] AD, I-Ar. The original bill is in Lincoln's handwriting except for bracketed passages. It was introduced by John T. Stuart from the committee on petitions to which had been referred the petition of sundry citizens of Peoria and Putnam counties, praying the establishment of a state road therein named. Introduced on January 12, the bill was passed on January 16. It appears in *Laws of Illinois*, 1835, pp. 112-13, with but minor changes, chiefly in punctuation.

[2] This wording was substituted for Lincoln's "and required."

Amendment to a Bill Concerning Marks and Brands[1]

[January 17, 1835]

Strike out all of the first section after the enacting clause.

Prefix the word "that" to the second section

Annex to the third Section the following (viz) That each certificate so made out shall be filed with the clerk of the county commissioners' court within ten days after obtaining the same

[1] AD, I-Ar. Lincoln's amendment, along with sundry others reported on January 17 by the select committee of which Lincoln was a member, came to naught. The bill was rejected in favor of a brief substitute reviving an earlier act of March 23, 1829, which was approved February 6, 1835 (*Laws of the State of Illinois*, 1835, p. 51).

[33]

Speech in Illinois Legislature
Concerning Apportionment of Representation in the State[1]

January 21, 1835

Mr. LINCOLN said, the reasons offered by the gentleman from Madison would certainly induce him to go against the resolution. The gentleman had said that there would be a difficulty in fixing the Senatorial districts; and, sir, in my humble opinion, there would be an insurmountable difficulty. The districts cannot be arranged, and with a full knowledge of this fact, I have no doubt the House will lay the resolution on the table until the 4th day of July—at least I will vote in that way.

[1] *Illinois Advocate and State Register*, January 28, 1835. Jesse B. Thomas, Jr., of Madison County, offered a preamble and resolution requiring the appointment of a joint select committee to report a bill fixing the ratio of apportionment of representation adapted to a census to be taken in 1835. Jacob Vandeventer of Schuyler County moved to lay the preamble and resolution on the table until July 4—the habitual motion when the matter was to be disposed of with finality—which was carried.

An Act of the Illinois Legislature
to Locate a State Road Therein Named, and for Other Purposes[1]

[January 22, 1835]

SEC 1st   Be it enacted by the People of the State of Illinois represented in the General Assembly. That so much of the State road, leading from Jacksonville in Morgan county to Quincy in Adams county established by an act entitled "An act to locate a state road from Jacksonville in Morgan county to Quincy in Adams county, and for other purposes, approved February 25—1833—as lies between[2] Illinois river and the Western boundry line of Schuyler county be and the same is hereby vacated.

SEC 2nd   Be it further enacted That John Taylor Senr. Benjamin Kindrick[3] and Harvey Luster of the county of Schuyler, be and they are hereby appointed commissioners to view, mark and locate a state road from a point on the West bank of Illinois river opposite Meredocia [sic]. Thence the nearest and best route through Mount Sterling to the Western boundry line of Schuyler county in the direction of Quincy, doing as little injury to private property as the public conveniance will permit.

[34]

Sec. 3rd. Said commissioners or a majority of them shall meet at Mount Sterling on the first Monday in May next, or within one month thereafter; and after being duly sworn by some Justice of the peace, faithfully to perform the duties required of them by this act, shall proceed to locate said road accordingly. Said road shall be marked in the prairy by suitable stakes well set in the earth, and in the timbered land by hacks, and blazes upon the trees—they shall make a return of the location thereof to the county commissioners court of Schuyler county, particularly noting all the principal places upon and near said road. Said commissioners shall receive for their services one dollar and fifty cents each per day for all the time necessarily employed in said work to gether with a reasonable compensation for one hand as a marker, which sum shall be paid by the county of Schuyler. Said road shall in all respects be deemed a public highway and shall be opened and kept in repair as other state roads are.

[1] AD, I-Ar. The original bill is in Lincoln's hand, but it was introduced by Jacob Vandeventer, representative from Schuyler County, on January 22. As passed and amended, it appears in *Laws of the State of Illinois*, 1835, pp. 103-104.

[2] As amended at this point, the act finally read "between Meridocia and John Wigle's in Adams county. . . ." (*Laws*, p. 103).

[3] Benjamin Kendrick.

Notice to Illinois Legislature of a Bill
Relative to a State Road Therein Named[1]

Mr. Speaker   [January 27, 1835]

I now give notice that on Thursday next I shall ask leave to introduce a bill for an act relative to a state road therein named

[1] AD, I-Ar. This notice refers to the bill introduced by John Dawson of Sangamon County on January 29, *infra*.

Bill Introduced in Illinois Legislature
Relative to a State Road Therein Named[1]

[January 29, 1835]

Sec 1 Be it enacted by the people of the state of Illinois represented in the General Assembly. That Reuben Harrison,[2] John Clary and Tandy James be and they are hereby appointed commissioners to view, mark and permanently locate so much of the state road, leading from Springfield in Sangamon county to Lewiston in Fulton county, as lies between Springfield and George G. Miller's ferry on the Sangamo river.

SEC 2. Said commissioners or a majority of them shall meet at the town of Springfield on the second Monday in March next or as soon thereafter as practicable and after being duly sworn by some officer authorized to administer oaths, shall proceed to perform the duties required of them by this act; avoiding as much as possible the injury of private property.

SEC 3 The said commissioners shall as soon thereafter as convenient, cause to be filed with the clerk of the county commissioner's court of the county of Sangamon a report and complete map of said road—which report and map shall be preserved and shall form a part of the record of said court. Said road when so established shall be kept in repair as other state roads are.

SEC 4 The county commissioners court of Sangamon county shall allow to said commissioners, out of the county treasury; such compensation, as, to them shall seem just and reasonable.

[1] AD, I-Ar. The bill was passed on February 2 as written and appears in *Laws of the State of Illinois,* 1835, p. 103. A copy made by Lincoln and forwarded to the Sangamon County Commissioners Court is also extant (IHi).

[2] Of these three friends of Lincoln's—all from New Salem vicinity—Reuben Harrison was the surveyor of New Salem and John Clary was the founder of nearby Clary's Grove. They were sworn in as commissioners on March 16.

Certificate of Survey for William McNeely[1]

1835 ⎱
March 10 ⎰ Surveyed for William McNeely a part of the of the [*sic*] South West fractional quarter of Section 30 in Township 18 North of Range 7 West. Begining at the middle of Gum's branch where the Eastern boundry line of said fraction crosses the same at an Ash 7 inches in diameter bearing N 28 W 48 links. Thence North 18 chains to the North East corner of said fraction at an Overcup 10 inches S 42 E 92 links. Thence West 8 chains & 95 links to a White Oak 10 inches S 36 E 43 links. Thence South 17 chains & 57 links to the middle of the aforesaid branch at a Hackberry 7 inches N 28 W 48 links. Thence up the branch with it's meanderings to the begining.

Also, the West half of the South West quarter of Section 21 in the afforesaid Township. Begining at the South West corner of the same at a Post & Mound. Thence East 20 chains to a Post & Mound. Thence North 40 chains to a Post & Mound. Thence West 20 chains to a Post & Mound. Thence South 40 chains to the begining.   John Calhoun s.s.c.

BY A. LINCOLN

[1] ADS, RPB. McNeely lived near New Salem, the two pieces of land described in the certificate being respectively about four and one-half miles west and one and one-half miles northeast of New Salem.

Certificate of Survey for Archibald Kincaid[1]

1835 }
March 24 } Surveyed for Archibald Kincaid the North West forth of the North East quarter of Section 33 in Township 18 North of Range 6 West. Begining at the North West corner of the same at a White Oak 12 inches in diameter bearing N 85 E 17 Links. White Oak 13 inches S 66 W 58 Links. Thence S 88 E 20 chains & 21 Links to a White Oak 9 inches S 25 W 27 Links. Thence South 20 chains to a White Oak 24 inches East side corner. Thence N 88 W 20 chains & 21 Links to a Spanish Oak 20 inches—corner. Thence North 20 chains to the begining.   J. Calhoun ssc

BY A. LINCOLN

[1] ADS-P, ISLA. Kincaid's land lay about three miles northwest of Athens, Illinois.

Certificate of Survey for John K. Kincaid[1]

1835 }
March 24 } Surveyed for John K. Kincaid, the following tracts of land 1st. The South East fourth of the South West quarter of Section 28. 2nd. A part of the East half of the South East quarter of Section 23—both in Township 18 North of Range 6 West. 1st. Begining at the South East corner of the same at a White Oak 12 inches in diameter bearing N 85 E. 17 Links White Oak 13 inches. S 66 W. 58 Links. Thence N 89 W 20 chains to a Burr Oak 11 inches N 59 W. 19 Links[.] Thence North 20 chains to a White Oak 12 inches S 27 W 55 Links. Thence S 89 E 20 chains to a White Oak 22 inches S 4 W. 51 Links. Thence South 20 chains to the begining.

2nd. Begining at the North East corner of the same at a White Oak 14 inches S 16 W. 78 Links White Oak 10 inches N 1 E. 66 Links. Thence N 88 W. 10 chains & 17 Links to a White Oak 24 inches S 76 E. 91 Links. Thence South 29 chains & 49 Links to a Lynn 14 inches S 51 E. 46 Links[.] Thence S 88 E. 10 chains & 17 Links to a Black Walnut 16 inches N 88 W. 32 Links. Thence North 29 chains & 49 Links to the begining.   J. Calhoun s.s.c.

BY—A. LINCOLN

[1] ADS, owned by J. Kennedy Kincaid, Athens, Illinois. John K. Kincaid was a brother of Archibald whose land was located in the same general vicinity.

To Francis P. Blair, Sr. and John C. Rives[1]

Messrs   New Salem Ills   Nov. 3. 1835.

Your subscriber at this place *John C Vance*,[2] is dead; and no person takes the paper from the office   Respectfully,

Blair & Rives.   A. LINCOLN P.M.

[1] ALS, ORB. Blair & Rives were publishers of the Washington, D. C. *Congressional Globe*.

[2] John C. Vance, a farmer living north of New Salem, Illinois, whose copy of Kirkham's *Grammar* Lincoln is purported to have studied.

To Joseph Duncan[1]

His Excellency Governer Duncan   New Salem.

Dear Sir   Nov. 10th. 1835

Understanding that Mr. Levi Davis[2] of Vandalia, is an applicant for the office of Auditor of Public Accounts, I take the liberty to say to you, that his appointment to that office would be entirely satisfactory to me, and, I doubt not, to most others who are the friends of quailification [*sic*] and—merit—   Your Obt. Servt.

A. LINCOLN

[1] ALS, ORB.

[2] Davis was appointed November 16.

To Thomas J. Nance[1]

Dear Sir   Vandalia. Decr. 10. 1835

In regard to the South half of Sec. 36. in Town 7 North Range 1 West the following is the only information that can be collected at the Auditors office. The S.W. quarter of said section was sold in 1823 to Daniel Hough for the tax of 1821 & 2. Half of the other quarter was sold in 1827 to Jesse Bartlett for the tax of 1826. The other 80 acres have not been sold for taxes. The residence of neither of the purchasers is known at the office.

There is but little of interest doing in the Legislature as yet: owing mostly to the census returns from several counties not having been made.   Respectfully   A. LINCOLN

[1] ALS, owned by Mrs. Fern Nance Pond. Nance was a prominent Democrat living near New Salem.

Notice to Illinois Legislature
of a Bill Supplemental to an Act Entitled
"An Act for the Relief of Insolvent Debtors . . ."[1]

Mr. Speaker   [December 10, 1835]

I now give notice that on saturday next[2] I shall ask leave to introduce a bill, for an act suplemental to an act entitled an act for the relief of insolvent debtors approved January 12th. 1829

[1] AD, I-Ar.
[2] Lincoln introduced the bill on schedule, Saturday, December 12 (*vide infra*).

Bill Introduced in Illinois Legislature
to Relocate Part of
State Road Leading from Crow's in Morgan County
to Musick's Bridge in Sangamon County[1]

[December 11, 1835]

A bill for "an act to relocate a part of the State road leading from Crow's,[2] in Morgan county to Musick's bridge in Sangamon county."

SEC 1   Be it enacted by the people of the State of Illinois represented in the General Assembly: That James Goldsby, David Batterton, and Charles Broadwell be, and they are hereby appointed commissioners to view mark, and locate so much of the state road leading from Crow's in Morgan county to Musick's bridge in Sangamon county, as lies between the head of Richland creek, and the Sangamo river.

SEC 2.   The said commissioners, or a majority of them, shall meet at the house of Peter Cartwright,[3] on the first monday in March next, or as soon there after as practicable, and after being duly sworn, shall proceed to perform the duties required of them by this act, avoiding as much as possible the injury of private property

SEC 3.   The said commissioners shall, as soon as convenient cause to be filed with the clerk of the county commissioner's court of Sangamon county a report & complete map of said road, which report and map shall be preserved, and shall form a part of the record of said court. Said road, when so established, shall be kept in repair as other State roads are

SEC 4.   The county commissioners court of Sangamon county,

shall allow to said commissioners, out of the county Treasury, such compensation as to them shall seem just and reasonable

[1] AD, I-Ar. Introduced by Lincoln on December 11, the bill was passed on December 15 and appears in *Laws of Illinois*, 1836, pp. 193-94.
[2] William Crow's place.
[3] Peter Cartwright was the well-known Methodist preacher whose political ambitions were later to bring him into rivalry with Lincoln.

Resolution Introduced in Illinois Legislature
Concerning the Incorporation of a Canal Company[1]

December 11, 1835

Resolved, That a select committee of five be appointed to inquire into the expediency of incorporating a company to construct a canal upon the valley of the Sangamon river, and that they report by bill or otherwise.

[1] *House Journal,* Ninth General Assembly, Second Session, p. 34. The resolution was adopted, and Lincoln was made a member of the select committee. On December 12, he reported a bill, not his own, to incorporate the Beardstown and Sangamon Canal Company (*vide infra,* Lincoln's amendment, December 12, 1835).

Amendment to an Act to Incorporate the
Beardstown and Sangamon Canal Company[1]

[December 12, 1835]

Sec 13. The State, or the counties through which the said canal shall pass, shall, at any time, after ten years shall have elapsed, from the completion of said canal, have the previlege of purchasing the same, by paying said company the original cost, together with any deficiency which may have accrued by a failure of said canal to produce twelve per cent per annum from the time of it's completion, upon the original cost

[1] AD, I-Ar. Although Lincoln reported the bill from the select committee, which had been appointed to inquire into the expediency of constructing a canal in the valley of Sangamon River, there is no evidence that he composed any part of it except this amended section 13. Presumably Lincoln's amendment was adopted in the committee, for he did not present it from the floor of the House. The original section 13, for which the amendment was substituted, read as follows: "The stock of said company shall be personal property, and shall be liable to be sold on execution,—said stock shall also be transferable & assignable in such manner as the Directors of said company shall prescribe." Although the bill became law, the canal never materialized (see *Laws of Illinois*, 1836, pp. 97-101).

[40]

Bill Introduced in Illinois Legislature
to Supplement "An Act for the Relief of
Insolvent Debtors . . ."[1]

[December 12, 1835]

A bill for an act suplemental to an act entitled an act for the relief of insolvent debtors approved January 12th. 1829

SEC. 1 Be it enacted by the people of the State of Illinois, represented in the General Assembly: That during the absence of the Judge of Probate from the county: and during the vacancy of the office of Judge of Probate, by death, resignation, or otherwise, in any county or counties of this State it shall be the duty of any Justice of the Peace of such county or counties, on application made to him, to perform all duties required of the Judges of Probate, by the act to which this is suplemental

SEC. 2 It shall be the duty of any sheriff or other officer having the custody of any person, to convey such person before some Justice of the Peace of the proper county, upon application made for that purpose: provided such person would have the right under the third section of the act to which this is suplemental, to demand his conveyance before the Judge of Probate

[1] AD, I-Ar. The bill passed without amendment on December 22, but died in the Senate judiciary committee.

Bill Introduced in Illinois Legislature
Concerning the County of Schuyler[1]

[December 15, 1835]

A bill for an Act concerning Schuyler County

SEC 1 Be it enacted by the people of the State of Illinois represented in the General Assembly: That the county commissioner's court, for the county of Schuyler, shall order the Judges of elections for the several precincts in said county, at the election to be holden on the first monday in August in the year one thousand eight hundred and thirty six, to open two columns, in their respective poll books, in addition to those necessary for the election of public officers: one of which columns shall be headed "Division" and the other "No division"

SEC 2 The qualified voters of said county, who may be in favour of a division of said county shall vote upon the column headed "Division" and all those opposed to such division, shall vote upon the column headed "No division"

[41]

SEC 3. The clerk of the county commissioner's court of the said county of Schuyler shall, on receiving full returns of the elections of said county, proceed to count the votes given upon the said additional columns, and if the number in favour of a division shall exceed the number against it, the said clerk shall certify and transmit an account of the same to the Secretary of State, whose duty it shall be to lay the same before this General Assembly at it's next session.

SEC 4 If the voters of said county shall vote the division contemplated by this act, the line of division shall be as follows (viz) Begining at the mouth of Crooked creek on the Illinois River. Thence up said creek with it's meanderings to the Northern boundry line of Township No. one North. Thence West with said line, to the line dividing Ranges Three and Four West. Thence North with said line to the Northern boundry line of Township No. Two North. Thence West with said line to the corner of Hancock and Adams counties: All that portion of the said county of Schuyler lying South and West of said division line, shall thence forward constitute and form a new county. Provided that said new county shall remain attached to the county of Schuyler for all county purposes until it's organization be provided for by law.

[1] AD, I-Ar. The bill was written by Lincoln for his colleague from Schuyler County, Jacob Vandeventer, who introduced the bill on December 15. Although it passed the House, the bill was tabled by the Senate.

Bill Introduced in Illinois Legislature
to Relocate a Part of a State Road Leading
from Springfield to Lewiston[1]

[December 15, 1835]

A bill for an Act to relocate a part of the State road leading from Springfield to Lewiston.

Be it enacted by the people of Illinois represented in the General Assembly, that so much of the State road leading from Springfield to Lewiston as lies between the Northern boundry of Township No. Eighteen North and the residence of John Jones, shall be so changed as to run due North from the point where said road now cross the afforesaid Township line, through the centre of the South West quarter of Section thirty four, Township Nineteen North Range Seven West, to the Northern boundry of said quarter: thence with the road as now traveled to the residence of the said John Jones.

[1] AD, I-Ar. The bill passed both houses and may be found in *Laws of Illinois*, 1836, p. 199. (See the bill of similar title, February 10, 1837, *infra*.)

Amendment Introduced in Illinois Legislature
to Section Eight of the Illinois and Michigan Canal Bill[1]

December 21, 1835

The Governor, during the recess of the General Assembly, for any good cause, shall have power to remove any or all of the said commissioners from office, and to supply vacancies occasioned by such removals, which appointments shall continue until other appointments are made by the General Assembly.

[1] *House Journal,* Ninth General Assembly, Second Session, p. 119. Section eight of the bill concerned the election of the canal commissioners. Lincoln's amendment failed.

Amendment to an Act
to Incorporate the Subscribers to the
Bank of the State of Illinois[1]

[December 22, 1835]

SEC 5 The said corporation shall, at the next session of this General Assembly, and at each subsequent general session, during the existence of it's charter, report to the same, the amount of debts due *from* said corporation, the amount of debts due *to* the same, the amount of specie in it's vaults, and and [*sic*] an account of all lands then owned by the same, and the amount for which such lands have been taken: and moreover, if said corporation shall, at any time neglect or refuse, to submit it's books, papers, and all and every thing necessary to a full and fair examination of it's affairs, to any person or persons appointed by the General Assembly for the purpose of making such examination, the said corporation shall forfeit it's charter.

[1] AD, I-Ar. The amendment was not adopted.

Amendment to Bill
Introduced in Illinois Legislature to Incorporate
the Sangamon Fire Insurance Company[1]

[December 22(?) 1835]

Amend by inserting these names

John Taylor.	Samuel Morris	Saml. H. Treat
John Williams	N. A. Rankin	Ninian W Edwards
George Pasfield	Joseph Klein	Elijah Iles
James Bell	Thomas Houghan	Nicholas A. Bryant

[1] AD, I-Ar. Only the amendment to the bill is in Lincoln's hand. The original bill introduced by William Carpenter of Sangamon County was entitled "An act to incorporate a Company therein named," with names of incorporators left blank. On the third reading of the bill, December 22, Lincoln moved to amend the title to "An act to incorporate the Sangamon Fire Insurance Company." The bill appears in *Laws of Illinois*, 1836, pp. 71-76, with Lincoln's title and the names of incorporators as listed in his amendment, with the exception of Nicholas Bryant, who was not named.

Resolution Introduced in Illinois Legislature
to Instruct Committee
on Public Accounts and Expenditures to Inquire
into the Publishing of State Laws[1]

[December 26, 1835]

Resolved, that the committee on public accounts and expenditures, be instructed to enquire into the expediency of authorizeing the publishing of the State laws, of a general nature, in the public Newspapers, and, that they report by bill or otherwise.

[1] AD, I-Ar. The resolution was adopted. John D. Hughes, representative from St. Clair County, reported on December 31 that ". . . in the opinion of the committee it is inexpedient to legislate on the subject. . . ." (AD, I-Ar.)

Notes of a Survey Made for David Hart[1]

1836

A part of the West half of the South East quarter of Section 13 in Township 17 North of Range 7 West of the 3rd Principal Meridian and bounded as follows (viz) Begining at the South East corner of said half quarter. Thence West, with the Southern boundary line, 10 chains and 7 links. Thence North 12 chains & 40 links to the centre of the channel of Rock creek. Thence down Rock creek with it's meanderings to the place where the line dividing the East & West halves of the above named quarter, crosses the same. Thence South with said dividing line to the begining. Containing 12 acres and 48 hundredths of an acre, more or less.

1836

[1] AD, CSmH. In a deposition taken before Thomas Moffett, September 2, 1837, in the case of Elijah Houghton *v.* Heirs of David Hart, Lincoln said that he had surveyed this tract for David Hart in the fall of 1834, and that Hart had sold the same to Houghton. Lincoln's endorsement on the verso of the document reads "Houghton. Notes for a 12 acre tract," which suggests that the document may have been made from the record in preparation for Houghton's suit against the heirs of Hart, no deed having been executed by Hart.

Report to Illinois Legislature
on State Expenses[1]

[January 2, 1836]

The committee on Public accounts and expenditures, who were required, by a resolution of the House,[2] to asscertain the probable amount of money necessary for defraying the expenses of the State for the succeeding year, report the following—

Contingent fund	$ 4.000
Penitentiary	750
Interest on Wiggins loan	6.000
Governor's salary	1.000
Auditor's do	1.600
Treasurer's do	1.600
Sec. State's do	1.100
Supreme Judges do	4.000
Circuit do do	4.500
Attorneys do	1.850
Agent of Ohio Salines—	200
Warden of Penitentiary	400
Public Printer	2.000
Counties on the Bounty tract—	4.150
Special appropriations and incidental expenses	6.000
General Assembly for Session of 1836, 7	37.000
Making in the whole	76.150
To which add the expenses of the present session of the General Assembly—	13 000
Total	$ 89 150

[1] AD, I-Ar. Lincoln wrote the report of the committee, but John D. Hughes delivered it to the House on January 2, 1836.
[2] Adopted on December 22, 1835.

Bill Introduced in Illinois Legislature
to Establish a State Road from Peoria to Pekin[1]

[January 9, 1836]

A bill for an act establishing a State road leading from Peoria via Pekin to the State road leading from Springfield to Peoria

SEC. 1 Be it enacted by the people of the state of Illinois represented in the General Assembly: That Madison Allen William Rankin & Theodorus Fisher be, and they are hereby appointed commissioners to view, mark, and locate a State road, begining at the town of Peoria, in the county of Peoria, Thence down the river on the North West side of the same crossing the same at Pekin in the county of Tazewell. Thence in a South Easterly direction till the same intersects the road leading from Springfield to Peoria.

SEC. 2 The said commissioners or a majority of them shall meet at the town of Peoria on the second monday of Aprile[2] next, or as soon thereafter as practicable, and after being duly sworn, shall proceed to perform the duties required of them by this act, avoiding, as much [as] the public good will permit, the injury of private property.

SEC 3 The said commissioners, shall, as soon thereafter as convenient, cause to be filed with the clerk of the county commissioner's court for the county of Peoria, a report, and correct map of so much of said road as may be located in the said county of Peoria and also, with the clerk of the county commissioners court for the county of Tazewell, a like report and map of so much of said road as may be located in the said county of Tazewell, and the said reports and maps shall be preserved and shall form parts of the records of said courts respectively[.] Said road, when so established, shall be kept in repair as other State roads are.

SEC. 4. The county commissioners courts of the said counties of Peoria and Tazewell may[3] allow to said commissioners, out of their county Treasuries respectively, such compensation as to them shall seem just and reasonable.

SEC. 5. Be it further enacted that the Commissioners Court of the County of Tazewell be and they are hereby authorized and directed to recieve and confirm the Report of Thomas Griffith Benjamin Briggs and Joshua Brown or a majority of them—Commissioners appointed by an Act entitled "An Act to change a State Road therein named,["] approved Feb 6. 1835. to review & relocate any part of the State Road leading from Pekin to Danville lying between the Towns of Pekin and Mackinaw.

Provided said Report has been or shall be presented to said Court on or before the first monday of June next

SEC 6. The Road when reported as aforesaid shall be considered a state Road in every respect as though said Report had been made within the time prescribed by the act aforesaid.

1 AD, I-Ar. The bill was introduced on January 9, 1836, by William Brown, representative from Tazewell and McLean counties, but was written for

Brown by Lincoln (sections 1-4) and John T. Stuart (sections 5-6). The bill was passed without amendment and appears in *Laws of Illinois*, 1836, pp. 206-207. [2] Stuart changed Lincoln's "May" to "Aprile." [3] Stuart changed Lincoln's "shall" to "may."

Petition to County Commissioners Concerning Benjamin Elmore[1]

February 3, 1836.

To the county commissioners court for the county of Sangamon.

We the undersigned being personally acquainted with the insane son of Travice Elmore for whose maintenance an allowance from the county treasury has already been made,[2] believe that the allowance is much too small, and therefore recommend that it be increased to a fair compensation for the maintenance and management of an absolute mad man.   Feb. 3rd. 1836

[1] ADS, IHi. The petition carries thirty names including Lincoln's. Many have become relatively illegible and all have been omitted here.
[2] *Vide supra*, February 9, 1833.

Advertisement for a Lost Horse[1]

STRAYED OR STOLEN

March 26, 1836

FROM a stable in Springfield, on Wednesday, 18th inst.[2] a large bay horse, star in his forehead, plainly marked with harness; supposed to be eight years old; had been shod all round, but is believed to have lost some of his shoes, and trots and paces. Any person who will take up said horse, and leave information at the Journal office, or with the subscriber at New-salem, shall be liberally paid for their trouble.   A. LINCOLN.

[1] *Sangamo Journal*, March 26, 1836.
[2] March 18, 1836 was on a Thursday.

To Levi Davis[1]

Dear Sir   New Salem Ills, April 4th. 1836

You will confer a favour on me by examining the Record kept by the old State Recorder, and ascertaining whether a deed for the N.W. quarter of Section 23. in Town 10 North Range 5 West in the Bounty tract, made by Williamson Trent to Michael Mcdierman has ever been recorded in that office, and if so, whether the record shows that the land has been transfered by Mcdierman, and if it has, who is the present owner under him. Also please to give me all the information in *your* office in regard to sales of said land for taxes, and who is the present owner by tax title. Verry respectfully, Your Obt. Servt.

Levi Davis Esqr. A. LINCOLN

¹ ALS, IHi. Davis was state auditor.

To the Editor of the *Sangamo Journal*¹

NEW SALEM, June 13, 1836.

To the Editor of the Journal:

In your paper of last Saturday, I see a communication over the signature of "Many Voters," in which the candidates who are announced in the Journal, are called upon to "show their hands." Agreed. Here's mine!

I go for all sharing the privileges of the government, who assist in bearing its burthens. Consequently I go for admitting all whites to the right of suffrage, who pay taxes or bear arms, (by no means excluding females.)

If elected, I shall consider the whole people of Sangamon my constituents, as well those that oppose, as those that support me.²

While acting as their representative, I shall be governed by their will, on all subjects upon which I have the means of knowing what their will is; and upon all others, I shall do what my own judgment teaches me will best advance their interests. Whether elected or not, I go for distributing the proceeds of the sales of the public lands to the several states, to enable our state, in common with others, to dig canals and construct rail roads, without borrowing money and paying interest on it.

If alive on the first Monday in November, I shall vote for Hugh L. White for President.³ Very respectfully, A. LINCOLN.

¹ *Sangamo Journal*, June 18, 1836.
² Lincoln received the highest vote of the seventeen Sangamon County candidates for the legislature on election day, August 1. The seven members elected from Sangamon were Whigs.
³ Hugh Lawson White, United States Senator from Tennessee, led Van Buren in New Salem 65 to 34; in Springfield 719 to 376; and in Sangamon County 1463 to 903. Van Buren carried the state 18,459 to 15,240. White received the electoral votes of only two states, Tennessee and Georgia.

To Robert Allen¹

Dear Col. New Salem, June 21. 1836

I am told that during my absence last week, you passed through this place, and stated publicly, that you were in possession of a

Survey of a School Section, May 10, 1836
Illinois State Historical Library

Survey of Huron, Illinois, May 21, 1836
New Salem, Illinois, State Park Museum

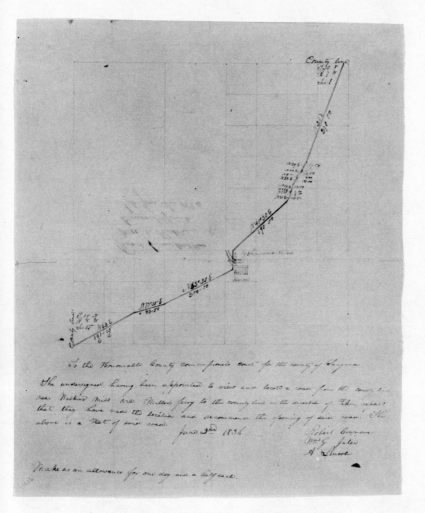

Survey of a Road near Watkins Mill, June 2, 1836
Illinois State Historical Library

Survey of Albany, Illinois, June 16, 1836
From Tarbell, *Life of Abraham Lincoln*

fact or facts, which, if known to the public, would entirely destroy the prospects of N. W. Edwards[2] and myself at the ensuing election; but that, through favour to us, you should forbear to divulge them.

No one has needed favours more than I, and generally, few have been less unwilling to accept them; but in this case, favour to me, would be injustice to the public, and therefore I must beg your pardon for declining it. That I once had the confidence of the people of Sangamon, is sufficiently evident, and if I have since done any thing, either by design or misadventure, which if known, would subject me to a forfeiture of that confidence, he that knows of that thing, and conceals it, is a traitor to his country's interest.

I find myself wholly unable to form any conjecture of what fact or facts, real or supposed, you spoke; but my opinion of your veracity, will not permit me, for a moment, to doubt, that you at least believed what you said.

I am flattered with the personal regard you manifested for me, but I do hope that, on more mature reflection, you will view the public interest as a paramount consideration, and, therefore, determine to let the worst come.

I here assure you, that the candid statement of facts, on your part, however low it may sink me, shall never break the tie of personal friendship between us.

I wish an answer to this, and you are at liberty to publish both if you choose   Verry Respectfully,   A. LINCOLN.

[1] ALS, IHi. Robert Allen was a resident of Springfield. There seems to be no record of any reply to Lincoln's communication. A number of references to Allen in Lincoln's later letters relate only to business dealings. This letter was first published by Allen's son, Major Robert Allen, in the *Illinois State Journal*, May 10, 1865, as an example of Lincoln's early "candor, honor, and high integrity."
[2] Ninian Wirt Edwards—whose father, Ninian Edwards the elder, had been the first governor of Illinois Territory, and later United States Senator from Illinois—was a well-to-do resident of Springfield and a Whig candidate for the legislature.

Speech at a Political Rally in the Court House at Springfield, Illinois[1]

July 11, 1836

Mr. Lincoln succeeded Mr. Calhoun.[2] At first he appeared embarrassed, and his air was such as modest merit always lends to one who speaks of his own acts. He claimed only so much credit as belonged to one of the members of the last Legislature, for getting the State out of debt. He next came to Mr. Calhoun and the land bill.[3] At one fell stroke, he broke the ice upon which we have seen Mr. Calhoun standing, and left him to contend with the chilling waters and merciless waves. His speech became more fluent, and his manner more easy as he progressed. In these degenerate days it seems to be the fashion of the day for all parties to admire even the frailties of the administration. The Van Buren men, particularly, are even taking shelter like ghosts under the rotten bones and tombstones of the dead acts of the administration. Mr. Lincoln, however, lifted the lid, and exposed to the eye the wretched condition of *some* of the acts of the Van Buren party. A girl might be born and become a mother before the Van Buren men will forget Mr. Lincoln. From beginning to end Mr. Lincoln was frequently interrupted by loud bursts of applause from a generous people.

[1] *Sangamo Journal*, July 16, 1836.
[2] John Calhoun of Sangamon County, Illinois.
[3] The bill in congress calling for distribution of the proceeds from the sale of public lands to the states. Like most Whigs, Lincoln followed Henry Clay in advocating distribution (see Lincoln's letter to the editor of the *Sangamo Journal*, June 13, 1836, *supra*). Democrats generally advocated the policy of preemption, the allowing of special privileges to actual settlers (squatters).

Petition to County Commissioners' Court Concerning Road Scrapers[1]

August, 1836

To the Honorable the County Commissioners' Court of Sangamon County Illinois.

Whereas, in the opinion of the under-signed petitioners the "public good" requires that said Court take suitable steps to furnish "Scrapers" on the public roads within the County,—not only for the purpose of economizing labor, but for the more necessary and laudable object of facilitating, cheapening and comforting the business and travelling operations of our common County. Your peti[ti]oners will not presume to extend remarks or argue the propriety of the above suggesting, believing that the Court will fully appreciate this hint, sanctioned alike by "Law" and the just claims of the road-laboring community.

And whereas, a "Road Tax" was laid on lands for 1836 by sd. Court the labor accruing to roads from which source will be applied this coming fall, we further suggest the propriety of attending forthwith to this request, that we may enjoy the use of such improvements as may be made in our roads. August 1836

[1] DS, IHi. The document, not in Lincoln's hand, carries one hundred and thirty-two signatures, including Lincoln's.

Will of Joshua Short[1]

In the name of God: Amen   August 22, 1836

I, Joshua Short, of the county of Sangamon and State of Illinois, being infirm in body but of sound mind and memory do ordain and establish the following as my *last will* and *testament* revoking all others.

It is my will that all my debts, if any there be, be immediately paid at my decease.

It is my will that all my property be disposed of at my decease, as follows (viz)

It is my will that my dearly beloved wife Parthena Short shall have and retain all the property that she had at the time of my marriage with her, or that she has since made.

It is further my will that, if she, my said wife, shall, at my decease, desire to go [to] her relations, she shall be conveyed thence at the expense of my estate.

It is my will that, after the above provisions are carried into effect, all the remaining part of my estate be equally divided between my three sons, Joseph Short, John Short, and William Short, and my three daughters, Sarah Bennett, Chloe Thomas and Elizabeth Short, and my grandson Allen Short, being the son of my deceased son James Short.

It is my will that my son John Short, and my son-in-law James Short be the executors of this my last will and testament

In testimony whereof I have hereunto set my hand and seal this twentysecond day of August, in the year of our Lord one thousand eight hundred and thirtysix.

                                   his

Attest   JOSHUA ✕ SHORT (SEAL)

  A. LINCOLN   mark

  John Tillie

         his

  Josiah ✕ Cook

         mark

[1] ADS-P, ISLA. A document entirely in Lincoln's hand, excepting signature of Tillie. Lincoln was studying law, but was not licensed to practice until seventeen days later, on September 9, 1836. Joshua Short was a farmer living a few miles north of New Salem, Illinois.

Petition to County Commissioners

Concerning Relocation of Road from Watkins Mill to the County Line[1]

[September 4, 1836]

To the county commissioner's court for the county of Sangamon, State of Illinois

We the undersigned respectfully request that your Honorable body pass an order relocating so much of the road leading from Watkin's Mill via Miller's ferry to the county line in the direction of Pekin, as lies between the Morgan county line and the Range line dividing Ranges 7 and 8 so as to make the same run from it's present begining on a right line to a point four poles North of the door of Charles Simmons' present dwelling. Thence on a right line to where said road now crosses the afforesaid Range line.

A. Lincoln	Julius Simmons	Moris Hutches
B, Winton	Henry Dick	William Edwards
B, Kilborne	A Conkey	Amos Ogden
R Simmons	Absalom Bowling	Charles Simmons
M L Hutches	Daniel Robinson	Jonathan Lowndsbury

[1] ADS, IHi.

To Ira I. Fenn[1]

Dr. Sir.   Springfield, Oct. 6. 1836

By direction of Judge Lockwood,[2] I send you this with it's contents   Yours &c.   A. LINCOLN

Ira I. Fenn Esqr.

[1] ALS, CSmH. Fenn was a resident of Columbia, Illinois.
[2] The document sent for Samuel D. Lockwood is not identified, but at this point the phrase "as per enclosed letter" was deleted by Lincoln.

Surveys for Alvin Ringo[1]

November 16, 17, 1836

1836 } Surveyed for   Ringo a tract of land composed of
Nov 16 } parts of Sections 30 & 31 in Township 18 North of Range 7 West and bounded as follows viz. Beginning on the line dividing Ranges 7 & 8 at a point 6 chains & 81 links North of the North West corner of the said Section 31 at a White Oak 16 inches in diameter bearing N. 43½ E. 48 links. Thence East 14 chains & 93 links to a White Oak 36 inches N 50 W 32 links.

Thence South 20 chains & 7 links to a sugar tree 14 inches N 29 W 53 links. Thence West 14 chains & 93 links to a Hickory 14 inches S. 22 E 19 links. Thence North 20 chains & 7 links to the beginning   T. M. Neale s. s. c.

BY A. LINCOLN

1836 } For the same a part of the North half of Section 5 in
Nov 17 } Township 17 North of Range 7 West and bounded as follows (viz) Begining at the most Northerly corner of a tract situated on the said Section 5, and sold to Lewis L Cooper by Robert Cownover.[2] Thence S 47 W 8 chains & 42 links to a Black Oak 11 inches corner. Thence S 70 E. 22 chains & 1 links to a White Oak 16 inches N 26 W 45 links. Thence N 29 E. 4 chains & 50 links to a White Oak 24 inches S 73 W 20 links. Thence N 61 W 19 chains & 2 links to the begining. Also a part of the East half of the South West quarter of the said Section 5, and bounded as follows. (viz) Begining at the South East corner of said half quarter at a White Oak 16 inches S 63 W 62 links. a White Oak 15 inches N 75 E 76 links. Thence N 89 W 19 chains & 71 links to a Post & Mound. Thence North 3 chains to a stake. Thence S 89 E. 19 chains & 71 links to a stake. Thence South 3 chains to the begining.   T. M Neale, s. s. c.

BY A. LINCOLN

[1] Although these surveys were at one time together, only the second has been located, in the Ford's Theatre Museum, Washington, D. C. Fortunately Herndon made copies of both, and the text of the first is taken from the copy in the Herndon-Weik Collection. A note in the same collection by William Green maintains that the survey of November 17 was the last Lincoln ever made.
[2] Robert Conover.

Petition to County Commissioners' Court
for a Road Commencing at Middletown[1]

[November 30, 1836]

To the Honorable the county commissioner's court for the county of Sangamon, Illinois.

We, the undersigned, citizens of Sangamon county respectfully request, that your Honorable body will pass an order for the establishment of a county road to commence at Middletown near Musick's bridge. Thence the nearest and best rout to Meaddows' Mill at the Sugar Grove. Thence, as near as the ground will permit, with the Section line runing one mile North of the Northern boundry of Townships Eighteen, to the county line.

1 AD, IHi. Lincoln drew up this petition before leaving for Vandalia to attend the legislature, which opened on December 5, 1836, and Coleman Smoot seems from the endorsement which appears on the verso of the document to have procured the fifty-nine signatures, including his own, and presented the petition to the court on December 5. November 30 is conjectured as the approximate date.

To Mary S. Owens[1]

Mary   Vandalia, Decr. 13 1836

I have been sick ever since my arrival here,[2] or I should have written sooner. It is but little difference, however, as I have verry little even yet to write. And more, the longer I can avoid the mortification of looking in the Post Office for your letter and not finding it, the better. You see I am mad about that *old letter* yet. I dont like verry well to risk you again. I'll try you once more any how.

The new State House[3] is not yet finished, and consequently the legislature is doing little or nothing. The Governor[4] delivered an inflamitory political Message, and it is expected there will be some sparring between the parties about [it as] soon as the two Houses get to business. Taylor[5] [deliv]ered up his petitions for the *New County* to one of [our me]mbers this morning. I am told that he dispairs [of its] success on account of all the members from Morg[an C]ounty opposing it. There are names enough on the petion[,] I think, to justify the members from our county in going for it; but if the members from Morgan oppose it, which they [say] they will, the chance will be bad.

Our chance to [take th]e seat of Government to Springfield is better than I ex[pected]. An Internal Improvement Convention was held here since we met, which recommended a loan of several milli[ons] of dollars on the faith of the State to construct Rail Roads. Some of the legislature are for it[,] and some against it; which has the majority I can not tell. There is great strife and struggling for the office of U.S. Senator here at this time. It is probable we shall ease their pains in a few days. The opposition men have no candidate of their own, and consequently they smile as complacently at the angry snarls of the contending Van Buren candidates and their respective friends, as the christain does at Satan's rage. You recollect I mentioned in the outset of this letter that I had been unwell. That is the fact, though I believe I am about well now; but that, with other things I can not account for, have conspired and have gotten my spirits so low, that I feel that I would rather be any place in the world than here. I really can not endure the thought of staying here ten weeks. Write back as soon as you get this, and if possible say something that will please me, for really I have not [been] pleased since I left you. This letter is so dry and [stupid] that I am ashamed to send it, but with my pres[ent feel]ings I can not do any better. Give my respects to M[r. and] Mrs. Abell[6] and family. Your friend

Miss Mary S. Owens   LINCOLN

[1] ALS, owned by James G. Vineyard of Kansas City, Missouri, grandson of Mary Owens. The manuscript is damaged in spots: portions of the text now illegible are bracketed as from NH.

Mary Owens first came to New Salem in 1833 to visit her sister, Mrs. Bennett Abell. Upon a later visit in 1836, brought about by the match-making activities of Mrs. Abell, who suggested to Lincoln that he marry her sister, Mary Owens and Lincoln reached some sort of understanding. That the prospects were not satisfactory to either party is evident from Lincoln's letters to Mary and from the letters which Mary wrote to William H. Herndon in 1866, answering queries about her side of the affair.

[2] Lincoln attended the opening session of the legislature on December 5.

[3] This was the third State House, begun in August, 1836, when the old building collapsed beyond repair.

[4] Governor Joseph Duncan, whose message denounced President Jackson's policies.

[5] John Taylor. The "new county" was named "Menard."

[6] Variant spellings in other sources are "Abel" and "Able."

Resolution in the Illinois Legislature
to Request Doorkeeper of the House to Make a Statement Concerning Need for an Assistant Doorkeeper[1]

[December 20, 1836]

Resolved that the door-keeper of this House, be now requested to state publicly to this body, whether, in his opinion, an assistant doorkeeper is necessary.

[1] AD, I-Ar. Along with several other resolutions concerning the position of assistant doorkeeper, Lincoln's resolution was tabled.

Speech in Illinois Legislature
Reporting a Bill with Amendments
to Establish a New County[1]

December 21, 1836

Mr. Lincoln said, that as a member of the committee, he would state that the bill before the House was a matter of compromise. He was willing to take the bill, because before any division of Sangamo could take place, the bill declared that the people of

Sangamo should themselves so decide. He would sustain the bill as it stood, the new county would be too small if lessened. He was opposed to offering to the people a territory too small for their acceptance.

[1] *Illinois State Register*, January 12, 1837. On the afternoon of December 21, Lincoln reported from the select committee to which Douglas' bill for the division of Sangamon County had been referred, with sundry amendments to the bill. Since Lincoln's amendments make up the bulk of the bill as finally passed by the House after Lincoln had rewritten it (*vide infra*, December 24), they have not been printed separately here.

Discussion in Illinois Legislature
Concerning the Division of Sangamon County[1]

December 21, 1836

Mr. Lincoln then moved that the report of the minority be spread upon the Journals, in order he said, that his constituents might see that report.

Mr. Linder[2] said, that for one, he should vote against the motion. He could see no advantage that could result to any body, by placing this minority report upon the pages of the journal. It was subjecting the State to needless expense in printing. There were many other ways by which the gentleman from Sangamon could get the report among his constituents, without putting it upon the journals of the House.

Mr. Lincoln replied that he claimed the right to know what was due to his constituents as much as any gentleman, and especially as much as one who was not their representative. He had made the motion to spread the report on the journal, because he thought it due to his constituents, and no more than a common act of courtesy from the House, to comply. Mr. L. said, he hoped that all that had been said on this subject, would go to his constituents. He thought it uncourteous, and a departure from the rules of etiquette, for the gentleman from Coles to meddle in the matter at all; but if the House chooses to go by the views of that gentleman, so be it; I am content. Mr. L. said he did not think the small expense to the State which the printing of the report would incur, the whole object of gentlemen, in opposing his motion. The intention is to affect my constituents.[3]

[1] *Illinois State Register*, January 12, 1837. On December 20, 1836, Stephen A. Douglas from the committee on petitions reported for the majority with a bill for the establishment of a new county out of part of Sangamon County (*vide infra*, December 24, as rewritten by Lincoln). John T. Stuart from the same committee reported for the minority against the bill. As customary,

the majority report delivered by Douglas was spread on the *Journal*, but the minority report was not printed. Hence on the morning of the following day Lincoln moved the printing of the minority report for the reasons indicated in this speech.

2 Usher F. Linder of Coles County.

3 After further discussion by other members, Lincoln's motion was lost, 44 to 24.

Bill Introduced in Illinois Legislature
to Organize the County of Van Buren[1]

[December 24, 1836]

SECTION 1 Be it enacted by the people of the state of Illinois represented in the General Assembly that all that tract of country lying within the following boundaries, to wit: Begining at the North West corner of Sangamon county on the Illinois river and runing from thence East along the North line of said county to the North East corner of Township No. 20 North of Range No. 5 West. Thence South along the Range line between Ranges four and five to the South East corner of Township No. Eighteen North of Range No. five West. Thence diagonally across Ranges, five, six, and seven West to the South West corner of Township No. Seventeen North of Range No. Seven West. Thence West along the line between Townships No. sixteen and seventeen to the line between Sangamon and Morgan counties. Thence North along the line between Sangamon and Morgan counties to the Sangamon river. Thence along the channel of the said Sangamon river to it's junction with the Illinois river; and thence following the meanders of Illinois river to the place of begining, shall constitute a new county to be called the county of Van Buren[2]

1 AD, I-Ar. In addition to the engrossed bill, which is in Lincoln's hand but dated and signed by the House clerk on December 24, there are two pages of amendments and two amendments on slips of paper, also in Lincoln's hand. These amendments, reported by Lincoln on December 21 from a select committee, make up more than half of the bill as passed. The original bill, introduced on December 20 by Stephen A. Douglas, representative from Morgan County, from the committee on petitions, was drawn in response to petitions signed by citizens of Morgan and Sangamon counties requesting the formation of a new county out of adjacent portions of the two counties. Remonstrances against the petitions had also been presented, and it was clear that Sangamon voters were by no means unanimously in favor of forming the new county. The bill was tabled by the Senate and failed to become law. (See Lincoln's "Report," February 13, 1837, *infra*.)

2 The name of the proposed county had been left blank throughout the original bill and remained so until Lincoln's amendment naming "Marshall" was changed on the motion of David Nowlin of Monroe County to read "Van Buren." The insertion of "Van Buren" in the title was done by amendment after the bill had been passed by the House.

SEC 2ND. The permanent seat of Justice for said county shall be the village of Petersburg, and the public buildings thereof shall be erected on the public square recorded in the plat of said town as public ground: Provided[3] that unless the proprietors of the said village of Petersburg shall convey to the said county of Van Buren for the purpose of the erection of public buildings, one fourth of all the lots of the said village, the seat of justice of said county shall not be located at the said village of Petersburg; but shall be located by commissioners hereinafter named, at some point not more than one mile and a half from the geographical centre of said county.

SEC 3RD. The county commissioners for said county, when elected under the provisions of this act, shall immediately appoint some suitable person, as agent, whose duty it shall be to call upon the proprietors of said village of Petersburg or their agent, and notify them or him, that he is ready to make the selection of the lots aforesaid, on behalf of the county; and if the said proprietors or their agent agree to said selection, the said agent for the county, shall proceed to make the selection by choosing one lot, and allowing the said proprietors or their agent to choose three, and so proceed till the whole selection is made: Provided that the paying over, by the proprietors of the said village of Petersburg, to the county commissioners of the said new county, one fourth of the proceeds of the sales of the lots already sold shall be deemed a sufficient compliance with the provisions of this act in regard to the lots so sold.[4]

SEC 4 If the said proprietors shall neglect or refuse, for a longer term than ten days after the said agent for the county has notified them that he is ready to make the selection as aforesaid, to convey to the county commissioners for the use of said county the lots selected, or offered to be selected, by said agent, the said county commissioners shall give notice to John Henry of Morgan county, Benjamin Mitchell of Tazewell county, and Samuel Hackelton of Fulton county, that they are appointed commissioners to locate the seat of Justice of said county, whose duty it shall be to meet at the said village of Petersburg on the second monday of August next, and after being duly sworn by some Justice of the Peace, faithfully and impartially to discharge their duties, shall proceed to locate the seat of justice of said county according to the provisions of this act; which location shall be the permanent seat of justice of said county.[5]

[3] This proviso was one of Lincoln's amendments.
[4] Section 3 was Lincoln's amendment.   [5] Section 4 was Lincoln's amendment.

SEC 5   The county commissioners of said county shall allow, out of the county treasury, the sum of three dollars to each of said commissioners for each day they may have been necessarily employed in making said location.[6]

SEC 6   The said new county of Van Buren shall constitute a part of first judicial circuit, and a circuit shall be held for said county at some convenient place in the village of Petersburg until the public buildings shall be erected. The time for holding said courts shall be appointed by the Judge presiding on said circuit.[7]

SEC 7   All Justices of the Peace and constables now commissioned in and for the county of Sangamon that now reside within the boundaries of the aforesaid county of Van Buren shall hold their offices in and for the said new county of Van Buren.

SEC 8   The legal voters of said county shall meet at the several precincts now organized for holding elections within the above boundaries on the first monday in July next, appoint Judges and clerks of elections, and proceed to elect three county commissioners, a Sheriff, a Coroner, a county surveyor and county Recorder for said county; and the returns of said election shall be made by said Judges and clerks to the Justices of the Peace in said new county of Van Buren, any three or more of whom shall meet at the village of Petersburg within seven days after said election and proceed to open said returns and in all things perform the duties required by law of the clerks of county commissioners courts and Justices of the Peace in like cases

SEC. 9   In all elections for officers, except county officers, the county shall vote with the county of Sangamon until the next census; and the returns of the elections shall be made to the county clerk of the new county of Van Buren, by whom a certified abstract of the returns of such election shall be made to the county commissioners clerk of Sangamon county within seven days thereafter.

SEC 10   Be it further enacted that the legal voters of the county of Sangamon shall meet at the several places of holding elections in said county, on the first monday of June next, and if a majority of said voters shall vote in favour of the organization of said new county of Van Buren under this act, then shall the county be organized as is in this act provided for; but if a majority of said voters shall vote against the organization of said new county, then shall this act be void and of none effect.

[6] Section 5 was Lincoln's amendment.
[7] Sections 6, 7, 8, 9, and 10 were in the original bill.

SEC 11 It shall be the duty of the Judges and clerks of the several election precincts in and for the county of Sangamon, to meet at the several places of holding elections, on the day prescribed in the tenth section of this act, and then and there proceed to open polls for the purpose contemplated in the said tenth section, and in all respects conduct the voting, and make the returns in the manner prescribed by the general election laws of this state. The official certificate of the clerk of the county commissioner's court of Sangamon county shall be evidence of the result of said voting.[8]

SEC 12 The clerk of the county commissioner's court for Sangamon county shall give notice of said voting in the same manner, and for the same length of time that he is required to do by law, of general elections.

[8] Sections 11 and 12 were amendments by Lincoln.

To John McNamar[1]

DEAR MACK: Vandalia, Dec. 24, 1836.

I write this to notify you that I have received the petition for the change of the state road, so as to make it run by Tilman Hornsecker's[2] and Bowman's,[3] and that unless you, who are opposed to the change, get up a remonstrance and send it on, I shall be forced to have a bill passed upon the petition. I might write you a long letter of political news but you will see that as soon in the newspapers, which will save me the trouble.

If you feel any particular interest in this affair don't fail to bestir yourself.[4] Your friend,   A. LINCOLN.

[1] *Illinois State Journal*, October 15, 1874. McNamar was a farmer residing seven miles northwest of New Salem. He is best known in the Lincoln story under the name of McNeil, the fiancé of Ann Rutledge, for whom Lincoln's attachment has become a legend.

[2] Surely a misreading for "Tilmon Hornbuckle."

[3] George W. Bowman.

[4] McNamar's explanation made in the interview accompanying the letter as published in the *Journal*, was that Lincoln had surveyed the state road so as to run in front of his farm, but that the petition would have relocated it two miles behind him. Evidently Lincoln's warning was effective, for the 1836-1837 session laws show no change of route.

Bond of Charles Gregory as Treasurer of Illinois[1]

December 30, 1836

Know all Men by These presents that We   Charles Gregory   Wm. Lane   Levi Davis   A. Lincoln   John Allen   R. B. Servant   Frank-

lin Wiitt   E. B. Webb   Wm. H. Davidson   Wm. J. Gatewood
Wm. Thomas   John Hogan are held and firmly bound unto Joseph
Duncan Governor of the State of Illinois and his successors in of-
fice in the sum of Fifty Thousand Dollars lawful money of the
State of Illinois for the true payment whereof, we bind ourselves,
our heirs, Executors and administrators jointly and severally,
firmly by these presents sealed with our seals and dated this 30th
Day of December Eighteen hundred and thirty six.

The condition of this obligation is such that whereas the above
bounden Charles Gregory has been appointed State Treasurer of
the State of Illinois, for the Term of the present Session of the
General Assembly, to commence on the 30th day of Dec: 1836.
Now if the said Charles Gregory, shall well and truly and faithfully discharge and perform the duties of his said office for and
during his said Term and shall give additional security whenever
such security shall at any time hereafter be required, then this
obligation shall be void, otherwise it shall be and remain in full
force.

	Charles Gregory (SEAL)	Franklin Witt (SEAL)
	Wm. Lane (SEAL)	E. B. Webb (SEAL)
Signed and delivered	Levi Davis (SEAL)	W. H. Davidson (SEAL)
in presence of	A. Lincoln (SEAL)	Wm. Gatewood (SEAL)
	John Allen (SEAL)	Wm. Thomas (SEAL)
	R. B. Servant (SEAL)	John Hogan (SEAL)

1 DS, I-Ar. The document bears Governor Joseph Duncan's approval signed
the next day, and countersigned by William H. Davidson, Speaker of the Senate,
and Levi Davis, Auditor of Public Accounts.

Speech in the Illinois Legislature
Concerning the State Bank[1]

January 11, 1837

REMARKS OF MR. LINCOLN,

In the House of Representatives, upon the resolution offered by
Mr. Linder, to institute an enquiry into the management of the
affairs of the State Bank.

MR. CHAIRMAN: Lest I should fall into the too common error,
of being mistaken in regard to which side I design to be upon, I
shall make it my first care to remove all doubt on that point, by
declaring that I am opposed to the resolution under consideration,
in toto. Before I proceed to the body of the subject, I will further

1 *Sangamo Journal*, January 28, 1837, reprinted from Vandalia *Free Press*.

remark, that it is not without a considerable degree of apprehension, that I venture to cross the track of the gentleman from Coles (Mr. Linder).[2] Indeed, I do not believe I could muster a sufficiency of courage to come in contact with that gentleman, were it not for the fact, that he, some days since, most graciously condescended to assure us that he would never be found wasting ammunition on *small game*. On the same fortunate occasion, he further gave us to understand, that he regarded *himself* as being decidedly the *superior* of our common friend from Randolph (Mr. Shields);[3] and feeling, as I really do, that I, to say the most of myself, am nothing more than the peer of our friend from Randolph, I shall regard the gentleman from Coles as decidedly my superior also, and consequently, in the course of what I shall have to say, whenever I shall have occasion to allude to that gentleman, I shall endeavor to adopt that kind of court language which I understand to be due to *decided superiority*. In one faculty, at least, there can be no dispute of the gentleman's superiority over me, and most other men; and that is, the faculty of entangling a subject, so that neither himself, or any other man, can find head or tail to it. Here he has introduced a resolution, embracing ninety-nine printed lines across common writing paper, and yet more than one half of his opening speech has been made upon subjects about which there is not one word said in his resolution.

Though his resolution embraces nothing in regard to the constitutionality of the Bank, much of what he has said has been with a view to make the impression that it was unconstitutional in its inception. Now, although I am satisfied that an ample field may be found within the pale of the resolution, at least for small game, yet as the gentleman has travelled out of it, I feel that I may, with all due humility, venture to follow him. The gentleman has discovered that some gentleman at Washington city has been upon the very eve of deciding our Bank unconstitutional, and that he would probably have completed his very authentic decision, had not some one of the Bank officers placed his hand upon his mouth, and begged him to withhold it. The fact that the individuals composing our Supreme Court have, in an official capacity, decided in favor of

2 Usher F. Linder (Democrat), who had offered a series of resolutions to institute an inquiry into the management of the State Bank, was elected attorney general soon after this speech. He remained in politics for many years, becoming a Whig in 1838 but returning to the Democratic fold when, as he said, "the Whigs were merged with the Abolitionists."

3 James Shields (Democrat), who during his term as state auditor challenged Lincoln to a duel in September, 1842. Shields' long political career included practically every state office; he was also elected a United States senator from Illinois (1849), Minnesota (1858), and Missouri (1879).

the constitutionality of the Bank, would, in my mind, seem a sufficient answer to this. It is a fact known to all, that the members of
the Supreme Court, together with the Governor, form a Council
of Revision, and that this Council approved this Bank Charter. I
ask, then, if the extra-judicial decision—not quite, but only almost
made, by the gentleman at Washington, before whom, by the way,
the question of the constitutionality of our Bank never has, nor
never can come—is to be taken as paramount to a decision officially
made by that tribunal, by which and which alone, the constitutionality of the Bank can ever be settled? But aside from this view
of the subject, I would ask, if the committee which this resolution
proposes to appoint, are to examine into the constitutionality of
the Bank? Are they to be clothed with power to send for persons
and papers, for this object? And after they have found the Bank
to be unconstitutional, and decided it so, how are they to enforce
their decision? What will their decision amount to? They cannot
compel the Bank to cease operations, or to change the course of its
operations. What good, then, can their labors result in? Certainly
none.

The gentleman asks, if we, without an examination, shall, by
giving the State deposites to the bank, and by taking the stock reserved for the State, legalize its former misconduct? Now I do not
pretend to possess sufficient legal knowledge to decide, whether a
legislative enactment, proposing to, and accepting from, the Bank,
certain terms, would have the effect to legalize or wipe out its
former errors, or not; but I can assure the gentleman, if such should
be the effect, he has already got behind the settlement of accounts;
for it is well known to all, that the Legislature, at its last session,
passed a supplemental Bank charter, which the Bank has since
accepted, and which, according to his doctrine, has legalized all the
alleged violations of its original charter in the distribution of its
stock.

I now proceed to the resolution. By examination it will be found
that the first thirty-three lines, being precisely one third of the
whole, relate exclusively to the distribution of the stock by the
commissioners appointed by the State. Now, sir, it is clear that no
question can arise on this portion of the resolution, except a question between capitalists in regard to the ownership of stock. Some
gentlemen have the stock in their hands, while others, who have
more money than they know what to do with, want it; and this,
and this alone, is the question, to settle which we are called on to
squander thousands of the people's money. What interest, let me
ask, have the people in the settlement of this question? What dif-

ference is it to them whether the stock is owned by Judge Smith,[4] or Sam. Wiggins?[5] If any gentleman be entitled to stock in the Bank, which he is kept out of possession of by others, let him assert his right in the Supreme Court, and let him or his antagonist, whichever may be found in the wrong, pay the costs of suit. It is an old maxim and a very sound one, that he that dances should always pay the fiddler. Now, sir, in the present case, if any gentlemen, whose money is a burden to them, choose to lead off a dance, I am decidedly opposed to the people's money being used to pay the fiddler. No one can doubt that the examination proposed by this resolution, must cost the State some ten or twelve thousand dollars; and all this to settle a question in which the people have no interest, and about which they care nothing. These capitalists generally act harmoniously, and in concert, to fleece the people, and now, that they have got into a quarrel with themselves, we are called upon to appropriate the people's money to settle the quarrel.

I leave this part of the resolution, and proceed to the remainder. It will be found that no charge in the remaining part of the resolution, if true, amounts to the violation of the Bank Charter, except one, which I will notice in due time. It might seem quite sufficient, to say no more upon any of these charges or insinuations, than enough to show they are not violations of the charter; yet, as that [they?] are ingeniously framed and handled, with a view to deceive and mislead, I will notice in their order, all the most prominent of them. The first of these, is in relation to a connexion between our Bank and several Banking institutions in other States. Admitting this connection to exist, I should like to see the gentleman from Coles, or any other gentleman, undertake to show that there is any harm in it. What can there be in such a connexion, that the people of Illinois are willing to pay their money to get a peep into? By a reference to the tenth section of the Bank charter, any gentleman can see that the framers of the act contemplated the holding of stock in the institutions of other corporations. Why, then, is it, when neither law nor justice forbids it, that we are asked to spend our time and money, in inquiring into its truth?

The next charge, in the order of time, is, that some officer, director, clerk or servant of the Bank, has been required to take an oath of secrecy in relation to the affairs of said Bank. Now, I do not know whether this be true or false—neither do I believe any honest man cares. I know that the seventh section of the charter ex-

---

[4] Theophilus W. Smith (Democrat), who wrote the bank's original charter.
[5] Samuel Wiggins was a Cincinnati financier, with whom a loan was negotiated in 1831.

pressly guarantees to the Bank the right of making, under certain restrictions, such by-laws as it may think fit; and I further know that the requiring an oath of secrecy, would not transcend those restrictions. What, then, if the Bank has chosen to exercise this right? Who can it injure? Does not every merchant have his secret mark? and who is ever silly enough to complain of it? I presume if the Bank does require any such oath of secrecy, it is done through a motive of delicacy to those individuals who deal with it. Why, sir, not many days since, one gentleman upon this floor, who, by the way I have no doubt is now ready to join this hue and cry against the Bank, indulged in a philippic against one of the Bank officers, because, as he said, he had *divulged a secret.*

Immediately following this last charge, there are several insinuations in the resolution, which are too silly to require any sort of notice, were it not for the fact, that they conclude by saying, *"to the great injury of the people at large."* In answer to this I would say, that it is strange enough, that the people are suffering these "great injuries," and yet are not sensible of it! Singular indeed that the people should be writhing under oppression and injury, and yet not one among them to be found, to raise the voice of complaint. If the Bank be inflicting injury upon the people, why is it, that not a single petition is presented to this body on the subject? If the Bank really be a grievance, why is it, that no one of the real people is found to ask redress of it? The truth is, no such oppression exists. If it did, our table would groan with memorials and petitions, and we would not be permitted to rest day or night, till we had put it down. The people know their rights; and they are never slow to assert and maintain them, when they are invaded. Let them call for an investigation, and I shall ever stand ready to respond to the call. But they have made no such call. I make the assertion boldly, and without fear of contradiction, that no man, who does not hold an office, or does not aspire to one, has ever found any fault of the Bank. It has doubled the prices of the products of their farms, and filled their pockets with a sound circulating medium, and they are all well pleased with its operations. No, Sir, it is the *politician* who is the first to sound the alarm, (which, by the way, is a false one.) It is he, [who,] by these unholy means, is endeavoring to blow up a storm that he may ride upon and direct. It is he, and he alone, that here proposes to spend thousands of the people's public treasure, for no other advantage to them, than to make valueless in their pockets the reward of their industry. Mr. Chairman, this movement is exclusively the work of politicians; a set of men who have interests aside from the interests of the people, and who, to say the most of them, are, taken as a mass, at least one long step removed from honest men. I say this with the greater freedom because, being a politician myself, none can regard it as personal.

Again, it is charged, or rather insinuated, that officers of the Bank have loaned money at usurious rates of interest. Suppose this to be true, are we to send a committee of this House to enquire into it? Suppose the committee should find it true can they redress the injured individuals? Assuredly not. If any individual had been injured in this way, is there not an ample remedy, to be found in the laws of the land? Does the gentleman from Coles know, that there is a statute standing in full force, making it highly penal, for an individual to loan money at a higher rate of interest than twelve per cent? If he does not he is too ignorant to be placed at the head of the committee which his resolution proposes; and if he does, his neglect to mention it, shows him to be too uncandid to merit the respect or confidence of any one.

But besides all this, if the Bank were struck from existence, could not the owners of the capital still loan it usuriously, as well as now? Whatever the Bank, or its officers, may have done, I know that usurious transactions were much more frequent and enormous, before the commencement of its operations, than they have ever been since.

The next insinuation is, that the Bank has refused specie payments. This, if true, is a violation of the charter. But there is not the least probability of its truth; because, if such had been the fact, the individual to whom payment was refused, would have had an interest in making it public, by suing for the damages to which the charter entitles him. Yet no such thing has been done; and the strong presumption is, that the insinuation is false and groundless.

From this to the end of the resolution, there is nothing that merits attention—I therefore drop the particular examination of it.

By a general view of the resolution, it will be seen that a principal object of the committee is, to examine into, and ferret out, a mass of corruption, supposed to have been committed by the commissioners who apportioned the stock of the Bank. I believe it is universally understood and acknowledged, that all men will ever act correctly, unless they have a motive to do otherwise. If this be true, we can only suppose that the commissioners acted corruptly, by also supposing that they were bribed to do so. Taking this view of the subject, I would ask if the Bank is likely to find it more difficult to bribe the committee of seven, which we are about to appoint, than it may have found it to bribe the commissioners?

(Here Mr. Linder called to order. The Chair decided that Mr.

Lincoln was not out of order. Mr. Linder appealed to the House; but before the question was put, withdrew his appeal, saying, he preferred to let the gentleman go on; he thought he would break his own neck. Mr. Lincoln proceeded)—

Another *gracious condescension.* I acknowledge it with gratitude. I know I was not out of order; and I know every sensible man in the House knows it. I was not saying that the gentleman from Coles could not be bribed, nor, on the other hand, will I say he could.[6] In that particular, I leave him where I found him. I was only endeavoring to show that there was at least as great a probability of *any* seven members that could be selected from this House, being bribed to act corruptly, as there was, that the twenty-four commissioners had been so bribed. By a reference to the ninth section of the Bank charter, it will be seen that those commissioners were John Tilson, Robert K. McLaughlin, Daniel Wann, A. G. S. Wight, John C. Riley, W. H. Davidson, Edward M. Wilson, Edward L. Pierson, Robert R. Green, Ezra Baker, Aquilla Wren, John Taylor, Samuel C. Christy, Edmund Roberts, Benjamin Godfrey, Thomas Mather, A. M. Jenkins, W. Linn, W. S. Gilman, Charles Prentice, Richard J. Hamilton, A. H. Buckner, W. F. Thornton, and Edmund D. Taylor.

These are twenty-four of the most respectable men in the State. Probably no twenty-four men could be selected in the State, with whom the people are better acquainted, or in whose honor and integrity, they would more readily place confidence. And I now repeat, that there is less probability that those men have been bribed and corrupted, than that *any* seven men, or rather any *six* men, that could be selected from the members of this House, might be so bribed and corrupted; even though they were headed and led on by "decided superiority" himself.

In all seriousness, I ask every reasonable man, if an issue be joined by these twenty-four commissioners, on the one part, and *any* other seven men, on the other part, and the whole depend upon the honor and integrity of the contending parties, to which party would the greatest degree of credit be due? Again: Another consideration is, that we have no right to make the examination. What I shall say upon this head, I design exclusively for the law-loving and law-abiding part of the House. To those who claim omnipotence for the Legislature, and who in the plenitude of their assumed powers, are disposed to disregard the Constitution, law, good faith, moral right, and every thing else, I have not a word to say.

[6] A superfluous "not," evidently a printer's error in the *Journal* text, has been deleted at the end of this sentence.

But to the law-abiding part I say, examine the Bank charter, go examine the Constitution; go examine the acts that the General Assembly of this State has passed, and you will find just as much authority given in each and every of them, to compel the Bank to bring its coffers to this hall, and to pour their contents upon this floor, as to compel it to submit to this examination which this resolution proposes. Why, sir, the gentleman from Coles, the mover of this resolution, very lately denied on this floor, that the Legislature had any right to repeal, or otherwise meddle with its own acts, when those acts were made in the nature of contracts, and had been accepted and acted on by other parties. Now I ask, if this resolution does not propose, for this House alone, to do, what he, but the other day, denied the right [of] the whole Legislature to do? He must either abandon the position he then took, or he must now vote against his own resolution. It is no difference to me, and I presume but little to any one else, which he does.

I am by no means the special advocate of the Bank. I have long thought that it would be well for it to report its condition to the General Assembly, and that cases might occur, when it might be proper to make an examination of its affairs by a committee. Accordingly, during the last session, while a bill supplemental to the Bank charter, was pending before the House, I offered an amendment to the same, in these words: "The said corporation shall, at the next session of the General Assembly, and at each subsequent General Session, during the existence of its charter, report to the same the amount of debts due *from* said corporation; the amount of debts due *to* the same; the amount of specie in its vaults, and an account of all lands then owned by the same, and the amount for which such lands have been taken; and moreover, if said corporation shall at any time neglect or refuse to submit its books, papers, and all and every thing necessary for a full and fair examination of its affairs, to any person or persons appointed by the General Assembly, for the purpose of making such examination, the said corporation shall forfeit its charter."

This amendment was negatived by a vote of 34 to 15. Eleven of the 34 who voted against it, are now members of this House; and though it would be out of order to call their names, I hope they will all recollect themselves, and not vote for this examination to be made without authority, inasmuch as they refused to reserve the authority when it was in their power to do so.

I have said that cases might occur, when an examination might be proper; but I do not believe any such case has now occurred; and if it has, I should still be opposed to making an examination without legal authority. I am opposed to encouraging that lawless and mobocratic spirit, whether in relation to the bank or any thing else, which is already abroad in the land; and is spreading with rapid and fearful impetuosity, to the ultimate overthrow of every institution, or even moral principle, in which persons and property have hitherto found security.

But supposing we had the authority, I would ask what good can result from the examination? Can we declare the Bank unconstitutional, and compel it to cease operations? Can we compel it to desist from the abuses of its power, provided we find such abuses to exist? Can we repair the injuries which it may have done to individuals? Most certainly we can do none of these things. Why then shall we spend the public money in such employment? O, say the examiners, we can injure the credit of the Bank, if nothing else. Please tell me, gentlemen, who will suffer most by that? You cannot injure, to any extent, the Stockholders. They are men of wealth—of large capital; and consequently, beyond the power of fortune, or even the shafts of malice. But by injuring the credit of the Bank, you will depreciate the value of its paper in the hands of the honest and unsuspecting farmer and mechanic, and that is all you can do. But suppose you could effect your whole purpose; suppose you could wipe the Bank from existence, which is the grand *ultimatum* of the project, what would be the consequence? Why, sir, we should spend several thousand dollars of the public treasure in the operation, annihilate the currency of the State; render valueless in the hands of our people that reward of their former labors; and finally, be once more under the comfortable obligation of paying the Wiggins' loan, principal and interest.[7]

[7] The Seventh General Assembly authorized the borrowing of $100,000 to redeem the outstanding circulation of the old State Bank, which fell due the next year.

Bill Introduced in Illinois Legislature
to Establish a State Road from Peoria to Hendersonville[1]

[January 21, 1837]

An act to establish a State road from Peoria to Hendersonville.

SEC. 1 Be it enacted by the People of the State of Illinois represented in the General Assembly: That Stephen French of Peoria county, and Henry McClenahan and Wilson Brown of Knox county, be, and they are hereby appointed commissioners, to view, mark and locate a state road from Peoria in Peoria county by way of Prince's mill to Hendersonville in Knox county.

Sᴇᴄ 2 Said commissioners shall meet at Hendersonville on the first monday in April next, or within six months thereafter, and, after being duly sworn by some Justice of the Peace, faithfully to perform the duties required of them by this act, shall proceed to locate said road, on the nearest and best route, avoiding, as much as the public convenience will permit, the injury of private property; and shall mark the same, by blazing the timber on the timbered land, and fixing stakes on the Pra[i]rie land.

Sᴇᴄ 3 Said commissioners shall make a map and report of so much of said road as lies in Peoria county, and file the same with the clerk of the county commissioner's court of said county; and a like map and report of so much as lies in Knox county and file the same with the clerk of the county commissioners court [of] said county. The county commissioners courts of Peoria and Knox counties shall allow said commissioners such compensation as they, respectively, shall deem just and reasonable

Sᴇᴄ 4 Said road shall be worked, and kept in repair, as other state roads are.

[1] AD, I-Ar. Lincoln wrote the bill, but it was introduced on January 21, 1837, by William McMurtry, representative from Warren, Knox, and Henry counties. The bill was passed and may be found in *Laws of Illinois*, 1837, pp. 267-68.

Amendments to Bill
Introduced in Illinois Legislature
to Establish a State Road
from Jacksonville to Syracuse and Bloomington[1]

[January 30, 1837]

Amend the third line of the first section, by striking out the name of William Montgomery and inserting that of John Armstrong.

Amend the seventh line of the same section, by inserting the words "by way of Greensburg" immediately after the word "thence"

Amend the fourth line of the second section, by striking out the word "Bloomington" and inserting "intersect the state road leading from Springfield to Bloomington, at or near the farm of Lemuel Foster"

[1] AD, I-Ar. The bill was introduced on January 27. On January 30, Lincoln reported it from the select committee to which it was referred with the amendments, which were adopted. The bill may be found in *Laws of Illinois*, 1837, pp. 280-81.

Amendment to an Amendment
Introduced in Illinois Legislature
to an Act Distributing
the School Funds to the Counties[1]

[February 7, 1837]

Provided that all counties which shall have been formed since the last taking of the census; shall for all school purposes, remain as though no division had been made, until the next taking of the census.

[1] AD, I-Ar. The engrossed bill "An act for distributing the school funds of this State among the counties, according to the number of children in each county under twenty years" was read for the third time on February 6, 1837. Several amendments were proposed and one adopted, but the House adjourned without voting on the bill. On the next day the question pending was taken up again and several amendments were proposed. One amendment proposed by James Craig, representative from Jo Daviess, Mercer and Rock Island counties, provided that "such counties as shall have been organized since the August election" should receive "a portion in the same ratio, on the number of votes given at their election for county officers, when organized respectively" (*House Journal*, Tenth General Assembly, First Session, p. 504). Lincoln's amendment to Craig's amendment was rejected, as was Craig's amendment also. After further discussion the bill was passed.

Bill Introduced in Illinois Legislature
to Relocate Part of a State Road
from Springfield to Lewiston[1]

[February 10, 1837]

An act to relocate a part of the State Road leading from Springfield to Lewiston.

Be it enacted by the People of the State of Illinois represented in the General Assembly: That Samuel Berry, James Pantier, and John Jones sen. be and they are hereby appointed commissioners to view, mark, and relocate so much of the State Road leading from Springfield to Lewiston as lies between the Southern boundary line of Township 19 North of Range 7 West, and the residence of the said John Jones sen.

The said commissioners shall meet at the house of Samuel Berry on the first monday of May next, or some convenient day thereafter, and after being duly sworn, shall proceed to make said relocation, and shall make return thereof to the county commissioners court for Sangamon county at their next term.

The said county commissioners court, shall allow said commissioners such compensation as they may deem reasonable.

¹ AD, I-Ar. The bill passed both houses and may be found in *Laws of Illinois*, 1837, pp. 203-204. Lincoln wrote this bill in response to a petition signed by James Pantier, John Jones, and other citizens who were dissatisfied with the bill which Lincoln had introduced in December, 1835. (See the bill by the same title, December 15, 1835, *supra*.)

Report to Illinois Legislature
on Petitions and Remonstrances Concerning
Establishment of New Counties¹

[February 13, 1837]

The select committee to whom was refered the petition of sundry citizens of Sangamon county, praying the establishment of three new counties, principally from the teritory of the said county of Sangamon; and to whom was also refered the remonstrance of sundry citizens of the same county, against *any* division or dismemberment of the same, have had the same under consideration and report: That 1437 names are found on the petition, and 2213 on the remonstrance.²

Upon this fact, the committee unanamously agree that the prayer of the petitioners ought not to be granted, and, therefore, ask to be discharged from the further consideration of the subject.

The same committee, to whom were also refered the petitions of sundry citizens of Montgomery & Shelby counties, praying the establishment of new counties, find that a majority of neither country [*sic*] has signed the said petitions, and they, therefore, ask to be discharged from the further consideration of the subject.

¹ AD, I-Ar.
² In connection with this report, see Lincoln's bill, December 24, 1836, *supra*.

Bill Introduced in Illinois Legislature
to Supplement "An Act to Erect Certain Bridges,
Approved January 22, 1831"¹

[February 13, 1837]

An Act Supplemental to an Act Entitled "An Act to Erect Certain Bridges" Approved Jan. 22, 1831

Be it enacted by the People of the State of Illinois represented in the General Assembly: That the county of Knox shall be entitled to all the benefits of the act to which this is supplemental; Provided the county commissioner's court of said county, shall comply with the requisites of said act, within two years from the passage of this act.

[1] AD, I-Ar. The bill was written by Lincoln, but introduced by William Mc-Murtry on February 13. It passed the House and was amended in the Senate to apply also to McDonough County. As amended, the bill appears in *Laws of Illinois*, 1837, p. 26.

Amendments Introduced in Illinois Legislature
to Senate Bill Permanently Locating the Seat of Government of the State of Illinois[1]

[February 14, 1837]

Strike out the word "twentieth" where it occurs, and insert "twenty third"

Fill the first blank with the word "fifty"

Fill the second blank with the word "three"

Add the following proviso to the 4th. section.

Provided that this act shall be null and void, unless the sum of fifty thousand dollars be donated by individuals, and secured by bonds and security to be approved of by the Governor, and made payable to, the State Treasurer, to become due at such time as the Governor shall direct, which bonds shall be executed and filed with the State Treasurer on or before the first day of May next; and which donation is especially designed to meet the appropriation herein before made, and shall be applied exclusively and immediately to that object; and also, unless a sufficient quantity of ground, not less than two acres, upon which to erect public buildings, be donated and conveyed to the State without expense to the State.

[1] AD, I-Ar. Although written by Lincoln, these amendments were moved by Alexander P. Dunbar, representative from Coles County. The amendments were adopted, but the first, calling for a change from "twentieth" to "twenty third," was later amended to "28th." The bill itself, calling for removal of the state capital from Vandalia to Springfield, was a project of the Sangamon "Long Nine" as a whole. Strategy called for its being introduced first in the Senate, probably because bills passed by the Senate usually had less trouble in the House. Although Lincoln did not write the bill, he was in a sense its author in a larger degree than he was of numerous bills which are preserved in his handwriting. Certainly it was Lincoln more than any other member of the legislature who was responsible for its final passage. Lincoln moved a final amendment, which passed on February 24, as follows: "The General Assembly reserves the right to repeal this act at any time hereafter" (*House Journal*, Tenth General Assembly, First Session, p. 702). The act appears in *Laws of Illinois*, 1837, pp. 321-22.

[73]

Report to Illinois Legislature
on Amount of Annual Revenue and Current Expenses[1]

[February 16, 1837]

The committee on Finance, who were required by a resolution to ascertain the amount of money annually receivable into the State Treasury by opperation of the existing revenue laws; and also, the amount necessary to meet the current expenses of the government, report:

That the amount receivable from all sources is	$ 57,895.15
And the amount required	55,151.97

The different items, forming the above amount of money are as follows (viz)

From non resident land tax	$ 44,395.15
From State Bank	12.000
From Shawaneetown [*sic*] Bank	1 500
Total as above	57,895.15

As to the amount necessary to meet the current expenditures of the government, the committee on Finance, have relied on a report made by the committee on Public Accounts and Expenditures, which, as above, is. $ 55.151.97

The committee on Finance, on looking over the report of the committee on Public Accounts and Expenditures, discover that, in their judgement, much too small a sum is allowed for a Contingent fund; they, therefore, think it prudent to add 15.000

Total	70.151 97
From which take the revenue	57.895 15
Leaving a deficit of.	12 256 82

[1] AD, I-Ar.

Protest in Illinois Legislature on Slavery[1]

March 3, 1837

The following protest was presented to the House, which was read and ordered to be spread on the journals, to wit:

"Resolutions upon the subject of domestic slavery having passed

[74]

both branches of the General Assembly at its present session, the undersigned hereby protest against the passage of the same.[2]

They believe that the institution of slavery is founded on both injustice and bad policy; but that the promulgation of abolition doctrines tends rather to increase than to abate its evils.

They believe that the Congress of the United States has no power, under the constitution, to interfere with the institution of slavery in the different States.

They believe that the Congress of the United States has the power, under the constitution, to abolish slavery in the District of Columbia; but that that power ought not to be exercised unless at the request of the people of said District.

The difference between these opinions and those contained in the said resolutions, is their reason for entering this protest."

DAN STONE,[3]

A. LINCOLN,

Representatives from the county of Sangamon.

[1] *House Journal,* Tenth General Assembly, First Session, pp. 817-18.
[2] The General Assembly had received from the States of Virginia, Alabama, Mississippi, New York, and Connecticut "Memorials . . . relative to the existence of domestic slavery . . ." A joint select committee of both houses reported to the House on January 12, 1837, deeply deploring "the unfortunate condition of our fellow men, whose lots are cast in thraldom in a land of liberty and peace," but holding that "the arm of the General Government has no power to strike their fetters from them," and spurning indignantly "an interference with the rights of property in other States." Following a diatribe against abolition societies, the committee recommended the adoption of the following resolutions:
"*Resolved by the General Assembly of the State of Illinois,* That we highly disapprove of the formation of abolition societies, and of the doctrines promulgated by them.
"*Resolved,* That the right of property in slaves, is sacred to the slave-holding States by the Federal Constitution, and that they cannot be deprived of that right without their consent.
"*Resolved,* That the General Government cannot abolish slavery in the District of Columbia, against the consent of the citizens of said District without a manifest breach of good faith.
"*Resolved,* That the Governor be requested to transmit to the States of Virginia, Alabama, Mississippi, New York, and Connecticut, a copy of the foregoing report and resolutions." (*Ibid.,* pp. 243-44.)
Considerable debate ensued and numerous amendments were offered, but no details of the debate, nor details of the amendments, are recorded in the *Journal* except those offered from the floor on the final reporting of the resolutions. Lincoln moved to amend the amendment proposed by the committee to the third resolution by inserting after the word "Congress," the following: "Unless the people of the said District petition for the same." The motion failed and after further debate the resolutions "as amended" were finally passed by the House on January 20. The Senate concurred on January 25. The resolutions as amended are not printed in the *Journal of the House,* but the degree to which the general sentiment of the resolutions was modified seems not to have impressed Lincoln and Stone, who presented their protest on March 3, after other

weighty legislation (notably the bill to remove the state capital from Vandalia to Springfield) had been safely passed.

[3] Daniel Stone was a Whig lawyer of Springfield, Illinois. Upon resigning his seat in the legislature after the adjournment of the session, he was succeeded by Edward D. Baker, elected at a special election on July 1.

Bond for Charles Oakley as Fund Commissioner[1]

March 4, 1837

Know all men by these presents that we Charles Oakley M. McConnel, Wm. Lane, Benjn. Mitchell, Richd. Bently [sic], A. Lincoln, R. L Wilson Jos. Naper, M. Aldrich, Robert Stuart, Asahel Ball, R. N. Cullum [sic], Jonas Rawalt, Jas. Craig Danl. Stone are held and firmly bound unto Joseph Duncan Governor of the State of Illinois, and his successors in office, for the use of said state in the penal sum of Fifty thousand dollars lawful money of the United States of America for which payment well and truly to be made, we bind ourselves, our heirs, executors and Administrators Jointly and severally, firmly by these presents, sealed with our seals and dated the Fourth day of March A. D. 1837.

The condition of the above obligation is such, that Whereas, the said Charles Oakley has been elected to the office of Fund Commissioner, under the provisions of an Act of the General Assembly of the State of Illinois, entitled "An Act to establish and maintain a General system of Internal improvement," approved the 27th. day of February A. D. 1837. Now if the said Charles Oakley, shall well, truly and faithfully discharge the duties of said office of Fund Commissioner as aforsaid [sic] according to the provisions of said act, and shall faithfully, account for all moneys that shall or may come into his hands as such Fund Commissioner and shall faithfully perform such other duties as shall from time to time be imposed upon him by Laws, as such Commissioner, then this obligation to be void otherwise to remain in full force and virtue.

Signed, Sealed and delivered in presence of[2]

[1] DS, I-Ar.
[2] The document carries a total of fifty-one signers, including the names of the persons named in the bond proper.

Bond for Benjamin S. Enloe
as Warden of State Penitentiary[1]

[March 13] 1837

Know all men by these Presents that we Ben S. Enloe, A. Lincoln, Andrew McCormick,[2] R. L. Wilson Dan Stone James Duncan

Jas A Whiteside   John Dement, Joseph E Watkins   Peter Warren
are held and firmly bound, unto Joseph Duncan, Governor of the
State of Illinois, and his successors in office for the use of the people
of said State in the penal sum of Ten Thousand dollars, for the payment of which, well and truly to be made, we bind, ourselves, our
heirs, Executors and administrators jointly—and severally firmly
by these presents, seale[d] with our seals, and dated this   day
of   1837.

The condition of the above obligation is such that whereas the
said Benjamin S. Enloe has been elected by the General Assembly
of the State of Illinois, Warden of the Penitentiary of said State,
Now if the said Benjamin S. Enloe, shall well and faithfully
discharge the duties of said office, according to Law, and deliver
over to his successor in office, all Books, records, vouchers, papers,
presses [?] and furniture appertaining to said office, whole safe
and undefaced, then this obligation to be void, otherwise to remain
in full force and virtue.

In presence of {

Ben. S. Enloe (Seal)	Dan Stone (Seal)
A. Lincoln (Seal)	Jos E Watkins (Seal)
Andrew McCormick (Seal)	James Duncan (Seal)
R. L. Wilson (Seal)	James A Whiteside (Seal)
Scanon Lane [?] (Seal)	John Dement (Seal)
Peter Warren (Seal)	

[1] DS, I-Ar. Governor Joseph Duncan's approval is dated March 13, 1837.
[2] Lincoln filled in his own name and that of McCormick.

To Levi Davis[1]

Friend Davis.   Springfield, April 19– 1837

The bearer of this, Dr. Henry,[2] visits you for the purpose of
drawing a small amount of money to enable the Commissioners to
commence the erection of a State House. He, as you probably
recollect, is one of the building commissioners. The bond for the
$50,000 required by the act locating the Seat of Government,[3] has
been executed by several of our citizens and duly approved by the
Governor;[4] and will be filed with the Treasurer, by Dr. Henry on
his arrival at your town. The Dr., being a stranger to you and the
Treasurer, and his duties being of a new kind, he has asked me to
request you, as a friend, to render him what assistance you con-
veniently can.

We have, generally in this country, peace, health, and plenty,
and no news. Verry respectfully: A. LINCOLN.

 ¹ ALS, CSmH. Davis, an attorney living in Vandalia, Illinois, was appointed state auditor by Governor Joseph Duncan, November 16, 1835.

² Anson G. Henry, a physician and Whig politician of Springfield, Illinois, was one of Lincoln's closest associates.

³ Passed by the legislature February 24-25, 1837, removing the state capital from Vandalia to Springfield.

⁴ Joseph Duncan.

To Mary S. Owens[1]

Friend Mary   Springfield, May 7. 1837

I have commenced two letters to send you before this, both of which displeased me before I got half done, and so I tore them up. The first I thought wasn't serious enough, and the second was on the other extreme. I shall send this, turn out as it may.

This thing of living in Springfield is rather a dull business after all, at least it is so to me. I am quite as lonesome here as [I] ever was anywhere in my life. I have been spoken to by but one woman since I've been here, and should not have been by her, if she could have avoided it. I've never been to church yet, nor probably shall not be soon. I stay away because I am conscious I should not know how to behave myself.

I am often thinking about what we said of your coming to live at Springfield. I am afraid you would not be satisfied. There is a great deal of flourishing about in carriages here, which it would be your doom to see without shareing in it. You would have to be poor without the means of hiding your poverty. Do you believe you could bear that patiently? Whatever woman may cast her lot with mine, should any ever do so, it is my intention to do all in my power to make her happy and contented; and there is nothing I can immagine, that would make me more unhappy than to fail in the effort. I know I should be much happier with you than the way I am, provided I saw no signs of discontent in you. What you have said to me may have been in jest, or I may have misunderstood it. If so, then let it be forgotten; if otherwise, I much wish you would think seriously before you decide. For my part I have already decided. What I have said I will most positively abide by, provided you wish it. My opinion is that you had better not do it. You have not been accustomed to hardship, and it may be more severe than you now immagine. I know you are capable of thinking correctly on any subject; and if you deliberate maturely upon this, before you decide, then I am willing to abide your decision.

You must write me a good long letter after you get this. You have nothing else to do, and though it might not seem interesting to you, after you had written it, it would be a good deal of company

to me in this "busy wilderness." Tell your sister I dont want to
hear any more about selling out and moving. That gives me the
hypo[2] whenever I think of it. Yours, &c.   LINCOLN.

[1] ALS, owned by Mrs. George H. Vineyard, St. Joseph, Missouri.
[2] Hypochondria.

Report Drawn for Road Commissioners[1]

May 23, 1837

We, the undersigned, being appointed by the county commissioner's court of Sangamon county, to view a road from the Public
Square in Springfield to Nathan Hussey's on the Fort Clark road,
report that we have viewed, marked, and located the road as follows (towit) Begining at the Public Square aforesaid, and running
from thence with the Peoria road as now traveled, to a point in the
middle of said road, from which one of the bearing trees of the
South West corner of Section one in Township 16 North of Range 5
West, being a Black Oak 12 inches in diameter, bears N 1¼ E 8
chains & 12 links, and thence according to the Plat & Field notes
returned herewith, to a point on the old road near to the North
West corner of the aforesaid Section one. Thence with the old road
as now traveled to the said Hussey's.

Given under our hands this 23rd of May. 1837
We report said road to be of public utility.

GEO PASFIELD
WASHINGTON ILES
JOHN WILLIAMS

[1] AD, IHi. Whether Lincoln made the survey as well as drew the report for
the Springfield commissioners is uncertain, since the plat and field notes mentioned in the report no longer accompany it.

To the Third Auditor of the United States Treasury[1]

Springfield, Illinois, May 30th. 1837–

If the claim, founded upon the enclosed papers, be allowed, the
money may be forwarded directly to the claimant, "Archelaus
Demmon, Springfield Illinois" If it be *not* allowed, on account of
insufficiency of evidence, or for other cause, and the defect, whatever it be, can be remedied, write back, stating particularly what
is lacking, and direct to A. Lincoln, place as above.

The Paymaster or disbursing officer, of whom this applicant received pay was, according to recollection, Major Wright of the

United States Army. In this there may be a mistake, as there is nothing but memory to refer to. At any rate it was the officer that paid Whiteside's Brigade. Respectfully   A. LINCOLN for
      Third Auditor[2]   the Applicant.

[1] ALS, IHi. According to endorsements on the letter and on the envelope, the claim was allowed in the amount of $32.68. Archelaus Demmon was a Black Hawk War veteran.
[2] Peter Hagner.

Resolution Adopted at a Public Meeting
Called by Anson G. Henry[1]

June 24, 1837

Whereas we have seen several publications in the "Illinois Republican," stating that Dr. A. G. Henry, one of the Commissioners appointed by the Legislature to superintend the building of the State House, is squandering disadvantageously and uselessly the public money appropriated by the citizens of this place for that object; and, whereas, if the charge be true, it is highly important to the interest of the State, that the trust now held by Dr. Henry should be immediately placed in other hands: therefore

Resolved, That a Committee of seven be appointed to examine the books and proceedings of the Commissioners appointed to superintend the building of the State House, and that said Committee make a full and complete Report of said proceedings, together with such remarks upon the facts disclosed as their acquaintance with such business may enable them to make, that may go to show whether the Commissioners are, or are not, progressing with the work in the most economical and judicious manner; and that said Report be published in the newspapers of this place.

[1] Sangamo Journal, July 1, 1837. The committee which was appointed at the meeting made its investigation and published a report completely vindicating Dr. Henry.

Notice to Illinois Legislature
of a Bill to Authorize Rhoda Hart and Others
to Sell Certain Real Estate[1]

Mr Speaker   [July 12, 1837]

I hereby give notice that on friday next or some day thereafter I shall ask leave to introduce a bill for an act to authorize Rhoda Hart and others to sell and convey certain real estate.

[1] AD, I-Ar. The bill was introduced on July 15 (vide infra).

Bill Introduced in Illinois Legislature
to Extend Corporate Powers of the President
and Trustees of the Town of Springfield[1]

[July 12, 1837]

SECTION 1 Be it enacted by the People of the State of Illinois represented in the General Assembly: That the President and trustees of the town of Springfield, in the county of Sangamon and state aforesaid, and their successors in office, or a majority of them, shall hereafter have authority in addition to the powers confered upon them by an act entitled "An act to incorporate the inhabitants of such towns as may wish to be incorporated," Approved February 12th. 1831, to extend the boundaries of said town one half mile in each direction beyond it's present limits, & to open, widen, and extend the streets and alleys of the same; and to levy and collect annually a tax on all the real estate in said town as extended, not exceeding four percent per annum on the assessed value thereof, and to borrow money, provided that at no time shall the amount so borrowed exceed one hundred thousand dollars.

SEC. 2 All moneys arising from the collection of taxes, or from the loan or loans above authorized shall be appropriated by the said President and Trustees and their successors in such manner as in their opinion will best promote the interests of the said town

SEC 3. The said President and Trustees shall have power to enforce their ordinances by authorizing the collection of taxes to sell any town lot or parcel of ground within the limit of said town or so much as will pay the tax due and in arrear from the owner thereof in such manner as is now authorized under the act approved Feb. 12. 1831 aforesaid.

SEC. 4. That when any street is opened, widened, or extended, the President and Trustees shall make the person or persons injured thereby, compensation; to ascertain which they shall cause to be summoned twelve good and lawful men, freeholders and inhabitants of said town, not directly interested, who being first duly sworn for that purpose, shall enquire in to and take into consideration, as well the benefit as the injury which may accrue, and estimate and assess the damage sustained by reason thereof, and shall moreover estimate the amount which other persons will be benefited thereby, all of which shall be returned to the board under their hands and seals, and the persons so benefited and assessed shall pay the same in such manner as shall be provided, and the residue if any shall be paid into the town Treasury.

[81]

Sec. 5. That upon the application of the owners of two thirds of the lots on any street or part of a street, it shall be lawful for the President and Trustees to levy and collect a special tax on the owners of the lots on said street or parts of a street according to their respective fronts, for the purpose of grading and paving the streets and side-walks in front thereof

Sec 6 This act to take effect from and after it's passage.

[1] AD, I-Ar. Although written by Lincoln, the bill was introduced in the Senate by Archer G. Herndon of Sangamon County. The bill became law and may be found in *Laws of Illinois*, 1837 (Special Session), pp. 94-95.

Notice to Illinois Legislature
of a Bill in Relation to State and County Roads[1]

Mr. Speaker.   [July 13, 1837]

I give notice that on monday next I shall ask leave to introduce a bill for an act in relation to State & County roads.

[1] AD, I-Ar. Although Lincoln wrote the notice, Richard N. Cullom, representative from Tazewell County, is recorded in the *House Journal* as the member giving the notice on July 13 (misprinted July 11). The bill was apparently never introduced.

Bill Introduced in Illinois Legislature
to Establish a State Road from Beardstown to Petersburg[1]

[July 13, 1837]

A bill for an act to establish a state road from Beardstown in Cass county to Petersburg in Sangamon county.

Section 1st. Be it enacted by the People of the state of Illinois represented in the General Assembly: That Henry McHenry, Solomon Penny and Myram Penny[2] be and they are hereby appointed commissioners to view, mark, and locate a state road from Beardstown in Cass county, thence as near as the ground will permit, by way of the town of Richmond, and Robinsons Mill to Petersburg in Sangamon county.

Sec 2. Said commissioners, or a majority of them shall meet at Beardstown on the first monday in September next, or on any other day which they may agree upon, within six months from the passage of this act, and after being duly sworn by some Justice of the Peace, faithfully to perform the duties herein required, shall proceed to view, mark, and locate said road as above described, avoiding as much as the public interest will permit, the injury of private property.

SEC. 3. Said commissioners shall make out a complete map and report of the location of so much of said road as lies in the county Cass, and file the same with the clerk of the county commissioners court of the said county of Cass; and a like map and report of so much as lies in the county of Sangamon and file the same with the clerk of the county commissioners court of said county of Sangamon.

SEC. 4. Said road shall be and remain a state road, and shall be opened and kept in repair as other state roads are.

SEC. 5. The county commissioners courts of the said counties of Cass and Sangamon shall allow said commissioners such compensation as they may deem reasonable

[1] AD, I-Ar. The bill became law and may be found in *Laws of Illinois*, 1837 (Special Session), p. 65.
[2] Upon the third reading of the bill, Lincoln moved the amendment of "Isham Reavis" to replace "Myram Penny," which was agreed to.

Bill Introduced in Illinois Legislature
to Authorize Rhoda Hart and Others
to Sell Certain Real Estate[1]

[July 15, 1837]

A bill for an act to authorize Rhoda Hart and others to sell and convey certain real estate.

SEC. 1 Be it enacted by the People of the state of Illinois represented in the the [sic] General Assembly: That Rhoda Hart, widdow, and Harvey B. Hart, Moses P. Hart, Nancy Hart, John F. Wilson, Martha Wilson, and Rhoda Hart, adult heirs of Moses Hart deceased, all of the county of Sangamon and state of Illinois, be and they are hereby authorized to sell and jointly convey, by a deed or deeds in feesimple, all the real estate of which the said Moses Hart deceased died seized, the same being the South West quarter of Section Twentyfour, the East half of the North West quarter of Section Twentyfour, and fifty acres of the South end or part of the East half of the South West quarter of [Sec]tion Thirteen all in Township Seventeen North of Range Seven West of the Third Principal Meridian, and lying in the said county of Sangamon.

Sec 2. The said conveyance shall be with this condition; that if the minor heirs of the said Moses Hart deceased shall not execute a release of all their right and title to said real estate, in favour of the purchaser or purchasers, his, her, or their heirs or assigns, within one year after the youngest of them shall arrive at the age of twentyone years, all the above named persons, selling and conveying said real estate as aforesaid, shall be jointly and severally bound to pay to the said purchaser or purchasers, his, her, or their heirs or assigns, double the sum for which the part of the said minor heirs may have been sold, to be recovered in an action of debt against them or either of them; and this act shall be sufficient evidence of said condition, without the same being set forth in the deed of conveyance or any other writing.

SECTION 3 The duly appointed guardian of the minor heirs of William Everly deceased, late of the county of Edwards and state of Illinois, be authorized to sell and convey the following described tracts of land, towit, the West half of the South West quarter of Section three, and the West half of the South East quarter of Section four, both in Township Seventeen North of Range two West of the Third Principal Meridian, and situated in the county of Sangamon and state aforesaid, the same being the property of the said minor heirs, and to apply the proceeds thereof to the maintainance and education of said heirs.

[1] AD, I-Ar. The bill was referred to the judiciary committee, whence it was reported without amendment and defeated on July 19, 1837.

Bill Amended in Illinois Legislature
Relative to the Building of a State House at Springfield[1]

[July 19, 1837]

SEC 1 Be enacted by the People of the state of Illinois represented in the General Assembly: That no money shall hereafter be drawn from the Treasury of the state for the purpose of erecting a State House, except such as may hereafter be paid into the said Treasury, by the citizens of Springfield, according to the provisions of a certain bond now on file in the Treasurer's office, executed by said citizens for the payment of fifty thousand dollars, to be applied to the erection of a State House, or otherwise

SEC 2. All moneyes that have heretofore been drawn from the Treasury by the acting commissioner, for the purpose of erecting a State House at Springfield shall be refunded so soon as the first instalment of the bond above mentioned becomes due.

[1] AD, I-Ar. The amended bill as written by Lincoln was reported on July 19 from a select committee to which had been referred a bill entitled "An act to repeal certain laws relative to the permanent location of the seat of Government of the State of Illinois, approved Feb. 25th and March 3rd, 1837." The original bill had been introduced by W. L. D. Ewing, representative from

Fayette and Effingham counties. When Ewing's bill was amended by "striking out all after the enacting clause," it was then referred to the select committee, from which emerged Lincoln's amended version, calculated to quiet the opposition in the House but with little chance of passing the Senate. Upon passage of the bill as amended, Lincoln moved to amend the title to read "An act relative to the building of a State House at Springfield," which was done. The bill died in the Senate.

Bill Introduced in Illinois Legislature
to Relocate a Part of State Road
Leading from William Crow's in Morgan County
to Musick's Bridge in Sangamon County[1]

[July 19, 1837]

A bill for an act to relocate a part of the state road leading from William Crow's in Morgan county to Musick's bridge in Sangamon county.[2]

SEC 1 Be it enacted by the People of the state of Illinois represented in the General Assembly: That Reuben Harrison, Dallis[3] Scott and Elihu Bone, be and they are hereby appointed commissioners to view mark and relocate so much of the state road leading from William Crow's in Morgan county to Musick's bridge in Sangamon county as lies between the head of Richland creek and the Sangamo river.

SEC 2. Said commissioners shall meet at the house of Peter Cartwright on the first monday in September next or on any other day agreed on by them within six months from the passage of this act, and after being duly sworn, shall proceed to relocate the part of the said road above mentioned, avoiding the injury of private property as much as the public convenience will permit.

SEC 3 said commissioners shall make a map and report of said relocation and file the same with the clerk of the county commissioners court of Sangamon county; and shall receive out of the treasury of said county such compensation as the county commissioners may deem reasonable.

SEC. 4 The road as now traveled from Springfield to Rochester both in Sangamon county, be and the same is hereby declared a state road and shall be worked and kept in repair as other state roads are.

SEC. 5. That Samuel K. Miller, James Fyffe, and James Lanterman be, and they are hereby appointed commissioners to view and locate a state road leading from Lawrenceville to Russelville, in Lawrence county.

SEC. 6. The said commissioners shall meet in Lawrenceville, on or before the second Monday in August next, or as soon thereafter as convenient, and after being sworn by some justice of the peace impartially to locate the same, they shall commence at Lawrenceville, thence by James Nabbs' bridge, across the Embarrass river, to the centre school house in Allison prairie, and from thence to Russelville on the most convenient and practicable ground, doing as little injury to private property as possible.

SEC. 7. The said commissioners shall, as soon as convenient, cause to be filed with the clerk of the county commissioners' court of Lawrence county, a report and complete map of said road, which report and map shall be preserved and shall form a part of the record of said court. Said road, when so established, shall be kept in repair as other state roads are; and the county commissioners' court of Lawrence county shall allow the said viewers not more than one dollar and fifty cents per day for their services.

SEC. 8. The inhabitants of the town of Petersburg, in Sangamon county, may hereafter be incorporated according to the provisions of the general town incorporation act, notwithstanding said town may not contain one hundred and fifty inhabitants.[4]

[1] AD, I-Ar. Introduced by Lincoln on July 19, the bill was immediately amended by Edward J. Oneille, representative from Lawrence County, with sections 5, 6, and 7, which do not appear in the bill in Lincoln's hand. Section 8 is in Lincoln's hand on the verso of the sheet containing sections 1 to 4, but was apparently not offered as an amendment. The inference is that Lincoln, in agreement with Oneille, left sections 5 to 7 for his colleague to provide. The bill became law and may be found in *Laws of Illinois*, 1837 (Special Session), pp. 71-72.

[2] The introduction of this bill, carrying a similar title to the bill introduced on December 11, 1835 (*supra*), was occasioned by a petition of sundry citizens of Sangamon County praying the review of the earlier bill, provisions of which were unsatisfactory.

[3] Dallas Scott.

[4] See letter to John Bennett, August 5, 1837, *infra*.

Amendment to an Act
Introduced in Illinois Legislature
to Locate a State Road[1]

[July 19, 1837]

SEC 4 That Bowling Green, Bennett Abell, and John Bennett, be and they are hereby authorized to meet at any time within six months from the passage of this act, and to relocate so much of the State road leading from Springfield to Lewiston, as lies between the towns of New-Salem and Petersburg, and are required to make a map and report of said relocation and file the same with the clerk of the county commissioner's court of Sangamon county; and for their services shall receive such compensation as the county commissioners of said county shall deem reasonable

1 AD, I-Ar. Lincoln's amendment was attached to a bill to locate a road in Vermilion County, introduced from the committee on petitions by John Wyatt, representative from Morgan County, in answer to a petition signed by sundry citizens of Vermilion. The bill died in the Senate.

Petition to Edward Smith[1]

Vandalia, Illinois July 21st 1837

To Edward Smith Esq—Understanding that you are about to leave the employ of the State We The undersigned members of the General Assembly, having the fullest confidence in your integrity; and ability as an Engineer would most earnestly request that you would continue, in the Employ of the Board of Public Works, of this State, until the Surveys contemplated in the Bill for an Act to Establish & Maintain a General System of Internal Improvements, are fully completed & that you by no means or from no cause retire from the state service.

1 DS, I-Ar. The petition carries forty-three names, including Lincoln's. Edward Smith, Democratic representative from Wabash County, was a leading figure in the internal improvements fight in which Lincoln was vitally interested. He continued in the legislature and was re-elected in 1838.

A Toast Volunteered at a Public Dinner at Springfield, Illinois[1]

July 25, 1837

By A. Lincoln, Esq.—All our friends.—They are too numerous to be now named individually, while there is no one of them who is not too dear to be forgotten or neglected.

1 *Sangamo Journal*, July 29, 1837. The dinner was held at Spottswood's Rural Hotel in celebration of the removal to Springfield of the state capital.

Petition for Pardon of Jesse E. Massie[1]

To His Excellency   Springfield Illinois
    The Governor of the State of Missouri   August 1837
The Undersigned Citizens of the County of Sangamon would most respectfully represent, that in the early part of 1836,

Massie a citizen of this county, of very respectable connexions and as many of us know, and all of us believe heretofore of good character and conduct, was convicted in the St. Louis Circuit Court of the crime of larceny, uppon three indictments for stealing property of very trivial value, and was sentenced to the Penitentiary for six years where he has ever since been confined. We are unwilling from the circumstances of the transaction to attach deliberate guilt to his conduct. The articles, were (as we are informed) alleged to have been taken from a steamboat on which he was employed—he was no doubt intoxicated. The hands—who were witnesses and himself had quarrelled, and he was taken into custody asleep and in liquor within a few steps of the boat, the property was in his trunk by his side—such we are informed were the circumstances. He was tried as appears from the record within a very few days of his arrest, without the presence of his friends—not without enemies, without means to employ counsel, and destitute of the knowledge to conduct a defence if innocent.

We incline to believe, from his friends—his early associations the manner in which he has been brought up, his previous fair character, and from the facts to which we have alluded—that he has been more imprudent than guilty and more unfortunate than criminal. But if guilty he has suffered a long confinement, and we most respectfully suggest that he is [rendered?] by the *uncertainty* of his guilt and the certainty of his punishment, a fit subject for the exercise of that clemency, which your excellency—is so happy as to be able to apply. We are very Respy Your obt Servants

[1] DS, Missouri State Archives. Lincoln was one of fifty-five signers. Endorsements on the document indicate that a pardon was issued March 8, 1838.

A Toast Volunteered at a Public Dinner at Athens, Illinois[1]

August 3, 1837

By A. Lincoln. Sangamon county will ever be true to her best interests and never more so than in reciprocating the good feelings of the citizens of Athens and neighborhood.

[1] *Sangamo Journal*, August 12, 1837. The dinner was given in honor of the Sangamon County delegation in the legislature, in expression of "approbation of their course in the Legislature."

Handbill: The Case of the Heirs of
Joseph Anderson *vs* James Adams[1]

August 5, 1837

TO THE PUBLIC

It is well known to most of you, that there is existing at this time, considerable excitement in regard to Gen. Adams's titles to certain

[1] *Sangamo Journal,* August 19, 1837. As reprinted in the *Journal,* this handbill carried the following editorial introduction:

TO THE PEOPLE

In accordance with our determination, as expressed last week, we present to the reader the articles which were published in hand-bill form, in reference to the case of the Heirs of Joseph Anderson vs. James Adams. These articles can now be read, uninfluenced by personal or party feeling, and with the sole motive of learning the truth. When that is done, the reader can pass his own judgment on the matters at issue.

We only regret in this case, that the publications were not made some weeks before the election. Such a course might have prevented the expressions of regret, which have often been heard since, from different individuals, on account of the disposition they made of their votes.

In an adjacent column appeared the following statement by the editor of the *Journal:*

It having been stated this morning that the subscriber had refused to give the name of the author of the hand bill above referred to (which statement is not true): to save any farther remarks on this subject, I now state that A. Lincoln, Esq. is the author of the handbill in question.   SIMEON FRANCIS.
August 7, 1837.

As in the instance of other pseudonymous and anonymous articles published in the *Journal,* the editors have excluded all but those which are incontrovertibly Lincoln's. Prior to the appearance of this handbill, there had appeared in the *Journal,* June 17, 24, and July 8, 15, 22, and 29, a series of six letters signed "Sampson's Ghost," which in view of subsequent developments seem possibly to have been the work of Lincoln and his colleagues, Edward D. Baker, Stephen T. Logan, and John T. Stuart. James Adams, the accused, attributed the letters to a group rather than to one individual. Charges which are explicit in the handbill and the subsequent "replies," were more veiled in the Sampson's Ghost letters, but it is obvious that only Lincoln and his associates as attorneys for the heirs of Joseph Anderson would have at that time been in possession of the evidence upon which the insinuations were based. Internal evidence in these letters, however, does not determine Lincoln's handiwork, and, as in the instance of a later series of pseudonymous letters in which Lincoln was one of several collaborators (see "The 'Rebecca' Letter," August 27, 1842, and footnote, *infra*), authorities have been somewhat precipitous in assigning Lincoln's authorship.

Subsequent to the appearance of the handbill and the "replies" to James Adams, there appeared in the *Journal* on September 30 and October 7 further communications signed "An Old Settler," which present additional accusations. These also may, or may not, have emanated from Lincoln's office, but they have been excluded here for the same reason as the earlier letters.

[89]

tracts of land, and the manner in which he acquired them. As I
understand, the Gen. charges that the whole has been gotten up
by a knot of lawyers to injure his election:[2] and as I am one of the
knot to which he refers—and as I happen to be in possession of
facts connected with the matter, I will, in as brief a manner as
possible, make a statement of them, together with the means by
which I arrived at the knowledge of them.

Sometime in May or June last,[3] a widow woman, by the name
of Anderson, and her son,[4] who reside in Fulton county, came to
Springfield, for the purpose, as they said, of selling a ten acre
lot of ground lying near town,[5] which they claimed as the property of the deceased husband and father.

When they reached town they found the land was claimed by
Gen. Adams. John T. Stuart and myself were employed to look
into the matter, and if it was thought we could do so with any prospect of success, to commence a suit for the land. I went immediately to the Recorder's office to examine Adams's title, and found
that the land had been entered by one Dixon,[6] deeded by Dixon[7]
to one Thomas, by Thomas[8] to one Miller, and by Miller[9] to Gen.
Adams. The oldest of these three deeds was about ten or eleven
years old, and the latest more than five, all recorded at the same
time, and that within less than one year.[10] This I thought a suspicious circumstance, and I was thereby induced to examine the
deeds very closely, with a view to the discovery of some defect by
which to overturn the title, being almost convinced then it was
founded in fraud. I finally discovered that in the deed from Thomas
to Miller, although Miller's name stood in a sort of a marginal note
on the record book, it was no where in the deed itself. I told the
fact to Talbott,[11] the Recorder, and proposed to him that he should
go to Gen. Adams' and get the original deed, and compare it with

[2] On August 7, Adams was elected over Dr. Anson G. Henry to the office of
probate justice of the peace by a vote of 1,025 to 792.

[3] May is correct.

[4] Mrs. Mary Anderson and son Richard.

[5] Almost two miles from the Statehouse in the hills upon which Oak Ridge
was subsequently located.

[6] John Dixon; entered November 17, 1823, Peoria County.

[7] Deeded November 29, 1825, to Joseph Thomas, Sangamon County "Deed
Book J.," 33-34.

[8] On September 17, 1825, Joseph Miller, Tazewell County, had given his
promissory note for $27 to Anderson for this land. Anderson agreed to get
Thomas to convey it to Miller, which was done November 1, 1826, *ibid.*, 34-35.

[9] On October 1, 1832, *ibid.*, 35-36. Miller conveyed the land to Adams in consideration of Anderson's judgment against him, which, Adams claimed, Anderson had assigned to Adams in discharge of a debt that Anderson owed Adams.

[10] Recorded June 18, 1836.

[11] Benjamin Talbott.

the record, and thereby ascertain whether the defect was in the original, or there was merely an error in the recording. As Talbott afterwards told me, he went to the General's, but not finding him at home, got the deed from his son,[12] which, when compared with the record, proved what we had discovered was merely an error of the Recorder. After Mr. Talbott corrected the record, he brought the original to our office, as I then thought and think yet, to show us that it was right. When he came into the room he handed the deed to me, remarking that the fault was all his own. On opening it, another paper fell out of it, which on examination, proved to be an assignment of a judgement in the Circuit Court of Sangamon County from Joseph Anderson, the late husband of the widow above named, to James Adams, the judgement being in favor of said Anderson against one Joseph Miller.[13] Knowing that this judgement had some connection with the land affair, I immediately took a copy of it, which is word for word, letter for letter and cross for cross as follows:

"Joseph Anderson vs. Joseph Miller.
Judgement in Sangamon Circuit Court *in favor of Joseph Anderson* against Joseph Miller obtained on a note originally 25 dolls. and interest thereon accrued.

"I assign all my right, title and interest *to the said Judgement,* to James Adams which is in consideration of a debt I owe the said Adams.

May 10th, 1827.   his
                                JOSEPH X ANDERSON.
                                        mark."[14]

As the copy shows, it bore date May 10th, 1827; although the judgement assigned by it was not obtained until the October afterwards, as may be seen by any one on the records of the Circuit Court. Two other strange circumstances attended it which cannot be represented by a copy. One of them was, that the date "1827" had first been made "1837" and without the figure "3" being fully obliterated, the figure "2" had afterwards been made on top of it; the other was that, although the date was ten years old, the writing on it, from the freshness of its appearance was thought by many, and I believe by all who saw it, not to be more than a week old. The paper on which it was written had a very old appearance; and

---

[12] Lucian Bonaparte Adams.
[13] Sangamon County Circuit Court records do not show any such judgment.
[14] The italicized words do not appear in the *Journal* on August 19, but were corrections in the September 30 issue.

there were some old figures on the back of it which made the freshness of the writing on the face [of?] it, much more striking than I suppose it otherwise might have been.

The reader's curiosity is no doubt excited to know what connection this assignment had with the land in question. The story is this: Dixon sold and deeded the land to Thomas;—Thomas sold it to Anderson; but before he gave a deed, Anderson sold it to Miller, and took Miller's note for the purchase money. When this note became due, Anderson sued Miller on it, and Miller procured an injunction from the Court of Chancery to stay the collection of the money until he should get a deed for the land.[15] Gen. Adams was employed as an attorney by Anderson in this chancery suit, and at the October term, 1827,[16] the injunction was dissolved, and a judgement given in favor of Anderson against Miller; and it was provided that Thomas was to execute a deed for the land in favor of Miller, and deliver it to Gen. Adams, to be held up by him till Miller paid the judgment, and then to deliver it to him. Miller left the county without paying the judgment. Anderson moved to Fulton county, where he has since died. When the widow came to Springfield last May or June, as before mentioned, and found the land deeded to Gen. Adams by Miller, she was naturally led to enquire why the money due upon the judgment had not been sent to them, inasmuch as he, Gen. Adams, had no authority to deliver Thomas' deed to Miller until the money was paid. Then it was the General told her, or perhaps her son, who came with her, that Anderson, in his life time, *had assigned the judgment to him*, Gen. Adams. I am now told that the General is exhibiting an assignment of the same judgment bearing date "1828"! and in other respects differing from the one described;[17] and that he is asserting that no such assignment as the one copied by me ever existed; or if there did, it was forged between Talbott and the lawyers, and slipped into his papers for the purpose of injuring him.[18] Now, I can only say that I know precisely such an one did exist, and that Ben. Talbott, Wm. Butler, C. R. Matheny, John T. Stuart, Judge Logan, Robert Irwin, P. C. Canedy and S. M. Tinsley, all saw and exam-

[15] Sangamon County Circuit Court Records, Book A, 323.

[16] On October 6, 1827, *ibid.*

[17] July 5, 1837, Adams filed what he claimed to be the original assignment, to which Anderson's name is signed in writing, *ibid.*, Book C, 421.

[18] Bill in chancery against Adams, filed by Lincoln & Stuart and Logan & Baker, attorneys for the heirs of Anderson, on June 22, 1837, makes no mention of either of these assignments, but charges fraudulent collusion between Adams and Miller. Joel Wright Admr. *et al. vs* Adams. MSS. Files, Clerk, Circuit Court, Sangamon County. Description of land (six and one-half lines) is only part of this eight-page bill written by Lincoln.

ined it, and that at least one half of them will swear that IT WAS
IN GENERAL ADAMS' HANDWRITING!! And further, I know
that Talbott will swear that he got it out of the General's possession, and returned it into his possession again. The assignment
which the General is now exhibiting purports to have been signed
by Anderson in writing. The one I copied was signed with a cross.
I am told that Gen. Neale[19] says that he will swear, that he heard
Gen. Adams tell young Anderson, that the assignment made by
his father, was signed with a cross.

The above are facts, as stated. I leave them without comment.
I have given the names of persons who have knowledge of these
facts, in order that any one who chooses may call on them and
ascertain how far they will corroborate my statements. I have only
made these statements because I am known by many to be one of
the individuals against whom the charge of forging the assignment
and slipping it into the General's papers, has been made; and because our silence might be construed into a confession of its truth.
I shall not subscribe my name: but I hereby authorise the editor
of the Journal to give it up to any one that may call for it.

[19] Thomas M. Neale, Springfield lawyer and surveyor.

To John Bennett[1]

Dear Sir.   Springfield, Aug. 5 1837
Mr. Edwards[2] tells me you wish to know, whether the act to
which your town incorporation provision was attached, passed into
a law. It did. You can organize under the general incorporation law
as soon as you choose.

I also tacked a provision on to a fellow's bill to authorize the
relocation of the road from Salem down to your town; but I am
not certain whether or not the bill passed; neither do I suppose I
can ascertain before the laws will be published. If it is a law, Bowling Green, Bennett Abell, and yourself are appointed to make the
change.[3]

No news. No excitement except a little about the election of
monday next. I suppose, of course, our friend Dr. Henry, stands
no chance in your "diggings"[4] Your friend and humble servant
John Bennett Esq.   A. LINCOLN

[1] ALS-F, ISLA. John Bennett was proprietor of a hotel in the new town of
Petersburg, Illinois, a few miles from New Salem, which Lincoln had surveyed
and planned in 1835-1836. Petersburg's success in drawing residents away
from New Salem marked the decline of that village, which became within a
few years a ghost town.
[2] Possibly Thomas Edwards, a farmer from near New Salem, or Ninian W.

Edwards of Springfield. The act referred to was passed July 19 (*vide supra*).

[3] The act was not passed. See Lincoln's amendment, July 19, *supra*.

[4] Dr. Anson G. Henry, Whig candidate for probate justice of peace, who two days later was defeated at the polls by General James Adams.

To Mary S. Owens[1]

Friend Mary.   Springfield Aug. 16th 1837

You will, no doubt, think it rather strange, that I should write you a letter on the same day on which we parted; and I can only account for it by supposing, that seeing you lately makes me think of you more than usual, while at our late meeting we had but few expressions of thoughts. You must know that I can not see you, or think of you, with entire indifference; and yet it may be, that you, are mistaken in regard to what my real feelings towards you are. If I knew you were not, I should not trouble you with this letter. Perhaps any other man would know enough without further information; but I consider it *my* peculiar right to plead ignorance, and your bounden duty to allow the plea. I want in all cases to do right, and most particularly so, in all cases with women. I want, at this particular time, more than any thing else, to do right with you, and if I *knew* it would be doing right, as I rather suspect it would, to let you alone, I would do it. And for the purpose of making the matter as plain as possible, I now say, that you can now drop the subject, dismiss your thoughts (if you ever had any) from me forever, and leave this letter unanswered, without calling forth one accusing murmer from me. And I will even go further, and say, that if it will add any thing to your comfort, or peace of mind, to do so, it is my sincere wish that you should. Do not understand by this, that I wish to cut your acquaintance. I mean no such thing. What I do wish is, that our further acquaintance shall depend upon yourself. If such further acquaintance would contribute nothing to your happiness, I am sure it would not to mine. If you feel yourself in any degree bound to me, I am now willing to release you, provided you wish it; while, on the other hand, I am willing, and even anxious to bind you faster, if I can be convinced that it will, in any considerable degree, add to your happiness. This, indeed, is the whole question with me. Nothing would make me more miserable than to believe you miserable—nothing more happy, than to know you were so.

In what I have now said, I think I can not be misunderstood; and to make myself understood, is the only object of this letter.

If it suits you best to not answer this—farewell—a long life and a merry one attend you. But if you conclude to write back, speak as plainly as I do. There can be neither harm nor danger, in saying, to me, any thing you think, just in the manner you think it.

My respects to your sister. Your friend   LINCOLN.

1 ALS, owned by Miss Lena Parrott, Augusta, Maine. This is the last of the letters written by Lincoln to Mary Owens. Apparently she did not reply. The conclusion of the affair, as Lincoln told it, may be found in his letter to Mrs. O. H. Browning, April 1, 1838, *infra*.

First Reply to James Adams[1]

September 6, 1837

Messrs. Lincoln and Talbott in reply to Gen. Adams.

In the Republican[2] of this morning a publication of Gen. Adams's appears, in which my name is used quite unreservedly. For this I thank the General. I thank him, because it gives me an opportunity, without appearing obtrusive, of explaining a part of a former publication of mine, which appears to me to have been misunderstood by many.

In the former publication alluded to, I stated, in substance, that Mr. Talbott got a deed from the son of Gen. Adams for the purpose of correcting a mistake that had occurred on the record of the said deed in the Recorder's office—that he corrected the record, and brought the deed and handed it to me—and that, on opening the deed, another paper, being the assignment of a judgment, *fell out* of it. This statement Gen. Adams and the editor of the Republican, have seized upon as a most palpable evidence of fabrication and falsehood. They set themselves gravely about proving, that the assignment could not have been in the deed when Talbott got it from young Adams, as he, Talbott, would have seen it when he opened the deed to correct the record. Now the truth is, Talbott *did* see the assignment when he opened the deed, or at least he told me he did on the same day; and I only omitted to say so, in my former publication, because it was a matter of such palpable and necessary inference. I had stated that Talbott had corrected the record by the deed; and of course he must have opened it; and, just as the General and his friends argue, must have seen the assignment. I omitted to state the fact of Talbott's seeing the assignment,

1 *Sangamo Journal,* September 9, 1837. Reprinted, *Sangamo Journal,* October 28, 1837.

2 Democratic organ founded in 1835. In 1839 it merged with the *Illinois State Register and People's Advocate* of Vandalia. Following the seat of government to Springfield, it became the *Illinois State Register.*

because its existence was so necessarily connected with other facts which I did state that I thought the greatest dunce could not but understand it. Did I say Talbott had not seen it? Did I say *any thing* that was *inconsistent* with his having seen it before? Most certainly I did neither; and if I did not, what becomes of the argument? These logical gentlemen cannot sustain their argument only by assuming that I *did* say *negatively* every thing that I *did not* say affirmatively; and upon the same assumption, we may expect to find the General, if a little harder pressed for argument, saying that I said Talbott came to our office with his head downwards, not that I actually said so, but because I omitted to say he came feet downward.

In his publication to-day, the Genl. produces the affidavit of Reuben Radford,[3] in which it is said that Talbott told Radford that he did not find the assignment in the deed in the recording of which the error was committed, but that he found it wrapped in another paper in the Recorder's office, upon which statement the Genl. comments, as follows, to wit:—"If it be true as stated by Talbott to Radford, that he found the assignment wrapped up in another paper at his office, that contradicts the statement of Lincoln that it fell out of the deed."

Is common sense to be abused with such sophistry? Did I say what Talbott found it in? If Talbott *did* find it in another paper at *his* office, is that any reason why he could not have folded it in a deed and brought it to *my* office? Can any one be so far duped, as to be made believe that what may have happened at *Talbott's* office at one time, is inconsistent with what happened at *my* office at another time?

Now Talbott's statement of the case as he makes it to me is this, that he got a bunch of deeds from young Adams, and that he knows he found the assignment in the bunch, but he is not certain which particular deed it was in, nor is he certain whether it *was* folded in the same deed out of which it was took, or another one, when it was brought to my office. Is this a mysterious story? Is there any thing suspicious about it?

But it is useless to dwell longer on this point. Any man who is not wilfully blind can see at a blush, that there is no discrepancy between Talbott and myself.

In regard to the Genl's. concluding statement, that "Having thus reviewed in my own way, the statements of Messrs. Talbott and Lincoln, and shown that they are not only inconsistent with

[3] Former storekeeper at New Salem whose stock Berry and Lincoln bought from William G. Greene in 1833.

truth, but each other"—I can only say, that I have shown that he has done no such thing; and if the reader is disposed to require any other evidence than the General's assertion, he will be of my opinion.

Excepting the General's most flimsy attempt at mystification, in regard to a discrepancy between Talbott and myself, he has not denied a single statement that I made in my handbill. Every material statement I made has been sworn to by men who, in former times, were thought as respectable as General Adams. I stated that an assignment of a Judgment, a copy of which I gave, had existed —Benj. Talbott, C. R. Matheny, Wm. Butler, and Judge Logan, swore to its existence, I stated that it was said to be in Gen. Adams's hand writing—the same men swore it was in his hand writing. I stated that Talbott would swear that he got it out of Gen. Adams's possession—Talbott came forward and did swear it.

Bidding adieu to the former publication, I now propose to examine the General's last gigantic production. I now propose to point out some discrepancies in the General's address; and such too, as he shall not be able to escape from. Speaking of the famous assignment, the Gen. says "This last charge, which was their last resort, their dying effort to render my character infamous among my fellow-citizens, was manufactured at a certain lawyer's office in the town, printed at the office of the Sangamon Journal, and found its way into the world some time between two days *just before the last election*." Now turn to Mr. Keys'[4] affidavit in which you will find the following, (viz:) "I certify that some time in May or the early part of June, 1837; I saw at Williams' corner a paper purporting to be an assignment from Joseph Anderson to James Adams, which assignment, was signed by a mark to Anderson's name," &c. Now mark, if Keys saw the assignment on the last of May or 1st of June, Gen. Adams tells a falsehood when he says it was *manufactured just before the election*, which was on the 7th of August; and if it was manufactured just before the election, Keys tells a falsehood when he says he saw it on the last of May or 1st of June. Either Keys or the General is irretrievably in for it; and in the General's very condescending language, I say, "let them settle it between them."

Now again, let the reader, bearing in mind that Gen. Adams has unequivocally said, in one part of his address, that the charge in relation to the assignment was *manufactured just before the*

---

[4] James W. Keyes, Springfield tailor. The *Journal* misspells the name throughout this reply.

election; turn to the affidavit of Peter S. Weber,[5] where the following will be found, (viz:) "I Peter S. Weber do certify, that from the best of my recollection on the day or day after Gen. Adams and wife started for the Illinois Rapids, in May last, that I was at the house of Gen. Adams, sitting in the Kitchen, situated on the back part of the house, it being in the afternoon, and that Benjamin Talbott came round the house, back into the Kitchen, and appeared wild and confused, and that he laid a package of papers on the kitchen table and requested that they should be handed to Lucian. He made no apology for coming to the kitchen, nor for not handing them to Lucian himself, but showed the token of being frightened and confused both in demeanor and speech, and for what cause I could not apprehend."

Commenting upon Weber's affidavit, Gen. Adams asks, "Why this fright and confusion?" I reply that this is a question for the General himself. Weber says that it was in May, and if so, it is most clear, that Talbott was not frightened on account of the assignment, unless the General lies when he says the assignment charge was manufactured *just before the election.* Is it not a strong evidence, that the General is not travelling with the pole-star of truth in his front, to see him in one part of his address roundly asserting, that the assignment was manufactured *just before the election,* and then, forgetting that position, procuring Weber's most foolish affidavit, to prove that Talbott had been engaged in manufacturing it *two months before?*

In another part of his address, Gen. Adams says, "That I hold an assignment of said judgement, dated the 20th of May, 1828, and signed by said Anderson, I have never pretended to deny or conceal, but stated that fact in one of my circulars previous to the election, and also in answer *to a Bill in Chancery.*" Now I pronounce this statement unqualifiedly false; and shall not rely on the word or oath of any man to sustain me in what I say; but will let the whole be decided by reference to the Circular and answer in Chancery of which the General speaks. In his circular he did speak of an assignment; but he *did not* say it bore date 20th of May 1828; nor did he say it bore any date. In his answer in chancery, he did say that he had an assignment; but he *did not* say that it bore date the 20th May 1828; but so far from it, he said on oath (for he swore to the answer) that as well as recollected, he obtained it in 1827. If any one doubts, let him examine the Circular and answer for himself. They are both accessible.

It will readily be observed that the principal part of Adams's

[5] Weber married a daughter of General Adams on November 14, 1837.

defence, rests upon the argument, that if he had been base enough to forge an assignment, he would not have been *fool enough* to forge one that would not cover the case. This argument he used in his circular before the election. The Republican has used it at least once, since then; and Adams uses it again in his publication of to-day. Now I pledge myself to show, that he is just such a *fool*, that he and his friends have contended it was impossible for him to be. Recollect—he says he has a genuine assignment; and that he got Joseph Klein's[6] affidavit, stating that he had seen it, and that he believed the signature to have been executed by the same hand, that signed Anderson's name to the answer in Chancery. Luckily Klein took a copy of this *genuine* assignment, which I have been permitted to see; and hence I know it *does not cover the case*. In the first place it is headed "Joseph Anderson vs. Joseph Miller," and leads off "Judgment in Sangamon Circuit Court." Now, mark, there never was a case in Sangamon Circuit Court entitled Joseph Anderson vs. Joseph Miller. The case mentioned in my former publication, and the only one between these parties that ever existed in the Circuit Court, was entitled Joseph Miller vs. Joseph Anderson, Miller being the plaintiff. What then becomes of all their sophistry about Adams not being *fool enough* to forge an assignment that would not cover the case? It is certain that the present one does not cover the case; and if he even got it honestly, it is still clear that he *was fool enough* to pay for an assignment that does not cover the case.

The General asks for the proof of disinterested witnesses. Who does he consider disinterested? None *can* be more so than those who have already testified against him. No one of them had the least interest on earth, so far as I can learn, to injure him. True, he says they had conspired against him; but if the testimony of an angel from heaven were introduced against him, he would make the same charge of conspiracy. And I now put the question to every reflecting man, do you believe that Benjamin Talbott, Charles R. Matheny, William Butler and Stephen T. Logan, all sustaining high and spotless characters, and justly proud of them, would deliberately perjure themselves, without any motive whatever, except to injure a man's election; and that too, a man who had been a candidate, time out of mind, and yet who had never been elected to any office?

Adams' assurance, in demanding disinterested testimony, is surpassing. He brings in the affidavit of his own son, and even of Peter S. Weber, with whom I am not acquainted, but who, I suppose, is

[6] A Springfield merchant, elected town trustee in 1838 and, later, alderman.

some black or mulatto boy, from his being kept in the Kitchen, to prove his points; but when such a man as Talbott, a man who, but two years ago run against Gen. Adams for the office of Recorder, and beat him more than four votes to one, is introduced against him, he asks the community, with all the consequence of a Lord, to reject his testimony.

I might easily write a volume, pointing out inconsistencies between the statements in Adams' last address with one another, and with other known facts; but I am aware the reader must already be tired with the length of this article. His opening statements, that he was first accused of being a tory, and that he refuted that; that then the Sampson's Ghost story was got up, and he reputed [refuted] that; and that as a last resort, a dying effort, the assignment charge was got up, is all as false as hell, as all this community must know. Sampson's Ghost first made its appearance in print, and that too, after Keys swears he saw the assignment, as any one may see by reference to the files of papers; and Gen. Adams himself, in reply to the Sampson's Ghost story, was the *first man* that raised the cry of *toryism*, and it was only by way of set-off, and never in seriousness, that it was bandied back at him. His effort is to make the impression that his enemies first made the charge of toryism, and he drove them from that, then Sampson's Ghost, he drove them from that, then finally the assignment charge was manufactured *just before the election*. Now the only general reply he ever made to the Sampson's Ghost and tory charges, he made *at one and the same time*, and not in succession as he states; and the date of that reply will show, that it was made at least a month *after* the date on which Keys swears he saw the Anderson assignment. But enough. In conclusion I will only say that I have a character to defend as well as Gen. Adams, but I disdain to *whine* about it as he does. It is true I have no children nor *Kitchen boys;* and if I had, I should scorn to lug them in to make affidavits for me.

Sept. 6, 1837.   A. LINCOLN.

To the Third Auditor
of the United States Treasury[1]

To the Third Auditor   Springfield Illinois,
Sir   Sept. 9th. 1837–

Enclosed are the proofs made for procuring payment for a horse lost by John W. Warnsing on the Black Hawk campaign. Warnsing has sold the claim to one Thomas Epperson; and both Warnsing at [*sic*] Epperson tell me there is a Power of attorney from Warnsing to Epperson now on file in your office. If this be true, I suppose the award & Draft may be made directly to Epperson; if not, let them be made to Warnsing. In either case, if not inconsistent with your regulations, let the letter, enclosing the Draft, be directed to me at [this?] place. The disbursing officer that paid [War]nsing was [the same that paid] Genl. Henry's Brigade [illegible word].[2] We do not recollect his name. Respectfully your Obt. Servt.   A. LINCOLN

[1] ALS, IHi. Peter Hagner was Third Auditor.
[2] Bracketed words are as deciphered from a damaged manuscript.

Second Reply to James Adams[1]

October 18, 1837

TO THE PUBLIC.

Such is the turn which things have lately taken, that when Gen. Adams writes a book, I am expected to write a commentary on it. In the Republican of this morning he has presented the world with a new work of six columns in length; in consequence of which I must beg the room of one column in the Journal. It is obvious that a minute reply cannot be made in one column to every thing that can be said in six; and, consequently, I hope that expectation will be answered, if I reply to such parts of the General's publication as are worth replying to.

It may not be improper to remind the reader that in his publication of Sept. 6th, General Adams said that the assignment charge was manufactured *just before the election;* and that in reply I proved that statement to be false by Keyes, his own witness. Now, without attempting to explain, he furnishes me with another witness (Tinsley) by which the same thing is proved, to wit, that the assignment *was not* manufactured *just before the election;* but that it was seen *some weeks* before. Let it be borne in mind that Adams made this statement—has himself furnished two witnesses to prove its falsehood, and does not attempt to deny or explain it. Before going farther, let a pin be stuck here, labelled "one lie proved and confessed." On the 6th of Sept. he said he had before stated in a handbill that he held an assignment dated May 20th, 1828, which in reply I pronounced to be false, and referred to the hand bill for the truth of what I said. This week he forgets to make any explanation of this. Let another pin be stuck here, labelled as before. I

[1] *Sangamo Journal,* October 28, 1837. Bracketed passages appear in the original.

mention these things, because, if, when I convict him in one falsehood, he is permitted to shift his ground, and pass it by in silence, there can be no end to this controversy.

The first thing that attracts my attention in the General's present production, is the information he is pleased to give to "those who are made to suffer at his (my) *hands.*" Under present circumstances, this cannot apply to me, for I am not a *widow* nor an *orphan:* nor have I a wife or children who by possibility might become such. Such, however, I have no doubt, have been, and will again be made to suffer at his *hands!! Hands!* yes, they are the mischievous agents. The next thing I shall notice is his favorite expression, "knot of lawyers, doctors and others," which he is so fond of applying to all who dare expose his rascality. Now, let it be remembered that when he first came to this country, he attempted to impose himself upon the community as a *lawyer,* and actually carried the attempt so far, as to induce a man who was under a charge of murder to intrust the defence of his life in his hands, and finally took his money and got him hanged. Is this the man that is to raise a breeze in his favor by abusing lawyers? If he is not himself a lawyer, it is for the lack of sense, and not of inclination. If he is not a lawyer, he *is* a liar, for he proclaimed himself a lawyer, and got a man hanged by depending on him.

Passing over such parts of the article as have neither fact nor argument in them, I come to the question asked by Adams whether any person ever saw the assignment in his possession. This is an insult to common sense. Talbott has swore once, and repeated time and again, that he got it *out* of Adams' possession and returned it *into* the same possession. Still, as though he was addressing fools, he has assurance to ask if any person ever saw it in his possession. Next I quote a sentence "Now my son Lucian swears that when Talbott called for the deed, that he, Talbott, opened it and *pointed out the error.*" True. His son Lucian did swear as he says; and in doing so, he swore what I will prove by his own affidavit to be a falsehood. Turn to Lucian's affidavit, and you will there see, that Talbott called for the deed by which to correct an error on the *record.* Thus it appears that the error in question was on the *record,* and not in the *deed.* How then could Talbott open the deed and point out the *error?* Where a thing *is not,* it cannot be pointed out. The error *was not* in the *deed,* and of course could not be pointed out there. This does not merely prove, that the error could not be pointed out, as Lucian swore it was; but it proves, too, that the deed was not opened in his presence with a special view to the error, for if it had been, he could not have failed to see that there was no error in it. It is easy enough to see why Lucian swore this. His object was to prove that the assignment *was not* in the deed, when Talbott got it: but it was discovered he could not swear this safely, without first swearing the deed was *opened*—and if he swore it was *opened*, he must show a *motive* for opening it, and the conclusion with him and his father was, that the pointing out the error, would appear the most plausible.

For the purpose of showing that the assignment was not in the bundle when Talbott got it, is the story introduced in Lucian's affidavit, that the deeds were *counted*. It is a remarkable fact, and one that should stand as a warning to all liars and fabricators, that in this short affidavit of Lucian's, he only attempted to depart from the truth, so far as I have the means of knowing, in two points, to wit, in *the opening the deed and pointing out the error;* and the *counting of the deeds,*—and in both of these he caught himself. About the counting, he caught himself thus—After saying the bundle contained *five* deeds and a lease, he proceeds, "and I saw no other papers than the *said deed* and lease." First he has *six* papers, and then he saw none but *two*. For "my son Lucian's" benefit, let a pin be stuck here.

Adams again adduces the argument, that he could not have forged the assignment, for the reason that he could have had no *motive* for it. With those that know the facts there is no absence of motive. Admitting the paper, which he has filed in the suit to be genuine, it is clear that *it* cannot answer the purpose for which he designs it. Hence his motive for making one that he supposed would answer, is obvious. His making the date too old is also easily enough accounted for. The records were not in his hands, and then there being some considerable talk upon this particular subject, he knew he could not examine the records to ascertain the precise dates without subjecting himself to suspicion; and hence he concluded to try it by guess, and as it turned out, missed it a little. About Miller's deposition, I have a word to say. In the first place, Miller's answer to the first question shows upon its face, that he had been tampered with, and the answer dictated to him. He was asked if he knew Joel Wright and James Adams; and above three-fourths of his answer consists of what he knew about Joseph Anderson, a man about whom nothing had been asked, nor a word said in the question—a fact that can only be accounted for upon the supposition, that Adams had secretly told him what he wished him to swear to.

Another of Miller's anwers I will prove both by common sense and the court of record is untrue. To one question he answers, "Anderson brought a suit against me before James Adams, then an acting Justice of the Peace in Sangamon County, before whom he obtained a judgment.

"Q. Did you *remove* the same by injunction to the Sangamon Circuit Court? Answer. I did remove it." Now mark—it is said he *removed* it by *injunction*. The word *"injunction"* in common language imports a command that some person or thing shall not *move* or be *removed;* in law it has the same meaning. An injunction issuing out of chancery to a Justice of the Peace, is a command to him to stop all proceedings in a name case till further orders. It is not an order to *remove*, but to *stop* or stay something that is already *moving*. Besides this, the records of the Sangamon Circuit Court show, that the judgement of which Miller swore was never removed into said court by injunction or otherwise.

I have now to take notice of a part of Adams' address which in the order of time should have been noticed before. It is in these words, "I have now shown, in the opinion of 2 competent judges that the hand writing of the forged assignment differed from mine, *and by one of them that it could not be mistaken for mine."* That is false. Tinsley no doubt is the judge referred to; and by reference to his certificate it will be seen, that he did not say the hand writing of the assignment could not be mistaken for Adams'—nor did he use any other expression substantially, or any thing near substantially the same. But if Tinsley had said the hand writing could not be mistaken for Adams', it would have been equally unfortunate for Adams: for it then would have contradicted Keyes, who says, "I looked at the writing and judged it the said Adams' or a good imitation."

Adams speaks with much apparent confidence of his success on the pending law suit, and the ultimate maintainance of his title to the land in question. Without wishing to disturb the pleasure of his dream, I would say to him that it is not impossible, that he may yet be taught to sing a different song in relation to the matter.

At the end of Miller's deposition, Adams asks, "Will Mr. Lincoln *now* say that he is almost convinced my title to this ten acre tract of land is founded in fraud?" I answer, I will not. I will *now* change the phraseology so as to make it run—I am *quite* convinced, &c. I cannot pass in silence Adams' assertion that he has proved that the forged assignment was not in the deed when it came from his house by *Talbott*, the Recorder. In this, although Talbott has sworn that the assignment was in the bundle of deeds when it came from his house, Adams has the unaccountable assurance to say that he has proved the contrary by Talbott. Let him, or his friends attempt to show, wherein he proved any such thing by Talbott.

In his publication of the 6th of Sept. he *hinted* to Talbott, that *he might be mistaken.* In his present, speaking of Talbott and me, he says *"They may have been imposed upon."* Can any man of the least penetration fail to see the object of this? After he has stormed and raved till he hopes or imagines that he has got us a little scared, he wishes to softly whisper in our ears, *"If you'll quit I will."* If he could get us to say, that some unknown, undefined being had slipped the assignment into our hands without our knowledge, not a doubt remains but that he would immediately discover, that we were the purest men on earth. This is the ground he evidently wishes us to understand he is willing to compromise upon. But we ask no such charity at his hands. We are neither *mistaken* nor *imposed upon.* We have made the statements we have, because we know them to be true—and we choose to live or die by them.

Esq. Carter,[2] who is Adams friend, personal and political, will recollect, that, on the 5th of this month, he, (Adams) with a great affectation of modesty, declared that he would never introduce his own child as a witness. Notwithstanding this affectation of modesty, he has in his present publication, introduced his child as a witness; and as if to show with how much contempt he could treat his own declaration, he has had this same Esq. Carter to administer the oath to him. And so important a witness does he consider him, and so entirely does the whole of his present production depend upon the testimony of his child, that in it he has mentioned "my son," "my son Lucian," "Lucian my son," and the like expressions no less than fifteen different times. Let it be remembered here, that I have shown the affidavit of "my darling son Lucian," to be false by the evidence apparent on its own face; and I now ask if that affidavit be taken away, what foundation will the fabric have left to stand upon?

General Adams' publications and out-door manoevring, taken in connection with the editorial articles of the Republican, are not more foolish and contradictory than they are ludicrous and amusing. One week the Republican notifies the public that Gen. Adams is preparing an *instrument* that will tear, rend, split, rive, blow up, confound, overwhelm, annihilate, extinguish, exterminate, burst asunder, and grind to powder all his slanderers, and particu-

2 William B. Carter, justice of the peace.

larly Talbott and Lincoln—all of which is to be done *in due time.* Then for two or three weeks all is calm—not a word said. Again the Republican comes forth with a mere passing remark that "public opinion has decided in favor of Gen. Adams," and intimates that he will give himself no more trouble about the matter. In the mean time Adams himself is prowling about, and as Burns says of the devil, *"For prey, a' holes and corners tryin,"* and in one instance, goes so far as to take an old acquaintance of mine several steps from a crowd, and apparently weighed down with the importance of his business, gravely and solemnly asks him if *"he ever heard Lincoln say he was a deist."* Anon the Republican comes again, "We invite the attention of the public to Gen. Adams' communication," &c, "The victory is a great one." "The triumph is overwhelming." [I really believe the editor of the Ill. Republican is fool enough to think General Adams is an honest man.] Then Gen. Adams leads off. *"Authors most egregiously mistaken,"* &c. *"most wofully shall their presumption be punished,"* &c. [Lord have mercy on us.] *"The hour is yet to come, yes nigh at hand—* (how long first do you reckon?)—*when the Journal and its junto shall say, I have appeared too early."—"then infamy shall be laid bare to the public gaze."* Suddenly the Gen. appears to relent at the severity with which he is treating us and he exclaims, *"The condemnation of my enemies is the inevitable result of my own defence."* For your health's sake, dear Gen. do not permit your tenderness of heart to afflict you so much on our account. For some reason (perhaps because we are killed so quickly) we shall never be sensible of our suffering.

Farewell, General. I will see you again at court, if not before— when and where we will settle the question whether you or the widow shall have the land.[3]

Oct. 18, 1837. A. LINCOLN.

[3] On October 17, 1837, Logan and Lincoln filed a replication (Sangamon County Circuit Court, Record C, 497). The case was never brought to trial; with the death of the defendant, Adams, on August 11, 1843, the suit was abated by the court, November 29, 1843 (*ibid.*, Record H, 219).

Bond of William Butler as Clerk of the Circuit Court of Sangamon County[1]

October 19, 1837

Know all men by these presents that we William Butler, Philip. C. Latham Garrett Elkin A. Lincoln & John T Stuart are held and firmly bound unto Joseph Duncan Governor of the State of Illinois and his successors in office, for the use of the People of the State of Illinois in the penal sum of Two Thousand Dollars, lawfull money of the United States, the payment of which, well and truly to be made, and performed, we and each of us, bind ourselves, our heirs, executors, and administrators, jointly & severally firmly by these presents, witness our hands and seals this 19th. day of October 1837

The condition of this obligation is such that if the above bounden William Butler shall faithfully discharge the duties of his office as Clerk of the Circuit Court in and for the County of Sangamon, and State of Illinois according to laws, and shall deliver up, when lawfully required so to do, the Papers, Books, Records, and Proceedings appertaining thereto, whole, safe, and undefaced, then the above obligation to be void, otherwise, to remain in full force and virtue

William Butler (Seal)	A. Lincoln (Seal)
P. C. Latham (Seal)	John T. Stuart (Seal)
Garrett Elkin (Seal)	

[1] DS, I-Ar. The document bears also the approval of Jesse B. Thomas, Judge of the First Judicial Circuit, dated the same day.

To William A. Minshall[1]

Friend Minshall.   Springfield, Dec. 7 1837

I write this to say that it is Stuart's intention to be a candidate for congress again; and that he will be publicly announced before long. I would suggest to you the propriety of your letting our friends in your parts know, that he is to be the candidate.

On the receipt of this, write me all you *know* and all you *think*, in regard to our prospects for the race.

I believe we have nothing here that would be news to you. I am ashamed to write so short a letter; but lack of *material*, you know, will [make?] any thing short. Your sincere friend

A. LINCOLN

P. S. We have adopted it as part of our policy here, to never speak of Douglass at all. Is'nt that the best mode of treating so small a matter?

[1] ALS, IHi. Minshall was a lawyer at Rushville, Illinois, and a Whig representative from Schuyler County in the legislature.

Address Before the Young Men's Lyceum of Springfield, Illinois[1]

January 27, 1838

THE PERPETUATION OF OUR POLITICAL INSTITUTIONS

As a subject for the remarks of the evening, *the perpetuation of our political institutions,* is selected.

In the great journal of things happening under the sun, we, the American People, find our account running, under date of the nineteenth century of the Christian era. We find ourselves in the peaceful possession, of the fairest portion of the earth, as regards extent of territory, fertility of soil, and salubrity of climate. We find ourselves under the government of a system of political institutions, conducing more essentially to the ends of civil and religious liberty, than any of which the history of former times tells us. We, when mounting the stage of existence, found ourselves the legal inheritors of these fundamental blessings. We toiled not in the acquirement or establishment of them—they are a legacy bequeathed us, by a *once* hardy, brave, and patriotic, but *now* lamented and departed race of ancestors. Their's was the task (and nobly they performed it) to possess themselves, and through themselves, us, of this goodly land; and to uprear upon its hills and its valleys, a political edifice of liberty and equal rights; 'tis ours only, to transmit these, the former, unprofaned by the foot of an invader; the latter, undecayed by the lapse of time, and untorn by [usurpation—to the latest generation that fate shall permit the world to know. This task of gratitude to our fathers, justice to][2] ourselves, duty to posterity, and love for our species in general, all imperatively require us faithfully to perform.

---

[1] *Sangamo Journal*, February 3, 1838. Preceding the address as printed in the *Journal*, appears the following notice:

Young Men's Lyceum,
Springfield, Jan. 27 1837 [1838].
"Resolved, That the thanks of this Lyceum be presented to A. Lincoln, Esq. for the Lecture delivered by him this evening, and that he be solicited to furnish a copy for publication."
Attest;   JAS H. MATHENY, SEC'Y.

The date 1837, as given in the resolution of thanks, is obviously a typographical error. The Young Men's Lyceum was organized in 1833 by a group which included Simeon Francis, John T. Stuart, and Dan Stone. It did not thrive, however, until the autumn of 1836. For the next few years it was one of the leading forces in the cultural activity of Springfield.
[2] Illegible portions of the text are bracketed as given by Nicolay and Hay.

How, then, shall we perform it? At what point shall we expect the approach of danger? By what means shall we fortify against it? Shall we expect some transatlantic military giant, to step the Ocean, and crush us at a blow? Never! All the armies of Europe, Asia and Africa combined, with all the treasure of the earth (our own excepted) in their military chest; with a Buonaparte for a commander, could not by force, take a drink from the Ohio, or make a track on the Blue Ridge, in a trial of a thousand years.

At what point then is the approach of danger to be expected? I answer, if it ever reach us, it must spring up amongst us. It cannot come from abroad. If destruction be our lot, we must ourselves be its author and finisher. As a nation of freemen, we must live through all time, or die by suicide.

I hope I am over wary; but if I am not, there is, even now, something of ill-omen amongst us. I mean the increasing disregard for law which pervades the country; the growing disposition to substitute the wild and furious passions, in lieu of the sober judgement of Courts; and the worse than savage mobs, for the executive ministers of justice. This disposition is awfully fearful in any community; and that it now exists in ours, though grating to our feelings to admit, it would be a violation of truth, and an insult to our intelligence, to deny. Accounts of outrages committed by mobs, form the every-day news of the times. They have pervaded the country, from New England to Louisiana;—they are neither peculiar to the eternal snows of the former, nor the burning suns of the latter;—they are not the creature of climate—neither are they confined to the slaveholding, or the non-slaveholding States. Alike, they spring up among the pleasure hunting masters of Southern slaves, and the order loving citizens of the land of steady habits. Whatever, then, their cause may be, it is common to the whole country.

It would be tedious, as well as useless, to recount the horrors of all of them. Those happening in the State of Mississippi, and at St. Louis, are, perhaps, the most dangerous in example, and revolting to humanity. In the Mississippi case, they first commenced by hanging the regular gamblers: a set of men, certainly not following for a livelihood, a very useful, or very honest occupation; but one which, so far from being forbidden by the laws, was actually licensed by an act of the Legislature, passed but a single year before. Next, negroes, suspected of conspiring to raise an insurrection, were caught up and hanged in all parts of the State: then, white men, supposed to be leagued with the negroes; and finally, strangers, from neighboring States, going thither on business, were, in many instances, subjected to the same fate. Thus went on this process of hanging, from gamblers to negroes, from negroes to white citizens, and from these to strangers; till, dead men were seen literally dangling from the boughs of trees upon every road side; and in numbers almost sufficient, to rival the native Spanish moss of the country, as a drapery of the forest.

Turn, then, to that horror-striking scene at St. Louis. A single victim was only sacrificed there. His story is very short; and is, perhaps, the most highly tragic, of any thing of its length, that has ever been witnessed in real life. A mulatto man, by the name of McIntosh, was seized in the street, dragged to the suburbs of the city, chained to a tree, and actually burned to death; and all within a single hour from the time he had been a freeman, attending to his own business, and at peace with the world.

Such are the effects of mob law; and such are the scenes, becoming more and more frequent in this land so lately famed for love of law and order; and the stories of which, have even now grown too familiar, to attract any thing more, than an idle remark.

But you are, perhaps, ready to ask, "What has this to do with the perpetuation of our political institutions?" I answer, it has much to do with it. Its direct consequences are, comparatively speaking, but a small evil; and much of its danger consists, in the proneness of our minds, to regard its direct, as its only consequences. Abstractly considered, the hanging of the gamblers at Vicksburg, was of but little consequence. They constitute a portion of population, that is worse than useless in a[ny community; and their death, if no perni]cious example be set by it, is never matter of reasonable regret with any one. If they were annually swept, from the stage of existence, by the plague or small pox, honest men would, perhaps, be much profited, by the operation. Similar too, is the correct reasoning, in regard to the burning of the negro at St. Louis. He had forfeited his life, by the perpetration of an outrageous murder, upon one of the most worthy and respectable citizens of the city; and had he not died as he did, he must have died by the sentence of the law, in a very short time afterwards. As to him alone, it was as well the way it was, as it could otherwise have been. But the example in either case, was fearful. When men take it in their heads to day, to hang gamblers, or burn murderers, they should recollect, that, in the confusion usually attending such transactions, they will be as likely to hang or burn some one, who is neither a gambler nor a murderer [as] one who is; and that, acting upon the [exam]ple they set, the mob of to-morrow, may, an[d] probably will, hang or burn some of them, [by th]e very same

mistake. And not only so; the innocent, those who have ever set
their faces against violations of law in every shape, alike with the
guilty, fall victims to the ravages of mob law; and thus it goes
on, step by step, till all the walls erected for the defence of the persons and property of individuals, are trodden down, and disregarded. But all this even, is not the full extent of the evil. By such
examples, by instances of the perpetrators of such acts going unpunished, the lawless in spirit, are encouraged to become lawless in
practice; and having been used to no restraint, but dread of punishment, they thus become, absolutely unrestrained. Having ever
regarded Government as their deadliest bane, they make a jubilee
of the suspension of its operations; and pray for nothing so much,
as its total annihilation. While, on the other hand, good men, men
who love tranquility, who desire to abide by the laws, and enjoy
their benefits, who would gladly spill their blood in the defence of
their country; seeing their property destroyed; their families insulted, and their lives endangered; their persons injured; and seeing nothing in prospect that forebodes a change for the better;
become tired of, and disgusted with, a Government that offers them
no protection; and are not much averse to a change in which they
imagine they have nothing to lose. Thus, then, by the operation of
this mobocratic spirit, which all must admit, is now abroad in the
land, the strongest bulwark of any Government, and particularly
of those constituted like ours, may effectually be broken down and
destroyed—I mean the *attachment* of the People. Whenever this
effect shall be produced among us; whenever the vicious portion of
population shall be permitted to gather in bands of hundreds and
thousands, and burn churches, ravage and rob provision stores,
throw printing presses into rivers, shoot editors,[3] and hang and
burn obnoxious persons at pleasure, and with impunity; depend on
it, this Government cannot last. By such things, the feelings of the
best citizens will become more or less alienated from it; and thus it
will be left without friends, or with too few, and those few too
weak, to make their friendship effectual. At such a time and under
such circumstances, men of sufficient tal[ent and ambition will not
be want]ing to seize [the opportunity, strike the blow, and over-

[3] Dwelling as he does on the horrors of lynch law in Mississippi and Missouri,
Lincoln may seem remiss in ignoring, save for this phrase, the lynching at
Alton, Illinois, on November 7, 1837, of the abolitionist editor Elijah Parish
Lovejoy. It is somewhat too obvious and naïve to assume that Lincoln was being
politic in avoiding reference to an episode so recent and so vivid in the recollection of his audience. Rather it seems possible that he chose a subtler way of
pricking the conscience of his audience than by direct denunciation. Members
of the Lyceum who listened to Lincoln without sensing the specter of Lovejoy
in their midst must have been obtuse indeed.

turn that fair fabric], which for the last half century, has been the fondest hope, of the lovers of freedom, throughout the world.

I know the American People are *much* attached to their Government;—I know they would suffer *much* for its sake;—I know they would endure evils long and patiently, before they would ever think of exchanging it for another. Yet, notwithstanding all this, if the laws be continually despised and disregarded, if their rights to be secure in their persons and property, are held by no better tenure than the caprice of a mob, the alienation of their affections from the Government is the natural consequence; and to that, sooner or later, it must come.

Here then, is one point at which danger may be expected.

The question recurs "how shall we fortify against it?" The answer is simple. Let every American, every lover of liberty, every well wisher to his posterity, swear by the blood of the Revolution, never to violate in the least particular, the laws of the country; and never to tolerate their violation by others. As the patriots of seventy-six did to the support of the Declaration of Independence, so to the support of the Constitution and Laws, let every American pledge his life, his property, and his sacred honor;—let every man remember that to violate the law, is to trample on the blood of his father, and to tear the character [charter?] of his own, and his children's liberty. Let reverence for the laws, be breathed by every American mother, to the lisping babe, that prattles on her lap—let it be taught in schools, in seminaries, and in colleges;—let it be written in Primmers, spelling books, and in Almanacs;—let it be preached from the pulpit, proclaimed in legislative halls, and enforced in courts of justice. And, in short, let it become the *political religion* of the nation; and let the old and the young, the rich and the poor, the grave and the gay, of all sexes and tongues, and colors and conditions, sacrifice unceasingly upon its altars.

While ever a state of feeling, such as this, shall universally, or even, very generally prevail throughout the nation, vain will be every effort, and fruitless every attempt, to subvert our national freedom.

When I so pressingly urge a strict observance of all the laws, let me not be understood as saying there are no bad laws, nor that grievances may not arise, for the redress of which, no legal provisions have been made. I mean to say no such thing. But I do mean to say, that, although bad laws, if they exist, should be repealed as soon as possible, still while they continue in force, for the sake of example, they should be religiously observed. So also in unprovided cases. If such arise, let proper legal provisions be made for them with the least possible delay; but, till then, let them if not too intolerable, be borne with.

There is no grievance that is a fit object of redress by mob law. In any case that arises, as for instance, the promulgation of abolitionism, one of two positions is necessarily true; that is, the thing is right within itself, and therefore deserves the protection of all law and all good citizens; or, it is wrong, and therefore proper to be prohibited by legal enactments; and in neither case, is the interposition of mob law, either necessary, justifiable, or excusable.

But, it may be asked, why suppose danger to our political institutions? Have we not preserved them for more than fifty years? And why may we not for fifty times as long?

We hope there is no *sufficient* reason. We hope all dangers may be overcome; but to conclude that no danger may ever arise, would itself be extremely dangerous. There are now, and will hereafter be, many causes, dangerous in their tendency, which have not existed heretofore; and which are not too insignificant to merit attention. That our government should have been maintained in its original form from its establishment until now, is not much to be wondered at. It had many props to support it through that period, which now are decayed, and crumbled away. Through that period, it was felt by all, to be an undecided experiment; now, it is understood to be a successful one. Then, all that sought celebrity and fame, and distinction, expected to find them in the success of that experiment. Their *all* was staked upon it:—their destiny was *inseparably* linked with it. Their ambition aspired to display before an admiring world, a practical demonstration of the truth of a proposition, which had hitherto been considered, at best no better, than problematical; namely, *the capability of a people to govern themselves*. If they succeeded, they were to be immortalized; their names were to be transferred to counties and cities, and rivers and mountains; and to be revered and sung, and toasted through all time. If they failed, they were to be called knaves and fools, and fanatics for a fleeting hour; then to sink and be forgotten. They succeeded. The experiment is successful; and thousands have won their deathless names in making it so. But the game is caught; and I believe it is true, that with the catching, end the pleasures of the chase. This field of glory is harvested, and the crop is already appropriated. But new reapers will arise, and *they*, too, will seek a field. It is to deny, what the history of the world tells us is true, to suppose that men of ambition and talents will not continue to spring up amongst us. And, when they do, they will as naturally seek the gratification of their ruling passion, as others have *so* done

[113]

before them. The question then, is, can that gratification be found in supporting and maintaining an edifice that has been erected by others? Most certainly it cannot. Many great and good men sufficiently qualified for any task they should undertake, may ever be found, whose ambition would aspire to nothing beyond a seat in Congress, a gubernatorial or a presidential chair; *but such belong not to the family of the lion, or the tribe of the eagle,*[.] What! think you these places would satisfy an Alexander, a Caesar, or a Napoleon? Never! Towering genius disdains a beaten path. It seeks regions hitherto unexplored. It sees *no distinction* in adding story to story, upon the monuments of fame, erected to the memory of others. It *denies* that it is glory enough to serve under any chief. It *scorns* to tread in the footsteps of *any* predecessor, however illustrious. It thirsts and burns for distinction; and, if possible, it will have it, whether at the expense of emancipating slaves, or enslaving freemen. Is it unreasonable then to expect, that some man possessed of the loftiest genius, coupled with ambition sufficient to push it to its utmost stretch, will at some time, spring up among us? And when such a one does, it will require the people to be united with each other, attached to the government and laws, and generally intelligent, to successfully frustrate his designs.

Distinction will be his paramount object; and although he would as willingly, perhaps more so, acquire it by doing good as harm; yet, that opportunity being past, and nothing left to be done in the way of building up, he would set boldly to the task of pulling down.

Here then, is a probable case, highly dangerous, and such a one as could not have well existed heretofore.

Another reason which *once was;* but which, to the same extent, is *now no more,* has done much in maintaining our institutions thus far. I mean the powerful influence which the interesting scenes of the revolution had upon the *passions* of the people as distinguished from their judgment. By this influence, the jealousy, envy, and avarice, incident to our nature, and so common to a state of peace, prosperity, and conscious strength, were, for the time, in a great measure smothered and rendered inactive; while the deep rooted principles of *hate,* and the powerful motive of *revenge,* instead of being turned against each other, were directed exclusively against the British nation. And thus, from the force of circumstances, the basest principles of our nature, were either made to lie dormant, or to become the active agents in the advancement of the noblest of cause[s?]—that of establishing and maintaining civil and religious liberty.

But this state of feeling *must fade, is fading, has faded,* with the circumstances that produced it.

I do not mean to say, that the scenes of the revolution *are now* or *ever will be* entirely forgotten; but that like every thing else, they must fade upon the memory of the world, and grow more and more dim by the lapse of time. In history, we hope, they will be read of, and recounted, so long as the bible shall be read;—but even granting that they will, their influence *cannot be* what it heretofore has been. Even then, they *cannot be* so universally known, nor so vividly felt, as they were by the generation just gone to rest. At the close of that struggle, nearly every adult male had been a participator in some of its scenes. The consequence was, that of those scenes, in the form of a husband, a father, a son or a brother, a *living history was* to be found in every family—a history bearing the indubitable testimonies of its own authenticity, in the limbs mangled, in the scars of wounds received, in the midst of the very scenes related—a history, too, that could be read and understood alike by all, the wise and the ignorant, the learned and the unlearned. But *those* histories are gone. They *can* be read no more forever. They *were* a fortress of strength; but, what invading foemen could *never do,* the silent artillery of time *has done;* the levelling of its walls. They are gone. They *were* a forest of giant oaks; but the all-resistless hurricane has swept over them, and left only, here and there, a lonely trunk, despoiled of its verdure, shorn of its foliage; unshading and unshaded, to murmur in a few more gentle breezes, and to combat with its mutilated limbs, a few more ruder storms, then to sink, and be no more.

They *were* the pillars of the temple of liberty; and now, that they have crumbled away, that temple must fall, unless we, their descendants, supply their places with other pillars, hewn from the solid quarry of sober reason. Passion has helped us; but can do so no more. It will in future be our enemy. Reason, cold, calculating, unimpassioned reason, must furnish all the materials for our future support and defence. Let those [materials] be moulded into *general intelligence,* [*sound*] *morality* and, in particular, *a reverence for the constitution and laws;* and, that we improved to the last; that we remained free to the last; that we revered his name to the last; [tha]t, during his long sleep, we permitted no hostile foot to pass over or desecrate [his] resting place; shall be that which to le[arn the last] trump shall awaken our Wash[ington.

Upon these] let the proud fabric of freedom r[est, as the] rock of its basis; and as truly as has been said of the only greater institution, *"the gates of hell shall not prevail against it."*

Application Written for James Wright[1]

[March, 1838]

James Wright hereby applies to the county commissioners' court of Sangamon county for a Writ of *ad quod damnum* to erect a mill dam on Brush creek on the South West quarter of Section number 18. Township 14 North of Range 4 West and the South East quarter of Section 13 in Township 14 North of Range 5 West, or either of them

[1] AD, IHi.

To Levi Davis[1]

Dear Sir: Springfield, March 15– 1838

We received yours of the 2nd. Inst. by due course of mail, and have only to offer in excuse for not answering it sooner, that we have been in a great state of confusion here ever since the receipt of your letter; and also, that your clients can not suffer by the delay. The suit is merely instituted to quiet a title which has passed through Dr. Stapp,[2] but to which he now lays no claim as we understand. He is a mere nominal party to the proceeding. More than all this, we believe nothing will or can be done with the case at this court.

We beg your pardon for our neglect in this business; if it had been important to you or your client we would have done better.

Yours sincerely   STUART & LINCOLN

[1] ALS, IHi. Entirely in Lincoln's hand.
[2] Probably James T. B. Stapp, former state auditor and cashier of the Bank of the State of Illinois at Vandalia.

Note for the Completion of the State Capitol[1]

$16,666.67.   Springfield, March 22, 1838.

One year after date, we, the undersigned, or either of us, promise to pay to the President, Directors and Company of the State Bank of Illinois, sixteen thousand, six hundred and sixty-six dollars and sixty-seven cents, for value received, negotiable and payable at the bank, in Springfield, with interest until paid, at the rate of six per centum per annum, payable semi-annually.

[1] John Carroll Power, *History of the Early Settlers of Sangamon County, Illinois* (1876), p. 48. The location of the original document is unknown. The note was signed by one hundred and one citizens of Springfield including Lincoln. The amount represented the unpaid third installment of the $50,000 pledged by citizens of Springfield to the building of the new capitol building,

which remained unpaid because many of the original bondsmen had met financial ruin in the panic of 1837. Lincoln had not signed the original bond, as sometimes maintained, but did sign the note of later date.

To Mrs. Orville H. Browning[1]

Dear Madam: Springfield, April 1. 1838.

Without appologising for being egotistical, I shall make the history of so much of my own life, as has elapsed since I saw you, the subject of this letter. And by the way I now discover, that, in order to give a full and inteligible account of the things I have done and suffered *since* I saw you, I shall necessarily have to relate some that happened *before*.

It was, then, in the autumn of 1836, that a married lady of my acquaintance,[2] and who was a great friend of mine, being about to pay a visit to her father and other relatives residing in Kentucky, proposed to me, that on her return she would bring a sister[3] of hers with her, upon condition that I would engage to become her brother-in-law with all convenient dispach. I, of course, accepted the proposal; for you know I could not have done otherwise, had I really been averse to it; but privately between you and me, I was most confoundedly well pleased with the project. I had seen the said sister some three years before, thought her inteligent and agreeable, and saw no good objection to plodding life through hand in hand with her. Time passed on, the lady took her journey and in due time returned, sister in company sure enough. This stomached me a little; for it appeared to me, that her coming so readily showed that she was a trifle too willing; but on reflection it occured to me, that she might have been prevailed on by her married sister to come, without any thing concerning me ever having been mentioned to her; and so I concluded that if no other objection presented itself, I would consent to wave this. All this occured upon my *hearing* of her arrival in the neighbourhood; for, be it remembered, I had not yet *seen* her, except about three years previous, as before mentioned.

[1] ALS, CSmH. The wife of Orville H. Browning of Quincy, Illinois, (nee Eliza Caldwell) was like her husband a native of Kentucky. The Brownings were married in 1836, and in the same year Browning was elected state senator from Adams County. Their political careers beginning only two years apart, Lincoln and Browning were to remain closely associated throughout Lincoln's life, and on the social side Mrs. Browning remained one of Lincoln's most valued friends.

[2] Mrs. Bennett Abell.

[3] Miss Mary S. Owens. See Lincoln's letters (*supra*) of December 13, 1836; May 7, 1837; August 16, 1837.

In a few days we had an interview, and although I had seen her before, she did not look as my immagination had pictured her. I knew she was over-size, but she now appeared a fair match for Falstaff; I knew she was called an "old maid", and I felt no doubt of the truth of at least half of the appelation; but now, when I beheld her, I could not for my life avoid thinking of my mother; and this, not from withered features, for her skin was too full of fat, to permit its contracting in to wrinkles; but from her want of teeth, weather-beaten appearance in general, and from a kind of notion that ran in my head, that *nothing* could have commenced at the size of infancy, and reached her present bulk in less than thirtyfive or forty years; and, in short, I was not all pleased with her. But what could I do? I had told her sister that I would take her for better or for worse; and I made a point of honor and conscience in all things, to stick to my word, especially if others had been induced to act on it, which in this case, I doubted not they had, for I was now fairly convinced, that no other man on earth would have her, and hence the conclusion that they were bent on holding me to my bargain. Well, thought I, I have said it, and, be consequences what they may, it shall not be my fault if I fail to do it. At once I determined to consider her my wife; and this done, all my powers of discovery were put to the rack, in search of perfections in her, which might be fairly set-off against her defects. I tried to immagine she was handsome, which, but for her unfortunate corpulency, was actually true. Exclusive of this, no woman that I have seen, has a finer face. I also tried to convince myself, that the mind was much more to be valued than the person; and in this, she was not inferior, as I could discover, to any with whom I had been acquainted.

Shortly after this, without attempting to come to any positive understanding with her, I set out for Vandalia, where and when you first saw me. During my stay there, I had letters from her, which did not change my opinion of either her intelect or intention; but on the contrary, confirmed it in both.

All this while, although I was fixed "firm as the surge repelling rock" in my resolution, I found I was continually repenting the rashness, which had led me to make it. Through life I have been in no bondage, either real or immaginary from the thraldom of which I so much desired to be free.

After my return home, I saw nothing to change my opinion of her in any particular. She was the same and so was I. I now spent my time between planing how I might get along through life after my contemplated change of circumstances should have taken place; and how I might procrastinate the evil day for a time, which I really dreaded as much—perhaps more, than an irishman does the halter.

After all my suffering upon this deeply interesting subject, here I am, wholly unexpectedly, completely out of the "scrape"; and I now want to know, if you can guess how I got out of it. Out clear in every sense of the term; no violation of word, honor or conscience. I dont believe you can guess, and so I may as well tell you at once. As the lawyers say, it was done in the manner following, towit. After I had delayed the matter as long as I thought I could in honor do, which by the way had brought me round into the last fall, I concluded I might as well bring it to a consumation without further delay; and so I mustered my resolution, and made the proposal to her direct; but, shocking to relate, she answered, No. At first I supposed she did it through an affectation of modesty, which I thought but ill-become her, under the peculiar circumstances of her case; but on my renewal of the charge, I found she repeled it with greater firmness than before. I tried it again and again, but with the same success, or rather with the same want of success. I finally was forced to give it up, at which I verry unexpectedly found myself mortified almost beyond endurance. I was mortified, it seemed to me, in a hundred different ways. My vanity was deeply wounded by the reflection, that I had so long been too stupid to discover her intentions, and at the same time never doubting that I understood them perfectly; and also, that she whom I had taught myself to believe no body else would have, had actually rejected me with all my fancied greatness; and to cap the whole, I then, for the first time, began to suspect that I was really a little in love with her. But let it all go. I'll try and out live it. Others have been made fools of by the girls; but this can never be with truth said of me. I most emphatically, in this instance, made a fool of myself. I have now come to the conclusion never again to think of marrying; and for this reason; I can never be satisfied with any one who would be block-head enough to have me.

When you receive this, write me a long yarn about something to amuse me. Give my respects to Mr. Browning. Your sincere friend
Mrs. O. H. Browning.   A. LINCOLN

Agreement and Note Drawn for James M. Crain[1]

April 20, 1838

Whereas John T. Stuart and Abraham Lincoln have engaged as attorneys in my behalf in a cause now pending in the chancery side of the Tazewell county circuit court in which I am complainant and the heirs of Lewis F. Crain deceased and others are defendants, therefore if I shall succeed to the full extent of my claim in said case, I promise to pay them, the said Stuart & Lincoln the sum of five hundred dollars; but if I should not succeed in the recovery of the property mentioned in said cause as having been purchased of Peter Menard; but shall succeed in the recovery of all the ballance claimed in said cause, then I promise to pay them the said Stuart & Lincoln the sum of three hundred dollars—

April 20. 1838— JAMES M. CRAIN

Tremont, April 20. 1838

Six months after date I promise to pay Stuart & Lincoln twentyfive dollars for value received— JAS. M. CRAIN

[1] AD, ORB. Crain and Menard were residents of Tazewell County.

Bill Rendered to Sangamon County[1]

[June 18, 1838]

The county of Sangamon. To Stuart & Lincoln Dr.

To furnishing room for Grand an[d] Petit Juries at July & October terms of 1837—and March term of 1838. $36.00.

[1] AD, IHi. The bill was for the use of the Stuart & Lincoln office.

To Jesse W. Fell[1]

Dear Fell. [July 23, 1838]

Yours on the reverse side of this sheet[2] is this moment received. Owing to my absence, the former letter of which you speak was not received until Saturday evening. I answered it yesterday,[3] and doubtless you will have received the answer ere you receive this. I again repeat that you may deny the charges made by Douglass against Stuart in relation to a government Bank. I hope Stuart will pay you the much deserved visit; he is, however, doing well, we are told, where he is. If we do our duty we shall succeed in the congressional election, but if we relax an *iota*, we shall be beaten.

Your friend A. LINCOLN

[1] Copy, IU-Illinois Historical Survey. The original in the Fell manuscripts was not available to the editors.

[2] Fell had written from Bloomington on July 20. Lincoln's reply indicates fully the content of Fell's letter.

[3] This letter of Lincoln's has never been located.

To Joseph Duncan[1]

To   Springfield 25 July 1838.

His Excellency Joseph Duncan
        Having learned that a vacancy has occured in the
board of Commissioners of public works—by the resignation of
J. W. Stephenson We take much pleasure in recommending to
your favorable consideration for the vacancy thus created our fellow citizen John Dickson[2] of Ogle county whom we consider in
every way fully qualified to discharge the duties of the office

Jesse B. Thomas Jr	C R Matheny	G. Elkin
J. Wright, Comr.	A.G Herndon	A. Lincoln
Pub. Works.	N W. Edwards	Gershom Jayne
	J. F. Speed	Th C Browne
Simeon Francis	William Butler	A. G. Henry[3]

[1] DS, ORB.   [2] John Dixon.
[3] Of the co-signers with Lincoln, not previously identified, Jesse B. Thomas,
Jr., was circuit judge; Joel Wright was a recently elected commissioner of public works; Charles R. Matheny was clerk of county commissioners' court; Joshua
F. Speed was a merchant and partner in James Bell & Co.; William Butler was
clerk of the circuit court; Garrett Elkin was sheriff; Gershom Jayne was a
Springfield physician; Thomas C. Browne was Illinois Supreme Court judge.

Inventory of Notes Due
Estate of George Spears[1]

September 3, 1838

The following is a correct list or inventory of the notes due the estate of George Spears sen: deceased—viz—

John Pemberton & T. J. Nance	$ 50
Joshua Nance & John M. Bingley	" 24
Jacob Bale & Benjamin Gibbs	200
Jacob Bale & Levi Summers	30
Jacob Bale & James Goldsby	45
Jacob Bale & Levi Summers	50
James Goldsby & Levi Summers	80
	$ 479
Also, one note paid	20
	" 499
[In addition to the above collected Interest	60
	$ 559][2]

Sept. 3. 1838.   GEORGE SPEARS JR.
                                  Executor of
                                  George Spears Sen. decd.

[1] AD, IHi.   [2] Bracketed portion not in Lincoln's hand.

[121]

Draft Prepared for James Wright[1]

Mr. Robert Allen: September 6, 1838
                     Please pay Stuart & Lincoln five dollars, and
charge to [James Wright]
Sept. 6th. 1838.
[Capt. Ransdell
                     will pay the above order
                                                     R. Allen][2]

[1] AD-P, ISLA. See the application written for Wright, March, 1838, *supra*.
[2] Bracketed portions not in Lincoln's hand.

Petition for Appointment of Antrim Campbell as Prosecuting Attorney[1]

[September 13, 1838]
We the undersigned do hereby certify that Antrim Campbell
has been engaged in the practice of the Law in Springfield for eight
months last past and from our knowledge of his character do believe him in every respect worthy of confidence and esteem, and
we do also cheerfully recommend him to his Excellency Joseph
Duncan Governor of the State of Illinois as fully qualified and
competent to fulfill the duties of Prosecuting Attorney and would
be much pleased to see him get the appointment to said office

Stephen T. Logan	Saml. H. Treat
E. D. Baker	J. Hewett
John T. Stuart	A Lincoln
Ninian W. Edwards	Cyrus Walker

[1] DS, I-Ar. Following on the same page begins the lettter of resignation
written by Josephus Hewett, dated September 13, 1838.

Remarks in Illinois Legislature
Concerning Resolutions Asking Information on Railroad and Fund Commissioners[1]

December 8, 1838
Mr. HARDIN[2] of Morgan, asked that certain resolutions presented by him on Monday, asking for detailed information upon
every subject connected with the duties of the Rail road and Fund
Commissioners, should be taken up. Several amendments were
offered to the resolution which were agreed to. Mr. LINCOLN in

[122]

reference to the resolutions said, that so far as he understood their object it was not an unfriendly one towards the Internal Improvement system. His own course was identified with the system. We had gone too far to recede, even if we were disposed to do so. He wished the resolution might pass, so as to enable the friends of the system to detect any errors which might be found in its prosecution, so as to prevent their recurrence.

[1] *Sangamo Journal,* December 15, 1838.
[2] John J. Hardin. His resolutions were adopted after considerable discussion (*House Journal,* Eleventh General Assembly, First Session, pp. 49-50).

Discussion in Illinois Legislature
Regarding an Act Concerning Judgments and Executions[1]

December 13, 1838

Upon the question shall the resolution[2] pass—ayes and nays called for—before being taken Lincoln rose and said that he hoped the resolution would pass, as it merely proposed an inquiry into the expediency of amending the law—or an examination into the fact whether the present law was defective. The resolution was amended by striking out the word "repealing" and inserting the word "amended."

Mr. Baker then spoke in opposition to the resolution on ground that it would give too much power to the creditor over those who are struggling to secure their homes. He was also opposed to this constant spirit of innovation.

Mr. Lincoln replied that he or Baker were mistaken, and explained his view of the proposed alteration. Under the present law, he said, few appeared at the sale of property, and the judgment creditor usually bids it in at half its value. The owner supposed that he would be able to redeem, but was frequently unable, and his property was thus sacrificed under the operation of this law. Baker admitted this true.

[1] Vandalia *Free Press,* December 27, 1838.
[2] A resolution proposed on December 12 by George Smith of Madison County, as follows: "That the committee on the Judiciary be instructed to inquire into the expediency of repealing so much of the 'Act concerning judgments and executions,' approved January 19th, 1825, as makes it lawful for any judgment creditor to redeem lands or tenements that may have been sold by virtue of any execution; and that they report by bill or otherwise" (*House Journal,* Eleventh General Assembly, First Session, p. 63). The resolution was rejected, but under a motion to reconsider on December 13, it was amended and passed.

Bill Introduced in Illinois Legislature
to Limit Justices of the Peace and Constables[1]

[December 14, 1838]

A bill for an act limiting Justices of the Peace and constables to their several Districts respectively.

SEC. 1 Be it enacted by the People of the State of Illinois represented in the General Assembly, that hereafter it shall not be lawful for any Justice of the Peace to issue any civil process to be served on any person in a different District from that in which such Justice shall reside, except in cases where the cause of action on which process is issued shall have accrued in the District where such Justice shall reside and the person against whom it shall issue shall reside in a different one.

SEC: 2. That hereafter no constable shall serve any civil process, issued by a Justice of the Peace unless the same shall have been issued by a Justice residing in the same District with such constable.

[1] AD, I-Ar. Although written by Lincoln, the bill was introduced by James T. Cunningham of Coles County. After much amending, the bill was finally rejected.

Remarks in Illinois Legislature
on Election of House Members to Office[1]

December 21, 1838

Mr. Lincoln moved its[2] reference to the committee on Internal Improvements. Mr. Smith of Wabash, and Mr. Thornton, both seemed to regard this as a direct attack on them. They were members of this committee, interested in the decision; and they would not allow the insinuation. They would hold the gentleman from Sangamon responsible, &c, &c. Mr. Lincoln replied, he did not move the reference with any such design as had been attributed to him. He had always been the friend of both the gentlemen; and at the last extra session he had voted against such a proposition, because his friend from Wabash was personally interested then in the decision, being at that time in the employ of the State. But he would now assure the gentlemen, that the proposition to refer did not originate with him. He was requested to make the motion by one of their especial friends, and a member of the same committee, viz: the gentleman from Perry (Mr. Murphy,) and to oblige him he had made the motion. But he was glad he had made it; the hydra was exposed; and all the talk about settling this matter at another tribunal, he had no objection to, if gentlemen insisted on it. He was always ready, and never shrunk from responsibility.

1 Alton *Telegraph*, December 29, 1838.

2 A resolution proposed by Archibald Williams, representative from Adams County, on December 20, as follows: "That we deprecate the practice of the General Assembly of electing members of their own body to fill State offices, as corrupting in its tendencies, by throwing around such members as intend to become candidates for such offices an influence adverse to impartial legislation" (*House Journal*, Eleventh General Assembly, First Session, p. 120). The resolution was adopted, with amendments, but on the following day a motion for reconsideration was made by Benjamin Johnson of Bond County. Lincoln's remarks were made, following acrimonious debate, on a motion to refer the resolution to the committee on the judiciary. Lincoln's motion and remarks are not recorded in the *House Journal*, but the motion to refer to the committee on the judiciary is recorded as decided in the negative, and hence the resolution remained as adopted the preceding day.

Additional Rule of the House of Representatives of Illinois[1]

[January 4, 1839]

No bill shall be referred or amended after its engrossment for the third reading, without the consent of two-thirds of the members present.

1 *House Journal*, Eleventh General Assembly, First Session, p. 167. The proposed rule was laid on the table, but see the rules submitted by Lincoln and adopted on January 5, 1839, *infra*.

Additional Rules Adopted by the House of Representatives of Illinois[1]

[January 5, 1839]

Rule — No Bill shall be committed or amended on the question of its passage, except by the consent of two thirds of all the members present

Rule — When any petition remonst[r]ance or claim is presented by a member and such member may not desire its reading, he may make the motion to dispense with its reading and ask its refer[e]nce at the time of presentation—and the chair may consider the motion as agreed to, unless some member should object and so state to the House

1 D, I-Ar. Although the original documents are not in Lincoln's handwriting, he moved their adoption on January 5, and considering his rule proposed the day before (*vide supra*) and the similar rule proposed on December 11, 1834 (*vide supra*), it seems likely that Lincoln may have composed the later statements as well as moved their adoption.

Remarks in Illinois Legislature
Concerning Resolutions in Relation to Fugitive Slaves[1]

January 5, 1839

Mr Lincoln, on the first reading of the resolutions, had inclined to vote in favor of concurring; but upon the second, he felt that he wanted more time for deliberation. He now thought it would be better to postpone the subject indefinitely; and accordingly, made a motion to this effect.

[1] Vandalia *Free Press*, January 10, 1839. The first resolution condemned the Governor of Maine for refusing to deliver two citizens accused of kidnapping a slave in Georgia, by condemning all such state executives. The second resolved that the citizens of non-slaveholding states ought not to interfere with the domestic relations of slaveholding states. Consideration of the resolutions was postponed.

Remarks in Illinois Legislature
Concerning Appropriation for Building the State House[1]

January 7, 1839

Mr Lincoln said, that as the Hon. Speaker[2] had confined his remarks to the expensiveness of the work under consideration, he would not wander from this point himself. And, indeed, it was unnecessary to say much upon that subject; for he believed that the majority would agree, that if the work was to be done [at] all, it had best be well done; that is, in a manner creditable to the State. He felt perfectly willing to submit the question to the House, without saying one word more.[3]

Mr. Lincoln, in reply, contended that the people of 1840 would have no better right to decide the question, than the people of 1839. True, the inhabitants of Vandalia had a right to retain the seat of government here twenty years, according to the provisions of the Constitution; but, on the other hand, if the people of Illinois at large had found that they had a hard bargain, they have a right to get out of it as soon as they can. Has not the corporation of Springfield faithfully performed her part of the contract? Two thirds of the stipulated sum is paid; and for the other third which is not paid, the bonds of twenty-five responsible men are put forward, which may be sued at any time, and are perfectly secure, so far as the interest of the State is involved. He could not say, indeed, with his colleague, that he considered *the faith of the State as pledged* to complete the State House at Springfield; but wished that work to go on, and that place to be made the permanent seat of government; because it was the place of his residence, and because he really believed that the people would thus be best accommodated. True, when the question of a Capitol was formerly submitted to the people at large, Springfield did not receive the highest number of votes; but this can furnish no evidence that if the question were now a second time submitted to the same tribunal, Springfield would not have a larger vote than any other point.

As to *making money* by locating the Capitol in some new place, and selling the lots of a city *that is to be,* he would simply ask how much money had been made, and how many State Houses had been built out of the land received here in Vandalia, as a donation from the General Government? Depend upon it, the idea of realizing such immense sums of money in this way, is all an illusion. As for the unconstitutionality of agitating this question at present, he hardly expected that those who bring forward a series of plans, of the same general nature with this now in progress at Springfield, would throw upon their opponents this charge; for each and all of these is equally unconstitutional.

[1] Vandalia *Free Press,* January 10, 1839. A less adequate account appears in the *Sangamo Journal,* January 19, 1839.   [2] William L. D. Ewing.
[3] Ewing then proposed other amendments, contending that it was unconstitutional to legislate on the subject until 1840, and that it would be better to locate the seat of government on vacant land.

Bill Introduced in Illinois Legislature
to Establish the Counties of Menard, Logan, and Dane[1]

[January 16-19, 1839]

A bill for an act to establish the counties of Menard, Logan and Dane.

SEC. 1st. Be it enacted by the People of the state of Illinois represented in the General Assembly that all that tract of country lying within the following boundaries to wit; Beginning at the North West corner of Section Twentyseven in Township Seventeen North of Range Eight West of the Third Principal Meridian; thence East to the centre of the Southern boundary of Section Twentyfour, in Township Seventeen North of Range Seven West; thence North to the middle of the Northern boundary of said sec-

[1] AD, I-Ar. The original bill which Lincoln introduced on January 16, was filed with amendments attached on January 19, as the engrossed copy. On February 6 a final amendment of the Senate amendments was adopted. The bill as amended may be found in *Laws of Illinois,* 1839, pp. 104-107. A supplemental act was also introduced by Lincoln on February 20 (*vide infra*).

tion; thence East to the middle of the Northern boundary of Section Nineteen in Township Seventeen North of Range Six West; thence North to the centre of Section Eighteen, Township and Range last aforesaid; thence East to the middle of the Eastern boundary line of said section; thence North to the channel of Rock Creek; thence down the channel of Rock Creek to where the Northern boundary line of section Nine, Township and Range last aforesaid, crosses the same; thence East to the South West corner of Section Two, Township & Range last aforesaid; thence North to the South East corner of Section Twentyseven in Township Eighteen North, Range aforesaid; thence East to the South East corner of Section Thirty in Township Eighteen North Range Four West; thence North to the South East corner of Section Eighteen in Township Nineteen North Range last aforesaid; thence West to the line between Ranges Four & Five; thence North to the Northern boundary line of Sangamon county; thence West with said line to the Illinois river; thence with the present boundary lines of Sangamon county to the place of begining, shall form and constitute the county of Menard.

SEC: 2nd. That all that tract of country lying within the following boundaries, towit; Begining at the North West corner of Township Twenty North of Range Four West; thence South to the South West corner of Section Eighteen, in Township Nineteen North of Range aforesaid; thence East one mile; thence South to the South East corner of the county of Menard; thence East to the line dividing Ranges Three and Four; thence South to the South West corner of Section Seven Township Seventeen North of Range Three West;[2] thence East to the Eastern boundary line of Sangamon county; thence with the present boundary lines of Sangamon county to the place of begining shall constitute the county of Logan.

SEC: 3rd. That all that tract of country lying within the following boundaries, towit; Begining where the Third Principal Meridian crosses the North Fork of the Sangamon river; thence down said river to the line between Sections Nine & Ten in Township Fifteen North of Range Three West; thence South to the South East corner of Section Four in Township Fourteen North Range last aforesaid; thence West three miles by the surveys; thence South three miles by the surveys; thence West three miles by the surveys; thence South to the Southern boundary of Township Eleven, Range last aforesaid; thence East with the surveys to the Third Principal Meridian; thence North to the place of begining shall constitute the county of Dane.

[2] See fifth amendment (*infra*), which was to be inserted at this point.

[128]

SEC: 4th. That Benjamin Mitchell of Tazewell county, John Henry of Morgan county, Newton Walker of Fulton county Richard O. Wariner[3] of Montgomery county, and Achilles Morris of Sangamon county be and they are hereby appointed commissioners to locate the seats of Justice of the counties of Menard and Dane. Said commissioners, or a majority of them shall meet at Petersburg in Menard county on the first monday of May next, or within twenty days thereafter, and after being first duly sworn by some one authorized to administer oaths, faithfully and impartially to discharge the duties imposed on them by this act, shall proceed to explore said county, and to locate the seat of Justice thereof with a view to present and future population; which location, when made, shall be and remain the Seat of Justice of the county of Menard.*[4]

SEC: 5th. Said commissioners, or a majority of them, shall meet at such place within the county of Dane as may be agreed on by them, and at such time as they may agree upon not exceeding twenty days after they shall have located the seat of justice of Menard county, and shall then and there proceed to make the location of the seat of justice of the said county of Dane, in all respects conformably with the fourth section of this act.

SEC: 6th. Said commissioners shall make out a certificate of the location of the seat of justice of each of the said counties of Menard and Dane, stating what tract of land, and what part of the tract each location is made upon; which certificates shall be signed by the said commissioners, and filed in the office of the clerk of the county commissioner's court of Sangamon county, and shall be evidence of the said locations respectively.

SEC 7th. Neither of said locations shall be made on private property unless the owner thereof shall either convey to the county, twenty acres of land, having the location at or near the centre thereof, or donate in money, to be applied to the erection of public buildings, the sum of three thousand dollars.

SEC: 8th. That Charles Emmerson of Macon county, Chenney Thomas of McLean county and Charles R. Matheny of Sangamon county, be, and they are hereby appointed commissioners to locate the seat of justice of Logan county; and who, or a majority of whom, shall, in all respects, perform their duties in the manner that the commissioners for the location of the county seats of the

---

[3] See first amendment (*infra*). Both Wariner (Warrener?) and Morris were omitted in the act as approved and printed.

[4] See fourth amendment marked by asterisk (*infra*), which was to be inserted at this point.

counties of Menard & Dane, are by this act required to do, and shall meet at the town of Postville in said county of Logan, on the first monday of May next, or within twenty days thereafter for the purpose of performing the same; and such location when so made, shall be and remain the seat of justice of the said county of Logan until the end of the session of the General Assembly in the year 1841.

SEC: 9th Each of said commissioners named in this act, shall receive out of the county treasuries respectively for which he may have served, such *per diem* allowance, as shall be paid the members of the present General Assembly.

SEC: 10th. An election shall be held on the first monday of April next in each of the counties established by this act, to elect for each of said counties, one Sheriff, one Coroner, one Recorder, one county surveyor, three county commissioners, one clerk of the county commissioner's court, and one Probate Justice of the Peace, who shall hold their offices until the next succeeding general election, and until their successors are elected and qualified; which elections shall be conducted in all respects agreeably to the law regulating elections. Said elections shall be held in the county of Menard, at Petersburg, Sugar-Grove, Huron, and Lynchburg; in the county of Logan, at at [*sic*] Postville and Pulaski; in the county of Dane, at Buck-Heart Grove, Allenton, and the house of John Durbin, and shall be held by the judges heretofore appointed by the authority of Sangamon county for those precincts respectively, provided, that where any place named in this act for holding said election, has not heretofore been an election precinct, the electors meeting there may choose their own judges and clerks, who shall be qualified according to law previous to entering upon the discharge of their duties.

SEC: 11th. The judges of elections, shall deliver to each officer elected a certificate of his election. The poll books shall be retained by them until the clerks of the county commissioner's courts, shall respectively be qualified, and then deliver such poll-books of each county to it's own clerk, who shall make and transmit to the Secretary of State an abstract of the votes given at such election in the same time, manner and form as is required of clerks of county commissioners courts in elections in other counties of this state.

SEC: 12th. The said counties hereby established shall be attached to, and form part of the first judicial circuit.

SEC: 13th The county of Menard shall be entitled to one representative in the General Assembly & the counties of Logan and Dane together one, the county of Sangamon, five, and the four together two senators; and, in case any vacancy shall occur previous to the next election, the four counties shall vote together to fill said vacancy in the same manner as if no division had taken place.

SEC: 14th. All bussiness now pending in the Sangamon circuit court, or which shall be commenced therein previous to the organization of the counties hereby established, shall be determined therein, as if no new counties had been established; and the sheriff of Sangamon county is hereby authorized to perform all duties within the boundaries of the said new counties, which may be necessary for the finishing of the aforesaid bussiness.[5]

SEC: 15th. The judges of the several election precincts within the aforesaid counties shall meet at the several places herein after named on the second day after said election to compare their respective polls—in the county of Menard, at the town of Petersburg; in the county of Logan at the town of Pulaski; in the county of Dane, at the town of Allenton.

1st. Amend the bill by striking out the names of Richard O. Warrener, and Achilles Morris wherever they occur.

2nd. amend the 14th. section by adding thereto the following towit: "and for the collection of the taxes already assessed. All bussiness now pending in the courts of the Justices of the Peace, or of the Probate Justice of the Peace, of Sangamon county, or which shall be commenced therein, previous to the organization of the new counties hereby established, shall be finished by said justices and their constables as though no division had taken place"

Amend by adding as a 16th Section the following: "The Justices of the Peace and constables now in office for Sangamon county, who reside in the boundaries of the new counties hereby established, shall continue in office in their respective new counties so long as they would have done if no division had taken place"

*Amend the 4th. section by adding the following proviso "Provided that if the said commissioners shall locate the seat of Justice of Menard county on the West or left side of the Sangamon river, then, and in that case, the lines of said county shall be changed as follows, towit: (Begining[6] at the South West corner of section thirty four in Township Eighteen North of Range Six West; thence North (*two*) miles) by the surveys; thence East with the surveys to the Eastern boundary line of said county as described in this act;

---

[5] See second amendment (*infra*), which was to be inserted at this point.

[6] This description was amended by the Senate and then further amended by Lincoln on February 6. (See final amendment to the amendment of the Senate, *infra*.)

thence with the before described boundaries throughout. Provided further, that said commissioner's [*sic*] in making the location of the seat of Justice of said county, shall pay no regard whatever, to the above contemplated change of lines.["]

Amend the Second Section in the 9th. line by inserting between the words *West* and thence—The following

> Thence east to the North east corner of
> Section fifteen township last afforesaid,
> thence South one Mile[7]

Amend the amendment of the Senate by striking out all from the word "Begining" to the word "miles" both inclusive, and insert the following—"Begining at the South West corner of Section Three in Township Seventeen North of Range Six West; thence North four miles"[8]

[7] This amendment is not in Lincoln's handwriting.
[8] This final amendment was adopted February 6.

Remarks in Illinois Legislature
Concerning Resolutions in Relation to
Purchase of Public Lands[1]

January 17, 1839

Mr. LINCOLN thought the resolutions ought to be seriously considered. In reply to the gentleman from Adams,[2] he said that it was not to enrich the State. The price of the lands may be raised, it was thought by some, by others that it would be reduced. The conclusion in his mind was that the Representatives in this Legislature from the country in which the lands lie would be opposed to raising the price, because it would operate against the settlement of the lands. He referred to the lands in the military tract. They had fallen into the hands of large speculators in consequence of the low price. He was opposed to a low price of land. He thought it was adverse to the interests of the poor settler, because speculators buy them up. He was opposed to a reduction of the price of public lands..

Mr. L. referred to some official documents emanating from Indiana, and compared the progressive population of the two States. Illinois had gained upon that State under the public land system as it is. His conclusion was that ten years from this time Illinois would

[1] *Illinois State Register*, February 5, 1839, and Vandalia *Free Press*, January 24, 1839. These remarks as reported in the press were part of a general discussion following the submission of the resolutions (*supra*).
[2] Archibald Williams of Quincy, Illinois.

have no more public land unsold than Indiana now has. He referred also to Ohio. That State had sold nearly all her public lands. She was but 20 years ahead of us, and as our lands were equally saleable, more so as he maintained, we should have no more 20 years from now than she has at present.

Mr. L. referred to the canal lands, and supposed that the policy of the State would be different in regard to them, if the Representatives from that section of country could themselves choose the policy, but the Representatives from other parts of the State had a veto upon it, and regulated the policy. He thought that if the State had all the lands, the policy of the Legislature would be more liberal to all sections.

He refered to the policy of the General Government. He thought that if the national debt had not been paid, the expenses of the Government would not have doubled, as they had done since that debt was paid.[3]

Mr. Lincoln said, that the arguments in favor of the plan now under consideration were briefly summed up in his report. He looked upon it as a hopeful means of meeting the burdens of government, and providing a future revenue for sustaining our system of Internal Improvement. Admit that the price of lands is not thus *diminished;* nay, admit that it is somewhat enhanced above that, at which the State may purchase them of the General Government, still, we shall gain *this* advantage—to keep these lands out of the grasp of speculators. Wherever lands are sold low, they invariably fall into the hands of the rich. Were the public lands to be put down to-day to the price of 50 cents an acre, speculators would get the best of them before the poor man could get the news. The question put by the gentleman from Morgan (Mr. Hardin) goes upon the supposition that we shall make a bad bargain with the General Government. But the plan is based upon the expectation of purchasing these lands at a reasonable rate. Illinois has some ten millions of unsold lands. Let us see what light we can obtain on this subject from Indiana and Ohio. Now, Indiana had, last year, only about four millions and one half of acres unsold; and Ohio, only about one million and three quarters. But Illinois is only 20 years younger than Ohio, and 10 years younger than Indiana; we may therefore conclude, that this State will in *ten* years have not more

[3] The "Report and Resolutions" lay on the table until January 28, when two amendments were offered and referred to a select committee with Lincoln as chairman. Lincoln's committee reported them back without amendment and recommended their adoption. Two amendments were then rejected and the resolutions adopted as written, on February 2, 1839.

than 4½ millions of acres remaining unsold; in *twenty* years, not more than 1¾ millions; and in this case, on the supposition that Illinois should now buy up all the lands, at a reduced price, she will have made a first rate bargain.

Now, the resources of the State *must be* husbanded. Economy is to be the order of the day. We must find some new sources of revenue. We need them, and shall need them, for many years to come. Our system of Internal Improvement requires them. The public debt is already enormous, and is augmenting every day. "This is the principal reason" said Mr. Lincoln in conclusion, "why I have persevered in opposition to the views of many of the committee, in bringing this subject before the House."

Discussion in Illinois Legislature
of Resolution Relative to Public Depositories[1]

January 17, 1839

Mr. Lincoln said if partiality shall be proven to exist, shall we say it does? or shall we rather use another word, which will not express our meaning, for fear we offend our MASTER; for his part, he wanted to call things by their right names, no matter who was offended.

There had been partiality; it was proven by the Secretary's report, and he believed we would be more thought of, if we said so, especially as it could not be denied.

Mr LINCOLN said, he would be willing that the word *partiality* should be stricken out if he thought it was not true. The Legislature would be more respected by the Government if it used plain language, whenever that language is true. Mr L. then summed up the arguments which had passed, and contended that the position was fully made out that the Government had been partial. He was willing to take the gentleman from Vermilion[2] by the hand. He says that by our course we strike our own party friends. Well, we are willing to go it. Let him do the same with his party friends. Gentlemen insist that they cannot pass on these resolutions without investigation. He had heard similar arguments often made to put off trial in court.[3]

[1] *Illinoisan* (Jacksonville), January 26, 1839; *Illinois State Register*, January 22, 1839. The resolution under discussion objected to the federal government's policy of depositing tax monies collected in Illinois in the Bank of Missouri, and complained that the policy was "unfair and partial."

[2] Isaac P. Walker, the one Democratic representative from that county.

[3] On Lincoln's motion the resolution was tabled.

Report and Resolutions Introduced
in Illinois Legislature in Relation to
Purchase of Public Lands[1]

January 17, 1839

The Committee on Finance, to which was referred a resolution of this House instructing them to inquire into the expediency of proposing to purchase of the Government of the United States all the unsold lands lying within the limits of the State of Illinois, have had the same under consideration, and report:

That, in their opinion, if such purchase could be made on reasonable terms, two objects of high importance to the State might thereby be effected—first, acquire control over all the territory within the limits of the State—and, second, acquire an important source of revenue.

We will examine these two points in their order, and with special reference to their bearing upon our internal improvement system.

In the first place, then, we are now so far advanced in a general system of internal improvements that, if we would, we cannot retreat from it, without disgrace and great loss. The conclusion then is, that we *must* advance; and if so, the first reason for the State acquiring title to the public lands is, that while we are at great expense in improving the country, and thereby enhancing the value of all the real property within its limits, that enhancement may attach exclusively to property owned by *ourselves* as a State, or to its citizens as individuals, and *not* to that owned by the Government of the United States. Again, it is conceded every where, as we believe, that Illinois surpasses every other spot of equal extent upon the face of the globe, in *fertility* of soil, and in the proportionable amount of the same which is sufficiently level for actual cultivation; and consequently that she is endowed by nature with the capacity of sustaining a greater amount of agricultural wealth and population than any other equal extent of territory in the world. To such an amount of wealth and population, our internal improvement system, now so alarming, in view of its having to be borne by our present numbers, and with our present means, would be a burden of no sort of consequence. How important, then, is it that all our energies should be exerted to bring that wealth and population among us as speedily as possible. But what, it may be asked, can the ownership of the land by the State do towards the

1 *House Journal*, Eleventh General Assembly, First Session, pp. 223-25.

[135]

accomplishment of that desirable object? It may be answered that the chief obstruction to the more rapid settlement of our country is found in the fact that so much of our best lands lie so remote from timber—an obstruction that, did our State but own those lands, our Legislature might do much towards removing, by extending encouragement in the shape of donations, exemptions from ordinary burdens, or otherwise, to the rearing and cultivating of timber, or to the invention of means of building and enclosure that might dispense with the present profuse use of timber. This, then, is another reason why the State should desire the control of all the lands within its limits.

Looking to these lands in the second point of view, to wit: as a source of revenue, your committee submit the following: There are now of unsold lands in the State of Illinois, twenty millions of acres, more or less. Should we purchase all of them, at 25 cents per acre, they would cost us five millions of dollars. This sum we might borrow, and the proceeds of the sales of the lands, at the present price of $1 25 per acre, would repay the principal, together with the interest thereon, at five per cent. for thirty years, and one half the lands still be left us.

In a very short time we shall have contracted a very heavy debt for the construction of public works; and yet those works will remain for a time so incomplete as to return us nothing; meanwhile the interest upon our debt must be paid. When this juncture shall arrive (as surely it will) we shall find ourselves at a point which may aptly be likened to the dead point in the steam-engine—a point extremely difficult of turning—but which, when once turned, will present no further difficulty, and all will again be well. The aid that we might derive in that *particular juncture*, by the purchase of the public lands, affords, in the opinion of the committee, the strongest reason for making that purchase. The annual proceeds of the sales of those lands, should the subsequent sales bear any proportion to those of former times, will pay the interest on the loan created for their own purchase, and also upon many millions of our internal improvement loans; and that, too, at that *particular time* when we shall have but *very small, if any* other, means of paying it. And finally, when our public works shall be completed, and consequently able to sustain themselves, the proceeds of the sales of the lands may be diverted to the payment of the original debt contracted for the purchase of them. To show that we are not mistaken in saying that the proceeds of the sales of the lands will annually pay the interest on their own loan, and also on a large amount of the internal improvement loan, it is only necessary to state that the interest on the land loan would be but five hundred thousand dollars, annually, and that the proceeds of the sales of the public lands in this State have, in one instance, been about three millions a year (the committee speak from memory only;) so that, should the average of the subsequent sales be half as large, we still should have left one million annually, to pay interest on our internal improvement debt.

The only remaining question is, whether there is any *probability* of the General Government accepting such a proposal. We think there are some reasons for believing it would. It would relieve the General Government from the perpetual source of expensive and vexatious legislation, which, perhaps, annually absorbs one-tenth of all it receives from that source of revenue. She would receive of us, at once, and without trouble, five millions of dollars—a sum one-third part as large as she paid a foreign government for the Louisiana territory, then including what are now the States of Louisiana, Arkansas, and Missouri—and receive it, too, after having received of us, for lands already sold, a sum equal to the whole sum paid for the Louisiana territory; and she would receive that five millions of dollars at a time when she is in most particular need of money.

But should your committee be mistaken; should there be no *probability* of the General Government accepting our proposal, still, it is believed no evil can follow the making it.

The committee, therefore, submit the following resolutions:[2]

Resolved by the General Assembly of the State of Illinois that the said State propose to purchase of the government of the United States, all the lands not sold or otherwise disposed of, within the limits of said State, at the rate of twentyfive cents per acre, to be paid (unless otherwise agreed upon) at such time, as the said Government of the United States, shall deliver over to the authorities of the said State of Illinois, all the plats, Field notes &c. &c. pertaining to the surveys of said lands.

Resolved, that the faith of the said State of Illinois is hereby irrevocably pledged, to carry into effect the foregoing proposal, if the Government of the United States shall accept the same within two years from the passage hereof.

Resolved, that our Senators in Congress be instructed and our Representatives requested, to use their best exertions to procure the

2 AD, I-Ar. Two copies of these resolutions are in the Illinois State Archives: one entirely in Lincoln's hand is apparently the original copy presented before the House; the other, partly in the hand of the clerk of the House, is apparently the copy sent to the Senate. The manuscript of the report preceding the resolutions has not been located.

passage of a law or resolution of Congress accepting the foregoing proposal.

Resolved, that the Governor be requested to transmit a copy of the foregoing resolutions to each of our Senators and Representatives in Congress.[3]

[3] The Senate copy carries this additional phrase: "in the adoption of which resolutions they ask the concurrence of the Senate."

Remarks in Illinois Legislature
Concerning Appointment of
Members of Legislature to Federal Office[1]

January 25, 1839

Mr. Lincoln would not like to see the abstract question of right to a seat in this legislature blinded with any personal interests. He should therefore vote against laying the resolution on the table till the 4th of July; and if this motion were lost, he would move to lay it on the table—with the intention of letting it lie there till near the close of the session; when it could be taken up without wearing the appearance of being a personal attack.

[1] Quincy *Whig*, February 2, 1839. A resolution offered by Vital Jarrot of St. Clair County called for an investigation of whether any member of the legislature had accepted a federal appointment in violation of the Illinois constitution, which prohibited members of the legislature from holding "any lucrative office under the United States, or this State," but excepting postmasters, and a few other offices. A Whig move aimed at William G. Flood's appointment to the Quincy Land Office, the resolution nevertheless dealt with a vital point, and Lincoln apparently wished to have the question settled in principle even though willing to avoid a clash over Flood's right to his seat in the legislature.

Letter Written for Edward D. Baker
to William Butler[1]

Wm Butler Esq Sir   Vandalia, Jany. 26. 1839

Yours of the 22nd. is duly received. Are you not ashamed of writing such a letter as that? If you believe the charges you make to be true, I say most flatly you are a fool. If you do not believe them, I do not see the necessity of your making them; they are not the sort of *jokes* that I Incline tamely to take. This is a short letter, but it is longer than one having so little truth, or reason or justice as yours, deserves as an answer. Yours with all proper respect.

E. D. BAKER

[1] AL, ICHi. Lincoln wrote the letter, probably at Baker's dictation, and Baker signed and addressed it. For the circumstances under which Baker wrote,

see Lincoln to Butler, February 1, *infra*. Although it is impossible to conjecture Butler's charges in detail, it is evident that they had to do with the controversial division of Sangamon County (see Lincoln's bill, January 16-19, *supra*), and Lincoln's letter to Butler (*infra*) illuminates the charges in part.

To William Butler[1]

Dear Butler: Vandalia, Jany. 26– 1839

Your letter of the 21st. Inst. is just received. You were in an ill-humor when you wrote that letter, and, no doubt, intended that I should be thrown into one also; which, however, I respectfully decline being done. All you have said about our having been bought up by Taylor, Wright, Turley,[2] enemies &c I *know you would not say, seriously, in your moments of reflection;* and therefore I do not think it worth while to attempt *seriously* to prove the contrary to you. I only now say, that I am willing to pledge myself in black and white to cut my own throat from ear to ear, if, when I meet you, you shall *seriously* say, that you believe me capable of betraying my friends for any price.

The grounds of your complaint I will answer seriously. First, then, as to Athens. We *have* Allen's[3] letter of which you speak; and although, he did not in that letter, pretend that he was specially authorized to speak for the people of Athens, he did *pretend,* that he *knew* their feelings, and that he fairly expressed them. And further; Hall & Francis[4] of Athens are now here, and I assure you, *they* say nothing about "giving us hell". They are as good-humored as I ever saw them. About Cowardin's[5] county. We passed the bill through the House with the lines precisely as Cowardin himself agreed they should pass. After Cowardin left, Turley insisted on having the Buffalo Heart Grove, insisting that the people of that Grove desired to go in the new county. We knew they desired no such thing; and to get rid of Turley's importunity, we promised him, that if he would get a majority of the people of the Grove to petition to go to the new county, we would let him have it. We immediately notified the people of the Grove of this promise; and we, on yesterday received a pe[ti]tion praying that the Grove may remain in the old county; and signed by every citizen in the grove

[1] ALS, ICHi.

[2] John Taylor, who had actively led the petitioners for the new county of Menard; John Wright and George W. Turley, of Mt. Pulaski, active petitioners for the new county of Logan.

[3] Probably James D. Allen, a merchant at Athens.

[4] Josiah N. Francis and Calvin Francis, brothers of Simeon Francis, both of whom resided at Athens at this time; Josiah was the more active in politics. "Hall" has not been identified.

[5] Peter G. Cowardin, who was active for the creation of Logan County.

but two; so that the grove neither is nor will be struck off to the new county. The lines, and every thing pertaining to that county are now, and will remain just as Cowardin agreed they should be. Wherein, then, has Cowardin, been betrayed, or your pledges to him violated?

Again; as to the Allenton county.[6] You know that we could not control the teritory proposed to be taken from Shelby & Montgomery counties. You complain that we run too far West. The justification for this is, that we *could* not get the teritory from Montgomery in any other shape, the legislature, recognizing the right of the member from that county, to divide the same as he pleased. And as to the part to be taken from Shelby, that, we could not get at all, Thornton,[7] refusing perem[p]torily to let his county be divided, or curtailed in any way. Since the bill passed the House, Frink[8] has been here (and here let me say, he is not half as mad as you would make us think) and obtained a pledge from Thornton, that if he can get a majority of Shelby county consenting to the curtailment he desires, he, Thornton, will go for it. Frink has gone to Shelby, to get petitioners, and the probability is, that we will yet be able to get from Shelby what Allenton desires. Nothing could do more credit to your heart, than the mortification you express at seeing the friends with whom you acted in getting up the remonstrance disappointed; but *surely* you ought not to blame us for being unable to accomplish impossibilities.

My respects to Mrs. Butler & Salome.[9] Your friend in spite of your ill-nature   LINCOLN

P.S. Judge Stone is here, and I am about to get him to help me about your Clerk-fee appropriation.[10]

[6] Allenton was the name of a community no longer in existence in what later became Christian County.

[7] William F. Thornton, representative from Shelby County.

[8] William S. Frink, a leading citizen of the Allenton community.

[9] Salome was Butler's oldest daughter.

[10] Judge Daniel Stone. See Lincoln's bill for the relief of the circuit clerk, February 6, *infra*.

To William Butler[1]

Friend Butler: Vandalia, Jany. 31th. 1839

I have just time before the bearer of this starts, to say that I want you to send me the *amount* of your claim for old State Bank fees. I can not find the old bill that Stone[2] introduced. You have heard before this, that we have passed Anti-Sub-Treasury resolutions thro' both Houses. Yesterday the Loco Focos, took it into their

heads that they would contend that Senate had amended the resolutions, and then the House had a right to try the whole question
over again. We commenced the fight at 9. A.M and kept it up most
fiercely till after candle-light, when on taking the final vote, we
beat them again 46 to 43.   LINCOLN

1 ALS, ICHi.   2 Daniel Stone.

To William Butler[1]

Friend Butler: Vandalia, Feb: 1. 1839
    Your letter enclosing one to Mr. Baker, was received on yester-
day evening.[2] There is no necessity for any bad feeling between
Baker & yourself. Your first letter to him was written while you
were in a state of high excitement, and therefore ought not to have
been construed as an emination of deliberate malice. Unfortunately
however it reached Baker while he was writhing under a severe
tooth-ache, and therefore he at that time was incapable of exercising that patience and reflection which the case required. The note
he sent you was written while in that state of feeling, and for that
reason I think you ought not to pay any serious regard to it. It is
always magnanamous to recant whatever we may have said in passion; and when you and Baker shall have done this, I am sure there
will no difficulty be left between you. I write this without Bakers
knowledge; and I do it because nothing would be more painful to me
than to see a difficulty between two of my most particular friends.
    About your dissatisfaction in relation to the South East county
I will now say that I all the while laboured under a mistake. When
I wrote to Frink & Murphy[3] that I would go for their county, I
only meant that I would go for giving them a county as against
Springfield & the old county; and it never occurred to me that I
was pledging myself to one party of the new-county men against
another, for I did not then know they were divided into parties.
When I consented for the lines to approach Springfield nearer than
the petition asked, I really thought I was confering a favour upon
the new-county. And, by the way, if you will compare Frink's petition with the lines as they now stand, you will see that there is but
three quarters of a township more taken from Sangamon county
than the petition asked for; and as to the part from Montgomery, I
have before told you we could not control that.
    No news here now. Your friend as ever   A. LINCOLN

1 ALS, ICHi.
2 A copy of Butler's letter to Baker, January 29, which is preserved with the
letters from Lincoln to Butler, makes apology and explains that the letter of

January 26 had been written under misapprehension. Butler continued, ". . . it was not my intention to insult you or any one of my friends though under the misapprehension I felt myself badly treated. . . ." Baker was apparently not satisfied, however, for a further letter from Butler, February 28, professed "I am willing to meet you as we parted at which time I hope for such mutual concessions as will enable us to remain as we ever have been if you still persist in a different co[u]rse I can regret it."

3 William S. Frink and Jesse Murphy of the Allenton community.

Bill Introduced in Illinois Legislature
for Relief of the Clerk of the Circuit Court
of Sangamon County[1]

[February 6, 1839]

A bill for an act for the relief of the clerk of the circuit court of Sangamon county.

SEC. 1 Be it enacted by the people of the state of Illinois represented in the General Assembly, that whenever the clerk of the circuit court of Sangamon county shall make out a fee bill in due form of law, for services rendered by him or by his predecessor in office, as clerk, in all cases in which the president and directors of the[2] State Bank of Illinois were a party, so far as said services were rendered for said Bank, and for which it is, or would be liable, as such party, and shall transmit the same to the Auditor of Public Accounts, said Auditor shall issue his warrant upon the Treasury in favour of said clerk for such an amount as may be so shown to be due him.

SEC: 2 Said clerk, in making out said fee-bill, shall be liable to the same penalties and forfeitures for any violation of the present law regulating fees as he would be in any other case.

Amend the first section by inserting immediately before the word "state" in the seventh line, the word "old"

Further amend by adding, as a third section, the following—

SEC: 3. The clerks of the circuit courts of Franklin, Fayette and Clinton counties shall be entitled to the same benefits, subject to the same pre-requisites and liabilities under this act, as the said clerk of Sangamon county.

1 AD, I-Ar. The bill with amendments was reported by Lincoln from the committee on finance on February 6. With an additional fourth section requiring that the clerk's fee bill be certified by the judges of the circuit courts in the respective counties, and with the title amended to include the names of the three additional counties, the act may be found in *Laws of Illinois*, 1840, p. 156.

2 See the first amendment requiring the insertion at this point of the word "old," in order to distinguish between the old and new institutions of the same name.

Discussion in Illinois Legislature
Concerning Protest of Resolutions on Sub-Treasury[1]

February 9, 1839

During the afternoon, some of the members, among whom was Mr. H. T. Pace of Jefferson, rose in his place and stated that when he signed it, he had not calculated that any other use was to be made of it than to send it to our members of Congress: but if it was to be placed on the journal . . . he would ask the privilege of expunging his name. . . .

Mr. Lincoln remarked, that if the gentleman from Jefferson wished to withdraw his name from that document, he for one was willing to admit it; but he would say to the member and the House, there were statements made in that document which were false and unfounded, and he would call on the authors of the protest, at the proper time, to retract. He would not deny the right of gentlemen to protest; but he would maintain his right to lay before the people a contradiction of their unfounded statements. Yet, while he wished to hold the signers of this document responsible to the people for what they had said, if the gentleman from Jefferson, or any one else, was ashamed of it, he hoped the House would permit them to withdraw their names.

[1] Alton *Telegraph*, March 2, 1839. Thirty-eight Democratic members had signed a protest against resolutions adopted instructing senators and requesting representatives to vote against the sub-treasury system of the federal administration.

To John T. Stuart[1]

Dear Stuart: Vandalia, Feb: 14th. 1839

I have a note in Bank which falls due some time between the 20th & last of this month. Butler[2] stands as principal, and I as security; but I am in reality the principal. It will take between 50 & 55 dollars to renew it. Butler has more than that much money in his hands which he collected on a debt of mine since I came away. I wish you to call at the Bank, have a note filled over my name signed below, get Butler to sign it, and also to let you have the money to renew it. Ewing[3] wont do any thing. He is not worth a damn. Your friend   A LINCOLN

[1] ALS-F, ISLA.   [2] William Butler.   [3] William L. D. Ewing.

Statement in Illinois Legislature
Concerning Internal Improvements[1]

February 15, 1839

Mr Lincoln admitted that *Sangamon county had received great and important benefits, at the last session of the Legislature, in return for giving support, thro' her delegation to the system of Internal Improvement;* and that though not *legally* bound, she is *morally* bound, to adhere to that system, through all time to come!

[1] Vandalia *Free Press*, February 21, 1839. The last phrase suggests some degree of exaggeration in this report.

Bill Introduced in Illinois Legislature
to Supplement Act Establishing Counties of
Menard, Logan and Dane[1]

[February 20, 1839]

A bill for an act supplemental to an act to establish the counties of Menard, Logan and Dane

Sec: 1st. Be it enacted by the People of the state of Illinois represented in the General Assembly: that the officers to be elected under the provisions of the act to which this is supplemental shall hold their offices respectively as long after the next August election as they would do under the general law if they had been elected at said August election.

Sec: 2. In all elections for a Senator or Senators in the district composed of the counties of Menard, Logan, Dane and Sangamon, the clerks of the county commissioners courts of the three first named counties, shall, within ten days after each election, return abstracts of the votes given for a Senator or Senators to the clerk of the county commissioner's court of Sangamon county, who shall, in presence of two Justices of the Peace, compare said abstracts, together with the votes given for such Senator or Senators in Sangamon county; and shall, as soon as convenient, make out, and deliver a certificate of election to the person so shown to be elected.

Sec. 3. In all elections for a Representative to the General assembly, in the counties of Logan and Dane, the clerks of the county commissioner's courts of said counties shall, within ten days after each election, meet at the county seat of Logan county, and shall, in the presence of two Justices of the Peace, proceed to compare the votes given in said counties for Representative; and also to

[144]

make out a certificate of election for the person so shown to be elected; which certificate shall be delivered to such person as soon thereafter as convenient.

SEC: 4. Militia duty shall be performed in the counties of Menard, Logan, Dane, and Sangamon, as if no division had been made.

1 AD, I-Ar. Introduced on February 20, the bill passed both houses without amendment. It may be found in *Laws of Illinois*, 1839, p. 205.

Resolution Introduced in Illinois Legislature
to Permit Citizens to Use the Hall of Representatives[1]

February 21, 1839

Resolved, That the use of the hall of the House of Representatives be tendered to the ladies and gentlemen resident at and visiting the town of Vandalia, on the evening of the 22d of February, instant, for the purpose of any public amusement they may choose to indulge in.

1 *House Journal*, Eleventh General Assembly, First Session, p. 476.

Amendments Introduced in Illinois Legislature
to an Act Dividing the State into Judicial Districts[1]

[February 21, 1839]

Amend by striking out "Ogle"[2] from the Sixth Circuit and inserting it in the ninth.

Amend further by striking out the word "first" in the eighth line of the first section and inserting the word "eighth"[3]

Amend further by striking out the word "eighth" in the twentieth line of the first section and inserting the word "first"

1 AD, I-Ar. The first amendment was adopted, the others rejected. The House had adopted another amendment, moved by Lincoln on February 19, adding the counties of Menard, Logan, and Dane to the Eighth Circuit. The entire act may be found in *Laws of Illinois*, 1839, pp. 155-56.   2 Ogle County.
3 This and the next amendment involved apparently a mere shift of names.

To William Butler[1]

Dear Butler: Vandalia, Feb. 23rd. 1839

Yours of the 16th enclosing a note for my signature is duly received. I am much obliged to you for your attention to this matter. I had not myself forgotten it. Before this reaches you, you will have learned that I had already sent a blank note with my name to

Stuart to fix this same bussiness.[2] I now sign the note you sent me, and enclose it to you. We have got a provision through the House attaching that part of Shelby to Dane county which was first petitioned for, which provision, we think will pass the Senate, as the Shelby Senator goes for it. We will adjourn on the 4th. of March. I would rather you should not be at the trouble of sending me a horse, as you kindly offered to do, in one of your former letters. I will get your clerk fee bill through, unless it shall be lost for want of time, which I some what fear. No news. Your friend as ever

A. LINCOLN

[1] ALS, ICHi.   [2] See Lincoln to Stuart, February 14, *supra.*

Resolution Adopted by Whig Meeting in Hall of House of Representatives[1]

February 27, 1839

Resolved, That a Committee of nine be appointed by the chair, to draft an address to the people of this State, setting forth the causes of our opposition to the present administration, and recommending all the opponents of the misrule of the government to unite upon the common platform of union and compromise.[2]

[1] Quincy *Whig,* March 9, 1839. Lincoln's resolution was one of several offered and adopted. The caucus was held for the purpose of organizing for the impending campaign. If the address was prepared and published, it has not been found.

[2] In pursuance of the resolution, the chair appointed the following: Abraham Lincoln, Orville H. Browning, William F. Thornton, William H. Davidson, Archibald Williams, Richard B. Servant, William B. Archer, George Churchill, and William Ross (*ibid.*).

Bill Introduced in Illinois Legislature
to Authorize a Survey Therein Named[1]

[February 28, 1839]

Strike out all after the enacting clause and insert the following—

"That the Board of Public Works shall so soon as convenience will permit, detail a competent engineer to survey a route commencing at or near the point where the present location of the Central Rail Road crosses Drury's Creek in Jackson county; thence via Frankfort in Franklin county, Mount Vernon in Jefferson county, and Salem in Marion county to a point on the present location of the aforesaid Rail Road at or near Vandalia. Said Board shall also detail a competent engineer to survey another route between the same starting and terminating points to pass at or near the coal banks on mudy—[2] thence through Pinckneyville in Perry county, Nashville in Washington county, and Carlyle in Clinton county.

SEC. 2. Said engineers shall make full and complete reports of the surveys of said routes respectively to the Board of Public Works; who, upon a full examination and comparison of the relative merits of the two said routes and the present location, with a view to the interest of the state, shall determine which of the three shall be the permanent location of the said Central Rail Road.

SEC: 3. The provisions of this act shall be carried into effect as speedily as possible; but while the same are in progress, the work on the said Central Rail Road shall proceed as though this act had never passed.

[1] AD, I-Ar. Lincoln wrote this bill to amend a Senate bill bearing the same title, but it was introduced in the House by John Crain, representative from Washington County. It passed the House, the Senate concurred, and the act may be found in *Laws of Illinois*, 1839, p. 242.

[2] Muddy River. The phrase "at or near the coal banks on mudy—thence" is an insertion not in Lincoln's hand.

Amendment Introduced in Illinois Legislature
to a Supplemental Act Incorporating
the Beardstown and Sangamon Canal Company[1]

[March 1, 1839]

Provided, that if said Canal shall not be commenced by the first of January 1841, the state shall have full right to the navigation of the Sangamon River.

[1] AD, I-Ar. Lincoln wrote the amendment, which was moved by his colleague Andrew McCormick of Sangamon County. The amendment was adopted by the House and the Senate concurred.

To William S. Wait[1]

Mr. William S. Wait: Vandalia, March 2. 1839

Sir: Your favour of yesterday was handed me by Mr. Dale.[2] In relation to the Revenue law, I think there is something [to] be feared from the argument you suggest, though I hope the danger is not as great as you apprehend. The passage of a Revenue law at this session, is *right* within itself; and I never despair of sustaining myself before the people upon any measure that will stand a full investigation. I presume I hardly need enter into an argument to prove to *you*, that our old revenue system, raising, as it did, all the state revenue from non-resident lands, and those lands rapidly *decreasing*, by passing into the hands of resident owners, whiles the wants of the Treasury were *increasing* with the increase of population, could not longer continue to answer the purpose of it's creation. That proposition is little less than self-evident. The only question is as to sustaining the change before the people. I believe it can be sustained, because it does not increase the tax upon the *"many poor"* but upon the *"wealthy few"* by taxing the land that is worth $50 or $100 per acre, in proportion to its value, insted of, as heretofore, no more than that which was worth but $5 per acre. This valuable land, as is well known, belongs, not to the poor, but to the wealthy citizen.

On the other hand, the wealthy can not *justly* complain, because the change is equitable within itself, and also a *sine qua non* to a compliance with the Constitution. If, however, the wealthy should, regardless of the justness of the complaint, as men often are, when interest is involved in the question, complain of the change, it is still to be remembered, that *they* are not sufficiently numerous to carry the elections. Verry Respectfully   A. LINCOLN

[1] ALS, owned by Mrs. Frank Davis, Hookdale, Illinois. William S. Wait was a prominent Democrat of Bond County.
[2] Michael G. Dale, also of Bond County.

Note Written in
Sangamon County Mortgage Record[1]

April 4, 1839

We do hereby enter full satisfaction on the within mortgage this 4th April 1839 Stuart & Lincoln attorneys for the administrator[2] of Nicholas Sintz deceased.

[1] ADS, Sangamon County Record (*Deed Book*, I, 473).
[2] Nicholas Moore was administrator. See receipt, May 10, 1839, *infra*. St. Clair Chrisman gave a mortgage to Nicholas Sintz on April 5, 1836, in consideration of $1,200 (*ibid.*).

Notice of a Public Meeting
to Discuss the Revenue Law[1]

April 5, 1839

TO THE PEOPLE OF SANGAMON COUNTY.

FELLOW CITIZENS:—We, a portion of the Sangamon delegation learning that great disatisfaction prevails among you, relative to the New Revenue Law, ask the favor of you, to attend a public discussion of the merits and demerits of that measure, on SATURDAY the 13th APRIL. inst., at Springfield. We invite every man in the County, who opposes the Revenue Law, to come armed with all the arguments against it that he can, and we confidently believe, we will be able to show, that none of them are well founded.

A. LINCOLN,   A. G. HERNDON.
A. McCORMIC[K],   J. CALHOUN.
                     N. W. EDWARDS.

P. S. We doubt not that the remainder of the delegation will concur with us in this call; but have not had the opportunity of seeing them since we concluded to make it.   April 5, 1839.

[1] *Sangamo Journal*, April 12, 1839. Some of Lincoln's arguments may be found in his letter to William S. Wait, March 2, 1839, *supra*.

Petition to Governor Thomas Carlin
for Appointment of Joseph Duncan to Negotiate Sale of Illinois and Michigan Canal Bonds[1]

[April 13, 1839]

The undersigned would respectfully recommend to the Governor of this State the appointment of JOSEPH DUNCAN, who is well known to have ever been an ardent and efficient friend of the Illinois and Michigan Canal, as a suitable and qualified person to negotiate the sale of the State Bonds authorised to be sold for the purpose of constructing the Illinois and Michigan Canal.

[1] Quincy *Whig*, April 13, 1839. The petition carries one hundred and seven names of prominent Whigs (65) and Democrats (42). Duncan was an ex-governor (1834) and a Whig. Governor Carlin had appointed ex-governor John Reynolds by the time the editorial including this protest appeared in print.

To Alexander P. Field[1]

Springfield, Illinois,
A. P. Field, Esq.   May 11, 1839.

Dear Sir: At the late session an act passed both Houses of legislature for the benefit of the clerks of the Circuit Courts of Sangamon, Hamilton, and Fayette counties.[2] I can see nothing of this act in the printed laws, one copy of which has reached us. I know it passed both Houses, but I am a little suspicious it has not been duly acted on by the Council of Revision. Will you please learn and write us what condition it is in, and also send us a copy of the act? Mr. Butler[3] will pay the charge on sight. Your friend,

A. LINCOLN.

[1] NH, I, 94-95. Field was secretary of state.
[2] The act for the relief of clerks of the circuit courts of Sangamon, Clinton, Fayette, and Franklin counties appears in *Laws of Illinois*, 1839-1840, p. 156.
[3] William Butler, circuit clerk of Sangamon County.

To Nathan Dresser[1]

Mr. Dresser: Springfield, May 30. 1839.

Enclosed are the papers to commence a suit for old man Summers against H. Sears.[2] You will find one of Butlers blank summons filled up by me which you can copy and it will be right in this case. It would do itself but for its having the Sangamon seal to it.

Also on the other side of this sheet you find a petition for an order to have the land involved in this matter conveyed to Sears. It, together with the bond, (also enclosed) you will file & docket among your Chancery cases. No process to issue on it.

[1] AL, DLC-HW. Dresser was clerk of the Menard County Circuit Court.
[2] Levi Summers, administrator of Alfred Summers *v.* Henry Sears, a trespass suit for $200 damages.

To John Rowan Herndon[1]

Dear Row: Springfield, June 11th. 1839—

Mr. Redman[2] informs me that you wish me to write you the particulars of a conversation between Dr. Felix[3] & myself relative to you. The Dr. overtook me between Rushville and Beardstown. He, after learning that I lived at Springfield, asked if I was acquainted with you. I told him I was. He said you had lately been elected constable in Adams, but that you never would be again. I asked him why? He said the people there, had found out, that you had been Sheriff or Deputy Sheriff in Sangamon county, and that you came off and left your securities to suffer. He then asked me if I did not know such to be the fact. I told him I did not think you had ever been Sheriff or Deputy Sheriff in Sangamon; but that I thought you had been constable. I further told him that if you had left your securities to suffer in that or any other case, I had never heard of it, and that if it had been so, I thought I would have heard it.

If the Dr. is telling that I told him *any* thing against you whatever, I authorize you to contradict it flatly. We have no news here. Your friend, as ever—   A. LINCOLN

1 ALS, InU. Herndon was known by his middle name. He was an old friend from New Salem, whose interest in the Herndon-Berry store Lincoln had purchased.

2 Probably George Redman.

3 Dr. Felix Regnier, brother of Dr. Francis Regnier, a young doctor from Ohio who settled in New Salem, later moving to Clary's Grove, then to Petersburg, Illinois.

To the Editor of the Chicago *American*[1]

Mr Editor,   Springfield June 24th. 1839

From present indications we have every reason to believe that Mr. Douglass[2] will contest the right of Mr Stuart[3] to a seat in Congress. We deem it a matter of great importance to the Whig party of this District that they should be prepared to meet such contest. The importance of the decision of that contest is increased by the doubt which at present exists as to which party will have the ascendency in the next Congress. In this state of uncertainty one vote may become of the utmost importance to the sustaining of those great principles for which the Whig party are now contending. To prepare ourselves for this contest and to solicit your aid in so doing by engaging your assistance in the collection of proofs to the following facts, are the objects of this communication

1st. Whether there are any mistakes for or against Mr Stuart in the addition of colum[n]s or otherwise, apparant on the face of the Poll Books of your County?

2nd. Whether any persons voted for Mr Douglass in your County who were *minors,* or who had not been *Residents* of the state *six months* preceeding the Election?

3rd. Whether any *unnaturalized foreigners* voted for Mr Douglass in your County?

After you shall have examined into the preceeding questions, we will thank you to write us the result without delay together with the *names* of the *illegal* voters refered to in the two last questions: the names of the individuals by whom the fact of their illegality can be proved and the name and the residence of a Justice of the Peace before whom Depositions can be taken and a proper place to take them. When informed by you of the fact we will immediately take steps to procure the proofs. We would suggest the propriety of your consulting the political Friends you may think proper in your County and solicit their assistance in procuring the above facts: or the appointment of precinct committees as you may think the most advisable. Respectfully yours &c.

Joshua F. Speed   James H. Matheny
E. D. Baker   A. Lincoln
Milton Hay

[151]

N.B. Would it not be as well to keep the knowledge of this investigation as well as any discoveries you may make, confined to as few as possible

P.S. Let letters on this subject, be addressed to "Stuart & Lincoln," as business letters.

¹ LS, RPB. This seems to have been a form letter which may have been sent to other Whig editors as well. The body of the letter is not in Lincoln's hand, but the date and salutation are partly in Lincoln's hand; the close and signatures, postscript, and envelope (addressed to the "Editor of the Chicago American" who was then William Stuart), are entirely in Lincoln's hand.

² In this early period Stephen A. Douglas spelled his name with the double "s."

³ John Todd Stuart, with whom Lincoln's association in the legislature had resulted in a law partnership which lasted until April, 1841.

Affidavit Concerning Isaac Anderson's Lost Horse¹

State of Illinois ⎱
Sangamon county ⎰   June 29, 1839

Abraham Lincoln, being first duly sworn, states on oath that he was the Captain of one of the companies [of] Illinois volunteers, on the expedition directed against the Sac & Fox Indians in the year 1832, that Isaac Anderson was a volunteer in said company, that said Anderson had a horse mustered into the service of the United States, and valued, (as affiant verrily believes, speaking from memory only, the original apraisement roll, being lost, mislaid or destroyed so that affiant, after diligent search he has not been able to find it) at fiftyfive dollars, that said horse was turned out to graze in consequence of sufficient forage not being furnished by the United states, and was thereby lost, that said horse was lost about the tenth of May 1832, and without any fault or negligence on the part of said Anderson. The army was marched from Dixons Ferry on Rock River, that being the point where said horse was lost, verry shortly after the loss of said horse. The affiant makes the above statements from memory only, but feels confident they are substantially correct.   A. LINCOLN

¹ ADS, IHi. Two subscriptions appear on the document, one signed by M. K. Anderson, Justice of the Peace, and the other by Charles R. Matheny, Clerk of the Sangamon County Commissioners Court.

Receipt to David Prickett¹

August 6, 1839

Received, Springfield, Aug: 6. 1839 of David Prickett, two hundred and fifty dollars, to be applied to the discharging of a judge-

ment in the Sangamon circuit court against said Prickett, & in favour of the surviving partners of the firm of A. & G. W. Kerr & Co.[2]   STUART & LINCOLN
                                                              Atty. for Plffs.

[1] ALS-P, ISLA. Prickett was a resident of Springfield who had been elected clerk of the House of Representatives in 1834 and 1836 and prosecuting attorney of the first judicial circuit in 1837. He had been defeated for judge of the eighth judicial circuit by Stephen T. Logan in February, 1839.
[2] The judgment was awarded to Kerr & Co. for $513.49 on July 13.

To Thomas Bohannon[1]

Mr. Thomas Bohannan   Springfield, Ills. Aug: 7. 1839
   Dr. Sir   Yours of the 29th ult. is duly received. It was our impression that we had acknowledged the receipt of the two notes of which you speak—one being on Allen & Stone[2] for $117.94 the other on J. Francis[3] for $50.35. We now do so.
   We have been receiving promises from time to time of the payment of those notes, but which payment has not yet been made. Unless payment is soon made we shall commence suits; though this course we shall regret; for they are honest and honorable men, but they are hard pressed. We regret to say that the entire certainty that we shall need all the means at our command, will not, in justice to ourselves, permit us to authorize you to draw upon us as you suggest. Yours &c.   STUART & LINCOLN

[1] ALS, IHi. Thomas Bohannon was a resident of Louisville, Kentucky.
[2] James D. Allen and William S. Stone, proprietors of a store in Athens, Illinois.
[3] Probably Josiah N. Francis, founder of the *Sangamo Journal* and brother of Simeon Francis, the editor. See the "Receipt to Josiah Francis," June 12, 1841, *infra*.

Note Concerning Remittance to Thomas Bohannon[1]

                                              October 23, 1839
   I hereby certify that I on this day deposited in the Post office at this place a letter of Stuart & Lincoln directed to Messrs Thos. Bohannan & Co of Louisville Ky—enclosing $126—
   Springfield, Ills. Oct. 23, 1839—   JOSHUA F. SPEED

[1] AD, DLC-HW. In Lincoln's hand, excepting signature. The letter to Bohannon has not been located, but the money referred to probably represented a collection on the notes against Allen & Stone and Josiah Francis. See letter to Bohannon, August 7, 1839, *supra*.

To William Doughty[1]

Mr. Doughty   Springfield Nov. 2nd. 1839

I understand my coat was left in your possession. Will you please get a yard or so of coarse domestic (for which I will pay you the first time I see you) and fold the coat in it and tie the card herein enclosed upon it, and hand the bundle to the Stage driver on his trip towards Springfield?

You will verry much oblige me by doing so. Your friend

A. LINCOLN

[1] ALS, owned by Edward Wallar Campbell. Major Doughty, a veteran of the War of 1812, was proprietor of the Franklin Tavern in Tremont, Illinois. Lincoln had attended court in Tremont September 23-27.

To John T. Stuart[1]

Dear Stuart: Springfield, Nov: 14. 1839–

I have been to the Secretary's office within the last hour; and find things precisely as you left them—no new arrivals of returns on either side. Douglass has not been here since you left. A report is in circulation here now, that he has abandoned the idea of going to Washington; though the report does not come in a verry authentic form, so far as I can learn. Though, by the way, speaking of authenticity, you know that if we had heard Douglass say that he had abandoned the contest, it would not be verry authentic. There is no news here. Noah,[2] I still think will be elected verry easily. I am afraid of our race for Representative. Dr. Knapp[3] has become a candidate; and I fear the few votes he will get will be taken from us. Also, some one has been tampering with old Esqr. Wycoff,[4] and induced him to send in his name to be anounced as a candidate. Francis refused to announce him without seeing him, and now I suppose there is to be a fuss about it. I have been so busy that I have not seen Mrs. Stuart since you left, though I understand she wrote you by to day's mail, which will inform you more about her than I could. The verry moment a Speaker is elected write me who he is. Your friend as ever—   A. LINCOLN

[1] ALS, CSmH.

[2] Noah W. Matheny, candidate to succeed his deceased father Charles R. Matheny, county clerk, won over Edmond Taylor, 966 to 653.

[3] Dr. Moses L. Knapp. The race for representative was won by Thomas J. Nance, Democrat of Petersburg, who defeated the Whig candidate John Bennett by 36 votes.

[4] Samuel Wyckoff announced his candidacy on November 11 (*Illinois State Register*, November 16, 1839) but withdrew on November 19.

[154]

Bill Introduced in Illinois Legislature
to Authorize the Collector of ——— County
to Collect Taxes[1]

[December 10, 1839]

A Bill for an act to authorize the Collector of   county to collect certain taxes therein named.

Be it enacted by the people of the state of Illinois represented in the General Assembly, that the collector of   county be authorized to collect all taxes now due from the inhabitants of that portion of Sangamon county lying within the following bounds towit: Begining at the South West corner of Section Three in Township Seventeen North of Range Six West thence North four miles by the surveys, thence East with the surveys ten miles; thence South with the surveys two miles; thence West with the surveys nine miles; thence South with the surveys two miles; then West with the surveys one mile to the begining.

---

[1] AD, I-Ar. Although drawn specifically to collect taxes due in a portion of Sangamon County which had not been incorporated in Menard as anticipated, Lincoln left the name of the county blank so that the committee to which the bill was referred might decide which county (Sangamon or Menard) collector should function. The bill was referred to a select committee with Lincoln as chairman. The bill as amended appears under an amended title, January 28-30, 1840, *infra.*

Resolutions Adopted
at a Whig Meeting at Springfield[1]

December 11, 1839

Whereas, the Van Buren State Convention, which adjourned on the 10th inst., passed various resolutions denouncing Whig individuals, Whig policy, and the Whig party in general. Therefore.

Resolved, That every member of that Convention, who introduced any such resolution or resolutions, or any amendment thereto, be respectfully requested to bring the same, or a correct copy thereof, into this Hall, and to attempt to sustain it by facts and arguments.

Resolved, That on the discussion of said resolutions, we will meet their authors, man for man, and speech for speech, in order that the public may see with whom are the facts, and with whom the arguments.

Resolved, That for the purpose of discussing said resolutions, we will meet their authors on to-morrow evening, at 7 o'clock, P.M.

[at] this Hall, or at any other time and place [which] may better suit their convenience.

1 *Sangamo Journal*, December 20, 1839.

To Mrs. Orville H. Browning[1]

To the Honorable Mrs. O. H. Browning— [December 11, 1839]

We the undersigned, respectfully represent to your *Honoress*, that we are in great need of your society in this town of Springfield; and therefore humbly pray that your *Honoress* will repair, forthwith to the Seat of Government, bringing in your train all ladies in general, who may be at your command; and all Mr. Browning's sisters in particular.[2] And as faithful & dutiful Petitioners we promise that if you grant this our request, we will render unto your Honoress due attention and faithful obedience to, your orders in general & to Miss Brownings in particular.

In tender consideration whereof we pray your Honoress, to grant your humble petitioners their above request, and such other and further relief in the premises as to your Honoress may seem right and proper. And your petitioners as in duty bound will ever pray &c.

A LINCOLN— J J HARDIN

E. B. WEBB JOHN DAWSON

1 ALS, owned by The Rosenbach Company, Philadelphia and New York. This communication was enclosed with another written by John J. Hardin as follows:

Dear Madam Springfield Decr 11th 1839

As the humble but honored instrument, selected to forward to your Honoress the for[e]going memorial of our grievances & petition for redress, I present therewith my most hearty congratulations at the prospect of your returning health, of your ability to undergo another seige at the seat of Government. The fact is madam, that in your absence business will not progress with its accustomed facility—and now when both yourself & my distinguished lady are away, they cannot even begin operations. There is no doubt if you were here, there would be extensive improvements in the important business, of visiting, conversation & amusement.

In consideration of our distressed situation Mr Butler has promised to give you up his parlor, but if there is any difficulty on that point I promise as a gallant knight to give you the privilege of hanging up on a peg in my closet, whenever it may suit your convenience.

I have been visiting the ladies this evening, they say it will be quite gay this winter—several ladies from a distance are here, with the intention of spending the winter. Mrs H will be here next week. The members are very much scattered in location, but we have quite a pleasant society in this House.

Many others besides your humble petitioners are inquiring for your Honoress & are anxiously awaiting your arrival. His Excellency will be considered, when you arrive, as the minor part of the Quincy Delegation. We trust therefore to have your Honoress here by the 25th inst, as a living Christmas present as large as life, twice as natural & three times as agreable.

With sentiments of the most profound respect and esteem I subscribe myself
y'r m't ob't, & very humble serv't.

                                                                J. J. HARDIN

Endorsed   [across the face of page 2 of the letter]
    A. LINCOLN
    E. B. WEBB
2 The manuscript is in Lincoln's hand to this point; the remainder seems to be
in that of John J. Hardin. Dawson was representative from Sangamon County;
Edwin B. Webb, representative from White County; John J. Hardin, representative from Morgan County.

Petition Written for John Bennett[1]

December 16, 1839

To the Honorable the General Assembly of the State of Illinois—
    The undersigned respectfully petitions that Blocks, two, three,
four and five in Bennett's addition to the town of Petersburgh in
the county of Menard be vacated.

Dec. 16 1839   JOHN BENNETT.

1 AD, I-Ar. This document, including the signature, is in Lincoln's hand and
was presented by him to the House of Representatives on December 17. The bill
answering the petition was introduced on December 27 (*vide infra*).

Resolution Introduced in Illinois Legislature
in Relation to Contested Election
in Pike County[1]

[December 17, 1839]

Resolved, that the final action upon the contested election from
the county of Pike, [be] defered until monday next; and that the
door keeper be directed to procure the attendance of George M.
Hanson of Coles county by that time.

1 AD, I-Ar. Lincoln wrote the resolution, but James T. Cunningham, representative from Coles County, moved its adoption, which was done. Oscar Love was
seated as representative from Pike County on December 10 on the supposition that
Richard Kerr had vacated his seat by removal from the state. Kerr contested the
election and replaced his opponent on December 24.

Speech at Springfield, Illinois[1]

December 18, 1839

. . . . On Wednesday evening, after many efforts on the part of
the Locos to GET OFF, the debate was opened on the part of the
Whigs, by a speech from Mr. Lincoln, characterized by that great

[157]

force and point for which he is so justly admired. He set out with a statement of three propositions, which he believed he could demonstrate to the satisfaction of every unprejudiced mind in the house. 1st, That there had been a total change in the administration of the Government, within the last ten years; and that change had been for the WORSE. 2d. That a new and corrupt system of tactics had been introduced into the National administration, unknown to former administrations: and thirdly, that the consummation and perfection of this whole scheme of fraud and corruption, was in the establishment of the SUB-TREASURY. These several propositions he sustained, not by rant, declamation and assertion, but by an array of documentary evidence, which could not be disputed.

[1] *Sangamo Journal,* January 3, 1840. Stephen A. Douglas replied for the Democrats.

Amendment Introduced in Illinois Legislature
to Bill Incorporating the Springfield Mechanics' Union[1]

[December 19, 1839]

Amend the bill by filling the blank in the first section with "Caleb Burchall [Birchall?], Thomas Lewis, Edmund R. Wiley, William D Herndon, Simeon Francis, George R. Weber Walter Davis, George Wood, and R F Coflin

[1] AD, I-Ar. As chairman of the select committee to which the petition of the Springfield mechanics asking incorporation had been referred, Lincoln introduced the bill, but did not write any part except the title and amendment. The men who are listed in Lincoln's amendment as incorporators all signed the petition under consideration. The bill passed both houses and may be found in *Laws of Illinois,* 1839-1840, pp. 74-75.

To John T. Stuart[1]

Dear Stuart: Springfield, Dec: 23rd. 1839–

Dr. Henry will write you all the political news. I write this about some little matters of business. You recollect you told me me [*sic*] you had drawn the Chicago Musick money & sent it to the claimants.[2] A d——d hawk billed yankee is here, besetting me at every turn I take, saying that Robt Kinzie never received the $80. to which he was entitled. Can you tell any thing about the matter?

Again Old Mr. Wright, who lives up South Fork some where, is teasing me continually about some *deeds* which he says he left

with you, but which I can find nothing of. Can you tell where they are?

The legislature is in session, and has suffered the Bank to forfeit it's charter without *Benefit* of *Clergy*. There seems to be but verry little disposition to resuscitate it. Whenever a letter comes from you to Mrs. Stuart, I carry it to her, and then I see Betty.[3] She is a tolerably nice *fellow* now. May be I will write again when I get more time. Your friend as ever   A. LINCOLN

P.S. The Democratic giant is here; but he is not now worth talking about.[4]   A.L.

[1] ALS, owned by heirs of Stuart Brown.

[2] In the Stuart & Lincoln fee book is the case of Kinzie & Forsythe *vs.* Samuel Musick: "Jan 28 1839 Sent Kinzie $75. by check" and "Oct 10 1839 By check on Chicago Bank $80." Robert A. Kinzie was a Chicago merchant and trader, son of the early Indian trader, John Kinzie. Jacob Forsyth was a Pittsburgh merchant.

[3] Bettie, daughter of John T. Stuart, born in July 1838.

[4] Stephen A. Douglas.

Speech on the Sub-Treasury[1]

December [26], 1839

FELLOW CITIZENS:— It is peculiarly embarrassing to me to attempt a continuance of the discussion, on this evening, which has been conducted in this Hall on several preceding ones. It is so, because on each of those evenings, there was a much fuller attendance than now, without any reason for its being so, except the greater *interest* the community feel in the *Speakers* who addressed them *then*, than they do in *him* who is to do so *now*. I am, indeed, apprehensive, that the few who have attended, have done so, more to spare me of mortification, than in the hope of being interested in any thing I may be able to say. This circumstance casts a damp upon my spirits, which I am sure I shall be unable to overcome during the evening. But enough of preface.[2]

The subject heretofore, and now to be discussed, is the Sub-

[1] Pamphlet (Monaghan 2), IHi. Also, *Sangamo Journal*, March 6, 1840. The pamphlet provides a superior text; it was printed in January or February, 1840, and received wide distribution during the ensuing campaign. The date upon which this speech was delivered has been a matter of some uncertainty, but it appears to be settled by a communication dated December 27, 1839, published in the Quincy *Whig*, January 4, 1840, which specifies that Lincoln spoke "last night in the Hall of the House of Representatives at Springfield, Illinois."

[2] There had been a debate held in November in which Lincoln took part. Again in December the debate was resumed, with many prominent Whigs and Democrats taking part, during Christmas week. Interest may have lagged by the time Lincoln's turn came to conclude the Whig argument on December 26, but certainly the day after Christmas was not calculated to draw many from their firesides who were not inveterate politicians.

Treasury scheme of the present Administration, as a means of collecting, safe-keeping, transferring and disbursing the revenues of the Nation, as contrasted with a National Bank for the same purposes. Mr. Douglass has said that we (the Whigs), have not dared to meet them (the Locos), in argument on this question. I protest against this assertion. I assert that we have again and again, during this discussion, urged facts and arguments against the Sub-Treasury, which they have neither dared to deny nor attempted to answer. But lest some may be led to believe that we really wish to avoid the question, I now propose, in my humble way, to urge those arguments again; at the same time, begging the audience to mark well the positions I shall take, and the proof I shall offer to sustain them, and that they will not again permit Mr. Douglass or his friends, to escape the force of them, by a round and ground-less assertion, that we "dare not meet them in argument."

Of the Sub-Treasury then, as contrasted with a National Bank, for the before enumerated purposes, I lay down the following propositions, to wit:

1st. It will injuriously affect the community by its operation on the circulating medium.

2d. It will be a more expensive fiscal agent.

3d. It will be a less secure depository of the public money.

To show the truth of the first proposition, let us take a short review of our condition under the operation of a National Bank. It was the depository of the public revenues. Between the collection of those revenues and the disbursements of them by the government, the Bank was permitted to, and did actually loan them out to individuals, and hence the large amount of money annually collected for revenue purposes, which by any other plan would have been idle a great portion of time, was kept almost constantly in circulation. Any person who will reflect, that money is only valuable while in circulation, will readily perceive, that any device which will keep the government revenues, in constant circulation, instead of being locked up in idleness, is no inconsiderable advantage.

By the Sub-Treasury, the revenue is to be collected, and kept in iron boxes until the government wants it for disbursement; thus robbing the people of the use of it, while the government does not itself need it, and while the money is performing no nobler office than that of rusting in iron boxes. The natural effect of this change of policy, every one will see, is to *reduce* the quantity of money in circulation.

But again, by the Sub-Treasury scheme the revenue is to be collected in specie. I anticipate that this will be disputed. I expect to hear it said, that it is not the policy of the Administration to collect the revenue in specie. If it shall, I reply, that Mr. Van Buren, in his message recommending the Sub-Treasury, expended nearly a column of that document in an attempt to persuade Congress to provide for the collection of the revenue in specie exclusively; and he concludes with these words. "It may be safely assumed, that no motive of *convenience* to the *citizen*, requires the reception of Bank paper." In addition to this, Mr. Silas Wright, Senator from New York, and the political, personal and confidential friend of Mr. Van Buren, drafted and introduced into the Senate the first Sub-Treasury Bill, and that bill provided for ultimately collecting the revenue in specie. It is true, I know, that that clause was stricken from the bill, but it was done by the votes of the Whigs, aided by a portion only of the Van Buren Senators. No Sub-Treasury bill has yet become a law, though two or three have been considered by Congress, some with and some without the specie clause; so that I admit there is room for quibbling upon the question of whether the administration favor the exclusive specie doctrine or not; but I take it, that the fact that the President at first urged the specie doctrine, and that under his recommendation the first bill introduced embraced it, warrants us in charging it as the policy of the party, until their head as publicly recants it, as he at first espoused it—I repeat then, that by the Sub-Treasury, the revenue is to be collected in *specie*. Now mark what the effect of this must be. By all estimates ever made, there are but between 60 and 80 millions of specie in the United States. The expenditures of the Government for the year 1838, the last for which we have had the report, were 40 millions. Thus it is seen, that if the whole revenue be collected in specie, it will take more than half of all the specie in the nation to do it. By this means more than half of all the specie belonging to the fifteen million of souls, who compose the whole population of the country, is thrown into the hands of the public office-holders, and other public creditors, composing in number, perhaps not more than one-quarter of a million; leaving the other fourteen millions and three-quarters to get along as they best can, with less than one-half of the specie of the country, and whatever rags and shin-plasters they may be able to put, and keep, in circulation. By this means, every office-holder, and other public creditor, may, and most likely will, set up shaver; and a most glorious harvest will the specie men have of it; each specie man, upon a fair division, having to his share, the fleecing of about 59 rag men.[3] In all candor, let me ask, was such a system for benefiting the few at the expense of the many, ever before devised? And was the sacred name of Democracy, ever before made to endorse such an enormity against the rights of the people?

I have already said that the Sub-Treasury will reduce the quantity of money in circulation. This position is strengthened by the recollection, that the revenue is to be collected in specie, so that the mere amount of revenue is not all that is withdrawn, but the amount of paper circulation that the 40 millions would serve as a basis to, is withdrawn; which would be in a sound state at least 100 millions. When 100 millions, or more, of the circulation we now have, shall be withdrawn, who can contemplate, without ter-

[3] Lincoln's footnote at this point is as follows:

"On the 4th of January 1839, the Senate of the United States passed the following resolution, to wit:

" *Resolved,* That the Secretary of the Treasury be directed to communicate to the Senate any information he may recently have received in respect to the mode of collecting, keeping and disbursing public monies in foreign countries.'

"Under this resolution the Secretary communicated to the Senate, a letter, the following extract from which, clearly shows that the collection of the revenue in *specie,* will establish a sound currency for the office holders, and a depreciated one for the people; and that the officeholders and other public creditors will turn shavers upon all the rest of the community. Here is the extract from the letter, being all of it that relates to the question:

" 'HAGUE, October 12, 1838.
" 'The financial system of Hamburg is, as far as is known, very simple, as may be supposed, from so small a territory.

" 'The whole amount of Hamburg coined money is about four and a half millions of marks current, or one million two hundred and eighty-two thousand five hundred dollars; and except under very extraordinary circumstances, *not more than one half that amount is in circulation,* and all duties, taxes, and excise, must be paid in Hamburg currency. *The consequence is that it invariably commands a premium of one to three per centum.* Every year one Senator and ten citizens are appointed to transact the whole of the financial concern, both as to receipt and disbursement of the funds, *which is always in cash,* and is every day deposited in the bank, to the credit of the chancery; and on being paid out the citizen to whose department the payment belongs must appear personally with the check or order, stating the amount and to whom to be paid. The person receiving very seldom keeps the money, *preferring to dispose of it to a money changer at a premium,* and taking other coin at a discount, of which there is a great variety and too large amount constantly in circulation, and on which in his daily payment *he loses nothing,* and those who have payments to make to the Government apply to the *money changers again for Hamburg currency,* which keeps it in constant motion; and I believe it frequently occurs that the bags which are sealed and labelled with the amount, are returned again to the bank without being opened.

" 'With great respect, your obedient servant,

" 'JOHN CUTHBERT.' "

" 'To the Hon. LEVI WOODBURY,
Secretary of the Treasury, Washington, D.C.' "

"This letter is found in Senate Document, p. 113, of the session of 1838-'39."

ror, the distress, ruin, bankruptcy and beggary, that must follow.

The man who has purchased any article, say a horse, on credit, at 100 dollars, when there are 200 millions circulating in the country, if the quantity be reduced to 100 millions by the arrival of pay-day, will find the horse but sufficient to pay half the debt; and the other half must either be paid out of his other means, and thereby become a clear loss to him; or go unpaid, and thereby become a clear loss to his creditor. What I have here said of a single case of the purchase of a horse, will hold good in every case of a debt existing at the time a reduction in the quantity of money occurs, by whomsoever, and for whatsoever it may have been contracted. It may be said, that what the debtor loses, the creditor gains by this operation; but on examination this will be found true only to a very limited extent. It is more generally true that *all* lose by it. The *creditor*, by losing more of his debts, than he gains by the increased value of those he collects; the *debtor* by either parting with more of his property to pay his debts, than he received in contracting them; or, by entirely breaking up in his business, and thereby being thrown upon the world in idleness.

The general distress thus created, will, to be sure, be *temporary*, because whatever change may occur in the quantity of money in any community, *time* will adjust the derangement produced; but while that adjustment is progressing, all suffer more or less, and very many lose every thing that renders life desirable. Why, then, shall we suffer a severe difficulty, even though it be *but temporary*, unless we receive some equivalent for it?

What I have been saying as to the effect produced by a reduction of the quantity of money, relates to the *whole* country. I now propose to show that it would produce a *peculiar* and *permanent* hardship upon the citizens of those States and Territories in which the public lands lie. The Land Offices in those States and Territories, as all know, form the great gulf by which all, or nearly all, the money in them, is swallowed up. When the quantity of money shall be reduced, and consequently every thing under individual control brought down in proportion, the price of those lands, being fixed by law, will remain as now. Of necessity, it will follow that the *produce* or *labor* that *now* raises money sufficient to purchase 80 acres, will *then* raise but sufficient to purchase 40, or perhaps not that much. And this difficulty and hardship will last as long, in some degree, as any portion of these lands shall remain undisposed of. Knowing, as I well do, the difficulty that poor people *now* encounter in procuring homes, I hesitate not to say, that when the price of the public lands shall be doubled or trebled; or, which is the same thing, produce and labor cut down to one-half or one-third of their present prices, it will be little less than impossible for them to procure those homes at all.

In answer to what I have said as to the effect the Sub-Treasury would have upon the currency, it is often urged that the money collected for revenue purposes will *not lie idle* in the vaults of the Treasury; and, farther, that a National Bank produces greater derangement in the currency, by a system of contractions and expansions, than the Sub-Treasury would produce in any way. In reply, I need only show, that experience proves the contrary of both these propositions. It is an undisputed fact, that the late Bank of the United States, paid the Government $75,000 annually, for the *privilege* of using the public money between the times of its collection and disbursement. Can any man suppose, that the Bank would have paid this sum, annually for twenty years, and then offered to renew its obligations to do so, if in reality there was no *time* intervening between the collection and disbursement of the revenue, and consequently no privilege of *using* the money extended to it?

Again, as to the contractions and expansions of a National Bank, I need only point to the period intervening between the time that the late Bank got into successful operation and that at which the Government commenced war upon it, to show that during that period, no such contractions or expansions took place. If before, or after that period, derangement occurred in the currency, it proves nothing. The Bank could not be expected to regulate the currency, either *before* it got into successful operation, or *after* it was crippled and thrown into death convulsions, by the removal of the deposits from it, and other hostile measures of the Government against it. We do not pretend, that a National Bank can establish and maintain a sound and uniform state of currency in the country, in *spite* of the National Government; but we do say, that it has established and maintained such a currency, and can do so again, by the *aid* of that Government; and we further say, that no duty is more imperative on that Government, than the duty it owes the people, of furnishing them a sound and uniform currency.

I now leave the proposition as to the effect of the Sub-Treasury upon the currency of the country, and pass to that relative to the additional *expense* which must be incurred by it over that incurred by a National Bank, as a fiscal agent of the Government. By the late National Bank, we had the public revenue received, safely kept, transferred and disbursed, not only without expense, but we actually received of the Bank $75,000 annually for its privileges, while rendering us those services. By the Sub-Treasury, according to the estimate of the Secretary of the Treasury, who is the warm advocate of the system and which estimate is the lowest made by any one, the same services are to cost $60,000. Mr. Rives,[4] who, to say the least, is equally talented and honest, estimates that these services, under the Sub-Treasury system, cannot cost less than $600,000. For the sake of liberality, let us suppose that the estimates of the Secretary and Mr. Rives, are the two extremes, and that their mean is about the true estimate, and we shall then find, that when to that sum is added the $75,000, which the Bank paid us, the difference between the two systems, in favor of the Bank, and against the Sub-Treasury, is $405,000 a year. This sum, though small when compared to the many millions annually expended by the General Government, is, when viewed by itself, very large; and much too large, when viewed in any light, to be thrown away once a year for nothing. It is sufficient to pay the pensions of more than 4,000 Revolutionary Soldiers, or to purchase a 40-acre tract of Government land, for each one of more than 8,000 poor families.

To the argument against the Sub-Treasury, on the score of additional expense, its friends, so far as I know, attempt no answer. They choose, so far as I can learn, to treat the throwing away $405,000 once a year, as a matter entirely too small to merit their democratic notice.

I now come to the proposition, that it would be less secure than a National Bank, as a depository of the public money. The experience of the past, I think, proves the truth of this. And here, inasmuch as I rely chiefly upon experience to establish it, let me ask, how is it that we know any thing—that any event will occur, that any combination of circumstances will produce a certain result—except by the analogies of past experience? What has once happened, will invariably happen again, when the same circumstances which combined to produce it, shall again combine in the same way. We all feel that we know that a blast of wind would extinguish the flame of the candle that stands by me. How do we know it? We have never seen this flame thus extinguished. We know it, because we have seen through all our lives, that a blast of wind extinguishes the flame of a candle whenever it is thrown fully upon it. Again, we all feel to *know* that we have to die. How? We have never died yet. We know it, because we know, or at least think we know, that of all the beings, just like ourselves, who have been coming into the world

4 William Cabell Rives, senator from Virginia, approved the removal of United States funds from the Bank.

for six thousand years, not one is now living who was here two hundred years ago.

I repeat then, that we know nothing of what will happen in future, but by the analogy of experience, and that the fair analogy of past experience fully proves that the Sub-Treasury would be a less safe depository of the public money than a National Bank. Examine it. By the Sub-Treasury scheme, the public money is to be kept, between the times of its collection and disbursement, by Treasurers of the Mint, Custom-house officers, Land officers, and some new officers to be appointed in the same way that those first enumerated are. Has a year passed since the organization of the Government, that numerous defalcations have not occurred among this class of officers? Look at Swartwout with his $1,200,000, Price with his $75,000, Harris with his $109,000, Hawkins with his $100,000, Linn with his $55,000, together with some twenty-five hundred lesser lights.[5] Place the public money again in these same hands, and will it not again go the same way? Most assuredly it will. But turn to the history of the National Bank in this country, and we shall there see, that those Banks performed the fiscal operations of the Government thro' a period of 40 years, received, safely kept, transferred, disbursed, an aggregate of nearly five hundred millions of dollars; and that, in all that time, and with all that money, not one dollar, nor one cent, did the Government lose by them. Place the public money again in a similar depository, and will it not again be safe?

But, conclusive as the experience of fifty years is, that individuals are unsafe depositories of the public money, and of forty years that National Banks are safe depositories, we are not left to rely solely upon that experience for the truth of those propositions. If experience were silent upon the subject, conclusive reasons could be shown for the truth of them.

It is often urged, that to say the public money will be more secure in a National Bank, than in the hands of individuals, as proposed in the Sub-Treasury, is to say, that Bank directors and Bank officers are more honest than sworn officers of the Government. Not so. We insist on no such thing. We say that public officers, selected with reference to their capacity and honesty, (which by the way, we deny is the practice in these days,) stand an equal chance, precisely, of being capable and honest, with Bank officers selected by

[5] Of these defalcators, Samuel Swartwout was collector at New York City; and William J. Linn, brother-in-law of Governor Duncan of Illinois, was receiver at Vandalia and Illinois State Bank Commissioner. The others were William M. Price of New York, W. P. Harris of Columbus, Mississippi, and L. Hawkins of Helena, Arkansas.

the same rule. We further say, that with however much care selections may be made, there will be some unfaithful and dishonest in both classes. The experience of the whole world, in all by-gone times, proves this true. The Saviour of the world chose twelve disciples, and even one of that small number, selected by superhuman wisdom, turned out a traitor and a devil. And, it may not be improper here to add, that Judas carried the bag—was the Sub-Treasurer of the Saviour and his disciples.

We then, do not say, nor need we say, to maintain our proposition, that Bank officers are more honest than Government officers, selected by the same rule. What we do say, is, that the *interest* of the Sub-Treasurer is *against his duty*—while the *interest* of the Bank is *on the side of its duty*. Take instances—a Sub-Treasurer has in his hands one hundred thousand dollars of public money; his *duty* says—"You ought to pay this money over"—but his *interest* says, "You ought to run away with this sum, and be a nabob the balance of your life." And who that knows anything of human nature, doubts that, in many instances, interest will prevail over duty, and that the Sub-Treasurer will prefer opulent knavery in a foreign land, to honest poverty at home? But how different is it with a Bank. Besides the Government money deposited with it, it is doing business upon a large capital of its own. If it proves faithful to the Government, it continues its business; if unfaithful, it forfeits its charter, breaks up its business, and thereby loses more than all it can make by seizing upon the Government funds in its possession. Its *interest*, therefore, is on the side of its duty—is to be faithful to the Government, and consequently, even the dishonest amongst its managers, have no temptation to be faithless to it. Even if robberies happen in the Bank, the losses are borne by the Bank, and the Government loses nothing. It is for this reason then, that we say a Bank is the more secure. It is because of that admirable feature in the Bank system, which places the *interest* and the *duty* of the depository both on one side; whereas that feature can never enter into the Sub-Treasury system. By the latter, the *interest* of the individuals keeping the public money, will wage an eternal war with their *duty*, and in very many instances must be victorious. In answer to the argument drawn from the fact that individual depositories of public money, have always proved unsafe, it is urged that even if we had a National Bank, the money has to *pass through* the same individual hands, that it will under the Sub-Treasury. This is only partially true in fact, and wholly fallacious in argument.

It is only partially true, in fact, because by the Sub-Treasury bill, four Receivers General are to be appointed by the President and Senate. These are new officers, and consequently, it cannot be true that the money, or any portion of it, has heretofore passed thro' their hands. These four new officers are to be located at New York, Boston, Charleston and St. Louis, and consequently are to be the depositories of all the money collected at or near those points; so that more than three-fourths of the public money will fall into the keeping of these four new officers, which did not exist as officers under the National Bank system. It is only partially true, then, that the money passes through the same hands, under a National Bank, as it would do under the Sub-Treasury.

It is true, that under either system, individuals must be employed as Collectors of the Customs, Receivers at the Land Offices, &c. &c. but the difference is, that under the Bank system, the receivers of all sorts, receive the money and pay it over to the Bank once a week when the collections are large, and once a month when they are small, whereas, by the Sub-Treasury system, individuals are not only to collect the money, but they are to *keep* it also, or pay it over to other individuals equally unsafe as themselves, to be by them kept, until it is wanted for disbursement. It is during the time that it is thus lying idle in their hands, that opportunity is afforded, and temptation held out to them to embezzle and escape with it. By the Bank system, each Collector or Receiver, is to deposit in Bank all the money in his hands at the end of each month at most, and to send the Bank certificates of deposite to the Secretary of the Treasury. Whenever that certificate of deposite fails to arrive at the proper time, the Secretary *knows* that the officers thus failing, is acting the knave; and if he is himself disposed to do his duty, he has him immediately removed from office, and thereby cuts him off from the possibility of embezzling but little more than the receipts of a single month. But by the Sub-Treasury System, the money is to lie month after month in the hands of individuals; larger amounts are to accumulate in the hands of the Receivers General, and some others, by perhaps ten to one, than ever accumulated in the hands of individuals before; yet during all this time, in relation to this great stake, the Secretary of the Treasury can comparatively know nothing. Reports, to be sure, he will have, but reports are often false, and always false when made by a knave to cloak his knavery. Long experience has shown, that nothing short of an actual demand of the money will expose an adroit peculator. Ask him for reports and he will give them to your heart's content; send agents to examine and count the money in his hands, and he will borrow of a friend, merely to be counted and then returned, a sufficient sum to make the sum square. Try what you will, it will all fail till you demand the money—then, and not till then, the truth will come.

The sum of the whole matter, I take to be this: Under the Bank system, while sums of money, by the law, were permitted to lie in the hands of individuals, *for very short periods only*, many and very large defalcations occurred by those individuals. Under the Sub-Treasury system, *much larger sums* are to lie in the hands of individuals *for much longer periods*, thereby multiplying *temptation* in proportion as the sums *are larger*; and multiplying *opportunity* in proportion as the periods *are longer* to, and for, those individuals to embezzle and escape with the public treasure; and, therefore, just in the proportion, that the *temptation* and the *opportunity* are greater under the Sub-Treasury than the Bank system, will the peculations and defalcations be greater under the former than they have been under the latter. The truth of this, independent of actual experience, is but little less than self-evident. I therefore, leave it.

But it is said, and truly too, that there is to be a *Penitentiary Department* to the Sub-Treasury. This, the advocates of the system will have it, will be a *"king-cure-all."* Before I go farther, may I not ask if the Penitentiary Department, is not itself an admission that they expect the public money to be stolen? Why build the cage if they expect to catch no birds? But to the question how effectual the Penitentiary will be in preventing defalcations. How effectual have Penitentiaries heretofore been in preventing the crimes they were established to suppress? Has not confinement in them long been the legal penalty of larceny, forgery, robbery, and many other crimes, in almost all the States? And yet, are not those crimes committed weekly, daily, nay, and even hourly, in every one of those States? Again, the gallows has long been the penalty of murder, and yet we scarcely open a newspaper, that does not relate a new case of that crime. If then, the Penitentiary has ever *heretofore* failed to prevent larceny, forgery and robbery, and the gallows and halter have likewise failed to prevent murder, by what process of reasoning, I ask, is it that we are to conclude the Penitentiary will *hereafter* prevent the stealing of the public money? But our opponents seem to think they answer the charge, that the money will be stolen, fully, if they can show that they will bring the offenders to punishment. Not so. Will the punishment of the thief bring back the stolen money? No more so than the hanging of a murderer restores his victim to life. What is the object desired? Certainly not the greatest number of thieves we can catch, but that the money may not be stolen. If, then, any plan can be devised for depositing the public treasure, where it will be never stolen, never embezzled, is not that the plan to be adopted? Turn, then, to a National Bank, and you have that plan, fully and completely successful, as tested by the experience of forty years.

I have now done with the three propositions that the Sub-Treasury would injuriously affect the currency, and would be more *expensive* and *less secure* as a depository of the public money than a National Bank. How far I have succeeded in establishing their truth is for others to judge.

Omitting, for want of time, what I had intended to say as to the effect of the Sub-Treasury, to bring the public money under the more immediate control of the President, than it has ever heretofore been, I now only ask the audience, when Mr. Calhoun[6] shall answer me, *to hold him to the questions*. Permit him not to escape them. Require him *either* to show, that the Sub-Treasury *would not* injuriously affect the *currency*, or that we should in some way, receive an equivalent for that injurious effect. Require him *either* to show that the Sub-Treasury *would not be more expensive* as a fiscal agent, than a Bank, or that we should, in some way be compensated for that additional expense. And particularly require him to show, that the public money *would be as secure* in the Sub-Treasury as in a National Bank, or that the additional *insecurity* would be overbalanced by some good result of the proposed change.

No one of them, in my humble judgment, will he be able to do; and I venture the prediction, and ask that it may be especially noted, *that he will not attempt to answer the proposition, that the Sub-Treasury would be more expensive than a National Bank as a fiscal agent of the Government.*

As a sweeping objection to a National Bank, and consequently an argument in favor of the Sub-Treasury as a substitute for it, it often has been urged, and doubtless will be again, that such a bank is unconstitutional. We have often heretofore shown, and therefore need not in detail do so again, that a majority of the Revolutionary patriarchs, whoever acted officially upon the question, commencing with Gen. Washington and embracing Gen. Jackson, the larger number of the signers of the Declaration, and of the framers of the Constitution, who were in the Congress of 1791, have decided upon their oaths that such a bank is constitutional. We have also shown that the votes of Congress have more often been in favor of than against its constitutionality. In addition to all this we have shown

[6] John Calhoun, Democrat of Sangamon County, who was to answer Lincoln's speech on Saturday night, December 28.

that the Supreme Court—that tribunal which the Constitution has itself established to decide Constitutional questions—has solemnly decided that such a bank is constitutional. Protesting that these authorities ought to settle the question—ought to be conclusive, I will not urge them further now. I now propose to take a view of the question which I have not known to be taken by anyone before. It is, that whatever objection ever has or ever can be made to the constitutionality of a bank, will apply with equal force in its whole length, breadth and proportions to the Sub-Treasury. Our opponents say, there is no *express* authority in the Constitution to establish a Bank, and therefore a Bank is unconstitutional; but we, with equal truth, may say, there is no *express* authority in the Constitution to establish a Sub-Treasury, and therefore a Sub-Treasury is unconstitutional. Who then, has the advantage of this *"express authority"* argument? Does it not cut equally both ways? Does it not wound them as deeply and as deadly as it does us?

Our position is that both are constitutional. The Constitution enumerates expressly several powers which Congress may exercise, superadded to which is a general authority "to make all laws necessary and proper," for carrying into effect all the powers vested by the Constitution of the Government of the United States. One of the express powers given Congress, is "To lay and collect taxes; duties, imposts, and excises; to pay the debts, and provide for the common defence and general welfare of the United States." Now, Congress is expressly authorized to make all laws necessary and proper for carrying this power into execution. To carry it into execution, it is indispensably necessary to collect, safely keep, transfer, and disburse a revenue. To do this, a Bank is "necessary and proper." But, say our opponents, to authorize the making of a Bank, the *necessity* must be so great, that the power just recited, would be nugatory without it; and that that *necessity* is expressly negatived by the fact, that they have got along *ten* whole years without such a *Bank.* Immediately we turn on them, and say, that that sort of *necessity* for a Sub-Treasury does not exist, because we have got along *forty* whole years without one. And this time, it may be observed, that we are not merely equal with them in the argument, but we beat them *forty* to *ten,* or which is the same thing, *four* to *one.* On examination, it will be found, that the absurd rule, which prescribes that before we can constitutionally adopt a National Bank as a fiscal agent, we must show an *indispensable necessity* for it, will exclude every sort of fiscal agent that the mind of man can conceive. A *Bank* is not *indispensable,* because we can take the *Sub-Treasury;* the *Sub-Treasury* is not indispensable because we can take the *Bank*. The rule is too absurd to need further comment. Upon the phrase *"necessary and proper,"* in the Constitution, it seems to me more reasonable to say, that *some* fiscal agent is *indispensably necessary;* but, inasmuch as no *particular sort* of agent is thus *indispensable,* because some *other* sort might be adopted, we are left to choose that sort of agent, which may be most *"proper"* on grounds of expediency.

But it is said the Constitution gives no power to Congress to pass acts of incorporation. Indeed! What is the passing [of] an act of incorporation, but the *making of a law?* Is any one wise enough to tell? The Constitution expressly gives Congress power *"to pass all laws necessary and proper,"* &c. If, then, the passing of a Bank charter, be the *"making a law necessary and proper,"* is it not clearly within the constitutional power of Congress to do so?

I now leave the Bank and the Sub-Treasury to try to answer, in a brief way, some of the arguments which, on previous evenings here, have been urged by Messrs. Lamborn[7] and Douglass. Mr. Lamborn admits that *"errors,"* as he charitably calls them, have occurred under the present and late administrations, but he insists that as great *"errors"* have occurred under all administrations. This we respectfully deny. We admit that errors may have occurred under all administrations; but we insist that there is *no parallel* between them and those of the two last. If they can show that their errors are no greater in number and magnitude, than those of former times, we call off the dogs.

But they can do no such thing. To be brief, I will now attempt a contrast of the "errors" of the two latter, with those of former administrations, in relation to the public expenditures only. What I am now about to say, as to the expenditures, will be, in all cases, exclusive of payments on the National debt. By an examination of authentic public documents, consisting of the regular series of annual reports, made by all the Secretaries of the Treasury from the establishment of the Government down to the close of the year 1838, the following contrasts will be presented.

1st. The last *ten* years under Gen. Jackson and Mr. Van Buren, cost more money than the first *twenty-seven* did, (including the heavy expenses of the late British war,) under Washington, Adams, Jefferson, and Madison.

2d. The last year of J. Q. Adams' administration cost, in round numbers, *thirteen* millions, being about *one* dollar to each soul in the nation; the last (1838) of Mr. Van Buren's cost *forty* millions,

---

[7] Josiah Lamborn, Democrat, who had spoken earlier in the week.

being about *two dollars and fifty cents* to each soul; and being larger than the expenditure of Mr. Adams in the proportion of *five* to *two*.

3d. The highest annual expenditure during the late British war, being in 1814, and while we had in actual service rising 188,000 militia, together with the whole regular army, swelling the number to greatly over 200,000, and they to be clad, fed and transported from point to point, with great rapidity and corresponding expense, and to be furnished with arms and ammunition, and they to be transported in like manner, and at like expense, was no more in round numbers than *thirty* millions; whereas, the annual expenditure of 1838, under Mr. Van Buren, and while we were at peace with every government in the world, was *forty* millions; being over the highest year of the late and very expensive war, in the proportion of *four* to *three*.

4th. Gen. Washington administered the Government *eight* years for *sixteen* millions. Mr. Van Buren administered it *one* year (1838) for *forty* millions; so that Mr. Van Buren expended *twice and a half* as much in *one* year, as Gen. Washington did in *eight*, and being in the proportion of *twenty* to *one*—or, in other words, had Gen. Washington administered the Government *twenty* years, at the same average expense that he did for *eight*, he would have carried us through the whole *twenty*, for no more money than Mr. Van Buren has expended in getting us through the single *one* of 1838.

Other facts, equally astounding, might be presented from the same authentic document; but I deem the foregoing abundantly sufficient to establish the proposition, that there is no parallel between the *"errors"* of the present and late administrations, and those of former times, and that Mr. Van Buren is wholly out of the line of all precedents.

But, Mr. Douglass, seeing that the enormous expenditure of 1838, has no parallel in the olden times, comes in with a long list of excuses for it. This list of excuses I will rapidly examine, and show, as I think, that the few of them which are true, prove nothing; and that the majority of them are wholly untrue in fact. He first says, that the expenditures of that year were made under the appropriations of Congress—*one branch of which was a Whig body*. It is true that those expenditures were made under the appropriations of Congress; but it is *untrue* that either branch of Congress was a *Whig* body. The Senate had fallen into the hands of the administration, more than a year before, as proven by the passage of the Expunging Resolution;[8] and at the time those appropriations were made, there were too few Whigs in that body, to make a respectable struggle, in point of numbers, upon any question. This is notorious to all. The House of Representatives that voted those appropriations, was the same that first assembled at the called session of September, 1838. Although it refused to pass the Sub-Treasury Bill, a majority of its members were elected as friends of the administration, and proved their adherence to it, by the election of a Van Buren Speaker, and two Van Buren clerks. It is clear then, that both branches of the Congress that passed those appropriations were in the hands of Mr. Van Buren's friends, so that the Whigs had no power to arrest them, as Mr. Douglass would insist. And is not the charge of extravagant expenditures, equally well sustained, if shown to have been made by a Van Buren Congress, as if shown to have been made in any other way? A Van Buren Congress passed the bill; and Mr. Van Buren himself approved them, and consequently the party are wholly responsible for them.

Mr. Douglass next says that a portion of the expenditures of that year was made for the purchase of public lands from the Indians. Now it happens that no such purchase was made during that year. It is true that some money was paid that year in pursuance of Indian treaties; but no more, or rather not as much as had been paid on the same account in each of several preceding years.

Next he says that the Florida war created many millions of this year's expenditure. This is true, and it is also true that during that and every other year that that war has existed, it has cost three or four times as much as it would have done under an honest and judicious administration of the Government. The large sums foolishly, not to say corruptly, thrown away in that war constitute one of the just causes of complaint against the administration. Take a single instance. The agents of the Government in connection with that war needed a certain Steamboat; the owner proposed to sell it for ten thousand dollars; the agents refused to give that sum, but hired the boat at one hundred dollars per day, and kept it at that hire till it amounted to ninety-two thousand dollars. This fact is not found in the public reports, but depends with me, on the verbal statement of an officer of the navy, who says he knows it to be true. That the administration ought to be credited for the *reasonable* expenses of the Florida war, we have never denied. Those *reasonable*

8 Resolution sponsored by Thomas H. Benton (Missouri Democrat) in January, 1837, which erased from the journal of the Senate the resolution of censure against the administration for the removal of the bank deposits.

charges, we say, could not exceed one or two millions a year. Deduct such a sum from the forty-million expenditure of 1838, and the remainder will still be without a parallel as an annual expenditure.

Again, Mr. Douglass says that the removal of the Indians to the country west of the Mississippi created much of the expenditure of 1838. I have examined the public documents in relation to this matter, and find that less was paid for the removal of Indians in that than in some former years. The whole sum expended on that account in that year did not much exceed one-quarter of a million. For this small sum, altho' we do not think the administration entitled to credit, because large sums have been expended in the same way in former years, we consent it may take one and make the most of it.

Next, Mr. Douglass says that five millions of the expenditures of 1838 consisted of the payment of the French indemnity money to its individual claimants. I have carefully examined the public documents, and thereby find this statement to be wholly untrue. Of the forty millions of dollars expended in 1838, I am enabled to say positively that not one dollar consisted of payments on the French indemnities. So much for that excuse.

Next comes the Post-office. He says that five millions were expended during that year to sustain that department. By a like examination of public documents, I find this also wholly untrue. Of the so often mentioned forty millions, not one dollar went to the Post-office. I am glad, however, that the Post-office has been referred to, because it warrants me in digressing a little to inquire how it is that that department of the Government has become a *charge* upon the Treasury, whereas under Mr. Adams and the Presidents before him it not only, to use a homely phrase, cut its own fodder, but actually threw a surplus into the Treasury. Although nothing of the forty millions was paid on that account in 1838, it is true that five millions are appropriated *to be so expended* in 1839; showing clearly that the department has become a *charge* upon the Treasury. How has this happened? I account for it in this way. The chief expense of the Post-office Department consists of the payments of Contractors for carrying the mail. Contracts for carrying the mails are by law let to the lowest bidders, after advertisement. This plan introduces competition, and insures the transportation of the mails at fair prices, so long as it is faithfully adhered to. It has ever been adhered to until Mr. Barry[9] was made

9 William Taylor Barry, appointed by President Jackson in March, 1829, resigned the office on April 10, 1835, under pressure of critics.

Postmaster-General. When he came into office, he formed the purpose of throwing the mail contracts into the hands of his friends, to the exclusion of his opponents. To effect this, the plan of letting to the lowest bidder must be evaded, and it must be done in this way: the favorite bid less by perhaps three or four hundred per cent. than the contract could be performed for, and consequently shutting out all honest competition, became the contractor. The Postmaster-General would immediately add some slight additional duty to the contract, and under the pretense of extra allowance for extra services run the contract to double, triple, and often quadruple what honest and fair bidders had proposed to take it at. In 1834 the finances of the department had become so deranged that total concealment was no longer possible, and consequently a committee of the Senate were directed to make a thorough investigation of its affairs. Their report is found in the Senate Documents of 1833-34, Vol. 5, Doc. 422; which documents may be seen at the Secretary's office, and I presume elsewhere in the State. The report shows numerous cases of similar import, of one of which I give the substance. The contract for carrying the mail upon a certain route had expired, and of course was to be let again. The old contractor offered to take it for $300 a year, the mail to be transported thereon three times a week, or for $600 transported daily. One James Reeside bid $40 for three times a week, or $99 daily, and of course received the contract. On the examination of the committee, it was discovered that Reeside had received for the service on this route, which he had contracted to render for less than $100, the enormous sum of $1,999! This is but a single case. Many similar ones, covering some ten or twenty pages of a large volume, are given in that report. The department was found to be insolvent to the amount of half a million, and to have been so grossly mismanaged, or rather so corruptly managed, in almost every particular, that the best friends of the Post Master General made no defence of his administration of it. They admitted that he was wholly unqualified for that office; but still he was retained in it by the President, until he resigned voluntarily about a year afterwards. And when he resigned it what do you think became of him? Why, he sunk into obscurity and disgrace, to be sure, you will say. No such thing. Well, then, what did become of him? Why the President immediately expressed his high disapprobation of his almost unequalled incapacity and corruption, by appointing him to a foreign mission, with a salary and outfit of $18,000 a year. The party now attempt to throw Barry off, and to avoid the responsibility of his sins. Did not the President endorse those sins, when on the very heel of their commission, he appointed their author to the very highest and most honorable office in his gift, and which is but a single step behind the very goal of American political ambition.

I return to another of Mr. Douglass' excuses for the expenditures of 1838, at the same time announcing the pleasing intelligence, that this is the last one. He says that ten millions of that years expenditure, was a contingent appropriation, to prosecute an anticipated war with Great Britain, on the Maine boundary question. Few words will settle this. First: that the ten millions appropriated was not *made* till 1839, and consequently could not have been expended in 1838; and, second: although it was appropriated, it has never been expended at all. Those who heard Mr. Douglass, recollect that he indulged himself in a contemptuous expression of pity for me. "Now he's got me," thought I. But when he went on to say that five millions of the expenditure of 1838, were payments of the French indemnities, *which I knew to be untrue;* that five millions had been for the Post Office, *which I knew to be untrue;* that ten millions had been for the Maine boundary war, *which I not only knew to be untrue, but supremely ridiculous also;* and when I saw that he was stupid enough to hope, that I would permit such groundless and audacious assertions to go unexposed, I readily consented, that on the score both of veracity and sagacity, the audience should judge whether he or I were the more deserving of the world's contempt.

Mr. Lamborn insists that the difference between the Van Buren party, and the Whigs is, that although, the former sometimes err in *practice*, they are always correct in *principle*—whereas the latter are wrong in *principle*—and the better to impress this proposition, he uses a figurative expression in these words: *"The Democrats are vulnerable in the heel, but they are sound in the head and the heart."* The first branch of the figure, that is that the Democrats are vulnerable in the heel, I admit is not merely figuratively, but literally true. Who that looks but for a moment at their Swartwouts, their Prices, their Harringtons, and their hundreds of others, scampering away with the public money to Texas, to Europe, and to every spot of the earth where a villain may hope to find refuge from justice, can at all doubt that they are most distressingly affected in their *heels* with a species of *"running itch."* It seems that this malady of their heels, operates on these *sound-headed* and *honest-hearted* creatures, very much like the cork-leg, in the comic song, did on its owner: which, when he had once got started on it, the more he tried to stop it, the more it would run away. At the hazard of wearing this point thread bare, I will relate an anecdote, which seems too strikingly in point to be omitted. A witty Irish soldier, who was always boasting of his bravery, when no danger was near, but who invariably retreated without orders at the first charge of an engagement, being asked by his Captain why he did so, replied: "Captain, I have as brave a *heart* as Julius Caesar ever had; but some how or other, whenever danger approaches, my *cowardly* legs will run away with it." So with Mr. Lamborn's party. They take the public money *into* their hand for the most laudable purpose, that *wise heads* and *honest hearts* can dictate; but before they can possibly get it *out* again their rascally *"vulnerable heels"* will run away with them.

Seriously: this proposition of Mr. Lamborn is nothing more or less, than a request that his party may be tried by their *professions* instead of their *practices*. Perhaps no position that the party assumes is more liable to, or more deserving of exposure, than this very modest request; and nothing but the unwarrantable length, to which I have already extended these remarks, forbids me now attempting to expose it. For the reason given, I pass it by.

I shall advert to but one more point.

Mr. Lamborn refers to the late elections in the States, and from their results, confidently predicts, that every State in the Union will vote for Mr. Van Buren at the next Presidential election. Address *that* argument to *cowards* and to *knaves;* with the *free* and the *brave* it will effect nothing. It *may* be true, if it *must*, let it. Many free countries have lost their liberty; and *ours may* lose hers; but if she shall, be it my proudest plume, not that I was the *last* to desert, but that I *never* deserted her. I know that the great volcano at Washington, aroused and directed by the evil spirit that reigns there, is belching forth the lava of political corruption, in a current broad and deep, which is sweeping with frightful velocity over the whole length and breadth of the land, bidding fair to leave unscathed no green spot or living thing, while on its bosom are riding like demons on the waves of Hell, the imps of that evil spirit, and fiendishly taunting all those who dare resist its destroying course, with the hopelessness of their effort; and knowing this, I cannot deny that all may be swept away. Broken by it, I, too, may be; bow to it I never will. The *probability* that we may fall in the struggle *ought not* to deter us from the support of a cause we believe to be just; it *shall not* deter me. If ever I feel the soul within me elevate and expand to those dimensions not wholly unworthy of its Almighty Architect, it is when I contemplate the cause of my country, deserted by all the world beside, and I standing up boldly and alone and hurling defiance at her victorious oppressors. Here, without contemplating consequences, before High Heaven, and in the face of the world, I swear eternal fidelity to the just cause, as I deem it, of the land of my life, my liberty and my love. And who, that thinks with me, will not fearlessly adopt the oath that I take. Let none faulter, who thinks he is right, and we may succeed. But, if after all, we shall fail, be it so. We still shall have the proud consolation of saying to our consciences, and to the departed shade of our country's freedom, that the cause approved of our judgment, and adored of our hearts, in disaster, in chains, in torture, in death, we NEVER faultered in defending.

To Thomas Mather[1]

Col. Thomas Mather,   Springfield, Illinois,
   President of State Bank: December 26, 1839.

Sir: You are herewith furnished with a copy of the joint resolution adopted by both branches of the General Assembly of Illinois, which has for its object the appointment of a joint committee to investigate the condition of the State Bank and Branches.

The undersigned have been appointed the committee, under the resolution, have organized, and are now ready to proceed with the examination contemplated by the aforesaid resolution.

You will have the goodness to advise the committee at what time you will be ready to receive them on the business aforesaid. With great respect, We have the honor to be, Your obedient servants,

Byrd Monroe,	Orlando B. Ficklin,
James H. Woodworth,	William W. Happy,
John D. Wood,	Richard Murphy,
Senate Committee.	Abraham Lincoln,
	John Moore,
	House Committee.

[1] *Reports Made To the Senate and House of Representatives of the State of Illinois,* 1840, I, 339. For the report of the committee, *vide infra* January 21, 1840.

Bill Introduced in Illinois Legislature
to Vacate Part of the Town Plat of
Bennett's Addition to the Town of Petersburg[1]

[December 27, 1839]

A Bill for an act to vacate a part of the town plat of Bennett's addition to the town of Petersburg:—

Be it enacted by the people of the state of Illinois represented in the General Assembly that the town plat for Blocks numbered two, three, four, and five, in Bennett's Addition to the town of Petersburg, be vacated; *Provided* that this act shall be null and void as against any individual proprietor or proprietors, (if any such there be) of the part of said town hereby proposed to be vacated.

¹ AD, I-Ar. Lincoln also wrote the petition to which this bill answers (December 16, 1839, *supra*). The bill passed the House, and passed the Senate with a lengthy amendment concerning the assessment and collection of taxes in certain counties. It failed to obtain approval before adjournment of the session.

Lincoln's Plan of Campaign in 1840¹

[c. January, 1840]

1st. Appoint one person in each county as county captain, and take his pledge to perform promptly all the duties assigned him.

Duties of the County Captain

1st. To procure from the poll-books a separate list for each Precinct of all the names of all those persons who voted the Whig ticket in August.

2nd. To appoint one person in each Precinct as Precinct Captain, and, by a personal interview with him, procure his pledge, to perform promptly all the duties assigned him.

3rd. To deliver to each Precinct Captain the list of names as above, belonging to his Precinct; and also a written list of his duties.

Duties of the Precinct Captain.

1st. To divide the list of names delivered him by the county Captain, into Sections of ten who reside most convenient to each other.

2nd. To appoint one person of each Section as Section Captain, and by a personal interview with him, procure his pledge to perform promptly all the duties assigned him.

3rd. To deliver to each Section Captain the list of names belonging to his Section and also a written list of his duties.

Duties of the Section Captain.

1st. To see each man of his Section face to face, and procure his pledge that he will for no consideration (impossibilities excepted) stay from the polls on the first monday in November; and that he will record his vote as early on the day as possible.

2nd. To add to his Section the name of every person in his vicinity who did not vote with us in August, but who will vote with us in the fall, and take the same pledge of him, as from the others.

3rd. To *task* himself to procure at least such additional names to his Section.

[1] AD, MoSHi. This document—contemporary with the campaign circular of January 31, 1840, but undated—was sent to Madison Miller, Whig candidate for representative from Monroe County. No accompanying letter has been found.

To John T. Stuart[1]

Dear Stuart: Springfield, Jany– 1st. 1840.

There is a considerable disposition on the part of both parties in the Legislature here, to reinstate the law bringing on the congressional elections next summer. What motive for this, the Locos have, I can not tell. The whigs say that the canal & other public works will stop, and consequently, we shall then be clear of the foreign votes, whereas by another year they may be brought in again. The whigs here of our district, say that every thing is in favour of holding the election next summer, except the fact of your absence, and several of them have requested me to ask your opinion on the matter. Write me immediately what you think of it.

On the other side of this sheet, I send you a copy of my Land Resolutions which passed both branches of our Legislature last winter.[2] Will you show them to Mr. Calhoun, informing him of the fact of their passage through our Legislature? Mr. Calhoun suggested a similar proposition last winter; and perhaps, if he finds himself backed by one of the states, he may be induced to take it up again. You will see by the resolutions, that you and the others of our delegation in Congress are instructed to go for them.[3]

[1] ALS, owned by heirs of Stuart Brown.
[2] See under date of January 17, 1839, *supra.* The copy which Lincoln sent to Stuart is not with this letter and may be presumed to have been turned over to Senator John C. Calhoun of South Carolina by Stuart according to Lincoln's suggestion.
[3] Since this one-page holograph bears no signature, it may be that the page bearing the resolutions carried also the close of the letter. Lincoln did not, however, write "on the other side of this sheet" as the text specifies.

Amendment Introduced in Illinois Legislature
to an Act to Amend an Act Concerning
the Public Revenue Approved February, 1837[1]

[January 2, 1840]

[Be it enacted by the People of the State of Ill]inois [represen]ted in [the General Assembly:][2] That hereafter all Revolutionary pensioners within this state, shall be permitted to loan all or any part of the money which they may have acquired exclusively by means of their pensions, without paying any tax whatever, therefor.

The assessors of the several counties within this state, shall take the production of the regular pension certificate from the War office of the United States, as sufficient evidence, that the person therein shown to be a Revolutionary pensioner is a Revolutionary pensioner; and shall then take the statement upon honor of such pensioner, as sufficient evidence of the facts whether he has any money loaned other than that acquired by means of his pension, and if so, how much, and on all other questions deemed necessary and proper under this act.

[1] AD, I-Ar. Lincoln wrote this as an individual bill bearing the title "A bill for an act exempting Revolutionary pensioners from taxation on loaned money," but immediately following the introduction of an "act to amend an act concerning the public revenue, approved February 1837," Lincoln moved his bill as an amendment in the form of an additional section. Both were referred to the committee on finance and died there, although a new bill bearing the title "An act to amend an act concerning the Public Revenue, approved 26th February, 1839" was reported from the committee on January 13 and finally became law without Lincoln's section providing for Revolutionary pensioners.

[2] The title and enabling statement have been torn off the document.

Bill Introduced in Illinois Legislature
to Establish a State Road from Petersburg to Waverly[1]

[January 10, 1840]

A bill for an act to establish a state road from Petersburg in Menard county to Waverly in Morgan county

SEC: 1st. Be it enacted by the People of the State of Illinois represented in the General Assembly: That John B. Broadwell, Franklin Minor[2] and Achilles Morris, be and they are hereby appointed commissioners to view mark, and locate a state road from Petersburg in Menard county by way of John B Broadwell's, Berlin, New Berlin and the rail road depot in Sangamon county to. Waverly in Morgan county.

SEC. 2nd. That said commissioners or a majority of them shall meet at Petersburg on the first monday of March next, or any time within sixty days thereafter—and after being first duly sworn, shall proceed to locate said said [sic] road, avoiding as much as possible all injury to private property.

SEC: 3rd. That said commissioners shall make out a separate report of so much of the location of said road as lies in each of said counties, and file the same with the clerk of the county commissioners court of the proper county.

SEC: 4th. That said commissioners shall have such compensation out of the Treasuries of said counties as shall be just and reasonable.[3]

[1] AD, I-Ar. Lincoln wrote and introduced the bill on January 10, 1840, from a select committee to which a petition requesting location of the road had been referred. Again referred to a second select committee of which Lincoln was a member, the bill was amended and reported on January 17, with sundry amendments, by Newton Cloud, representative from Morgan County. The bill as amended and passed by both houses may be found in *Laws of Illinois*, 1840, p. 64.

[2] The name of John J. Lemon has been deleted and the name of Franklin Minor inserted, not in Lincoln's hand.

[3] Sections 4, 5, and 6 as printed in *Laws of Illinois* were amendments reported by Cloud on January 17.

Bill Introduced in Illinois Legislature
to Legalize Survey and Town Plat of Mount Auburn[1]

[January 15, 1840]

A bill for an act legalizing the Survey and plat of the town of Mount Auburn in the county of Dane.

Be it enacted by the People of the state of Illinois represented in the General Assembly: That the Survey and Town Plat of the town of Mount Auburn in the county of Dane, as certified by T. R. Skinner, Surveyor Logan county, are hereby made as legal as if they had been made by the Surveyor of Dane county.

[1] AD, I-Ar. Lincoln wrote the bill, but his colleague Edward D. Baker introduced it on January 15. The bill passed the House but died in the Senate.

Amendment Introduced in Illinois Legislature
to an Act for Relief of Incorporated Towns[1]

[January 18, 1840]

Strike out the second Section,[2] and insert the following—

SEC. 2. The collector of each county shall pay over to the President and Trustees of each incorporated town within his county one half of the county tax collected by him off of property real and personal within the limits of such incorporated town.

[1] AD, I-Ar. Lincoln wrote the amendment, which was reported from the committee on finance along with the bill. Bill and amendment were tabled.

[2] The second section in the original bill read as follows:

"Real estate situated in incorporated towns shall pay a state tax but shall not hereafter be taxed for county purposes. And it shall be lawful for the President &

Trustees of towns to assess such taxes on the real estate situated within the limits of their respective incorporated towns as to them may seem proper not exceeding one half of one per cent."

To John T. Stuart[1]

Dear Stuart: Springfield, Jany. 20th. 1840.

Yours of the 5th. Inst. is recd. It is the first from you for a great while. You wish the news from here. The Legislature is in session yet, but has done nothing of importance. The following is my guess as to what *will be* done. The Internal Improvement System will be put down in a lump, without benefit of clergy. The Bank will be resusitated with some trifling modifications. Whether the canal will go ahead or stop is verry doubtful. Whether the State House will go ahead, depends upon the laws already in force.

A proposition made in the House today to throw off to the Teritory of Wisconsin about 14 of our Northern counties—decided. Ayes 11. Noes. 70.

Be sure to send me as many copies of the life of Harrison, as you can spare from other uses.

Be verry sure to procure and send me the Senate Journal of New York of September 1814. I have a newspaper article which says that that document proves that Van Buren voted against raisin[g] troops in the last war.

And, in general, send me every thing you think will be a good *"war-club."* The nomination of Harrison takes first rate. You know I am never sanguine; but I believe we will carry the state. The chance for doing so, appears to me 25 per cent better than it did for you to beat Douglass. A great many of the grocery sort of Van Buren men, as formerly, are out for Harrison. Our Irish Blacksmith Gregory,[2] is for Harrison. I believe I may say, that all our friends think the chance of carrying the state, verry good.

You have heard that the Whigs and Locos had a political discussion shortly after the meeting of the Legislature. Well, I made a big speech, which is in progress of printing in pamphlet form.[3] To enlighten you and the rest of the world, I shall send you a copy when it is finished.

I cant think of any thing else now. Your friend, as ever—

A. LINCOLN

[1] ALS, CSmH.   [2] George Gregory.
[3] See under date of December 26, 1839.

Committee Report in Illinois Legislature on Condition of the State Bank[1]

[January 21, 1840]

The undersigned members of the Committee to which was re-fered the Joint Resolution of both branches of the Legislature, submit the following report to the Senate

In obedience to the joint resolution of both branches of the General Assembly, the undersigned[2] proceeded to examine into the condition of the State Bank of Illinois, and into such charges preferred against the Bank, as they deemed of sufficient importance, in their bearing upon the interests of the community, to claim the time and attention of the undersigned

As a reason for not going more minutely into an examination of the condition and conduct of the several branches of this institution, the undersigned would state, that time has not been afforded them to visit the several branches, and their information, therefore, relative to the branches, is derived, in part, from witnesses called before and examined by the undersigned, but mainly from the statements under oath of the President and Cashier of the Parent Bank.

It will be recollected, that, during the session of 1836-7, a joint select committee was appointed by the Legislature of Illinois, to examine into the condition of the State Bank, with a view of ascertaining, among other things, whether said said [sic] institution would constitute a safe depository for the funds of the State.

On the 18th. day of February 1837, that committee submitted a report to the House of Representatives, and about the same time a report was also submitted to the Senate, which reports occupied most of the ground, from the organization of the Bank in 1835 to the then present time.

The undersigned deemed it an act of inutility, not to say of supererogation, to re-investigate and re-examine the same charges, examined and reported upon by the former committee: and have therefore directed their attention more particularly to the actings and doings of the Bank since February 1837.

---

1 AD, I-Ar. The document carries Lincoln's signature, but is not otherwise in his hand. It is probable that Lincoln had relatively little to do with the actual composition of the report. He attended but few of the committee meetings, as indicated in the proceedings of the committee. Orlando B. Ficklin, probably the principal author, delivered the report to the House on January 21, 1840.

2 Where "undersigned" appears, the original word "committee" has been deleted, as the result of the fact that a minority of the committee disagreed and chose to make a separate report.

After a laborious and attentive investigation, the undersigned have prepared the following report, which they beg leave to submit.

As the undersigned believed, that the Legislature wished information, to enlighten their judgment, and to assist them in coming to a conclusion, as to the propriety of renewing the forfeited charter of the Bank, they deemed it not improper to bestow most of their attention upon the following inquiries—

1. Whether there had been any circumstances of mismanagement of the affairs of the Bank, or mal-practices on the part of her officers, or any of them, against which future legislation might guard, or which would render the institution unworthy of public confidence?

2. Whether the stock in said Bank, owned by the state, is safe: and, whether the interest of the state, and the interests of the people, would be consulted, by a renewal of the charter of the Bank?

By reference to the the [sic] joint resolution of both houses, it will be seen, that the first inquiry is, "whether the Bank has forfeited its charter?"

The 25th. section of the charter, as amended, provides—That if the Bank shall, for sixty days after demand, neglect or refuse to pay its evidences of debt in specie, it shall forthwith close all its business, except the collecting and securing its debts, and the charter shall be forfeited.

More than sixty days have elapsed, since the Bank announced that it had suspended specie payments, and, as applications for the specie redemption of its liabilities have doubtless since been made and refused, the undersigned have no doubt, that the charter of the Bank would be declared forfeited by the proper court, on proof of such demand and refusal. The forfeiture, they believe, would date on the sixtieth day from the day of refusal. The charter, therefore, although not yet adjudicated upon, must certainly be forfeited, when the subject is brought before the proper tribunal.

The next inquiry, which the committee is directed to make, is— "what rates, of the discounts of the Bank, have been to persons living out of the state?"

The examination of the statements of the Bank has produced in our minds some surprize, at the smallness of the business, which the Bank has done with non-residents. The amount, now due the Bank, on loans and discounts to non residents, amounts to but 4 per cent of the whole sum of the debt due the Bank. The documents, which form a part of this report, give information, as to the distribution and character of this debt.

The committee are next instructed to inquire, as to the character

[186]

of the transactions of the Bank, with the House of Nevins, Townsend & Co, of New York.

The object of the inquiries on this subject appears to be, to ascertain, if the Bank, in its transactions with this House, has loaned them money, either without, or at a low rate of, interest; or has suffered any portion of the stock, which they own in the Bank, to remain unpaid; and, whether the Bank did not keep in their hands, for their advantage, large sums of money, while our citizens, who applied to the Bank for funds in New York, were refused them.

A full examination of the accounts of this house, with the Bank, has assured the undersigned, that none of these abuses have existed.

This house has been employed by the Bank, as its agent in New York, for the transaction of most, if not all, of its business, to be done through an agent in that City. Their agency commenced, as appears from the documents herewith submitted, by the transfer to them from the Phoenix Bank of New York, out of the funds received by that bank, in payment of the Capital Stock of the State Bank, paid in by individuals, of One Hundred Thousand Dollars: which they were instructed to vest in Gold Coin for the use of the Bank, and one half of which they shortly afterwards forwarded to the Bank in gold. The funds of the Bank having accumulated at this time in New York, from the paying in of the capital stock, and the Phoenix Bank having refused to allow any Interest thereon, a portion of it was deposited with Nevins, Townsend & Co, who gave security, and allowed six per cent interest on it. It did not remain long in their hands, however—a demand for eastern exchange arising at home, which occasioned its withdrawal. For some time past, this House has constantly been the creditor of the Bank, for large sums of money paid on the checks of the Bank; and, at the present time, the Bank is their debtor in the sum of $150,000.

The undersigned have not been able to discover any thing objectionable in these transactions. It would seem that this house was not only able, but willing, to make large advances to the Bank, and that some advantage must have resulted to those, whom the Bank was, by these means, enabled to accommodate with checks on New York. The necessity of some agency of the Bank in New York is obvious: and no reason is seen, for the preference of a Bank over private bankers, if they are able to give satisfactory security, as is the case with the house of Nevins, Townsend & Co, who are bankers of high character.

The committee are next instructed to inquire, if the capital stock, subscribed by Samuel Wiggins of Cincinnati, has been paid in?—

In prosecuting this inquiry, they have ascertained, that Samuel

[187]

Wiggins was the original holder of the stock of the Bank, to the amount of nearly $200,000—; on which he paid several of the earlier instalments: but, that, being disappointed in the sale of his stock, he applied to the Bank, and obtained loans to the amount of $108,000, for the refunding of which he pledged his Bank stock: which money, so obtained, was applied in paying up the calls made by the Bank, on the purchasers of its stock. This is said to be the only instance, except an am[oun]t of about $3000. to other individuals in which this odious practice has been resorted to. A subterfuge and evasion of the law of this character has been practised in other states to an alarming extent, so as to make the capital of particular banks rest upon a paper, instead of a metallic, basis. While the undersigned regret, that any, even a solitary, case of this sort, should have been tolerated by the Directors of the State Bank, and do not incline to offer for it any palliation whatever, they at the same time feel highly gratified, that this practice, so obnoxious to well founded objection, has not been general; but that all the other payments of subscriptions upon stock have been made in gold and silver, or in such funds as were authorized to be received by the charter of the Bank

It has also been made the duty of the committee to ascertain the nature of the transactions of the Bank with the house of Denman of Philadelphia—whether any loans were made them, whether they were permitted the free use of money, collected by the falling due of bills drawn on them, on account of pork, bacon, lard & lead, shipped them by the Bank—and whether any bills, drawn on them, have been renewed to prevent protest.

The undersigned have not been able, in their examination to find the slightest trace of any connexion between the Bank and the house in question, other than that, which has grown out of the purchase, by the Parent Bank and the Alton Branch, from our citizens, of bills of exchange drawn on said house. Mr. Denman is believed, by the undersigned, to be a responsible and wealthy commission merchant, a part of whose business is, dealing in western produce as agent for the shippers and they feel it is due to him to state— that all the bills on him, held by the bank, have been fully paid, when due.

The next subject of enquiry is the transaction of the Bank with the house of Gregg & Weld of Boston

It appears that the bank was the holder of about 70,000$ of the acceptances of this House of Dfts. drawn on them at Alton and negotiated by the Branch of the bank there when they failed and since that time this debt has been reduced to $23000 which sum is considered by the officers of the bank as being pretty well secured.

Intimately connected with this branch of the inquiry is the transactions of the bank with the house of Godfrey Gilman & Co of Alton.

The tabular statement of the Cashier shows the amount of the liabilities of this house, as drawers discounters and endorsers, to have swolen to the immense amount of $800.748.00 which has since been reduced to the sum of $419.358.00. This debt also is considered to be made safe by collateral security.

The undersigned feel less reluctance in introducing the names of these individuals, and their private accounts with the Bank from the fact that public rumor was rife with reports and charges against them, and had not failed to set forth the facts in as glowing colors at least as they meritted

These two cases are deemed sufficient to demonstrate the impolicy, of the bank extending such large accomodations to individuals or firms—many objections might be urged to this course, the undersigned however will proceed to notice only a few of them

1st. It deprives the bank of the power of fulfiling one of its important functions towit the extending its accomodations to the community generally

2d. It is exceedingly hazardous to risk so much upon the solvency of a single individual or firm, as a single failure may result in the loss of the entire debt

3d. The individual or firm having access to the Bank and being permitted the free use of its funds may monopolize the trade in any speculation or enterprise in which he chooses to embark

4th. Nothing is better calculated to engender heartburnings and to enlist enemies of the most hostile character against a bank than for the community to entertain the belief that the institution is used for the benefit of the few to the exclusion of the many. It will be recollected that a charge similar to this—was made against the late bank of the United States and to sustain that charge it was urged that Mr. T Biddle in Oct. 1830 was indebted to that institution in the sum of $1.120.000—if the objection had any weight in it as applied to the United States Bank with its immense capital and circulation—with how much greater force does the objection apply to our Bank having a circulation less than $3,000,000.

It is understood that the Directors of the Parent board aware of the impropriety of this course have adopted measures to restrain directors of branches in again making such excessive loans. While the undersigned decidedly disapprobate this practice of extending such large accomodations to individuals or firms, they are gratified to have the opportunity to bear testimony that the bank in a large majority of cases has made her discounts to dealers wanting small sums for immediate use, as will be seen by reference to a tabular statement furnished by the Bank and herewith presented

For the nature and extent of the loan to the Bank of Missouri—reference is made to the copy of contract between the two banks which is herewith submitted

The transaction was not fully carried out and the amount loaned was soon returned.

The arrangement seems to have been made from a desire on the part of this Bank to cultivate friendly relations with a neighboring institution which was about to go into operation

It was a part of the contract with the Missouri bank that she should redeem in specie if necessary the paper of the State Bank loaned to her. The undersigned see nothing objectionable in this transaction

The undersigned is also charged with the enquiry whether the Bank has dealt or speculated in lead land or any other commodity. So far as the undersigned have been able to hear and ascertain the facts the bank has not engaged in speculating in lead, land or any other commodity. In relation to this charge the undersigned have availed themselves of the testimony of the officers of the Bank of the correspondence touching these transactions and of the testimony of respectable gentlemen residing at the point where these abuses are said to have occured.

The bank professing to be desirous to enhance the price of lead, in the hand of the miner or smelter and to give the profits incident to its reshipment, to the commission merchants of Alton rather than to those of Saint Louis, who had hitherto monopolized the trade, made arrangements to have the lead shipped to J. G. Lamb of Alton—who was to act as the mutual agent of the owner of the lead and the Bank in its reshipment and sale. Upon the sale of the lead after refunding the money advanced, when the shipment was first made to the agent, say about three fourths of the market price of the lead together with interest commissions and other costs—and charges incident to the operation, the overplus accruing from the sale thereof, was to be paid to the former owner—thereby making the bank neither gaining [sic] or looser [sic] by the fluctuation in price of the article so shipped.

The statements of the officers of the bank is coroborated by the testimony of the other witnesses examined as to this point as will more fully appear by the accompanying depositions

While the undersigned fully acquit the bank of the charge of speculating or dealing in lead, they are constrained to animadvert upon this course as being unwise and improper on the part of the Bank. It is most obvious that so soon as the arrangement above aluded to was made public, (and its publicity could not easily be prevented) the commission merchants of Saint Louis and the keen-eyed speculator of the mineral region whose interests would be affected injuriously by this operation of the Bank, would wage a simultanious war against the institution, and prompted by the ever living principle of cupidity each would try to excell the other in the malignity of the attack, and in the ferocity of its procecution.

Experience has shewn us that such was the result of this enter-prise and the avowed good intentions of the Bank have not only been thwarted but much odium has been brot to bear against that institution in consequence of the lead operation

The undersigned believe that a Bank should pursue the "even tenor of her way" without lending her influence and her funds to stimulate any particular individual, in any particular branch of business, and whenever she departs from her plain path of duty, she is likely to awaken the vigilant jealousy of the people, and bring upon her own head either ruin or a loss of confidence which to a Bank is infinitely worse

In relation to the charge of the Bank dealing in Pork the under-signed would say that they have no evidence of that fact, but on the contrary if such has been the case, those cognisant of it have failed to make the proof, there is one circumstance however connected with this charge to which the undersigned will advert

The cashier of the Chicago Branch with a view of entering en-gaging in the purchase of pork with Mr. E K Hubbard and Mr. Dole[3] procured their note to be discounted and obtained funds for the purpose aforesaid.

Altho. the undersigned do not deny the right of any officer of the Bank in common with other citizens to receive accomodations yet they deem it imprudent to embark in speculations of the staple commodities of the country, and more especially so when the Bank is not prepared to accomodate all who might desire to obtain its paper

If the Bank at the time refered to had been prepared to discount the notes of all who applied this circumstance would probably have excited no remark, but so soon as the notes of others were rejected the disappointed applicants bitterly complain of favoriteism being extended to bank officers

If there is any one subject of which the people are more easily

[3] George W. Dole was a director of the bank.

[191]

excited than any other—and in regard to which their jealousy never slumbers, it is as to the priveliges and powers of Banks[,] therefore every precaution should be used by those institutions to guard against such charges or at least to furnish them no foundation to rest upon.

The undersigned have not been able to asscertain that the bank has dealt or speculated in lands further than was absolutely necessary for the erection of her Banking houses

The next enquiry relates to the suspended debts of the Bank at the branches of Alton, Galena and Chicago, as the examination in prosecution of this enquiry necessarily involves an exhibition to the undersigned of the transaction of the bank with a number of private individuals and as a publication of their names and accounts would effect no public good they have declined doing so & will only state the general results of the examination

A considerable amount of debt exists at these Branches which at the present is unproductive and must require much time in the collection—although a portion of this debt will in all probability be lost it is not believed that the loss will be sufficiently heavy to empair eventually the capital stock of the Bank

It will be seen by a refference to an exhibit furnished by the Bank that a contingent fund of about 170.000$ has been set apart which the undersigned believe will indemnify the Bank in any losses on her suspended debt and the other debts due the bank and branches are believed to be well secured

In answer to the enquiry what portions of the loans of the bank have been made to bank directors the undersigned refer to a statement made by the officers of the Bank and accompanying this report

The amount due from bank directors was heretofore larger than it now is, and has been reduced by the going out of office of some who were largely indebted, the undersigned do not believe that the liability of the present directors is greater than might be safely extended to other individuals of equal number and responsibility not connected with the Bank

The committee next proceeded to investigate the charge contained in the following portion of the resolution to wit "also the character of the transaction between the acting fund commissioner and the President of the Bank" in the negociation of the Bonds sold to constitute the stock owned by the state in that institution and if the Bonds at or since the time of their purchase by the Bank could not have been sold for cash at or above par and whether any money has been paid in to represent the stock of the state

The answer of the officers of the Bank to this enquiry is that after fruitless efforts to sell the stock at par it was offered to the bank in payment of the subscription of the state stock and was accepted by that institution and that the Bonds have ever since been offered at par but have not been sold

The amount of stock so sold to the Bank was $1765.000 and the sum of 335.000 Dollars was paid in cash making in all $2,000,000.

While it is granted that the sale of the state bonds owned by the bank would have enabled that institution to enlarge her circulation and thereby accomodate more persons it is deemed very questionable whether in the present crisis the stockholders and note holders of the bank are not in a better condition than if the state bonds had been sold for the reason that they can be used to obtain funds either by sale or hypothecation

The next inquiry is "whether the bank has not dealt unfairly in declaring dividends and reporting means as available which are in reality unavailable and in bad Debts"

The question of the propriety or impropriety of dividends of the bank must depend on the amount of its bad debts as compared with its surplus fund and reserved profits.

These latter the officers of the bank have stated on their oaths they believe to equal or exceed the former & the undersigned have no reason to differ from them in opinion on this subject

Some of the committee are aware that their has been a great anxiety with some persons connected with the public works that the dividends should be as large as possible and were fearful that this influence might have operated on the directors but they have no evidence of such a result

The last enquiry which the committee are directed to make is "whether houses connected with some of the principle officers of the Bank have not been accomodated largely to the exclusion of others equaly solvent"

The undersigned feel it to be their duty to state without hesitation that there is not the slightest evidence to support a charge of this character

The undersigned before passing on will offer some reflections upon the causes of the suspension of specie payments by the bank. It will be recollected that when the Banks of Phila. and New York suspended specie payments in 1837, that the western and southern Banks almost simultaneously followed in their train

When the Phila. banks suspended specie payments last fall, many of the western and southern banks also found it necessary to close business. Their is a chain of connexion between the banks of the interior and those of the Atlantic cities which obliges the former to follow the course of the latter and the suspension of the banks located at the center of trade is felt by all the banks in the union

This is not attributable to any organic defects of the institutions themselves but to the irresistable law of trade and exchange which cannot be controaled [*sic*] by country banks

The position of our banks is doubly unfortunate[;] they have not only to guard against the accumulation of their paper in the eastern cities but have also to keep an eye upon Saint Louis, at which point much of the trade of the west centres

When we super-add to those causes the fact, that the funds (mostly gold and silver) of the General Government collected in the land offices in this state have (with the exception of a limited deposite in the branch at Chicago) been transported to and deposited in the banks of Kentucky and the Bank of Missouri. It must therefore be admitted that the banks of this State have had a peculiarly difficult task to perform in keeping up the credit of their paper.

Under this view of the subject unless it is first shewn that our banks had some agency in bringing about the suspension by the Banks of the Atlantic cities in 1837 & '39 your committee perceives but little cause to visit any very heavy denunciations upon our institutions for doing an act which they were urged to by the most imperious necessity

An opinion as to the solvency of the Bank to meet and to pay all demands against it, will no doubt be expected from the committee.

It will be perceived from the statement of the condition of the bank filed herewith, that her entire circulation amounts to $2,786.-315 and that her whole liabilities are $3.924.002.84/100 while she has on hand $2,464,750. of Illinois State Bonds— $2.710.476 76/100 of notes Discounted and due from individuals to the Bank 440,182 10/100 Dollars of money loaned to individuals by the Bank and secured by mortgage on real estate— Bills of Exchange $786.974 89/100 Real Estate 72 600.33/100 Dollars—due from other Banks. 435.624.27/100 dollars due by state of Illinois 141.-089 46/100 notes of other Banks 152.275 dollars— of Gold and Silver Coin 473.869 32/100 dollars making in all 7.677.794 13/100 Dollars this sum your committee deems amply sufficient to indemnify not only note holders & other creditors of the bank but also to secure the State for all the Stock which she owns in the institution and in the event of the bank not being resuscitated your committee apprehend no danger of the state sustaining any loss upon its bank stock

Before closing this report it is but an act of justice due from the undersigned to the officers of the parent bank to state, that they afforded the committee every facility in their power to aid them in a free & full investigation into the condition of the bank and into the conduct of its various officers.

B. MONROE[4] ⎱ of the Sen   of H R   ORLANDO B. FICKLIN,
JNO. D. WOOD ⎰   A. LINCOLN

[4] Byrd Monroe, senator from Coles County; John D. Wood, senator from Washington County; Orlando B. Ficklin, representative from Coles County.

To John T. Stuart[1]

Dear Stuart: Springfield, Jany. 21st. 1840.

A bill bringing on the congressional elections in this state, next summer, has passed the House of Representatives this minute.[2] As I think it will also pass the Senate, I take the earliest moment to advise you of it. I do not think any one of our political friends, wishes to push you off the track.

Anticipating the introduction of this bill, I wrote you, for your feelings on the subject, several weeks since; but have received no answer. It may be, that my letter miscarried; if so, will you, on the receipt of this, write me what you think and feel about the matter.

Nothing new, except I believe I have got our Truett[3] debt secured. I have Truetts note at twelve months, with his brother Myers as surety. Your friend, as ever—   A. LINCOLN

[1] ALS-P, ISLA.
[2] The bill would have changed the date of congressional elections to August, 1840. In 1839 the legislature, because of the census of 1840, had moved the 1840 election forward one year. The Senate tabled the bill.
[3] Henry B. Truett and Myers Truett of Galena, Illinois.

Amendments Introduced in Illinois Legislature
to an Act for Further Prosecution of
the Illinois and Michigan Canal[1]

January 22, 23, 1840

Amend the eighth section by adding there to the following, towit:

"nor upon any contracts except those existing at the passage of this act." *Provided* that contracts which may be transfered from

one contractor to another, without any change in their terms, shall not be construed to be new contracts

& *Provided* that no more than five hundred thousand dollars of said certificates shall at any one time be outstanding.

[1] AD, I-Ar. The first amendment never came to a vote; the second was adopted; but the bill failed to pass.

Remarks in the Illinois Legislature
Concerning the Illinois and Michigan Canal[1]

January 22, 23, 1840

Mr. LINCOLN, from the select committee to which was referred the Canal bill,[2] reported the same back to the House, with the following amendment: "the scrip hereby authorized to be issued, shall be applied to existing contracts."

Mr. LINCOLN said that although he voted for its engrossment before, yet he did it somewhat reluctantly. He was under the impression that the scrip would be paid out for less than its nominal value; but as it was to be paid out for contracts made in view of money, and if paid with scrip at its nominal value, no loss would result therefrom; but on the contrary, the State would make something. Upon the scrip which is now propos[ed, to be issued, . . . would be . . .][3] whereas, we would have to pay interest upon money. Contracts had been made when the prices for labor, provisions, &c., were high; and hence contractors were willing to take scrip, as they would not thereby sustain as much loss as they would, were they to abandon entirely their contracts. He thought that we should lose much by stopping the work on the Canal— that a mutual injury would result to the State by suspending all operations there. It would be, continued Mr. L., very much like stopping a skift in the middle of a river—if it was not going up, it *would* go down. The embankments upon the Canal would be washing away, and the excavations filling up. He, for these reasons, was for the bill as amended; and, in conclusion, would humbly express the hope that it might pass.

Mr. LINCOLN[4] said he had not examined to see what amount of scrip would probably be needed. The principal point in his mind was this, that no body was obliged to take these certificates. It is altogether voluntary on their part, and if they apprehend it will fall on their hands, they will not take it.

Further—the loss, if any there be, will fall on the citizens of that section of the country. This scrip is not going to circulate over an extensive range of country, but will be confined chiefly to the vicinity of the canal. Now we find the representatives of that section of the country are all in favor of the bill. When we propose to protect their interests, they say to us, leave us to take care of ourselves—we are willing to run this risk. And this is reasonable; we must suppose they are competent to protect their own interests, and it is only fair to let them do it.

1 *Sangamo Journal*, January 28, 1840, and *Illinois State Register*, January 29, 1840.

2 A bill providing for the continuation of the Illinois and Michigan Canal.

3 Practically all of one line is cut off top of newspaper at this point.

4 The report continues from the *Illinois State Register*. Daniel T. Moore, Democrat from St. Clair County, had expressed fear that holders of the scrip would lose. Joseph Naper, Democrat from Cook County, thought there was no danger of this.

Bill Introduced in Illinois Legislature
to Authorize Purchase of a House for the Use
of the Governor[1]

[January 24, 1840]

A bill for an act authorizing the purchase of a house for the use of the Governor.

Sec: 1st. Be it enacted by the People of the state of Illinois represented in the General Assembly: That the Auditor of Public Accounts be and he is hereby authorized to purchase a suitable house and lot, within the town of Springfield, for a residence for the Governor of the state, *Provided* the same shall not cost more than eight thousand dollars.

Sec: 2nd. The Auditor shall issue his warrant on the Treasury for the amount agreed on by him for said purchase, in favour of the person or persons of whom said purchase shall have been made.

Sec: 3rd. Before issuing his warrant as aforesaid, the Auditor shall particularly enquire into and ascertain that a clear and unencumbered title to the house and lot so purchased can be made; and moreover shall actually take a conveyance of such title to the Governor of the state of Illinois for the use of the People of said state.

Sec: 4th. Upon the completion of such purchase and conveyance, the Auditor shall notify the Governor thereof; and after one month subsequent to said notice, no allowance for house rent, or traveling expenses shall be made to the Governor.

1 AD, I-Ar. Several amendments to the bill were offered on the second reading, January 29, and the bill and proposed amendments were indefinitely postponed.

Bill Introduced in Illinois Legislature
to Dissolve the Bonds of Matrimony Between
Nathaniel B. and Sarah Martin[1]

[January 25, 1840]

A bill for an act to dissolve the bands of matrimony between Nathaniel B. Martin, and Sarah Martin his wife.

Be it enacted by the people of the state of Illinois represented in the General Assembly: That the bands of matrimony existing between Nathaniel B. Martin and Sarah Martin, his wife, be, and they are hereby forever dissolved.

[1] AD, I-Ar. Lincoln reported the bill on January 25 from the select committee to which Sarah Martin's petition had been referred. Her petition bears minor emendations in Lincoln's hand. The bill passed the House but died in the Senate.

Resolution Introduced in Illinois Legislature
Concerning Election of a Treasurer
of the Board of Canal Commissioners[1]

[January 27, 1840]

Resolved by the House of Representatives (the Senate concurring herein) that the two houses will meet in the Hall of the House of Representatives on tuesday the 28th. Inst. at 2 o'clock P.M and proceed to the election of a Treasurer of the Board of Canal Commissioners.

[1] AD, I-Ar. The resolution was adopted by the House, but the joint session did not concur until February 1, when David Prickett, clerk of the House, was elected treasurer.

Bill Introduced in Illinois Legislature
in Relation to Taking of Depositions
and in Relation to Menard and Logan Counties[1]

[January 28-30, 1840]

A bill for an act relative to the taking of depositions, and to the Collector of Menard county.

Be it enacted by the People of the State of Illinois represented in the General Assembly. That hereafter in any suit at law or in Equity wherein the defendant or defendants shall reside without the limits of this state, or shall have gone without the limits of this state with the intention of removing himself or themselves, or his or their personal property and effects without the limits of the same, and shall have no attorney known to the plaintiff or complainant within the limits of this state, it shall be lawful for the plaintiff or complainant in such suit to take depositions to be used in the same, in the same manner, as is now provided by law, excepting that the notice now required by law to be served on such defendant or defendants shall not be required to be given; *Provided* that in every such case the plaintiff or complainant shall, before taking such depositions, file with the clerk of the court wherein such suit shall be depending the affidavit of himself or some other credible person, stating that he verrily believes that said defendant or defendants resides without the limits of this state, or has gone beyond the limits of this state with the intention of removing himself, or his personal property or effects beyond the limits of the same, and has no known attorney residing in this state

Sec: 2nd. That the Collector of Menard county be authorized to collect all taxes now due for the year 1839 1839 [*sic*] from the inhabitants of, or on real estate situated within that portion of Sangamon county, which lies within the following boundaries, towit: Begining at the South West corner of Section Three in Township Seventeen North of Range Six West, thence North four miles by the surveys; thence East ten miles by the surveys; thence South two miles by the surveys; thence West nine miles by the surveys; thence South two miles by the surveys; thence West one mile by the surveys to the begining.[2]

Sec. 3rd. That said collection shall be made in accordance with the assessment heretofore made under the authority of Menard county; and said collector shall pay over the state revenue collected in said district to the state as in other cases; and shall pay one half colle[c]ted therefrom, for county purposes into the county Treasury of Sangamon county, and the other half, into the county Treasury of Menard county.

[1] AD, I-Ar. This bill was a revision of the bill introduced by Lincoln on December 10, 1839 (*vide supra*). In addition to the portion of the revised bill given here as written by Lincoln, other amendments, not Lincoln's, were adopted. Lincoln's amendment of the title, after the bill's passage on January 30, was adopted as follows: "An act in relation to taking depositions, and in relation to Menard and Logan counties." The original document has the first two sentences marked for deletion.

[2] Section two of the present bill constituted the original bill introduced on December 10, 1839.

To John T. Stuart[1]

Dear Stuart: Springfield, Jany. 29th. 1840

You recollect I mentioned to you that I had secured our Truett debt by taking a new note with Myers as security. You also recollect that the old note was in your individual name, and was sent to Gilbreath at Dixon's.[2] Myers came through Springfield and left the new note, and I sent an order to Truett[3] on Gilbreath, to deliver up the old note, which Gilbreath refuses to do, as appears by the enclosed letter from Truett, upon the ground that *you*, and not I, have control of the matter. Will you, on the receipt of this, immediately send an order to Truett at Dixon's on Gilbreath for the old note, framing it so that Truett will have to pay all cost and expense that may have accrued, before he gets the note. Dont neglect this, because Truett, as you will see by his letter, is verry anxious about it.

The outlines of things here are—

Internal Improvement down—

Canal down—

Bank up—

Harrison going ahead—

Your friend as ever
A. LINCOLN

1 ALS-P, ISLA.

2 Probably Dixon's Ferry, Illinois. Gilbreath has not been further identified.

3 Henry B. Truett and Myers Truett (*vide supra*, Lincoln to John T. Stuart, January 21, 1840).

Amendment Introduced in Illinois Legislature
to an Act in Relation to Promissory Notes[1]

[January 30, 1840]

Provided that nothing herein shall be construed to legalize the taking of more than twelve per cent interest per annum in any case whatever.

1 AD, I-Ar. Lincoln's amendment was adopted and the bill passed the House on January 30, but died in the Senate.

Remarks in Illinois Legislature
Concerning an Act to Modify the System of Internal Improvements[1]

January 30, 1840

Mr. LINCOLN said, he thought this a question of sufficient importance to justify this last effort in behalf of a proposition, to save something to the State, from the general wreck. It was very true that similar propositions had before been voted down in this House by large majorities; but it might be a returning sense of justice, would induce this House to acknowledge, upon this last opportunity, that at least some portion of our Internal Improvements should be carried on. That after the immense debt, we have incurred in carrying these works almost to completion, at least one work calculated to yield something towards defraying its expense, should be finished and put in operation. Every body acknowledged that this much, if no more, should be done; and why not come up to the question here, with the same candor, that we do out of doors?

[1] *Sangamo Journal*, February 7, 1840. Lincoln's remarks were in reply to John J. Hardin's observation that he hoped the bill "would be pressed upon the attention of the House no longer."

Campaign Circular from Whig Committee[1]

January [31?], 1840

CONFIDENTIAL.

To Messrs. ——

Gentlemen:—In obedience to a resolution of the Whig State Convention,[2] we have appointed you the Central Whig Committee of your county. The trust confided to you will be one of watchfulness and labor: but we do hope the glory of having contributed to the overthrow of the corrupt powers that now control our beloved country, will be a sufficient reward for the time and labor you will devote to it. Our whig brethren throughout the Union have met in convention,[3] and after due deliberation and mutual concessions have elected candidates for the Presidency and Vice presidency, not only worthy of our cause, but worthy of the support of every true patriot, who would have our country redeemed, and her institutions honestly and faithfully administered.

To overthrow the *trained bands* that are opposed to us, whose salaried officers are ever on the watch, and whose misguided followers are ever ready to obey their smallest commands, every Whig must not only know his duty, but must firmly resolve, whatever of time and labor it may cost, boldly and *faithfully* to do it.

Our intention is to organize the whole State, so that every Whig can be brought to the polls in the coming presidential contest. We

[1] *Illinois State Register*, February 21, 1840. An inferior printing appears in the *Sangamo Journal* of the same date. Although bearing the January date, as printed in the *Register*, the circular seems not to have been put in the mail before February 4. The editor of the Democratic *Register* was responsible for the italicization of certain passages.　　[2] Held in Springfield, October 7-8, 1839.
[3] At Harrisburg, Pennsylvania, December 4, 1839.

cannot do this, however, without your co-operation; and as we do our duty, so we shall expect you to do yours[.]

After due deliberation, the following is the plan of organization, and the duties required of each county committee.

1st. To divide their county into small districts, and to appoint in each a sub-committee, whose duty it shall be to make a perfect list of all the voters in their respective districts, and to ascertain with certainty for whom they will vote. If they meet with men who are doubtful as to the man they will support, such voters should be designated in separate lines, with the name of the man they will probably support.

2nd. It will be the duty of said sub-committee to keep a CONSTANT WATCH on the DOUBTFUL VOTERS, and from time to time have them TALKED TO by those IN WHOM THEY HAVE THE MOST CONFIDENCE, and also to place in their hands such documents as will enlighten and influence them.

3d. It will also be their duty to report to you, at least once a month, the progress they are making, and on election days see that every Whig is brought to the polls.

4th. The sub-committees should be appointed immediately; and by the last of April, at least, they should make their first report.

5th. On the first of each month hereafter, we shall expect to hear from you. After the first report of your sub-committees, unless there should be found a great many doubtful voters, you can tell pretty accurately the manner in which your county will vote. In each of your letters to us, you will state the number of certain votes, both for and against us, as well as the number of doubtful votes, with your opinion of the manner in which they will be cast.

6th. When we hear from all the counties, we shall be able to tell with *similar* accuracy, the political complexion of the State. This information will be forwarded to you as soon as received.

7th. Enclosed is a prospectus for a newspaper[4] to be published until after the Presidential election. It will be SUPERINTENDED BY OURSELVES, and every Whig in the State MUST take it. It will be published so low that every one can afford it. YOU MUST RAISE A FUND AND FORWARD US FOR EXTRA COPIES—every county ought to send FIFTY or ONE HUNDRED DOLLARS,—and the copies will be forwarded to you for distribution among our POLITICAL OPPONENTS. The paper will be devoted exclusively to the *great cause* in which

[4] *The Old Soldier*, edited by the Whig State Central Committee, was printed by Simeon Francis and Company, publishers of the *Sangamo Journal*. The first number appeared February 1, and eighteen issues appeared before the November election. On February 17 *Old Hickory*, the Democratic campaign paper, made its initial appearance.

we are engaged. Procure subscriptions and forward them to us immediately.⁵

8th. Immediately after any election in your county, you must inform us of its results; and as early as possible after any general election, we will give you the like information.

9th. A Senator in Congress is to be elected by our next Legislature. Let no local interests divide you, but select candidates that can succeed.

10th. Plan of operations will of course be CONCEALED FROM EVERY ONE except OUR GOOD FRIENDS, who of right ought to know them.⁶

Trusting much in our good cause, the strength of our candidates, and the determination of the Whigs every where, to do their duty, we go to the work of organization in this State, confident of success[.] We have the numbers, and if properly organized and exerted, with the gallant HARRISON at our head, we shall meet our foes, and conquer them in all parts of the Union.

Address your letters to Dr. A. G. Henry.

A. G. HENRY,	E. D. BAKER,
R. F. BARRETT,	J. F. SPEED.⁷
A. LINCOLN,	

⁵ On February 25, Judge Thomas C. Browne of the Illinois Supreme Court wrote to Henry Eddy that *The Old Soldier* had eight thousand subscribers, and that he expected twenty thousand (transcript, Eddy MSS., IHi).

⁶ The object of secrecy was not very well achieved. The Democratic press gave wide and somewhat exaggerated publicity to the circular within a few weeks. The Whig committee's secrecy seems to have been intended to take the opposition by surprise. The Democrats had used a tight state organization to such good purpose that the Whigs were driven to it in self-defense. See the communication "To the Readers of the Old Soldier," February 28, 1840 (*infra*).

⁷ Of these Whig leaders not previously identified, Dr. Richard F. Barrett was a physician who had migrated to Sangamon County from Green County, Kentucky, in 1831-1832. Joshua F. Speed, also a Kentuckian, was a merchant of Springfield whose close friendship with Lincoln had begun upon Lincoln's removal to Springfield from New Salem in 1837.

Communication to the Readers of
*The Old Soldier*¹

February 28, 1840

TO THE READERS OF THE OLD SOLDIER.

Some time since the undersigned sent a Circular² to particular individuals in several Counties of this State, urging them to use their best exertions to organize, and form into "battle array" the

¹ *Sangamo Journal,* February 28, 1840.   ² *Vide supra,* January [31?] 1840.

friends of Gen. Harrison, for the approaching contest. This Circular we marked "Confidential." We did so, because we knew, that nothing short of the utmost secrecy, on the part of even our own friends, could enable it to "clear the clutches" of the Post Office, and reach any tolerable portion of its points of destination. As we anticipated, it has been pirated from the mail, and published in the Van Buren papers. Of course, all copies of it, which have not reached their addresses, will not *now* be permitted to do so. We therefore urge upon our friends in those counties, which this circular has never reached, (if the paper containing this article shall ever reach them) to go to work and organize themselves in the most efficient manner, for routing the enemies of the country and of Gen. Harrison, from the councils of the nation.

The Van Buren papers raise many objections to the Circular in question. They affect the greatest horror, that it should have been marked "Confidential." Had they not better reserve their horror for the contemplation of the fact, that *their friends* "robbed the mail" to get hold of it? And does not the fact that they did thus rob the mail, justify, nay, even imperiously require, every honest man to use every possible precaution, to enable his communications to pass unembezzled through the post offices, to their destination?

But, again, it is objected that we, the undersigned, are the editors of "The Old Soldier," as it is urged appears from this confidential Circular. This assumption the Circular does not warrant. In it, we say "the Old Soldier" will be *superintended* by us. Of course we are responsible for its contents; and we desire to shun no part of the responsibility, arising from its management. But while we say this, we also say to the friends of Gen. Harrison every where, that they, as well as we, are the editors of "the Old Soldier." And we now invite them—particularly those who have seen Gen. Harrison, where cowards dared not show their heads—where storms of "leaden rain and iron hail" carried death and desolation in their course—where his erect figure, stationed on the loftiest rampart, and seen from every part of the theatre of action; and his voice, rising in trumpet tones above the roaring of the death-dealing tempest,—gave "form and spirit to the war"; them, we invite to aid us in filling its columns with such "burning truths" and "confounding arguments" as may sear the eye-balls, and stun the ears of the Old hero's thousand-tongued calumniators.

What credit or discredit "the Old Soldier" may derive from *our names*, is not for us to determine. *We* have not thrust those *names* upon the public; but now that our enemies have, we only say: "Then they are; let those assail them who can." Upon the authority of those names, (whether that authority be good or bad,) we assure the readers of "the Old Soldier," that nothing shall appear in its columns, *as facts*, which we do not, on the fullest investigation in our power to make, believe to be true. No *"vile falsehood"* shall enter them. It is our intention, that our friends every where may, without fear of successful contradiction, repeat whatever they may find, *stated as a fact*, in the columns of "the Old Soldier."

But the Van Buren papers object to the friends of Gen. Harrison organizing. We urge that organization; and we insist that it is not for our opponents to inveigh against it. *They* set us the example of organization; and we, in self defence, are driven into it. If *they* now wish *disbanding*, let them again set the example. Let them *disband* their double-drilled-army of "forty thousand office holders," a part of whose regular tactics it is, to pilfer letters and papers from the mails, lest the old soldiers, who have fought and bled with Gen. Harrison, may all learn that he is now a candidate for the Presidency.

With our own friends, we justify—we urge—organization on the score of necessity. A disbanded yeomanry cannot successfully meet an organized soldiery.

The old soldiers of the war of 1812-13-and '14, remember, that previous to that war, there was no organization amongst them; but that, immediately on learning that an organized foe was invading their land, they, too, organized—met—conquered—killed and drove the foe beyond the "world of waters." To those old soldiers we say—An organized army of office-holders is now fitting out an expedition against your old commander. They are coming armed— (not with bristling steel, because that bedazzles their eyes—not with powder and balls, because the smell of sulphur offends their nostrils, but) with falsehood, slander, and detraction, upon the characters of yourselves and your chieftain, established in the hard and bloody conflicts with your country's invading enemies. That army too, must be met. Organization must again be had. We, your sons and younger brothers, will form the rank and file; you shall be the generals, and commanders-in-chief. Thus organized, we will meet, conquer and disperse Gen. Harrison's and the country's enemies, and place him in the chair, now disgraced by their effeminate and luxury-loving chief.

A. G. HENRY,	J. F. SPEED,
R. F. BARRETT,*	A. LINCOLN.
E. D. BAKER,	

*Dr. BARRETT having taken the office of Fund Commissioner, does not think it proper for him to longer participate in the superintendence of the "Old Soldier," and he, therefore, withdraws from it.[3]

[3] Footnote in the source.

To John T. Stuart[1]

Springfield, March 1, 1840.

Dear Stuart: I have never seen the prospects of our party so bright in these parts as they are now. We shall carry this county by a larger majority than we did in 1836, when you ran against May.[2] I do not think my prospects individually are very flattering, for I think it is probable I shall not be permitted to be a candidate; but the party ticket will succeed triumphantly. Subscriptions to the "Old Soldier" pour in without abatement. This morning I took from the post-office a letter from Dubois[3] inclosing the names of sixty subscribers; and on carrying it to Francis, I found he had received one hundred and forty more from other quarters by the same day's mail. That is but an average specimen of every day's receipts. Yesterday Douglas, having chosen to consider himself insulted by something in the "Journal," undertook to cane Francis in the street.[4] Francis caught him by the hair and jammed him back against a market-cart, where the matter ended by Francis being pulled away from him. The whole affair was so ludicrous that Francis and everybody else (Douglas excepted) have been laughing about it ever since.

I send you the names of some of the Van Buren men who have come out for Harrison about town, and suggest that you send them some documents: Moses Coffman (he let us appoint him a delegate yesterday), Aaron Coffman, George Gregory, H. M. Briggs, —— Johnson[5] (at Birchall's book-store), Michael Glynn, —— Armstrong[6] (not Hosea, nor Hugh, but a carpenter), Thomas Hunter, Moses Pilcher (he was always a Whig, and deserves attention), Matthew Crowder, Jr., Greenberry Smith, John Fagan, George Fagan, William Fagan (these three fell out with us about Early, and are doubtful now),[7] John Cartmel, Noah Rickard, John Rickard, Walter Marsh (the foregoing should be addressed at Springfield). Also send some to Solomon Miller and John Auth at Saulsbury;[8] also to Charles Harper, Samuel Harper, and B. C. Harper; and T. J. Scroggins, John Scroggins,[9] at [Mount] Pulaski, Logan County.

Speed says he wrote you what Jo. Smith[10] said about you as he passed here. We will procure the names of some of his people here and send them to you before long. Speed also says you must not fail to send us the New York journal he wrote for some time since. Evan Butler[11] is jealous that you never send your compliments to him. You must not neglect him next time. Your friend, as ever,

A. LINCOLN.

[206]

1 NH, I, 148-50.   2 William L. May, Democrat.
3 Jesse Kilgore Dubois, state representative from Lawrence County.
4 Simeon Francis, editor.   5 J. H. Johnson, partner of Caleb Birchall.
6 John Armstrong.
7 William Fagan, a Kentuckian who settled on a farm near Springfield in 1831, and his two sons, John, who was Lincoln's age, and George, who was a few years younger. Probably Lincoln refers to the defense by Stuart & Lincoln which brought about the acquittal of Henry B. Truett for the murder of Dr. Jacob M. Early on March 7, 1838.   8 Salisbury, Illinois.   9 Thomas J. Scroggin.
10 Joseph Smith, the founder of Mormonism.
11 Evan T. Butler, deputy circuit clerk, Sangamon County.

Notice of an Election[1]

March 18, 1840

Notice is hereby given,

THAT in pursuance of law an election will be held in the City of Springfield, on the third Monday of April next, for the election of one Mayor of the City, and one Alderman from each Ward.

The election in the First Ward shall be held at the house of W. W. Watson.

The election in the Second Ward shall be held at the house of Michael Glynn.

The election in the Third Ward shall be held at the Court Room.

The election in the Fourth Ward shall be held at the American House.

Should the city charter not be accepted by the citizens, the above notice will be null and void.

The polls for said elections will be opened at 8 A. M. and closed at 12 M.

Springfield, March 18, 1840.

	P. C. CANEDY,	P. C. LATHAM,
	J. WHITNEY,	A. LINCOLN,
SIMEON FRANCIS, Clerk.	J. KLEINE,	Trustees.

1 *Sangamo Journal,* March 20, 1840.

Notice of an Election[1]

March 18, 1840

Notice is hereby given,

THAT, in pursuance of law, an election will be held at the Court Room, in the town of Springfield, on the first Monday of April next for the election of five Trustees for said town.

Also, that in pursuance of a law of this State, approved February 3d, 1840, incorporating the city of Springfield, the votes of the citizens of Springfield, will be received on the same day at the same place, as aforesaid, for the adoption or rejection of the aforesaid city charter or law incorporating the town of Springfield.

The polls for said elections shall be opened at 8 A.M. and closed at 2 P.M.

Springfield, March 18, 1840.

	P. C. CANNEDY,	A. LINCOLN,
	J. WHITNEY,	P. C. LATHAM,
SIMEON FRANCIS, Clerk.	J. KLEINE,	Trustees.

[1] *Sangamo Journal*, March 20, 1840.

To John T. Stuart[1]

Dear Stuart: Springfield, March 26 1840

In relation to the Kinzie matter,[2] I can say no more than this, that the check was taken from the Bank by you, and on the same day you made a note in our memorandum book, stating you had sent it by mail to Kinzie; but there is no memorandum concerning it at Irwin's.[3] Kinzie has ceased writing about it, and consequently I have some hope that he has received it.

We have had a convention for nominating candidates in this county. Baker[4] was put on the track for the Senate, and Bradford,[5] Brown[6] of the Island Grove, Josiah Francis, Darnielle,[7] & I for the House. Ninian[8] was verry much hurt at not being nominated; but he has become tolerably well reconciled. I was much, verry much, wounded myself at his being left out. The fact is, the country delegates made the nominations as they pleased; and they *pleased* to make them all from the country, except Baker & me, whom they supposed necessary to make stump speeches. Old Col. Elkin[9] is nominated for Sheriff. That's right.

The Locos have no candidates on the track yet, except Dick Taylor[10] for the Senate. Last saturday he made a speech, and May[11] answered him. The way May let the wind out of him, was a perfect wonder. The court room was verry full, and neither you nor I ever saw a crowd in this county so near all one side, and all feeling so good before. You will see a short account of it in the Journal.

LINCOLN

Japh. Ball[12] has come out for Harrison. Ain't that a caution?

[1] ALS, owned by heirs of Stuart Brown.
[2] Robert A. Kinzie. See n. 2, letter to Stuart, *supra*, December 23, 1839.
[3] Robert Irwin & Co., of Springfield, Illinois. [4] Edward D. Baker.
[5] James M. Bradford. [6] James N. Brown. [7] John Darneille.
[8] Ninian W. Edwards. [9] William F. Elkin. [10] Edmund Dick Taylor.
[11] William L. May. [12] Japhet A. Ball.

To Richard F. Barrett[1]

Dear Doctor: Springfield, Ills. April 17th. 1840

Do not fail to procure a copy of the *Journal* of the New York Convention of 1821. I sometimes see the *Debates* of the New York Convention refered to, and I am not sure whether the *Journal & Debates* are one & the same, or distinct. If they are distinct, try to procure both. I would not miss your getting them for a hundred dollars. If they can not be found in New York City,[2] they certainly can in Albany. I would be glad if you could also procure the Journal of the New York Senate for the fall session of 1812.

If you get the Journals mentioned, bring them with you on your return, unless you can send them sooner by some entirely safe conveyance.

I attended the Carlinville & Bellville meetings and find things going on swimingly in both places.

The City Charter is accepted by 226 to 121. Nothing else new. Write me on the receipt of this. Your friend, as ever

A. LINCOLN

P.S. Your Brother[3] has been nominated for the Legislature by the Locos, after all. Whether he will accept or not is not yet certain; but I presume he will. A.L.

1 ALS, The Rosenbach Company, Philadelphia and New York.
2 Barrett was probably in New York on state business as Fund Commissioner, to which office he had been elected by the legislature on February 1, 1840.
3 James W. Barrett.

Bill to Sangamon County[1]

[May, 1840?]

County of Sangamon
            To Stuart & Lincoln Dr.
  To use of Room for juries from
  May 1839 to May 1840 $36.00

1 AD, IHi.

Speech at Tremont, Illinois[1]

May 2, 1840

Immediately after dinner, the large Court House was filled to overflowing, and the debate was opened by Mr. Lincoln, who after some general and appropriate remarks concerning the design and object of all Governments, drew a vivid picture of our prosperous and happy condition previous to the time of the war which was waged against the U.S. Bank, the constitutionality, as well as the great utility of which he vindicated in a most triumphant manner. He next turned his attention to the Sub-Treasury, the hideous deformity and injurious effects of which were exposed in a masterly style. He then reviewed the political course of Mr. Van Buren, and especially his votes in the New York Convention in allowing Free Negroes the right of suffrage, and his Janus-faced policy in relation to the war. In this part of his speech Mr. Lincoln was particularly felicitous, and the frequent and spontaneous bursts of applause from the People, gave evidence that their hearts were with him. He related many highly amusing anecdotes which convulsed the house with laughter; and concluded his eloquent address with a successful vindication of the civil and military reputation of the Hero of Tippecanoe.

[1] *Sangamo Journal*, May 15, 1840.

To Jonathan G. Randall[1]

Jonathan G. Randall,   Springfield, Ill.,
Rushville, Ill.   June 16, 1840.

My Dear Sir—Your son Richard has just told me of his great loss. The rascally Whigs, through a mistake, took his trunk containing all his clothes off to Chicago, and his heart is almost broken. Make him up some new ones just as you know he needs and make his heart glad. Yours respectfully   A. LINCOLN.

[1] Printed by Howard F. Dyson, "Lincoln in Rushville," *Transactions of the Illinois State Historical Society For the Year 1903*, Publication No. 8. Illinois State Historical Library (1904), p. 226. According to Dyson, Richard Randall was apprenticed to Simeon Francis in the *Sangamo Journal* printing office. A delegation of Chicago Whigs had stored their baggage in the office during a convention which coincided with young Richard's first days in Springfield, and on departing took Richard's trunk by mistake.

Receipt to John Hogan,
Commissioner of Public Works[1]

Received Springfield June 17th 1840 of John Hogan Comr of the Board of Public Works, One Hundred and fifty Dollars in full for the above order of the Board Pub Works.

$150.   SCHUYLER STRONG
                                          A. LINCOLN

1 D, I-Ar. The receipt appears on the bottom of an order by William Prentiss, Secretary of the Board of Public Works, directing that one hundred dollars be allowed to Strong and fifty dollars to Lincoln for professional services rendered the board. Lincoln's name was signed, apparently, by Strong, a Springfield attorney with whom we infer Lincoln must have collaborated. The nature of the services has not been discovered. A similar document may be found in Auditor's records, State of Illinois.

To William G. Anderson[1]

W. G. Anderson   Lawrenceville, Oct. 31st. 1840.

Dear Sir   Your note of yesterday is received.[2] In the difficulty between us, of which you speak, you say you think I was the aggressor. I do not think I was. You say my "words imported insult." I meant them as a fair set-off to your own statements, and not otherwise; and in that light alone I now wish you to understand them. You ask for my "present" feelings on the subject." I entertain no unkind feeling to you, and none of any sort upon the subject, except a sincere regret that I permitted myself to get into such an altercation. Yours, &c   A. LINCOLN

1 ALS, THi. William G. Anderson, Democrat; representative, Wabash County, 1832, and Lawrence County 1842, 1844.

2 This letter is also in the library of the Tennessee Historical Society. The background of the altercation is obscure. Lincoln was actively campaigning for the Whig ticket in the southern counties of Illinois during the latter half of October. Doubtless in a political discussion on October 28, sharp words passed between the two partisans, for Anderson wrote as follows:

A. Lincoln Esqr.   Lawrenceville, Oct. 30– 1840–

Dr. sir: On our first meeting on Wednesday last, a difficulty in words, ensued between us, which I deem it my duty to notice further. I think you were the aggressor. Your words imported insult; and whether you meant them as such is for you to say. You will therefore please inform me on this point and if you designed to offend me, please communicate to me your present feelings on the subject, and whether you persist in the stand you took. Your obt. servt.

W. G. ANDERSON

Resolution Introduced in Illinois Legislature[1]

November 24, 1840

Resolved, That the Clerk of this House inform the Senate that they have met, elected Wm. Lee D. Ewing their Speaker, John Calhoun their principal Clerk, George Davis their Assistant Clerk, Robert Smith their Engrossing and Enrolling Clerk, Wm. C. Murphy principal Door keeper, and Benjamin Roberts Assistant Door-keeper, and are now ready to proceed to Legislative business.

1 *House Journal*, Twelfth General Assembly, First Session, p. 7.

Remarks in Illinois Legislature
on Printing of Governor's Message[1]

November 26, 1840

Mr. Lincoln said he had moved for the ayes and noes on this motion to print 8,000 copies, from a higher consideration than the saving of 30 or 40 dollars, which the member from Cook [Ebenezer Peck] had said would be the *only* additional expense. He would grant that 30 or 40 dollars were not worth quarreling about. But when we reflected, that if we now quarrel about 40 dollars, and it is nevertheless allowed, would not the presumption be very strong, that hereafter, many such sums, will be allowed without a quarrel, and without objection.

Some experience in this matter had convinced him that it was altogether useless to print so much as we had even been in the habit of doing. He would appeal to the experience of every member who had served in the Legislature if one half of them were ever distributed. No sir; from the time they are printed, until the end of the session, they can be found every where in places nameable and unnameable—in short, every where, but amongst the people.

[1] *Sangamo Journal,* November 27, 1840.

Remarks in Illinois Legislature
Concerning Election Frauds[1]

November 28, 1840

Mr. Lincoln said without granting for a moment the truth of any of the gentleman's charges and surmises, from Gallatin yet he was willing for the purposes of his Resolution, to assume that all these stupendous frauds of which the gentleman had been speaking, had been committed; and if so it showed the necessity of the adoption of the Resolution offered by himself. If it was a fact that Legislative action was necessary to protect the elective franchise from abuse in this state, he was willing to go as far as any,—and to provide any punishment within the bounds of humanity, for those who could abuse such a right. It was for that reason he had submitted his resolution. He was afraid of no investigation that might be instituted into the recent election in this state, for himself or his friends. But he could see no good that could result from such an investigation as that proposed by the gentleman. He had every reason to believe that all this hue and cry about frauds, was entirely groundless, and raised for other than honest purposes.

[212]

As to the instance which the gentleman had given of the Steamboat on the Wabash river,[2] he would state that he was near the Wabash at the time and place mentioned by the gentleman, and after making diligent inquiry for a Steam Boat, could hear of none. Again, he believed as much fraud had been charged to have taken place in Sangamon county as any where else—he was willing for the purpose of testing the truth and character of these charges, that a special investigation should be instituted into the election in this county, that every vote should be scrutinized and the result, whatever it might be should be taken as conclusive as to whether these charges were well founded or not. This investigation would cost the State but little;—it would be here, where we had every facility for enquiring into the facts, without expense, and here too where the greatest frauds are alleged to have been perpetrated, and surely no gentleman who was honest in the belief of these frauds, could object to the proposition.

[1] Quincy *Whig*, December 12, 1840. These remarks occurred during the debate on Lincoln's resolution (*vide supra*), which John A. McClernand of Gallatin County moved to strike out and replace with a somewhat different resolution.

[2] One of several instances of election fraud narrated by McClernand concerned a steamboat which plied up and down the Wabash voting a large number of people at various towns.

Resolution Introduced in Illinois Legislature on Election Frauds[1]

[November 28, 1840]

Resolved, that so much of the Governors Message as relates to fraudulent voting, and other fraudulent practices at elections, be refered to the committee on elections, with instructions to said committee to prepare and report to this House, a Bill for such an act as may, in their judgement, afford the greatest possible protection of the elective franchise, against all frauds of all sorts whatever.

[1] AD, I-Ar. Lincoln's resolution was amended by John A. McClernand, representative from Gallatin County, to refer the investigation to a joint select committee instead of the committee on elections, and was adopted as amended.

Resolution Introduced in Illinois Legislature Concerning Teachers' Examinations[1]

[December 2, 1840]

Resolved, that the Committee on Education be instructed to enquire into the expediency of providing by law for the examination, as to their qualifications, of persons offering themselves as School-teachers, and that no teacher shall receive any part of the Public School Funds, who shall not have successfully passed such examination; and that they report by Bill or otherwise.

[1] AD, I-Ar. Several attempts to amend failed, and the resolution was adopted as written. This became Section 81 of the act organizing and maintaining common schools as ultimately passed. (See *Laws of Illinois*, 1841, pp. 259-87.)

Remarks in Illinois Legislature Concerning Petition of Norman H. Purple[1]

December 4, 1840

Mr. LINCOLN moved that the reports[2] be referred to a committee of the whole House, and that the House do now resolve itself into committee of the whole on the subject. . . . Mr. LINCOLN considered the question of the highest importance, whether an individual had a right to sit in this House or not. The course he should propose would be to take up the evidence and decide upon the evidence and decide upon the facts seriatim. . . .

Mr. DRUMMOND[3] was opposed to taking up: he wished for time to investigate the matter thoroughly. . . .

[Mr. LINCOLN said it would afford him pleasure to oblige his friend from Joe Davies, (Mr. Drummond) but he thought his objections to taking up the matter now, were not well founded. His objection was, that he had not heard the testimony. This is the very reason why we should now go into the testimony—we should go into it like a jury without prepossessions, and be the better prepared to arrive at correct conclusions from the testimony. The gentleman had deprecated party feeling. He confessed he had this much feeling about it, honestly. The gentleman who held his seat, was a political friend of his, and if, after an investigation, it is shown that he is fairly the representative, he should feel gratified. But he did not believe that his mind would be swayed by party feeling, from deciding honestly and justly in this case. The sooner we could decide this matter, the better—there was less party excitement now than there would be to-morrow, and less to-morrow, than there would be the day after.][4]

Mr. LINCOLN thought that the question had better be gone into now. In courts of law Jurors were required to decide on evidence without previous study or examination. They were required to know nothing of the subject untill the evidence was laid before them for their immediate decision. He thought that the heat of party would be augmented by delay.

The Speaker called Mr. L. to order as being irrelevant no mention had been made of party-heat.

Mr. DRUMMOND said he had spoken only of debate.

Mr. LINCOLN asked what caused the heat, if it was not party? Mr. L. concluded by urging that the question would be decided now better than hereafter, and he thought with less heat and excitement.

1 *Illinois State Register,* December 11, 1840.

2 Partisanship split the select committee into a majority (Democrat) reporting in favor of Norman H. Purple (Democrat) and a minority (Whig) reporting in favor of William J. Phelps (Whig). Phelps had won over Purple by a slim majority of seven votes. Purple's contest of the election hinged on a claim that fifteen illegal votes had been cast for Phelps, whereas only eight illegal votes had been cast for Purple. Also, Purple maintained that two of his would-be supporters had been rejected at the polls without proper cause. These two votes provided the margin of victory for Purple, upon which the Democratic majority report sought to seat him in place of Phelps. The upshot of the contest was that Phelps retained his seat and the testimony in the case was ordered to be printed.

3 Thomas Drummond, Whig, Jo Daviess County.

4 *Sangamo Journal,* December 8, 1840. The *Journal* report is less adequate than the report taken from the *Register* except for this paragraph which gives Lincoln's argument somewhat more in detail.

Remarks in Illinois Legislature
Amending a Bill Providing Interest on State Debt[1]

December 4, 1840

Mr. LINCOLN moved to strike out the bill and amendment and insert the following:

AN ACT providing for the payment of interest on the State debt.

SEC. 1st. Be it enacted by the people of the State of Illinois, represented in the General Assembly, That the Governor be authorized and required to issue, from time to time, such an amount of State bonds, to be called the "Illinois Interest Bonds," as may be absolutely necessary for the payment of the interest upon the lawful debts of the State, contracted before the passage of this act.

SEC. 2d Said bonds shall bear interest at the rate of   per cent annum, payable half yearly at   and be reimbursable in   years from their respective issuings.

SEC. 3d. That the State's portion of the tax hereafter arising from all lands which were not taxable in the year one thousand eight hundred and forty, is hereby set apart as an exclusive fund for the payment of interest on the said "Illinois Interest Bonds";

1 *Sangamo Journal,* December 11, 1840. The House was sitting as a committee of the whole on a bill and amendments to provide for the interest on the public debt.

and the faith of the State is hereby pledged, that said fund shall be applied to that object and to no other, except at any time there should be a surplus, in which case such surplus shall become a part of the general funds of the Treasury.

SEC. 4th. That hereafter the sum of thirty cents for each hundred dollars' worth of all taxable property shall be paid into the State Treasury; and no more than forty cents for each hundred dollars worth of such taxable property shall be levied and collected for county purposes.

Mr. LINCOLN said he submitted this proposition with great diffidence. He had felt his share of the responsibility devolving upon us in the present crisis, and after revolving in his mind every scheme which seemed to afford the least prospect of relief, he submitted this as the result of his own deliberations. The details of the bill might be imperfect, but he relied upon the correctness of its general features. By the plan proposed in the original bill, of hypothecating our bonds, he was satisfied we could not get along more than two or three months before some other step would be necessary—another session would have to be called, and new provisions made.

It might be objected that these bonds would not be saleable, and the money could not be raised in time. He was no financier, but he believed these bonds thus secured, would be equal to the best in market. A perfect security was provided for the interest, and it was this characteristic that inspired confidence and made bonds saleable. If there was any distrust, it could not be because enough had not been promised; it must be because our means of fulfilling our promises were distrusted. He believed it would have the effect to raise our other bonds in market. There was another objection to this plan, which applied to the original bill, and that was as to impropriety of borrowing money to pay interest on borrowed money —that we are hereby paying compound interest. To this he would reply, that if it were a fact that our population and wealth were increasing in a ratio greater than the increased interest hereby incurred, then this was not a good objection. If our increasing means would justify us in deferring to a future time the resort to taxation, then we had better pay compound interest, than resort to taxation now. He was satisfied that, by a direct tax now, money enough could not be collected to pay our accruing interest. The bill proposed to provide in this way for interest not otherwise provided for. It was not intended to apply to those bonds, for the interest on which, a security had already been provided. He hoped the House would seriously consider the proposition. He had no pride in its success, as a measure of his own, but submitted it to the wisdom of the House, with the hope, that if there was any thing objectionable in it, it would be pointed out and amended.[2]

Mr. LINCOLN replied at considerable length, and repeated his former arguments in favor of the amendment offered by himself. In conclusion, Mr. L. said that his plan had been termed an expedient. He considered this an unfortunate expression for those who advocated the original bill. That [was?] emphatically an expedient—a mere shift, which could but answer a temporary purpose, and might lead to further difficulty.[3]

Mr. Lincoln went into the reasons which appeared to him to render this plan preferable to that of hypothecating the State bonds. By this course we could get along till the next meeting of the Legislature, which was of great importance. To the objection which might be urged that, these interest bonds could not be cashed, he replied, that if our other bonds could, much more could these which offered a perfect security, a fund being irrevocably set aside to provide for their redemption. To another objection, that we should be paying compound interest he would reply, that the rapid growth and increase of our resources was in so great a ratio as to outstrip the difficulty; that his object was to do the best that could be done in the present emergency; all agreed that the faith of the State must be preserved; this plan appeared to him preferable to an hypothecation of bonds, which would have to be redeemed and the interest paid. How this was to be done he could not see; therefore he had after turning the matter over in every way devised this measure, which would carry us on till the next Legislature.[4]

[2] At this point the argument for and against Lincoln's proposal was taken over by other members of the House.

[3] Further discussion by other members followed until John J. Hardin moved that the committee rise, report progress, and ask leave to sit again, which was agreed to.

[4] *Illinois State Register*, December 11, 1840. This report covers the same series of remarks as the more detailed account in the *Journal*, but is reproduced for the slight additional details of what Lincoln said. On December 7 Lincoln introduced the revised bill (*vide infra*), and further advocated his measure on December 11 and 12.

Bill Introduced in Illinois Legislature
to Provide for Payment of Interest on the Public Debt[1]

[December 7, 1840]

Sec: 1st. Be it enacted by the People of the state of Illinois represented in the General Assembly: That hereafter, in addition to the revenue now raised by taxation, there shall be levied and collected, for state purposes, a tax at the rate of ten cents on each one hundred dollars worth of all property.

Sec: 2nd. Said additional revenue, so raised, shall be set apart exclusively for the payment of interest on the state indebtedness—and be called the "Interest Fund"

Sec: 3rd. That the minimum valuation of all lands for the purpose of taxation, shall be four dollars per acre. And each assessor, shall, in addition to the oath now required by law, be required to swear particularly, that he will, in no instance, value any land at four dollars per acre, that he, in his conscience, believes to be worth more.

Sec: 4th. The Governor shall from time to time issue such an amount of state bonds, to be called the "Illinois Interest Bonds" as may be absolutely necessary to raise funds for the payment of interest on the state debts, that there is no other means of paying—and also sufficient to redeem all state bonds now hypothecated.

Sec: 5th. Said Interest Bonds shall be sold by the Fund Commissioner, for the best price they will command, and the proceeds by him faithfully applied to the foregoing objects

Sec 6th. Said Bonds shall be reimbursable after the year 1865, and bear interest at the rate of six per cent per annum, payable half yearly.

Sec: 7th. A sufficiency of the said "Interest Fund" is hereby irrevocably pledged, for the payment of interest upon the said "Illinois Interest Bonds" and the same shall be applied to that object in preference to all other objects.

---

[1] AD, I-Ar. Although the bill was first introduced on December 7, it underwent numerous changes and the text as given is undoubtedly of a later date. The original bill seems not to be extant and the record of debates concerning it as given in the *House Journal* becomes confused. On December 8, however, Lincoln proposed the following amendments to his original bill, neither of which appear in the text: "Mr. Lincoln, proposed to amend the bill by inserting into the 9th line, at the end of the word 'next' the words following, to wit:

" 'And also, sufficient to pay freights, duty and other necessary charges upon railroad iron, which has been received, and to be received under contracts heretofore made, and also sufficient to pay the necessary charges of the prosecution of certain suits prosecuting and to be prosecuted on behalf of this State, in the State of New York. And if it shall become necessary to prevent a forfeiture of the bonds so hypothecated, said Fund Commissioner is hereby empowered to re-hypothecate said bonds for that purpose, and for no other whatever.'

"Also, to amend said bill further, by adding the following proviso at the end of the bill, viz:

" '*And provided further,* That the Fund Commissioner shall not be authorized to pay interest upon any bonds sold for which a consideration has not been received by the State whenever such bonds shall be found in the hands, custody, power or possession of the original purchasers or contracting powers.' " *House Journal*, pp. 89-90. The bill passed both houses substantially as above, and may be found in *Laws of Illinois*, 1841, pp. 165-66.

Remarks in Illinois Legislature
Concerning Unfinished Business of the Last Session[1]

December 7, 1840

Mr. TURNEY[2] offered a resolution, that the unfinished business of the last session of the Legislature be taken from the files, and placed in the same stage of forwardness in this session of the Legislature, that it occupied at the adjournment of the former session.

Mr. LINCOLN demanded the ayes and noes. . . .[3]

Mr. LINCOLN would state why he had called the ayes and noes on the resolution. If it were a fact that there was no illegality in the proposed measure, then it was certainly desirable on the grounds of expedience, that the resolution should be adopted. But our constitution had provided that every bill should be read three times on three different days, unless three-fourths should dispense with the rules, before it became a law. Now, was it not a matter of serious doubt whether this House could take up a bill which had been twice read during the last session and by reading it once now, pass it into a law?

[1] *Sangamo Journal*, December 11, 1840.
[2] Daniel Turney of Wayne County.   [3] The resolution was adopted.

Remarks in Illinois Legislature
Concerning Payment of Interest on the Public Debt[1]

December 11, 1840

Mr. LINCOLN said he was already committed to the principle contained in the amendment proposed by the gentleman from Morgan.[2] The only difference between the measure he had formerly proposed, and that now proposed by the gentleman, was that by his plan, a provision was made for increasing our means for defraying the ordinary expenses of the State, as well as to meet our accruing interest. It was just as bad to be bankrupt in one respect as in the other, and while we were adjusting the one, the other had as well be attended to at the same time.

[1] *Sangamo Journal*, December 15, 1840. Lincoln's remarks also appear in *Illinois State Register*, December 18, 1840.
[2] John J. Hardin had offered an amendment to Lincoln's bill (*vide supra*, December 7, 1840), calling for a direct tax exclusively to pay interest. The amendment was tabled.

Remarks in Illinois Legislature
Concerning Payment of Interest on State Debt[1]

December 12, 1840

Mr. LINCOLN had thought at first that some permanent provision ought to have been made for the bonds to be hypothecated. He was in favor of such a permanent fund, but he was soon convinced that if we connect with the question at this moment matters of finance, of revenue and taxation, nothing could be done. He was willing to go for the naked proposition, simply to pay the interest due. Mr. L. therefore, now proposed to adopt this amendment, without clogging it with revenue questions. *He* wished to see by a direct vote if the house would adopt the naked proposition. He for one was for it; if any details required amendment, it could be done hereafter.

[1] *Illinois State Register*, December 18, 1840. Lincoln's remarks were in favor of an amendment offered by Alfred W. Cavarly of Greene County, to a bill providing payment of interest on the state debt. The amendment called for "the simple proposition to pay the interest unembarrassed with a multitude of other questions." The amendment lost 47 to 41.

Amendments Introduced in Illinois Legislature
to an Act to Vacate Town Plat of Livingston[1]

[December 12, 1840]

Amend the Bill by adding the following additional sections, towit:

Sec. 2nd. That the town plat of the town of Cicero in the county of Sangamon be vacated *Provided* that John Latham and Archibald Constant, or the heirs of them or either of them, be the sole proprietors of said town at the passage of this act.

Sec: 3rd. That Blocks numbered Six, Seven, eight, and nine, of the Plat of the town of Caledonia in the county of Putnam, are hereby vacated, Provided that P. G. Young be the sole proprietor of said Blocks at the passage of this act.

Sec: 4. That the south end of Charles Street from first to Second South Streets in Coleman's addition to the Town of Belleville in the County of St. Clair is hereby vacated.

[1] AD, I-Ar. These amendments to a Senate bill were adopted by the House on December 12, 1840. The council of revision turned the bill down, objecting to Lincoln's fourth section. Whereupon the fourth section was removed and the amended bill passed both houses. It may be found in *Laws of Illinois*, 1841, pp. 315-16.

Remarks in Illinois Legislature
Concerning Bill to Provide Payment of Interest on the Public Debt[1]

December 14, 1840

Mr. LINCOLN wished to know if there was any provision providing for the increase of the State Revenue; we had no funds to set aside out of that Revenue, which was not more than enough for present requirements. Mr. L explained how he had contrived that the measure he had proposed on a former occasion would not take away from the necessary supplies.

[1] *Illinois State Register*, December 18, 1840. Stephen G. Hicks of Jefferson County had introduced a substitute for Lincoln's bill introduced December 7, 1840. Hicks' bill was rejected.

To John T. Stuart[1]

Springfield, December 17, 1840.

Dear Stuart: McRoberts[2] was elected senator yesterday. The vote stood: McRoberts, seventy-seven; Cyrus Edwards, fifty; E. D. Baker, one; absent, three. This affair of appointment to office is very annoying—more so to you than to me, doubtless. I am, as you know, opposed to removals to make places for our friends. Bearing this in mind, I express my preference in a few cases, as follows: For marshal, first, John Dawson; second, Dr. B. F. Edwards. For postmaster here, Dr. Henry;[3] Carlinville, Joseph C. Howell. There is no question of the propriety of removing the postmaster at Carlinville. I have been told by so many different persons as to preclude all doubt of its truth, that he boldly refused to deliver from his office during the canvass all documents franked by Whig members of Congress. Yours,   LINCOLN.

[1] NH, I, 156.
[2] Samuel McRoberts, first native Illinoisan elected to the U. S. Senate, succeeded General John M. Robinson and served until his death in March, 1843.
[3] Anson G. Henry.

Resolution Introduced in Illinois Legislature
Concerning Expenditures for Public Printing[1]

December 19, 1840

Resolved, That a select committee be appointed to enquire into the causes which have produced the very large expenditure for the item of public printing, and they be instructed to report a bill to the House having for its object the reduction of that item of expenditure, if in their judgment such reduction can be had without detriment to the public interest.

[1] *House Journal*, Twelfth General Assembly, First Session, p. 137. After considerable discussion (*vide infra*) the resolution was adopted and Lincoln was made a member of the select committee.

Discussion in Illinois Legislature
Concerning Expenditures for Public Printing[1]

December 19, 1840

Mr LINCOLN offered for adoption a resolution for a select committee to enquire into the causes of the large amount of the item of public printing, and to enquire into the possibility of reducing the expense &c.

Mr. LINCOLN in offering this resolution distinctly stated that he contemplated and intended no attack on any individual: his only object was to ascertain if it might be in the power of the House to reduce this heavy item of public expenditure.

Mr BENTLEY[2] suggested that the committee on public accounts and expenditures was the proper committee to entrust with this enquiry, and moved to amend accordingly.

Mr LINCOLN objected to the shuffling off of responsibility, and said that as for himself, he would prefer not to be on the select committee to be appointed. He was not inclined to believe that more printing was done than was ordered, or that more was charged for than the law allowed. He was disposed to believe if there was any fault, it was at our own door. He had just read the message of the Governor of Indiana, in which he called the attention of their Legislature to the enormous expenditure of 12,000 dollars for public printing. Thus it would be seen that in our sister state, with a population doubling ours, 12,000 was called an *enormous* expenditure, whilst we, with only half the population, and doubly more embarrassed, were paying $23,000 for the same object! So far was he from wishing to make this matter a party business, that he would distinctly say, it was his desire that he himself should not be placed upon the committee to be appointed.

Mr ORMSBEE[3] referred the House to a resolution now before the committee of which he was chairman, and which covered the whole ground of the resolution now offered.

[1] *Illinois State Register*, January 1, 1841.
[2] Richard Bentley of Bond County.   [3] Joseph W. Ormsbee of Scott County.

Mr OLDS[4] said he could view this resolution in no other light than as an effort to get up political capital; it must be evident that this was the sole motive of bringing forward such a proposition at such a time as this, when gentlemen reflect that a resolution for an inquiry upon this very subject had already been committed to one of the standing committees of the House. What, he would ask, was the use of the Speakers appointing committees, if gentlemen should be permitted to take out of their hands the proper and legitimate objects submitted to them, in order to get up special committees for the mere purpose of making flaming reports intended to produce false impressions among the people. He (Mr O) was as strenuous an advocate of economy as the gentleman could be who had offered this resolution, but he must say that it appeared somewhat suspicious to him that this resolution should be bro't forward at this time. The House must well remember that the item of printing expense has been incurred mainly if not altogether by the party which is known as the whig party. How is it, that if they are sincere in their present movement, they did not make enquires and aim at a curtailment of expenses when they had a majority in the House? The very fact that they did not, plainly proved to his mind what was the true object and intent of this resolution. He would therefore oppose it, not because he was willing to sustain any unnecessary or profuse expenditure—far from it; but because he considered it an unnecessary and wanton waste both of time and money to take up such a resolution as this, when already there was before the House a resolution of the very same nature, having the same object in view, and fully adequate to every purpose required. He would therefore move to lay the resolution on the table.

Mr O subsequently withdrew his motion to afford Mr Lincoln an opportunity to explain.

Mr LINCOLN, in reply to the gentleman from Macoupin, said that the gentleman was a stranger to him, as he had never been introduced to him, but he hoped the gentleman would give him the credit of being candid in the statement of the motives which had induced him to offer this resolution; he would repeat, that he had no motive which he had not expressed; he had not introduced this resolution in a fault finding spirit, he was only desirous of doing his duty, and in reply to the gentleman from Scott he would say that if he considered it as a slur on his committee he would candidly and sincerely assure him that he (Mr L) did not mean or contemplate any such thing. His view was that if a change could be brought about advantageous to the people, it was our duty to set

4 Francis A. Olds of Macoupin County.

about the correction of abuses, and he would ask if this was not becoming and honest to the people of the country? He had put the resolution into its present form because he considered that the resolution offered some days ago did not cover all the ground: he was for bringing in the best bill that could be brought in, on the subject: if the gentleman from Macoupin thought otherwise, and supposed he (Mr L) was for making an attack on the public printer, he hoped the House would believe him when he said that he did not believe that the public printer got more work or more pay than the law allowed him, or that he made more than he was warranted by that law. Mr L had proposed a select committee, because he thought it could be done without casting imputations on the committee, which had been referred to by the gentleman from Scott. Mr L had no right to think that it had not been as faithful in the performance of its duties as any other committee. If gentlemen would reflect that the appointment of the select committee as proposed would be within the power of the Speaker, he thought that would afford a sufficient guarantee that no political movement had been contemplated by him.

Discussion in Illinois Legislature
of Bill for Relief of William Dormady[1]

December 21, 1840

Mr. LINCOLN said, as wholesale charges of fraud had been dealt out by the gentleman from Cook, which involved many of his constituents, he felt it his duty to say something in regard to this case.

It was not true, as the gentleman had stated, that the petitioner had been defrauded through the chicanery of the law, or of the courts. He would inform the House that since this Legislature had met, the naked question of fact, of the actual destruction of these notes, accompanied by any question of law, had been submitted to a jury, of the petitioner's own choice, and that a majority of this jury had solemnly decided that it was an attempt on the part of Dormady to impose upon the Bank. Under such circumstances, was it not assuming too much for the gentleman from Cook to get up here and tell us, without examination on his part, that the facts were as he had stated them, and that there was fraud and perjury on the part of the Bank, the court, and the jury?

Mr. MURPHY, in reply, said, it was somewhat strange the gentleman should impute fraud to one of his own constituents. He supposed Mr. Dormady was a loco, and did not vote for the gen-

tleman, (Mr. Lincoln) which accounted for his offering the petition. He did not charge the jury with perjury—it was nothing
unusual for a jury to disagree about a just claim, especially where
they had the instructions of a judge to help them, against right. It
might be that Mr. Dormady was unable to procure such testimony
as was necessary in a court of law. Mr. M. recapitulated the circumstances of the case which he contended were sufficient to justify
the House in passing the bill.

Mr. LINCOLN said, he did not know whether Mr. D. voted for
him or not—he presumed he did not. If there were those in this
House who thought this fact would have any influence on his conduct in regard to this bill, he should not stop to enlighten them as
to his motives; he was careless of the opinion of such. The gentleman from Cook persisted in reciting what he termed the *facts* of
this case. He would say to the House that the trial, to which he had
before alluded, was presided over by Judge Breese, whom the gentleman would not charge with partiality to the Bank—that this
jury was composed in part by Mr. D.'s own political friends—that
he had able counsel to assist him, and that upon the naked question, as to whether these notes were burnt or not, a majority of
that jury had determined, after hearing under oath all the testimony, and the arguments of counsel, that these notes were not
burnt. And yet the gentleman, without investigation, assumed that
for granted, which the jury found otherwise, and upon this assumption charged fraud and dishonesty upon the Bank, and all who had
any thing to do with the case. He thought it better that one man
should rest under the imputation of fraud than one hundred.

1 *Sangamo Journal*, December 25, 1840. Richard Murphy of Cook County
had introduced a bill to remunerate Dormady (also spelled Dormandy) for certain bank notes which were purportedly destroyed by fire.

Remarks in Illinois Legislature
Concerning Apportionment[1]

January 7, 1841

Mr. Lincoln said there was always in agreeing upon the ratio
of an apportionment, no number we could fix upon that could suit
all. Our counties ranged in population from 750 to 16,000. If we
adopt the idea of the gentleman from Hamilton, and give each
county a representative, we must begin with the county which has
750 inhabitants; and as the republican principle of representation
according to numbers, will not be denied as proper for the basis of

our action, we must then give a representative, according to the gentleman from Hamilton (Mr. Carpenter) for every 750 in the state. This by calculating, would be found to give a house of representatives of about 650 members. Such a proposition he was satisfied would not be tolerated by the house. He was disposed to go for the resolution as it came from the senate.

[1] Peoria *Register and North-Western Gazetteer*, January 15, 1841. An inferior report of Lincoln's remarks appears in the *Illinois State Register* of the same date. The resolution under discussion proposed 12,000 as the ratio for apportionment. Lincoln's remarks were made in opposition to a motion by Milton Carpenter of Hamilton County, who wished to substitute a lower figure and who expressed the opinion that "every county should have a representative in one branch of the legislature."

Remarks in Illinois Legislature
Concerning Commemoration of the Battle of New Orleans[1]

January 8, 1841

Mr. LINCOLN said that as that jumping scrape had become so celebrated it appeared necessary that he should say something about it.

The Speaker called Mr. Lincoln to order.

Mr. LINCOLN said that as to jumping, he should jump when he pleased and no one should hinder him. *He* thought this Resolution ought to pass. Mr. L. proceeded to advocate it, as a national subject, not on party grounds: he was proud of the victory of New-Orleans, and the military fame of Gen. Jackson, though he could never find in his heart to support him as a politician. He had sat for 6 years in the Legislature, and this day had always been observed as a matter of course, with no view whatever to politics.

[1] *Illinois State Register*, January 15, 1841. Speaking on a resolution to adjourn for a half-day in commemoration of the Battle of New Orleans, William H. Bissell of Monroe County had referred to the notorious incident which had occurred on December 5, 1840, when Lincoln and other Whigs had jumped out of the windows in an unsuccessful effort to prevent a quorum.

Remarks in Illinois Legislature
Concerning a Burlesque Petition[1]

January 9, 1841

Mr. LINCOLN thought as the subject had come up, and seemed likely to be a painful one, the best course would be to dispose of the matter in a manner the least painful. He would be sorry to see a resolution of this kind pass, calculated to wound the feelings of him who had presented the petition. He hoped the resolution would be so modified.

Mr. LINCOLN then moved to strike out that portion of the resolution requiring the petition to be returned to the member presenting it.

1 *Illinois State Register,* January 22, 1841. A burlesque petition had been presented by Asahel Gridley, McLean County Whig, in reference to a speech of Alpheus Wheeler, Democrat of Pike County. In order to place the shoe on the other foot, John A. McClernand, Democrat of Gallatin County, offered a resolution condemning the petition and its presentation by Gridley as insulting to the House. Lincoln's effort was to terminate the affair.

Speech in Illinois Legislature
Concerning Apportionment[1]

[January 9, 1841?]

Mr. Lincoln replied. He appealed to every old member in the House, if it was not a fact, that when this body consisted of but fifty five members,[2] business was conducted with twice the facility that it now was. The reason was obvious enough to any reflecting mind. It required double the journalizing and double the length of time to call and record every vote which was put to the House; but a stronger reason was, that amongst ninety members the proposition of members, who, in the language of the gentleman from Monroe, (Mr. Bissell)[3] were disposed to protract business, was just double that in a House of half the number. It was perfectly plain that if each of the ninety-one members, now on this floor, make speeches on any subject, that it would require just double the time of half that number. The gentleman from Monroe, (Mr. Bissell) accused his friend from St. Clair, (Mr. Trumbull)[4] of attaching some peculiar magic to the number 100. He did not understand his objection to exceeding that number to arise from any magic in it, but from the fact that it was large enough, and expensive enough for any legislative body.

The gentleman had accused old women of being partial to the number 9; but this he presumed was without foundation. A few years since, it would be recollected by the House, that the delegation from this county were dubbed, by way of eminence the "long nine," and by way of further distinction, he had been called the "longest" of the nine. Now, said Mr. L. I desire to say to my friend from Monroe (Mr. Bissell) that if any woman, old or young, ever thought there was any peculiar charm in this distinguished specimen of number 9, I have, as yet, been so unfortunate as not to have discovered it, (loud applause.).[5]

[1] D, CSmH. This document is a longhand copy, preserved in the Herndon manuscripts of the Lamon Papers, of what is apparently a contemporary newspaper report of a discussion in the legislature concerning apportionment. The discussion of the Senate resolution which took place in the House on January 7 (*vide supra*), as reported in the newspapers, does not seem to have included this speech. On January 9 further discussion took place, but newspaper reports are not available, the *Sangamo Journal* for January 12, the issue in which the report might be expected, not being extant.

[2] In 1835 the number of representatives was increased to ninety-one.

[3] William H. Bissell.   [4] Lyman Trumbull.

[5] The manuscript contains two further paragraphs reporting discussion by other members of the House.

To John T. Stuart[1]

Dear Stuart: Springfield, Jany. 20th. 1841

I have had no letter from you since you left. No matter for that. What I wish now is to speak of our Post-Office. You know I desired Dr. Henry[2] to have that place when you left; I now desire it more than ever. I have, within the last few days, been making a most discreditable exhibition of myself in the way of hypochondriaism[3] and thereby got an impression that Dr. Henry is necessary to my existence. Unless he gets that place he leaves Springfield. You therefore see how much I am interested in the matter.

We shall shortly forward you a petition in his favour signed by all or nearly all the Whig members of the Legislature, as well as other whigs.

This, together with what you know of the Dr.'s position and merits I sincerely hope will secure him the appointment. My heart is verry much set upon it.

Pardon me for not writing more; I have not sufficient composure to write a long letter. As ever yours   A. LINCOLN

[1] ALS, owned by Mrs. Logan Hay, Springfield, Illinois.

[2] Anson G. Henry, who did not get the postmastership which went to G. W. Spottswood.

[3] Lincoln was absent from the legislature January 13 to 19 because of illness of a psychopathic nature, brought on in all probability by what he later would refer to as "that fatal first of Jany. '41" (letter to Joshua F. Speed, March 27, 1842; see also other letters to Speed written in 1841-1842). What occurred has been variously reported by Lincoln's contemporaries, but general agreement has been reached among modern scholars to the effect that on this date Lincoln asked

to be released from his engagement to Mary Todd. It is clear from his later references to the event and to his ensuing emotional chaos, that Lincoln underwent misery of no mild variety as the result, not merely of his own indecision and instability, but also of his awareness that he was the cause of an injury to Mary Todd no less severe and humiliating than his own. That his condition was common knowledge is indicated by several references in contemporary letters, among them the following, written on January 22, by Martin McKee to John J. Hardin: "We have been very much distressed, on Mr. Lincoln's account; hearing that he had two Cat fits and a Duck fit since we left." (*Hardin MSS.*, ICHi.)

To John T. Stuart[1]

Dear Stuart: Jany. 23rd. 1841– Springfield, Ills.

Yours of the 3rd. Inst. is recd. & I proceed to answer it as well as I can, tho' from the deplorable state of my mind at this time,[2] I fear I shall give you but little satisfaction. About the matter of the congressional election, I can only tell you, that there is a bill now before the Senate adopting the General Ticket system;[3] but whether the party have fully determined on it's adoption is yet uncertain. There is no sign of opposition to you among our friends, and none that I can learn among our enemies; tho', of course, there will be, if the Genl. Ticket be adopted. The Chicago American, Peoria Register, & Sangamo Journal, have already hoisted your flag upon their own responsibility; & the other whig papers of the District are expected to follow immediately. On last evening there was a meeting of our friends at Butler's;[4] and I submitted the question to them & found them unanamously in favour of having you announced as a candidate. A few of us this morning, however, concluded, that as you were already being announced in the papers, we would delay announcing you, *as by your own authority* for a week or two. We thought that to appear too keen about it might spur our opponents on about their Genl. Ticket project. Upon the whole, I think I may say with certainty, that your reelection is sure, if it be in the power of the whigs to make it so.

For not giving you a general summary of news, you *must* pardon me; it is not in my power to do so. I am now the most miserable man living. If what I feel were equally distributed to the whole human family, there would not be one cheerful face on the earth. Whether I shall ever be better I can not tell; I awfully forebode I shall not. To remain as I am is impossible; I must die or be better, it appears to me. The matter you speak of on my account, you may attend to as you say, unless you shall hear of my condition forbidding it. I say this, because I fear I shall be unable to attend to any bussiness here, and a change of scene might help me. If I could be myself, I would rather remain at home with Judge Logan. I can write no more. Your friend, as ever—

A. LINCOLN

¹ ALS, owned by heirs of Stuart Brown.
² Probably the result of his reputed breaking of his engagement to Mary Todd on the "fatal first of Jany."
³ "An act fixing the manner of Congressional elections" ordered to a second reading January 5, 1841; consideration indefinitely postponed February 10, 1841.
⁴ William Butler.

Speech in Illinois Legislature
on Bill to Provide Payment for Work on State House¹

January 25, 1841

Mr. LINCOLN addressed the House in support of the bill and amendment. He was anxious that the bill should pass, whether the amendment was adopted or not; but he would be gratified if the amendment should also prevail.

It was hardly necessary for him to say, that in common with the rest of the community, the citizens of Springfield felt the severity of the times, and that this was calculated further to distress them, and that too for a claim which many of the disinterested citizens of this state thought of very questionable propriety. But this he would not now discuss. He wished to say in reply to the gentleman from Fulton (Mr. Ross)² who had stated that better accommodations were promised as an inducement to the removal of the seat of Government to this place, that so far, as himself and the representatives from this county were concerned, such was not the fact; nor did he believe it was removed from such miserable motives. There was not a member of that Legislature, that would confess that he was influenced by such unworthy considerations. It was from the fact that the great body of population being North, that a more central location was desired, and this it could not be doubted was the governing consideration with the Legislature. If the gentleman from Fulton thought that he was paying too high for his bread and meat, let him go home and invite his constituents to come over and set up a competition in this line of business. This was a matter that would always regulate itself. He hoped the amendment would prevail, but if it did not the bill should pass by all means, as the laborers had been waiting in need for some time.

¹ *Sangamo Journal*, January 29, 1841. Prior to Lincoln's speech, John J. Brown of Vermilion County had moved to amend the bill by striking out the passage

requiring $16,666.66 to be collected by suit in court from the citizens of Spring-
field. Further consideration of Brown's amendment was postponed until the next
day (*vide infra*).   [2] Lewis W. Ross.

Amendments Introduced in Illinois Legislature
Concerning Bill to Provide Payment for
Work on State House[1]

January 26, 1841

Mr LINCOLN moved to amend by inserting a proviso, that if any
one of the obligors in the bond shall pay his proportionate share of
indebtedness, he or they shall be free from all further obligation
on the bond.

Mr Ross moved to lay the above amendment on the table; which
was negatived. Yeas 36, nays 39.

Mr CAVARLY moved to refer the bill and amendments to a select
committee. . . .

Mr LINCOLN deprecated delay; the wants of the workmen were
most urgent, and he hoped no delay would take place.

Mr PECK spoke against delay. . . .

Mr LINCOLN moved to strike out $20,000 and insert $30,000,
which was agreed to; and the bill ordered to a third reading.

[1] *Illinois State Register*, February 5, 1841. The *Sangamo Journal*, January 29,
1841, merely mentions this debate, which ensued upon the tabling of John J.
Brown's amendment, supported by Lincoln on the preceding day (*vide supra*).
The *House Journal* does not record the full discussion and omits reference to the
first of Lincoln's amendments.

Debate in Illinois Legislature
on Resolution to Adjourn[1]

January 27, 1841

Messrs. CAVARLY and PARSONS[2] spoke against the resolution, and
Messrs. Hardin and Lincoln, supported it.

Mr LINCOLN denied that his party had attempted to delay any
measure brought forward by the other party.

[1] *Sangamo Journal*, February 2, 1841; *Illinois State Register*, February 12,
1841.
[2] Alfred W. Cavarly, representative from Greene and Jersey counties; Solomon
Parsons of Pike County.

Bill Introduced in Illinois Legislature

to Authorize Certain State Debtors to Discharge Their Indebtedness in Illinois Internal Improvement Scrip[1]

[January 27, 1841]

An act authorizing certain Debtors of the State to discharge their indebtedness in Illinois Internal Improvement Scrip.

Be it enacted by the People of the state of Illinois represented in the General Assembly: That the obligors upon a certain bond executed by sundry citizens of the City of Springfield, in favour of the State of Illinois, for the sum of fifty thousand dollars, be authorized to discharge the same or the ballance due thereon, in whole or in part, in Illinois Internal Improvement Scrip.

[1] AD, I-Ar. The bill passed both houses and may be found in *Laws of Illinois*, 1841, p. 300.

Discussion in Illinois Legislature

Concerning Bill to Authorize Certain State Debtors
to Discharge Their Indebtedness
in Illinois Internal Improvement Scrip[1]

February 1, 1841

Mr LINCOLN, from the committee on Finance, reported back the bill authorizing certain state debtors to discharge their debts in Illinois State scrip,[2] recommending its passage.

Mr Ross moved to amend by adding a proviso, that the payment be made without suit.

Mr LINCOLN replied in opposition to this amendment. . . .

[1] *Illinois State Register*, February 12, 1841.
[2] *Vide supra*, January 27, 1841.

Discussion in Illinois Legislature

of Bill to Create a Board of Auditors[1]

February 4, 1841

The bill was further discussed by Messrs. Trumbull and Kitchell,[2] in opposition, and by Messrs. Archer, Lincoln, and Gillespie,[3] in favor of the bill.

[1] *Sangamo Journal*, February 9, 1841.
[2] Lyman Trumbull of St. Clair County and Wickliff Kitchell of Montgomery County.
[3] William B. Archer of Clark County and Joseph Gillespie of Madison County.

To John T. Stuart[1]

Dear Stuart: Springfield, Feb: 5th. 1841

Some of us here have concluded, that if it be agreeable, Bat Webb[2] shall be our District Attorney. He would accept the place; but will not enter into a scramble for it. We here, or at least I, know of no other applicant. I will add, that I really have my heart set upon Webb's appointment to this place; and that I believe the whole party would be gratified with it.

What the Locos will do about the Congressional election no man can tell. I heard Herndon[3] say on yesterday, that he was in favour of taking Jersey, Green, Scott, Morgan, Cass, Menard, Sangamon, Logan and Tazewell, from your District & adding them to Reynolds, and leaving all else in *statu quo*. Something like this I think more probable than the District system; because our opponents are somewhat afraid of the latter themselves. As ever your friend

A. LINCOLN

[1] ALS-P, ISLA.   [2] Edwin B. Webb.
[3] Probably Archer G. Herndon, the father of William H. Herndon.

Discussion in Illinois Legislature
Concerning Bill to Incorporate
the Springfield and Alton Railroad Company[1]

February 6, 1841

Mr EDWARDS,[2] from the committee on Internal Improvement, reported back the bill to incorporate the Springfield and Alton Rail Road company, with an amendment providing for the use of the State property.

The question being on ordering the bill to a third reading,

Mr. MUNSELL[3] opposed the bill on the ground that the State property should not be given without conditions, to one section of the country more than another.

Mr LINCOLN replied, and shewed in substance that the State property would all be lost and go to ruin, if the principle be adopted that no one shall have any, for fear all shall not have some.

[1] *Illinois State Register*, February 19, 1841.
[2] Cyrus Edwards of Madison County.
[3] Leander Munsell of Edgar County.

Circular from Whig Committee Against the Judiciary Bill[1]

February [8?], 1841

Appeal to the People of the State of Illinois.

FELLOW-CITIZENS:

When the General Assembly, now about adjourning, assembled in November last, from the bankrupt state of the public Treasury, the pecuniary embarrassments prevailing in every department of society, the dilapidated state of the public works, and the impending danger of the degradation of the State, you had a right to expect that your Representatives would lose no time in devising and adopting measures to avert threatened calamities, alleviate the distresses of the people, and allay the fearful apprehensions in regard to the future prosperity of the State. It was not expected by you, that the spirit of party would take the lead in the councils of the State, and make every interest bend to its demands. Nor was it expected that any party would assume to itself the entire control of legislation, and convert the means and offices of the State, and the substance of the people, into aliment for party subsistence. Neither could it have been expected by you, that party spirit, however strong its desires and unreasonable its demands, would have passed the sanctuary of the Constitution, and entered, with its unhallowed and hideous form into the formation of the Judiciary system.

At an early period of the session, measures were adopted by the dominant party to take possession of the State, to fill all public offices with party men, and make every measure effecting the interests of the people and the credit of the State, operate in furtherance of their party views. The merits of men and measures therefore became the subject of discussion in caucus, instead of the halls of legislation, and decisions there made, by a minority of the Legislature, have been executed and carried into effect by the force of party discipline, without any regard whatever to the rights of the people, or the interests of the State.

The Supreme Court of the State was organized and judges appointed, according to the provisions of the Constitution, in 1824.

1 *The Illinoian* (Jacksonville), March 27, 1841. The date can be estimated from a reference in the *Illinois State Register*, February 12, 1841: "We learn that the members of the Federal party met in caucus one night last week, concocted a remonstrance against the judiciary bill, filled with the most unheard of misrepresentations, have since printed ten thousand copies thereof, and sent them to the various secret committees in different parts of the State which were organized previous to the fall elections. The object is to create a panic amongst the people."

The people have never complained of the organization of that court—no attempt has ever before been made to change that department. Respect for public opinion and regard for the rights and liberties of the people have hitherto restrained the spirit of party from attacks upon the independence and integrity of the Judiciary. The same Judges have continued in office since 1824; their decisions have not been the subject of complaint among the people; the integrity and honesty of the court has not been questioned and it has never been supposed that the court has ever permitted party prejudice or party considerations to operate upon their decisions. The court was made to consist of four judges, and by the Constitution, two forms a quorum for the transaction of business. With this tribunal thus constituted, the people have been satisfied for near sixteen years. The same law which organized the Supreme court in 1824 also established and organized circuit courts, to be held in each county in the State, and five circuit judges were appointed to hold those courts. In 1826 the legislature abolished these circuit courts, repealed the Judges out of office, and required the judges of the Supreme court to hold the circuit courts. The reasons assigned for this change were, 1st, that the business of the country could be better attended to by the four judges of the supreme court, than by the two sets of judges; and, 2d, the state of the public treasury forbade the employment of unnecessary officers. In 1828 a circuit was established north of the Illinois river, in order to meet the wants of the people, and a circuit judge was appointed to hold the courts in that circuit.

In 1834 the circuit court system was again established throughout the State, circuit Judges appointed to hold the courts, and the judges of the supreme court were relieved from the performance of circuit court duties. This change was recommended by the then acting Governor of the State, Gen. W. L. D. Ewing, in the following terms:

"The augmented population of the State—the multiplied number of organized counties, as well as the increase of business in all has long since convinced every one conversant with this department of our government, of the indispensable necessity of an alteration in our Judiciary system, and the subject is therefore recommended to the earnest patriotic consideration of the Legislature. The present system has never been exempt from serious and weighty objections. The idea of appealing from the circuit court to the same judges in the supreme court, is recommended by little hopes of redress to the injured party below. The duties of the circuit, too, it may be added, consume one half of the year, leaving a small and inadequate portion of time, when that required for domestic purposes is deducted, to erect, in the decisions of the supreme court, a judicial monument of legal learning and research, which the talent and ability of the court might otherwise be entirely competent to."

With this organization of circuit courts, the people have never complained. The only complaints which we have heard have come from circuits which were so large that the judges could not dispose of the business, and the circuits in which judges Pearson and Ralston lately presided.

Whilst the honor and credit of the State demanded legislation upon the subject of the public debt, the Canal, the unfinished public works, and the embarrassments of the people, the Judiciary stood upon a basis which required no change—no legislative action. Yet the party in power, neglecting every interest requiring legislative action, and wholly disregarding the rights, wishes, and interests of the people, has, for the unholy purpose of providing places for its partizans and supplying them with large salaries, disorganized that department of the Government. Provision is made for the election of five party Judges of the Supreme Court—the proscription of four circuit Judges, and the appointment of party Clerks in more than half the counties in the State. Men, professing respect for public opinion and acknowledged to be leaders of the party, have avowed in the halls of legislation, that the change in the judiciary was intended to produce political results favorable to their party & party friends. The immutable principles of justice are to make way for party interests, and the bonds of social order are to be rent in twain, in order that a desperate faction may be sustained at the expense of the people. The change proposed in the judiciary was supported upon grounds so destructive to the institutions of the country, and so entirely at war with the rights and liberties of the people, that the party could not secure entire unanimity in its support—three democrats of the Senate and five of the House voting against the measure. They were unwilling to see the temples of justice and the seats of independent judges occupied by the tools of faction. The declarations of the party leaders, the selection of party men for judges, and the total disregard for the public will, in the adoption of the measure, prove conclusively that the object has been, not reform, but destruction, not the advancement of the highest interests of the State, but the predominance of party.

We cannot in this manner undertake to point out all the objections to this party measure—we present you with those stated by the Council of Revision, upon returning the bill, and we ask for them a candid consideration.

Believing that the independence of the Judiciary has been destroyed—that hereafter our courts will be independent of the people, and entirely dependent upon the Legislature—that our rights of property and liberty of conscience can no longer be regarded as safe from the encroachments of unconstitutional legislation—and knowing of no other remedy which can be adopted consistently with the peace and good order of society—we call upon you to avail yourselves of the opportunity afforded, and, at the next general election, vote for a Convention of the People.

S. H. Little,[2]	E. B. Webb,
E. D. Baker,	A. Lincoln,
J. J. Hardin,	J. Gillespie,

Committee on behalf of the Whig members of the Legislature.

[2] Lincoln's fellow-committeemen were: Sidney H. Little, senator, McDonough and Hancock Counties; Edward D. Baker, senator, Sangamon County; John J. Hardin, representative, Morgan County; Edwin B. Webb, representative, White County; Joseph Gillespie, representative, Madison County.

Remarks in Illinois Legislature
Reporting Bill for Election of a Public Binder[1]

February 9, 1841

Mr. LINCOLN, from a select committee, reported back the bill for election of a Public Binder, with an amendment, securing the future work under the present General Assembly to Birchall and Johnson under contract made with them.

After some remarks by Messrs Lincoln, Kitchell, and Brown,[2] of Vermilion, without taking the question, the House adjourned.

[1] *Illinois State Register*, February 19, 1841.
[2] Wickliff Kitchell, Montgomery County; and John J. Brown.

Speech in Illinois Legislature
Concerning the State Bank[1]

February 11, 1841

A very interesting debate sprung up in the House yesterday upon a bill to repeal the act making the State Bank the fiscal agent of the State. The discussion took a wide range and was viewed with a good deal of interest, as involving, indirectly, the question whether the Bank should be sustained in a further suspension of specie payments. There is a manifest disposition on the part of some of the Van Buren men to prop up the Bank, and it is perfectly apparent that the party are prepared to detach a fraction of themselves to go with the Whigs in sustaining the Bank—their usual policy—and then throw the odium of suspension upon the Whigs. Mr. Lincoln said that he was tired of this business. If there was to be this continual warfare against the Institutions of the State, the sooner it was brought to an end the better. If the great body of the party would act upon conservative principles, he was willing to go with them, but this scheme of detaching a fragment from their party to help the Whigs pass a measure and then turn around and kick and cuff us for it, he had seen practiced long enough. The Bill was finally referred to the committee on Banks and Corporations. The debate was exceedingly interesting and occupied nearly the whole of the day. The chief speakers were Messrs. McClernand[2] and Lincoln, and the encounter between them was peculiarly sharp and personal.

[1] *North Western Gazette and Galena Advertiser,* February 17, 1841.
[2] John A. McClernand of Gallatin County.

Debate in Illinois Legislature
Concerning Sale of State Bonds[1]

February 15, 1841

The first section of the bill providing for the sale of bonds for payment of the July interest was taken up and considered: several amendments were proposed by Messrs. Kitchell, Henderson[2] and Lincoln, and a lengthy debate took place on the question whether bonds should be sold at par value only, or whether they should be sold at such value as they might bear in the money market. Messrs Lincoln, McClernand, Peck, and Brown,[3] of Vermilion, contended that to restrict them to be sold at par value only, was tantamount to prohibiting their sale, and would, therefore, defeat the whole object of the bill, and amount to an entire abandonment of the good faith of the State. . . .

[1] *Illinois State Register,* February 26, 1841. Brief mention also in *Sangamo Journal* of same date.   [2] Wickliff Kitchell and William H. Henderson.
[3] John A. McClernand, Ebenezer Peck, and John J. Brown.

Amendment Introduced in Illinois Legislature
to an Act to Amend an Act
to Incorporate the City of Springfield[1]

[February 17, 1841]

Amend said Bill by striking out all of the first section after the word "repealed" in the eighth line thereof, and inserting the following towit:

"and hereafter every Inhabitant of said City who is intitled to vote for state officers, and who has the requisite length of residence according to the act to which this is an amendment, shall be[2] eligible to the office of Mayor or Alderman of said City."

[1] AD, I-Ar. The Senate bill introduced by Archer G. Herndon of Sangamon County, "An act to amend an act to incorporate the City of Springfield, approved February 3, 1840," passed the House with Lincoln's amendment on February 17, 1841, and the Senate concurred. The entire act may be found in *Laws of Illinois*, 1841, pp. 61-62.

[2] Deletion at this point: "entitled to vote at all City elections, and also be."

Discussion in Illinois Legislature
Concerning Bill to Reorganize the Judiciary[1]

February 18, 1841

Mr DRUMMOND moved to strike out Judge Brown from the 6th, and Judge Treat from the 8th circuit, and transpose them.

Messrs Trumbull and White opposed the amendment, which was supported by Messrs Brown, of Vermilion, Drummond and Lincoln. . . .

Mr LINCOLN resumed the argument in favor of sending Judge Treat to Jo Daviess, and Judge Brown to the Sangamo Circuit.

Mr Trumbull replied. . . .

Mr LINCOLN replied, and was followed by Mr White on the other side.

[1] *Illinois State Register*, February 26, 1841. Brief mention also in *Sangamo Journal* of same date.

Amendment Introduced in Illinois Legislature
to an Act Making Appropriations for the
Years 1841 and 1842[1]

[February 18, 1841]

To William W Watson the sum of eightyone dollars for the use of a room for the Supreme Court twentyseven days at their June term 1840.

[1] AD, I-Ar. Written by Lincoln but moved by Ebenezer Peck, representative from Cook County, the amendment was adopted, making the twelfth part of section three of the bill as printed in the *Laws of Illinois*, 1841, pp. 28-31.

Remarks in Illinois Legislature
Concerning Relief of William Dormady[1]

February 19, 1841

Mr LINCOLN explained a curious experiment which he said had been tried in the presence of a Jury: a pocket book filled with blank bills had been exposed to the action of fire, and the bills had not been burnt, which same bills afterwards burnt freely when subjected to the flame of a candle, hence a jury had concluded, and Mr L. also believed that the notes could not have been burnt in the manner stated in the affidavit. (The affidavit stated that the notes had, together with the pocket book been carbonized, *not inflamed*, and that on handling them they had crumbled to pieces.)[2]

[1] *Illinois State Register*, March 5, 1841.
[2] See also Lincoln's remarks, December 21, 1840 (*supra*).

Debate in Illinois Legislature
Concerning Bill to Change Lines of Menard County[1]

February 22, 1841

Mr. LINCOLN was in favor of the reference. If, as his colleague[2] had stated, the people directly interested in this matter were opposed to the measure, he should most certainly oppose the bill—he would obey the will of his constituents. He hoped the reference would be had.

[1] *Sangamo Journal*, February 26, 1841.
[2] Josiah Francis of Sangamon had moved to refer the bill to a select committee. The motion failed and the bill was ordered to be engrossed.

Bill Introduced in Illinois Legislature
in Relation to the State Bank of Illinois[1]

[February 22, 1841]

SEC. 1st. Be it enacted by the People of the state of Illinois: That the twentyfifth section of an act entitled an act to incorporate the subscribers to the Bank of the state of Illinois Approved February 12th. 1835 be and the same is hereby repealed; and any and all forfeiture or forfeitures, which may have accrued under said section, hereby set aside.

SEC: 2nd. That the said Bank be authorized to receive interest at the rate of eight per cent per annum, on all indebtedness hereafter created for shorter time than seven months, and on all other indebtedness, as now fixed by law.

[240]

SEC: 3rd. That said Bank be authorized to issue and circulate bills or notes of less denomination than five dollars.

SEC: 4th. If the said Bank shall avail itself of the foregoing provisions, it shall do so upon the condition, that it advance to the state the sum of two hundred thousand dollars before the next regular meeting of the General Assembly, for which advances it shall receive six per cent. state bonds at par— said advances to be made at such times, and in such sums not exceeding the whole, as may be necessary for the redemption of bonds hypothecated and for paying interest on the state indebtedness, other than that due said Bank; to which purposes, and no other said advances shall be faithfully applied.

SEC: 5th. To avail said Bank of the provisions of this act, the President and Directors thereof shall pass an order accepting the same at their first meeting after the passage of this act.

Amend[2] the bill by striking out the 3rd section and inserting in lieu thereof the following—

"The said Bank shall not be entitled to the benefits of this act, until it shall have entered into contract with the Governor, to purchase of the state six per cent bonds at par as follows viz: On the first day of July next the amount of fifty thousand dollars, on the first day of January 1842 fifty thousand dollars; on the first day of July 1842 fifty thousand dollars, and on the first day of January 1843 fifty thousand dollars. And the purchase money of such bonds shall be advanced, at the times named, by said Bank, and applied exclusively to the redemption of Bonds heretofore hypothecated by the Fund Commissioner, and to the payment of interest due on state indebtedness, other than to said Bank."

[1] AD, I-Ar. Lincoln wrote the bill, but it was introduced by Peter Green, representative from Clay County. The bill was so completely changed by amendments of both House and Senate that Lincoln voted against its passage. Under the title "An act concerning the State Bank of Illinois," the revised bill may be found in *Laws of Illinois*, 1841, pp. 40-42. See discussion, February 24, 1841, *infra*.

[2] This amendment in Lincoln's hand is part of the original document.

Suggestion in Illinois Legislature
Concerning Printing a Report[1]

February 23, 1841

Mr. LINCOLN suggested that the printing be dispensed with,— without taking the question on the printing.

[1] *Sangamo Journal*, March 5, 1841. The report under discussion concerned the "best means of further providing for the payment of interest on the State debt,"

and was presented by Cyrus Edwards of Madison County from a Select Committee of nine of which Lincoln was a member. It was printed in full in the *Sangamo Journal*, May 28, 1841.

Discussion in Illinois Legislature
Concerning the State Bank[1]

February 24, 1841

On motion of Mr HENDERSON,[2] the bill in relation to the State Bank was again taken up. . . .

Mr McCLERNAND[3] moved to lay the bill on the table, which motion was lost, yeas 26, nays 51.

The bill was then ordered to a second reading.

Mr LINCOLN moved to dispense with the rules, and read it a second time by its title.

Mr LINCOLN expressed his views of the necessity of an immediate settlement of the question: it was he said so connected with the great measure of providing for the interest and credit of the State that he hoped it would be passed without further delay.

Mr KITCHELL[4] said, he hoped the bill would not be read again, nor at all: he believed the bill was calculated to ruin the State.

Mr LOGAN[5] said, that some gentlemen were total destructives, they wished to destroy the canal, the Bank and every thing—but he would like to know how could the people pay taxes if the whole circulation was destroyed? now, it depended on this Bank: if it was destroyed the currency of the State would be cut off.

The motion of Mr LINCOLN was then carried, and the bill was read a second time. . . .

Mr McCLERNAND moved to refer the bill to the committee on Finance. . . .

Mr MURPHY[6] of Perry, moved its reference to a select committee.

Messrs. LINCOLN and BROWN,[7] of Vermilion, opposed the reference.

Mr McCLERNAND supported the reference, and referred to Mr Lincoln's having on a former occasion expressed his intention of going against the Bank, as a mark of inconsistency.

Mr LINCOLN replied and explained: that he had deprecated the efforts made to crush the Bank and only acted consistently in recommending what he thought the best means of saving both it and the state.

[1] *Illinois State Register*, March 5, 1841. See Lincoln's bill introduced February 22, 1841, *supra*.   [2] William H. Henderson of Putnam County.
[3] John A. McClernand of Gallatin County.
[4] Wickliff Kitchell of Montgomery County.

Discussion in Illinois Legislature
Concerning Payment of the State Debt[1]

February 24, 1841

On motion of Mr. BALDWIN,[2] the bill to provide for the payment of the State debt, was taken up and read a second time. . . .

Mr KITCHELL[3] offered to amend by requiring that the Bonds shall not be parted with at a less sum than their expressed value.

Mr LINCOLN thought that to maintain the credit of the State, the best plan was to provide for making bonds good and valuable by raising a revenue to meet them, and having done so, then to dispose of them without restrictions and forcing them to an unnatural maximum. . . .

Messrs Lincoln and Henderson,[4] in reference to the amendment, shewed the absurdities of pretending to sell bonds to pay interest and fixing upon them a price at which they never could be sold.

[1] *Illinois State Register*, March 5, 1841.
[2] Daniel Baldwin of St. Clair County.
[3] Wickliff Kitchell of Montgomery County.
[4] William H. Henderson of Putnam County. Kitchell's amendment was tabled.

Remarks in Illinois Legislature
Concerning a Bill for Completion of
the Illinois and Michigan Canal[1]

February 26, 1841

Mr. LINCOLN offered an amendment, allowing the State to pay in Bonds at par for all work hereafter done, and to issue therefor $3,000,000 bonds.

Mr. BISSELL[2] moved to strike out 3 and insert $1,500,000. Mr. LINCOLN accepted the amendment.

Messrs. Lincoln and Dodge[3] supported the bill and Mr. Ormsbee and Kitchell[4] opposed it.

Mr. KITCHELL was surprised at the course of the gentleman from Sangamon (Mr. Lincoln). We were already prostrated by debt, and that gentleman thought it would be for the interest of the State to go still deeper. Mr. K. said it reminded him of an anecdote, which he would relate. A drunkard in Arkansas took so much of the *cretur*, that he lost his reason and remained for some time in a state of insensibility. His wife tried every experiment to cure him;

but it was of no avail, until a neighbor came to the house and recommended some *brandy toddy*. The insensible man rose at the word *toddy*, and said "that is the stuff." It was so with the gentleman from Sangamon—more debt would be for the better.

Mr. LINCOLN replied. He begged leave to tell an anecdote. The gentleman's course the past winter reminded him of an eccentric old bachelor who lived in the Hoosier State. Like the gentleman from Montgomery, he was very famous for seeing *big bugaboos* in every thing. He lived with an older brother, and one day he went out hunting. His brother heard him firing back of the field, and went out to see what was the matter. He found him loading and firing as fast as possible in the top of a tree.

Not being able to discover any thing in the tree, he asked him what he was firing at. He replied a squirrel—and kept on firing. His brother believing there was some humbug about the matter, examined his person, and found on one of his eye lashes a *big louse* crawling about. It is so with the gentleman from Montgomery. He imagined he could see squirrels every day, when they were nothing but *lice*.

[The House was convulsed with laughter.]

[1] *Sangamo Journal*, March 5, 1841. Brackets are in the source. The *Illinois State Register*, March 12, 1841, summarizes this discussion and states that Lincoln's argument showed "that to prosecute the work now was in fact the most economical plan that could be adopted: to stop it, would involve the State in much more debt and ruin." [2] William H. Bissell of Monroe County.

[3] Abram R. Dodge of LaSalle County.

[4] Joseph W. Ormsbee of Scott County and Wickliff Kitchell of Montgomery County.

Whig Protest in Illinois Legislature Against the Reorganization of the Judiciary[1]

February 26, 1841

PROTEST.

The genius and the policy of Republican institutions alike indicate the wisdom and the necessity of a frequent appeal to the

[1] *Journal of the House of Representatives of the Twelfth General Assembly of the State of Illinois* (1840-1841), pp. 539-43. Lincoln, like all Whig members, opposed this reorganization bill. How much hand he had in the composition of this protest is, however, extremely problematical. Albert J. Beveridge expresses the opinion that it was written by John J. Hardin (*Abraham Lincoln, 1809-1858*, I, 297), but this possibility is strengthened chiefly by the fact that Hardin made the formal presentation before the House. Probably both the "Protest" and the "Circular" (*supra*, February [8?], 1841), as well as earlier documents which bear Lincoln's name along with those of several Whig collaborators, were drawn by several hands.

people. It is thus, and thus only that the misconduct of their Representatives may be rebuked, and when the guards of our Constitution, and the sacred rights of minorities are trampled under foot, the time has arrived for the appeal and the decision.

The undersigned, members of the present General Assembly, have witnessed with regret and indignation, the passage of the law for the re-organization of the Judiciary. Their earnest and repeated efforts to defeat it have been unavailing, and already the din of the degrading contest for its offices and emoluments, sounds mournfully in the ear of patriotism.

To the majority of a Legislature whose idol is party supremacy, we have addressed our reasons in vain. Announced as a party measure for party purposes, it has been strengthened by the startling admission, and it only remains for us to present to the people and the country, the causes of our opposition, and our opinion of the results.

Our great objection to this bill is, that it is uncalled for by public opinion, or public convenience. The bill provides for the repeal of all the circuit courts, and for the election of five additional Supreme Judges, who, together with the present Supreme Judges, are required to hold circuit courts.

This is an entire change in our Judiciary system. By what necessity is it justified, or by what emergency is it required? Does it cause more courts to be held, or more causes to be decided? Will delays of justice be obviated, or justice brought nearer to any man's door? To all these questions, the answer must be, no. There are still but nine circuit judges. They at least can perform no more duty by being Supreme Judges. They can travel no further, endure no more, sleep no less; for at best they are but men; and whoever for a moment examines, will see, that this bill, so far from aiding the speedy administration of justice, must, by imposing new and increased duties upon the judges presiding on the circuits, most materially delay and impede it.

Since the adoption of the circuit system in 1834, the need of additional circuits has been constantly increasing, and gradually supplied. Our population has doubled, our business has increased in a still greater proportion, and the creation of new circuits, so as to keep pace with this advance, has been demanded by the people, and performed by the Legislature. There can be no doubt that a continuance in this course would have proved for the future, as it has done for the past, convenient, economical, and satisfactory.

But if this change has not been called for by public convenience, still less has it been demanded by public opinion. When the Legislature assembled in advance of the usual time, the public mind was turned with feverish anxiety to the condition of the State, and the course of its rulers; an increased debt; an empty treasury. Our internal improvement system a wretched skeleton, railroads half finished, or half decayed; iron without roads, and roads without iron; the canal so surrounded with difficulties that even its truest friends were almost found "to stop, too fearful, and too faint to go." Our scrip, issued on the faith of the State, spreading like leaves, every where, and like leaves almost valueless. These were some of the difficulties of our condition, and these it was supposed, required our utmost wisdom and patriotism. But while thus surrounded by clouds of misfortune, there was one part of the State administration against which there was no complaint, and in which almost alone, no change was required. Need we say this was our system of circuit courts, established after various trials, conforming itself to the condition and increase of our population, and approved by the experience of all the surrounding States. How strange, how unaccountable must it appear, that while all the rest of these great interests remaining unprotected, almost untouched, this system of circuit courts has been attacked and destroyed. Yet, if unjust and unwise as we believe it to be, public opinion, the great moving principle of free government, had indicated this change, we would have yielded obedience to its dictates, or at least bowed in submission to its authority. But this was not the case. In the canvass preceding the late election, excited and heated as it was, the subject was undiscussed, the change was not proposed, and even when it was known that there was a large majority of Van Buren men in either branch of the Legislature. Up to this moment, no petition, no complaint upon this subject has invited the attention of this body, or asked for its Legislation to destroy our Judiciary system.

Thus unasked, unrequired, the bill has been ushered into existence, not merely in advance, but in defiance of that public will for which its supporters always profess such profound respect.

Nor is the manner in which this bill has been sustained, less remarkable. It was preceded by the statement that the destruction of the existing system was to be followed by the creation of inferior tribunals, by which the public interests would be advanced. Their jurisdiction, their judges, their location, were left to the imaginations of those whose votes were necessary; and if visions of judicial dignity burst upon their excited fancy, and furnished powerful reasons in support of the bill they were called upon to pass, it might well be called a master stroke of policy, if not of morals, to suggest the idea. Nor were the spoils of victory to be disregarded. Scattered in every county of the State, the new clerkships might tempt avarice, and excite ambition, or at least afford a safe, if not honorable retreat from the indignation of the people.

But, as if these reasons were still insufficient, the genius of its friends were called into brilliant exercise in rousing the spirit of party; and the dominant party were called to its support in the name of Democracy, as if the spirit of Democracy could animate a measure remarkable only for its supreme contempt for the popular will, or stern determination to usurp power. It was thus the Democracy were called on to rally to its support, and it was unblushingly avowed as its object, to obtain a Democratic majority in the Supreme Court, that they might decide questions of law according to the principles of Democracy, or in other words, according to the will of the party in power. It was by these and kindred means that the bare constitutional majority was obtained, and thus the independence of the Judiciary, the surest shield of public welfare and private right, has been brought to abject submission at the feet of Legislative authority.

We have not been neglectful of our duty in warning the majority of the dangers of these violations of the spirit of the Constitution. We have pointed to the care with which the Constitution has guarded the rights of the Judiciary. We have remonstrated against this evasive mode of removing Judges who are expressly required by the Constitution to be commissioned during good behaviour. We have asked that if criminal or incompetent, they should be removed by address or impeachment, the only modes known to the Constitution; and we have deprecated in earnest but respectful terms, an arbitrary exercise of power which may soon become the precedent for still more flagrant violations of right and justice. But we have striven in vain; the torrent of party prejudices has borne down our objections, and we can only hope that in the majesty of the popular will it may find a barrier sufficient to impede its course and stay its mischief.

We desire to say also that we consider this a fit occasion to express our conviction of the great injury this bill will cause to our character as a State. We have arrived at a critical period in our history; we seem to be surrounded by adverse circumstances well fitted to try our public faith and individual virtue. It would be the greatest, as we trust it may be the last evil we could endure, to lose our rank among States, and stand disgraced amid the fair sisters of our confederacy. But if, to the calamities to which we are already subject, and which direct painful attention to our course, is to be added a party Judiciary, made by one party, and for one party, and

[247]

of one party, who that loves his country does not painfully perceive the deep but certain degradation which awaits us.

Nor do we think the influence of this bill less pernicious in its more immediate results; that there will be a lamentable want of confidence in our courts, we firmly believe; nor indeed can it be otherwise. Whoever may be selected as Judges under this bill must feel that they receive their offices from party domination, for party purposes, and the lofty independence so becoming to a judge cannot exist; the will of the party and the success of the party must be in their thoughts, and if it were possible to suppose it otherwise, how will they stand with the community? Will they not be subject to the galling but continual imputation, to the burden of a suspicion, justified, if not by their conduct, at least by their position; baneful and miserable must the tendencies of this measure be, since our courts, if not corrupt, must be suspected, and the streams of justice tinged, if not by the impurity of the fountain, by the jaundiced vision of the beholder.

There are some of the undersigned who witnessed in another State[2] the fearful consequences of a similar interference with the courts by the Legislative authority. They saw there a contest thus produced which for bitterness and ferocity has seldom been equalled; they witnessed the whole framework of society shaken, justice denied, delayed, and brought into disrepute; crime stalking unrebuked and unpunished, and the best interests of a community shattered or crushed, and they cannot remain silent when an attempt is made which being intended for similar purposes, may produce similar results.

For the reasons thus presented, and for others no less apparent, the undersigned cannot assent to the passage of the bill, or permit it to become a law without this evidence of their disapproval; and they now protest against the passage of a bill for the re-organization of the Judiciary; because,

First. It violates the great principles of the government by subjecting the Judiciary to the Legislature;

Second. It is a fatal blow at the independence of the Judges, and the constitutional term of their office;

Third. It is a measure not asked for, or wished for by the people;

Fourth. It will greatly increase the expense of our courts, or else greatly diminish their utility;

Fifth. It will give our courts a political and partizan character, thereby imparing public confidence in their decisions;

2 Kentucky.

Sixth. It will impair our standing in the opinion of other States, and the world;

Seventh. It is a party measure, for party purposes, from which no practical good to the people can possibly arise, but which may be the source of innumerable evils.

The undersigned are well aware that this protest will be altogether unavailing with the majority of this body. The blow has already fallen, and we are compelled to stand by the mournful spectators of the ruin it will cause. But we cannot do otherwise than point out the danger of this measure, its impolicy and its usurpation, in order, at least, that the despotism of a momentary majority may not become a precedent for succeeding enormities, or future crimes.

We have thus accomplished our only remaining duty on this painful subject, and we commit the final decision of this great question to the judgment and justice of the people. We have struggled ineffectually to guard the principles of our government from unhallowed innovation, and we now submit this great question to our constituents, and the country. As Representatives, we can do no more; as citizens, we shall be found where we have ever been, contending for the supremacy of the Constitution.

Nor are we without our great consolation; there is a spirit in the people, sometimes slumbering, but never extinct, which, when thoroughly aroused by usurpation or tyranny, will overwhelm the usurper and his devices in an undistinguished ruin; nor can they long escape this generous indignation, who prostitute the power bestowed by the people to unworthy ends or selfish purposes. When that spirit shall kindle in its might, and rebuke the authors and abettors of this plan, we may rely upon this protest as a proof of our fidelity to the cause of the country, and a shield against the indignation of the people.

Joseph Gillespie,	Thomas Threlkeld,	D. M. Woodson,
John J. Brown,	A. Lincoln,	E. B. Webb,
Leander Munsell,	J. M. McLean,	John Denny,
Wm. B. Archer,	H. W. Thornton,	Isaac Froman,
John F. Charles,	Wm. A. Minshall,	James H. Beall,
Isaac Funk,	Jas. M. Bradford,	Josiah Francis,
Alden Hull,	John J. Hardin,	Daniel Troy,
John Darnielle,	Jeremiah Cox,	James Parkinson,
Geo. W. Waters,	Peter Menard, Jr.,	John Canady,
Cyrus Edwards,	Wm. H. Henderson,	Alexander Phillips,
James T. Cunningham,	James Reynolds,	Jas. N. Brown,
John Bennett,	Wm. W. Bailey,	

Bill Introduced in Illinois Legislature
Supplemental to Charter of
the Springfield and Alton Turnpike Company[1]

[February 27, 1841]

SEC. 1. *Be it enacted by the People of the State of Illinois, represented in the General Assembly,* That the Springfield and Alton turnpike road company be, and they are hereby authorized to take and appropriate the work and materials on so much of the western division of the Alton and Mount Carmel railroad, as extends from the public landing in the city of Alton, to the juncture of said railroad with the Alton and Shelbyville railroad, together with all the timber and other materials that have been furnished and not used for the first mentioned railroad, and so much of the work done and materials furnished upon the Alton and Shelbyville railroad as extends from the juncture aforesaid, towards its contemplated intersection with the Central railroad, and to continue along the line of said railroad towards the Central railroad so far as they may deem proper, and also to connect the turnpike or railroad contemplated in the charter of said turnpike road company, with the Northern Cross railroad at Berlin in Sangamon county; or at such other point on said Cross railroad between Berlin and Springfield as may be most beneficial for the interest of said company, and for the public, and to use so much of the said Cross railroad between Jacksonville and Springfield as they shall deem necessary in common with the State, or any company to whom the same may be granted; and said Springfield and Alton turnpike road company shall pay to the State or company a proportionate amount for the necessary repairs of the road, and such further sum for the use of so much of said Cross railroad as shall be used as may be agreed upon by the parties; or in case of disagreement, such further sum as shall be decreed by the judge of the circuit court of Sangamon county sitting as chancellor: *Provided, always,* That the State or companies to whom the same may be granted, shall have the free and full use and enjoyment of the aforesaid State works without cost or charge, in common with the said Springfield and Alton turnpike road company: *Provided further,* That the said Springfield and Alton turnpike road company, shall enter into bond with sufficient security to the Governor, conditioned for the faithful application of the

[1] *Laws of Illinois,* 1841, pp. 353-55. Lincoln introduced the bill on February 4, but since the original document cannot be found, the act as amended and approved is reproduced from the source indicated. It is not certain that Lincoln wrote, as well as introduced, the original bill.

materials aforesaid, and for the efficient commencement of their said road within two years, and for the final completion of the same within ten years from the passage of this act.

SEC. 2. The said Springfield and Alton turnpike road company are hereby further authorized to use so much of the railroad iron now owned by the State, as will be sufficient to lay down a single or double railroad track, from the end or diverging point of the State works on the Alton and Shelbyville railroad, to the point of intersection with the Northern Cross railroad contemplated in this act, for which iron so to be used, the said company shall pay a fair value, to be determined by the company, and the proper agent of the State, which sum or value so agreed upon shall be paid by said company to the State, when it is required to pay its bonds given for said iron; the interest on the amount of iron so purchased is to be paid at such time and times as the interest is required to be paid on the bonds given as aforesaid, and the rate of interest to be the same; the final payment for said iron to be secured by pledging to the State the railroad to be constructed by the company, and by giving additional security to the satisfaction of the State.

SEC. 3. The Governor upon the filing a bond in the amount sufficient to cover all damages which may be sustained by the State, shall authorize the said Springfield and Alton turnpike road company to have and take the work and materials aforesaid, and use the same as hereby directed.

SEC. 4. That the proviso in the ninth section of the act to which this is an amendment, be, and the same is hereby repealed.

SEC. 5. That at any time after fifteen years from the completion of said Springfield and Alton turnpike road, or a railroad in lieu thereof as authorized by the charter of said company, the State shall have the privilege of purchasing said road by paying to said company the original cost of said road exclusive of the value of the work and materials obtained from the State, as herein before provided, together with such a sum by way of interest, as may, when added to the profits, the company may have received from said road equal in annual interest of six per centum on said original cost, in case said profits shall have fallen short of such annual rate of interest.

SEC. 6. That Thomas G. Hawley, Benjamin K. Hart, Jonathan T. Hudson, Jeremiah A. Townsend, John W. Buffum, S. M. Tinsley, S.B. Opdycke, F.A. Olds and Cyrus Edwards shall be commissioners in connection with the present directors of said Springfield and Alton turnpike road company, the duty of whom, or a majority of whom, shall be to open the books in the city of Springfield and Alton, or wheresoever they may deem proper after giving such notice as is required by the original charter of said company; to receive subscriptions for a sufficient amount of stock in said company over and above the present capital stock, as will enable said company, without delay, to proceed to complete said road; and the said commissioners are further authorized to receive subscriptions for so much of the original capital stock of said company as has been previously subscribed for, and on which no part of the subscription money or any instalments have been *bona fide* paid.

SEC. 7. That all acts and parts of acts inconsistent with the provisions of this act, be, and the same are hereby repealed.

SEC. 8. This act to take effect from and after its passage.

Approved, February 27, 1841.

Discussion in Illinois Legislature
of a Bill for Taxing Doctors and Lawyers[1]

February 27, 1841

Mr LINCOLN moved to amend the Lawyers tax by striking out all that part of the bill taxing lawyers $15 in every county of the State in which they attend to any suit, (besides also $15 in their own county,) the amendment was carried.

Mr. DOLLINS[2] moved to amend by substituting 10 for $15, agreed to.

Mr BISSELL[3] moved to reduce the Doctors tax from 10 to $5 agreed to.

Mr KITCHELL[4] moved to tax all the members of the Legislature $5.

Mr LINCOLN suggested that there was a rule preventing them from voting in cases in which they were interested, and it appeared to him they were interested in this case, (a laugh)

[1] *Illinois State Register*, March 12, 1841.   [2] Achilles D. Dollins.
[3] William H. Bissell.   [4] Wickliff Kitchell.

Letter Written to Silas Reed for John M. Neale[1]

Hon: Silas Reed   Springfield, Illinois,
    Surveyor General &c.   June 3rd. 1841

My object in trou[bling you] with this is to procure a contract of the [?] Surveying. You are favourably known by ma[ny promin]ent citizens of this city, and, in case you [shall be] disposed to treat my application favourably, I will procure any sort of recommendation from them that you may require.[2] Yours with respect

JOHN M. NEALE

P.S. I have concluded to send two or three recommendations at this time, thinking it might enable you to decide on my application without further delay.   J.M.N.

[1] ALS, ORB. This letter, including even the signature, is in Lincoln's hand. The document is mutilated, the editors having endeavored to supply the missing words in brackets.   [2] See Lincoln's endorsement (*infra*).

Endorsement: John T. Stuart to Silas Reed[1]

June 3, 1841

I most cheerfully endorse the foregoing recommendations of Col. Neale.   A. LINCOLN

[1] AES, ORB. Lincoln's endorsement is on the bottom of Stuart's letter to Reed, June 3, 1841, enclosed with Neale's letter to Reed of the same date (*supra*).

To William H. Davidson[1]

Dear Col: Springfield, June 4th. 1841—

Yours of the 23rd. ult: is duly received and I have most cheerfully complied with the request you make in relation to Col: Servant.[2] I have written to Mr. Tyler[3] saying all for the Col: that I could say for the best man on earth. Baker[4] will do the same to-day.

About the matter you and I spoke of at our last parting, I can say nothing which would be news to you. My feelings, and those of Baker, on that subject, are precisely the same as when we last saw you; but the question is *how* to effect any thing. If you see any way that we can do any thing you ought to write us; there is no indelicacy in it. Baker and I were with Webb[5] at Vermillion, and talked the matter over with him; and he will tell you the particulars of what we thought.

With my best respects to Mrs. Davidson and Mrs. Wilson,[6] I remain Your friend, as ever   A. LINCOLN

[1] ALS, IHi. Davidson lived at Carmi in White County, Illinois.
[2] Richard B. Servant of Chester, Illinois, who was appointed receiver of the Land Office at Kaskaskia in 1843.   [3] President John Tyler.
[4] Edward D. Baker.   [5] Edwin B. Webb.
[6] Mrs. William Wilson (nee Mary S. Davidson), sister of Davidson, and wife of the Chief Justice of Illinois.

Receipt to Josiah N. Francis[1]

June 12th. 1841–

This may certify that I have this day received of Josiah Francis[2] four notes, hereafter described, upon the following conditions that I am to keep them forty days unless the makers or any of them call and pay, and at the end of that time or any time afterwards am to return them or so many of them as remain unpaid, when said Francis may demand them of me at my office; and any money I may receive upon s[ai]d notes is to be applied to one or the other or both of two judgements obtained against sd Francis in one case & against him and others in the other, before Thomas Moffett a Justice of the Peace of Sangamon county. The constable who has the executions in those cases, if they will expire before the said forty days, may return them and take out new, & if they will not so expire, he may suspend acting upon them for that length of time.
The notes are as follows—

1 on Wesley Eads for.	$73.58
1 on William Boyd for.	34.06
1 on William Ramsay for.	20.00
1 on Bondurant & Primm for.	12.37.

A. LINCOLN

All responsibility of A. Lincoln on this receipt is discharged by receipt & application of money & by return of notes.
Nov. 17. 1845   JOSIAH FRANCIS

[1] ADS, owned by Mrs. Logan Hay, Springfield, Illinois.
[2] See letter to Thomas Bohannon, August 7, 1839, n. 3, *supra*.

To Joshua F. Speed[1]

Dear Speed: Springfield, June 19th. 1841
We have had the highest state of excitement here for a week past that our community has ever witnessed; and, although the public feeling is now somewhat allayed, the curious affair which aroused it, is verry far from being, even yet, cleared of mystery. It would take a quire of paper to give you any thing like a full account of it; and I therefore only propose a brief outline.[2] The chief personages in the drama, are Archibald Fisher, supposed to be murdered; and

[1] ALS, ORB. Speed had sold his store on January 1, 1841, and two or three months later had gone home to the Speed plantation near Louisville, Kentucky.
[2] For a more complete account see *infra*, "Remarkable Case of Arrest for Murder," April 15, 1846.

Archibald Trailor, Henry Trailor, and William Trailor, supposed to have murdered him. The three Trailors are brothers; the first, Arch: as you know, lives in town; the second, Henry, in Clary's Grove, and the third, Wm., in Warren county; and Fisher, the supposed *murderee*, being without a family, had made his home with William. On saturday evening, being the 29th. of May, Fisher and William came to Henry's in a one horse dearborn, and there staid over sunday; and on monday all three came to Springfield, Henry on horseback, and joined Archibald at Myers'[3] the dutch carpenter. That evening at supper Fisher was missing, and so next morning. Some ineffectual search was made for him; and on tuesday at 1 o'clock PM. Wm. & Henry started home without him. In a day or so Henry and one or two of his Clary Grove neighbours came back and searched for him again, and advertised his disappearance in the paper. The knowledge of the matter thus far, had not been general; and here it dropped entirely till about the 10th. Inst. when Keys[4] received a letter from the Post Master[5] in Warren [County], stating that Wm. had arrived at home, and was telling a verry mysterious and improbable story about the disappearance of Fisher, which induced the community there to suppose that he had been disposed of unfairly. Key's made this letter public, which immediately set the whole town and adjoining country agog; and so it has continued until yesterday. The mass of the People commenced a systematic search for the dead body, while Wickersham was dispatched to arrest Henry Trailor at the Grove; and Jim Maxey, to Warren to arrest William.[6] On monday last Henry was brought in, and showed an evident inclination to insinuate that he knew Fisher to be dead, and that Arch: & Wm. had killed him. He said he guessed the body could be found in Spring Creek between the Beardstown road bridge and Hickoxes[7] mill. Away the People swept like a herd of buffaloes, and cut down Hickoxes mill dam *nolens volens*, to draw the water out of the pond; and then went up and down, and down and up the creek, fishing and raking, and ducking and diving for two days, and after all, no dead body found. In the mean time a sort of scuffling ground had been found in the brush in the angle or point where the road leading into the woods past the brewery, and the one leading in past the brick-yard join. From this scuffle ground, was the sign of something about the size of a man having been dragged to the edge of the thicket, where it

3 Probably William H. Myer.
4 James W. Keyes, at the time postmaster at Springfield.
5 Probably Charles Stice, postmaster at Greenbush, near where Trailor lived.
6 Josiah Wickersham and James Maxcy were deputy sheriffs.
7 Addison and Horace Hickox operated a mill on Spring Creek.

joined the track of some small wheeled carriage which was drawn
by one horse, as shown by the horse tracks. The carriage track led
off towards Spring Creek. Near this drag trail, Dr. Merryman[8]
found *two hairs*, which after a long scientific examination, he pronounced to be triangular human hairs, which term, he says includes within it, the whiskers, the hairs growing under the arms
and on other parts of the body; and he judged that these two were
of the whiskers, because the ends were cut, showing that they had
flourished in the neighbourhood of the razor's opperations. On
thursday last, Jim: Maxey brought in William Trailor from Warren. On the same day Arch: was arrested and put in jail. Yesterday
(friday) William was put upon his examining trial before May
and Lavely.[9] Archibald and Henry were both present. Lamborn[10]
prossecuted, and Logan,[11] Baker,[12] and your humble servant, de-
fended. A great many witnesses were introduced and examined;
but I shall only mention those whose testimony seemed to be the
most important. The first of these was Capt. Ransdell.[13] He swore,
that when William and Henry left Springfield for home on the
tuesday before mentioned, they did not take the direct route, which,
you know, leads by the butcher shop, but that they followed the
street North untill they got opposite, or nearly opposite May's new
house, after which he could not see them from where he stood; and
it was afterwards proven than in about an hour after they started,
they came into the street by the butcher's shop from towards the
brick yard. Dr. Merryman & others swore to what is before stated
about the scuffle-ground, drag-trail, whiskers, and carriage tracks.
Henry was then introduced by the prossecution. He swore, that
when they started for home, they went out North as Ransdell
stated, and turned down West by the brick yard into the woods,
and there met Archibald; that they proceeded a small distance further, where he was placed as a sentinel to watch for, and announce
the approach of any one that might happen that way; that William
and Arch: took the dearborn out of the road a small distance to the
edge of the thicket, where they stopped, and he saw them lift the
body of a man into it; that they then moved off with the carriage
in the direction of Hickoxes mill, and he loitered about for something like an hour, when William returned with the carriage, but
without Arch: and said that they had put *him* in a safe place; that
they then went some how, he did not know exactly how, into the

8 Dr. Elias H. Merryman.
9 William L. May, mayor, and William Lavely, justice of the peace.
10 Josiah Lamborn.   11 Stephen T. Logan.   12 Edward D. Baker.
13 Wharton Ransdell, tavern keeper.

road close to the brewery, and proceeded on to Clary's Grove. He also stated that sometime during the day, William told him, that he and Arch: had killed Fisher the evening before; that the way they did it was by him (William) knocking him down with a club, and Arch: then choking him to death. An old man from Warren, called Dr. Gilmore, was then introduced on the part of the defence. He swore that he had known Fisher for several years; that Fisher had resided at his house a long time at each of two different spells; once while he built a barn for him, and once while he was doctored for some chronic disease; that two or three years ago, Fisher had a serious hurt in his head by the bursting of a gun, since which he has been subject to continual bad health, and occasional abberations of mind. He also stated that on last tuesday, being the same day that Maxey arrested William Trailor, he (the Dr) was from home in the early part of the day, and on his return about 11 o'clock, found Fisher at his house in bed, and apparantly verry unwell; that he asked how he had come from Springfield; that Fisher said he had come by Peoria, and also told [of] several other other [*sic*] places he had been at not in the direction of Peoria, which showed that he, at the time of speaking, did not know where he had been, or that he had been wandering about in a state of derangement. He further stated that in about two hours he received a note from one of William Trailor's friends, advising him of his arrest, and requesting him to go on to Springfield as a witness, to testify to the state of Fisher's health in former times; that he immediately set off, catching up two of his neighbours, as company, and riding all evening and all night, overtook Maxey & William at Lewiston in Fulton county; that Maxey refusing to discharge Trailor upon his statement, his two neighbors returned, and he came on to Springfield. Some question being made whether the doctor's story was not a fabrication, several acquaintances of his, among whom was the same Post Master who wrote to Key's as before mentioned, were introduced as sort of compurgators, who all swore, that they knew the doctor [to] be of good character for truth and veracity, and generally of good character in every way. Here the testimony ended, and the Trailors were discharged, Arch: and William expressing, both in word and manner their entire confidence that Fisher would be found alive at the doctor's by Galaway [*sic*], Mallory,[14] and Myers, who a day before had been dispached for that purpose; while Henry still protested that no power on earth could ever show Fisher alive. Thus stands this curious affair now. When the doctor's story was first made public, it was amusing

14 Andrew J. Galloway, Egbert M. Mallory.

to scan and contemplate the countenances, and hear the remarks of those who had been actively engaged in the search for the dead body. Some looked quizical, some melancholly, and some furiously angry. Porter, who had been very active, swore he always knew the man was not dead, and that *he* had not stirred an inch to hunt for him; Langford,[15] who had taken the lead in cuting down Hickoxes mill dam, and wanted to hang Hickox for objecting, looked most awfully wo-begone; he seemed the "*wictim of hun-requited haffection*" as represented in the comic almanic [*sic*] we used to laugh over; and Hart,[16] the little drayman that hauled Molly[17] home once, said it was too *damned* bad, to have so much trouble, and no hanging after all.

I commenced this letter on yesterday, since which I received yours of the 13th. I stick to my promise to come to Louisville. Nothing new here except what I have written. I have not seen Sarah[18] since my long trip, and I am going out there as soon as I mail this letter. Yours forever   LINCOLN.

15 James R. Langford, carpenter and joiner.
16 Ellis Hart.   17 Mary Todd.
18 Sarah A. Rickard, sister-in-law of William Butler, who made her home with the Butlers.

Statement Regarding Harry Wilton[1]

June 25, 1841

It having been charged in some of the public prints, that HARRY WILTON,[2] late United States Marshal for the District of Illinois, had used his office for political effect, in the appointment of Deputies for the taking of the census for the year 1840, we, the undersigned, were called upon by Mr. Wilton to examine the papers in his possession relative to these appointments, and to ascertain therefrom the correctness or incorrectness of such charge. We accompanied Mr. Wilton to a room, and examined the matter as fully as we could with the means afforded us. The only sources of information, bearing on the subject, which were submitted to us, were the *letters*, &c. recommending and opposing the various appointments made, and Mr. Wilton's *verbal statements* concerning the same. From these letters, &c., it appears that in some instances appointments were made in accordance with the recommendations of leading whigs, and in opposition to those of leading democrats; among which instances, the appointments in Scott, Wayne, Madison and Lawrence are the strongest. According to Mr. Wilton's statement, of the 76 appointments we examined, 54 were of democrats, 11 of whigs, and 11 of unknown politics.

The chief ground of complaint against Mr. Wilton, as we had understood it, was because of his appointment of so many democratic candidates for the legislature; thus giving them a decided advantage over their whig opponents—and consequently our attention was directed rather particularly to that point. We found that there were many such appointments, among which were those in Tazewell, McLean, Iriquois [*sic*], Coles, Menard, Wayne, Washington, Fayette, &c.; and we did not learn that there was ONE instance in which a whig candidate for the legislature had been appointed. There was no written evidence before us, showing us at what *time* those appointments were made; but Mr. Wilton stated that they all, with one exception, were made before those appointed became candidates for the legislature; and the letters, &c. recommending them all bear date before, and most of them long before those appointed were publicly announced as candidates.

We give the foregoing naked facts, and draw no conclusions from them.   BENJ. S. EDWARDS,[3]

June 25, 1841.   A. LINCOLN.

[1] *Sangamo Journal*, July 2, 1841.

[2] Appointed U. S. Marshal on June 28, 1833, and reappointed May 24, 1838. The *Sangamo Journal* had made the charge May 7, 1841.

[3] Benjamin Stephenson Edwards, youngest son of Ninian Edwards and brother of Ninian W. Edwards, was apparently not satisfied with this joint statement. Immediately following the joint statement in the *Journal* appears Edwards' individual statement, dated June 24, in which he specifies, "*I* am convinced that in no case has he [Wilton] used the office of Marshal for party or *political* purposes." The *Journal*, however, comments at length on "the facts here presented, and others of a similar character, to which we might refer, [which] led the whig party to believe that the office was used for political purposes."

To Mary Speed[1]

Miss Mary Speed,   Bloomington, Illinois,
Louisville, Ky.   Sept. 27th. 1841

My Friend: Having resolved to write to some of your mother's family, and not having the express permission of any one of them [to] do so, I have had some little difficulty in determining on which to inflict the task of reading what I now feel must be a most dull and silly letter; but when I remembered that you and I were something of cronies while I was at Farmington,[2] and that, while there, I once was under the necessity of shutting you up in a room to pre-

[1] ALS, DLC. Mary Speed was the daughter of John Speed by his first wife, and a half sister to Joshua.

[2] Lincoln visited Joshua Speed from early August to the middle of September, at the Speed plantation in Jefferson County, Kentucky, near Louisville, called Farmington.

vent your committing an assault and battery upon me, I instantly decided that you should be the devoted one.

I assume that you have not heard from Joshua & myself since we left,[3] because I think it doubtful whether he has written.

You remember there was some uneasiness about Joshua's health when we left. That little indisposition of his turned out to be nothing serious; and it was pretty nearly forgotten when we reached Springfield. We got on board the Steam Boat Lebanon, in the locks of the Canal about 12. o'clock. M. of the day we left, and reached St. Louis the next monday at 8 P.M. Nothing of interest happened during the passage, except the vexatious delays occasioned by the sand bars be thought interesting. By the way, a fine example was presented on board the boat for contemplating the effect of *condition* upon human happiness. A gentleman had purchased twelve negroes in diferent parts of Kentucky and was taking them to a farm in the South. They were chained six and six together. A small iron clevis was around the left wrist of each, and this fastened to the main chain by a shorter one at a convenient distance from, the others; so that the negroes were strung together precisely like so many fish upon a trot-line. In this condition they were being separated forever from the scenes of their childhood, their friends, their fathers and mothers, and brothers and sisters, and many of them, from their wives and children, and going into perpetual slavery where the lash of the master is proverbially more ruthless and unrelenting than any other where; and yet amid all these distressing circumstances, as we would think them, they were the most cheerful and apparantly happy creatures on board. One, whose offence for which he had been sold was an over-fondness for his wife, played the fiddle almost continually; and the others danced, sung, cracked jokes, and played various games with cards from day to day. How true it is that "God tempers the wind to the shorn lamb," or in other words, that He renders the worst of human conditions tolerable, while He permits the best, to be nothing better than tolerable.

To return to the narative. When we reached Springfield, I staid but one day when I started on this tedious circuit where I now am. Do you remember my going to the city[4] while I was in Kentucky, to have a tooth extracted, and making a failure of it? Well, that same old tooth got to paining me so much, that about a week since I had it torn out, bringing with it a bit of the jawbone; the consequence of which is that my mouth is now so sore that I can neither

3 Joshua returned with Lincoln and stayed until the first of the year.
4 Probably Louisville, Kentucky.

talk, nor eat. I am litterally "subsisting on savoury remembrances" —that is, being unable to eat, I am living upon the remembrance of the delicious dishes of peaches and cream we used to have at your house.

When we left, Miss Fanny Henning[5] was owing you a visit, as I understood. Has she paid it yet? If she has, are you not convinced that she is one of the sweetest girls in the world? There is but one thing about her, so far as I could perceive, that I would have otherwise than as it is. That is something of a tendency to melancholly. This, let it be observed, is a misfortune not a fault. Give her an assurance of my verry highest regard, when *you* see her.

Is little Siss Eliza Davis[6] at your house yet? If she is kiss her "o'er and o'er again" for me.

Tell your mother that I have not got her "present"[7] with me; but that I intend to read it regularly when I return home. I doubt not that it is really, as she says, the best cure for the "Blues" could one but take it according to the truth.

Give my respects to all your sisters (including "Aunt Emma")[8] and brothers. Tell Mrs. Peay,[9] of whose happy face I shall long retain a pleasant remembrance, that I have been trying to think of a name for her homestead, but as yet, can not satisfy myself with one. I shall be verry happy to receive a line from you, soon after you receive this; and, in case you choose to favour me with one, address it to Charleston, Coles Co. Ills as I shall be there about the time to receive it. Your sincere friend   A. LINCOLN

[5] The future wife of Joshua Speed.

[6] Since Lincoln's reference seems to imply a child, this is probably the two-year-old daughter of Joshua's younger sister Susan Fry Speed Davis. However, Mary's own younger sister (also a child of John Speed's first wife) was named Eliza Davis Speed.   [7] An "Oxford" Bible.

[8] Inquiry among descendants of the Speed family elicits the possibility that Lincoln refers to Emma Keats who married Joshua's younger brother Philip. This would account for Lincoln's use of quotation marks to set off the name. Emma Keats was a daughter of George Keats, the brother of the poet John Keats.

[9] Mrs. Peachy Walker Speed Peay (wife of Austin Peay), Joshua's older sister.

Call for Whig State Convention[1]

October 20, 1841

WHIG STATE CONVENTION.

The undersigned, acting as is believed, in accordance with the wishes of the whig party, and in compliance with their duties as the Whig Central Committee of this State, appoint the third Monday of December next, for the meeting of a Whig State Convention, at Springfield, for the purpose of nominating candidates for the offices of Governor and Lieutenant Governor of this State for the coming election.

It is recommended that the number of Delegates to the Convention shall conform to the number of Representatives to which the Counties are respectively entitled under the new apportionment; but that in all cases every County shall be entitled to one Delegate.

We would urge upon our political friends in the different Counties to call meetings immediately for the election of Delegates.

It is ardently hoped that the Counties will be fully represented, in order that the will of the people may be expressed in the selection of candidates.   A. G. HENRY,   E. D. BAKER,

Springfield, Oct. 20, 1841.   J. F. SPEED,   WM. L. MAY,

          A. LINCOLN,

          Whig State Central Committee.

1 *Sangamo Journal*, October 22, 1841.

Indenture: Thomas and Sarah Lincoln to Abraham Lincoln[1]

October 25, 1841

This Indenture made this twentyfifth day of October in the year of our Lord one thousand eight hundred and fortyone by and between Thomas Lincoln and Sarah his wife, of the county of Coles and State of Illinois, party of the first part, and Abraham Lincoln of the county of Sangamon and State aforesaid, party of the second part, Witnesseth:

That the said party of the first part, for, and in consideration of the sum of two hundred dollars to them in hand paid by the said party of the second part, the receipt whereof is hereby acknowledged, have granted, bargained, and sold; and by these presents do grant, bargain and sell unto the said party of the second part, his heirs and assigns forever, all their right, title, interest, and estate in and to the North East fourth of the South East quarter of Section Twentyone, in Township Eleven North, Range Nine East containing forty acres, more or less; reserving, however the ocupation, use, and entire control of said tract of land, and the appurtenances thereunto belonging, to the said party of the first part, and to the survivor of them, during both and each of their natural-lives.

To have and to hold to the said party of the second part, his heirs and assigns forever, subject to the reservation aforesaid, the above described tract or parcel of land, aforesaid together with all and singular the previleges and appurtenances thereunto belonging.

In testimony whereof the said party of the first part have hereunto set their hands and seals, the day and year above written.

THOMAS LINCOLN (SEAL)

her

SARAH ✕ LINCOLN (SEAL)

mark

[1] AD-P, ISLA. Document is in Lincoln's hand except for Thomas Lincoln's signature. Lincoln was in Charleston, Coles County, Illinois, October 25-26.

Acknowledgment of Deed[1]

State of Illinois ⎱ ss.   October 25, 1841
Coles County ⎰

Personally appeared before the undersigned, an acting Justice of the Peace, in and for the county aforesaid, Thomas Lincoln, and Sarah Lincoln his wife, who are personally known to me to be the identical persons by whom, and in whose names the within deed is executed, and acknowledged the same to be their voluntary act and deed for the purposes therein expressed.

Given under my hand and seal this 25th. day of October. A.D. 1841— DAVID DRYDEN J. P. (SEAL)

[1] AD-P, ISLA. In Lincoln's hand except for signature.

Bond[1]

October 25, 1841

Whereas I have purchased of Thomas Lincoln and his wife, the North East fourth of the South East quarter of Section Twentyone in Township Eleven North of Range Nine East, for which I have paid them the sum of two hundred dollars, and have taken their deed of conveyance for the same, with a reservation of a life estate therein to them and the survivor of them. Now I bind myself, my heirs and assigns, to convey said tract of land to John D. Johnston, or his heirs, at any time after the death of the survivor of the said Thomas Lincoln & wife, provided he shall pay me, my heirs or assigns, the said sum of two hundred dollars, at any time within one year after the death of the survivor of the said Thomas Lincoln & wife, and the same may be paid without interest except after the death of the survivor as aforesaid.[2]

Witness my hand and seal this 25th. of October A.D. 1841.

A. LINCOLN (SEAL)

[1] ADS, DLM.

[2] Lincoln never sold or disposed of this forty-acre tract. According to an affidavit filed May 7, 1888, John J. Hall, a second cousin, had become the owner by undisputed possession for more than twenty years.

Receipt to John Brodie[1]

November 17, 1841

Received, Springfield, Nov. 17th. 1841 of John Brodie, administrator of Archibald Hood deceased, ten dollars, being in full for a fee which said Hood owed me, and also the only debt he owed me.

A. LINCOLN

[1] ADS-P, ISLA. John Brodie and Archibald Hood were stonecutters, residents of Springfield, Illinois.

Resolutions Adopted at a Whig Meeting[1]

November 22, 1841

Whereas, a State Whig Convention has been called to reconcile conflicting claims to the nomination of a Whig candidate for Governor; and whereas Col. Wm. H. Davidson has declined being a candidate for that office—leaving no other candidate before the people than Gen. Joseph Duncan—

Resolved, As the opinion of this meeting, that the necessity of holding a State Convention seems to be obviated, and that we will cordially unite in the support of Joseph Duncan for Governor of this State—but that on the subject of holding a State convention, as on all others connected with the interests of the Whig party and the maintenance of its principles, we will abide the decision of our friends in other portions of the State.

Resolved, That we respectfully suggest the name of Hon. JUSTIN HARLAN, of Clark county—late a Judge of the Circuit Court—as a suitable candidate for the office of Lieutenant Governor.

Resolved, That the following named persons be delegates for this county to the State Whig Convention, provided it is deemed necessary to hold one: Wm. Caldwell, of Sugar Creek; S. B. Eaty of Athens; John Dawson, of Wolf Creek; H. Yates, of Island Grove; and A. Lincoln of Springfield.

[1] *Sangamo Journal,* November 26, 1841. Lincoln, Simeon Francis, and William Porter reported the resolutions as a committee.

Receipt to A. H. Kellar[1]

Decr. 6th. 1841. Received of A. H. Kellar $12.50. the ballance of his note to Stuart & Lincoln, and for one half of which I am to account to Stuart.

A. LINCOLN

[1] ADS, IHi. Probably Abram H. Keller a justice of peace in Macon County.

To Joshua F. Speed[1]

My Dear Speed: [January 3? 1842]

Feeling, as you know I do, the deepest solicitude for the success of the enterprize you are engaged in, I adopt this as the last method I can invent to aid you, in case (which God forbid) you shall need any aid. I do not place what I am going to say on paper, because I can say it any better in that way than I could by word of mouth; but because, were I to say it orrally, before we part,[2] most likely you would forget it at the verry time when it might do you some good. As I think it reasonable that you will feel verry badly some time between this and the final consummation of your purpose, it is intended that you shall read this just at such a time.

Why I say it is reasonable that you will feel verry badly yet, is, because of *three special causes,* added to the *general one* which I shall mention.

The general cause is, that you are *naturally of a nervous temperament;* and this I say from what I have seen of you personally, and what you have told me concerning your mother at various times, and concerning your brother William at the time his wife died.

The first special cause is, *your exposure to bad weather* on your journey, which my experience clearly proves to be verry severe on defective nerves.

The second is, *the absence of all business and conversation of friends,* which might divert your mind, and give it occasional rest from that *intensity* of thought, which will some times wear the sweetest idea thread-bare and turn it to the bitterness of death.

The third is, *the rapid and near approach of that crisis on which all your thoughts and feelings concentrate.*

If from all these causes you shall escape and go through triumphantly, without another "twinge of the soul," I shall be most happily, but most egregiously deceived.

If, on the contrary, you shall, as I expect you will at some time, be agonized and distressed, let me, who have some reason to speak with judgement on such a subject, beseech you, to ascribe it to the causes I have mentioned; and not to some false and ruinous suggestion of the Devil.

"But" you will say "do not your causes apply to every one engaged in a like undertaking?"

By no means. *The particular causes,* to a greater or less extent, perhaps do apply in all cases; but the *general one,* nervous debility, which is the key and conductor of all the particular ones, and without which *they* would be utterly harmless, though it *does* pertain to you, *does not* pertain to one in a thousand. It is out of this, that the painful difference between you and the mass of the world springs.

I know what the painful point with you is, at all times when you are unhappy. It is an apprehension that you do not love her as you should. What nonsense!—How came you to court her? Was it because you thought she desired it; and that you had given her reason to expect it? If it was for that, why did not the same reason make you court Ann Todd,[3] and at least twenty others of whom you can think, & to whom it would apply with greater force than to *her*? Did you court her for her wealth? Why, you knew she had none. But you say you *reasoned* yourself *into* it. What do you mean by that? Was it not, that you found yourself unable to *reason* yourself *out of* it? Did you not think, and partly form the purpose, of courting her the first time you ever saw or heard of her? What had reason to do with it, at that early stage? There was nothing *at that time* for reason to work upon. Whether she was moral, aimiable, sensible, or even of good character, you did not, nor could not then know; except perhaps you might infer the last from the company you found her in. All you then did or could know of her, was her *personal appearance and deportment;* and these, if they impress at all, impress the *heart* and not the head.

Say candidly, were not those heavenly *black eyes,* the whole basis of all your early *reasoning* on the subject?

After you and I had once been at her residence, did you not go and take me all the way to Lexington and back, for no other purpose but to get to see her again, on our return, [in that] seeming to take a trip for that express object?

What earthly consideration would you take to find her scouting and despising you, and giving herself up to another? But of this you have no apprehension; and therefore you can not bring it home to your feelings.

I shall be so anxious about you, that I want you to write me every mail. Your friend   LINCOLN

[1] ALS, ORB.

[2] Speed had returned to Springfield with Lincoln in September, 1841, but was now returning to Kentucky to live and to marry Miss Fanny Henning. The date given to this letter by Nicolay and Hay has been followed as presumably the date assigned to it by Speed for the *Complete Works,* but Speed wrote Herndon, September 17, 1866, that he remained in Springfield until the "1st of Jany. 1842" (DLC-HW). In any event, Lincoln wrote the letter before Speed's departure and presumably gave it to him before he left. There is no postmark to indicate that the letter went through the mail.

[3] Younger sister of Mary Todd.

Memorandum Concerning Bank Account
of Stuart & Lincoln[1]

Jany. 24th. 1842.

I this day drew $71.70 cents being the ballance of Stuart & Lincoln's deposit in Bank,[2] and deposited $60.41 cents thereof to the credit of Logan & Lincoln, $20. of which is for the use of Stout, Ingoldsby & Co[3] and $40.41 for the use of Daniel Stafford Jr.[4] The remaining $11.29, not knowing exactly to whom it belongs, I have put in my pocket, holding myself responsible to whomever may hereafter prove to be the owner.   A. LINCOLN

1842—Feb 28—$50 of the above this day drawn from Bank and loaned to Noah Rickard,[5] with Noah Matheny as surety
    LINCOLN

[1] Copy, ISLA.
[2] The partnership of Stuart & Lincoln was dissolved and the firm of Logan & Lincoln began doing business April 14, 1841.
[3] Unidentified.   [4] Son of Daniel Sattley Stafford?
[5] Noah M. Rickard, an older brother of Sarah Rickard. (See Lincoln to Speed, June 19, 1841, *supra*.)

To Joshua F. Speed[1]

Dear Speed: Springfield, Ills. Feby. 3– 1842–

Your letter of the 25th. Jany. came to hand to-day. You well know that I do not feel my own sorrows much more keenly than I do yours, when I know of them; and yet I assure you I was not much hurt by what you wrote me of your excessively bad feeling at the time you wrote. Not that I am less capable of sympathising with you now than ever; not that I am less your friend than ever, but because I hope and believe, that your present anxiety and distress about *her*[2] health and *her* life, must and will forever banish those horid doubts, which I know you sometimes felt, as to the truth of your affection for her. If they can be once and forever removed, (and I almost feel a presentiment that the Almighty has sent your present affliction expressly for that object) surely, nothing can come in their stead, to fill their immeasurable measure of misery. The death scenes of those we love, are surely painful enough; but these we are prepared to, and expect to see. They happen to all, and all know they must happen. Painful as they are, they are not an unlooked-for-sorrow. Should she, as you fear, be destined to an early grave, it is indeed, a great consolation to know that she is so well prepared to meet it. Her religion, which you

[267]

once disliked so much, I will venture you now prize most highly.

But I hope your melancholly bodings as to her early death, are not well founded. I even hope, that ere this reaches you, she will have returned with improved and still improving health; and that you will have met her, and forgotten the sorrows of the past, in the enjoyment of the present.

I would say more if I could; but it seems I have said enough. It really appears to me that you yourself ought to rejoice, and not sorrow, at this indubitable evidence of your undying affection for her. Why Speed, if you did not love her, although you might not wish her death, you would most calmly be resigned to it. Perhaps this point is no longer a question with you, and my pertenacious dwelling upon it, is a rude intrusion upon your feelings. If so, you must pardon me. You know the Hell I have suffered on that point, and how tender I am upon it. You know I do not mean wrong.

I have been quite clear of hypo[3] since you left,—even better than I was along in the fall.

I have seen Sarah[4] but once. She seemed verry cheerful, and so, I said nothing to her about what we spoke of.

Old uncle Billy Herndon[5] is dead; and it is said this evening that uncle Ben Ferguson[6] will not live. This I believe is all the news, and enough at that unless it were better.

Write me immediately on the receipt of this. Your friend, as ever   LINCOLN

[1] ALS, ORB.   [2] Fanny Henning.   [3] Hypochondria.
[4] Sarah Rickard.   [5] An uncle of William H. Herndon.
[6] See *infra*, Lincoln's eulogy delivered February 8, 1842.

Eulogy on Benjamin Ferguson[1]

February 8, 1842

Mr. PRESIDENT:—The solemn duty has been assigned to me, of announcing to this Society,[2] the sudden and melancholy death of its much respected member, BENJAMIN FERGUSON.

After an illness of only six days, he closed his mortal existence, at a quarter past seven on the evening of the 3d inst., in the bosom of his family at his residence in this city.

Mr. FERGUSON was one who became a member of this society without any prospect of advantage to himself. He was, though not totally abstinent, strictly temperate before; and he espoused the cause solely with the hope and benevolent design of being able, by his efforts and example, to benefit others. Would to God, he had been longer spared to the humane work upon which he had so disinterestedly entered.

In his intercourse with his fellow men, he possessed that rare uprightness of character, which was evidenced by his having no disputes or bickerings of his own, while he was ever the chosen arbiter to settle those of his neighbors.

In very truth he was, the noblest work of God—an honest man.

The grateful task commonly vouchsafed to the mournful living, of casting the mantle of charitable forgetfulness over the faults of the lamented dead, is denied to us: for although it is much to say, for any of the erring family of man, we believe we may say, that he whom we deplore was faultless.

To Almighty God we commend him; and, in his name, implore the aid and protection, of his omnipotent right arm, for his bereaved and disconsolate family.

1 *Sangamo Journal*, February 11, 1842.
2 The eulogy was delivered before the Washington Temperance Society, the same before which Lincoln was to deliver his "Temperance Address" two weeks later.

To Joshua F. Speed[1]

Dear Speed: Springfield, Ills. Feby. 13. 1842–

Yours of the 1st. Inst. came to hand three or four days ago. When this shall reach you, you will have been Fanny's husband several days.[2] You know my desire to befriend you is everlasting— that I will never cease, while I know how to do any thing.

But you will always hereafter, be on ground that I have never ocupied, and consequently, if advice were needed, I might advise wrong.

I do fondly hope, however, that you will never again need any comfort from abroad. But should I be mistaken in this—should excessive pleasure still be accompanied with a painful counterpart at times, still let me urge you, as I have ever done, to remember in the dep[t]h and even the agony of despondency, that verry shortly you are to feel well again. I am now fully convinced, that you love her as ardently as you are capable of loving. Your ever being happy in her presence, and your intense anxiety about her health, if there were nothing else, would place this beyond all dispute in my mind. I incline to think it probable, that your nerves will fail you occasionally for a while; but once you get them fairly graded now, that trouble is over forever.

I think if I were you, in case my mind were not exactly right, I would avoid being *idle*; I would immediately engage in some business, or go to making preparations for it, which would be the same thing.

If you went through the ceremony *calmly*, or even with sufficient composure not to excite alarm in any present, you are safe, beyond question, and in two or three months, to say the most, will be the happiest of men.

I hope with tolerable confidence, that this letter is a plaster for a place that is no longer sore. God grant it may be so.

I would desire you to give my particular respects to Fanny, but perhaps you will not wish her to know you have received this, lest she should desire to see it. Make her write me an answer to my last letter to her at any rate.[3] I would set great value upon another letter from her.

Write me whenever you have leisure. Yours forever.

A. LINCOLN

P.S. I have been quite a man ever since you left.

[1] ALS, ORB.   [2] The marriage took place February 15.
[3] The letter was apparently not preserved.

To Garland B. Shelledy[1]

G. B. Shelody: Esqr.   Springfield, Ills., Feby. 16– 1842–

Yours of the 10th. is duly received. Judge Logan[2] & myself are doing bussiness together now and we are willing to attend to your cases as you propose. As to the terms, we are willing to attend each case you prepare and send us for $10—(when there shall be no opposition,) to be sent in advance, or you to know that it is safe. It takes $5.75 of cost to start upon, that is, $1.75 to clerk, and $2— to each of two publishers of papers. Judge Logan thinks it will take the ballance of $20 to carry a case through. This must be advanced from time to time as the services are performed, as the officers will not act without. I do not know whether you can be admitted an attorney of the Federal court in your absence or not; nor is it material, as the business can be done in our names.

Thinking it may aid you a little, I send you one of our blank forms of Petitions. It, you will see, is framed to be sworn to before the Federal court clerk, and, in your cases, will have [to] be so far changed, as to be sworn to before the clerk of your circuit court; and his certificate must be accompanied with his official seal. The schedules too, must be attended to. Be sure that they contain the creditors *names*, their *residences*, the *amounts* due each, the *debtors names*, their *residences*, and the *amounts* they owe, also all *property* and *where* located.

Also be sure that the Schedules are *signed* by the applicants as well as the Petition.

Publication will have to be made here in one paper, and in one nearest the residence of the applicant. Write us in each case where this last advertisement is to be sent—whether to you or to what paper.

I believe I have now said every thing that can be of any advantage. Your friend, as ever   A. LINCOLN

1 ALS, owned by Garland B. Shelledy, Paris, Illinois.
2 According to William H. Herndon, Lincoln's partnership with John T. Stuart ended on April 14, 1841, and Lincoln became the junior partner of Stephen T. Logan, who was nine years his senior and an outstanding member of the bar. Logan and Lincoln were associated perhaps a few weeks earlier than the date given, since they appeared together in the case of Webb *v.* Parrin on March 23 and in several other cases in this spring term of court.

Temperance Address[1]

AN ADDRESS,

Delivered before the Springfield Washington Temperance
Society, on the 22d February, 1842–

BY ABRAHAM LINCOLN, ESQ.,

And published by direction of the Society.

Although the Temperance cause has been in progress for near twenty years, it is apparent to all, that it is, *just now,* being crowned with a degree of success, hitherto unparalleled.

The list of its friends is daily swelled by the additions of fifties, of hundreds, and of thousands. The cause itself seems suddenly transformed from a cold abstract theory, to a living, breathing, active, and powerful chieftain, going forth "conquering and to conquer." The citadels of his great adversary are daily being stormed and dismantled; his temples and his altars, where the rites of his idolatrous worship have long been performed, and where human sacrifices have long been wont to be made, are daily desecrated and deserted. The trump of the conqueror's fame is sounding from hill to hill, from sea to sea, and from land to land, and calling millions to his standard at a blast.

For this new and splendid success, we heartily rejoice. That that success is so much greater *now* than *heretofore,* is doubtless owing to rational causes; and if we would have it to continue, we shall do well to enquire what those causes are. The warfare heretofore

1 *Sangamo Journal,* March 25, 1842. The address was delivered at noon in the Second Presbyterian Church.

waged against the demon of Intemperance, has, some how or other, been erroneous. Either the champions engaged, or the tactics they adopted, have not been the most proper. These champions for the most part, have been Preachers, Lawyers, and hired agents. Between these and the mass of mankind, there is a want of *approachability*, if the term be admissible, partially at least, fatal to their success. They are supposed to have no sympathy of feeling or interest, with those very persons whom it is their object to convince and persuade.

And again, it is so easy and so common to ascribe motives to men of these classes, other than those they profess to act upon. The *preacher*, it is said, advocates temperance because he is a fanatic, and desires a union of Church and State; the *lawyer*, from his pride and vanity of hearing himself speak; and the *hired agent*, for his salary. But when one, who has long been known as a victim of intemperance, bursts the fetters that have bound him, and appears before his neighbors "clothed, and in his right mind," a redeemed specimen of long lost humanity, and stands up with tears of joy trembling in eyes, to tell of the miseries *once* endured, *now* to be endured no more forever; of his once naked and starving children, now clad and fed comfortably; of a wife long weighed down with woe, weeping, and a broken heart, now restored to health, happiness, and renewed affection; and how easily it all is done, once it is resolved to be done; however simple his language, there is a logic, and an eloquence in it, that few, with human feelings, can resist. They cannot say that *he* desires a union of church and state, for he is not a church member; they can not say *he* is vain of hearing himself speak, for his whole demeanor shows, he would gladly avoid speaking at all; they cannot say *he* speaks for pay for he receives none, and asks for none. Nor can his sincerity in any way be doubted; or his sympathy for those he would persuade to imitate his example, be denied.

In my judgment, it is to the battles of this new class of champions that our late success is greatly, perhaps chiefly, owing. But, had the old school champions themselves, been of the most wise selecting, was their *system* of tactics, the most judicious? It seems to me, it was not. Too much denunciation against dram sellers and dram-drinkers was indulged in. This, I think, was both impolitic and unjust. It was *impolitic*, because, it is not much in the nature of man to be driven to any thing; still less to be driven about that which is exclusively his own business; and least of all, where such driving is to be submitted to, at the expense of pecuniary interest, or burning appetite. When the dram-seller and drinker, were incessantly told, not in the accents of entreaty and persuasion, diffidently addressed by erring man to an erring brother; but in the thundering tones of anathema and denunciation, with which the lordly Judge often groups together all the crimes of the felon's life, and thrusts them in his face just ere he passes sentence of death upon him, that *they* were the authors of all the vice and misery and crime in the land; that *they* were the manufacturers and material of all the thieves and robbers and murderers that infested the earth; that *their* houses were the workshops of the devil; and that *their persons* should be shunned by all the good and virtuous, as moral pestilences—I say, when they were told all this, and in this way, it is not wonderful that they were slow, *very slow*, to acknowledge the truth of such denunciations, and to join the ranks of their denouncers, in a hue and cry against themselves.

To have expected them to do otherwise than as they did—to have expected them not to meet denunciation with denunciation, crimination with crimination, and anathema with anathema, was to expect a reversal of human nature, which is God's decree, and never can be reversed. When the conduct of men is designed to be influenced, *persuasion*, kind, unassuming persuasion, should ever be adopted. It is an old and a true maxim, that a "drop of honey catches more flies than a gallon of gall." So with men. If you would win a man to your cause, *first* convince him that you are his sincere friend. Therein is a drop of honey that catches his heart, which, say what he will, is the great high road to his reason, and which, when once gained, you will find but little trouble in convincing his judgment of the justice of your cause, if indeed that cause really be a just one. On the contrary, assume to dictate to his judgment, or to command his action, or to mark him as one to be shunned and despised, and he will retreat within himself, close all the avenues to his head and his heart; and tho' your cause be naked truth itself, transformed to the heaviest lance, harder than steel, and sharper than steel can be made, and tho' you throw it with more than Herculean force and precision, you shall no more be able to pierce him, than to penetrate the hard shell of a tortoise with a rye straw.

Such is man, and so *must* he be understood by those who would lead him, even to his own best interest.

On this point, the Washingtonians greatly excel the temperance advocates of former times. Those whom *they* desire to convince and persuade, are their old friends and companions. They know they are not demons, nor even the worst of men. *They* know that generally, they are kind, generous and charitable, even beyond the example of their more staid and sober neighbors. *They* are practical philanthropists; and *they* glow with a generous and brotherly zeal, that mere theorizers are incapable of feeling. Benevolence and charity possess *their* hearts entirely; and out of the abundance of their hearts, their tongues give utterance. "Love through all their actions runs, and all their words are mild." In this spirit they speak and act, and in the same, they are heard and regarded. And when such is the temper of the advocate, and such of the audience, no good cause can be unsuccessful.

But I have said that denunciations against dram-sellers and dram-drinkers, are *unjust* as well as impolitic. Let us see.

I have not enquired at what period of time the use of intoxicating drinks commenced; nor is it important to know. It is sufficient that to all of us who now inhabit the world, the practice of drinking them, is just as old as the world itself,—that is, we have seen the one, just as long as we have seen the other. When all such of us, as have now reached the years of maturity, first opened our eyes upon the stage of existence, we found intoxicating liquor, recognized by every body, used by every body, and repudiated by nobody. It commonly entered into the first draught of the infant, and the last draught of the dying man. From the sideboard of the parson, down to the ragged pocket of the houseless loafer, it was constantly found. Physicians prescribed it in this, that, and the other disease. Government provided it for its soldiers and sailors; and to have a rolling or raising, a husking or hoe-down, any where without it, was *positively insufferable.*

So too, it was every where a respectable article of manufacture and of merchandize. The making of it was regarded as an honorable livelihood; and he who could make most, was the most enterprising and respectable. Large and small manufactories of it were every where erected, in which all the earthly goods of their owners were invested. Wagons drew it from town to town—boats bore it from clime to clime, and the winds wafted it from nation to nation; and merchants bought and sold it, by wholesale and by retail, with precisely the same feelings, on the part of seller, buyer, and bystander, as are felt at the selling and buying of flour, beef, bacon, or any other of the real necessaries of life. Universal public opinion not only tolerated, but recognized and adopted its use.

It is true, that even *then*, it was known and acknowledged, that many were greatly injured by it; but none seemed to think the injury arose from the *use* of a *bad thing*, but from the *abuse* of a *very good thing*. The victims to it were pitied, and compassionated, just as now are, the heirs of consumptions, and other hereditary diseases. Their failing was treated as a *misfortune*, and not as a *crime*, or even as a *disgrace*.

If, then, what I have been saying be true, is it wonderful, that *some* should think and act *now*, as *all* thought and acted *twenty years ago*? And is it *just* to assail, *contemn*, or despise them, for doing so? The universal *sense* of mankind, on any subject, is an argument, or at least an *influence* not easily overcome. The success of the argument in favor of the existence of an over-ruling Providence, mainly depends upon that sense; and men ought not, in justice, to be denounced for yielding to it, in any case, or for giving it up slowly, *especially*, where they are backed by interest, fixed habits, or burning appetites.

Another error, as it seems to me, into which the old reformers fell, was, the position that all habitual drunkards were utterly incorrigible, and therefore, must be turned adrift, and damned without remedy, in order that the grace of temperance might abound to the temperate *then*, and to all mankind some hundred years *thereafter*. There is in this something so repugnant to humanity, so uncharitable, so cold-blooded and feelingless, that it never did, nor ever can enlist the enthusiasm of a popular cause. We could not love the man who taught it—we could not hear him with patience. The heart could not throw open its portals to it. The generous man could not adopt it. It could not mix with his blood. It looked so fiendishly selfish, so like throwing fathers and brothers overboard, to lighten the boat for our security—that the noble minded shrank from the manifest meanness of the thing.

And besides this, the benefits of a reformation to be effected by such a system, were too remote in point of time, to warmly engage many in its behalf. Few can be induced to labor exclusively for posterity; and none will do it enthusiastically. Posterity has done nothing for us; and theorise on it as we may, practically we shall do very little for it, unless we are made to think, we are, at the same time, doing something for ourselves. What an ignorance of human nature does it exhibit, to ask or expect a whole community to rise up and labor for the *temporal* happiness of *others* after *themselves* shall be consigned to the dust, a majority of which community take no pains whatever to secure their own eternal welfare, at a no greater distant day? Great distance, in either time or space, has wonderful power to lull and render quiescent the human mind. Pleasures to be enjoyed, or pains to be endured, *after* we shall be dead and gone, are but little regarded, even in our *own* cases, and much less in the cases of others.

Still, in addition to this, there is something so ludicrous in *promises* of good, or *threats* of evil, a great way off, as to render the whole subject with which they are connected, easily turned into ridicule. "Better lay down that spade you're stealing, Paddy,—if you don't you'll pay for it at the day of judgment." "By the powers, if ye'll credit me so long, I'll take another, jist."

By the Washingtonians, this system of consigning the habitual drunkard to hopeless ruin, is repudiated. *They* adopt a more enlarged philanthropy. *They* go for present as well as future good. *They* labor for all *now* living, as well as all *hereafter* to live. *They* teach *hope* to all—*despair* to none. As applying to *their* cause, *they* deny the doctrine of unpardonable sin. As in Christianity it is taught, so in this *they* teach, that

> "While the lamp holds out to burn,
> The vilest sinner may return."

And, what is matter of the most profound gratulation, they, by experiment upon experiment, and example upon example, prove the maxim to be no less true in the one case than in the other. On every hand we behold those, who but yesterday, were the chief of sinners, now the chief apostles of the cause. Drunken devils are cast out by ones, by sevens, and by legions; and their unfortunate victims, like the poor possessed, who was redeemed from his long and lonely wanderings in the tombs, are publishing to the ends of the earth, how great things have been done for them.

To these *new champions*, and this *new* system of tactics, our late success is mainly owing; and to *them* we must chiefly look for the final consummation. The ball is now rolling gloriously on, and none are so able as *they* to increase its speed, and its bulk—to add to its momentum, and its magnitude. Even though unlearned in letters, for this task, none others are so well educated. To fit them for this work, they have been taught in the true school. *They* have been in *that* gulf, from which they would teach others the means of escape. *They* have passed that prison wall, which others have long declared impassable; and who that has not, shall dare to weigh opinions with *them*, as to the mode of passing.

But if it be true, as I have insisted, that those who have suffered by intemperance *personally*, and have reformed, are the most powerful and efficient instruments to push the reformation to ultimate success, it does not follow, that those who have not suffered, have no part left them to perform. Whether or not the world would be vastly benefitted by a total and final banishment from it of all intoxicating drinks, seems to me not *now* to be an open question. Three-fourths of mankind confess the affirmative with their *tongues,* and, I believe, all the rest acknowledge it in their *hearts.*

Ought *any,* then, to refuse their aid in doing what the good of the *whole* demands? Shall he, who cannot do *much,* be, for that reason, excused if he do *nothing?* "But," says one, "what good can I do by signing the pledge? I never drink even without signing." This question has already been asked and answered more than millions of times. Let it be answered once more. For the man to suddenly, or in any other way, to break off from the use of drams, who has indulged in them for a long course of years, and until his appetite for them has become ten or a hundred fold stronger, and more craving, than any natural appetite can be, requires a most powerful moral effort. In such an undertaking, he needs every moral support and influence, that can possibly be brought to his aid, and thrown around him. And not only so; but every moral prop, should be taken *from* whatever argument might rise in his mind to lure him to his backsliding. When he casts his eyes around him, he should be able to see, all that he respects, all that he admires, and all that [he?] loves, kindly and anxiously pointing him onward; and none beckoning him back, to his former miserable "wallowing in the mire."

But it is said by some, that men will *think* and *act* for themselves; that none will disuse spirits or any thing else, merely because his neighbors do; and that *moral influence* is not that powerful engine contended for. Let us examine this. Let me ask the man who would maintain this position most stiffly, what compensation he will accept to go to church some Sunday and sit during the sermon with his wife's bonnet upon his head? Not a trifle, I'll venture. And why not? There would be nothing irreligious in it: nothing immoral, nothing uncomfortable. Then why not? Is it not because there would be something egregiously unfashionable in it? Then it is the influence of *fashion;* and what is the influence of fashion, but the influence that *other* people's actions have [on our own?] actions, the strong inclination each of us feels to do as we see all our neighbors do? Nor is the influence of fashion confined to any particular thing or class of things. It is just as strong on one subject as another. Let us make it as unfashionable to withhold our names from the temperance pledge as for husbands to wear their wives bonnets to church, and instances will be just as rare in the one case as the other.

"But," say some, "we are no drunkards; and we shall not acknowledge ourselves such by joining a reformed drunkard's society, whatever our influence might be." Surely no Christian will adhere to this objection. If they believe, as they profess, that

Omnipotence condescended to take on himself the form of sinful man, and, as such, to die an ignominious death for their sakes, surely they will not refuse submission to the infinitely lesser condescension, for the temporal, and perhaps eternal salvation, of a large, erring, and unfortunate class of their own fellow creatures. Nor is the condescension very great.

In my judgment, such of us as have never fallen victims, have been spared more from the absence of appetite, than from any mental or moral superiority over those who have. Indeed, I believe, if we take habitual drunkards as a class, their heads and their hearts will bear an advantageous comparison with those of any other class. There seems ever to have been a proneness in the brilliant, and the warm-blooded, to fall into this vice. The demon of intemperance ever seems to have delighted in sucking the blood of genius and of generosity. What one of us but can call to mind some dear relative, more promising in youth than all his fellows, who has fallen a sacrifice to his rapacity? He ever seems to have gone forth, like the Egyptian angel of death, commissioned to slay if not the first, the fairest born of every family. Shall he now be arrested in his desolating career? In that arrest, all can give aid that will; and who shall be excused that *can*, and will not? Far around as human breath has ever blown, he keeps our fathers, our brothers, our sons, and our friends, prostrate in the chains of moral death. To all the living every where, we cry, "come sound the moral resurrection trump, that these may rise and stand up, an exceeding great army" —"Come from the four winds, O breath! and breathe upon these slain, that they may live."

If the relative grandeur of revolutions shall be estimated by the great amount of human misery they alleviate, and the small amount they inflict, then, indeed, will this be the grandest the world shall ever have seen. Of our political revolution of '76, we all are justly proud. It has given us a degree of political freedom, far exceeding that of any other of the nations of the earth. In it the world has found a solution of that long mooted problem, as to the capability of man to govern himself. In it was the germ which has vegetated, and still is to grow and expand into the universal liberty of mankind.

But with all these glorious results, past, present, and to come, it had its evils too. It breathed forth famine, swam in blood and rode on fire; and long, long after, the orphan's cry, and the widow's wail, continued to break the sad silence that ensued. These were the price, the inevitable price, paid for the blessings it bought.

Turn now, to the temperance revolution. In *it*, we shall find a stronger bondage broken; a viler slavery, manumitted; a greater tyrant deposed. In *it*, more of want supplied, more disease healed, more sorrow assuaged. By *it* no orphans starving, no widows weeping. By *it*, none wounded in feeling, none injured in interest. Even the dram-maker, and dram seller, will have glided into other occupations *so* gradually, as never to have felt the shock of change; and will stand ready to join all others in the universal song of gladness.

And what a noble ally this, to the cause of political freedom. With such an aid, its march cannot fail to be on and on, till every son of earth shall drink in rich fruition, the sorrow quenching draughts of perfect liberty. Happy day, when, all appetites controled, all passions subdued, all matters subjected, *mind*, all conquering *mind*, shall live and move the monarch of the world. Glorious consummation! Hail fall of Fury! Reign of Reason, all hail!

And when the victory shall be complete—when there shall be neither a slave nor a drunkard on the earth—how proud the title of that *Land*, which may truly claim to be the birth-place and the cradle of both those revolutions, that shall have ended in that victory. How nobly distinguished that People, who shall have planted, and nurtured to maturity, both the political and moral freedom of their species.

This is the one hundred and tenth anniversary of the birth-day of Washington. We are met to celebrate this day. Washington is the mightiest name of earth—*long since* mightiest in the cause of civil liberty; *still* mightiest in moral reformation. On that name, an eulogy is expected. It cannot be. To add brightness to the sun, or glory to the name of Washington, is alike impossible. Let none attempt it. In solemn awe pronounce the name, and in its naked deathless splendor, leave it shining on.

Promissory Note of James Gambrel[1]

Springfield. Feby. 24th. 1842

On or before the first day of November next I promise to pay A. Lincoln twenty dollars in good fire wood about four feet in length, at the selling price when delivered, to be delivered at any place designated by said Lincoln, in the city of Springfield—for value received. JAMES GAMBREL

[1] AD, owned by Gordon A. Block, Philadelphia, Pennsylvania. Document is in Lincoln's hand excepting the signature. On March 18, Logan & Lincoln appeared as solicitors for Gambrel in the United States District Court, in his petition to be declared bankrupt. The promissory note probably represents the fee for this service.

To Joshua F. Speed[1]

Dear Speed: Springfield, Feb: 25– 1842–

I received yours of the 12th. written the day you went down to William's place, some days since; but delayed answering it, till I should receive the promised one, of the 16th., which came last night. I opened the latter, with intense anxiety and trepidation—so much, that although it turned out better than I expected, I have hardly yet, at the distance of ten hours, become calm.

I tell you, Speed, our *forebodings*, for which you and I are rather peculiar, are all the worst sort of nonsense. I fancied, from the time I received your letter of *saturday*, that the one of *wednesday* was never to come; and yet it *did* come, and what is more, it is perfectly clear, both from it's *tone* and *handwriting*, that you were much *happier*, or, if you think the term preferable, *less miserable*, when you wrote *it*, than when you wrote the last one before. You had so obviously improved, at the verry time I so much feared, you would have grown worse. You say that "something indescribably horrible and alarming still haunts you.["] You will not say *that* three months from now, I will venture. When your nerves once get steady now, the whole trouble will be over forever. Nor should you become impatient at their being even verry slow, in becoming steady. Again; you say you much fear that that Elysium of which you have dreamed so much, is never to be realized. Well, if it shall not, I dare swear, it will not be the fault of her who is now your wife. I now have no doubt that it is the peculiar misfortune of both you and me, to dream dreams of Elysium far exceeding all that any thing earthly can realize. Far short of your dreams as you may be, no woman could do more to realize them, than that same black eyed Fanny. If you could but contemplate her through my immagination, it would appear ridiculous to you, that any one should for a moment think of being unhappy with her. My old Father used to have a saying that "If you make a bad bargain, *hug* it the tighter"; and it occurs to me, that if the bargain you have just closed can possibly be called a bad one, it is certainly the most *pleasant one* for applying that maxim to, which my fancy can, by any effort, picture.

I write another letter enclosing this, which you can show her, if she desires it.[2] I do this, because, she would think strangely perhaps should you tell her that you receive no letters from me; or, telling her you do, should refuse to let her see them.

I close this, entertaining the confident hope, that every successive letter I shall have from you, (which I here pray may not be few, nor far between,) may show you possessing a more steady hand, and cheerful heart, than the last preceding it. As ever, your friend   LINCOLN

1 ALS, ORB.   2 *Vide infra.*

To Joshua F. Speed[1]

Dear Speed: Springfield, Feby. 25– 1842–

Yours of the 16th. Inst. announcing that Miss Fanny[2] and you "are no more twain, but one flesh," reached me this morning. I have no way of telling how much happiness I wish you both; tho' I believe you both can conceive it. I feel som[e]what jealous of both of you now; you will be so exclusively concerned for one another, that I shall be forgotten entirely. My acquaintance with Miss Fanny (I call her thus, lest you should think I am speaking of your mother) was too short for me to reasonably hope to long be remembered by her; and still, I am sure, I shall not forget her soon. Try if you can not remind her of that debt she owes me; and be sure you do not interfere to prevent her paying it.

I regret to learn that you have resolved to not return to Illinois. I shall be verry lonesome without you. How miserably things seem to be arranged in this world. If we have no friends, we have no pleasure; and if we have them, we are sure to lose them, and be doubly pained by the loss. I did hope she and you would make your home here; but I own I have no right to insist. You owe obligations to her, ten thousand times more sacred than any you can owe to others; and, in that light, let them be respected and observed. It is natural that she should desire to remain with her relatives and friends. As to friends, however, *she* could not need them any where; she would have them in abundance here.

Give my kind rememberance to Mr. Williamson and his family, particularly Miss Elizabeth[3]—also to your Mother, brothers, and sisters. Ask little Eliza Davis[4] if she will ride to town with me if I come there again.

And, finally, give Fanny a double reciprocation of all the love she sent me. Write me often, and believe me Yours forever

LINCOLN

P.S. Poor Eastham[5] is gone at last. He died a while before day this morning. They say he was verry loth to die.

No clerk is appointed yet.   L.

1 ALS, ORB.   2 Speed's bride, Fanny Henning.
3 Probably an uncle of Fanny's and his daughter.
4 See note 6, letter to Miss Mary Speed, September 27, 1841.
5 Marvellous Eastham, clerk of the Sangamon County Circuit Court.

To Joshua F. Speed[1]

Dear Speed: Springfield, March 27th. 1842

Yours of the 10th. Inst. was received three or four days since. You know I am sincere, when I tell you, the pleasure it's contents gave me was and is inexpressible. As to your farm matter, I have no sympathy with you. *I* have no farm, nor ever expect to have; and, consequently, have not studied the subject enough to be much interested with it. I can only say that I am glad *you* are satisfied and pleased with it.

But on that other subject, to me of the most intense interest, whether in joy or sorrow, I never had the power to withhold my sympathy from you. It can not be told, how it now thrills me with joy, to hear you say you are *"far happier than you ever expected to be."* That much I know is enough. I know you too well to suppose your expectations were not, at least sometimes, extravagant; and if the reality exceeds them all, I say, enough, dear Lord. I am not going beyond the truth, when I tell you, that the short space it took me to read your last letter, gave me more pleasure, than the total sum of all I have enjoyed since that fatal first of Jany. '41[2]. Since then, it seems to me, I should have been entirely happy, but for the never-absent idea, that there is *one* still unhappy whom I have contributed to make so. That still kills my soul. I can not but reproach myself, for even wishing to be happy while she is otherwise. She accompanied a large party on the Rail Road cars, to Jacksonville last monday; and on her return, spoke, so that I heard of it, of having enjoyed the trip exceedingly. God be praised for that.

You know with what sleepless vigilance I have watched you, ever since the commencement of your affair; and altho' I am now almost confident it is useless, I can not forbear once more to say that I think it is even yet possible for your spirits to flag down and leave you miserable. If they should, dont fail to remember that they can not long remain so.

One thing I can tell you which I know you will be glad to hear; and that is, that I have seen Sarah,[3] and scrutinized her feelings as well as I could, and am fully convinced, she is far happier now, than she has been for the last fifteen months past.

You will see by the last Sangamo Journal that I made a Temperance speech on the 22. of Feb. which I claim that Fanny and

[1] ALS, ORB.
[2] The date on which Lincoln asked to be released from his engagement to Mary Todd.   [3] Sarah Rickard.

you shall read as an act of charity to me; for I can not learn that any body else has read it, or is likely to. Fortunately, it is not very long and I shall deem it a sufficient compliance with my request, if one of you listens while the other reads it. As to your Lockridge matter, it is only necessary to say that there has been no court since you left, and that the next, commences to-morrow morning, during which I suppose we can not fail to get a judgement.[4]

I wish you would learn of Everett[5] what he will take, over and above a discharge for all trouble we have been at, to take his business out of our hands and give it to somebody else. It is impossible to collect money on that or any other claim here now; and altho' you know I am not a very petulant ma[n,] I declare I am almost out of patience with [Mr.] Everett's endless importunity. It seems like [he n]ot only writes all the letters he can himself; b[ut] gets every body else in Louisville and vicinity to be constantly writing to us about his claim.

I have always [h]eard that Mr. Evere[tt is] a very clever fellow, and I am very [sorry] he can not be obliged; but it does seem to me he ought to know we are interested [to] collect his money, and therefore *would* do [it] if we could. I am neither joking nor in a [pet] when I say we would thank him to transfer h[is] business to some other, without any compensation for what we have done, provided he will see the court cost paid, for which we are security.

The sweet violet you enclosed, came safely to hand, but it was so dry, and mashed so fla[t,] that it crumbled to dust at the first attempt to handle it. The juice that mashed out of it, stained a [place] on the letter, which I mean to preserve and ch[erish] for the sake of her who procured it to be se[nt.] My renewed good wishes to her, in particula[r,] and generally to all such of your relatives as know me. As ever   LINCOLN

4 On March 28, Logan & Lincoln obtained judgment for $312.09 in James Bell & Company *v.* John Lockridge. Speed had been a partner in Bell & Company.
5 A friend of Speed's who lived in Louisville, Kentucky.

Petition for Pardon of Michael Hill[1]

April 2, 1842

To his Excellency, Thomas Carlin, Governor of the State of Illinois—

The undersigned, your petitioners, respectfully represent that Michael Hill has, at the March term (now in session) of the Sangamon circuit court, been tried on an indictment for manslaughter, and a verdict of guilty, and that he be confined in the penitentiary for the term of one year and ten days found against him; that your petitioners are the jurors that rendered the verdict; that, under their oaths, they felt it their duty to render such verdict as they did, but that, considering the circumstances, they deem Mr. Hill a most fit subject for the Executive clemency; that he is an elderly, respectable, and peaceful citizen, with a large and respected family; that he was highly provoked, by oft repeated and long continued abuse, to strike the fatal blow, and that, when he did strike, it is agreed by all, he had no intention of killing, or very seriously hurting the unfortunate deceased. They therefore respectfully request, that your Excellency will grant him a full pardon of the entire punishment imposed by the law in the case.

April 2. 1842.

[1] AD, I-Ar. In addition to the signatures of the jurors, attested by John Calhoun as clerk, there are 147 signatures of citizens of Springfield and Sangamon County, including those of "A. Lincoln" and "S. T. Logan" (both signed by Lincoln).

To Joshua F. Speed[1]

Dear Speed   Springfield April 13, 1842

Your letter to the judge and me in relation to some claims of yours to be put in our hands by Mr. Hurst[2] was received some days since. The notes have not yet been handed over to us, tho they will be at any moment we desire them.

The best information we can give as to the solvency of the men you mention—is that so far as we can learn, they stand precisely as they did, when you left. We have got a judgment against Lockridge as you anticipate, and Bell,[3] by some conversational arrangement with him, has been induced to direct us to stay the execution a few months. As to Mr. Richards note, the judge I presume will attend to it, but for me I cannot even dun him. John Bran[s]on called on me to-day and begged to not be sued.[4] He says he admits it to have been owing long enough—to be paid but that he will positively pay sooner than collection could be made by law—and that he will give most any security we will ask, write us what we shall do with him. On saturday last we had a whig county convention to nominate candidates, and now guess who compose the ticket. For Representatives Wm. Caldwell, Sugar Creek, James Brown Island grove, Wm. Hickman Mechanicsburg, and judge Logan[5] in town. Col. Elkin[6] for sheriff again. Billy Herndon[7] & Dr. McNeil[8] are candidates for the legislature on their own hooks, & Harvey[9] in like manner for sheriff. Our ticket is very popular—and will certainly succeed with great ease. Edwards[10] is a little mortified tho' he is quite quiet—and has permitted no one but me to know his feelings—he goes for the ticket without complaint. Give my love to your dear Fanny and remind her once more of that letter she owes me. Are not she and you going to pay us a visit during the summer or autumn. As ever yours

A. LINCOLN

[1] Copy, DLC-HW. The original has not been located.
[2] Charles R. Hurst, clerk in James Bell & Company, who purchased Speed's share of the store in 1841.   [3] James Bell.
[4] Lincoln obtained judgment against Branson, November 17, 1843, and collected the amount on January 4, 1844.   [5] Stephen T. Logan.
[6] William F. Elkin.
[7] Probably William D. Herndon who withdrew his candidacy before the election.   [8] Francis A. McNeill.   [9] William Harvey.
[10] Ninian W. Edwards.

To G. W. Hawley[1]

Mr. G. W. Hawley   Springfield, April 18. 1842

Inclosed are the papers in your case, which together with your property and credits must be delivered up to the assignee at once. We have written the letters and sent them to your distant creditors according to the rule. You must give the personal notices to your creditors residing in your own county. Your cash account with us stands as follows. To your credit.   State Bank $10.00
                                  "   Shawneetown   10.00
                                                          ─────────
                                                            20.00

Of this we have expended of state Bank $6.00 leaving on hand $4.00.

Of the Shawnee, we have expended for these papers $3.00, for postage on your letter 37½ cents; for 70 day publication $4.00. in all $7.37½ leaving on hand $2.62½. Yours &c.

LOGAN & LINCOLN

[1] ALS, ORB. G. W. Hawley, a resident of Dixon, Illinois, was represented by Logan & Lincoln in the United States District Court, in a bankruptcy suit.

To Frederick A. Thomas[1]

Friend Thomas: Springfield, April 21 1842—

Yours of the 11th Inst. was received some days since. As to the Rules, it would be useless to send you copy; in asmuch as the Supreme court of the U.S. have adopted a set of Rules, which supercede, the rules adopted by the District court. The Supreme court Rules have not yet reached us. The personal attendance here of your friend Dr. Flanders[2] is not absolutely necessary. When you get hold of the rules, make out his papers according to them, and send them to me, and I will do my part here, for whatever you charge him for doing your part there. One thing bear constantly in mind; that is, that unless I am furnished with money to pay cost as the case progresses, I can not move an inch—and State Bank paper will not do, at that.[3] The whole cost, exclusive of lawyer's fees, will be, as we think, about $20. in something at least as good as Shawnee. Yours &c.

A. LINCOLN

P.S. Tell J. K. Dubois[4] he must come to the Legislature again; that I am off the track, and that the wheels of government will inevitably stop without the aid of one of us.

A. L.

[1] ALS-P, ISLA. Frederick A. Thomas was an attorney in Lawrenceville, Illinois.   [2] John L. Flanders.

[3] State Bank paper fell to forty-four cents on the dollar in April. Shawneetown bank paper was discounted less than ten per cent.

[4] Jesse K. Dubois of Lawrence County was a fellow committee member with Lincoln (Public Accounts and Expenditures) while in the legislature. He was reelected on August 1, 1842.

Document Drawn for Joseph Torrey and F. L. King to William Butler and Thomas Moffett[1]

April 27, 1842

Whereas William Butler and Thomas Moffett are sureties on a certain promissory note for the sum of three hundred dollars with twelve per cent interest from date until paid payable to P. C. Latham three weeks after date, and bearing date Sept. 22, 1839 to which note Joseph Torr[e]y & Co. are principals, and of which firm I am a member, and have assumed to pay said note. Now therefore to secure said Butler and Moffett from paying said note or any part thereof I transfer all book accounts due to me to them; and for this same purpose I assign to [them the?] notes of which the following is a list, towit. [Here is omitted a list of seventy-three debtors with the amount due from each of them].

And for the same purpose I transfer to said Moffett and Butler a judgement in the Sangamon circuit court in favour of said Joseph Torr[e]y & Co against Folsom Dorset, for the sum of $636.21 cents rendered Nov. 17, 1841.

Said accounts, notes, and judgement, are to be in the custody and control of Turner R. King as the mutual agent of the parties who is to collect the money due thereon as fast as possible, and apply the same to the payment of the note first, mentioned, and to return the overplus if any to me.

In testimony whereof I hereunto set my hand this 27th. day of April 1842.   F. L. KING
                                                                    By T. R. King

1 AD, IHi. Document in Lincoln's hand excepting signatures.

Petition for an Increase of the Tariff[1]

[May 12, 1842]

To the Honorable Senate and House of Representatives in Congress assembled:

The undersigned citizens of Sangamon County[2] of the State of Illinois, respectfully request Congress to establish by law a TARIFF of duties, so as to prevent excessive importations of goods, and excessive exportations of specie; to create a Home market for agricultural productions; a Home demand for the skill and industry of our people; to raise revenue enough to relieve the nation from debt and to support the government, and so to foster our manufactures as to make our nation PROSPEROUS in Peace and INDEPENDENT in War.

1 DS, DNA RG 233 HR 27A, Committee on Manufactures. The printed petition, probably clipped from a newspaper, is pasted at the top of the first of several pages of signatures, numbering 271 including Lincoln's. The petition was referred to the Committee on Manufactures May 12, 1842.
2 The words "of Sangamon County" were inserted in the printed form.

Circular to Henry E. Dummer and Others[1]

(CONFIDENTIAL)

Gentlemen   Springfield July 2d 1842

Some difficulty arises under the apportionment Bill of the last session as to the number of Senators to be elected, and the districts which they are to represent.

The Locofoco party, availing themselves as usual of every opportunity to secure and increase their power, are running a Senator from Cook and one from Will, while that district has a Senator (Pearson)[2] still in office. In the County of Green[e] they run a Senator for Green[e] and Jersey to fill a Vacancy (Allen)[3] and a Senator for Green[e] & Calhoun under the new Law. It is very much to be feared, that having already a majority assured in the Senate they would if the votes should be wanted give these Senators to be elected their seats right or wrong. There are difficulties in

[287]

a good construction of the Law and it may be a matter of much doubt, as to what the decision may be. At any rate your District (Cass & Scott) is entitled equally with the others to a Senator, if they receive them they must receive yours, and if both should be rejected, things will be as they were. We take the liberty therfore to suggest the propriety of running a whig in your new district for a Senator, as it will be done here, and we shall at any rate either get an equal number of Senators by it or prevent them from getting any.[4]

The chances of a majority for us on joint ballot are so good that we ought not to permit ourselves to loose it by negligence on our part, or fraud on theirs. Yours Sincerely

H. E. DUMMER Esqr	A. G. HENRY	S. T. LOGAN
& other good Whigs	E. D. BAKER	A. LINCOLN
	N. W. EDWARDS	J. SMITH

P.S. It will of course be better for the Clerk to give notices of the elections, but want of time in the notice, will by no means Vitiate the Election.

[1] D, IHi. The manuscript is not in Lincoln's hand, nor is the signature, but the preservation of the original in the Henry E. Dummer papers certifies that the document originated with the "Whig Junto" of Springfield over whose names it was sent out, and for whose direction Lincoln was largely responsible. Henry E. Dummer was an attorney residing at Beardstown in Cass County. He had been the law partner of John T. Stuart while living in Springfield, his place in the firm being taken by Lincoln upon his removal to Beardstown.

[2] John Pearson.   [3] John Allen.

[4] Dummer followed the advice of the circular, became a candidate for the senate from the Cass and Scott district and was defeated by the Democrat James Gillham, who was not seated, however, since Scott County was already represented under the old law.

To Joshua F. Speed[1]

Dear Speed: Springfield, Ills. July 4th. 1842–

Yours of the 16th. June was received only a day or two since. It was not mailed at Louisville till the 25th. You speak of the great time that has elapsed since I wrote you. Let me explain that. Your letter reached here a day or two after I started on the circuit; I was gone five or six weeks, so that I got the letter only a few days before Butler started to your country.[2] I thought it scarcely worth while to write you the news, which he could and would tell you more in detail. On his return, he told me you would write me soon; and so I waited for your letter. As to my having been displeased with your advice, surely you know better than that. I know you do; and

[1] ALS, ORB.   [2] William Butler, at whose home Lincoln was boarding.

therefore I will not labour to convince you. True, that subject is painfull to me; but it is not your silence, or the silence of all the world that can make me forget it. I acknowledge the correctness of your advice too; but before I resolve to do the one thing or the other, I must regain my confidence in my own ability to keep my resolves when they are made. In that ability, you know, I once prided myself as the only, or at least the chief, gem of my character; that gem I lost—how, and when, you too well know. I have not yet regained it; and until I do, I can not trust myself in any matter of much importance. I believe now that, had you understood my case at the time, as well as I understood yours afterwards, by the aid you would have given me, I should have sailed through clear; but that does not now afford me sufficient confidence, to begin that, or the like of that, again.

You make a kind acknowledgement of your obligations to me for your present happiness. I am much pleased with that acknowledgement; but a thousand times more am I pleased to know, that you enjoy a degree of happiness, worthy of an acknowledgement. The truth is, I am not sure there was any merit, with me, in the part I took in your difficulty; I was drawn to it as by fate; if I would, I could not have done less than I did. I always was superstitious; and as part of my superstition, I believe God made me one of the instruments of bringing your Fanny and you together, which union, I have no doubt He had fore-ordained. Whatever he designs, he will do for *me* yet. "Stand *still* and see the salvation of the Lord" is my text just now. If, as you say, you have told Fanny *all*, I should have no objection to her seeing this letter, but for it's reference to our friend here. Let her seeing it, depend upon whether she has ever known any thing of my affair; and if she has not, do not let her.

I do not think I can come to Kentucky this season. I am so poor, and make so little headway in the world, that I drop back in a month of idleness, as much as I gain in a year's rowing. I should like to visit you again. I should like to see that "Sis" of yours, that was absent when I was there; tho' I suppose she would run away again, if she were to hear I was coming.

About your collecting business. We have sued Branson; and will sue the others to the next court, unless they give deeds of trust as you require.[3] Col Allen happened in the office since I commenced this letter, and promises to give a deed of trust. He says he had made the arrangement to pay you, and would have done it, but for

---

[3] Lincoln got judgment for $344.79 and costs in Speed *v.* Branson & Branson in Sangamon County Circuit Court, November 17, 1843.

the going down of the Shawanee [sic] money.[4] We did not get the note in time to sue Hall at the last Tazewell court.[5] Lockridge's property is levied on for you.[6] John Irwin[7] has done nothing with that Baker & Van Bergen matter. We will not fail to bring the suits for your use, where they are in the name of James Bell & Co. I have made you a subscriber to the Journal; and also sent the number containing the temperance speech. My respect and esteem to all your friends there; and, by your permission, my love to your Fanny. Ever yours— LINCOLN

[4] Robert Allen (see letter dated June 21, 1836), proprietor of stage lines operating out of Springfield, gave his note for $900 at 12 per cent to James Bell & Company, January 1, 1842. On July 5, he gave a trust deed to 200 acres in Christian County to Lincoln for use and benefit of Speed. The Bank of Illinois (at Shawneetown) failed in February, 1842, but was expected to resume in June. Having passed the day set for resumption, June 15, the value of its paper declined further.

[5] Lincoln got judgment by default for $149.65 in James Bell & Company v. William Hall in Tazewell County Circuit Court on September 16, 1842.

[6] Supra, letter of March 27.

[7] Brother and partner of Robert Irwin. Robert Irwin & Company operated the store next door to James Bell & Company. Lincoln got judgment for $1,155 in Peter Van Bergen v. William Walters in Sangamon County Circuit Court, November 26, 1842.

To Frederick A. Thomas[1]

Friend Thomas: Springfield, July 11– 1842–

Enclosed you find your License by which you will see I have had you regularly enrolled as an attorney. The clerk is entitled to a fee of one dollar, which I have promised to see paid in one month. I therefore wish you to send me the money. It will take two dollars of State Bank or Shawneetown.

As to the customary fee in Bankruptcy for which you enquire, I can not say there is any custom on the subject. On the reverse side hereof, is a commission to Ryan[2] as Bankrupt commissioner. Your friend   A. LINCOLN

[1] ALS, original owned by Scott Thomas, Lafayette, Indiana.
[2] The commission is not available on the original document.

To Samuel D. Marshall[1]

Friend Sam: Springfield, July 14. 1842–

Yours of the 15th. June, relative to the suit of Grable vs Margrave[2] was duly received, and I have delayed answering it till now, when I can announce the result of the case. The judgement is affirmed. So soon as the clerk has liesure to make out a copy of the mandate of the court, I will get him to do so, and send it to you, by force of which, your clerk will issue an execution.

As to the fee, if you are agreed, let it be as follows. Give me credit for two years subscription to your paper,[3] and send me five dollars in good money or the equivalent of it in our Illinois paper.

There is nothing new here. Bennett's[4] Mormon disclosiers [*sic*] are making some little stir here, but not very great. Ever your friend   A. LINCOLN

1 ALS, ICHi. Marshall was an attorney practicing in Shawneetown, Illinois.
2 Lincoln argued the case before the State Supreme Court the day before.
3 *Illinois Republican*, published by Marshall.
4 General John C. Bennett, upon being cast out of the Mormon church for immoral conduct, testified copiously both as to the immorality and dangers of Mormonism to the state. His testimony has been widely discounted by historians.

To [Isaac P.?] Walker[1]

Springfield, August 15, 1842.

Friend Walker: Enclosed you have an order of court allowing your assignee to sell your property on a credit. Nothing is said in it about allowing your creditors pay for what they may purchase without money. We however, think this a matter of no consequence; as it will be a matter of course to take their *bonds* and security, as of other purchasers, and then, in the final settlement, to set off their dividends against those bonds in whole or as far as they will go. Yours, &c.,   LOGAN & LINCOLN.

1 Tarbell (Appendix), p. 288. Not being able to identify the court order or the transaction mentioned in this letter, the editors cannot be sure to which of several "Walkers" this letter was addressed. Isaac P. Walker, lawyer, Democrat, was representative in the legislature from Vermilion County in 1838.

The "Rebecca" Letter[1]

LETTER FROM THE LOST TOWNSHIPS.

Dear Mr. Printer: Lost Townships, Aug. 27, 1842.

I see you printed that long letter I sent you a spell ago[2]—I'm quite encouraged by it, and can't keep from writing again. I think

1 *Sangamo Journal*, September 2, 1842.
2 The first of the letters signed "Rebecca" dated August 10, 1842, appeared in the *Journal*, on August 19, 1842. The author of this first letter was not Lincoln. In all probability the same pen produced it which had produced an earlier series of letters from "Lost Townships," printed in the *Journal* on February 10, May 5, May 26, and September 15, 1838. The first of this series, dated January 20, 1838, has a number of interesting parallels in style to the first of the "Rebecca" series,

the printing of my letters will be a good thing all round,—it will give me the benefit of being known by the world, and give the world the advantage of knowing what's going on in the Lost Townships, and give your paper respectability besides. So here come³ another. Yesterday afternoon I hurried through cleaning up the dinner dishes, and stepped over to neighbor S—— to see if his wife Peggy was as well as mought be expected, and hear what they called the baby. Well, when I got there, and just turned round the corner of his log cabin, there he was setting on the door-step reading a newspaper.

'How are you Jeff,' says I,—he sorter started when he heard me, for he hadn't seen me before. 'Why,' says he, 'I'm mad as the devil, aunt Becca.'

'What about,' says I, 'aint its hair the right color? None of that nonsense, Jeff—there aint an honester woman in the Lost Township than—'

'Than who?' says he, 'what the mischief are you about?'

I began to see I was running the wrong trail, and so says I, 'O nothing, I guess I was mistaken a little, that's all. But what is it you're mad about?'

'Why,' says he, 'I've been tugging ever since harvest getting out wheat and hauling it to the river, to raise State Bank paper enough to pay my tax this year, and a little school debt I owe; and now just as I've got it, here I open this infernal Extra Register, expecting to find it full of "glorious democratic victories," and "High

---

³ The editors have been chary of correcting typographical errors, since the intent of semi-literacy is part of Lincoln's satire.

and reiterates the correspondent's intention of sending the editor a present (a pot of butter in the 1838 letter, a jar of pickles in the 1842 letter) in such a way that one may suspect the editor of the *Journal* of bending his literary talent to stimulate rural subscribers, notoriously in arrears, to pay in produce.

Be this as it may, there is no satisfactory evidence that Lincoln wrote the earlier series of letters from Lost Townships, and Lincoln's own testimony is against his having written any of the second series except the second letter, which is printed here.

Two more letters appeared in the *Journal* on September 9: one dated August 29 was comparatively mild in its satire and written in the same vein as the first letter of August 10; the other dated September 8 was somewhat amateurish and made even more offensive personal allusions than those contained in Lincoln's letter. This fourth letter, written by Mary Todd and Julia Jayne, and a piece of doggerel signed "Cathleen," which appeared in the *Journal* on September 16, presumably had much to do with James Shields' decision to demand from the editor, Simeon Francis, the name of the pseudonymous author. Francis may have given Shields Lincoln's name only, or Shields may have concluded on his own responsibility that only Lincoln could give him satisfaction.

In any event, the remainder of the story is told in the duel correspondence (*vide infra*).

Comb'd Cocks," when, lo and behold, I find a set of fellows calling themselves *officers of State*, have forbidden the tax collectors and school commissioners to receive State paper at all; and so here it is, dead on my hands.[4] I don't now believe all the plunder I've got will fetch ready cash enough to pay my taxes and that school debt.'

I was a good deal thunderstruck myself; for that was the first I had heard of the proclamation, and my old man was pretty much in the same fix with Jeff. We both stood a moment, staring at one another without knowing what to say. At last says I, 'Mr. S—— let me look at that paper.' He handed it to me, when I read the proclamation over.

'There now,' says he, 'did you ever see such a piece of impudence and imposition as that?' I saw Jeff was in a good tune for saying some ill-natured things, and so I tho't I would just argue a little on the contrary side, and make him rant a spell if I could.

'Why,' says I, looking as dignified and thoughtful as I could, 'it seems pretty tough to be sure, to have to raise silver where there's none to be raised; but then you see *"there will be danger of loss"* if it aint done.'

'Loss, damnation!' says he, 'I defy Daniel Webster, I defy King Solomon, I defy the world,—I defy—I defy—yes, I defy even you, aunt Becca, to show how the people can lose any thing by paying their taxes in State paper.' 'Well,' says I, 'you see what the *officers of State* say about it, and they are a desarnin set of men.' 'But,' says I, 'I guess you're mistaken about what the proclamation says; it don't say *the people* will lose any thing by the paper money being taken for taxes. It only says *"there will be danger of loss,"* and though it is tolerable plain that the people can't lose by paying their taxes in something they can get easier than silver, instead of having to pay silver; and though it is just as plain, that the State can't lose by taking State Bank paper, however low it may be, while she owes the Bank more than the whole revenue, and can pay that paper over on her debt, dollar for dollar; still *there is danger of loss* to the *"officers of State,"* and you know Jeff, we can't get along without *officers of State.'*

'Damn officers of State,' says he, 'that's what you whigs are always hurraing for.' 'Now don't swear so Jeff,' says I, 'you know I belong to the meetin, and swearin hurts my feelins.' 'Beg pardon,

---

4 The failure of the State Bank in February, 1842, put a premium on "sound" money. State Bank currency was accepted only at a discount, and since other legal tender was scarce many transactions were carried on by barter. That Shields as State Auditor was acting in the best interests of the State in refusing to honor the currency of the State Bank was beside the point so far as Whig political tactics were concerned.

aunt Becca,' says he, 'but I do say its enough to make Dr. Goddard[5] swear, to have tax to pay in silver, for nothing only that Ford[6] may get his two thousand a year, and Shields his twenty four hundred a year, and Carpenter[7] his sixteen hundred a year, and all without "danger of loss" by taking it in State paper.' 'Yes, yes, it's plain enough now what these *officers of State* mean by "danger of loss." Wash,[8] I 'spose, actually lost fifteen hundred dollars out of the three thousand that two of these "officers of State" let him steal from the Treasury, by being compelled to take it in State paper. Wonder if we don't have a proclamation before long, commanding us to make up this loss to Wash in silver.'

And so he went on, till his breath run out, and he had to stop. I couldn't think of any thing to say just then: and so I begun to look over the paper again. 'Aye! here's another proclamation, or something like it.' 'Another!' says Jeff, 'and whose egg is it, pray?' I looked to the bottom of it, and read aloud, 'Your obedient servant, Jas Shields, Auditor.'

'Aha!' says Jeff, 'one of them same three fellows again. Well read it, and let's hear what of it.' I read on till I came to where it says, *"The object of this measure is to suspend the collection of the revenue for the current year."* 'Now stop, now stop,' says he, 'that's a lie aready, and I don't want to hear of it.' 'O may be not,' says I.

'I say it—is—a—lie. — Suspend the collection, indeed! Will the collectors that have taken their oaths to make the collection DARE to suspend it? Is there any thing in the law requiring them to perjure themselves at the bidding of Jas. Shields? Will the greedy gullet of the penitentiary be satisfied with swallowing *him* instead of all *them* if they should venture to obey him? And would he not discover some "danger of loss" and be off, about the time it came to taking their places?

'And suppose the people attempt to suspend by refusing to pay, what then? The collectors would just jerk up their horses, and cows, and the like, and sell them to the highest bidder for silver in hand, without valuation or redemption. Why, Shields didn't believe that story himself—it was never meant for the truth. If it was true, why was it not writ till five days after the proclamation? Why didn't Carlin[9] and Carpenter sign it as well as Shields? Answer me that, aunt Becca. I say its a lie, and not a well told one

[5] Probably Dr. Addison S. Goddard, Methodist minister.
[6] Thomas Ford, Democrat, governor 1842-1846.
[7] Milton Carpenter, state treasurer, Democrat.
[8] Milton H. Wash, clerk in Shields' office, who had embezzled $1161 of state funds.   [9] Thomas Carlin, Democrat, governor 1838-1842.

at that. It grins out like a copper dollar. Shields is a fool as well as
a liar. With him truth is out of the question, and as for getting a
good bright passable lie out of him, you might as well try to strike
fire from a cake of tallow. I stick to it, its all an infernal whig lie.'

'A *whig* lie,—Highty! Tighty!!'

'Yes, a *whig* lie; and its just like every thing the cursed British
whigs do. First they'll do some devilment, and then they'll tell a
lie to hide it. And they don't care how plain a lie it is; they think
they can cram any sort of a one down the throats of the ignorant
loco focos, as they call the democrats.'

'Why, Jeff, you're crazy—you don't mean to say Shields is a
whig.'

'*Yes I do.*'

'Why, look here, the proclamation is in your own democratic
paper as you call it.'

'I know it, and what of that? They only printed it to let us democrats see the deviltry the whigs are at.'

'Well, but Shields is the Auditor of this loco—I mean this democratic State.'

'So he is, and Tyler appointed him to office.'

'Tyler appointed him?'

'Yes (if you must chaw it over) Tyler appointed him, or if it
wasn't him it was old granny Harrison, and that's all one. I tell
you, aunt Becca, there's no mistake about his being a whig—why
his very looks shows it—every thing about him shows it—if I was
deaf and blind I could tell him by the smell. I seed him when I
was down in Springfield last winter. They had a sort of a gatherin
there one night, among the grandees, they called a fair. All the
galls about town was there, and all the handsome widows, and
married women, finickin about, trying to look like galls, tied as
tight in the middle, and puffed out at both ends like bundles of
fodder that hadn't been stacked yet, but wanted stackin pretty bad.
And then they had tables all round the house kivered over with
baby caps, and pin-cushions, and ten thousand such little nick-
nacks, tryin to sell 'em to the fellows that were bowin and scrapin,
and kungeerin about 'em. They wouldn't let no democrats in, for
fear they'd disgust the ladies, or scare the little galls, or dirty the
floor. I looked in at the window, and there was this same fellow
Shields floatin about on the air, without heft or earthly substance,
just like a lock of cat-fur where cats had been fightin.

'He was paying his money to this one and that one, and tother
one, and sufferin great loss because it wasn't silver instead of
State paper; and the sweet distress he seemed to be in,—his very

features, in the exstatic agony of his soul, spoke audibly and distinctly—"Dear girls, *it is distressing*, but I cannot marry you all. Too well I know how much you suffer; but do, *do* remember, it is not my fault that I am *so* handsome and *so* interesting."

'As this last was expressed by a most exquisite contortion of his face, he seized hold of one of their hands and squeezed, and held on to it about a quarter of an hour. O, my good fellow, says I to myself, if that was one of our democratic galls in the Lost Township, the way you'd get a brass pin let into you, would be about up to the head. He a democrat! Fiddle-sticks! I tell you, aunt Becca, he's a whig, and no mistake: nobody but a whig could make such a conceity dunce of himself.'

'Well,' says I, 'may be he is, but if he is, I'm mistaken the worst sort.

'May be so; may be so; but if I am I'll suffer by it; I'll be a democrat if it turns out that Shields is a whig; considerin you shall be a whig if he turns out a democrat.'

'A bargain, by jingoes,' says he, 'but how will we find out.'

'Why,' says I, 'we'll just write and ax the printer.' 'Agreed again,' says he, 'and by thunder if it does turn out that Shields is a democrat, I never will ————'

'Jefferson,—Jefferson—'

'What do you want, Peggy.'

'Do get through your everlasting clatter some time, and bring me a gourd of water; the child's been crying for a drink this livelong hour.'

'Let it die then, it may as well die for water as to be taxed to death to fatten *officers of State*.'

Jeff run off to get the water though, just like he hadn't been sayin any thing spiteful; for he's a rall good hearted fellow, after all, once you get at the foundation of him.

I walked into the house, and 'why Peggy,' says I, 'I declare, we like to forgot you altogether.' 'O yes,' says she, 'when a body can't help themselves, every body soon forgets 'em; but thank God by day after to-morrow I shall be well enough to milk the cows and pen the calves, and wring the contrary one's tails for 'em, and no thanks to nobody.' 'Geod evening, Peggy,' says I, and so I sloped, for I seed she was mad at me, for making Jeff neglect her so long.

And now Mr. Printer, will you be sure to let us know in your next paper whether this Shields is a whig or a democrat? I don't care about it for myself, for I know well enough how it is already, but I want to convince Jeff. It may do some good to let him, and others like him, know *who* and *what* these *officers of State* are. It may help to send the present hypocritical set to where they belong, and to fill the places they now disgrace with men who will do more work, for less pay, and take a fewer airs while they are doing it. It aint sensible to think that the same men who get us into trouble will change their course; and yet its pretty plain, if some change for the better is not made, its not long that neither Peggy, or I, or any of us, will have a cow left to milk, or a calf's tail to wring. Yours, truly,   REBECCA———.

To Henry Clay[1]

Hon. Henry Clay,   Springfield, Illinois,
Lexington, Kentucky.   August 29, 1842.

Dear Sir: We hear you are to visit Indianapolis, Indiana, on the 5th of October next. If our information in this is correct, we hope you will not deny us the pleasure of seeing you in our State. We are aware of the toil necessarily incident to a journey by one circumstanced as you are; but once you have embarked, as you have already determined to do, the toil would not be greatly augmented by extending the journey to our capital. The season of the year will be most favorable for good roads and pleasant weather; and although we cannot but believe you would be highly gratified with such a visit to the prairie-land, the pleasure it would give us, and thousands such as we, is beyond all question. You have never visited Illinois, or at least this portion of it; and should you now yield to our request, we promise you such a reception as shall be worthy of the man on whom are now turned the fondest hopes of a great and suffering nation.

Please inform us at the earliest convenience whether we may expect you.[2] Very respectfully, your obedient servants,

A. G. Henry,[3]	P. A. Saunders,	A. Lincoln,
C. Birchall,	J. N. Francis,	Robt. Irwin,
J. M. Cabaniss,	A. T. Bledsoe,	J. M. Allen,

Executive Committee, "Clay Club."

[1] NH, I, 231-32.   [2] Clay declined with thanks on September 6, 1842.
[3] Anson G. Henry, Caleb Birchall, John M. Cabaniss, Presley A. Saunders, J. Newton Francis, Albert T. Bledsoe, Robert Irwin, James M. Allen.

Tabulation of Votes in Sangamon County for State Representatives 1832-1836[1]

[September 9, 1842]

Elections in Sangamon county Illinois, for State Representatives, in the years 1832-1834 & 1836—

1832

E. D. Taylor—	Dem.	1127	⎫
J. T. Stuart	Whig.	991	⎬ Elected
Achs. Morris.	Dem.	945	⎪
Peter Cartwright	Dem.	815	⎭
A.G. Herndon	Dem.	806	
Wm. Carpenter	Dem.	774	
John Dawson	Dem.	717	
A. Lincoln	Whig.	657	
T. M. Neale	Whig	593	
Richard Quinton	Dem.	485	
Zach. Peter	Whig	216	
Edw. Robinson	Whig	169	
Wm Kirkpatrick	Dem.	44—	

1834—

John Dawson—	Dem—	1390	⎫
A. Lincoln.	Whig	1376	⎬ Elected—
Wm. Carpenter	Dem.	1170	⎪
J. T. Stuart	Whig	1164	⎭
Richd. Quinton	Dem.	1038	
Andw. McCormick	Whig—	694	
Wm. Alvey	Whig.	613	
T. M. Neale	Whig—	514	
S. J. Campbell	Dem	192	
James Shepherd	Dem.	154	
James Baker	Whig	130	
John Durley	Whig	92	
Wm. Kendall	Whig—	42.	

1836—

A. Lincoln	Whig—	1716	⎫
W. F. Elkin	Whig.	1694	⎪
N W Edwards—	Whig—	1659	⎪
John Dawson	Whig.	1641	⎬ Elected
Dan Stone—	Whig.	1438	⎪
R. L. Wilson.	Whig.	1353	⎪
Andw. McCormick	Whig.	1306	⎭
John Calhoun	Dem.	1278	
J. M. Early	Dem.	1194	
Richd. Quinton	Dem.	1137	
Thos. Wynne.	Dem.	972	
Aaron Vandaveer	Dem.	922	
Uriah Mann	Dem.	913	
Geo. Power	Dem.	905	
James Baker—	Whig—	101	
J. L. Thompson	Dem—	38	
T. Young	Whig—	12—	

1 AD, ORB. The document carries at the bottom a certification by N. W. Matheny, Clerk, County Commissioners Court, dated September 9, 1842. It is laced together with pink ribbon tied in a bow at the top, as it was prepared for Mary Todd on the day when her satiric contribution to the Rebecca letters was published in the *Sangamo Journal* (*vide supra*). It is difficult to avoid the conjecture that Lincoln produced this prosaic but obviously sentimental document as a result of his meetings with Mary at the home of Simeon Francis during the letter-writing episode (Beveridge, I, 343-44).

To James Shields[1]

Jas. Shields, Esq.   Tremont, Sept. 17, 1842.

Your note of to-day was handed me by Gen. Whiteside.[2] In that note you say you have been informed, through the medium of the editor of the Journal,[3] that I am the author of certain articles in that paper which you deem personally abusive of you: and without stopping to enquire whether I really am the author, or to point out what is offensive in them, you demand an unqualified retraction of all that is offensive; and then proceed to hint at consequences.

Now, sir, there is in this so much assumption of facts, and so much of menace as to consequences, that I cannot submit to answer that note any farther than I have, and to add, that the consequence to which I suppose you allude, would be matter of as great regret to me as it possibly could to you.[4] Respectfully,

                                                       A. LINCOLN.

1 *Sangamo Journal*, October 14, 1842. Shields' letters also appear in this issue of the *Journal*. Lincoln was in Tremont attending court. Shields and friend John D. Whiteside went to Tremont specifically to see Lincoln.

2 The text of the note follows:

A. Lincoln, Esq.   TREMONT, Sept. 17th, 1842.

I regret that my absence on public business compelled me to postpone a matter of private consideration a little longer than I could have desired. It will only be necessary, however, to account for it by informing you that I have been to Quincy on business that would not admit of delay. I will now state briefly the reasons of my troubling you with this communication, the disagreeable nature of which I regret—as I had hoped to avoid any difficulty with any one in Springfield, while residing there, by endeavoring to conduct myself in such a way amongst both my political friends and opponents, as to escape the necessity of any. Whilst thus abstaining from giving provocation, I have become the object of slander, vituperation and personal abuse, which were I capable of submitting to, I would prove myself worthy of the whole of it.

In two or three of the last numbers of the Sangamo Journal, articles of the most personal nature and calculated to degrade me, have made their appearance. On enquiring I was informed by the editor of that paper, through the medium of my friend, Gen. Whiteside, that you are the author of those articles. This information satisfies me that I have become by some means or other, the object of your secret hostility. I will not take the trouble of enquiring into the reason of all this, but I will take the liberty of requiring a full, positive and absolute retraction of all offensive allusions used by you in these communications, in relation to my private character and standing as a man, as an apology for the insults conveyed in them.

This may prevent consequences which no one will regret more than myself. Your ob't serv't,   JAS. SHIELDS.

³ Simeon Francis.

⁴ According to Dr. Elias H. Merryman, Lincoln's second, who published the full account of the circumstances in the *Journal* on October 14 in reply to an account, published in the *Journal* on October 7, by General John D. Whiteside, Shields' second, the following note from Shields was prepared in about an hour. Whiteside conferred "two or three hours" with Lincoln's friend William Butler without presenting the note to Lincoln. "This was in consequence of an assurance from Mr. Butler that Mr. Lincoln could not receive any communication from Mr. Shields unless it were a withdrawal of his first note or a challenge. Mr. Butler further stated to Gen. Whiteside that on the withdrawal of the first note and a proper and gentlemanly request for an explanation, he had no doubt one would be given." Whiteside agreed to take the suggestion to Shields and wait until Monday (it being Saturday the seventeenth) before taking further action. Merryman continues, "On Monday morning he called and presented Mr. Lincoln the same note as Mr. Butler says he had brought on Saturday evening. It was as follows:

A. Lincoln, Esq.   TREMONT, Sept. 17, 1842.

In your reply to my note of this date, you intimate that I assume facts, and menace consequences, and that you cannot submit to answer it further. As now, sir, you desire it, I will be a little more particular. The editor of the Sangamo Journal gave me to understand that you are the author of an article which appeared I think in that paper of the 2d Sept. inst, headed the Lost Townships, and signed Rebecca or Becca. I would therefore take the liberty of asking whether you are the author of said article or any other over the same signature, which has appeared in any of the late numbers of that paper. If so, I repeat my request of an absolute retraction of all offensive allusion contained therein in relation to my private character and standing. If you are not the author of any of the articles, your denial will be sufficient. I will say further, it is not my intention to menace, but to do myself justice. Your obd't serv't,   JAS. SHIELDS."

Merryman's account continues: "This Mr. Lincoln perused, and returned to Gen. Whiteside, telling him verbally, that he did not think it consistent with his honor to negociate for peace with Mr. Shields, unless Mr. Shields would withdraw his former offensive letter." Shields, however, replied by designating Whiteside as his second, and Lincoln promptly designated Merryman as his. These gentlemen, mutually agreed to "endeavor to settle the matter amicably," returned to Springfield Monday night only to discover that much excitement prevailed and that an arrest was probable. "To prevent this," Merryman continues, "it was agreed by Mr. Lincoln and myself that he should leave early on Tuesday morning. Accordingly he prepared the following instructions for my guide, on a suggestion from Mr. Butler, that he had reason to believe that an attempt would be made by the opposite party to have the matter accommodated."

Memorandum of Duel Instructions
to Elias H. Merryman¹

[September 19, 1842]

In case Whitesides² shall signify a wish to adjust this affair without further difficulty, let him know that if the present papers be withdrawn, & a note from Mr. Shields asking to know if I am the author of the articles of which he complains, and asking that I shall make him gentlemanly satisfaction, if I am the author, and this without menace, or dictation as to what that satisfaction shall be, a pledge is made, that the following answer shall be given—

"I did write the 'Lost Township' letter which appeared in the Journal of the 2nd. Inst. but had no participation, in any form, in any other article alluding to you. I wrote that, wholly for political effect. I had no intention of injuring your personal or private character or standing as a man or a gentleman; and I did not then think, and do not now think that that article, could produce or has produced that effect against you, and had I anticipated such an effect I would have forborne to write it. And I will add, that your conduct towards me, so far as I knew, had always been gentlemanly; and that I had no personal pique against you, and no cause for any."

If this should be done, I leave it with you to arrange what shall & what shall not be published.

If nothing like this is done—the preliminaries of the fight are to be—

1st. Weapons—Cavalry broad swords of the largest size, precisely equal in all respects—and such as now used by the cavalry company at Jacksonville.

2nd. Position—A plank ten feet long, & from nine to twelve inches broad to be firmly fixed on edge, on the ground, as the line between us which neither is to pass his foot over upon forfeit of his life. Next a line drawn on the ground on either side of said plank & paralel with it, each at the distance of the whole length of the sword and three feet additional from the plank; and the passing of his own such line by either party during the fight shall be deemed a surrender of the contest.

3. Time—On thursday evening at five o'clock if you can get it so; but in no case to be at a greater distance of time than friday evening at five o'clock.

4th. Place—Within three miles of Alton on the opposite side of the river, the particular spot to be agreed on by you.

Any preliminary details coming within the above rules, you are at liberty to make at your discretion; but you are in no case to swerve from these rules, or to pass beyond their limits.

1 AD, DLC-RTL. The peaceable conclusion of the matter seemed unlikely when Whiteside refused to convey Lincoln's condition of withdrawal of the first letter written by Shields. Under threat of impending arrest all parties proceeded to Alton. At this point John J. Hardin and Revel W. English intervened as mutual friends of Shields and Lincoln, in a letter addressed to Whiteside and Merryman, proposing that "the whole difficulty be submitted to four or more gentlemen, to

be selected by yourselves, who shall consider the affair, and report thereupon for your consideration."

In spite of further disagreement and recrimination among the "friends" of the two principals in the duel, Shields finally accepted Lincoln's "explanation," through the arbitrament of seconds and mutual friends.

2 Lincoln's use of the final "s" in Whiteside's name is erroneous. John D. Whiteside was a Democrat, representative in the legislature from Monroe County 1832-1836, and state senator from Madison, St. Clair and Monroe counties, 1836-1837.

Statements Concerning the Whiteside-Merryman Affair[1]

October [4], 1842

Upon presenting this note[2] to Gen. Whiteside, and stating verbally that it was an agreement to meet him at the time he mentioned, at Louisiana, Missouri, he replied:—

"Lincoln, I can not accept any thing from him now. I have business at St. Louis: and it is as near as Louisiana."

A. LINCOLN.

Dr. Merryman requests me, as he understands you are going away, to give you notice, that he will publish the correspondence which has passed between you and him, with such comments as he shall think proper.

Upon making the above statement verbally to Gen. Whiteside, he replied:—"I am going away when it suits my convenience; but I expect Dr. Merryman, as an honorable man, to meet me at St. Louis. We then shall be untrammeled by the laws of this State."

A. LINCOLN.

1 *Sangamo Journal*, October 7, 1842. For the circumstances connected with this aftermath of the Shields-Lincoln duel, see Lincoln's letter to Speed, October 5, 1842.

2 The final note of several exchanged between six A.M. and seven P.M. on October 4. Lincoln was now acting as "friend" of Dr. Merryman, with about as much success as Merryman had had when their roles were reversed. The note denied Whiteside's "right to name time and place" and specified Louisiana, Missouri, "on Friday next." Whiteside refused to receive the note and Lincoln's first statement covers what passed between them verbally. Lincoln's second statement covers the verbal message which Merryman then requested him to deliver to Whiteside. Being unable to agree upon a meeting place, Whiteside and Merryman did not consummate their reluctant desires.

To Joshua F. Speed[1]

Dear Speed: Springfield, Oct. 5 1842—

Your have heard of my duel with Shields, and I have now to inform you that the duelling business still rages in this city. Day-before-yesterday Shields challenged Butler, who accepted, and proposed figh[t]ing next morning at sun-rising in Bob. Allen's meadow, one hundred yards distance with rifles. To this, Whitesides, Shields' second, said "No" because of the law. Thus ended, duel No. 2. Yesterday, Whitesides chose to consider himself insulted by Dr. Merryman, and so, sent him a kind of *quasi* challenge inviting him to meet him at the planter's House in St. Louis on the next friday to settle their difficulty. Merryman made me his friend, and sent W. a note enquiring to know if he meant his note as a challenge, and if so, that he would, according to the law in such case made and provided, prescribe the terms of the meeting. W. Returned for answer, that if M. would meet him at the Planter's House as desired, he would challenge him. M. replied in a note, that he denied W's right to dictate time and place; but that he, M, would would [sic] waive the question of *time*, and meet him at Louisiana Missouri. Upon my presenting this note to W. and stating verbally, it's contents, he declined receiving it, saying he had business at St. Louis, and it was as near as Louisiana. Merryman then directed me to notify Whitesides, that he should publish the correspondence between them with such comments as he thought fit. This I did. Thus it stood at bed time last night. This morning Whitesides, by his friend Shields, is praying for a new— trial, on the ground that he was mistaken in Merrymans proposition to meet him at Louisiana Missouri thinking it was the State of Louisiana. This Merryman hoots at, and is preparing his publication—while the town is in a ferment and a street fight somewhat anticipated.

But I began this letter not for what I have been writing; but to say something on that subject which you know to be of such infinite solicitude to me. The immense suffering you endured from the first days of September till the middle of February you never tried to conceal from me, and I well understood. You have now been the husband of a lovely woman nearly eight months. That you are happier now than you were the day you married her I well know; for without, you would not be living. But I have your word for it too; and the returning elasticity of spirits which is manifested in your letters. But I want to ask a closer question—"Are you now, in *feeling* as well as *judgement*, glad you are married as you are?" From any body but me, this would be an impudent question not to be tolerated; but I know you will pardon it in me. Please answer it quickly as I feel impatient to know.[2]

I have sent my love to your Fanny so often that I fear she is getting tired of it; however I venture to tender it again. Yours forever   LINCOLN

[1]ALS, ORB.   [2] Lincoln and Mary Todd were married on November 4.

To James S. Irwin[1]

Jas. S. Irwin Esqr.   Springfield, Nov. 2 1842.

Owing to my absence, yours of the 22nd. ult. was not received till this moment.

Judge Logan & myself are willing to attend to any business in the Supreme Court you may send us. As to fees, it is impossible to establish a rule that will apply in all, or even a great many cases. We believe we are never accused of being very unreasonable in this particular; and we would always be easily satisfied, provided we could see the money—but whatever fees we earn at a distance, if not paid *before*, we have noticed we never hear of after the work is done. We therefore, are growing a little sensitive on that point. Yours &c.   A. LINCOLN

[1] ALS, ORB. James S. Irwin was a native of Kentucky and a graduate of Centre College who had moved to Jacksonville, Illinois, where he studied law. Licensed to practice January 1, 1842, he moved to Mount Sterling, to which place Lincoln's letter was addressed.

Family Record in Abraham Lincoln's Bible[1]

November 4, 1842—April 4, 1853

Abraham Lincoln and Mary Todd, married, November 4—1842[2]—

Robert Todd Lincoln, born August 1—1843—

Edward B. Lincoln, born March 10—1846—

William Wallace Lincoln born December 21—1850—

Thomas Lincoln, born April 4. 1853.[3]

Edward B. Lincoln died February 1—1850[4]

[1] AD, DLC. The date of the first entry is arbitrarily selected for placing this document chronologically. This record should not be confused with the record which Lincoln wrote in the Thomas Lincoln family Bible in 1851.

[2] Entered by Robert T. Lincoln under marriages: "Robert Todd Lincoln and Mary Harlan, married September 24th 1868."

[3] Entered by Robert T. Lincoln under births: "Mary Lincoln born October 15—1869. Abraham Lincoln born August 14—1873/ Jessie Harlan Lincoln born November 6—1875."

[4] Entered by Robert T. Lincoln under deaths: "William Wallace Lincoln died February 20th. 1862/ Abraham Lincoln died April 15th 1865/ Thomas Lincoln died July 15th. 1871./ Mary Todd Lincoln died July 16th. 1882."

To Samuel D. Marshall[1]

Dear Sam.   Springfield, Nov. 11th. 1842–

Yours of the 10th. Oct. enclosing five dollars was taken from the office in my absence by Judge Logan[2] who neglected to hand it to

me till about a week ago, and just an hour before I took a wife. Your other of the 3rd. Inst. is also received. The Forbes & Hill case, of which you speak has not been brought up as yet.

I have looked into the Dorman & Lane case,[3] till I believe I understand the facts of it; and I also believe we can reverse it. In the last I may be mistaken, but I think the case, at least worth the experiment; and if Dorman will risk the cost, I will do my best for the "biggest kind of a fee" as you say, if we succeed, and nothing if we fail. I have not had a chance to consult Logan since I read your letters, but if the case comes up, I can have the use of him if I need him.

I would advise you to procure the Record and send it up immediately. Attend to the making out of the Record yourself, or most likely, the clerk will not get it all together right.

Nothing new here, except my marrying,[4] which to me, is matter of profound wonder. Yours forever   A. LINCOLN

[1] ALS, ICHi.   [2] Stephen T. Logan.

[3] After considerable litigation the case was reversed by the State Supreme Court. Lincoln settled his fee for $100 more than ten years later on April 8, 1853. The case involved the attempt of William Dorman and his wife to recover property obtained by her guardian John Lane during her minority.

[4] November 4, 1842.

To Joshua F. Speed[1]

Dear Speed: Springfield, Ills. Jany. 18– 1843–

It has been a long time since I wrote you last, but you have not been forgotten nevertheless. Hurst[2] called on me yesterday, and as he said by your direction paid me $72. State Bank paper, $42. Shawneetown paper, and $2.59 cents silver. What shall I do with it? The Nesbitts[3] have let the time of redemption run out on the land you bought on their execution, so that the land falls to you, and the cost is to be paid to the officer's somehow. Van Bergen[4] placed his debt on Walters[5] in our hands to collect and pay you. We foreclosed on Walter's house and lots and sold them & bought them in in [sic] your name. This sale, owing to the peculiarity of the case, was made without valuation or redemption, so that the property is now yours absolutely. But we suppose you would still prefer the money, and that Walters, (as he is reelected Public Printer) will wish to redeem it. We therefore suggest the propriety of your signing the blank document at the end of this sheet, authorizing Col: Elkin[6] to deed the property to Walters in case he shall redeem it. If he shall not so redeem it, there will be the cost to pay in that case too. It was sold for about $1200, the amount of

Van's debt; but although you are the ostensible purchaser, we have a secret contract with Van that he is purch[as]er for so much of the purchase money as is over and above what will pay you.

I have just called on judge Browne,[7] & find that he will pay nothing but Auditors warrants, which of course I can not receive. I wish you would direct me to bring a suit against him at once

Your brother James sent us a note on Bell & Boice,[8] which you had assigned to your Brother William. Ask James to write me whether we shall sue Boice, now that Bell is dead.

Mary is very well and continues her old sentiments of friendship for you. How the marriage life goes with us I will tell you when I see you here, which I hope will be very soon. Ever your friend   A. LINCOLN

Of course the order below is not to be used unless Walters pays the money.

Whereas at a sale of Lots 14—15 & 16 in Block 7 in E. Ile's addition to the late town now city of Springfield Illinois, made by William F Elkin as commissioner under a Decree of the Sangamon circuit court, I became the purchaser of said lots, now therefore for value received of William Walters, I authorize and direct said Elkin to convey said lots by deed to said Walters, or to any other person that said Walters may direct. Witness my hand and seal this   day of   A.D. 1843   (SEAL)

[1] ALS, ORB.
[2] Charles R. Hurst, clerk in James Bell & Company, who purchased Speed's share of the store in 1841.
[3] Lincoln got judgment for $60 for Bell & Speed v. James Nesbitt on November 24, 1841.   [4] Peter Van Bergen.
[5] William Walters, editor of the Democratic *Illinois State Register*. Lincoln had obtained judgment for $1,155 in Peter Van Bergen v. William Walters on November 26, 1842. Speed's endorsement on verso of last page reads: "replied to 27 Jany 1843/ gave Walters right to redeem if done immedyetly."
[6] William F. Elkin.   [7] Thomas C. Browne.   [8] Unidentified.

To Alden Hull[1]

Friend Hull: Springfield, Feby. 14– 1843.

Your county and ours are almost sure to be placed in the same congressional district. I would like to be it's Representative; still circumstances may happen to prevent my even being a candidate. If, however, there are any whigs in Tazewell who would as soon I should represent them as any other person, I would be glad they would not cast me aside until they see and hear further what turn things take.

Do not suppose, Esqr. that in addressing this letter to you, I assume that you will be for me against all other whigs; I only mean, that I know you to be my personal friend, a good whig, and an honorable man, to whom I may, without fear, communicate a fact which I wish my particular friends (if I have any) to know.

There is nothing new here now worth telling. Your friend as ever   A. LINCOLN

1 ALS-F, ISLA. Alden Hull had represented Tazewell County in the legislature 1838-1842.

To Richard S. Thomas[1]

Springfield, Ills., Feb. 14, 1843.

Friend Richard: . . . Now if you should hear any one say that Lincoln don't want to go to Congress, I wish you as a personal friend of mine, would tell him you have reason to believe he is mistaken. The truth is, I would like to go very much. Still, circumstances may happen which may prevent my being a candidate.

If there are any who be my friends in such an enterprise, what I now want is that they shall not throw me away just yet. Yours as ever,   A. LINCOLN.

1 Tracy, pp. 9-10. Richard S. Thomas was a lawyer of Virginia, Illinois, and an active Whig.

Resolutions at a Whig Meeting[1]

March 1, 1843

Resolved, That a Tariff of duties on imported goods, producing sufficient Revenue, for the payment of the necessary expenditures of the National Government, and so adjusted as to protect American Industry, is indispensably necessary to the prosperity of the American people.

Resolved, That we are opposed to Direct Taxation for the support of the National Government.

Resolved, That a National Bank, properly restricted, is highly necessary and proper to the establishment and maintainance of a sound currency; and for the cheap and safe collection, keeping, and disbursing the public revenue.

Resolved, That the distribution of the proceeds of the sales of Public Lands, upon the principles of Clay's bill,[2] accords with the best interests of the Nation, and particularly with those of the State of Illinois.

Resolved, That we recommend to the whigs of each Congressional District of the State, to nominate and support, at the approaching election, a candidate of their own principles, regardless of the chances of success.

Resolved, That we recommend to the whigs of all portions of this State to adopt, and rigidly adhere to, the Convention System of nominating candidates.

Resolved, That we recommend to the whigs of each Congressional District to hold a District Convention on or before the first Monday of May next, to be composed of a number of delegates from each county equal to double the number of its Representatives in the General Assembly, *provided* each county shall have at least one delegate. Said delegates to be chosen by primary meetings of the whigs, at such times and places as they in their respective counties may see fit. Said District Conventions, each, to nominate one candidate for Congress, and one delegate to a National Convention, for the purpose of nominating candidates for President and Vice President of the United States. The seven delegates so nominated to a National Convention, to have power to add two delegates to their own number, and to fill all vacancies.

Resolved, That A. T. Bledsoe,[3] S. T. Logan, and A. Lincoln, be appointed a committee to prepare an address to the People of the State.

Resolved, That N. W. Edwards, A. G. Henry, James H. Matheny, John C. Doremus, and James C. Conkling,[4] be appointed a Whig Central State Committee, with authority to fill any vacancy that may occur in the committee.

[1] Quincy *Whig,* March 15, 1843. The meeting was held in the hall of representatives in the Statehouse (see letter to John Bennett, March 7, 1843). Although Lincoln specifies the printing of the resolutions in the *Journal,* no files of the *Journal* are available for the specified date (March 9).

[2] Henry Clay's distribution bill, first introduced in 1832, provided that 10 per cent of the net proceeds of the sale of public lands be distributed to the states in which they were located. Before the bill was adopted a provision was added for pre-emption—a policy sponsored by Thomas H. Benton for the protection of so-called "squatters." A further provision made distribution contingent upon maintenance of tariff rates at a level below 20 per cent. When the 20 per cent level was reached in 1841, Clay's measure was automatically suspended. See Lincoln's discussion in the "Campaign Circular from Whig Committee," March 4, 1843.

[3] Albert Taylor Bledsoe, whose law office adjoined Lincoln's, and whose later varied career included the ministry, a professorship at the University of Virginia, and the position of assistant secretary of war in the Confederacy.

[4] Of these, two perhaps require initial identification: John Caldwell Doremus and James Cook Conkling were Springfield attorneys active in Whig politics. Conkling married Mercy Levering, close friend of Mary Todd Lincoln, and was among Lincoln's closest associates.

To Richard S. Thomas[1]

Friend Richard: Springfield, March 2. 1843–

I received yours of the 27th. ult., in due course, for which I thank you. The fact mentioned by you that an impression was being made that I did not wish to be a candidate was precisely the reason of my writing you before.

The Bill forming the Districts is now a law, and our District is composed of Putnam, Marshall, Woodford, Tazewell, Logan, Mason, Menard, Cass, Scott, Morgan and Sangamon.

Last night the Whigs of the State, now here, held a meeting and recommended that a convention be held in each District on or before the first Monday of May, to nominate candidates for congress. By this recommendation your county will have two delegates in our convention. Why might you not be one of those Delegates?

You will see the full length proceedings of the meeting in the *Journal*. The meeting was large, and every resolution passed unanimously; and I do hope the principles & recommendations put forth by them may be responded to with the same unanimity by our friends every where.

If they shall be so responded to, we shall yet, and at no very distant day, be of the majority in the State.

Write me again, if it is not too troublesome. Yours as ever,

A. LINCOLN—

[1] Copy, DLC-HW.

Campaign Circular from Whig Committee[1]

March 4, 1843

ADDRESS TO THE PEOPLE OF ILLINOIS.

FELLOW-CITIZENS: By a resolution of a meeting of such of the Whigs of the State, as are now at Springfield, we, the undersigned, were appointed to prepare an address to you.[2] The performance of that task we now undertake.

Several resolutions were adopted by the meeting; and the chief object of this address is, to show briefly, the reasons for their adoption.

The first of those resolutions declares a tariff of duties upon foreign importations, producing sufficient revenue for the support of

[1] *North Western Gazette and Galena Advertiser*, March 17, 1843. This seems the best source available for the text of this circular. However, certain variations merit attention in the printing which appears in the Quincy *Whig*, March 22, 1843. Bracketed passages are from the *Whig*, which is, however, in general an inferior printing.   [2] *Supra*, March 1, 1843.

the General Government, and so adjusted as to protect American industry, to be indispensably necessary to the prosperity of the American People; and the second declares Direct Taxation for a National Revenue to be improper. Those two resolutions are kindred in their nature, and therefore proper and convenient to be considered together. The question of protection is entirely too broad to be crowded into a few pages only, together with several other subjects. On that point, we therefore content ourselves with giving the following extracts from the writings of Mr. Jefferson, Gen. Jackson, and the speech of Mr. Calhoun:

"To be independent for the comforts of life, we must fabricate them ourselves. We must now place the manufacturer by the side of the agriculturalist. The grand inquiry now is, shall we make our own comforts, or go without them at the will of a foreign nation? He, therefore, who is now against domestic manufactures must be for reducing us either to dependence on that foreign nation, or to be clothed in skins and to live like wild beasts in dens and caverns. I am not one of those; experience has taught me that manufactures are now as necessary to our independence as to our comfort."—*Letter of Mr. Jefferson to Benjamin Austin.*[3]

"I ask, what is the real situation of the agriculturalist? Where has the American farmer a market for his surplus produce? Except for cotton, he has neither a foreign nor a home market. Does not this clearly prove, when there is no market at home or abroad, that there is too much labor employed in agriculture? Common sense at once points out the remedy. Take from agriculture 600,000 men, women and children, and you will at once give a market for more breadstuffs than all Europe now furnishes. In short, we have been too long subject to the policy of British merchants. It is time we should become a little more *Americanized,* and instead of feeding the paupers and laborers of England, feed our own; or else, in a short time, by continuing our present policy, we shall all be rendered paupers ourselves."—*Gen. Jackson's letter to Dr. Coleman.*[4]

"When our manufactures are grown to a certain perfection, as they soon will be, under the fostering care of Government, the farmer will find a ready market for his surplus produce, and, what is of equal consequence, a certain and cheap supply of all he wants; his prosperity will diffuse itself to every class of the community."
—*Speech of Hon. J. C. Calhoun on the tariff.*[5]

[3] Date of this letter is January 9, 1816.
[4] Date of this letter to Dr. Littleton Coleman, a member of the Virginia legislature and a Jackson supporter who had professed opposite views, is April 26, 1824.
[5] Speech of April 6, 1816.

The question of Revenue we will now briefly consider. For several years past, the revenues of the Government have been unequal to its expenditures, and consequently, loan after loan, sometimes directly, and sometimes indirectly in form, have been resorted to. By this means a new National debt, has been created, and is still growing on us with a rapidity fearful to contemplate—a rapidity only reasonably to be expected in time of war. This state of things has been produced by a prevailing unwillingness, either to increase the tariff, or resort to direct taxation. But the one or the other must come. Coming expenditures must be met, and the present debt must be paid; and money cannot always be borrowed for these objects. The system of loans is but temporary in its nature, and must soon explode. It is a system, not only ruinous while it lasts, but one that must soon fail and leave us destitute. As an individual who undertakes to live by borrowing, soon finds his original means devoured by interest, and next no one left to borrow from—so must it be with a government.

We repeat, then, that a tariff sufficient for revenue, or a direct tax, must soon be resorted to; and, indeed, we believe this alternative is now denied by no one. But which system shall be adopted? Some of our opponents, in theory, admit the propriety of a tariff sufficient for revenue; but even they, will not in *practice* vote for such a tariff; while others boldly advocate direct taxation. Inasmuch, therefore, as some of them boldly advocate direct taxation, and all the rest, or so nearly all, as to make exceptions needless, refuse to adopt the tariff—we think it is doing them no injustice to class them all as advocates of direct taxation. Indeed, we believe, they are only delaying an open avowal of the system, till they can assure themselves that the people will. Let us then briefly compare the two systems. The tariff is the cheaper system, because the duties, being collected in large parcels at a few commercial points, will require comparatively few officers in their collection; while by the direct tax system, the land must be literally covered with assessors and collectors, going forth like swarms of Egyptian locusts, devouring every blade of grass and other green thing. And again, by the tariff system, the whole revenue is paid by the consumers of foreign goods, and those chiefly, the luxuries, and not the necessaries of life. By this system, the man who contents himself to live upon the products of his own country, pays nothing at all. And surely, that country is extensive enough, and its products abundant and varied enough, to answer all the real wants of its people. In short, by this system, the burthen of revenue falls almost entirely on the wealthy and luxurious few, while the substantial and laboring many who live at home, and upon home products, go entirely free.

By the direct tax system, none can escape. However strictly the citizen may exclude from his premises, all foreign luxuries—fine cloths, fine silks, rich wines, golden chains, and diamond rings; still, for the possession of his house, his barn, and his homespun, he is to be perpetually haunted and harassed by the tax-gatherer. With these views we leave it to be determined, whether we or our opponents are the more truly democratic on this subject.

The third resolution declares the necessity and propriety of a National Bank. During the last fifty years so much has been said and written both as to the constitutionality and expediency of such an institution, that we could not hope to improve in the least on former discussions of the subject, were we to undertake it. We, therefore, upon the [question of?] constitutionality, content ourselves with remarking the facts, that the first National Bank was established chiefly by the same men who formed the constitution, at a time when that instrument was but two years old, receiving the sanction, as President, of the immortal Washington; that the second received the sanction, as President, of Mr. Madison, to whom common consent has awarded the proud title of "Father of the Constitution"; and subsequently the sanction of the Supreme Court, the most enlightened judicial tribunal in the world.

Upon the question of the expediency, we only ask you to examine the history of the times, during the existence of the two Banks, and compare those times with the miserable present.

The fourth resolution declares the expediency of Mr. Clay's Land Bill.[6] Much incomprehensible jargon is often urged against the constitutionality of this measure. We forbear, in this place, attempting to answer to it, simply because, in our opinion, those who urge it, are, through party zeal, resolved not to see or acknowledge the truth.

The question of expediency, at least so far as Illinois is concerned, seems to us the clearest imaginable. By the bill, we are to receive annually a large sum of money, no part of which we otherwise receive. The precise annual sum cannot be known in advance; it doubtless will vary in different years; still it is something to know, that in last year,—a year of almost unparalleled pecuniary pressure—it amounted to more than forty thousand dollars.

This annual income, in the midst of our almost insupportable difficulties, in the days of our severest necessity, our political opponents are furiously resolving to take and keep from us. And for

6 See "Resolutions at a Whig Meeting," March 1, 1843, *supra*, n. 2.

what? Many silly reasons are given, as is usual in cases when a single good one is not to be found. One is, that by giving us the proceeds of the public lands, we impoverish the National Treasury, and thereby render necessary an increase of the tariff. This may be true, but if so, the amount of it only is, that those whose pride, whose abundance of means, prompt them to spurn the manufactures of our own country, and to strut in British cloaks, and coats, and pantaloons, may have to pay a few cents more on the yard for the cloth that makes them. A terrible evil, truly, to the Illinois farmer, who never wore, nor never expects to wear, a single yard of British goods in his whole life.

Another of their reasons is, that by the passage and continuance, of Mr. Clay's bill, we prevent the passage of a bill which would give us more. This if it were sound, in itself, is waging destructive war with the former position; for if Mr. Clay's bill impoverishes the Treasury too much, what shall be said of one that impoverishes it still more? But it is not sound in itself. It is not true that Mr. Clay's bill prevents the passage of one more favorable to us of the new States. Considering the strength and opposite interest of the old States; the wonder is, that they ever permitted one to pass so favorable as Mr. Clay's. The last twenty odd years' efforts to reduce the price of the lands, and to pass graduation bills, and cession Bills, prove the assertion to be true; and even if there were no experience in support of it, the reason itself is plain. The States in which none, or few, of the public lands lie, and those consequently interested against parting with them, except for the best price, are the majority; and a moment's reflection will show, that they must ever continue the majority—because by the time one of the original new States (Ohio for example) becomes populous, and gets weight in Congress, the public lands in her limits are [so] nearly sold out, that in every point material to this question, she becomes an old State. She does not wish the price reduced, because there is none left for her citizens to buy; she does not wish them ceded to the States in which they lie, because they no longer lie in her limits, and she will get nothing by the cession. In the nature of things, the States interested in the reduction of price, in graduation, in cession, and in all similar projects, never can be the majority. Nor is there reason to hope that any of them can ever succeed as a democratic party measure, because we have heretofore seen that party in full power, year after year, with many of their leaders making loud professions in favor of these projects, and yet doing nothing. What reason then is there, to believe they will hereafter do better? In every light in which we can view this question, it amounts simply to this. Shall we accept our share of the proceeds, under Mr. Clay's bill; or shall we rather reject that, and get nothing?

The fifth resolution recommends that a Whig candidate for Congress be run in every District, regardless of the chances of success.

We are aware that it is sometimes a temporary gratification, when a friend cannot succeed, to be able to choose between opponents; but we believe that that gratification is the seed time which never fails to be followed by a most abundant harvest of bitterness. By this policy we entangle ourselves. By voting for our opponents, such of us as do it, in some measure estop ourselves to complain of their acts, however glaringly wrong we may believe them to be. By this policy, no one portion of our friends, can ever be certain as to what course another portion may adopt; and by this want of mutual and perfect understanding, our political identity is partially frittered away and lost. And again, those who are thus elected by our aid, ever become our bitterest prosecutors [persecutors]. Take a few prominent examples: In 1830 Reynolds[7] was so elected Governor; in 1835, we exerted our whole strength to elect Judge Young[8] to the United States Senate, which effort, though failing, gave him the prominence that subsequently elected him; in 1836 Gen. Ewing[9] was so elected to the United States Senate, and yet let us ask what three men have been more perseveringly vindictive in their assaults upon all our men and measures than they. During the last summer the whole State was covered with pamphlet editions of misrepresentations against us, methodized into chapters and verses, written by two of these same men, Reynolds and Young; in which they did not stop at charging us with error merely, but roundly denounced us as the designing enemies of human liberty itself. If it be the will of Heaven that such men shall politically live, be it so, but never, never again permit them to draw a particle of their sustenance from us.

The sixth resolution recommends the adoption of the convention system for the nomination of candidates.[10]

This we believe to be of the very first importance. Whether the system is right in itself, we do not stop to enquire; contenting ourselves with trying to show, that while our opponents use it, it is madness in us not to defend ourselves with it. Experience has shown that we cannot successfully defend ourselves without it. For examples, look at the election last year. Our candidate for

[7] John Reynolds.   [8] Richard Montgomery Young.
[9] William L. D. Ewing.
[10] See letter to John Bennett, March 7, 1843, where Lincoln specified his authorship of this argument in favor of conventions.

Governor, with the approbation of a large portion of the party, took the field without a nomination, and in open opposition to the system. Wherever in the counties the whigs had held Conventions and nominated candidates for the Legislature, the aspirants, who were not nominated, were induced to rebel against the nominations, and to become candidates, as is said, "on their own hook." And go where you would into a large whig county, you were sure to find the whigs, not contending shoulder to shoulder against the common enemy, but divided into factions, and fighting furiously with one another. The election came, [and] what was the result? The Governor beaten, the whig vote being decreased many thousands since 1840, although the democratic vote had not increased any. Beaten almost every where for members of the Legislature. Tazewell, with her four hundred whig majority, sending a delegation half democratic. Vermillion, with her five hundred, doing the same. Coles, with her four hundred, sending two out of three; Morgan, with her two hundred and fifty, sending her three out of four; and this, to say nothing of the numerous other less glaring examples; the whole winding up with the aggregate number of twenty-seven democratic representatives sent from whig counties. As to the Senators, too, the result was of the same character. And it is most worthy to be remembered, that of all the whigs in the State, who ran against the regular nominees, a single *one only* was elected. Although they succeeded in defeating the nominees almost by scores, they too, were defeated, and the spoils chucklingly borne off by the common enemy.

We do not mention the fact of many of the whigs opposing the Convention System heretofore, for the purpose of censuring them. Far from it. We expressly protest against such a conclusion. We know they were generally, perhaps universally, as good and true whigs, as we ourselves claim to be. We mention it merely to draw attention to the disastrous result it produced, as an example forever hereafter to be avoided.

That "union is strength" is a truth that has been known, illustrated and declared, in various ways and forms in all ages of the world. That great fabulist and philosopher, Aesop, illustrated it by his fable of the bundle of sticks; and he whose wisdom surpasses that of all philosophers, has declared that "a house divided against itself cannot stand." It is to induce our friends to act upon this important, and universally acknowledged truth, that we urge the adoption of the Convention System. Reflection will prove, that there is no other way of practically applying it. In its application, we know there will be incidents temporarily painful; but, after all, we believe those incidents will be fewer and less intense, with, than without, the system. If two friends aspire to the same office, it is certain both cannot succeed. Would it not, then, be much less painful to have the question decided by mutual friends some time before, than to snarl and quarrel till the day of election, and then both be beaten by the common enemy?

Before leaving this subject, we think proper to remark that we do not understand the resolution as intended to recommend the application of the Convention System to the nomination of candidates for the small offices no way connected with politics; though we must say, we do not perceive that such an application of it would be wrong.

The seventh resolution recommends the holding of District Conventions in May next, for the purpose of nominating candidates for Congress.

The propriety of this, rests upon the same reasons with that of the sixth, and therefore needs no further discussion.

The eighth and ninth also, relate merely to the practical application of the foregoing, and therefore need no discussion.

Before closing, permit us to add a few reflections on [the present condition and future prospects of] the whig party. In almost all the States we have fallen into the minority, and despondency seems to prevail universally among us. Is there just cause for this? In 1840 we carried the nation by more than a hundred and forty thousand majority. Our opponents charged that we did it by fraudulent voting; but whatever *they* may have *believed, we knew* the charge to be untrue. Where now is that mighty host? Have they gone over to the enemy? Let the results of the late elections answer. Every State which has fallen off from the whig cause since 1840 has done so, not by giving *more* democratic votes than they did then, but by giving *fewer* Whig. Bouck,[11] who was elected democratic Governor of New York last fall by more than 15,000 majority, had not then as many votes as he had in 1840, when he was beaten by seven or eight thousand. And so has it been in all the other States which have fallen away from our cause. From this, it is evident, that tens of thousands, in the late elections, have not voted at all. Who and what are they? is an important question, as respects the future. They *can* come forward and give us the victory again. That all, or nearly all of them, are whigs, is most apparent. Our opponents, stung to madness by the defeat of 1840, have ever since rallied with more than their usual unanimity. It has not been *they* that have been staid from the polls. These facts show what the result must be, once the people again rally in their entire strength.

11 William C. Bouck.

Proclaim these facts and predict this result, and, although unthinking opponents may smile at us, the sagacious ones will "believe and tremble." And why shall the whigs not all rally again? Are their principles less dear now than in 1840? Have any of their doctrines, since then, been discovered to be untrue? It is true, the victory of 1840 did not produce the happy results anticipated, but it is equally true, as we believe, that the unfortunate death of Gen. Harrison[12] was the cause of the failure. It was not the election of Gen. Harrison that was expected to produce happy effects, but the measures to be adopted by his administration. By means of his death, and the unexpected course of his successor, those measures were never adopted. How could the fruits follow? The consequences we always predicted, would follow the failure of those measures, have followed, and are now upon us in all their horrors. By the course of Mr. Tyler the policy of our opponents has continued in operation; still leaving them with the advantage of charging all its evils upon us as the results of a whig administration. Let none be deceived by this somewhat plausible, tho' entirely false charge. If they ask us for the sufficient and sound currency we promised, let *them* be answered, that we only promised it, through the medium of a National Bank, which, they aided by Mr. Tyler, prevented our establishing. And, let them be reminded too, that their own policy in relation to the currency, has all the time been, and still is, in full operation. Let us then again come forth in our might, and by a second victory, accomplish that, which death only prevented in the first. We can do it. When did the whigs ever fail if they were fully aroused and united? Even in single States and Districts, under such circumstances, defeat seldom overtakes them. Call to mind the contested elections within the last few years, and particularly those of Moore and Letcher from Kentucky;[13] Newland [*sic*] and Graham from North Carolina,[14] and the famous New Jersey case.[15] In all

[12] President Harrison died on April 4, 1841, one month after his inauguration, and was succeeded by John Tyler.

[13] Robert P. Letcher, Whig, contested the election of Thomas P. Moore, Democrat, to the Twenty-third Congress, but the House of Representatives did not seat either candidate and declared a new election necessary. Letcher won and took his seat on December 1, 1834.

[14] James Graham, Whig, presented credentials to the Twenty-fourth Congress, served March 4, 1835 to March 29, 1836, when his seat was declared vacant by a Democratic House, but was not given to his competitor, David Newlands. Graham was subsequently reelected.

[15] Ephraim Bateman, Whig, presiding in the joint convention of the General Assembly of New Jersey in 1826, cast the deciding vote to elect himself United States Senator against Theodore Frelinghuysen, Democrat. A select committee of five senators considered a remonstrance against the legality of his election, reported on May 22, 1828, that he had only exercised a legal right by thus voting, and discharged the remonstrance.

those districts Loco Focoism had stalked omnipotent before; but when the whole people were aroused by its enormities, on those occasions, they put it down never to rise again.

We declare it to be our solemn conviction, that the whigs are always a majority of this Nation; and that to make them always successful, needs but to get them all to the polls, and [to] vote unitedly. This is the great desideratum. Let us make every effort to attain it. At every election, let every whig act as though he knew the result to depend upon his action. In the great contest of 1840, some more than twenty-one hundred thousand votes were cast— and so surely as there shall be that many, with the ordinary increase added, cast in 1844, that surely will a whig be elected President of the United States.

A. LINCOLN.

March, 4, 1843

S. T. LOGAN.

A. T. BLEDSOE.

To John Bennett[1]

Friend Bennett: Springfield March 7– 1843–

Your letter of this day was handed me by Mr. Miles.[2] It is too late now to effect the object you desire. On yesterday morning the most of the whig members from this District got together and agreed to hold the convention at Tremont in Tazewell county. I am sorry to hear that any of the whigs of your county, or, indeed of any county, should longer be against conventions.

On last Wednesday evening a meeting of all the whigs then here from all parts of the State was held, and the question of the propriety of conventions was brought up and fully discussed, and at the end of the discussion, a resolution reccommending the system of conventions to all the whigs of the State, was unanamously adopted.[3] Other Resolutions also were passed, all of which will appear in the next Journal. The meeting also appointed a committee to draft an address to the People of the State which address will also appear in the next Journal.[4] In it, you will find a brief argument in favour of conventions; and although I wrote it myself, I *will* say to you, that it is conclusive upon this point—that it, can not be reasonably answered.

The right way for you to do, is to hold your meeting and appoint delegates any how; and if there be any who will not take part, let it be so. The matter will work so well this time that even they who now oppose will come in next time.

The convention is to be held at Tremont on the 5th. April, and according to the rule we have adopted your county is to have two delegates—being double the number of your representatives.[5]

If there be any good whig who is disposed still to stick out against conventions, get him at least to read the argument in their favour in the address. Yours as ever   A. LINCOLN

1 ALS-F, ISLA. Bennett was a friend of Lincoln's in New Salem and now resided at Petersburg.   2 George U. Miles, Menard County Whig.
3 *Supra*, under date of March 1.   4 *Supra*, under date of March 4.
5 The convention was postponed to May 1 and the meeting place changed to Pekin, Illinois.

To Joshua F. Speed[1]

Dear Speed: Springfield, March 24. 1843–
Hurst tells me that Lockridge has redeemed the land in your case, & paid him the money; and that he has written you about it.[2] I now have the pleasure of informing you that Walters has paid me $703.25 (in gold) for you.[3] There is something still due you from him,—I think near a hundred dollars, for which I promised him a little additional time. The gold, (except the toll) we hold subject to your order.

We had a meeting of the whigs of the county here on last monday to appoint delegates to a district convention, and Baker beat me[4] & got the delegation instructed to go for him. The meeting, in spite of my attempt to decline it, appointed me one of the delegates;[5] so that in getting Baker the nomination, I shall be "fixed" a good deal like a fellow who is made groomsman to the man what has cut him out, and is marrying his own dear "gal." About the prospect of your having a namesake at our house cant say, exactly yet.   [Signature removed.]

1 ALS, IHi.
2 Charles R. Hurst. For the Lockridge case, see Lincoln to Speed, March 27, 1842.   3 William Walters. See Lincoln to Speed, January 18, 1843 (*supra*).
4 The convention was held on March 20 in the Statehouse to select delegates to the Seventh Congressional District convention. Lincoln withdrew after seven ballots and Baker was chosen as Sangamon's candidate for the nomination.
5 Lincoln was one of eight delegates to the district convention.

To Martin S. Morris[1]

Friend Morris: Springfield March 26th. 1843
Your letter of the 23rd. was received on yesterday morning, and for which (instead of an excuse which you thought proper to ask)

1 Copy, DLC-HW. Martin Sims Morris of Petersburg was one of two delegates from Menard County. The county convention instructed delegates to vote first for Lincoln and second for Hardin. The other Menard delegate was George U. Miles. Morris, rather than Lincoln, is responsible for the errors in spelling which appear in the copy.

I tender you my sincere thanks. It is truly gratifying to me to learn that while the people of Sangamon have cast me off, my old friends of Menard who have known me longest and best of any, still retain there confidence in me. It would astonish if not amuse, the older citizens of your County who twelve years ago knew me a strange[r], friendless, uneducated, penniless boy, working on a flat boat—at ten dollars per month to learn that I have been put down here as the candidate of pride, wealth, and arristocratic family distinction. Yet so chiefly it was. There was too the strangest combination of church influence against me. Baker is a Campbellite, and therefore as I supose, with few acceptions got all that church. My wife has some relatives in the Presbyterian and some in the Episcopal Churches, and therefore, whereever it would tell, I was set down as either the one or the other, whilst it was every where contended that no ch[r]istian ought to go for me, because I belonged to no church, was suspected of being a deist, and had talked about fighting a duel. With all these things Baker, of course had nothing to do. Nor do I complain of them. As to his own church going for him, I think that was right enough, and as to the influences I have spoken of in the other, though they were very strong, it would be grossly untrue and unjust to charge that they acted upon them in a body or even very nearly so. I only mean that those influences levied a tax of a considerable per cent. upon my strength throughout the religious comunity.

But enough of this. You say that in choosing a candidate for Congress you have an equal right with Sangamon, and in this you are undoubtedly correct. In agreeing to withdraw if the whigs of Sangamon should go against me I did not mean that they alone were worth consulting; but that if she with her heavy delegation should be against me, it would be impossible for me to succeed—and therefore I had as well decline. And in relation to Menard having rights, permit me to fully recognize them—and to express the opinion that if she and Mason act circumspectly they will in the convention be able so far to enforce there rights as to decide absolutely which *one* of the candidates shall be successful. Let me show you the reason of this. Hardin or some other Morgan Candidate will get Morgan, Scott, & Cass—14 Baker has Sangamon already, and he or he and some [one] else not the Morgan man will get Putnam, Marshall, Woodford, Taz[e]well & Logan—which with Sangamon make 16. Then you & Mason having three, can give the victory to either man. You say you shall instruct your delegates to go for me unless I object. I certainly shall not object. That would be too plesant a compliment for me to tread in the dust. And besides if any thing

[320]

should hapen (which however is not probable) by which Baker should be thrown out of the fight, I would be at liberty to accept the nomination if I could get it. I do however feell myself bound not to hinder him in any way from getting the nomination.[2] I should dispise myself were I to attempt it. I think it would be proper for your meeting to appoint three delegates, and instruct them to go for some one as first choice, some one else as second choice, and perhaps some one as *third*—and if in those instructions I were named as the first choice, it would gratify me very much. If you wish to hold the ballance of power, it is important for you to attend too, and secure the vote of Mason also. You should be sure to have men appointed delegates, that you know you can safely confide in. If yourself & James Short[3] were appointed for your County all would be safe. But whether Jims woman afair a year ago might not be in the way of his appointment is a question. I dont know whether you know it, but I know him to be as honorable a man as there is in the world. You have my permission and even request to show this letter to Short; but to no one else unless it be a very particular friend who you know will not speak of it. Yours as ever

A. LINCOLN

P.S. Will you write me again?　　A. L—

[2] Neither Edward D. Baker nor Lincoln were successful. John J. Hardin was nominated at the Pekin convention on May 1.
[3] An old friend who lived on a farm near New Salem.

To Martin S. Morris[1]

Friend Morris:　　　　　　　　　　April 14th 1843.

I have heard it insinuated that Baker has been attempting to get you or Miles[2] or both of you to violate the instructions of the meeting that appointed you, and to go for him. I have insisted, and still insist, that this can not be true. Surely Baker would not do the like. As well might Hardin ask me to vote for him, in the convention.

Again, it is said there will be an attempt to get up instructions in your county, requiring you to go for Baker. This is all wrong again. Upon the same rule, why might not I fly from the decision against me in Sangamon and get up instructions to their delegation to go for me. There are at least twelve hundred whigs in the county, that took no part. And yet I would as soon put my head in the fire as to attempt it. I should feel myself strongly dishonored by it.

Besides, if any one should get the nomination by such extraordinary means, all harmony in the district would inevitably be lost. Honest whigs (and very nearly all of them are honest) will not

[321]

quietly abide such enormities. I repeat, such an attempt on Baker's part can not be true. Write, me at Springfield, how this matter is. Dont show or speak of this letter. As ever yours   A. LINCOLN

[1] ALS, IHM.

[2] Lincoln was away attending court at Versailles, Woodford County. George U. Miles was the other delegate from Menard. See Lincoln to Morris, March 26, 1843, and note. Morris was taken ill and Francis Regnier was appointed in his place.

Resolution Adopted at Whig Convention at Pekin, Illinois[1]

May 1, 1843

Resolved, That this convention, as individuals, recommend E. D. Baker as a suitable person to be voted for by the whigs of this district, for Representative to Congress, at the election in 1844, subject to the decision of a District Convention, should the whigs of the district think proper to hold one.

[1] *Illinois Gazette* (Lacon), May 6, 1843. Lincoln had previously withdrawn Baker's name as a current candidate so that John J. Hardin would have no opposition before the convention.

Proposal of a Barbecue[1]

May 11, 1843

A Proposition.

We have a proposition to make to our friends of Morgan, that, in case the locos run a candidate for Congress in that county at the August election, the majority of votes in SANGAMON COUNTY for HARDIN shall DOUBLE the number of his majority in MORGAN COUNTY. The losing County shall give a free BARBACUE to the whigs of the other county—the said Barbacue to be provided at some place most convenient for the accommodation of the whigs of the two Counties.

Whigs of Morgan, will you go it?

[1] *Sangamo Journal,* May 11, 1843. That Lincoln wrote this notice seems evident from his letter to John J. Hardin, May 11, 1843 (*infra*).

To John J. Hardin[1]

Friend Hardin: Springfield, May 11th, 1843.

Butler[2] informs me that he received a letter from you, in which you expressed some doubt whether the whigs of Sangamon will support you cordially. You may, at once, dismiss all fears on that subject. We have already resolved to make a particular effort to give you the very largest majority possible in our county. From this, no whig of the county dissents. We have many objects for doing it. We make it a matter of honor and pride to do it; we do it, because we love the whig cause; we do it, because we like you personally; and last, we wish to convince you, that we do not bear that hatred to Morgan county, that you people have so long seemed to imagine. You will see by the journal of this week, that we propose, upon pain of losing a Barbecue, to give you twice as great a majority in this county as you shall receive in your own. I got up the proposal.[3]

Who of the five appointed, is to write the District address? I did the labor of writing one address this year; and got thunder for my reward.[4] Nothing new here. Yours as ever.　　A. LINCOLN.

P.S.—I wish you would measure one of the largest of those swords, we took to Alton, and write me the length of it, from tip of the point to tip of the hilt, in feet and inches, I have a dispute about the length.[5]　　A. L.

[1] Tarbell (Appendix), pp. 289-90.
[2] William Butler. Hardin had been nominated the Whig candidate for congress in the Seventh District by the convention at Pekin on May 1.
[3] At Jacksonville, on October 6, Morgan County Whigs paid the election bet at a barbecue. Sangamon County gave Hardin a majority twice as large as his majority in Morgan County.
[4] See "Address to the People of Illinois," March 4, 1843.
[5] Lincoln refers to the cavalry broadswords which were to have been used in his duel with Shields. See "Memorandum," September 19, 1842, *supra.*

To Joshua F. Speed[1]

Dear Speed:　　　　　　　　Springfield, May 18th. 1843–

Yours of the 9th. Inst. is duly received, which I do not meet as a "bore," but as a most welcome visiter. I will answer the business part of it first. The note you enclosed on Cannan & Harlan, I have placed in Moffett's[2] hands according to your directions. Harvey[3] is the constable to have it. I have called three times to get the note, you mention, on B. C. Webster & Co; but did not find Hurst.[4] I will yet get it, and do with it, as you bid. At the April court at Tazewell, I saw Hall; and he then gave me an order on Jewett to draw of him, all rent which may fall due, after the 12th. day of Jany. last,

[1] ALS, ORB.　　[2] Thomas Moffett (?), a justice of the peace.
[3] William Harvey (?), Whig.
[4] Charles R. Hurst. B. C. Webster & Company was a general merchandise store in Springfield.

till your debt shall be paid.[5] The rent is for the house Ransom did live in just above the Globe;[6] and is $222 per year payable quarterly, so that one quarter fell due the 12th. April. I presented the order to Jewett, since the 12th. and he said it was right, and he would accept, it, which, however, was not done in writing for want of pen & ink at the time & place. He acknowledged that the quarter's rent was due, and said he would pay it in a short time but could not at the moment. He also said that he thought, by some former arrangement, a portion of that quarter would have to be paid to the Irwins.[7] Thus stands the Hall matter. I think we will get the money on it, in the course of this year. You ask for the amount of interest on your Van Bergen note of $572.32,[8] and also upon the judgement against Van assigned by Baker. The note drew 12 per cent from date, and bore date Oct. 1st. 1841. I suppose the 12 per cent ceased, at the time we bought in Walters' house which was on the 23rd. Decr. 1842. If I count right, the interest up to that time, was $78.69 cents, which added to the principal makes $651.01. On this aggregate sum you are entitled to interest at 6 per cent only, from the said 23rd. Decr. 1842 until paid. What that will amount to, you can calculate for yourself. The judgement assigned by Baker to you for $219.80, was so assigned on the 2nd. of April 1841, and of course draws 6 per cent from that time until paid. This too you can calculate for yourself. About the 25th. of March 1843 (the precise date I dont now remember) Walters paid $703.25. This, of course must be remembered in counting interest. According to my count, there was due you of principal & interest on both claims on the 25th. of March 1843—$906.70. Walters then paid $703.25—which leaves still due you, $203.45, drawing 6 per cent from that date. Walters is promising to pay the ballance every day, but still has not done it. I think he will do it soon. Allen has gone to nothing, as Butler tells you.[9] There are 200 acres of the tract I took the deed of trust on. The improvements I should suppose you remember as well as I. It is the stage stand on the Shelbyville road, where you always said I would'nt pay Baker's[10] tavern bill. It seems to me it must be worth much more than the debt; but whether any body will redeem it in these hard times, I can not say.

In relation to our congress matter here, you were right in sup-

[5] Logan & Lincoln obtained judgment for $149.65 in Bell & Company *v.* Hall, September 16, 1842.

[6] The Globe Tavern where the Lincolns resided from November, 1842, until shortly after August 1, 1843.   [7] Robert Irwin & Company.

[8] See note 7 of letter to Speed, July 4, 1842 (*supra*).

[9] Robert Allen; William Butler. For the failure of Allen's business, see note 4 of letter to Speed, July 4, 1842.   [10] Edward D. Baker.

posing I would support the nominee. Neither Baker or I, however is the man; but *Hardin*. So far as I can judge from present appearances, we shall have no split or trouble about the matter; all will be harmony. In relation to the "coming events"[11] about which Butler wrote you, I had not *heard* one word before I got your letter; but I have so much confidence in the judgement of a Butler on such a subject, that I incline to think there may be some reality in it. What *day* does Butler appoint? By the way, how do "events" of the same sort come on in your family? Are you possessing houses and lands, and oxen and asses, and men-servants and maidservants, and begetting sons and daughters? We are not keeping house; but boarding at the Globe tavern, which is very well kept now by a widow lady of the name of Beck.[12] Our room (the same Dr. Wallace[13] occupied there) and boarding only costs four dollars a week. Ann Todd[14] was married something more than a year since to a fellow by the name of Campbell, and who Mary says, is pretty much of a "dunce" though he has a little money & property. They live in Boonville, Mo; and have not been heard from lately enough, to enable me to say any thing about her health. I reckon it will scarcely be in our power to visit Kentucky this year. Besides poverty, and the necessity of attending to business, those "coming events" I suspect would be some what in the way. I most heartily wish you and your Fanny would not fail to come. Just let us know the time a week in advance, and we will have a room provided for you at our house, and all be merry together for awhile. Be sure to give my respects to your mother and family. Assure her, that if I ever come near her I will not fail to call and see her. Mary joins in sending love to your Fanny and you. Yours as ever

A. LINCOLN

P.S. Since I wrote the above I saw Hurst and discover that the note on B. C. Webster & Co does not fall due till the 9th. June. Hurst says it will be paid when due.

[11] Robert Todd Lincoln was born August 1, 1843.
[12] Sarah Beck (Mrs. James).
[13] Dr. William S. Wallace, brother-in-law of Mary Todd Lincoln.
[14] Sister of Mary.

Resolutions Adopted by a Whig Meeting at the Capitol[1]

June 10, 1843

Resolved, That we recommend to the Whigs of all the counties of this State, to hold meetings, and appoint delegates to meet in Convention on the second Monday of December next, in Springfield, and select nine persons as a Whig electoral ticket to be voted for by all the Whigs of the State at the Presidential election in 1844.

Resolved, That all the Whig papers of this State be requested to publish the above resolution.

Resolved, That we invite our democratic brethren to select two or three members of their party to meet a like number of ours to discuss the question of difference between the two political parties of the Nation, during all the evenings of next week; each Speaker to occupy one evening, the parties to take evening and evening about, and the speaker whose lot it shall be to open the debate, to have the privilege of making the closing speech on his own side of the question.

Resolved, That the President of the Clay Club, be directed to present a copy of the above resolution to the President of the Democratic Association.

[1] *Sangamo Journal,* June 15, 1843.

Arbitration Award to Samuel Wyckoff[1]

July 3, 1843

Whereas we the undersigned, Samuel Wycoff, and Dennis Forrest, the former being owner of the North West quarter of Section Eight, and the latter being owner of the South West quarter of Section Five, both tracts of Township Fourteen North of Range Six West, in Sangamon county, have a dispute concerning a small strip of land, each claiming it, as being part of his tract aforesaid; therefore we submit said dispute to the arbitrament of Abraham Lincoln, who is to hear the evidence adduced by both parties, and thereupon, decide which is the owner of the disputed land, and what line is hereafter to be the dividing line between us, and we hereby mutually bind ourselves in the penal sum of five hundred dollars, as liquidated damages, to abide by the decision he shall make, and each to give and allow the other peacable possession and enjoyment of his own side of the line so to be designated.

Witness our hands and seals this 19th. day of June A.D. 1843.

SAMUEL WYCKOFF

DENNIS FORREST

In pursuance of the above agreement, having fully heard the evidence, I decide that the land in dispute between said Wycoff and Forrest, belongs to said Wycoff, and that the old United States Surveyor's line, beginning at the West end thereof, and running thence Easterly as marked through the timber by said U.S. Surveyor, so far as the timber extends, and continuing the same course as so marked, the proper distance to reach the East side of the lands of said Wycoff and Forrest above described, shall hereafter be the dividing line between the said lands of the parties.

July 3rd. 1843—   A. LINCOLN

1 ADS, IHi. The document is in Lincoln's hand except for Wyckoff's and Forrest's signatures. Lincoln misspelled Wyckoff's name.

Arbitration Award to the State of Illinois
Against Anson G. Henry[1]

July 14, 1843

State of Illinois ⎫ We the Undersigned Arbitrators having care-
        vs   ⎬ fully examined the accounts in refference to the
A. G. Henry   ⎭ matters within Submitted between the State of
Illinois and A. G. Henry late Treasurer of the Board of State house commissioners do find and award in favour of the State of Illinois against the Said Henry the Sum of Two hundred and Seventy One Dollars

Witness Our hands & Seals at Springfield this 14h day of July A D 1843   STEPHEN J. IANKIEWICZ[2] (SEAL)

                                        A. LINCOLN (SEAL)

                                        N. H. PURPLE (SEAL)

12 days Each Services for Arbitrators

1 DS, I-Ar. Henry was administrator of funds during building of the state house in Springfield.
2 Iankiewicz was an employee in the state auditor's office.

Speech at Hillsboro, Illinois,
in Reply to Orlando B. Ficklin[1]

July 15, 1843

. . . . It was a little amusing to see how cautiously, this deputy and "spokesman" of the whig candidate in this district, came into the doctrine of the assumption of the State debts; endeavoring first to show that all the whigs were not for it; that it was not a question at issue; that he never had heard a speech on it before? [sic] and finally, that it was not a bad thing at any rate, and the people had better go for it. It is impossible to follow through his answer—but all were amused at the speech.

1 Illinois State Register, July 28, 1843. This fragmentary report is the only one available and is excerpted from a letter to the editor which is signed "A Democrat."

To Robert S. Blackwell[1]

Dear Bob: Springfield, July 24th. 1843
    Yours of the 18th. inclosing your license is received. I have had
it perfected, and herewith return it to you.
    Nothing new here. God bless you.   A. LINCOLN

[1] ALS-P, ISLA. Blackwell was a prominent Whig of Rushville, Illinois.

To Joshua F. Speed[1]

Dear Speed: Springfield, July 26th. 1843.
    Yours of the 17th. Inst. is received. Your former letter of the 9th.
of June was also received. The note on Butler,[2] I did not wish to
collect, for reasons well understood by you; and I therefore handed
it to Hurst.[3] Butler has not been at home since it was received. He
is, I suppose, this moment in New York city.
    The B. C. Webster & Co money, you have got, as I see by a letter
of yours to Hurst. We received the ballance of the Walters[4] money
three or four days ago. We received an overplus for Van.[5] at the
same time, and we take out of the gross sum for you, what, according to our calculation, is your due. That we make to be $212.95[.]
We retain the $12.95, as you see, and send you enclosed two one
hundred dollar Missouri bills. You often direct us & Hurst to deposite for you in St. Louis; but this is more difficult than it would
be to deposite for you at Knob-view; because, every other thing
being equal, we do not know who to deposite with in St. Louis
whereas we do at Knob-view. We therefore enclose the present re-
mittance to you direct. I was talking with Allen[6] a few days ago,
and he said he would like still to try to sell the farm for something
more than your debt; but that he would deed it to you outright at
any time, you desired it, provided you would take it, and discharge
his debt. You know that under the deed of trust you may sell it for
what it will bring, and hold him bound for the ballance, provided
it does not sell for enough to pay the whole debt. I told him I would
write you.
    We shall look with impatience for your visit this fall. Your
Fanny can not be more anxious to see my Molly[7] than the latter is
to see her; nor as much so as I am. Dont fail to come. We are but
two, as yet. Your friend as ever   A. LINCOLN
    P.S. Since I wrote the above, I have seen John Irwin, who starts
to the East within a week from now, and by whom I have concluded to send the money in preference to enclosing it. He will
leave it with your brother James in the city.   A. L.

[1] ALS, ORB.   [2] William Butler.   [3] Charles R. Hurst.
[4] William Walters.   [5] Peter Van Bergen.   [6] Robert Allen.
[7] Mary Todd Lincoln.

To a Gentleman in Tremont[1]

July 31, 1843

Dear Sir—Your letter of the 27th inst. is received. I have consulted with Judge LOGAN on the question whether the 20 acres deeded by Harris will revert in case the county seat is removed, and after a good deal of reflection he thinks it a doubtful question. *He says* that where land is conveyed for the purpose of erecting public buildings on it, if those buildings are removed from it or abandoned as public buildings, the land reverts—but if not conveyed for that purpose, it will not revert by such removal or abandonment. Now in this case the deed does not show the land to have been conveyed for the purpose of erecting public buildings on it, while the law to which the deed refers provides for receiving the donation *for the express purpose of erecting public buildings on it,* —so that if the object of the conveyance is to be collected from the deed, it will not revert—while, if it be collected from the law, it will revert. *My own impression is,* that the object of the conveyance is properly collected from a consideration of the deed and the law both together, and consequently that *the land will revert, in case the county seat shall be removed.* Yours, &c.

A. LINCOLN.

[1] D, RPB. A broadside addressed "To the Electors of Tazewell County" argues for the retention of the county seat at Pekin on the ground that the public square and buildings on it would revert to the original owners if not used for public purposes for which it was donated. The name of the "gentleman in Tremont" to whom Lincoln's letter "dated Springfield, July 31, 1843," was addressed is not indicated in the broadside. The land had been deeded by John H. Harris of Tremont.

Speech at Whig Barbecue
at Jacksonville, Illinois[1]

October 6, 1843

. . . . After Mr. Baker sat down, Mr. Lincoln was again called upon.[2] He took up the three prominent principles of the Whig Party—The Tariff, a sound and uniform National Currency and the Distribution of the proceeds of the Public Lands. All these he illustrated so plainly and so forcibly, as to show that he not only

[329]

understood these principles thoroughly himself and their beneficial bearing on the American people, but that he also possessed a most happy faculty of vindicating them and of urging their adoption before an audience in such a manner as to convince all present of their necessity.[3]

[1] Burlington, Iowa, *Hawk Eye*, October 19, 1843. From a long account of the proceedings at which Morgan County Whigs paid the bet proposed by Lincoln on May 11, 1843 (*vide supra*).

[2] Lincoln's speech in the afternoon is described as "most excellent" but is not reported.

[3] Six lines cut off the bottom of the page apparently contained the conclusion of the summary of Lincoln's speech.

To John McNamar[1]

Friend McNamar: November [9?], 1843

You see the object of the above letter. As it speaks of the Tax of 1842. I had supposed the land was already sold, but, so far as the Returns in the Auditors Office shows, it has not. It may be that James meant the year 1843. I wish you would examine; and if the taxes have been paid up to this year, apply the enclosed money, or enough of it, to the payment of the tax of this year & send me the receipt by mail.

Write the condition in which it stands at any rate. Yours as ever

A. LINCOLN

[1] ALS-P, ISLA. McNamar was in 1843 Menard County assessor. The approximate date of this letter can be inferred from the fact that it is written on the bottom of the letter from Josiah L. James, dated Tremont, November 3, 1843. Since Lincoln was attending court in Petersburg November 6-8, he would not have had to write McNamar about this matter if he had received the letter before his return to Springfield. November 9 is the earliest probable date, but the letter may have been written somewhat later. James' letter requested Lincoln to pay "taxes on the land herein described for the year 1842—Viz—N.W. ¼ & E ½ of S W ¼ of S. 28—Town 19 — R 5 West." (ALS-P, ISLA.)

To Henry E. Dummer[1]

Friend Dummer: Springfield, Jany. 2. 1844

In reply to yours of the 14th. ult. I say that if you can get a clear title to the 40 acres of land, together with costs, and a reasonable fee to yourself, I reckon you had better do it.

Have the deed made to me. Yours as ever—   A. LINCOLN

[1] ALS, IHi.

Sale Contract by Charles Dresser
and Abraham Lincoln[1]

January 16, 1844

This memorandum witnesseth that Charles Dresser and Abraham Lincoln of Springfield Illinois, have contracted with each other as follows:

The said Dresser is to convey to, or procure to be conveyed to, said Lincoln, by a clear title in fee simple, the entire premises (ground and improvements) in Springfield, on which said Dresser now resides, and give him possession of said premises, on or before the first day of April next—for which said Lincoln, at or before the same day, is to pay to said Dresser twelve hundred dollars, or what said Dresser shall then at his own option, accept as equivalent thereto; and also to procure to be conveyed to said Dresser, by a clear title in fee simple, the entire premises (ground and building) in Springfield, on the block immediately West of the Public square, the building on which is now occupied by H. A. Hough[2] as a shop, being the same premises, some time since conveyed by N. W. Edwards & wife to said Lincoln & Stephen T. Logan. Said Dresser takes upon himself to arrange with said Hough for the possession of said shop and premises.

Jany. 16th. 1844   CHARLES DRESSER
(signed duplicates.)   A. LINCOLN

Received[3] of A Lincoln on the within seven hundred and fifty dollars, on which he is to be allowed interest at the rate of twelve per cent per annum, until the within contract is complied with, or performance offered by said Dresser; and in case said Dresser, shall fail to comply with the within, we hereby bind ourselves to refund said seven hundred and fifty dollars to said Lincoln with interest at the rate of twelve per cent per annum from date.

February 5th. 1844—   CHARLES DRESSER
                                                    S. M. TINSLEY[4]

---

[1] ADS, owned by Mrs. Katherine Dresser White, Springfield, Illinois. The property described contained a story and a half house, built in 1839 by the Reverend Charles Dresser, D.D., who was the first Episcopal clergyman in Springfield (rector, St. Paul's, 1838-1855), who performed Lincoln's wedding ceremony on November 4, 1842. The house was later made into a full two-story dwelling. It is now owned by the State of Illinois and maintained as a memorial.

[2] A cabinetmaker.

[3] This receipt, written on the back of the contract, is also in Lincoln's hand, except for the signatures. The deed was given to Lincoln on May 3, 1844.

[4] Seth M. Tinsley, storekeeper and owner of the building where the Logan & Lincoln law office was located.

To Richard S. Thomas[1]

Friend Richard: Springfield, Feby. 14th. 1844.–

I am sorry to have to say I can find but one copy of President's Messages in town; and that one, belongs to the State Library, and, of course, can not be had. If alive and well, I am sure to be with you on the 22nd. I will meet the *trio* of mighty adversaries[2] you mention, in the best manner I can. No news here. Yours forever,
R S. Thomas   A. LINCOLN
       Virginia, Ills

[1] ALS, original owned by James Shepard Dennis, Bennington, Vermont.
[2] Judge John Pearson was probably one of those mentioned. See speeches in Virginia, Illinois, February 22-23, *infra.*

To Simeon Ryder[1]

Mr. Simeon Ryder: Springfield, Feby. 16th. 1844

Yours of the 14th. Inst. is received. The decree taken against Stringer at the last term of our court was not a *final*, but only an *interlocutory* decree.[2] The substance of it is, that Stringer pay to you on or before the first day of the next term, your debt & interest, and that Stringer should have ten days to file an answer, to enable him to contest the claim of Mitchells heirs, and the cause continued. Stringer's ten days have long since expired long ago, and he has filed no answer. At next court, I suppose a decree will [be] rendered, ordering the sale of the property to pay your debt, subject to the claim of Mitchell's heirs.[3]

No Injunction has been obtained in the case. Yours &c.
                                               A. LINCOLN

[1] ALS, Hayner Memorial Library, Alton, Illinois. Simeon Ryder was a resident of Madison County.
[2] On November 30, 1843, against Daniel Stringer and the heirs of Edward Mitchell.
[3] The case was continued at the March term of court and the final decree rendered on July 29, 1844. By its terms Ryder was awarded $479.25 and the heirs of Mitchell $716.45.

Speeches in Virginia, Illinois[1]

February 22, 1844

The Cass County Clay Club met at Virginia on the 22d. T. M. Kilpatrich[2], Esq. addressed the meeting. Subsequently John Pierson,[3] Esq. appeared, and asked the privilege of setting forth the beauties of Locoism in a speech; which was acceded to.—Mr. Lincoln replied to him, and if any thing was left of Pierson's state-

[332]

ments or arguments unanswered or unrefuted, our informant, after the most minute examination, was not able to make the discovery.

He [Judge John Pearson] was followed by A. LINCOLN, Esq. in an able and eloquent speech, characterised by his well known ability. He made a clean shucking of the Judge, pointing out the fallacy of his arguments and disproving most of his statements. Mr. L. made a most able and conclusive argument on the Bank question, proving that it was no new fangled scheme, but one advocated and carried out by the fathers of the Republican school. His speech was received by repeated and rapturous applause.

Mr. Lincoln commenced and tried to show that because Washington and Madison signed the U.S. Bank Bill, therefore it was constitutional. He labored hard to prove that Washington never done a wrong thing in his life; that Clay was honest in changing his party and his bank notions; he launched into the State Bank system, and said that the democrats chartered our State Bank, and all the State Banks were chartered by the democrats; that the majority of the directors (of democrats) had authorized the suspension in 1837, and intimated that the democrats had been for it, (the State Bank) ever since, and told his old calf story and made up his hour. Judge Pearson claimed his right of reply. . . .

In the evening, I am told, the whigs had a meeting of the Clay Club, and the speakers let themselves out, for they were under no restraint. Lincoln talked of the tariff, though in the day he carefully avoided that subject, and said, in conclusion, that a good argument might be made on both sides, when he got thro' he told his brethren he wanted to meet with them in the morning before he took his departure. . . .

1 *Sangamo Journal*, February 29, 1844; March 28, 1844. *Illinois State Register*, March 15, 1844 (last two excerpts).
2 Thomas M. Killpatrick, Whig state senator from Scott County.
3 Judge John Pearson.

Speech in Virginia, Illinois[1]

February 23, 1844

We had a meeting at night, and on the morning of the 23d, addresses were received from Mr. Killpatrick[2] and Mr. Lincoln. They portrayed the absurdities of loco focoism, and the soundness of whig principles, with great success.

1 *Sangamo Journal*, March 28, 1844.   2 Thomas M. Killpatrick.

Speech at Sugar Creek, Illinois[1]

March 1, 1844

. . . . The poor ignorant people were enlightened by speeches (if they were worthy of the name) from Messrs Lincoln, Baker, Henry and McNeil.[2] Mr. Lincoln made some large statements, but I suppose they were true, for he had the document with him. He attempted to make the farmer believe that the high pressure tariff made every thing they bought cheaper, but said also he could not tell the reason, but that it was so, and I suppose that is enough for the huge farmer to know. Now, the little boys who Mr. Lincoln enlightened as to what the tariff was, could have told him better than to make such a statement. He then proceeded along very calmly, until Mr. Baker handed him a State Register, containing some extracts from the papers of Alex. Hamilton; then he rolled his eyes and shook his head, as if he had seen an Irishman.

[1] *Illinois State Register*, March 15, 1844. This only available report of the speech occurs in a letter to the editor.
[2] Edward D. Baker, John Henry of Morgan County, and Francis A. McNeill of Sangamon County.

Debates with John Calhoun and Alfred W. Cavarly in Springfield, Illinois[1]

March 20-25, 1844

This being the first week of our Circuit Court, arrangements have been made by the public speakers, of both parties, to devote the evening hours, to the discussion of the great questions involved in the coming Presidential election. . . . Judge CAVARLY. . . . quoted . . . from a speech of Mr. Stuart,[2] made in Congress, an admission that the *consumer* of imported articles paid the duty. . . . This only bright spot in Mr. Stuart's speech, so disturbed Mr. Lincoln, that he promised to forfeit his "ears" and his "legs" if he did not demonstrate, that protected articles have been cheaper since the late Tariff than before. . . .

. . . . Mr. Calhoun's first speech on Wednesday evening was . . . unanswerable. . . . Though Mr. Calhoun triumphantly established the first proposition, yet Mr. Lincoln had the hardihood to assert that it might *probably* fall upon the manufacturer, after Mr. Calhoun had shown that it positively fell upon the consumer. . . . Mr. Lincoln very candidly acknowledged his inability to prove that the tariff had anything to do with the *late* low prices throughout this country and Europe. . . .

[334]

There has been an interesting public discussion at the Court Room, on the political questions which divide the country, every evening of last week and Monday evening of this week. Mr. Cavarly of Green, lead off; and was followed by Wm. Brown, Esq. of Morgan—the two occupying two evenings. Mr. Calhoun followed Mr. Brown, and he by Mr. Lincoln, and these gentlemen continued the discussion five evenings.

The discussion has been well attended, and we readily accord to Mr. Calhoun due praise for making most of a bad cause. The efforts of Mr. Lincoln, were distinguished for ability, and in all candor we must say, that we did not discover a single position raised by Mr. Calhoun, that he did not entirely demolish.

1 *Illinois State Register,* March 22, 29, 1844; *Sangamo Journal,* March 28, 1844.
2 John T. Stuart.

To Rowland, Smith & Company[1]

Messrs Rowland, Smith & Co. Springfield, Ills.
Gent. April 24th. 1844–

Since the Supreme court of the United States have decided our property laws to be unconstitutional; and our own courts have ascertained, and concluded to follow the decision, we have become a little encouraged to make some further attempts to make some collections. Your case in our hands against Francis, Allen, & Stone stands about thus.

1841. March 26th. Judgement for $887.64. & costs.
1842. April 18th. Real estate sold and bought in for you at the sum of $666.67. and not redeemed.

This sale, if we calculate the interest correctly, left still due you on that date $277.55, which with interest from that date amounts now to about $310.85. This last amount & the cost are still to pay. [We sup]pose you would be pleased to have it collected[, but in] as much as the officers have never received any thing [yet] for what they have already done, we apprehend they will be loth to proceed. The precise amount of cost already incurred we have not now at hand, but it will not greatly vary from $40. We will direct the Sheriff to collect the ballance.

As to the real estate, we can not attend to it, as agents, & we therefore recommend that you give the charge of it, to Mr. Isaac S. Britton,[2] a trust-worthy man, & one whom the Lord made on purpose for such bussiness. Yours &c LOGAN & LINCOLN

1 ALS, DLC-HW. Notations on verso are not in Lincoln's hand.
2 Lincoln voted for Isaac S. Britton for school commissioner August 2, 1841.

To Horatio M. Vandeveer[1]

Friend Vandaveer: Springfield, April 28th. 1844[2]

On the other half of this sheet is a little Bill for a Divorce. I wish you would fill the blank in the proper place, with Taylor's christian name, file the Bill, and issue the subpoena in chancery for the woman immediately.[3] Yours as ever   A. LINCOLN

[1] ALS-P, ISLA. Vandeveer was clerk of the Christian County Circuit Court.
[2] Postmarked May 3.
[3] Andrew J. Wilson charged his wife Susan with adultery and named Edward Taylor co-respondent. The case was dismissed May 27, 1844, costs ordered assessed against the plaintiff.

To John J. Hardin[1]

Dear Hardin: Springfield, May 21, 1844.

Knowing that you have correspondents enough, I have forborne to trouble you heretofore; and I now only do so, to get you to set a matter right which has got wrong with one of our best friends. It is old uncle Thomas Campbell of Spring Creek—(Berlin P.O.) He has received several documents from you, and he says they are old newspapers and documents, having no sort of interest in them. He is, therefore, getting a strong impression that you treat him with disrespect. This, I know, is a mistaken impression; and you must correct it. The way, I leave to yourself. Rob't W. Canfield,[2] says he would like to have a document or two from you.

The Locos here are in considerable trouble about Van Buren's letter on Texas,[3] and the Virginia electors. They are growing sick of the Tariff question;[4] and consequently are much confounded at V. B.'s cutting them off from the new Texas question. Nearly half the leaders swear they wont stand it. Of those are Ford, T. Campbell, Ewing, Calhoun and others.[5] They don't exactly say they won't vote for V. B., but they say he will not be the candidate,[6] and that *they* are for Texas anyhow. As ever yours,

A. LINCOLN.

[1] Tarbell (Appendix), pp. 290-91.
[2] Delegate to Sangamon County Whig convention in 1843 from one of the rural precincts.
[3] Probably the "Hammet letter" (Washington *Globe*, April 27, 1844). Van Buren took a negative position on the question of annexation, on the ground of our neutral obligations to Mexico.
[4] Van Buren had come out for tariff for revenue only.
[5] Thomas Ford, governor; Thompson Campbell, secretary of state; William L. D. Ewing, auditor; John Calhoun, circuit clerk and Democratic candidate for congress.
[6] James K. Polk received the Democratic nomination on May 27, 1844, pledging the party to immediate "re-annexation" of Texas.

Speech on Annexation of Texas[1]

May 22, 1844

A meeting was held at the State House on Wednesday evening, the 22d ult. for the purpose of considering the letters of Mr. Clay, Mr. Van Buren and Mr. Benton upon the question of immediate Annexation. The meeting was addressed by Mr. Lincoln, who briefly reviewed the grounds taken by those distinguished gentlemen, concurring with them in the opinion, that Annexation at this time upon the terms agreed upon by John Tyler was altogether inexpedient. . . .

[1] *Sangamo Journal*, June 6, 1844.

Speech and Resolutions Concerning Philadelphia Riots[1]

June 12, 1844

PUBLIC MEETING.

At a meeting holden in the city of Springfield, on the evening of the 12th June; on motion of E. D. BAKER, Esq, DAVID J. BAKER, Esq. of Kaskaskia, was unanimously chosen to side over this meeting; and on motion of Dr. HENRY, BENJ F. JAMES, Esq of Tremont, was chosen Secretary.

The object of the meeting being stated by ABRAHAM LINCOLN, Esq. of Springfield,—to be a desire, that the subject of the recent Philadelphia riots, as connected with, and promoted by the whig party, should be fairly discussed, and understood by the citizens of this State and country. On his motion, the following Preamble and Resolutions were submitted for the action of the meeting—supporting them by able and forcible arguments:

WHEREAS, There seems to be a determined effort making, by the so called democratic party, to charge the blame of the late riots in Philadelphia, upon the Whigs; and to ascribe that blame to a supposed hostility of the Whig party in general to *foreigners and Catholics*; and, WHEREAS, truth, and justice to ourselves, demand that we should repel the charge; therefore,

Resolved, That in admitting the foreigner to the rights of citizenship, he should be put to some reasonable test of his fidelity to our country and its institutions; and that he should first dwell among us a reasonable time to become generally acquainted with the nature of those institutions; and that, consistent with these requisites, naturalization laws, should be so framed, as to render admission to citizenship under them, as convenient, cheap, and expeditious as possible.

Resolved, That we will now, and at all times, oppose as best we may, all attempts to either destroy the naturalization laws or to so alter them, as to render admission under them, less convenient, less cheap, or less expeditious than it now is.

Resolved, That the guarantee of the rights of conscience, as found in our Constitution, is most sacred and inviolable, and one that belongs no less to the Catholic, than to the Protestant; and that all attempts to abridge or interfere with these rights, either of Catholic or Protestant, directly or indirectly, have our decided disapprobation, and shall ever have our most effective opposition.

Resolved, That we reprobate and condemn each and every thing in the Philadelphia riots, and the causes which led to them, from whatever quarter they may have come, which are in conflict with the principles above expressed.

Mr. Lincoln . . . at a meeting of the whigs convened for the purpose of investigating the causes of the Philadelphia riots, said that he had not yet seen an account of this affair which he could rely upon as *true*—(I should like to know how *he* is to judge of the correctness of any report.). . . . Mr. Lincoln however was incorrect in stating that the Catholics demanded the exclusion of the Bible from the public schools . . . all they wanted was the privilege . . . of introducing and using their own translation.

Mr. Lincoln expressed the kindest, and most benevolent feelings towards foreigners; they were, I doubt not, the sincere and honest sentiments of *his heart;* but they were not those of *his party.* . . . Mr. Lincoln also alleged that the whigs were as much the friends of foreigners as democrats; but he failed to substantiate it in a manner satisfactory to the foreigners who heard him. . . .

[1] *Sangamo Journal,* June 20, 1844 (resolutions); *Illinois State Register,* June 21, 1844.

Resolutions Adopted by the Whig Convention at Peoria, Illinois[1]

June 19, 1844

Resolved, That the Whigs of Illinois respond to the nomination of HENRY CLAY as the Whig candidate for the Presidency, by the Whig National Convention, with an enthusiasm only equalled by that [with] which it was made; that the great statesman of the

West commands not only our admiration, for his brilliant and eminently practical talents, our respect and gratitude for his invaluable and ever patriotic services to our country, but the warmest and deepest feelings of our hearts for the noble and generous qualities so peculiarly characteristic of our gallant HARRY OF THE WEST.

Resolved, That in THEODORE FRELINGHUYSEN, the nominee of the vice-presidency, we recognize an able and eloquent advocate of Whig principles, a statesman whose talents have given lustre to our national councils, a man whose pure life and active philanthropy commend him to the esteem of every good citizen, and who, in all the varied relations of life through which he has passed, has shown himself to be "without fear and without reproach."

Resolved, therefore, That the Whigs of Illinois in Convention assembled, hereby cordially ratify and confirm the nominations of the Whig National Convention, and pledge themselves to use all honorable efforts to insure their favorable reception and ratification at the polls in November next.

Resolved, That thus responding to the nomination of HENRY CLAY for the Presidency, we hereby cordially adopt and affirm the principles which have guided, and have been so proverbially illustrated by that great man, in his long and brilliant career as an American Statesman.

That foremost in importance among these principles we recognize and affirm, that of providing a national revenue by a tariff of duties on foreign importations, so adjusted that while it will yield no more than is necessary for an economical and efficient administration of the federal government, will at the same time afford equal protection and encouragement to every branch of American Industry.

That, next in importance, in its effects upon the interests and welfare of the whole country, we regard the plan of distributing the proceeds of the public lands among the several States, as well on account of its intrinsic justice and expediency, as of its tendency to produce uniformity and stability in our National Legislature in regard to the revenue.

That the establishment of a sound currency, the practical restriction of the veto power, so that it may not be wielded to the centralization of all power in the hands of a corrupt and despotic Executive; the limitation of the presidential office to one term; the non-interference of all officers of the government as such, in elections; an economical, faithful and impartial administration of the government—and reform of all those abuses which have sprung out of the corrupt use of the power of appointments, are also objects which claim our approval, and challenge our untiring efforts to secure their accomplishments.

That the Whigs of Illinois, although often beaten in their political battles, have never yet been conquered, and that at the *ides* of November next, at the polls, we will fall into the phalanx of the Whig States, with a majority that shall show that in "every peril" *the Suckers* are willing to "divide the danger."

¹ Quincy *Whig*, June 26, 1844. The committee on resolutions was composed of Lincoln, William Kellogg, Jonathan Y. Scammon, William F. Bryan, Lincoln B. Knowlton, J. R. Cooper, Samuel H. Davis, John M. Smith, and William Broaddus. Lincoln's individual contribution to the resolutions is problematical. Lincoln also spoke at the convention, but no report of his speech is available, except for the statement that he "made an able argument in defence of whig principles."

To John W. Vance¹

My dear old Friend: Springfield, July 7th. 1844.—

Your letter of the 27th. June was received on yesterday. You remember taking the horse back from Karr, and receipting all of the debt except four hundred dollars and some interest. Well, at the last Decr. term of the U.S. court, we got a judgement for the $400. & interest according to your receipt. Kilgore was then in jail, and had been for three or four months. I had always had doubts about the legality of the transfer of the horse back to you, by Karr; and was fearful Kilgore might sue you, & recover either the horse or the value of him. I therefore made a written contract with Kilgore, in which he ratified the transfer of the horse to you by Karr, and I let him "slope" from the jail. His lying in jail so long, made a pretty big bill of cost. I presume near a hundred dollars—perhaps more. The whole cost, including this jail bill, you are liable for, though you have a judgement against the defendants for it. You personally, being security for costs, for your brother, in the suit, are liable any moment to be sued for the cost; and I may as well mention, that the jailor in particular, is continually deviling me to have his bill paid. I do wish you could do something for him. The judgement I think will be ultimately paid, but not speedily.

Van Bergen, the deputy Marshall, who has the execution is out of town now, so that I can not give you particulars as to the prospect of collecting the debt. I believe this is about all the information I can give you. Your friend as ever   A. LINCOLN

¹ ALS, IHi. Vance was a wealthy salt manufacturer who lived at Danville, Vermilion County, Illinois. He had served both as state senator and representative during Lincoln's terms in the legislature. Lincoln filed suit in Vance *v.* Kilgore *et al* on December 1, 1843, and on December 6 the court awarded Vance $1,765.66.

Resolutions Adopted by Springfield Clay Club on the Death of John Brodie[1]

August 7, 1844

Whereas, we the Springfield Clay Club, impelled by a profound respect for the character of our late and lamented friend, JOHN BRODIE, and by the peculiarly afflictive manner of his death, are desirous of expressing in some appropriate way our deep and lasting regard for his memory: therefore

Resolved, That we deeply mourn the loss we have sustained in the death of our fellow citizen, JOHN BRODIE, whose honesty and worth have endeared him to our whole community.

Resolved, That we will cherish his memory with affectionate respect.

Resolved, That a committee of five persons be appointed by the President to ascertain whether it will be agreeable to his family for us to place upon his grave a stone monument, with a suitable inscription, to his memory, and that they report to the next meeting of the Club.

Resolved, That the members of this Club stand ready to render any assistance to the family of the deceased, which may be necessary and acceptable, and that said committee be instructed to inquire and report to this Club, from time to time, in what manner we may be able to assist the widow and the family of the deceased, in the settlement of their business, or in any other way that may contribute to the comfort or consolation of the bereaved family.

Resolved, That said committee communicate to the afflicted wife of the deceased a copy of this Preamble and these resolutions.

[1] *Sangamo Journal*, August 8, 1844. Brodie was killed on August 3 when struck by the fall of a derrick with which a Liberty Pole was being raised for the Whig rally scheduled on that day. The Whig Liberty Pole, 214 feet 6 inches high, was erected on August 23.

Speech at Rockport, Indiana[1]

October 30, 1844

Mr. Lincoln, of Springfield, Ill., addressed a large and respectable audience at the court house on Wednesday evening last, upon the whig policy. His main argument was directed in pointing out the advantages of a Protective Tariff. He handled that subject in a manner that done honor to himself and the whig cause. Other subjects were investigated in a like manner. His speech was plain, argumentative and of an hour's duration.

¹ *The* (Rockport, Indiana) *Herald*, November 1, 1844. Following Lincoln's speech, according to *The Herald*, John Pitcher, a friend of Lincoln's boyhood, delivered a speech in which "he exhibited the democratic policies in an unenviable light . . ." Lincoln's trip to Indiana extended from October 24 through election day, November 4. Of several speeches made in Indiana, the one at Rockport is the only one for which a report has been found.

To Samuel D. Marshall¹

Dear Sam: Springfield, Decr 6. 1844.

In your last letter, you incline to complain, that in mine, I did not notice what you had said about the case of Stickney vs Cassell, nor the cases against the Shawneetown Bank. The truth is, when I received your letter, I glanced it over, stuck it away, postponed the consideration of the cases, above mentioned, and forgot them alltogether. I now give you some account of all your cases, in detail.

Dorman vs Lane, stands as it did, & I will do the best I can with it according to your instructions. Gatewood vs. Wood & Wood we would have failed entirely to get into court but for an agreement with Mr. Eddy,² which saved us. By the agreement we altered the record so as to make it appear that it had been sent to the circuit court, also agreeing that at the next term of the Galatin circuit court, all the papers & orders are to be altered there accordingly *nunc pro tunc.* Stickney vs Cassell, I have just examined, & I think I can get the judgement affirmed. I'll try. The cases against the Bank, neither Logan nor I can engage in with you; we being to some extent standing counsel for Dunlap,³ & also specially retained by him in these cases. Mr. Eddy has retained me in a case for your father, for the Supreme court, which, however, I have not yet examined.

Give my respects to your Father and believe me as ever Your sincere friend   A. LINCOLN

¹ ALS, ICHi. References to the several supreme court cases mentioned in this letter may be traced in Lincoln's subsequent letters to Marshall, *infra.*
² Henry Eddy, attorney and fellow townsman of Samuel Marshall.
³ Probably James T. Dunlap of Springfield, Illinois.

To John J. Hardin¹

Dear John J.   Springfield, Ills. Decr. 17– 1844

You perhaps know of the great scramble going on here about our Post-office. Upon general principles, you know this would be no concern of the whigs, but in this particular case, if it be in your power to do any thing, you may thereby do a favour to some of your friends here, without disobliging any of them, so far as I believe.

The man we wish appointed is J. R. Diller—the reason is, that Major Spotswood's[2] family, now comparatively destitute, will be favoured by it. I write this by an understanding with Diller himself, who has seen it's contents. I do not perceive *how* you can effect any thing; but if you *can* and *will*, you will oblige at least Your sincere friend   A. LINCOLN

P.S. Let this be confidential.   LINCOLN.

[1] ALS, owned by David S. Lansden, Cairo, Illinois.
[2] George W. Spottswood, deceased postmaster. Jonathan R. Diller was appointed and held office until 1849.

Request for Use of Hall of Representatives for a Temperance Lecture[1]

To the Honorable,   Springfield
The House of Representatives,   25th. Jan. 1845–

At a very large and respectable meeting of ladies and gentlemen, held in this City on yesterday evening, it was resolved that the undersigned be appointed a committee to request of your Honorable body that Mr. Fairchild be permitted to deliver an address on Temperance this evening and also on monday evening next in the Representative Hall. Mr. Fairchild is a talented and eloquent young gentleman, eminently qualified to advance the cause of virtue and temperance & to promote the best interests of society. By permitting your Hall thus to be used your Honorable body will confer a great favor upon the whole community. All expences for keeping up fires, cleaning the Hall &c. shall be paid by private contribution. Most respectfully, Yours &c,   J. LAMBORN.

A. LINCOLN.

J. DOUGHERTY.

Committee

&c

[1] D, I-Ar. Lamborn wrote and signed for the committee.

Recommendation for Admittance of Stanislaus P. Lalumiere to the Practice of Law[1]

February 12, 1845

We the undersigned, having examined Stanislaus P. LaLumiere, touching his qualification to practice law, do recommend that he be allowed a license for the same.   A. LINCOLN.

Feby. 12. 1845.   J. GILLESPIE

[1] ADS, Marquette University. Accompanying the recommendation is the license issued by Samuel H. Treat and the oath signed by Lalumiere. Following a term as clerk of the United States Court in Springfield, Lalumiere went to St. Louis, Missouri, to take a similar position. While there he entered the novitiate of the Society of Jesus, and upon being ordained priest in 1857, was sent to Milwaukee, Wisconsin, where he later founded Marquette University.

To Archibald Williams[1]

Friend Williams: Springfield, March 1, 1845.

The supreme court adjourned this morning for the term. Your cases of Reinhardt vs. Schuyler, Bunce[2] vs. Schuyler, Dickhut vs. Dunell, and Sullivan vs. Andrews are continued. Hinman vs. Pope I wrote you concerning some time ago. McNutt et al. vs. Bean and Thompson is reversed and remanded.

Fitzpatrick vs. Brady et al. is reversed and remanded with leave to complainant to amend his bill so as to show the real consideration given for the land.

Bunce[3] against Graves, the court confirmed, wherefore, in accordance with your directions, I moved to have the case remanded to enable you to take a new trial in the court below. The court allowed the motion; of which I am glad, and I guess you are.

This, I believe, is all as to court business. The canal men have got their measure through the legislature pretty much or quite in the shape they desired.[4] Nothing else now. Yours, as ever,

A. LINCOLN.

[1] Tarbell (Appendix), p. 292. Williams was a lawyer of Quincy, Illinois.
[2] Bruen is the correct spelling.
[3] Graves *v.* Bruen. The Supreme Court allowed Lincoln's motion the same day this letter was written.
[4] The new act repeated the provisions of the act passed in the previous session. The Illinois and Michigan Canal is too long a story to summarize in a footnote. See T. C. Pease, *The Frontier State.*

Endorsement: Thomas Clements to Logan & Lincoln[1]

March 19, 1845

We accept the within, on condition that Burtle's account is not to exceed ten dollars, and agree to pay accordingly, when the amount of the judgement comes to our hands.

March 19. 1845.   LOGAN & LINCOLN

[1] AES, IHi. Thomas Clements on March 19, 1845, requested Logan & Lincoln to pay, out of funds to be collected on his judgment against John C. Cloyd, the amount of James Burtle's account against Clements. Clements, Cloyd, and Burtle were all residents of Sangamon County.

To Samuel D. Marshall[1]

Dear Sam: Springfield, June 20. 1845–

I have wondered very much why you never wrote me, concerning the Dorman & Lane case, since I wrote you, as to the decision of it in the Supreme court. I learn this morning at the clerk's office, that Lane has not, as yet, taken out the order remanding it; and I think it possible, he may have abandoned it. You, perhaps, know his intention. The case of Gatewood vs. Wood & Wood—has that been settled? or how stands it?

At the request of Mr. Eddy,[2] I attended a case in the Supreme court of Rawlings against Field,[3] your father, Mr. Eddy & some others, and got the judgment reversed. This was no business of yours, and I now only ask, as a favor of you, that if Mr. Eddy is well you say to him I would like to have the little fee in the case, if convenient.

Please write me on the receipt of this. Yours forever

                           A. LINCOLN.

[1] ALS, ICHi.   [2] Henry Eddy.

[3] Lincoln won this case before the Illinois Supreme Court when judgment was reversed on February 24, 1845.

To J. McDowell[1]

Dear Sir: Springfield, August 8. 1845

I hope you will excuse me for not sooner answering Mr. Constable's[2] letter, inclosing also one from you, when I assure you that I have not until now, had an oppertunity to examine the case.

Mr. Constable has stated or rather propounded several interrogatories, but I think I can express my views better without following them strictly. Whatever your uncle could do, if he were now alive, in relation to this contract, I think these devisees can now do—that is, your uncle, if now alive, could tender the remaining payment and interest, and have a specific performance, or damages in lieu, unless he should be barred by the Statute of limitations; but he would be barred by the Statute, unless there is some great length of time allowed by the terms of the bond for the payment of the money. The terms of the bond, in this particular you have not aforded me the means of knowing. But these devisees may stand on better ground than your uncle would if alive, as against the Statute of limitations; that is to say, if your uncle was not, by the terms of the bond, in default of payment, before his death, then the time of the minority of the devisees will not be counted against them otherwise, if he was so in default.

[345]

My opinion upon the whole case is about this: If your uncle was in default of payment, by the terms of the bond, before his death, these devisees can maintain no sort of suit in relation to the matter; if he was not so in default, they can, by tendering or paying the remaining payment, with interest, have the land, or damages in lieu.

Mr. Constable has said something about these devisees having no more than a life-estate. My view of our Statute on this subject is, that these devisees take a life-estate, and *their* heirs male, the title in in [*sic*] fee—nothing ever returning to your fathers heirs so far as this question is concerned.

I will say farther that, if I were you, I would not compromise the case at any cost; but let them sue if they will. Even if the main point of the case is against you, there will be so many little breaker's in their way, as to prevent their ever getting through safely. Respectfully   A. LINCOLN

1 ALS, IHi. J. McDowell was a resident of Mount Carmel, Illinois.
2 Charles H. Constable, attorney and state senator of Mount Carmel. There is no further record of Lincoln's connection with this case.

Petition for Pardon of a Person Unknown[1]

September [15?] 1845

To His Excellency Thomas Ford Governor of the State of Illinois

The undersigned would respectfully represent, that at the last term of the McLean circuit court held in the month of September, AD 1845, a person to said court unknown, was indicted, plead guilty to the charge and was by said court sentenced to the Penitentiary for the term of one year for the crime of Larceny. That said person was apprehended about five month[s] previous to the sitting of said court during all which time he has been confined in the Jail for the county of McLean. That during his said confinement he has in all respects behaved and conducted himself as one worthy of a better fate. That he has at all times acknowledged the taking of the watch with which he has been charged, and upon which he has been sentenced. That he was destitute of money at the time he took the watch and we have been told that he tried repeatedly on the road to obtain employment as a labouring hand, but was not successful in getting work.

We would therefore humbly suggest that in consideration of the punishment, which he has already received, together with his conduct, destitution & youth, that in our opinions he is a fit object for executive clemency.

[346]

We therefore petition your excellency, that he may be reprieved, and as in duty bound your Petitioners will ever pray.

[1] DS, I-Ar. Lincoln and John T. Stuart were among the fifty-two signers, mostly citizens of Bloomington, Illinois. The circuit court met in Bloomington, September 15-20, 1845. Although accompanied by letters from the presiding judge Samuel H. Treat and Lieutenant Governor John Moore, the petition seems not to have impressed Governor Ford.

To Williamson Durley[1]

Friend Durley: Springfield, Octr. 3. 1845

When I saw you at home,[2] it was agreed that I should write to you and your brother Madison.[3] Until I then saw you, I was not aware of your being what is generally called an abolitionist, or, as you call yourself, a Liberty-man; though I well knew there were many such in your county. I was glad to hear you say that you intend to attempt to bring about, at the next election in Putnam, a union of the whigs proper, and such of the liberty men, as are whigs in principle on all questions save only that of slavery. So far as I can perceive, by such union, neither party need yield any thing, on *the* point in difference between them. If the whig abolitionists of New York had voted with us last fall, Mr. Clay would now be president, whig principles in the ascendent, and Texas not annexed; whereas by the division, all that either had at stake in the contest, was lost. And, indeed, it was extremely probable, beforehand, that such would be the result. As I always understood, the Liberty-men deprecated the annexation of Texas extremely; and, this being so, why they should refuse to so cast their votes as to prevent it, even to me, seemed wonderful. What was their process of reasoning, I can only judge from what a single one of them told me. It was this: "We are not to do *evil* that *good* may come." This general, proposition is doubtless correct; but did it apply? If by your votes you could have prevented the *extention*, &c. of slavery, would it not have been *good* and not *evil* so to have used your votes, even though it involved the casting of them for a slaveholder? By the *fruit* the tree is to be known. An *evil* tree can not bring forth *good* fruit. If the fruit of electing Mr. Clay would have been to prevent the extension of slavery, could the act of electing have been *evil*?

But I will not argue farther. I perhaps ought to say that individually I never was much interested in the Texas question. I never could see much good to come of annexation; inasmuch, as they were already a free republican people on our own model; on the other hand, I never could very clearly see how the annexation would augment the evil of slavery. It always seemed to me that slaves would be taken there in about equal numbers, with or without annexation. And if more *were* taken because of annexation, still there would be just so many the fewer left, where they were taken from. It is possibly true, to some extent, that with annexation, some slaves may be sent to Texas and continued in slavery, that otherwise might have been liberated. To whatever extent this may be true, I think annexation an evil. I hold it to be a paramount duty of us in the free states, due to the Union of the states, and perhaps to liberty itself (paradox though it may seem) to let the slavery of the other states alone; while, on the other hand, I hold it to be equally clear, that we should never knowingly lend ourselves directly or indirectly, to prevent that slavery from dying a natural death—to find new places for it to live in, when it can no longer exist in the old. Of course I am not now considering what would be our duty, in cases of insurrection among the slaves.

To recur to the Texas question, I understand the Liberty men to have viewed annexation as a much greater evil than I ever did; and I, would like to convince you if I could, that they could have prevented it, without violation of principle, if they had chosen.

I intend this letter for you and Madison together; and if you and he or either shall think fit to drop me a line, I shall be pleased. Yours with respect
A. LINCOLN

[1] ALS, IHi.   [2] Probably on or near September 13.
[3] Madison G. Durley. Both brothers were Lincoln supporters at Hennepin, Putnam County.

Release of Judgment Against Francis Regnier[1]

October 24, 1845

For and in consideration of the sum of twenty five dollars received of Francis Regnier,[2] I do hereby transfer and release to said Regnier all my right, title and interest in and to a judgment obtained in the Morgan circuit court in the year 1844 in favor of Eliza S. Cabbott[3] (since married to   Torry)[4] against said Regnier in being my individual interest and believed to be one eighth part of said judgment, be the same more or less. Witness my hand this 24th. day of October 1845; as one of the attornies of the plaintiff.
A. LINCOLN

[1] ADS-P, ISLA.
[2] Dr. Francis Regnier, formerly of New Salem, at this date residing in Petersburg, Illinois.
[3] Cabot *v.* Regnier, a slander suit, on change of venue from Menard County, March 14-15, 1844.   [4] E. C. Torrey.

Petition for Pardon of Samuel Smith[1]

[November, 1845]

To the Honorable the Governor of the State of Illinois

Thomas Ford

Your Petitioners would respectfully represent that Samuel Smith a citizen of this State and of Sangamon, was at the last Term of the Circuit court, indicted for an assault by the Grand jurors of said County and convicted by the petit jurors of an assault and sentenced by the Honorable Judge of the Circuit, Samuel H. Treat, to three days imprisonment and ten dollars fine and pay the cost of suit. Your petitioners would further respectfully represent that the Said Saml. Smith has lain in the county jail all the said term and several days more and that he is still in jail and is a poor man and is unable to pay the fine and costs of suit and they would most respectfully ask of Your Excellency to release him from prison, so that he may pay the fine and cost of suit

[1] DS, I-Ar. Lincoln was one of twenty signers. Samuel Smith was sentenced in November, 1845, and pardoned on December 2, 1845.

To Benjamin F. James[1]

Friend James: Springfield, Nov: 17, 1845.

The paper at Pekin[2] has nominated Hardin for Governor; and, commenting on this, the Alton paper,[3] indirectly nominates him for Congress. It would give Hardin a great start, and perhaps use me up, if the whig papers of the District should nominate him for *Congress*. If your feelings towards me are the same as when I saw you (which I have no reason to doubt) I wish you would let nothing appear in your paper which may opperate against me. You understand.

Matters stand just as they did when I saw you. Baker is certainly off of the track, and I fear Hardin intends to be on it.

In relation to the business you wrote me of, some time since, I suppose the Marshall called on you; and we think it can be adjusted, at court, to the satisfaction of you & friend Thompson.[4]

[A. LINCOLN][5]

[1] ALS, MH.
[2] Lincoln was in error. See his correction in the next letter to James (*infra*). James was editor of the *Tazewell Whig* published at Tremont, near Pekin, Illinois.   [3] The Alton *Telegraph and Democratic Review*.
[4] Philo Hale Thompson, a merchant of Pekin.
[5] Signature has been cut off the original manuscript.

To Henry E. Dummer[1]

Friend Dummer: Springfield, Nov: 18th. 1845

Before Baker[2] left, he said to me, in accordance with what had long been an understanding between him and me, that the track for the next congressional race was clear to me, so far as he was concerned; and that he would say so publicly in any manner, and at any time I might desire. I said, in reply, that as to the manner and time, I would consider a while, and write him. I understand friend Delahay[3] to have already informed you of the substance of the above.

I now wish to say to you that if it be consistent with your feelings, you would set a few stakes for me. I do not certainly know, but I strongly suspect, that Genl. Hardin[4] wishes to run again. I know of no argument to give me a preference over him, unless it be "Turn about is fair play."

The Pekin paper[5] has lately nominated or suggested Hardin's name for Governor, and the Alton paper,[6] noticing that, indirectly nominates him for Congress. I wish you would, if you can, see that, while these things are bandied about among the papers, the Beardstown paper[7] takes no stand that may injure my chance, unless the conductor really prefers Genl. Hardin, in which case, I suppose it would be fair.

Let this be confidential, and please write me in a few days. Yours as ever A. LINCOLN

[1] ALS, IHi.   [2] Edward D. Baker.
[3] Mark W. Delahay, attorney and newspaper editor whose association with Lincoln was of long standing and who married a distant relative of Lincoln's mother. Delahay was located at this time in Cass County.
[4] John J. Hardin.
[5] See letter to Benjamin F. James, November 17, 1845, *supra.*
[6] *Telegraph and Democratic Review.*   [7] *Gazette.*

To Benjamin F. James[1]

Friend James: Springfield, Novr. 24th. 1845

Yours of the 19th. was not received till this morning. The error I fell into in relation to the *Pekin* paper, I discovered myself the day after I wrote you.[2] The way I fell into it was, that Stuart (John T) met me in the court & told me about a nomination having been made in the Pekin paper, and about the comments upon it in the Alton paper; and without seeing either paper myself, I wrote you. In writing to you, I only meant to call your attention to the matter; and that done, I knew all would be right with you. Of course I should not have thought this necessary, if, at the time, I had known that the nomination had been made in your paper. And let me assure you, that if there is any thing in my letter indicating an opinion that the nomination for *Governor,* which I supposed to have been made in the Pekin paper, was opperating, or could opperate against me, such was not my meaning. Now, that I know that nomination was made by you,[3] I say that it *may* do me good while I do not see that it *can* do me harm. But, while the subject is in agitation, should any of the papers in the District nominate the same man[4] for *Congress* that would do me harm; and it was that which I wished to guard against. Let me assure that I do not, for a moment, suppose, that what you *have* done is ill-judged; or that any thing you shall do, will be. It was not to object to the course of the *Pekin* paper (as I then thought it) but to guard against any falling into the wake of the *Alton* paper, that I wrote.

You, perhaps, have noticed the Journal's article of last week, upon the same subject. It was written without any consultation with me, but I was told by Francis[5] of it's purport before it was published. I chose to let it go as it was, lest it should be suspected that I was attempting to juggle Hardin out of a nomination for congress by juggleing him into one for Governor. If you, and the other papers, a little more distant from me, choose, to take the same course you have, of course I have no objection. After you shall have received this, I think we shall fully understand each other, and that our views as to the effects of these things are not dissimilar. Confidential of course Yours as ever   A. LINCOLN

[1] ALS, MH.   [2] See letter of November 17, *supra.*
[3] In James' paper, *Tazewell Whig,* November 1, 1845.   [4] John J. Hardin.
[5] Simeon Francis, editor. This would have been the November 20 issue of the *Sangamo Journal.*

To Benjamin F. James[1]

B. F. James Esq.   Springfield, Ills., Dec. 6, 1845.

Dear Sir: To succeed, I must have 17 votes in convention. To secure them, I think I may safely claim Sangamon 8, Menard 2, Logan 1, making 11, so that if you and other friends can secure Dr. Boal's[2] entire senatorial district, that is, Tazewell 4, Woodford 1, and Marshall 1, it just covers the case. . . .

Upon the whole, it is my intention to give him the trial, unless clouds should rise, which are not yet discernible. This determination you need not, however, as yet, announce in your paper, at least not as coming from me. . . .

In doing this, let nothing be said against Hardin . . . nothing deserves to be said against him. Let the pith of the whole argument be "Turn about is fair play." Yours very truly,   A. LINCOLN
P.S. . . .   A. L.

¹ Tracy, p. 16.   ² Robert S. Boal of Lacon, Illinois.

To Samuel D. Marshall¹

Friend Sam: Springfield Decr. 30. 1845
I learned to day, that Lane,² to avoid paying the cost of taking the case between Dorman and him, back from the Supreme Court, has commenced a new proceeding in your circuit court. Write me, if this is so; and I together with judge Logan, will try to frame a plea either in bar or in abatement, out of the fact of the pendency of the old case, that shall blow them up with their new case.

By the way, if they fail for more than year (which they have nearly done already) to take the old case down from here, I think we can plead limitation on them, so that it will stick for good and all. Dont speak of this, lest they hear it, and take the alarm.

Write me on receipt of this. Yours as ever—   A. LINCOLN

¹ ALS-P, ISLA.
² See letter of November 11, 1842, and subsequent correspondence.

Endorsement¹

[1846-1847?]
At the request of Mr. Crosby,² I most cheerfully state that I concur fully in the foregoing certificate of Judge Treat. It is thought not improper for me to add, that I am the Representative to Congress for the District in which Mr. Crosby resides.

A. LINCOLN

¹ AES, IHi. The date is conjectural from the contents.   ² J. W. Crosby.

To Robert Boal¹

Dear Doctor   Springfield Jany. 7 1846.
Since I saw you last fall, I have often thought of writing you as it was then understood I would, but on reflection I have always found that I had nothing new to tell you. All has happened as I then told you I expected it would—Baker's declining, Hardin's taking the track, and so on.

If Hardin and I stood precisely equal—that is, if *neither* of us had been to congress, or if we *both* had—it would only accord with what I have always done, for the sake of peace, to give way to him; and I expect I should do it. That I *can* voluntarily postpone my pretentions, when they are no more than equal to those to which they are postponed, you have yourself seen. But to yield to Hardin under present circumstances, seems to me as nothing else than yielding to one who would gladly sacrifice me altogether. This, I would rather not submit to. That Hardin is talented, energetic, usually generous and magnanimous, I have, before this, affirmed to you, and do not now deny. You know that my only argument is that "turn about is fair play". This he, practically at least, denies.

If it would not be taxing you too much, I wish you would write me, telling the aspect of things in your county, or rather your district; and also send the names of some of your whig neighbours, to whom I might, with propriety write. Unless I can get some one to do this, Hardin with his old franking list, will have the advantage of me. My reliance for a fair shake (and I want nothing more) in your county is chiefly on you, because of your position and standing, and because I am acquainted with so few others. Let this be strictly confidential, & any letter you may write me shall be the same if you desire. Let me hear from you soon. Yours truly

A. LINCOLN

1 ALS-F, ISLA.

To Benjamin F. James[1]

Friend James: Springfield, Jany. 14– 1846.

Yours of the 10th. was not received until this morning. I can not but be pleased with it's contents. I saw Henry's communication[2] in your paper, as also your editorial remarks, neither of which, in my opinion, was in any way misjudged—both quite the thing. I think just as you do concerning the dictation of the course of the Alton paper, and also, concerning it's utter harmlessness.

As to the proposition to hold the convention at Petersburg, I will at once tell you all I know, and all I feel. A good friend of ours there, John Bennett, wrote me that he thought it would do good with the whigs of Menard, to see a respectable convention conducted in good style. They are a little disinclined, to adopt the convention system; & Bennett thinks some of their prejudices would be done away by their having the convention amongst them. At his request, therefore I had the little paragraph put in the Journal.[3] This is all I know. Now, as to what I *feel*,—I feel a desire that they

of Petersburg should be gratified, if it can be done without a sacrafice of the wishes of others, and without detriment to the cause—
nothing more. I can gain nothing in the contest by having it there.
I showed your letter to Stuart, and he thinks there is something in
your suggestion of holding it at your town. I should be pleased if
I could concur with you in the hope that my name would be the
only one presented to the convention—but I can not. Hardin is a
man of desparate energy and perseverance; and one that never
backs out; and, I fear, to think otherwise, is to be deceived in the
character of our adversary.

I would rejoice to be spared the labour of a contest; but "being
in" I shall go it thoroughly, and to the bottom. As to my being able
to make a break in the lower counties, I tell you that I can *possibly*
get Cass, but I do not think I will. Morgan & Scott are beyond my
reach. Menard is safe to me. Mason—neck and neck. Logan is
mine. To make the matter sure, your entire Senatorial District
must be secured. Of this I suppose Tazewell is safe; and I have
much done in both the other counties. In Woodford I have Davenport,[4] Simms, Willard,[5] Bracken,[6] Perry[,][7] Travis,[8] Dr. Hazzard
[*sic*],[9] and the Clarks [*sic*],[10] & some others all specially committed. At Lacon, in Marshall the very most active friend I have in
the District (If I except yourself) is at work.[11] Through him I have
procured their names, and written to three or four of the most
active whigs in each precinct of the county. Still I wish you all in
Tazewell, to keep your eyes continually on Woodford and Marshall. Let no oppertunity of making a mark escape. When they shall
be safe, all will be safe—*I think.*

The Beardstown paper[12] is entirely in the hands of my friends.
The editor is a whig, and personally dislikes Hardin. When this
Supreme court shall adjourn, (which it is thought will be about the
15th. of February) it is my intention to take a quiet trip through
the towns and neighbourhoods of Logan county, Delevan [*sic*],
Tremont,[13] and on to & through the upper counties. Dont speak of
this, or let it relax any of your vigilance.

When I shall reach Tremont, we will talk over every thing at
large. Yours truly A. LINCOLN

[1] ALS, MH.
[2] Dr. Anson G. Henry who was then a resident of Pekin, Illinois; the communication favoring Lincoln was signed "A Whig," and appeared in the *Tazewell
Whig*, December 27, 1845.
[3] "A whig of Menard county, speaking on behalf of himself and others, expresses a wish, that the Convention for the nomination of a Whig candidate for
Congress in this District, be held at Petersburgh. We know no reason why it
should not; and if others are agreed, so are we." *Sangamo Journal*, January
1, 1846. [4] Reverend William Davenport, minister of the Christian Church.

⁵ Peter H. Willard, prominent merchant at Metamora, Illinois.
⁶ Matthew Bracken, of Walnut Grove.   ⁷ John J. Perry.
⁸ Daniel Travis.   ⁹ Dr. John Hazard.
¹⁰ Henry J. and Robert M. Clarke.   ¹¹ Dr. Robert Boal.
¹² *Gazette,* edited by Sylvester Emmons.
¹³ Delavan and Tremont are in Tazewell County.

To John Bennett[1]

Friend John: Springfield, Jany. 15– 1846

Nathan Dresser[2] is here, and speaks as though the contest between Hardin & me is to be doubtful in Menard county. I know he is candid, and this alarms me some. I asked him to tell me the names of the men that were going strong for Hardin; he said Morris[3] was about as strong as any. Now tell me, is Morris going it openly? You remember you wrote me, that he would be neutral. Nathan also said that some man (who he could not remember) had said lately, that Menard county was again to decide the contest; and that that made the contest very doubtful.[4] Do you know who that was?

Dont fail to write me instantly on receiving this, telling me all —particularly the names of those who are going strong against me.

Yours as ever,   A. LINCOLN

¹ ALS-F, ISLA.   ² Circuit clerk, Menard County.
³ Martin S. Morris.
⁴ Dresser was made chairman of the District Whig Convention held at Petersburg on May 1 which endorsed Lincoln unanimously.

To John Bennett[1]

Dear John: Springfield, Jany. 16– 1846.

The enclosed letters I wrote last night, but when I went to the Post-office this morning your mail had left about half an hour. So I send them by Mr. Harris.[2] Will you please take out the one addressed to you,[3] and drop the others in your Post-office, unless you see the men to hand them to in person, in which case please do that.

Yours as ever   A. LINCOLN

¹ ALS, RPB.
² Thomas L. Harris, Democrat, state senator from Menard County, and later, Lincoln's successor in congress.   ³ See preceding letter, January 15.

To Benjamin F. James[1]

Dear James: Springfield, Jany. 16. 1846–

A plan is on foot to change the mode of selecting the candidate for this district.[2] The movement is intended to injure me, and if effected, most likely would injure me to some extent. I have not time to give particulars now; but I want you to let nothing prevent your getting an article in your paper, of *this week*[3] taking strong ground for the old system, under which Hardin & Baker were nominated, without seeming to know or suspect, that any one desires to change it. I have written Dr. Henry more at length; and he will probably call & consult with you, in getting up the article; but whether he does or not dont fail, on any account, to get it in *this week*.

[A. LINCOLN][4]

[1] ALS, MH.   [2] See Lincoln to John J. Hardin, January 19, 1846.
[3] An editorial appeared in the *Tazewell Whig*, January 24, 1846.
[4] Signature has been removed from the original manuscript.

To John J. Hardin[1]

Dear Genl.[2]   Springfield, Jany. 19th. 1846

I do not wish to join in your proposal[3] of a new plan for the selection of a whig candidate for congress, because

1st. I am entirely satisfied with the old system[4] under which you and Baker were successively nominated and elected to congress; and because the whigs of the District are well acquainted with that system, and, so far as I know or believe, are universally satisfied with it. If the old system be thought to be vague, as to all the delegates of a county, voting the same, way; or as to instructions to them, as to whom they are to vote for; or as to filling vacancies, I am willing to join in a provision to make these matters certain.

2nd. As to your proposals that a poll shall be opened in *every* precinct, and that the whole shall take place on the *same* day, I do not personally object. They seem to me to not be unfair; and I forbear to join in proposing them, only because I rather choose to leave the decision in each county to the whigs of the county, to be made as their own judgment and convenience may dictate.

3rd. As to your proposed stipulation that all the candidates shall remain in their own counties, and restrain their friends to the same, it seems to me that on reflection you will see, the fact of your having been in congress, has, in various ways, so spread your name in the district, as to give you a decided advantage in such a stipulation. I appreciate your desire to keep down excitement; and I promise you to "keep cool" under all circumstances.

4th. I have already said I am satisfied with the old system, under which such good men have triumphed; and that I desire no departure from its principles. But if there must be a departure from it, I shall insist upon a more accurate and just apportionment of delegates, or representative votes, to the constituent body, than exists by the old; and which you propose to retain in your new plan.

If we take the entire population of the counties as shown by the late census, we shall see that by the old plan, and by your proposed new plan

Morgan county with a population of 16.541 has		8 votes
while Sangamon with 18.697—2156 greater has but		8 do
So, Scott, with 6553—has		4 do
while Tazewell with 7615—1062 greater—	has but	4 do—
So, Mason with 3135 has		1. do
while Logan with 3907—772 greater has but		1. do—

And so, in a less degree, the matter runs through all the counties; being not only wrong in principle, but the advantage of it being all manifestly in your favour, with one slight exception in the comparison of two counties not here mentioned.

Again: If we take the *whig votes* of the counties as shown by the late presidential election as a basis, the thing is still worse. Take a comparison of the same six counties—

Morgan, with her 1443 whig votes has			8 votes
Sangamon with her 1837—	394 greater only		8 do.
Mason with her 255—	has		1 do
Logan do do 310—	55 greater only.		1. do
Scott do do 670—		has	4. do
Tazewell do do 1011.	341 greater—only		4. do—

It seems to me most obvious that the old system needs adjustment in nothing so much as in this; and still by your proposal, no notice is taken of it.

I have always been in the habit of acceding to almost any proposal that a friend would make; and I am truly sorry I can not in this.

I perhaps ought to mention that some friends at different places, are endeavouring to secure the honor of the sitting of a convention at their towns respectively; and I fear they would not feel much complimented, if we were to make a bargain that it shall sit no where. Yours as ever   A. LINCOLN

1 ALS, ICHi.
2 Hardin was made a brigadier general of militia on November 9, 1840.

[3] As published in the *Sangamo Journal*, February 26, 1846, Hardin's proposals were as follows:

Proposals for the selection of a candidate for Congress by the Whig voters of this District:

1. Each county to have double as many voters as it has members in the House of Representatives—being the same number allowed in the two last Conventions—that is:

Sangamon,	8 votes	Logan,	1 vote
Morgan,	8 do	Mason,	1 do
Tazewell,	4 do	Woodford,	1 do
Scott,	4 do	Marshall,	1 do
Cass,	2 do	Putnam,	1 do
Menard,	2 do		

2. The Whigs to meet at the various precincts in the District, and appoint two Judges (who shall have power to select a third in case of difference of opinion on any question) and vote by ballot for the person they prefer for candidate.

3. The Judges to take a list of the names of voters, and keep and open the ballots after all the votes are given, and then to return a written or printed statement of the number of votes for each candidate to a central committee at Springfield.

4. A central committee of three persons at Springfield, shall open and examine the returns, and within two weeks after the vote is taken, or sooner if all the returns are in, or any person has a majority of the votes, they shall make out and publish the result, and state who has been selected as the Candidate of the Whigs of the district.

5. The election to be held on one day, and no person to vote by proxy. And in counting the votes, the Central Committee to exclude no vote for informality, if they can fairly ascertain for whom it was intended to be given.

6. Whoever gets the most votes in a county shall be entitled to the vote in that county in the general result made out by the central committee.

7. Should it happen that no candidate has a majority of the thirty-three votes, by reason of there being more than two candidates—then the hindermost candidate is to decline or be dropped, and the committee shall order a new election in those counties which voted for the hindermost candidate.

8. The central committee to prepare a handbill stating this plan, and to circulate it in every precinct of the District.

9. All whig voters to be entitled to vote.

10. Each person who is spoken of as a candidate to give a pledge to the committee and the public, that he will not go into any other county than the one in which he resides for the purpose of influencing the voters—and to further pledge himself that as far as is practicable he will restrain his friends from going out of their counties to electioneer, or attempt to influence voters. The object of this being to prevent excitement between the candidates and their friends, and to leave the voters of the counties to their unbiased choice.

11. The expenses of the central committee in printing circulars, and in postage, shall be paid by the person getting the nomination.

12. The vote to be taken on Saturday the —— day of March.

[4] The convention system, for which Lincoln had labored so heartily and which many Whigs, Hardin among them, had opposed as undemocratic because it restricted party candidacy. Prior to the adoption of the system, any Whig could announce, as a Whig, for any office. Consequently, the Democrats, who had first adopted the convention system, were often able to elect candidates even in Whig territory, by reason of their uniting on one candidate while Whig support was divided among several. Hardin was nominated by convention in 1843, Edward D. Baker in 1845, and Lincoln now regarded it to be his turn. That Hardin's proposals were not merely in the interest of party harmony is obvious.

To N. J. Rockwell[1]

N. J. Rockwell: Springfield, January 21, 1846.

Dear Sir: You perhaps know that General Hardin and I have a contest for the Whig nomination for Congress for this district. He has had a turn and my argument is "Turn about is fair play." I shall be pleased if this strikes you as a sufficient argument. Yours truly,   A. LINCOLN.

[1] Tarbell (Appendix), p. 295. Rockwell was a resident of Havana and Whig candidate for the state senate.

Receipt for H. C. Gibson's Pockets[1]

We have found in H C Gibsons Pokets ten dollars and fifteen cts in cash   JOHN ALLEN

Jan 25th. 1846   A. LINCOLN

[1] DS, owned by J. Colby Beekman, Petersburg, Illinois. Lincoln was campaigning in Petersburg on this date. John Allen was a physician of Petersburg, who attended H. C. Gibson, a citizen of Aurora, Illinois, who died in Petersburg while traveling (*Sangamo Journal*, January 29, 1846).

To Benjamin F. James[1]

Dear James: Springfield, Jany. 27. 1846

Yours enclosing the article[2] from the Whig is received. In my judgment you have hit the matter exactly right. I believe it is too late to get the article in the Journal of this week;[3] but Dickinson[4] will understand it just as well from your paper, knowing, as he does, your position towards me. More than all, I wrote him at the same time I did you. As to suggestions for the committee, I would say appoint the convention for the first monday of May—as to the *place,* I can hardly make a suggestion, so many points desiring it. I was at Petersburg saturday and sunday; and they are very anxious for it there. A friend has also written me, desiring it at Beardstown.[5]

I would have the committee leave the mode of choosing delegates to the whigs of the different counties, as may best suit them respectively. I would have them propose, for the sake of uniformity that the delegates should all be instructed as to their man, and the delegation of each county should go as a unit. If, without this, some counties should send *united* delegations & others *divided* ones, it might make bad work.

Also have it proposed, that when the convention shall meet, if there shall be any absent delegates, the members present may fill the vacancies, with persons to act under the same instructions, which may be known to have been given to such absentees. You understand. Other particulars I leave to you. I am sorry to say I am afraid I can not go to Mason, so as to attend to your business; but if I shall determine to go there, I will write you.

Do you hear any thing from Woodford & Marshall? Davenport,[6] ten days ago, passed through here, and told me Woodford is safe; but, though in hope, I am not entirely easy about Marshall. I have so few personal acquaintances in that county, that I can not get at [it?] right. Dickinson is doing all that any one man can do; but it seems like it is an over-task for one.

I suppose Dr. Henry will be with you on saturday. I got a letter from him to-day on the same subject as yours; and shall write him before saturday. Yours truly,   A. LINCOLN

[1] ALS, MH.
[2] An editorial which Lincoln had requested in his letter of January 16, and which appeared in the *Tazewell Whig*, January 24, 1846.
[3] Appeared in the issue for February 5, 1846.   [4] B. F. Dickinson.
[5] It was held at Petersburg on May 1.   [6] Reverend William Davenport.

To John J. Hardin[1]

Genl. J. J. Hardin: Springfield.
Dear Sir: Feb. 7. 1846–

Your second letter[2] was duly received and, so far as it goes, it is entirely satisfactory.

I had set apart the leisure this day affords, to write you the long letter alluded to by me in my last; but on going to the Post-office, and seeing the communication in the Morgan Journal,[3] I am almost discouraged of the hope of doing any good by it; especially when I reflect that most probably that communication was written with your knowledge, in as much as it proceeds partly on information which could only have been furnished by you.

However, as I suppose it can do no *harm*, I will proceed. Your letter, admiting my right to seek, or desire, a nomination for congress, opens with an expression of dissatisfaction with the *manner*

[1] ALS, ICHi.
[2] This letter is not extant, Lincoln's quotations from it being the only source for its contents.
[3] The *Morgan Journal* for this date is not extant, but the article referred to was copied by the *Illinois Gazette*, February 14, 1846. It argued against Lincoln's principle of rotation in office and published the fact that Hardin had proposed a district Whig poll to replace the convention system, and also the fact of Lincoln's having declined to support the proposal—which facts could have come to light only through Hardin's having revealed the content of Lincoln's letter of January 19.

in which you think I have endeavoured to obtain it. Now, *if I have*, sought the nomination in an *improper* manner; you have the right, to the extent, to be dissatisfied. But I deny all *impropriety* on my part, in the matter.

In the early part of your letter, you introduce the proposition made by me to you and Baker, that we should take a turn a piece; and alluding to the principle you suppose [to] be involved in it, in an after part of your letter, you say—"As a whig I have constantly combatted such practices when practiced among the Locos; & I do not see that they are any more praise worthy, or less anti-republican, when sought to be adopted by whigs." Now, if my proposition had been that we (yourself, Baker & I) should be candidates by turns, and that we should unite our strength throughout to keep down all other candidates, I should not deny the justice of the censurable language you employ; but if you so understood it, you wholly misunderstood it. I never expressed, nor meant to express, that by such an arrangement, any one of us should be, in the least restricted in his right to support any person he might choose, in the District; but only that he should not *himself*, be a candidate out of his turn. I felt then, and it seems to me I *said* then, that even with such an arrangement, should Governor Duncan be a candidate, when you were not, it would be your *previlege* and perhaps your *duty* to go for him.

In this, the true sense of my proposition, I deny that there is any thing censurable in it—any thing but a spirit of mutual concession, for harmony's sake.

In this same connection you say, "It is, in effect, acting upon the principle that the District is a horse which each candidate may mount and ride a two mile heat without consulting any body but the grooms & Jockeys." Well, of course, you go the contrary of this principle; which is, in effect acting on the principle that the District is a horse which, the first jockey that can mount him, may whip and spur round and round, till jockey, or horse, or both, fall dead on the track. And upon your principle, there is a fact as fatal to your clcaims as mine, which is, that neither you nor I, but *Baker* is the jockey now in the stirrups.

"Without consulting any body but the grooms & Jockeys" is an implied charge that I wish, in some way to interfere with the right of the people to select their candidate. I do not understand it so. I, and my few friends say to the people that "Turn about is fair play." You and your friends do not meet this, and say "Turn about is *not* fair play"—but insist the argument itself, ought not to be used. Fair or unfair, why not trust the people to decide it?

In the early part of your letter you say "It is also true that you did come to my house early in September to know whether I desired to run, stating that you wanted to give Baker a race." In this you are mistaken. I did not state to you that I wanted to give Baker a race; but on the contrary I told you I believed I could get Baker off the track. I do not know that you attached any importance to what I am disavowing; but, on the contrary, I do not know but you mean it as the basis of an inference that I acted deceitfully with you, in pretending to expect a contest with Baker, when in fact I did not expect it.

It is true, that after Baker's interview with you in September, he did send a letter, by a messenger, to me at Tremont; in which letter he detailed what passed at the interview, and the result, precisely as you do, in substance; and in which letter he did urge me to relinquish my my [sic] pretensions. He had before told me that he would not be a candidate, if I desired he should not; and he then repeated it; but at the same time argued that you, by having been in congress, and having taken a high stand then, would in all probability beat me; so that the sacrafice he made for me, in declining, would, in the end, do me no good. And this is as near as I ever came of hearing Baker express the determination that I should beat you, if he could not; which you say you have learned he did. When he finally determined to decline, he did express the wish that I might succeed; and he has since written his letter of declension; and when *that* is told; all I know, or believe, as to him, *is told*. If he has ever, in any way, attempted to dictate to any friend of his to go for me in preference of you, it is more than I know or believe. That he has a part assigned him to act in the drama, I know to be untrue. What I here say, is not in its nature capable of very certain proof; but it may be said, that being where he is, he can only opperate against you by letters. If he attempts this to any considerable extent, some of them will fall into the hands of your friends who will apprize you of them. Have you yet seen or heard of any?

I now quote from your letter again. "You well knew I would not be a candidate for Governor. Yet during the fall courts, whilst I learn you were obtaining pledges from all the whigs you could to support you for the next candidate, my name was run up as a candidate for Governor by one of your friends under circumstances which now leave no room for doubt that the design was to keep my name out of view for congress, so that the whigs might be more easily influenced to commit themselves to go for you."

Now this is a direct imputation that I *procured*, or *winked at*, or in some way directly or indirectly, *had a hand in*, the nominating of you for Governor;[4] and the imputation is, to the utmost hair-breadth of it, unjust. I never *knew*, or *believed*, or had any *suspicion*, that it *was done*, or *was to be done*, until it was out, had gone to Alton, and been commented upon in the Alton paper, and came back to Springfield, and my attention was called to it by Stuart, in our circuit court room, a few days, as I remember it, after you had been here attending to the case of Thayer vs Farrell, and had left. I went immediately to the Journal office, and told them it was my wish that they should not fall in with the nomination for Governor. They showed me a little paragraph, which they had already prepared, and which was published, and seen by you, as I suppose.

The reason I had not seen the nomination in the Tazewell paper was, as I suppose, because I did not then, as I do not now, take that paper. That I was wholly *innocent* and *ignorant* of that movement, I believe, if need be, I can prove more conclusively than is often in the power of man to prove any such thing.

In the paragraph last quoted you say that the design was to keep your name out of view &c. In the general disavowal I have made, this last is, of course included; and I now go farther, and declare, that to my recollection, I have not, in a single instance, presented my name as a candidate for congress, without, at the same time presenting yours for the same place. I have some times met a man who would express the opinion that you would yield the track to me; and some times one who believed you would be a candidate for Governor; and I invariably assured such, that you would, in my opinion, be a candidate *for congress*. And while I have thus kept your name *in view* for congress, I have not reproached you for being a candidate, or for any thing else; on the contrary I have constantly spoken of you in the most kind and commendatory terms, as to your talents, your past services, and your goodness of heart. If I falsify in this, you can convict me. The witnesses live, and can tell.

And now tell me: If you think so harshly of me because a paper under the control of one of my friends nominated *you* for Governor, *what*, or *how*, ought I to think of you because of your paper at Jacksonville doing the same thing for *me* twice? Why, you will say you had nothing [to] do with it; and I shall believe you; but why am I to be judged less charatably?

In another part of your letter you attempt to convict me of giving a double account as to my motive in introducing the resolution to the convention at Pekin. You say "You then told me the object was to soothe Baker's mortified feelings, and that it did not amount

4 See letters to Benjamin F. James, November 17, 24, 1845.

to a committal of any body." "Now you say the object was to give Baker the field for the next race, so as to keep the party together." I kept no copy of my letter; but I *guess* if you will turn to it, you will find that I have not, any where in it, said "the object was to give Baker the field for the next race &c" and then if you will allow that you may have committed as great a mistake, as to what I told you at Pekin, you will find yourself a good deal short of the conviction you intended. What I told you at Pekin I do not precisely recollect; but I am sure of some things I did *not* tell you or any one else. If you shall say that I told you it was *an* object with me, in introducing the resolution, to soothe Baker's feelings, I shall admit it; but if you shall say I told you that, that was *the sole* object, I deny it.

If you shall say I then told you that the passage of the resolution amounted to a committal of no one, I deny that also; but if you shall say I then told you, it amounted to a committal of no one, except the delegates, generally who voted for it, and me, particularly, who introduced it, I shall not deny it.

This much, and no more, as a committal, I always supposed it to amount to; and I guess you will be able to find nothing in my late letter to you that is inconsistent with this. And I here add, that I have not since entering this contest with you, or at any time, sought to appropriate to myself any benefit from that resolution, e[i]ther as settling the succession to pass through me, or as settling a principle that shall give the succession that direction. I have said that "Turn about is fair play"; but this I have said just as I would, if that resolution had never been thought of. I should not hesitate to say publicly, that I claim nothing, in any form, through the Pekin convention, were it not that some friends have thought and spoken differently, and I dislike to rebuke them for what they have not supposed to be injustice to you, while they have meant it in kindness to me—yet, ⸱rather than be over-delicate, if you desire it, I will do it any how. I repeat, I desire *nothing* from the Pekin convention. If I am not, (in services done the party, and in capacity to serve in future) near enough your equal, when added to the fact of your having had a turn, to entitle me to the nomination, I scorn it on any and all other grounds. The question of capacity, I opine your Morgan Journal correspondent will find little difficulty in deciding; and probably the District may concur, with quite as little.

A good long paragraph of your letter is occupied in an argument to prove that struggles for the succession will break down the party. It is certain that struggles between candidates, do not strengthen a party; but who are most responsible for these struggles, those who are willing to live and let live, or those who are resolved, at all hazzards, to take care of "number one"? Take, as an example, the very case in hand. You have (and deservedly) many devoted friends; and they have been gratified by seeing you in congress, and taking a stand that did high credit to you and to them. I also have a few friends (I fear not enough) who, as well as your own, aided in giving you that distinction. Is it natural that they shall be greatly pleased at hearing what they helped to build up, turned into an argument, for keeping their own favourite down? Will they grow, and multiply on such grateful food? Is it by such exclusiveness that you think a party will gain strength?

In my letter to you,⁵ I reminded you that you had first at Washington, and afterwards at Pekin, said to me that if Baker succeeded he would most likely hang on as long as possible, while with you it would be different. If I am not mistaken in your having said this (and I am sure I am not) it seems you *then* thought a little more favourably of "turn about" than you seem to now. And in writing your letter you seem to have felt this; for that is about the only part of mine, that you have failed to notice.

After, by way of imputations upon me, you have used the the [*sic*] terms "management" "manoevering" and "combination" quite freely, you, in your closing paragraph say: "For it is mortifying to discover that those with whom I have long acted & from whom I expected a different course, have considered it all fair to prevent my nomination to congress." Feeling, as I do, the utter injustice of these imputations, it is somewhat difficult to be patient under them—yet I content myself with saying that if there is cause for mortification any where, it is in the readiness with which you believe, and make such charges, against one with whom you truly say you have long acted; and in whose conduct, you have heretofore marked nothing as dishonorable.

I believe you do not mean to be unjust, or ungenerous; and I, therefore am slow to believe that you will not yet think *better* and think *differently* of this matter. Yours truly   A. LINCOLN.

⁵ January 19, 1846, *supra.*

To Benjamin F. James¹

Dear James: Springfield, Feb. 9. 1846

You have seen, or will see what I am inclined to think you will regard as rather an extraordinary communication in the Morgan Journal.² The "excessive modesty" of it's tone is certainly admirable. As an excuse for getting before the public, the writer sets out with a pretence of answering an article which I believe appeared in the Lacon paper some time since; taking the ground that the Pekin convention had settled the rotation principle. Now whether the Pekin convention did or did not settle that principle, I care not. If I am not, in what I *have done*, and am *able to do*, for the party, near enough the equal of Genl. Hardin, to entitle me to the nomination, now that he has one, I scorn it on *any* and *all* other grounds.

So far then, as this Morgan Journal commun[ic]ation may relate to the Pekin convention, I rather prefer that your paper shall let it "stink and die" unnoticed.

There is, however, as you will see, another thing in the communication which is, an attempt to injure me because of my declining to reccommend the adoption of a *new plan*, for the selecting a candidate. The attempt is to make it appear that I am unwilling to have a *fair* expression of the whigs of the District upon our respective claims. Now, nothing can be more false in fact; and if Genl. Hardin, had chosen, to furnish his friend with my *written reason* for declining that part of his plan; and that friend had chosen to publish that *reason*, instead of his own construction of the act, the falsehood of his insinuation would have been most apparant. That written reason was as follows, towit:

"As to your proposals that a poll shall be opened in *every* precinct, and that the whole shall take place on the *same* day, I do not personally object. They seem to me to not be unfair; and I forbear to join in proposing them, only because I rather choose to leave the decision in each county, to the whigs of the county, to be made as their own judgment and convenience may dictate."[3]

I send you this as a weapon with which to demolish, what I can not but regard as a mean insinuation against me. You may use it as you please; I prefer however that you should show it to some of our friends, and not publish it, unless in your judgment it becomes rather urgently necessary.

The reason I want to keep all points of controversy out of the papers, so far as possible, is, that it will be *just all we can do*, to keep out of a quarrel—and I am resolved to do my part to keep peace. Yours truly   A. LINCOLN

[1] ALS, MH.   [2] February 6, 1846.
[3] See letter to Hardin, January 19, 1846.

To Andrew Johnston[1]

Dear Johnston: Springfield, Ills., Feb. 24, 1846.
Feeling a little poetic this evening, I have concluded to redeem my promise this evening by sending you the piece you expressed

the wish to have.[2] You find it enclosed. I wish I could think of something else to say; but I believe I can not. By the way, how would you like to see a piece of poetry of my own making? I have a piece that is almost done, but I find a deal of trouble to finish it.

Give my respects to Mr. Williams,[3] and have him, together with yourself, to understand, that if there is any thing I can do, in connection with your business in the courts, I shall take pleasure in doing it, upon notice. Yours forever,   A. LINCOLN.

[1] Hertz, II, 553, as given in Madigan, *A Catalogue of Lincolniana* (1929), item No. 1. Johnston was a lawyer practicing in Quincy, Illinois. Little is known about his friendship with Lincoln beyond what may be inferred from the letters in which Lincoln sent his literary compositions.
[2] A copy of William Knox's "Mortality." See letter of April 18, 1846, *infra*.
[3] Archibald Williams, leading attorney of Quincy, Illinois.

"My Childhood-Home I See Again"[1]

[February 25?] 1846

My childhood-home I see again,
    And gladden with the view;
And still as mem'ries crowd my brain,
    There's sadness in it too.

O memory! thou mid-way world
    'Twixt Earth and Paradise,
Where things decayed, and loved ones lost
    In dreamy shadows rise.

And freed from all that's gross or vile,
    Seem hallowed, pure, and bright,
Like scenes in some enchanted isle,
    All bathed in liquid light.

[1] AD, DLC. The date of this manuscript is uncertain. The editors have dated it the day following Lincoln's letter (*supra*) to Andrew Johnston because in that letter Lincoln specifies that the poem is "almost done." The first ten stanzas, with some minor corrections or variations, were enclosed in the letter to Johnston, April 18, 1846 (*infra*), and the remainder, excepting the last two, but including an additional stanza, were sent to Johnston in a letter of September 6, 1846 (*infra*). Since Lincoln refers in his letter of April 18 to the poem's having four cantos, it seems obvious that this manuscript is incomplete. It is possible that "The Bear Hunt," mentioned in the letter of September 6, 1846, and hence printed under that date, may be one of the cantos. But this accounts for only three of the four cantos mentioned by Lincoln. Possibly Lincoln did not complete the poem as planned, or the manuscript may not have been preserved in its entirety.

As distant mountains please the eye,
   When twilight chases day—
As bugle-tones, that, passing by,
   In distance die away—

As leaving some grand water-fall
   We ling'ring, list it's roar,
So memory will hallow all
   We've known, but know no more.

Now twenty years have passed away,
   Since here I bid farewell
To woods, and fields, and scenes of play
   And school-mates loved so well.

Where many were, how few remain
   Of old familiar things!
But seeing these to mind again
   The lost and absent brings.

The friends I left that parting day—
   How changed, as time has sped!
Young childhood grown, strong manhood grey,
   And half of all are dead.

I hear the lone survivors tell
   How nought from death could save,
Till every sound appears a knell,
   And every spot a grave.

I range the fields with pensive tread,
   And pace the hollow rooms;
And feel (companions of the dead)
   I'm living in the tombs.

A[nd] here's an object more of dread,
   Than ought the grave contains—
A human-form, with reason fled,
   While wretched life remains.

Poor Matthew! Once of genius bright,—
   A fortune-favored child—
Now locked for aye, in mental night,
   A haggard mad-man wild.

Poor Matthew! I have ne'er forgot
   When first with maddened will,
Yourself you maimed, your father fought,
   And mother strove to kill;

And terror spread, and neighbours ran,
   Your dang'rous strength to bind;
And soon a howling crazy man,
   Your limbs were fast confined.

How then you writhed and shrieked aloud,
   Your bones and sinnews bared;
And fiendish on the gaping crowd,
   With burning eye-balls glared.

And begged, and swore, and wept, and prayed,
   With maniac laughter joined—
How fearful are the signs displayed,
   By pangs that kill the mind!

And when at length, tho' drear and long,
   Time soothed your fiercer woes—
How plaintively your mournful song,
   Upon the still night rose.

I've heard it oft, as if I dreamed,
   Far-distant, sweet, and lone;
The funeral dirge it ever seemed
   Of reason dead and gone.

To drink it's strains, I've stole away,
   All silently and still,
Ere yet the rising god of day
   Had streaked the Eastern hill.

Air held his breath; the trees all still
   Seemed sorr'wing angels round.
Their swelling tears in dew-drops fell
   Upon the list'ning ground.

But this is past, and nought remains
   That raised you o'er the brute.
Your mad'ning shrieks and soothing strains
   Are like forever mute.

Now fare thee well: more thou the cause
Than subject now of woe.
All mental pangs, but time's kind laws,
Hast lost the power to know.

And[2] now away to seek some scene
Less painful than the last—
With less of horror mingled in
The present and the past.

The very spot where grew the bread
That formed my bones, I see.
How strange, old field, on thee to tread,
And feel I'm part of thee!

[2] This stanza and the next seem obviously to mark the beginning of a third canto.

To Samuel D. Marshall[1]

Dear Sam: Springfield March 3– 1846
I herewith send you the draft of a plea for our case. By consultation with Judge Logan, I draw it in the form I do, to compel Lane, in order to get round it, to reply that the case has been brought to, and reversed & remanded by the Supreme court, upon his doing which, you join issue with him, and that will compel him to pay the cost in the Supreme court in order to get the Record to prove his replication with. If I were to set out the whole facts in a plea in abatement, we should have to pay the Supreme court cost, in order to get the record to prove the plea with. This we wish to avoid. This, that I send, is a plea in bar. You will, of course, put in all and all manner, of other pleas in bar—particularly as to lapse of time. Yours, as ever—   A. LINCOLN

Dorman & wife ⎫
        ads   ⎬ Petition to sell real estate—
Lane, admr. &c ⎭

                            And the said defendants come and defend, when, where &c. and say, that the said Petitioner to have and maintain his petition, or to have the prayer thereof granted, by said court, ought not, because they say, that heretofore towit, on the   day of   A.D.   the said petitioner filed his petition in this court, against these defendants, praying an order for the sale of the identical same land, for the purpose of paying the identical same debt, as in the petition herein; and that such proceedings were had on that petition, that at the⁣ term of said court, the final order was made by said court, directing the sale of said land, for the object in that petition stated—and this the said defendants are ready to verify; wherefore they pray judgment &c.

MARSHALL p.d.

¹ ALS-P, ISLA.

The Trailor Murder Case[1]

April 15, 1846

REMARKABLE CASE OF ARREST FOR MURDER.

In the year 1841,[2] there resided, at different points in the State of Illinois, three brothers by the name of Trailor. Their Christian names were William, Henry and Archibald. Archibald resided at Springfield, then as now the Seat of Government of the State. He was a sober, retiring and industrious man, of about thirty years of age; a carpenter by trade, and a bachelor, boarding with his partner in business—a Mr. Myers. Henry, a year or two older, was a man of like retiring and industrious habits; had a family and resided with it on a farm at Clary's Grove, about twenty miles distant from Springfield in a North-westerly direction. William, still older, and with similar habits, resided on a farm in Warren county, distant from Springfield something more than a hundred miles in the same North-westerly direction. He was a widower, with several children. In the neighborhood of William's residence, there was, and had been for several years, a man by the name of Fisher, who was somewhat above the age of fifty; had no family, and no settled home; but who boarded and lodged a while here, and a while there,

---

¹ Quincy *Whig*, April 15, 1846. Lincoln's authorship of this narrative, published anonymously, was well known to his associates—see Ward H. Lamon, *The Life of Abraham Lincoln from His Birth to His Inauguration as President* (1872), p. 317. Its publication in the Quincy *Whig*, whence it was copied a week later by the *Sangamo Journal*, was doubtless connected with the literary friendship between Lincoln and Andrew Johnston which brought about the publication of the only verse Lincoln is known to have published, in the *Whig* on May 5, 1847. As published in the *Whig*, the narrative was provided with the following editorial preface: "The following narrative has been handed us for publication by a member of the bar. There is no doubt of the truth of every fact stated; and the whole affair is of so extraordinary a character as to entitle it to publication, and commend it to the attention of those at present engaged in discussing reforms in criminal jurisprudence, and the abolition of capital punishment. ED. WHIG."

² See the letter to Joshua F. Speed, June 19, 1841, *supra*, for an account of this "strange affair" written shortly after the case was closed. Identification of the several officials participating in the affair is given in the notes to this letter.

[371]

with the persons for whom he did little jobs of work. His habits were remarkably economical, so that an impression got about that he had accumulated a considerable amount of money. In the latter part of May in the year mentioned, William formed the purpose of visiting his brothers at Clary's Grove, and Springfield; and Fisher, at the time having his temporary residence at his house, resolved to accompany him. They set out together in a buggy with a single horse. On Sunday Evening they reached Henry's residence, and staid over night. On Monday Morning, being the first Monday of June, they started on to Springfield, Henry accompanying them on horse back. They reached town about noon, met Archibald, went with him to his boarding house, and there took up their lodgings for the time they should remain. After dinner, the three Trailors and Fisher left the boarding house in company, for the avowed purpose of spending the evening together in looking about the town. At supper, the Trailors had all returned, but Fisher was missing, and some inquiry was made about him. After supper, the Trailors went out professedly in search of him. One by one they returned, the last coming in after late tea time, and each stating that he had been unable to discover any thing of Fisher. The next day, both before and after breakfast, they went professedly in search again, and returned at noon, still unsuccessful. Dinner again being had, William and Henry expressed a determination to give up the search and start for their homes. This was remonstrated against by some of the boarders about the house, on the ground that Fisher was somewhere in the vicinity, and would be left without any conveyance, as he and William had come in the same buggy. The remonstrance was disregarded, and they departed for their homes respectively. Up to this time, the knowledge of Fisher's mysterious disappearance, had spread very little beyond the few boarders at Myers', and excited no considerable interest. After the lapse of three or four days, Henry returned to Springfield, for the ostensible purpose of making further search for Fisher. Procuring some of the boarders, he, together with them and Archibald, spent another day in ineffectual search, when it was again abandoned, and he returned home. No general interest was yet excited. On the Friday, week after Fisher's disappearance, the Postmaster at Springfield received a letter from the Postmaster nearest William's residence in Warren county, stating that William had returned home without Fisher, and was saying, rather boastfully, that Fisher was dead, and had willed him his money, and that he had got about fifteen hundred dollars by it. The letter further stated that William's story and conduct seemed strange; and desired the Postmaster at Springfield to ascertain and write what was the truth in the matter. The Postmaster at Springfield made the letter public, and at once, excitement became universal and intense. Springfield, at that time had a population of about 3500, with a city organization. The Attorney General of the State resided there. A purpose was forthwith formed to ferret out the mystery, in putting which into execution, the Mayor of the city, and the Attorney General took the lead. To make search for, and, if possible, find the body of the man supposed to be murdered, was resolved on as the first step. In pursuance of this, men were formed into large parties, and marched abreast, in all directions, so as to let no inch of ground in the vicinity, remain unsearched. Examinations were made of cellars, wells, and pits of all descriptions, where it was thought possible the body might be concealed. All the fresh, or tolerably fresh graves at the grave-yard were pried into, and dead horses and dead dogs were disinterred, where, in some instances, they had been buried by their partial masters. This search, as has appeared, commenced on Friday. It continued until Saturday afternoon without success, when it was determined to dispatch officers to arrest William and Henry at their residences respectively. The officers started on Sunday Morning, meanwhile, the search for the body was continued, and rumors got afloat of the Trailors having passed, at different times and places, several gold pieces, which were readily supposed to have belonged to Fisher. On Monday, the officers sent for Henry, having arrested him, arrived with him. The Mayor and Attorney Gen'l took charge of him, and set their wits to work to elicit a discovery from him. He denied, and denied, and persisted in denying. They still plied him in every conceivable way, till Wednesday, when, protesting his own innocence, he stated that his brothers, William and Archibald had murdered Fisher; that they had killed him, without his (Henry's) knowledge at the time, and made a temporary concealment of his body; that immediately preceding his and William's departure from Springfield for home, on Tuesday, the day after Fisher's disappearance, William and Archibald communicated the fact to him, and engaged his assistance in making a permanent concealment of the body; that at the time he and William left professedly for home, they did not take the road directly, but meandering their way through the streets, entered the woods at the North West of the city, two or three hundred yards to the right of where the road where they should have travelled entered them; that penetrating the woods some few hundred yards, they halted and Archibald came a somewhat different route, on foot, and joined them; that William and Archibald then stationed him (Henry) on an old and disused road that ran near by, as a sentinel, to give warning of the approach of any intruder; that William and Archibald then removed the buggy to the edge of a dense brush thicket, about forty yards distant from his (Henry's) position, where, leaving the buggy, they entered the thicket, and in a few minutes returned with the body and placed it in the buggy; that from his station, he could and did distinctly see that the object placed in the buggy was a dead man, of the general appearance and size of Fisher; that William and Archibald then moved off with the buggy in the direction of Hickox's mill pond, and after an absence of half an hour returned, saying they had put him in a safe place; that Archibald then left for town, and he and William found their way to the road, and made for their homes. At this disclosure, all lingering credulity was broken down, and excitement rose to an almost inconceivable height. Up to this time, the well known character of Archibald had repelled and put down all suspicions as to him. Till then, those who were ready to swear that a murder had been committed, were almost as confident that Archibald had had no part in it. But now, he was seized and thrown into jail; and, indeed, his personal security rendered it by no means objectionable to him. And now came the search for the brush thicket, and the search of the mill pond. The thicket was found, and the buggy tracks at the point indicated. At a point within the thicket the signs of a struggle were discovered, and a trail from thence to the buggy track was traced. In attempting to follow the track of the buggy from the thicket, it was found to proceed in the direction of the mill pond, but could not be traced all the way. At the pond, however, it was found that a buggy had been backed down to, and partially into the water's edge. Search was now to be made in the pond; and it was made in every imaginable way. Hundreds and hundreds were engaged in raking, fishing, and draining. After much fruitless effort in this way, on Thursday Morning, the mill dam was cut down, and the water of the pond partially drawn off, and the same processes of search again gone through with. About noon of this day, the officer sent for William, returned having him in custody; and a man calling himself Dr. Gilmore, came in company with them. It seems that the officer arrested William at his own house early in the day on Tuesday, and started to Springfield with him; that after dark awhile, they reached Lewiston in Fulton county, where they stopped for the night; that late in the night this Dr. Gilmore arrived, stating that Fisher was alive at his house; and that he had followed on to give the information, so that William might be released without further trouble; that the officer, distrusting Dr.

Gilmore, refused to release William, but brought him on to Spring-field, and the Dr. accompanied them. On reaching Springfield, the Dr. re-asserted that Fisher was alive, and at his house. At this the multitude for a time, were utterly confounded. Gilmore's story was communicated to Henry Trailor, who, without faltering, re-affirmed his own story about Fisher's murder. Henry's adherence to his own story was communicated to the crowd, and at once the idea started, and became nearly, if not quite universal that Gilmore was a confederate of the Trailors, and had invented the tale he was telling, to secure their release and escape. Excitement was again at its zenith. About 3 o'clock the same evening, Myers, Archibald's partner, started with a two horse carriage, for the purpose of ascer-taining whether Fisher was alive, as stated by Gilmore, and if so, of bringing him back to Springfield with him. On Friday a legal examination was gone into before two Justices, on the charge of murder against William and Archibald. Henry was introduced as a witness by the prosecution, and on oath, re-affirmed his state-ments, as heretofore detailed; and, at the end of which, he bore a thorough and rigid cross-examination without faltering or expo-sure. The prosecution also proved by a respectable lady, that on the Monday evening of Fisher's disappearance, she saw Archibald whom she well knew, and another man whom she did not then know, but whom she believed at the time of testifying to be Wil-liam, (then present;) and still another, answering the description of Fisher, all enter the timber at the North West of town, (the point indicated by Henry,) and after one or two hours, saw Wil-liam and Archibald return without Fisher. Several other witnesses testified, that on Tuesday, at the time William and Henry pro-fessedly gave up the search for Fisher's body and started for home, they did not take the road directly, but did go into the woods as stated by Henry. By others also, it was proved, that since Fisher's disappearance, William and Archibald had passed rather an un-usual number of gold pieces. The statements heretofore made about the thicket, the signs of a struggle, the buggy tracks, &c., were fully proven by numerous witnesses. At this the prosecution rested. Dr. Gilmore was then introduced by the defendants. He stated that he resided in Warren county about seven miles distant from William's residence; that on the morning of William's arrest, he was out from home and heard of the arrest, and of its being on a charge of the murder of Fisher; that on returning to his own house, he found Fisher there; that Fisher was in very feeble health, and could give no rational account as to where he had been during his absence; that he (Gilmore) then started in pursuit of the officer as before stated, and that he should have taken Fisher with him only that the state of his health did not permit. Gilmore also stated that he had known Fisher for several years, and that he had understood he was subject to temporary derangement of mind, owing to an injury about his head received in early life. There was about Dr. Gilmore so much of the air and manner of truth, that his statement prevailed in the minds of the audience and of the court, and the Trailors were discharged; although they attempted no explanation of the circumstances proven by the other witnesses. On the next Monday, Myers arrived in Springfield, bringing with him the now famed Fisher, in full life and proper person. Thus ended this strange affair; and while it is readily conceived that a writer of novels could bring a story to a more perfect climax, it may well be doubted, whether a stranger affair ever really occurred. Much of the matter remains in mystery to this day. The going into the woods with Fisher, and returning without him, by the Trailors; their going into the woods at the same place the next day, after they professed to have given up the search; the signs of a struggle in the thicket, the buggy tracks at the edge of it; and the location of the thicket and the signs about it, corresponding precisely with Henry's story, are circumstances that have never been explained.

William and Archibald have both died since—William in less than a year, and Archibald in about two years after the supposed murder. Henry is still living, but never speaks of the subject.

It is not the object of the writer of this, to enter into the many curious speculations that might be indulged upon the facts of this narrative; yet he can scarcely forbear a remark upon what would, almost certainly have been the fate of William and Archibald, had Fisher not been found alive. It seems he had wandered away in mental derangement, and, had he died in this condition, and his body been found in the vicinity, it is difficult to conceive what could have saved the Trailors from the consequence of having murdered him. Or, if he had died, and his body never found, the case against them, would have been quite as bad, for, although it is a principle of law that a conviction for murder shall not be had, unless the body of the deceased be discovered, it is to be remembered, that Henry testified he saw Fisher's dead body.[3]

---

[3] Of several published "speculations" on the facts which Lincoln narrates, one seems to the editors worth quoting at some length as a rationalization that takes into account nearly all of the unanswered questions and provides a plausible explanation for them. Roger W. Barrett, who edited Lincoln's narrative in a brochure entitled *A Strange Affair* (1933) concludes as follows:

"The real mystery of the case is why Archibald and William Trailor would never reveal what occurred, nor the circumstances under which they parted

To Andrew Johnston[1]

Tremont, April 18, 1846.

Friend Johnston: Your letter, written some six weeks since,[2] was received in due course, and also the paper with the parody. It is true, as suggested it might be, that I have never seen Poe's "Raven";[3] and I very well know that a parody is almost entirely dependent for its interest upon the reader's acquaintance with the original. Still there is enough in the polecat, self-considered, to afford one several hearty laughs. I think four or five of the last stanzas are decidedly funny, particularly where Jeremiah "scrubbed and washed, and prayed and fasted."

I have not your letter now before me; but, from memory, I

---

[1] NH, I, 288-92.

[2] The parody entitled "The Pole-Cat" did not appear in the Quincy *Whig* until March 18, 1846. Hence Lincoln's estimate of "six weeks" is somewhat inaccurate.

[3] "The Raven" was first published in N. P. Willis' *Evening Mirror*, January, 1845. Later Lincoln read and memorized the poem.

---

from Fisher, nor tell why, after leaving the searching party on the following day ostensibly to go to their homes, they again returned to the thicket and remained there for an hour or so while Henry stood guard. In the silence of the three brothers, these questions have remained unanswered for almost a century and there is no voice that can 'provoke the silent dust' to reveal their secret.

"But, subject to information that may yet be discovered, and to any more plausible explanation which may be suggested, the following is offered as a solution which is consistent with all the facts and circumstances of the case as now known.

"Lincoln, in his letter to Speed, relates that 'Fisher had a serious hurt in his head by the bursting of a gun, since which he had been subject to continued bad health and occasional aberration of mind.' Such an injury may cause mental aberration or epileptic fit, followed by catalepsy, leaving the sufferer in a state closely resembling, and occasionally mistaken for death.

"Entering the thicket—either to meet the young lady or with a premonition of the impending attack—Fisher, seized with a fit, or mental aberration, may have struggled with the brothers, or, if he went in alone, may in falling, have sustained some visible mark of injury before the Trailors followed him into the thicket. The brothers, mistaking the unconscious or cataleptic state of Fisher for the sign of death, and fearing that because of the evidence of the struggle, or the possession of his money, they would be suspected of foul play, concealed the body in order to gain time to determine what course to pursue. Fisher may have turned his money over to them, or they may have taken it from his person to safeguard it.

"Returning the following day and finding the body as they had left it, they apparently determined to dispose of it in the mill pond, so that when found it would be supposed that Fisher had accidentally drowned. Presumably the Trailors drove hastily away and Fisher, regaining consciousness through the effect of his sudden immersion, escaped drowning to wander in a daze over the prairies.

"The Trailors must have been puzzled when the pond was drained and no body found, and bewildered when Fisher turned up alive. After their acquittal and vindication at the town meeting, it is not to be wondered that Archibald and William would never reveal their part in this strange affair."

think you ask me who is the author of the piece I sent you,[4] and that you do so ask as to indicate a slight suspicion that I myself am the author. Beyond all question, I am not the author. I would give all I am worth, and go in debt, to be able to write so fine a piece as I think that is. Neither do I know who is the author. I met it in a straggling form in a newspaper last summer, and I remember to have seen it once before, about fifteen years ago, and this is all I know about it. The piece of poetry of my own which I alluded to, I was led to write under the following circumstances. In the fall of 1844, thinking I might aid some to carry the State of Indiana for Mr. Clay, I went into the neighborhood in that State in which I was raised,[5] where my mother and only sister were buried, and from which I had been absent about fifteen years. That part of the country is, within itself, as unpoetical as any spot of the earth; but still, seeing it and its objects and inhabitants aroused feelings in me which were certainly poetry; though whether my expression of those feelings is poetry is quite another question. When I got to writing, the change of subjects divided the thing into four little divisions or cantos, the first only of which I send you now and may send the others hereafter. Yours truly,

A. LINCOLN.

My childhood's home I see again,[6]
  And sadden with the view;
And still, as memory crowds my brain,
  There's pleasure in it too.

O Memory! thou midway world
  'Twixt earth and paradise,
Where things decayed and loved ones lost
  In dreamy shadows rise,

And, freed from all that's earthly vile,
  Seem hallowed, pure, and bright,
Like scenes in some enchanted isle
  All bathed in liquid light.

[4] See Lincoln's letter to Johnston, February 24, 1846. The poem was "Mortality" by William Knox.

[5] Now Spencer County, then Perry County, Indiana.

[6] In the absence of the original manuscript of this canto which was enclosed with the letter to Johnston, it is impossible to know which variations from the complete manuscript are Lincoln's emendations. The version sent to Johnston seems, however, to be a revision of the first canto as preserved in the complete manuscript printed *supra* (February 25? 1846). A second canto was sent in Lincoln's letter of September 6, 1846. Both cantos were published in the Quincy *Whig*, May 5, 1847. See letter of February 25, 1847, *infra*.

As dusky mountains please the eye
    When twilight chases day;
As bugle-notes that, passing by,
    In distance die away;

As leaving some grand waterfall,
    We, lingering, list its roar—
So memory will hallow all
    We've known, but know no more.

Near twenty years have passed away
    Since here I bid farewell
To woods and fields, and scenes of play,
    And playmates loved so well.

Where many were, but few remain
    Of old familiar things;
But seeing them, to mind again
    The lost and absent brings.

The friends I left that parting day,
    How changed, as time has sped!
Young childhood grown, strong manhood gray,
    And half of all are dead.

I hear the loved survivors tell
    How nought from death could save,
Till every sound appears a knell,
    And every spot a grave.

I range the fields with pensive tread,
    And pace the hollow rooms,
And feel (companion of the dead)
    I'm living in the tombs.

To Isaac Williams[1]

Friend Williams: Springfield, April 24th. 1846
    When I saw you at Washington, I understood that it might be
inconvenient for you to attend the Petersburg convention.[2] I have
come a little more anxious since I saw you, that the convention
shall be full; and I write this to let you know that if it is inconvenient for you to attend, our friend, B. F. James, will willingly

go as a substitute for you. Please be sure to attend, *"or send a hand"* Yours truly   A. LINCOLN

¹ ALS-P, ISLA. Williams was a resident of Washington, Tazewell County, Illinois.   ² May 1, 1846.

To James Berdan¹

Jas. Berdan, Esqr.   Springfield,
Dear Sir: April 26th 1846
    I thank you for the promptness with which you answered my letter written from Bloomington.² I also thank you for the frankness with which you comment upon a certain part of my letter; because that comment affords me an oppertunity of trying to express myself better than I did before, seeing, as I do, that in that part of my letter, you have not understood me as I intended to be understood. In speaking of the *"dissatisfaction* of men who yet mean to do no wrong &c."* I meant no special application of what I said, to the whigs of Morgan, or of Morgan & Scott. I only had in my mind the fact, that previous to Genl. Hardin's withdrawal, some of his friends and some of mine, had become a little warm; and I felt, and meant to say, that for them now to meet face to face and converse together, was the best way to efface any remnant of unpleasant feeling, if any such existed. I did not suppose, that Genl. Hardin's friends were in any greater need of having their feelings corrected than mine were. Since I saw you at Jacksonville, I have had no more suspicion of the whigs of Morgan than of those of any other part of the District.
    I write this only to try to remove any impression that I distrust, you & the other whigs of your county.³ Yours truly

                                                        A. LINCOLN

¹ ALS-P, ISLA. Berdan was a lawyer of Jacksonville, Illinois.
² Lincoln was in Bloomington attending court, April 20-23.
³ Morgan County Whigs continued, however, to rebel against the convention system of nominating candidates which their favorite son John J. Hardin opposed.

To James Berdan¹

Jas. Berdan Esqr.   Springfield,
Dear Sir: May 7th. 1846
    It is a matter of high moral obligation, if not of necessity, for me to attend the Coles & Edgar courts. I have some cases in both of them, in which the parties have my promise, and are depending upon me. The court commences in Coles on the second monday, and in Edgar on the third. Your court in Morgan commences on

the fourth monday; and it is my purpose to be with you then, and make a speech. I mention the Coles & Edgar courts, in order, that if I should not reach Jacksonville at the time named, you may understand the reason why. I do not, however, think there is much danger of my being detained; as I shall go with a purpose not to be, and consequently shall engage in no new cases that might delay me. Yours truly   A. LINCOLN

1 ALS, IHi.

To John J. Hardin[1]

Dear Hardin: Springfield, May 29th. 1846
Dr. F. A. McNeil, is desirous of going the campaign to Mexico, as a surgeon,[2] and he thinks that you, more probably than any one else, may have the power to give him the place. If it shall turn out that you hold the power, and can, consistantly with the claims of others, give him the appointment, it would very much gratify many of us here, and dissatisfy none. We regard him as a very sensible, and very clever man; and an excellent physician & surgeon.

Genl. Covell[3] has just arrived here direct from Washington. I infer from some things he says, that some Loco foco rascality is in contemplation in relation to officering the army. He says that Shields, as well as Semple, is coming on, and doubtless he came on himself with his eye upon a military office. He says, moreover, that a supplemental bill, to the army bill, had been introduced into one branch of congress, authorizing the President to appoint two Majors general, and four Brigadiers. This, in connection, with his expressions of doubt, as to whether Genl. Scott, will proceed to the seat of war, induces me to think they even contemplate placing these new made heroes over the heads of Scott, Gaines, Taylor & others. *You* will understand, while *I* do not, whether, by the organization of the army, this is possible. If it is *possible*, it is, in my opinion, decidedly *probable*. Let these conjectures of mine be confidential. Yours as ever   A. LINCOLN

1 ALS, IHi.
2 Dr. Francis A. McNeill was also a minister of the gospel, which perhaps accounts for the seeming redundance of Lincoln's stipulation.
3 Merritt L. Covell of McLean County was a general of militia.

Speech at Lacon, Illinois[1]

July 18, 1846
However, there was a respectable gathering of the citizens of our village, and Mr. Lincoln gave us a good speech. The Tariff was

[381]

the principal subject, with which he showed himself to be thoroughly acquainted. In a most logical, argumentative effort, he demonstrated the necessity of a discriminating tariff, and the excellence of that adopted by the whig congress of 1842; and also that the consumer does not usually pay the tariff, but the manufacturer and importer. Mr. L. closed with some general observations on the Mexican war, annexation of Texas, and the Oregon question.

1 *The Illinois Gazette* (Lacon), July 25, 1846. Lincoln's speech had received no advance announcement, according to the *Gazette.*

Handbill Replying to Charges of Infidelity[1]

July 31, 1846

To the Voters of the Seventh Congressional District.

FELLOW CITIZENS:

A charge having got into circulation in some of the neighborhoods of this District, in substance that I am an open scoffer at Christianity,[2] I have by the advice of some friends concluded to notice the subject in this form. That I am not a member of any Christian Church, is true; but I have never denied the truth of the Scriptures; and I have never spoken with intentional disrespect of religion in general, or of any denomination of Christians in particular. It is true that in early life I was inclined to believe in what I understand is called the "Doctrine of Necessity"—that is, that the human mind is impelled to action, or held in rest by some power, over which the mind itself has no control; and I have sometimes (with one, two or three, but never publicly) tried to maintain this opinion in argument. The habit of arguing thus however, I have, entirely left off for more than five years. And I add here, I have always understood this same opinion to be held by several of the Christian denominations. The foregoing, is the whole truth, briefly stated, in relation to myself, upon this subject.

I do not think I could myself, be brought to support a man for office, whom I knew to be an open enemy of, and scoffer at, religion. Leaving the higher matter of eternal consequences, between him and his Maker, I still do not think any man has the right thus to insult the feelings, and injure the morals, of the community in which he may live. If, then, I was guilty of such conduct, I should blame no man who should condemn me for it; but I do blame those, whoever they may be, who falsely put such a charge in circulation against me.

July 31, 1846.   A. LINCOLN.

[382]

1 *Illinois Gazette,* August 15, 1846. The handbill likewise appears in the *Taze-well Whig,* August 22, 1846.
2 See Lincoln's letter to Allen Ford, August 11, 1846, *infra.*

To Allen N. Ford[1]

Springfield, August 11th, 1846.

Mr. Ford:—I see in your paper of the 8th inst. a communication in relation to myself, of which it is perhaps expected of me to take some notice.[2]

Shortly before starting on my tour through yours, and the other Northern counties of the District, I was informed by letter from Jacksonville that Mr. Cartwright was whispering the charge of infidelity against me in that quarter. I at once wrote a contradiction of it, and sent it to my friends there, with the request that they should publish it or not, as in their discretion they might think proper, having in view the extent of the circulation of the charge, as also the extent of credence it might be receiving. They did not publish it. After my return from your part of the District, I was informed that he had been putting the same charge in circulation against me in some of the neighborhoods in our own, and one or two of the adjoining counties.[3] I believe nine persons out of ten had not heard the charge at all; and, in a word, its extent of circulation was just such as to make a public notice of it appear uncalled for; while it was not entirely safe to leave it unnoticed. After some reflection, I published the little hand-bill,[4] herewith enclosed, and sent it to the neighborhoods above referred to.

I have little doubt now, that to make the same charge—to slyly sow the seed in select spots—was the chief object of his mission through your part of the District, at a time when he knew I could not contradict him, either in person or by letter before the election. And, from the election returns in your county, being so different from what they are in parts where Mr. Cartwright and I are both well known, I incline to the belief that he has succeeded in deceiving some honest men there.[5]

As to Mr. Woodward, "our worthy commissioner from Henry," spoken of by your correspondent, I must say it is a little singular that he should know so much about me, while, if I ever saw *him,* or heard of him, save in the communication in your paper, I have forgotten it. If Mr. Woodward has given such assurance of my character as your correspondent asserts, I can still suppose him to be a worthy man; he may have believed what he said; but there is, even in that charitable view of his case, one lesson in morals which he might, not without profit, learn of even me—and that is, never to add the weight of his character to a charge against his fellow man, without *knowing* it to be true. I believe it is an established maxim in morals that he who makes an assertion without knowing whether it is true or false, is guilty of falsehood; and the accidental truth of the assertion, does not justify or excuse him. This maxim ought to be particularly held in view, when we contemplate an attack upon the reputation of our neighbor. I suspect it will turn out that Mr. Woodward got his information in relation to me, from Mr. Cartwright; and I here aver, that he, Cartwright, never heard me utter a word in any way indicating my opinions on religious matters, in his life.

It is my wish that you give this letter, together with the accompanying hand-bill, a place in your paper.[6] Yours truly,

A. LINCOLN.

[1] *Illinois Gazette*, August 15, 1846. Ford was editor of the *Gazette*, published at Lacon, Illinois.

[2] Since the election was over (August 3), Lincoln's motive seems to have been to set the record straight, perhaps with an eye on his future political career. The issue of the *Gazette* for August 8 is not in the files of the Illinois State Historical Library.

[3] Lincoln spoke in Lacon on July 18. His Democratic opponent, the Reverend Peter Cartwright, was the famed Methodist circuit rider. Dr. Robert Boal of Lacon, writing to Richard Yates on August 25, 1860, recalled this episode of the campaign in 1846, and commented, "Cartwright *sneaked* through this part of the district after Lincoln, and grossly misrepresented him." Yates MSS., IHi.

[4] *Supra*, July 31, 1846.

[5] Lincoln received 6,340 votes to Cartwright's 4,829 in the district as a whole, but in Marshall County he received only 250 against Cartwright's 323, and in adjacent Woodford County, 215 against Cartwright's 300.

[6] The handbill was printed in the same column immediately following the letter, but by reason of its prior date, July 31, it will be found *supra*.

To Andrew Johnston[1]

Friend Johns[t]on:[2]   Springfield, Sept. 6th. 1846

You remember when I wrote you from Tremont last spring,[3] sending you a little canto of what I called poetry, I promised to bore you with another some time. I now fulfil the promise. The subject of the present one is an insane man. His name is Matthew Gentry. He is three years older than I, and when we were boys we went to school together. He was rather a bright lad, and the son of *the* rich man of our very poor neighbourhood. At the age of nineteen he unaccountably became furiously mad, from which condition he gradually settled down into harmless insanity. When, as I told you in my other letter I visited my old home in the fall of

[1] ALS, PHi.   [2] Lincoln misspells the name.
[3] See letter of April 18, 1846, *supra*.

1844, I found him still lingering in this wretched condition. In my poetizing mood I could not forget the impressions his case made upon me. Here is the result—[4]

> But here's an object more of dread
>   Than ought the grave contains—
> A human form with reason fled,
>   While wretched life remains.
>
> Poor Matthew! Once of genius bright,
>   A fortune-favored child—
> Now locked for aye, in mental night,
>   A haggard mad-man wild.
>
> Poor Matthew! I have ne'er forgot,
>   When first, with maddened will,
> Yourself you maimed, your father fought,
>   And mother strove to kill;
>
> When terror spread, and neighbours ran,
>   Your dange'rous strength to bind;
> And soon, a howling crazy man
>   Your limbs were fast confined.
>
> How then you strove and shrieked aloud,
>   Your bones and sinews bared;
> And fiendish on the gazing crowd,
>   With burning eye-balls glared—
>
> And begged, and swore, and wept and prayed
>   With maniac laugh[ter?] joined—
> How fearful were those signs displayed
>   By pangs that killed thy mind!
>
> And when at length, tho' drear and long,
>   Time soothed thy fiercer woes,
> How plaintively thy mournful song
>   Upon the still night rose.
>
> I've heard it oft, as if I dreamed,
>   Far distant, sweet, and lone—
> The funeral dirge, it ever seemed
>   Of reason dead and gone.

[4] Johnston published these stanzas anonymously in the Quincy *Whig*, May 5, 1847. See letter of February 25, 1847, *infra*.

To drink it's strains, I've stole away,
  All stealthily and still,
Ere yet the rising God of day
  Had streaked the Eastern hill.

Air held his breath; trees, with the spell,
  Seemed sorrowing angels round,
Whose swelling tears in dew-drops fell
  Upon the listening ground.

But this is past; and nought remains,
  That raised thee o'er the brute.
Thy piercing shrieks, and soothing strains,
  Are like, forever mute.

Now fare thee well—more thou the *cause*,
  Than *subject* now of woe.
All mental pangs, by time's kind laws,
  Hast lost the power to know.

O death![5] Thou awe-inspiring prince,
  That keepst the world in fear;
Why dost thou tear more blest ones hence,
  And leave him ling'ring here?

If I should ever send another, the subject will be a "Bear hunt."
Yours as ever   A. LINCOLN

[5] This stanza, apparently written for this letter only, does not appear in the manuscript containing both cantos (*supra*, February 25?, 1846).

The Bear Hunt[1]

[September 6, 1846?]

A wild-bear chace, didst never see?
  Then hast thou lived in vain.
Thy richest bump of glorious glee,
  Lies desert in thy brain.

When first my father settled here,
  'Twas then the frontier line:
The panther's scream, filled night with fear
  And bears preyed on the swine.

[1] AD, NNP. The probable date of this document is *circa* September 6, 1846, as indicated in the last paragraph of the preceding letter to Andrew Johnston. See also the letter to Johnston, *infra* February 25, 1847, note 3.

But wo for Bruin's short lived fun,
　　When rose the squealing cry;
Now man and horse, with dog and gun,
　　For vengeance, at him fly.

A sound of danger strikes his ear;
　　He gives the breeze a snuff:
Away he bounds, with little fear,
　　And seeks the tangled *rough.*

On press his foes, and reach the ground,
　　Where's left his half munched meal;
The dogs, in circles, scent around,
　　And find his fresh made trail.

With instant cry, away they dash,
　　And men as fast pursue;
O'er logs they leap, through water splash,
　　And shout the brisk halloo.

Now to elude the eager pack,
　　Bear shuns the open ground;
Th[r]ough matted vines, he shapes his track
　　And runs it, round and round.

The tall fleet cur, with deep-mouthed voice,
　　Now speeds him, as the wind;
While half-grown pup, and short-legged fice,
　　Are yelping far behind.

And fresh recruits are dropping in
　　To join the merry *corps:*
With yelp and yell,—a mingled din—
　　The woods are in a roar.

And round, and round the chace now goes,
　　The world's alive with fun;
Nick Carter's horse, his rider throws,
　　And more, Hill drops his gun.

Now sorely pressed, bear glances back,
　　And lolls his tired tongue;
When as, to force him from his track,
　　An ambush on him sprung.

[387]

Across the glade he sweeps for flight,
  And fully is in view.
The dogs, new-fired, by the sight,
  Their cry, and speed, renew.

The foremost ones, now reach his rear,
  He turns, they dash away;
And circling now, the wrathful bear,
  They have him full at bay.

At top of speed, the horse-men come,
  All screaming in a row.
"Whoop! Take him Tiger. Seize him Drum."
  Bang,—bang—the rifles go.

And furious now, the dogs he tears,
  And crushes in his ire.
Wheels right and left, and upward rears,
  With eyes of burning fire.

But leaden death is at his heart,
  Vain all the strength he plies.
And, spouting blood from every part,
  He reels, and sinks, and dies.

And now a dinsome clamor rose,
  'Bout who should have his skin;
Who first draws blood, each hunter knows,
  This prize must always win.

But who did this, and how to trace
  What's true from what's a lie,
Like lawyers, in a murder case
  They stoutly *argufy*.

Aforesaid fice, of blustering mood,
  Behind, and quite forgot,
Just now emerging from the wood,
  Arrives upon the spot.

With grinning teeth, and up-turned hair—
  Brim full of spunk and wrath,
He growls, and seizes on dead bear,
  And shakes for life and death.

And swells as if his skin would tear,
And growls and shakes again;
And swears, as plain as dog can swear,
That he has won the skin.

Conceited whelp! we laugh at thee—
Nor mind, that not a few
Of pompous, two-legged dogs there be,
Conceited quite as you.

To William Brown[1]

Dear Judge   Springfield, Octr. 22. 1846

I have just returned from Coles, where I saw Ficklin,[2] who handed me a note on Anthony Thornton[3] and somebody else, with $25— in money, which he directed me to pass over to you upon presentation of his receipt (for the note I suppose).

I want to get the matter off of my hands. What shall be done about it? Yours truly   A. LINCOLN

[1] ALS, owned by E. Warfield Brown, Jacksonville, Illinois. William Brown, law partner of Richard Yates at Jacksonville, Illinois, was successor to Stephen T. Logan as judge of the first circuit, but resigned in 1837 after serving four months.
[2] Orlando B. Ficklin, state representative from Coles County in 1838 and 1842, congressman from the third district elected in 1843, 1844, and 1846.
[3] A Whig lawyer of Moultrie County.

To Joshua F. Speed[1]

Dear Speed: Springfield, Octr. 22nd. 1846

Owing to my absence,[2] yours of the 10th. Inst. was not received until yesterday. Since then I have been devoting myself to arive [sic] at a correct conclusion upon your matter of business. It may be that you do not precisely understand the nature and result of the suit against you and Bell's estate. It is a chancery suit, and has been brought to a final decree, in which, you are treated as a nominal party only. The decree is, that Bell's administrator pay the Nelson Fry debt, out of the proceeds of Bell's half of the store.[3] So far, you are not injured; because you are released from the debt, without having paid any thing, and Hurst[4] is in no way left liable

[1] ALS, ORB.   [2] Lincoln had been on the circuit attending court.
[3] Nelson Fry got a judgment for $810 against William H. Herndon, administrator of James Bell, and Joshua F. Speed, on July 28, 1846.
[4] Charles R. Hurst who had bought Speed's interest in Bell & Company.

to you, because the debt he & Bell undertook to pay, is, or will be, paid without your paying it, or any part of it. The question, then, is, "How are you injured?" By diverting so much of the assets of Bell's estate, to the payment of the Fry debt, the general assets are lessened, and so, will pay a smaller dividend to general creditors; one of which creditors I suppose you are, in effect, as assignor of the note to W. P. Speed.[5] It incidentally enlarges your liability to W. P. Speed; and to that extent, you are injured. How much will this be? I think, $100– or $120– being the dividend of 25 or 30 per cent, that Hurst's half of the Fry debt, would would [sic] pay on the W. P. S. debt. Hurst's undertaking was, in effect, that he would pay the *whole* of the Fry debt, if Bell did not pay any part of it; but it was not his undertaking, that if Bell should pay the whole of it, he would refund the whole, so that Bell should be the better able to pay his other debts. You are not losing on the Fry debt, because that is, or will be paid; but your loss will be on the W. P. S. debt,—a debt that Hurst is under no obligation to indemnify you against. Hurst is bound to account to Bell's estate, for one half of the Fry debt; because he owed half, and Bell's estate pays all; and if, upon such accounting any thing is due the estate from Hurst, it will swell the estate, and so far enlarge the dividend to the W. P. S. debt. But when Bell's estate shall call Hurst to account, he will will [sic] I am informed show that the estate, after paying the whole of the Fry debt is still indebted to him. If so, not much, if any thing can come from that quarter—nothing, unless it can be so turned, as to compel him [to?] pay *all* he owes the estate, and take a *dividend* only, upon what the estate owes him. If you had paid the Fry debt yourself, you could then turn on Hurst and make him refund you; but this would only bring [you?] where you started from, excepting it would leave Bell's estate able to pay a larger dividend; and Hurst would then turn upon the estate to contribute one half, which would enlarge the indebtedness of the estate in the same proportion, and so reduce the dividend again. I believe the only thing that can be done for your advantage in the matter, is for Bell's administrator to call Hurst to account for one half the Fry debt, and then fight off, the best he can, Hurst's claim of indebtedness against the estate.

I should be much pleased to see [you?] here again; but I must, in candour, say I do not perceive how your personal presence would do any good in the business matter.

You, no doubt, assign the suspension of our correspondence to

5 William Pope Speed, a brother.

the true philosophical cause, though it must be confessed, by both of us, that this is rather a cold reason for allowing a friendship, such as ours, to die by degrees. I propose now, that, on the receipt of this, you shall be considered in my debt, and under obligation to pay soon, and that neither shall remain long in arrears hereafter. Are you agreed?

Being elected to Congress, though I am very grateful to our friends, for having done it, has not pleased me as much as I expected.

We have another boy, born the 10th. of March last.[6] He is very much such a child as Bob[7] was at his age—rather of a longer order. Bob is "short and low," and, I expect, always will be. He talks very plainly—almost as plainly as any body. He is quite smart enough. I some times fear he is one of the little rare-ripe sort, that are smarter at about five than ever after. He has a great deal of that sort of mischief, that is the offspring of much animal spirits. Since I began this letter a messenger came to tell me, Bob was lost; but by the time I reached the house, his mother had found him, and had him whip[p]ed—and, by now, very likely he is run away again.

Mary has read your letter, and wishes to be remembered to Mrs. S. and you, in which I most sincerely join her. As ever Yours—

A. Lincoln

[6] Edward Baker Lincoln, named for Edward D. Baker.
[7] Robert Todd Lincoln.

To Hezekiah M. Wead[1]

Friend Wead: Springfield, Decr. 6th. 1846

Yours by the hand of Mr. Davidson[2] was duly received. I will have your declaration filed and rule taken to-morrow, according to *Gunter*.[3]

Your case of Nicholas vs Herbert, stands on the Docket No. 57— assigned to no particular day for trial. If the opposite party will be ready to try it, as soon as the court will, my opinion is you may come right along. My recollection is, that I have never known the trial of a case in this court, delayed beyond the first week, where both parties were ready for trial. Yours truly   A. Lincoln

[1] ALS-P, ISLA. Wead was an attorney of Lewistown, Illinois.
[2] William H. Davidson (?), of Carmi, Illinois.
[3] Unable to identify any legal authority by this name, the editors suspect that Lincoln is using a bit of surveyors' lingo, the equivalent of "according to Hoyle," Edmund Gunter being the surveyor's authority.

To Henry E. Dummer[1]

Friend Dummer: Springfield, Feb. 8, 1847

Yours of the 3rd was duly received. I have procured Judge Lockwood's[2] part to be performed and now mail the record to St. Louis as you desired. I write you merely to relieve you of any anxiety as to the matter having in any way miscarried. Yours sincerely,

A. LINCOLN

[1] Angle, p. 32.   [2] Samuel D. Lockwood of the Illinois Supreme Court.

To Andrew Johnston[1]

Springfield, February 25, 1847.

Dear Johnston: Yours of the 2d of December was duly delivered to me by Mr. Williams.[2] To say the least, I am not at all displeased with your proposal to publish the poetry, or doggerel, or whatever else it may be called, which I sent you. I consent that it may be done, together with the third canto, which I now send you.[3] Whether the prefatory remarks in my letter shall be published with the verses, I leave entirely to your discretion; but let names be suppressed by all means. I have not sufficient hope of the verses attracting any favorable notice to tempt me to risk being ridiculed for having written them.

Why not drop into the paper, at the same time, the "half dozen stanzas of your own"? Or if, for any reason, it suit your feelings better, send them to me, and I will take pleasure in putting them in the paper here. Family well, and nothing new. Yours sincerely,

A. LINCOLN.

[1] NH, I, 298-99.   [2] Archibald Williams of Quincy.

[3] In the Quincy *Whig* for May 5, 1847, Johnston published anonymously the first two cantos, giving them as a main title "The Return" and as subtitles "Part I—Reflection," "Part II—The Maniac." Quotations from Lincoln's letter provided the "prefatory remarks." The third canto mentioned by Lincoln does not appear in the *Whig*. If, as may be supposed, the third canto consisted of "The Bear Hunt," *supra*, [September 6, 1846?], Johnston may well have concluded that it was unsuitable for printing as a companion piece to the other cantos.

Resolutions Adopted
at John J. Hardin Memorial Meeting[1]

April 5, 1847

The Hon. Mr. Lincoln then explained the objects of the meeting in a few appropriate remarks, when he offered the following resolutions, which were unanimously adopted:

[392]

Resolved: That, while we sincerely rejoice at the signal triumph of the American arms at Buena Vista, and contemplate with the highest pride, the imperishable honor won by our Illinois brethren, upon that bloody field, it is with the deepest grief we have learned of the fall of the many brave and generous spirits there, and especially, of that of Col. J. J. HARDIN.

Resolved: That William Pope, Mason Brayman, John Calhoun, Antrim Campbell and Geo. L. Huntington be a committee to correspond with the people, or committees of other counties, and especially with Col. Hardin's immediate neighbors at Jacksonville, on the subject embraced in these resolutions; and that said committee have power to fill vacancies, and to call subsequent meetings, when, in their judgment it becomes proper.

Resolved: That the proceedings of this meeting be published in both the papers in this city.

[1] *Sangamo Journal,* April 8, 1847. Colonel John J. Hardin was killed in the Battle of Buena Vista (February 22-23, 1847).

Petition Concerning Jacob Hoffman[1]

April [19?] 1847

To the Honorable Augustus C French Governor of the State of Illinois.

The undersigned would respectfully represent, that at the April Term of the McLean county circuit court one Jacob Hoffman was indicted for the crime of Forgery. That to said indictment said Hoffman plead guilty, and was by the court sentenced to the Penitentiary for the term of one year. That they believe that this is the first offence of which said Hoffman has been guilty. They would further state that he has been confined in the Jail for the county of McLean for about five months. That he is yet quite a young man, and connected with a large and respectable, *though poor family* who [reside?] in Fulton county Illinois. That the Father of said Hoffman is an old, and infirm [man?] and that he and his family, have depended for subsistance to a considerable extent, upon the labour of said Jacob Hoffman.

That in consideration of the premises they would humbly petition your Honor that the punishment may be remitted, and said Hoffman set at liberty, and as in duty bound your petitioners would ever pray &c

[1] DS, I-Ar. Lincoln was merely one of the signers, nearly two hundred, of this petition.

Petition for Pardon of Sigler H. Lester[1]

May 19, 1847

To the Honorable the Governor of the State of Illinois—

Whereas Sigler H. Lester was, at the May Term 1847 of the Cumberland circuit court, by said court, convicted of an assault with intent to commit murder, and sentenced to confinement in the Penitentiary for the term of one year, and whereas there are circumstances, which in our opinion, render it proper, that the Executive clemency should be extended to him, therefore We, the undersigned, respectfully recommend that Your Excellency, grant a pardon of said offence to said Lester.

May 19th. 1847.

[1] ADS, I-Ar. The petition carries one hundred ninety-one signatures including Lincoln's. Two other copies of the petition, not in Lincoln's hand, carry one hundred three and sixty signatures, respectively, of Coles County citizens and friends of Lester.

To Orville H. Browning[1]

Dear Browning: Springfield, June 24th. 1847.

Yours of the 19th. Inst. is received, and I have filed a plea for you, in the case of Moore vs Latourette.

Dont *fret* yourself about the trouble you give me; when I get tired, I'll tell you.

I am glad you sent this letter, because it reminds me to write you the result of your two cases of Moore vs Brown, & God knows who all, the charge of which you sent to Logan, and into which he drew me with him. We tried one of them, in which, after the plaintiff proved title, we offered the Auditors deed, as the first link of connected title and seven years possession, which was objected to, and the judges divided in opinion, which division is certified for the Supreme court. The other case stands over to abide &c.

Indeed, *indeed*, I do not know what they are doing in the Convention.[2] It is considered as almost settled, that they will *not* prohibit Banks; that they *will* establish a poll tax; *will* restrict the number of members of both Houses of the Legislature to 100; *will* limit their *per diem* to $2 or 2.50– and make it still less after the first forty days of the session. So far as I have mentioned, I am pleased. Some other things I have fears for. I am not easy about the *Courts*. I am satisfied with them as they are; but shall not care *much* if the judges are made elective by the People, and their terms of office limited. I fear, however, something more; and, as I think, much worse than all this, towit "A Puppy Court" that is, a Judge

[394]

in each county, with civil jurisdiction in all cases up to a thousand dollars, and criminal, in all cases not capital. "A Migratory Supreme Court" and *Salaries* so low as to exclude all respectable talent. From these, may God preserve us.

As to what I, Baker,[3] and every body else are doing, *I* am preparing to go to the Chicago River & Harbor Convention.[4] *Baker* has gone to Alton, as is thought, to be Colonel of the Sixth Regiment, and *every body* is doing pretty much what every body is always doing.

I hope this may find you well, and Mrs. Browning recovered from her hurt. I dont believe Mary & I can visit Quincy, although it would be very pleasant to do so.

My Chicago trip and *"Several other gentlemen"* (Bob. & Ed)[5] are very much in the way of it. Our love to Mrs. Browning and yourself.   A. LINCOLN

[1] ALS, IHi.
[2] The constitutional convention met in Springfield from June through August. Lincoln's report of the probabilities of the new constitution were borne out in the constitution finished on August 31 and ratified by the people in March, 1848.
[3] Edward D. Baker.   [4] July 5-7.   [5] Lincoln's sons, Robert and Edward.

Open Letter on Springfield and Alton Railroad[1]

June 30, 1847

To the People of Sangamon County:

An effort is being made to build a Railroad from Springfield to Alton. A charter has been granted by the Legislature, and books are now open for subscriptions to the stock. The *chief* reliance for taking the stock must be on the Eastern capitalists; yet, as an inducement to them, we, here, must do something. We must stake something of our own in the enterprise, to convince them that we believe it will succeed, and to place ourselves between them and subsequent unfavorable legislation, which, it is supposed, they very much dread.

The whole is a matter of pecuniary interest; and the proper question for us is, whether, with reference to the present and the future, and to direct and indirect results, it is our *interest* to subscribe. If it can be shown that it is, we hope few will refuse.

The shares in the stock are one hundred dollars each. Whoever takes a share is required to advance five dollars on it, which will be returned to him, unless the whole stock is taken, so that the work

[1] *Sangamo Journal*, July 6, 1847. Construction work on the Alton and Sangamon was not begun until 1852, and the line was opened from Alton to Springfield the following year. A connection to Chicago was established in 1854.

may certainly go on. If the whole shall be taken, the fund created by the five dollar advances will be used to begin the work; and as it progresses, additional calls will be made until it is finished. It is believed it can be completed in about three years. Up to its completion, the shareholders will have lost the *use* of their money, from the times of the respective advances. The questions occur, "What will the road be *worth* when completed?" "How will it pay for the use of the money—how return the principal?" Many who have already subscribed, and who therefore, if they deceive others also deceive themselves, are satisfied that the road can be built for something less than seven hundred thousand dollars. No actual survey has been made; but a good engineer, well acquainted with the route, and the subject, estimates it at this. Now, if the nett income shall be seven or eight—say eight—per cent per annum upon this sum, in the aggregate $56,000, the stock will be *very* good; and the shareholder who does not wish to have money out at eight per cent. interest, can readily sell at par, or above it, and so have a return of his principal.

But will the road nett $56,000 a year? Will it make repairs, bear expenses, and still leave this much? These are questions which no one can, beforehand, answer with precise accuracy. The more difficult it is to make a road at first, the more difficult it is to keep [it] in repair, and *vice versa;* so that the expenses and cost of repairs of railroads, have been found very nearly uniform at about ten per cent. per annum on the capital expended in building them. This, on our road, would be $70,000 a year. Now, if we can insure a gross income of the $56,000 and the $70,000 together; that is, $126,000 —all is safe.

This gross income must, of course, depend upon the amount of business done upon the road. We suppose it is quite fair to assume that all the transportation now done, directly and indirectly, between Saint Louis and Springfield, together with its increase, will be done upon the road when completed. We learn it as an unquestionable fact, that the merchants of Springfield now pay, annually, for carrying goods *from* Saint Louis *to* Springfield, something more than $22,000. This being so, how much does the country produce, that pays for these goods, cost in carriage *from* Springfield *to* Saint Louis? Certainly *more,* in the same proportion as the produce *weighs* more than the goods. But what is this proportion? One of our largest dealers, who has, at our request, made an estimate, and has taken some pains to be accurate, assures us that the average of country produce is *five* times as heavy as the average of the articles in his business, in proportion to value. His business, too, is exclusively of *dry goods*, between which and produce the difference in weight, in proportion to value, is still greater. Another merchant tells us that a barrel of flour is quite equal in weight to a hundred dollars' worth of average dry goods articles. We suppose, then, we are far within bounds, in estimating that the transportation of produce from here to St. Louis costs *five* times as much as the transportation of goods from there here. This gives us $132,000 as the present annual cost of transportation of goods and produce between St. Louis and Springfield. And this does not include the trade of the villages of the county, nor of the counties above and adjoining; nor of the intermediate country; nor anything for the mail, nor for passengers. These must, on a moderate estimate, double the amount, swelling it to $264,000! Assuming this as the gross income, and it makes repairs, pays expenses, and leaves a nett sum of $194,000; being nearly 28 per cent. on the capital. This sum, however, is arrived at as the assumption that transportation is to remain as *dear* as it now is; while the chief reason for desiring the road is that transportation may be *cheapened*. Reduce, then, the cost of carriage to one third its present rates, and it still leaves more than nine per cent. as the profits of the stockholders. This the *distant* holder will be abundantly satisfied with; while the resident will have the same, and more than as much additional, in the cheapening what he buys, enhancing what he sells, and greatly increasing the value of his real property.

Another important matter, already alluded to, is the certain and large increase of business which must occur on the line of the road; and this, whether the road shall or shall not be built; greater, however, if it shall. Increase of business would naturally follow, the building of a good road in any country; and this applies especially to this road, by the facts that the country of its line is unequalled in natural agricultural resources, is new, and only yet very partially brought into cultivation. Not one tenth of the land fitted for the plough has yet been subjected to it. Add the *new* fact, that the use of Indian corn has, at length, been successfully introduced into Europe, under circumstances that warrant the hope of its continuance, and the amount of means of transportation which the people of this country must need, is beyond calculation.

Again: at no distant day, a railroad, connecting the Eastern cities with some point on the Mississippi, will surely be built. If we lie by till this be done, it may pass us in such a way as to do us harm rather than good; while, if we complete, or even begin, our road first, it will attract the other, and so become, not merely a local improvement, but a link in one of a great national character, retaining all its local benefits, and superadding many from its general connection.

In view of the foregoing considerations, briefly stated, is it not the interest of us all to *act*, and to act *now;* in this matter?

It is encouraging, in a double aspect, to know that near a hundred thousand dollars of the stock has already been taken, by some four hundred farmers, mechanics, merchants, and members of all classes, resident in the counties of Madison, Jersey, Macoupin, Morgan, and Sangamon. It is encouraging, in the *amount* taken, and also in the evidence of *confidence* in the success of the undertaking, entertained by so great a number of men, well acquainted with the country through which the road is to pass.

Committee:

A. Lincoln,	John T. Stuart,
J. N. Brown,	William Pickrell,
John Calhoun,	J. Bunn,
B. C. Webster,	John Williams,
P. P. Enos;	S. B. Opdycke.

Springfield, June 30, 1847.

Report on Alton and Springfield Railroad[1]

August 5, 1847

ALTON AND SPRINGFIELD RAIL ROAD.

ADDRESS OF THE COMMITTEE.

At a meeting of the citizens of Sangamon County, the undersigned were appointed a committee to collect facts and report an address on the project of connecting Alton and Springfield by means of a Rail Road. A portion of the committee have examined the subject with great zeal and industry, and submit the following as the result of their labors:

Constructing a rail road from Alton to Springfield, is viewed but as a link in a great chain of rail road communication which shall unite Boston and New York with the Mississippi. Whatever interest Illinois has in this great improvement, and whatever advantages this particular route through Illinois may possess, is necessarily connected with the proposed work from Alton, on the Mississippi, to Springfield. A rail road commencing from the Mississippi, and

[1] *Sangamo Journal,* August 5, 1847. How much Lincoln contributed to the composition of the report is uncertain. The Democratic *Illinois State Register* designated the same document as the "address of John Calhoun," but that Democrat Calhoun was solely responsible seems unlikely.

running through Springfield to the eastern boundary of the State, in the direction of Lafayette, was marked out many years ago in a system adopted by the State, and a million or more of dollars were expended upon it before it was abandoned. This route commenced at Quincy, on the Mississippi, and crossing the Illinois at Meredosia, extended through Springfield east to the State line. The work from the Illinois river to Springfield, a distance of fifty-seven miles, was completed by the State. More than two hundred thousand dollars were expended east of Springfield in the direction to Lafayette in Indiana.

Since the abandonment of the Internal Improvement system by the State, several acts of incorporation have been passed by the legislature, the object of which was to secure to the people of the State, if possible, the construction of the most important of these works by individual enterprise and capital. These acts of incorporation have looked to no general plan, such as is now contemplated, and the great work of connecting the Mississippi with the eastern cities, through Indiana and other States, can now be commenced only by blending some two or three charters. Of these acts of incorporation, one was passed last winter to construct a rail road from Alton to Springfield. The route proposed in this act is from Alton through Carlinville, in Macoupin county, and New Berlin to Springfield, a distance of about eighty miles. The company is authorised to use fifteen miles of the grade already completed, or nearly so, by the State, from Alton in the direction to Carlinville, and fifteen miles of the Springfield and Meredosia rail road, from Springfield to New Berlin, under certain stipulations named in the law. The capital stock of the company is $500,000, and may be increased under the law to $1,000,000.

In 1845 the legislature passed a law incorporating the Sangamon and Morgan rail road company with a capital of $1,000,000. This act required the company to purchase the road from Springfield to the Illinois river at a stipulated price before it could organize. No company was organized under this act, and at the late session of the legislature a law was passed authorizing the Governor to sell the road from Springfield to the Illinois river at public auction to the highest bidder. The purchaser or purchasers under this law were to be entitled to all the benefits of the act for the incorporation of the Sangamon and Morgan rail road company, and were to be held by this law to be the subscribers to the whole capital stock of said company of $1,000,000. A law was also passed at the late session, supplemental to the act incorporating the Sangamon and Morgan rail road company. By this supplemental act the company was authorized to construct the cross rail road east from Springfield to the Indiana State line, on the route previously located by the State, and all the materials, grade, and work done by the State east of Springfield, amounting in value to more than two hundred thousand dollars, were given to the company for that purpose. The capital stock of the company was also increased, $1,000.000. The road from Springfield to the Illinois river has been advertised and sold by the Governor, and the purchasers, N. H. Ridgley and others, have thus secured the benefits of the laws for the incorporation of the Sangamon and Morgan rail road company. A company is therefore organized for the construction of a rail road from the Illinois river to the line dividing the States of Illinois and Indiana; and for about eight thousand dollars, the sum given for the road from Springfield to the Illinois river, all the work on this route, which cost the State more than $1,000,000, is made available to the company. These advantages ought, by all means, in the course of a few years, to secure the completion of the road from Springfield to the line of Indiana. Thus the two or three acts of incorporation above alluded to, fully authorize, with an aggregate capital of $3,000,000, the construction of the great work, so far as Illinois is concerned, which proposes to connect the Mississippi with eastern cities by means of rail road. The citizens of Indiana are now actively engaged in doing whatever is necessary to forward the work in that State; and the proceedings of a meeting in Lafayette show that the proper measures are being taken to secure, so far as Indiana is concerned, the energetic prosecution of the work to completion.

So far as the acts of the Illinois Legislature are concerned, but one difficulty presents itself. The road from Alton to Springfield passes for fifteen miles over the road from the Illinois river to Springfield. The Sangamon and Morgan company own the road from the Illinois river to Springfield, and such work as is done between Springfield and the Indiana line; and possesses, also, the sole right to complete the road from Springfield to the eastern line of the State. If the company had also the sole right of making the road from Springfield to Alton, no difficulty could possibly occur. But if the road from Alton to Springfield should fall into the hands of other individuals, then would they be compelled, under the laws, to use that portion of the road lying between New Berlin and Springfield, which belongs to the Sangamon and Morgan company. This might be embarrassing to the Alton and Springfield company, and could be fully obviated only by the Sangamon and Morgan company taking stock in the Alton and Springfield rail road, to the full and fair value of the portion of their road lying between Springfield and New Berlin.

But the money which is to make the road from Alton to Spring-field, and from Springfield to Lafayette, is principally to come from eastern capitalists. Boston and New York can, and probably will, furnish the funds necessary to connect those cities with the Missis-sippi river; and as the same interests will be blended in the prose-cution of the work through its whole extent, so is it probable that the same interests will ultimately get possession of and control the entire work through this State. No eastern capitalist, therefore, will be likely to take stock in the Alton and Springfield rail road but with a view of its extension so as to form a complete connection between the eastern cities and the Mississippi river. In this view, the apparent difficulty between two works running over the same ground, as probably productive of disagreement between two com-panies, would ultimately disappear. In presenting, therefore, the Alton and Springfield rail road to the consideration of capitalists, as a distinct work, it will be understood as a matter of course, to be only the beginning of a great work, the construction of a single link in the great chain of improvement; and if we can show that this link can now be profitably undertaken, we apprehend that no existing obstacle, growing out of the laws of this State, will prevent such subscriptions of stock as will be necessary to the speedy com-mencement of the work. That the business of this country, its pro-ductions, its population, its demands, would justify the making a good rail road from Alton to Springfield, independent of its connec-tion with a great chain of improvement, is the object of this com-mittee reasonably to show.

The distance from Alton to Springfield, by way of Carlinville and New Berlin, is about eighty miles. Of this distances, fifteen miles from Alton to Brighton, is graded. This fifteen miles em-braces by very far, the heaviest grade on the whole route, passing over the bluffs of the Mississippi river to the table land. The ex-penditure by the State on this fifteen miles was very heavy, and though the law provides that the State shall receive a price to be estimated in State indebtedness and paid by the company, yet there can be no doubt that the legislature will, as in other cases, surren-der the work done to the company without compensation. The State will find an ample inducement to do this in the advantages she will derive in the completion of the road.

Fifteen miles of the road from Springfield to New Berlin, is com-pleted. Deducting, therefore, thirty miles, but fifty remain to be graded. These 50 miles pass over a level prairie country, with a natural grade, almost fitting it for a rail road, and upon which the expenditure for grading would be very light. In the whole fifty miles there is but one place where the expenditure for grading would be considerable. This is the crossing of Macoupin creek. Here a considerable embankment with a bridge and cutting through the bluffs is required. The whole grade from Alton to New Berlin, could easily be contracted for a sum less than three thousand dollars per mile, and the whole sixty-five miles could be fully completed with a T rail, at a cost not exceeding ten thousand dollars per mile, or an aggregate cost of $650,000. (Locomotives, cars, engines-houses, depots and all other fixtures, together with the right of way, would not probably exceed the sum of $150,000—making the total cost of the work $800,000.)

The road proposed would either pass through or drain the products from the counties of Madison, Macoupin, Sangamon, Logan, Macon, DeWitt, Christian and Morgan. As Madison is situated on the Mississippi river, and will probably do the greater portion of its business independent of the rail road, it is entirely left out of the following calculations, though very much of the business of the parts remote from the river must be done on the road. One-third of Morgan county is also deducted from the estimates, it being presumed that at least one-third of its business will be done independent of the road in the direction of the Illinois river.

The population of the eight counties, Madison, Macoupin, Sangamon, Logan, Macon, DeWitt, Christian and Morgan, in 1840, was 69,019, and in 1845, was 75,609. By the same ratio of increase, the population of these counties is estimated in 1850 at 96,526. Deducting the estimated population of Madison and one-third of Morgan, leaves the estimated population of the counties, whose business will all be done on the rail road, in 1850, at 67,073.

The productions of the above counties, except Madison, in 1840, were as follows:

Horse and Mules, ...	23,383
Neat Cattle, ...	69,086
Swine, ...	196,679
Bushels of Wheat, ...	245,890
do of Indian Corn, ...	3,582,659

Estimating the increase of production from 1840 to '45, and from 1845 to '50, in the proportion to the increase of population, we have the production of 1845 as follows:

Horses and Mules, ...	26,866
Neat Cattle, ...	80,150
Swine, ...	237,777
Bushels of Wheat, ...	284,334
do of Indian Corn, ...	4,231,455

And for 1850, we have the following results:

Horses and Mules, ...	34,599
Neat Cattle, ...	104,120
Swine, ...	308,584
Bushels of Wheat, ...	363,840
do of Indian Corn, ...	5,459,274

Deducting from the above the one-third of the population and products of Morgan, and the following table will furnish a true exhibit of the country immediately dependent on the rail road:

		per ct.	Surplus.
Population, ...	67,000		
Horses and Mules, ...	32,211	20	6,442
Neat Cattle, ...	97,921	20	19,444
Hogs, ...	296,152	33⅓	98,717
Bushels of Wheat, ...	342,363	50	171,181
Bushels of Indian Corn,	5,177,231	20	1,035,446

The right hand column of the above table exhibits the surplus of production in those articles which this country produces in the greatest abundance, and is carefully prepared from information obtained of persons well qualified by their business pursuits to judge accurately. For instance, the surplus of hogs is put down at one third. This leaves one-third for home consumption and one third for stock. That one-third is abundant for home consumption is evident from the fact that it will furnish more than a pound of pork per day to every man, woman and child in the district. That the stock is ample when put at one third every farmer in the country will attest.

The horses, mules and neat cattle will go to market principally on foot: and in estimating production for rail road transportation, they are left out of the calculation entirely, though the completion of the rail road would probably lead to beef packing, to a very considerable extent, in this city. In 1850, therefore, the surplus production of the country dependent on this road, and on which reliance can be placed for rail road transportation, will be 98,717 hogs, 171,-181 bushels of wheat, and 1,025,447 bushels of Indian corn. Oats, barley, rye and potatoes, though produced in large quantities, are not taken into the estimate, the object of this address being to show the reliable results, which the rail road transportation of the great staples of the country will furnish. The great demand for corn for foreign exportation is relied upon to justify its production and sending to market at the cheapest rates of rail road transportation. It will always be exported when the price in Alton and St. Louis is twenty-five cents or more a bushel; and the counties embraced in this rail road district, could produce an immensely greater quantity than is at present estimated, if a market at fair prices could be always expected with any degree of certainty.

Nine-tenths of all the produce for this rail road will be furnished at Springfield and New Berlin, as all the counties but Macoupin will centre their produce at those points. In estimating therefore the value of freights, the sum assumed for transportation from Springfield has been applied to all the products estimated to pass over the road. A price, however, has been assumed so low as to leave no doubt that the average will fully equal, if not exceed it.

If the rail road should, therefore, be completed in 1850 the following results might be anticipated:

Transportation of 1,206,628 bushels of Wheat and Corn at 6½ cts. per bushel,	$75,441 25
98,717 head of hogs at an average weight of 200 lbs. would yield at 25 cts. per cwt.	49,358 00
The amount now paid in the above counties for bringing supplies from the river, estimated from the actual amounts paid in Springfield, and at the actual cost of transportation from the river to Springfield is $74,180. We estimate the rail road rates at one-third the common rates, and find that bringing the necessary supplies for the above counties will yield to the rail road,	24,726 66
We estimate that 30 passengers will travel over the road each day for 300 days in the year, which at $2 each will produce,	18,000 00

Producing for 1850, $167,498 91

The estimated cost of the road is $800,000.

The annual interest on this sum at 6 per ct.   48 000 00

Leaving a balance of $119,498 00 or nearly fifteen per cent. on the estimated cost to keep the road, fixtures, engines, &c., in repair, and to pay the costs of running trains and furnishing necessary materials. We think this sum most ample, but whether it be too large or too small, we have not now here the means of determining. Those who may be disposed in the East to take stock in this company, will easily be able from the above estimates to arrive at tolerably accurate conclusions. If that portion of this proposed road, between Springfield and New Berlin, should continue in the hands of the present owners, or if some company, other than the Alton and Springfield company should continue to control it, an additional expenditure on that account will be required. The estimate of costs have been made only for the sixty-five miles, from New Berlin to Alton. We think, as we have suggested in another part of this report, that the whole of this great route will ultimately get into the hands of one company, and that those who are really interested in prosecuting to completion this grand scheme of improvement, will soon overcome the difficulty arising from conflicting ownership and interests.

John Calhoun,	John T. Stuart,
A. Lincoln,	William Pickerell,
J. N. Brown,	J. Bunn,
P. P. Enos,	John Williams,
S. B. Opdycke,	Virgil Hickox.

To Converse & Priest[1]

October 1st. 1847.

Messrs. Converse & Priest: If you will let Mr. E. G. Johns[2] have any amount of oil not exceeding ten dollars in value, I will pay you the money for it in three months from date.

A. LINCOLN

[1] Tracy, p. 24. Lincoln probably addressed this letter to the proprietors of an establishment advertised in the *Sangamo Journal*, October 21, 1847, as "Priest's Oil Factory." Probably John W. Priest.

[2] Edmund G. Johns, house and sign painter in Springfield, Illinois.

To Buckner S. Morris and John J. Brown[1]

Friends Morris & Brown: Springfield, Octr. 19– 1847

Your letter of the 15th. was received this morning. The Governor is not here, and will not be, it is thought, for about ten days. Unfortunately for my attending to the business you sent, I start for Washington, by way of Kentucky, on next monday. I will try, however, to have the only objection that can be made, presented to the Governor. I suppose it is the true construction of the act of Congress, for the Governor, on whom the requisition is made, to look to the sufficiency of the affidavit; otherwise the provision of the act, that a copy of the indictment or affidavit, shall accompany the requisition, is mere foolishness. What view, however, our Governor will take, no man can tell. If he shall make the order surrendering the defendants, you will have, then, to do the best you can by a *Habeas Corpus*.[2] Yours in haste, A. LINCOLN

[1] ALS-P, ISLA. Buckner S. Morris and John J. Brown, attorneys of Chicago.

[2] Apparently this letter and the subsequent one dated October 21 are concerned with the extradition to New York of Joseph Thornton, Andrew Pringle, Samuel Stead, and John Davidson. Governor Augustus C. French of Illinois de-

clined to award his warrant for the apprehension of the parties named, on the very ground suggested in Lincoln's letter—namely, the insufficiency of the affidavit upon which the purported fugitives from justice were demanded. See *Governors' Letter-Books, 1840-1853*, edited by Evarts B. Greene and Charles M. Thompson (1911), pp. 146-47.

To Buckner S. Morris and John J. Brown[1]

Messrs. Morris & Brown: Springfield,
Gentlemen   Oct. 21. 1847

Your second letter on the matter of Thornton & others,[2] came to hand this morning. I went at once to see Logan, and found that he is not engaged against you, and that he had so sent you word by Mr. Butterfield,[3] as he says. He says that some time ago, a young man (who he knows not) came to him, with a copy of the affidavit, to engage him to aid in getting the Governor to grant the warrant; and that he, Logan, told the man, that in his opinion, the affidavit was clearly insufficient, upon which the young man left, without making any engagement with him. If the Governor shall arrive before I leave, Logan & I will both attend to the matter, and *he* will attend to it, if he does not come till after I leave; all upon the condition that the Governor shall not have acted upon the matter, *before* his arrival here. I mention this condition because, I learned this morning from the Secretary of State, that he is forwarding to the Governor, at Palestine, all papers he receives in the case, as fast as he receives them. Among the papers forwarded will be your letter to the Gov: or Sec. of, I believe, the same date & about the same contents of your last letter to me; so that the Gov: will, at all events have your points and authorities. The case is a clear one on our side; but whether the Gov. will view it so is another thing.
Yours as ever   A. LINCOLN

[1] ALS, IHi.
[2] Joseph Thornton. See note to letter to Morris and Brown, October 19, 1847, *supra.*   [3] Justin Butterfield, Chicago attorney.

Lease Contract Between Abraham Lincoln and Cornelius Ludlum[1]

October 23, 1847

It is hereby agreed by and between Abraham Lincoln of the City of Springfield, Illinois, and Cornelius Ludlum of the same place, that the said Lincoln lets to the said Ludlum the dwelling house in which said Lincoln now lives, in said city, together with the lot on which it stands, and the other appurtenances of said lot, for the term of one year, to commence on the first day of November next; for which the said Ludlum agrees to pay said Lincoln the sum of ninety dollars, in quarter yearly payments, to be especially careful to prevent any destruction by fire, to allow said Lincoln, the use of the North-up-stairs room, during the term, in which to store his furniture, and to return the premises at the end of the year in as good repair as he may receive them ordinary decay only excepted.

    October 23rd. 1847.   A. LINCOLN
                                        C LUDLUM

February 1st. 1848. Recd. of C Ludlum Twenty two Dollars Fifty cents for Three months Rent   JOHN IRWIN & Co[2]

August 4th. 1848. Recd. of M Brayman[3] Twenty two & 50/100 Dollars for three months Rent ending April 30th. 1848
                                  JOHN IRWIN & Co

Novr. 18th. 1848. Received of M. Brayman, fiftyfive dollars, including five allowed for repairing fence, which is in full of rent, on the above up to the first instant, [a]nd ten dollars on the next quarte[r . . . .]

    R[ec]eived, May 9. 1849. of M. [Brayman . . . .]
    [. . . .]nes for rent of house up to [. . . . .]
    [. . . . .] the same, & all other accounts [. . . . .]

[1] ADS, Thomas Condell estate, Springfield, Illinois, and ADS, ORB. Lincoln wrote out this lease in duplicate leaving blanks where the name "Ludlum" appears, and later inserted the correct name. Ludlum was a brick contractor of Jacksonville, Illinois.

[2] The first two of these endorsements are not, of course, in Lincoln's hand, but the last two are. Portions of the last endorsement are torn away. The endorsements appear only on the Barrett copy, which is presumably the one kept by Lincoln, while the Condell copy is the one retained by Ludlum.

[3] Brayman was a prominent lawyer with whom Lincoln came to be associated as attorney for the Illinois Central Railroad.

Fragments of a Tariff Discussion[1]

[December 1, 1847?]

Whether the protective policy shall be finally abandoned, is now the question.

[1] AD, DLC-RTL. The order in which these fragments are printed follows the arrangement of Nicolay and Hay. The date subscribed by Nicolay and Hay has been kept, but it is obvious from Lincoln's own parenthetical note at the end that these "scraps" were not all written at the same time.

Discussion and experience already had; and question now in greater dispute than ever.

Has there not been some great error in the mode of discussion?

Propose a single issue of fact, namely—"From 1816 to the present, have protected articles [co]st us more, of labour, during the *higher*, than during the *lower* duties upon them?"

Introduce the evidence.

Analyze this issue, and try to show that it embraces the *true* and the whole question of the protective policy.

Intended as a test of *experience*.

The *period* seclected [*sic*], is fair; because it is a period of peace —a period sufficiently long to furnish a fair average under all other causes operating on prices—a period in which various modifications of higher and lower duties have occurred.

Protected articles, only are embraced. Show that *these only* belong to the question.

The *labour* price only is embraced. Show this to be correct.

I suppose the true effect of duties upon prices to be as follows: If a certain duty be levied upon an article which, by nature can not be produced in this country, as three cents a pound upon coffee, the effect will be, that the consumer will pay one cent more per pound than before, the producer will take one cent less, and the merchant one cent less in profits—in other words, the burthen of the duty will [be] distributed over consumption, production, and commerce, and not confined to either. But if a duty amounting to full protection be levied upon an article which can be produced here with as little labour, as elsewhere, as iron, that article will ultimately, and at no distant day, in consequence of such duty, be sold to our people cheaper than before, at least by the amount of the cost of *carrying* it from abroad.

. . . as to useless labour.[2] Before proceeding however, it may be as well to give a specimen of what I conceive to be useless labour. I say, then, that all *carrying*, & incidents of carrying, of articles from

[2] Another draft of this particular fragment is not included in Nicolay and Hay. It reads as follows: "First, then, as to useless labour. But what is useless labour? I suppose, then, that all labour done *directly* and *incidentally* in carrying articles from the place of their production to a *distant* place for consumption, which articles, could be produced of as good quality, and sufficient quantity, with as little labour at the place of consumption, as at the place carried from, is useless labour. Applying this principle to our own country b[y] an example, let us suppose that A and B are a Pennsylvania farmer, and a Pennsylvania iron-maker, whose lands are adjoining. Under the protective policy A is furnishing B. with bread and meat, and vegetables and fruits, and food for horses and oxen, and fresh supplies of horses and oxen themselves occasionaly,

the place of their production, to a *distant* place for consumption, which articles could be produced of as good quality, in sufficient quantity, and with as little labour, at the place of consumption, as at the place carried from, is useless labour. Applying this principle to our own country by an example, let us suppose that A and B, are a Pen[n]sylvania farmer, and a Pennsylvania iron-maker, whose lands are adjoining. Under the protective policy A is furnishing B with bread and meat, and vegetables, and fruits, and food for horses and oxen, and fresh supplies of horses and ox[en] themselves occasionally, and receiving, in exchange, all the iron, iron utensils, tools, and implements he needs. In this process of exchange, each receives the *whole* of that which the other parts with —and the reward of labour between them is perfect; each receiving the product of just so much labour, as he has himself bestowed on what he parts with for it. But the change comes. The protective policy is abandoned, and A determines to buy his iron and iron manufactures of C. in Europe. This he can only do by a direct or an indirect exchange of the produce of his farm for them. We will suppose the direct exchange is adopted. In this A desires to exchange ten barrels of flour the precise product of one hundred days labour, for the largest quantity of iron &c that he can get; C, also wishes to exchange the precise product, in iron, of one hundred days labour, for the greatest quantity of flour he can get. In intrinsic value the

---

and receiving, in exchange all the iron, iron utensils, tools and implements he needs. In this process of exchange, each receives the *whole* of what the other parts with. But the change comes. The protective policy is abandoned (how, and under what expect[at]ion, I will hereafter try to show) and A. determines, for the future, to buy his supply of iron and iron fabrics of C an ironmaker in England. This he can only do by a *direct* or an *indirect* exchange of the products of his farm for them. The direct exchange is supposed to be adopted. In a certain instance of this sort, A desires to exchange ten barrels of flour, the precise product of one hundred days labour, for the greatest quantity of iron he can get; C, also wishes to exchange the precise product of one hundred days labour, in iron, for the greatest quantity of flour he can get. But before the exchange can take place, the flour must be *carried* from Penna. to England, and the iron from England to Pennsylvania. The flour starts. The waggoner who hauls it to Philadelphia, takes a part of it to pay him for his labour; then a merchant there, takes a little more for storage and forwarding commission, and another takes a little more for insurance; and then the shipowner carries it across the water, and takes a little more of it for his trouble; still before it reaches C it is tolled two or three times more for storage, drayage, commission and so on; so that when C gets [it, there are] but seven barrels and a half of it left. The iron, too, in it's transit from England to Pennsylvania, goes through the same process of tolling; so that when it reaches A, there are but three qua[rters] of it left. Now, this carrying labour, was generally useless in this that it diminished the *quantity*, while it added nothing to the *quality* of the articles carried; and it was useless to A because, by continuing to buy of B, it needed not to be done."

things to be so exchanged are precisely equal. But before this exchange can take place, the flour must be carried from Pennsylvania to England, and the iron from England to Pennsylvania. The flour starts; the waggoner who hauls it to Philadelphia, takes a part of it to pay him for his labour; then a merchant there takes a little more for storage and forwarding commission, and another takes a little more for insurance; and then the ship-owner carries it across the water, and takes a little more of it for his trouble; still before it reaches C. it is tolled two or three times more for storage, drayage, commission and so on, so that when C. gets it, there are but seven & a half barrels of it left. The iron too, in its transit from England to Penna., goes through the same process [of] tolling, so that when it reaches A there is but three quarters of it left. The result of this case is, that A. and C. have each parted with one hundred days labour, and each received but seventyfive in return. That the carrying in this case, was introduced by A ceasing to buy of B, and turning [to] C; that it was utterly useless; and that it is ruinous in its effects, upon A, are all little less than self evident. "But," asks one, "if A is now only getting three quarters as much iron from C for ten barrels of flour as he used to get of B, why does he not turn back to B?" The answer is "B has quit making iron, and so, has none to sell." "But why did B quit making?" ["]Because A quit buying of him, and he had no other customer to sell to.["] "But surely A. did not cease buying of B. with the *expectation* of buying of C. on harder terms?" ["]Certainly not. Let me tell you how that was. When B was making iron as well as C, B had but *one* customer, this farmer A. C had *four* customers in Europe.["]

It seems to be an opinion very generally entertained, that the condition of a nation, is *best*, whe[ne]ver it can *buy cheapest*; but this is not necessarily true, because if, at the same time, and by the same cause, it is compelled to *sell* correspondingly cheap, nothing is gained. Then, it is said, the best condition is, when we can *buy cheapest*, and *sell dearest*; but this again, is not necessarily true; because, with both these, we might have scarcely any thing to sell—or, which is the same thing, to buy with. To illustrate this, suppose a man in the present state of things is labouring the year round, at ten dollars per month, which amounts in the year to $120—a change in affairs enables him to buy supplies at half the former price, to get fifty dollars per month for his labour; but at the same time deprives him of employment during all the months of the year but one. In this case, though goods have fallen one half, and labour risen five to one, it is still plain, that at the end of the year, the labourer is twenty dollars poorer, than under the old state of things.

These reflections show, that to reason and act correctly on this subject, we must look not merely to *buying* cheap, nor yet to buying cheap *and* selling dear; but also to having constant employment, so that we may have the largest possible amount of something to sell. This matter of employment can only be secured by an ample, steady, and certain market, to sell the products of labour in.

But let us yield the point, and admit that, by abandoning the protective policy, our farmers can purchase their supplies of manufactured articles *cheaper* than by continuing it; and then let us see whether, even at that, they will, upon the whole, be gainers by the change. To simplify this question, let us suppose the whole agricultural interest of the country to be in the hands of one man, who has one hundred labourers in h[is e]mploy; the whole manufacturing interest, to be in the hands of [one] other man, who has twenty labourers in his employ. The farmer [own]s all the plough and pasture land, and the manufacturer, all the iron-mines, and coal-banks, and sites of water power. Each is pushing on in his own way, and obtaining supplies from the other so far as he needs—that is, the manufacturer, is buying of the farmer all the cotten he can use in his cotten factory, all the wool he can use in his woollen establishment, all the bread and meat, as well as all the fruits and vegetables which are necessary for himself and all his hands in all his departments; all the corn, and oats, and hay, which are necessary for all his horses and oxen, as well as fresh supplies of horses and oxen themselves, to do all his heavy hauling about [his] iron works and generally of every sort. The farmer, in turn, is buy[ing] of the manufacturer all the iron, iron tools, wooden tools, cotten goods, woolen goods &c &c. that he needs in his business and for his hands. But after awhile farmer discovers that, were it not for the protective policy, he could buy all these supplies cheaper from a European manufacturer, owing to the fact that the price of labour is only one quarter as high there as here. He and his hands are a majority of the whole; and therefore have the legal and moral right to have their interest first consulted. They throw off the protective policy, and farmer ceases buying of home manufacturer. Verry soon, however, he discovers, that to *buy*, even at the cheaper rate, requires something to buy with, and some how or other, he is falling short in this particular.

In the early days of the world, the Almighty said to the first of our race "In the sweat of thy face shalt thou eat bread"; and since then, if we except the *light* and the *air* of heaven, no good thing has been, or can be enjoyed by us, without having first cost labour. And, inasmuch [as] most good things are produced by labour, it follows that [all] such things of right belong to those whose labour has produced them. But it has so happened in all ages of the world, that *some* have laboured, and *others* have, without labour, enjoyed a large proportion of the fruits. This is wrong, and should not continue. To [secure] to each labourer the whole product of his labour, or as nearly as possible, is a most worthy object of any good government. But then the question arises, how can a government best, effect this? In our own country, in it's present condition, will the protective principle *advance* or *retard* this object? Upon this subject, the habits of our whole species fall into three great classes— *useful* labour, *useless* labour and *idleness*. Of these the first only is meritorious; and to it all the products of labour rightfully belong; but the two latter, while they exist, are heavy pensioners upon the first, robbing it of a large portion of it's just rights. The only remedy for this is to, as far as possible, drive *useless* labour and *idleness* out of existence. And, first, as to useles labour. Before making war upon this, we must learn to distinguish it from the *useful*. It appears to me, then, that all labour done *directly* and *incidentally* in *carrying* articles to their place of consumption, which could have been produced in sufficient abundance, *with as little labour, at the place of consumption*, as at the place they were carried from, is useless labour. Let us take a few examples of the application of this principle to [our] own country. Iron & every thing made of iron, can be produced, in sufficient abundance, [and] with as little labour, in the United States, as any where else in the world; therefore, all labour done in bringing iron & it's fabrics from a foreign country to the United States, is useless labour. The same precisely may be said of cotten, wool, and of their fabrics respectively, as well as many other articles. While the uselessness of the carrying labour is [equally true] of all the articles mentioned, and of many others not men[tioned,] it is, perhaps, more glaringly obvious in relation to the cotten [goods we] purchase from abroad. The raw cotten, from which they are made, itself grows in our own country; is carried by land and by water to England, [is] there spun, wove, dyed, stamped &c; and then carried back [again] and worn in the very country where it grew, and partly by the very persons who grew it. Why should it not be spun, wove &c. in the very neighbourhood where it both grows and is consumed, and the carrying [about?] thereby dispensed with? Has nature interposed any obstacle? Are not all the agents—animal power, water power, and steam power—

as good and as abundant here as elsewhere? Will not as small an amount of human labour answer here as elsewhere? We may easily see that the cost of this useless labour is very heavy. It includes, not only the cost of the actual carriage, but also the insurances of every kind, and the profits the merchants through whose hands it passes. All these create a heavy burthen necessarily falling upon the useful labour connected w[ith] such articles, either *depressing* the price to the *producer,* or enhancing it to the *consumer,* or, what is more probable, doing both in part. A supposed case, will serve to illustrate several points now to the p[ur]pose. A, in the interior of South Carolina, has one hundred pounds of cotten, which we suppose to be the precise product of one mans labour for twenty days; B, in Manchester, England, has one hundred yards of cotten cloth, the precise product of the same amount of labour. This lot of cotten, and lot of cloth are precisely equal to each other in their intrinsic value. But A. wishes to part with his cotten for the largest quantity of cloth he can get; B, also wishes to part with his cloth for the greatest quantity of c[otten] he can get. An exchange is therefore necessary; but before this can be effected, the cotten must be carried to Manchester, and the cloth to South Carolina. The cotten starts to Manchester; the man that hauls it to Charleston in his waggon, takes a little of it out to pay him for his trouble; the merchant, who stores it a while before the ship is ready to sail, takes a little out, for his trouble; the ship-owner, who carries it across the water, takes a little out for his trouble, still before it gets to Manchester, it is tolled two or three times more for drayage, storage, commission, and so on; so that when it reaches B's hands there are but seventyfive pounds of it left. The cloth, too, in it's transit from Manchester to South Carolina goes through the same process of tolling, so that when it reaches A there are but seventyfive yards of it. Now, in this case, A. and B. have each parted with twenty days labour; and each received but fifteen in return. But now let us suppose that B. has removed to the side of A's farm, in South Carolina, and has there made his lot of cloth. Is it not clear that he and A. can then exchange their cloth & cotten, each getting the *whole* of what the other parts with?

This supposed case shows the utter uselessness of the carrying labour in all similar cases, and also the direct burthen it imposes up[on] useful labour. And whoever will take up the train of reflection suggested by this case, and run it out to the full extent of it's just application, will be astonished, at the amount of useless labour [he] will thus discover to be done in this very way. I am mistaken, if it is not in fact many times [over] equal to all the real want in

[413]

the world. This useless labour I would have discontinued, and those engaged in it, added to the class of useful labourers. If I be asked whether I would destroy all commerce, I answer "Certainly not"— I would continue it where it is *necessary*, and *discontinue* it, where it is not. An instance: I would continue commerce so far as it is employed in bringing us coffee, and I would discontinue it so far as it is employed in bringing us cotten goods.

But let us yield the point, and admit that, by abandoning to protective policy, our farmers can purchase their supplies of manufactured articles *cheaper* than before; and then let us see whether, even at that, the farmers will, upon the whole, be gainers by the change. To simplify this question, let us suppose our whole population to consist of but twenty men. Under the prevalence of the protective policy, fifteen of these are farmers, one is a miller, one manufactures iron, one, implements from iron, one cotten goods, and one woolen goods. The farmers discover, that, owing to labour only costing one quarter as much in Europe as here, they can buy iron, iron implements, cotten goods, & woolen goods cheaper, when brought from Europe, [tha]n when made by their neighbours. They are the majority, and [ther]efore have both the legal and moral right to have their in[tere]st first consulted. They throw off the protective policy, [an]d cease buying these articles of their neighbours. But they [soo]n discover that to buy, and at the cheaper rate, requires [som]ething to buy with. Falling short in this particular, one of [th]ese farmers, takes a load of wheat to the miller, and [g]ets it made into flour, and starts, as had been his cus[to]m, to the iron furnace; he approaches the well known spot, [bu]t, strange to say, all is cold and still as death—no [sm]oke rises, no furnace roars, no anvil rings. After some search [h]e finds the owner of the desolate place, and calls out to him, "Come, Vulcan, dont you want to buy a load of flour?" "Why" says Vulcan "I am hungry enough, to be sure—have'nt tasted bread for a week— but then you see my works are stopped, and I have nothing to give for your flour.["] ["]But, Vulcan, why dont you go to work and get something?["] ["]I am ready to do so; will you hire me, farmer?["] ["]Oh, no; I could only set you to raising wheat, and you see I have more of that already than I can get any thing for.["] ["]But give me employment, and send your flour to Europe [for a] market.["] ["]Why, Vulcan, how silly you talk. Dont you [know] they raise wheat in Europe as well as here, and that *labour* is so cheap there as to fix the price of flour there so low as scarcely to pay the long carriage of it from [here,] leaving nothing whatever to me." ["]But, farmer, could'nt you pay to raise and prepare garden stuffs, and fruits, such as radishes, cabages, irish and sweet potatoes, cucumbers, water-melons and musk-melons, plumbs [*sic*], pears, peaches, apples, and the like; all these are good things and used to sell well.["] ["]So they did use to sell well, but it was to *you* we sold them, and now you tell us you have nothing to buy with. Of course I can not sell such things to the other farmers, because each of them raises enough for himself, and, in fact, rather wishes to sell than to buy. Neither can I send them to Europe for a market; because, to say nothing of European markets being stocked with such articles at lower prices than I can afford, they are of such a nature as to rot before they could reach there. The truth is, Vulcan, I am compelled to quit raising these things altogether, except a few for my own use, and this leaves part of my own time idle on my hands, instead of my finding employment for you.["]

If at any time all *labour* should cease, and all existing provisions be equally divided among the people, at the end of a single year there could scarcely be one human being left alive—all would have perished by want of subsistence.

So again, if upon such division, all that *sort* of labour, which produces provisions, should cease, and each individual should take up so much of his share as he could, and carry it continually around his habitation, although in this carrying, the amount of labour going on might be as great as ever, so long as it could last, at the end of the year the result would be precisely the same—that is, none would be left living.

The first of these propositions shows, that universal *idleness* would speedily result in universal *ruin;* and the second shows, that *useless labour* is, in this respect, the same as idleness.

I submit, then, whether it does not follow, that *partial* idleness, and partial *useless labour*, would, in the proportion of their extent, in like manner result, in partial ruin—whether, if *all* should subsist upon the labour that *one half* should perform, it would not result in very scanty allowance to the whole.

Believing that these propositions, and the [conclusions] I draw from them can not be successfully controverted, I, for the present, assume their correctness, and proceed to try to show, that the abandonment of the protective policy by the American Government, must result in the increase of both useless labour, and idleness; and so, in pro[por]tion, must produce want and ruin among our people.

(The foregoing scraps about protection were written by Lincoln, between his election to Congress in 1846, and taking his seat in Dec. 1847)[3]

[3] This parenthetical comment in Lincoln's own hand was presumably written during the summer of 1860, at which time these scraps seem to have been sent to Simon Cameron by David Davis. Nicolay's list of "The Carpet-Bag Papers," preserved in the Robert Todd Lincoln Collection, lists these "Eleven foolscap halfsheets of notes and memoranda with two endorsements as follows:

" 'The foregoing paper was written by Lincoln in 1848 as being what he thought Genl. Taylor ought to say.' also

" 'The foregoing scraps about protection were written by Lincoln between his election to Congress in 1846 and taking his seat in 1847.'

"They were enclosed in an envelop addressed to Hon David Davis, Bloomington Ill. under frank of 'Simon Cameron U.SS.' "

The first of these endorsements applies to the fragment printed *infra* under date of [July 1, 1848]; the second applies to the document under consideration here.

To [David A.?] Smith[1]

Friend Smith: Washington, Decr. 3. 1847

This is my first day at this place, & on reaching here I found your letter in relation to your business with Douglass. I met him afterwards, but disliking to dunn him at the first meeting with him, I let it pass, for the time. I will attend to it shortly however & write you.

You intimate there is some danger of my neglecting the business; but if you will get me as good a fee as you got for Jo. Gillespie[2] in the case he tells of, I'll never desert you. Yours truly

A. LINCOLN

[1] ALS, ICHi. It seems probable that the person addressed was David A. Smith, an attorney of Jacksonville, Illinois, with whom Lincoln had long been acquainted in law practice. The possibility of its being Robert Smith of Alton, Illinois, seems less likely, in view of the fact that he was like Lincoln a member of the Thirtieth Congress, and being in Washington could very well have attended to the business indicated in the letter for himself.

[2] Joseph Gillespie of Edwardsville, Illinois.

To William H. Herndon[1]

Washington, December 5, 1847.

Dear William: You may remember that about a year ago a man by the name of Wilson (James Wilson, I think) paid us twenty dollars as an advance fee to attend to a case in the Supreme Court for him, against a Mr. Campbell,[2] the record of which case was in the hands of Mr. Dixon[3] of St. Louis, who never furnished it to us.[4] When I was at Bloomington last fall, I met a friend of Wilson, who mentioned the subject to me, and induced me to write to Wilson, telling him I would leave the ten dollars with you which had been left with me to pay for making abstracts in the case, so that the case may go on this winter; but I came away, and forgot to do it. What I want now is to send you the money, to be used accordingly, if any one comes on to start the case, or to be retained by you if no one does.

There is nothing of consequence new here. Congress is to organize to-morrow. Last night we held a Whig caucus for the House, and nominated Winthrop of Massachusetts for speaker,[5] Sargent of Pennsylvania for sergeant-at-arms,[6] Homer [Horner] of New Jersey doorkeeper,[7] and McCormick of District of Columbia postmaster.[8] The Whig majority in the House is so small [9] that, together with some little dissatisfaction, [it] leaves it doubtful whether we will elect them all.

This paper is too thick to fold, which is the reason I send only a half-sheet. Yours as ever,   A. LINCOLN.

[1] NH, I, 315-16. The Lincolns arrived in Washington December 2.
[2] James Campbell.   [3] George C. Dixon.
[4] Case dismissed for want of prosecution, January 21, 1846.
[5] Robert C. Winthrop of Boston was elected on the third ballot.
[6] Nathan Sargent, elected.   [7] Robert E. Horner, elected.
[8] William J. McCormick, defeated by John M. Johnson, incumbent.
[9] The Whig majority was four.

Endorsement: Chester Butler *et al* to Robert E. Horner[1]

December 7, 1847

I concur, on the faith of what the above named gentlemen have said   A. LINCOLN

[1] AES, ORB. On December 7, 1847, Chester Butler, Whig congressman from Pennsylvania, and eleven of his colleagues recommended to Robert E. Horner the retention of John Raub as a laborer in the House building. Lincoln and thirty-eight other members also signed the petition.

To James K. Polk[1]

House of Representatives. Decr. 8. 1847

His Excellency the President of the U. States

Dear Sir: We, the undersigned, members of the H.R. and being one Democrat and one Whig, respectfully solicit the appointment of Thomas Graham Jr. of Beardstown, Illinois, to a first Lieutenancy in the U.S. Infantry. Mr. Graham is a Democrat, but is reccommended, as we personally know, by most respectable men of both parties. Under these circumstances, we are sincerely desirous that he should receive the appointment. Accompanying this, are the letters which have been forwarded to us on the subject. Very Respectfully   Your Obt. Servts.   W A RICHARDSON[2]

A. LINCOLN

[1] ALS, owned by Edward C. Stone, Boston, Massachusetts.
[2] William A. Richardson, a Democrat of Schuyler County, Illinois, was elected to Congress from the Fifth District in 1847 (special election).

To James K. Polk[1]

House of Representatives, Decr. 8– 1847
His Excellency, the President of the U. States.

Dear Sir: Mr. Franklin L Rhoads, of Pekin, Illinois, desires the appointment to a Lieutenancy in the U.S. Army, as you perceive by the Pe[ti]tion, accompanying this. Mr. Rhoads is a Whig; but of the fifteen persons who sign his Petition, I personally know five to be influential Democrats, five whigs, and the remaining five to be respectable men, though their politics are unknown to me. The Mr. Jones, who writes the accompanying letter, addressed to me, has received a military education, and was Mr. Rhoads' captain in the battle of Cerro Gordo. If the appointment could be confered on Mr. Rhoads, I should be personally grateful for it. Very Respectfully Your Obt. Servt.   A. LINCOLN

[1] ALS, IHi. See also the letter of December 11, 1847, *infra*.

Petition to Robert E. Horner
Concerning Abram O. Bowen[1]

December 9, 1847
Mr R. E. Horner Esqr Door Keeper of House of Reps

I understand that Mr Abram O. Bowen of Missouri who has been for some time Fireman of the House was the first person appointed to that place & that he was not used as an instrument of proscription to any other person.

Mr Bowen is *gentlemanly* & courteous in his deportment & I believe discharges his duties faithfully. I *should* be *pleased* to see him retained & recommend him to your consideration. Respy

9th Dec. 1847

[1] DS, InU. The petition was drawn up by Caleb B. Smith of Indiana and bears the signatures of fifteen other members of the House, including Lincoln.

To Richard Yates[1]

Friend Yates: Washington, December 10, 1847.

I presented your claim to Douglass[2] this morning; he says it is all right and that he will pay it in a few days. When he shall have done so, you will hear from me at once.

Things have not advanced far enough to enable me to tell you much in the way of politics, more than you see in the papers. I believe Mr. Calhoun[3] and what force he can control are preparing to support Gen. Taylor[4] for the Presidency. I get this impression from conversations with Duff Greene,[5] who boards at the same house I do. There are, however, a great many Whigs here who do not wish to go for Taylor, and some of whom I fear can not be brought to do it. There are still many others of them who are strong for him, among whom I class Mr. Crittenden,[6] although he does not expressly say so. I shall be pleased to have a line from you occasionally. Yours truly,   A. LINCOLN.

[1] Printed in "Lincoln," a speech of Honorable Richard Yates of Illinois in the House of Representatives, February 12, 1921.
[2] Stephen A. Douglas gave Lincoln a check for $167.00, on December 21, 1847, drawn on Corcoran & Riggs.
[3] John C. Calhoun of South Carolina.   [4] Zachary Taylor.
[5] Politician and editor, member of Andrew Jackson's "Kitchen Cabinet," but a supporter of Henry Clay in 1832 and John C. Calhoun in 1836.
[6] Senator John J. Crittenden of Kentucky.

To James K. Polk[1]

His Excellency, the President.   Washington, Decr. 11. 1847

Some days since I transmitted to you the application of Mr. Rhoads of Pekin Illinois, for a Lieutenancy. Since then I have received the enclosed letter of Hon: E. D. Baker, in his behalf, which I now take the liberty of submitting to you. Your Obt. Servt.

A. LINCOLN

[1] ALS, IHi. See also letter of December 8, 1847, *supra*. The army records do not show that Rhoads was ever appointed.

To William H. Herndon[1]

Dear William: Washington, Dec. 12. 1847

As soon as the Congressional Globe and Appendix begins to issue, I shall send you a copy of it regularly. I wish you to read it, or as much of it as you please, and be careful to preserve all the numbers, so that we can have a complete file of it

There is nothing new here, but what you see in the papers. Yours as ever—   A. LINCOLN

[1] ALS, IHi.

To William H. Herndon[1]

Dear William: Washington, Dec. 13. 1847

Your letter advising me of the receipt of our fee in the Bank case, is just received, and I dont expect to hear another as good a piece of news from Springfield while I am away. I am under no obligation to the Bank; and I therefore wish you to buy Bank certificates and pay my debt there, so as to pay it with the least money possible. I would as soon you should buy them of Mr. Ridgley[2] or any other person at the Bank, as of any one else, provided you can get them as cheaply. I suppose after the Bank debt shall be paid, there will be some money left, out of which I would like to have you to pay Lavely & Stout[3] $20– and Priest & somebody[4] (oil makers) $10– for materials got for house painting. If there shall still be any left, keep it till you see, or hear from me.

I shall begin sending documents so soon as [I] can get them. I wrote you yesterday about a Congressional Globe. As you are all so anxious for me to distinguish myself, I have concluded to do so, before long. Yours truly,   A. LINCOLN

[1] ALS, MHi.   [2] Nicholas H. Ridgely, cashier, Illinois State Bank.
[3] William Lavely and Ebenezer Stout, wholesale and retail groceries, provisions, etc.
[4] John W. Priest and Leighton G. Moore. See note to Converse & Priest, October 1, 1847, *supra*.

"Spot" Resolutions
in the United States House of Representatives[1]

December 22, 1847

Whereas the President of the United States, in his message of May 11th. 1846, has declared that "The Mexican Government not only refused to receive him" (the envoy of the U.S.) "or listen to his propositions, but, after a long continued series of menaces, have at last invaded *our teritory*, and shed the blood of our fellow *citizens* on *our own soil*"

And again, in his message of December 8, 1846 that "We had ample cause of war against Mexico, long before the breaking out of

[1] AD, DNA RG 233 HR 30 A B 3 (1); *Congressional Globe*, Thirtieth Congress, First Session, 1848, p. 64. The resolutions were read and laid on the table. The text of the resolutions as printed in the *Globe* was considerably altered from Lincoln's original, which is here followed in detail.

[420]

hostilities. But even then we forbore to take redress into our own hands, until Mexico herself became the aggressor by invading *our soil* in hostile array, and shedding the blood of our *citizens*"

And yet again, in his message of December 7– 1847 that "The Mexican Government refused even to hear the terms of adjustment which he" (our minister of peace) "was authorized to propose; and finally, under wholly unjustifiable pretexts, involved the two countries in war, by invading the teritory of the State of Texas, striking the first blow, and shedding the blood of our *citizens* on *our own soil*"

And whereas this House desires to obtain a full knowledge of all the facts which go to establish whether the particular spot of soil on which the blood of our *citizens* was so shed, was, or was not, *our own soil*, at that time; therefore

Resolved by the House of Representatives, that the President of the United States be respectfully requested to inform this House—

First: Whether the spot of soil on which the blood of our *citizens* was shed, as in his messages declared, was, or was not, within the teritories of Spain, at least from the treaty of 1819 until the Mexican revolution

Second: Whether that spot is, or is not, within the teritory which was wrested from Spain, by the Mexican revolution.

Third: Whether that spot is, or is not, within a settlement of people, which settlement had existed ever since long before the Texas revolution, until it's inhabitants fled from the approach of the U.S. Army.

Fourth: Whether that settlement is, or is not, isolated from any and all other settlements, by the Gulf of Mexico, and the Rio Grande, on the South and West, and by wide uninhabited regions on the North and East.

Fifth: Whether the *People* of that settlement, or a *majority* of them, or *any* of them, had ever, previous to the bloodshed, mentioned in his messages, submitted themselves to the government or laws of Texas, or of the United States, by *consent*, or by *compulsion*, either by accepting office, or voting at elections, or paying taxes, or serving on juries, or having process served upon them, or in *any other way*.

Sixth: Whether the People of that settlement, did, or did not, flee from the approach of the United States Army, leaving unprotected their homes and their growing crops, *before* the blood was shed, as in his messages stated; and whether the first blood so shed, was, or was not shed, within the *inclosure* of the People, or some of them, who had thus fled from it.

Seventh: Whether our *citizens*, whose blood was shed, as in his messages declared, were, or were not, at that time, *armed* officers, and *soldiers*, sent into that settlement, by the military order of the President through the Secretary of War—and

Eighth: Whether the military force of the United States, including those *citizens*, was, or was not, so sent into that settlement, after Genl. Taylor had, more than once, intimated to the War Department that, in his opinion, no such movement was necessary to the defence or protection of Texas.

To the Commissioner of Pensions[1]

Commissioner of Pensions   House of Representatives
Dear Sir: Decr. 26. 1847

Will you please inform me, as soon as convenient, whether the claims of John Huckleberry and Thomas Collins,[2] of Illinois, for Land warrants, have been presented at your office; and if they have, what is their condition. Respectfully   A. LINCOLN

1 ALS, PHC.
2 John W. Huckleberry and Thomas Collins were Sangamon County veterans of the Mexican War.

To Blair & Rives[1]

Messrs Blair & Rives   [1848?]

Gentlemen: The copies of the Globe and Appendix to which I am entitled, I shall thank you to retain and deliver to me at the end of the session. Respectfully   A. LINCOLN

1 ALS, owned by Stratford Lee Morton, St. Louis, Missouri. This letter is undated, but is written on the bottom of the printed circular which Blair & Rives distributed to members of congress with information concerning the printing of the *Congressional Globe*. One infers that the circular was distributed in December, 1847, or January, 1848, and that Lincoln's reply was probably penned shortly thereafter.

To Richard S. Thomas[1]

Dear Richard: Washington, Jany. 1– 1848.

Your letter of the 23rd. Decr. is received, as also the Petition you mention. When documents become plenty, which they have not yet, I will send them to you. There is a good deal of diversity among the whigs here, as to who shall be their candidate for the Presidency; but I think it will result in favor of Genl. Taylor.

As to Mr. Graham's[2] application for a Lieutenancy, I have already submitted it to the President, in the best way I could think of to give it chance of success. I wrote him about it; and do not know any thing more that I can do for him. You know I can have no intimacy with the President, which might give me personal influence with him. In great haste Yours as ever—   A. LINCOLN

[1] ALS, IHi.   [2] See letter to President Polk, December 8, 1847, *supra.*

Remarks in
United States House of Representatives
Concerning Postal Contracts[1]

January 5, 1848

Mr. LINCOLN said that he had made an effort some few days since to obtain the floor in relation to this measure[2], but had failed. One of the objects he had then had in view was now in a great measure superseded by what had fallen from the gentleman from Virginia[3] who had just taken his seat. He begged to assure his friends on the other side of the House, that no assault whatever was meant upon the Postmaster General; and he was glad that what the gentleman had now said, modified to a great extent the impression which might have been created by the language he had used on a previous occasion. He wanted to state to gentlemen who might have entertained such impressions, that the Committee on the Post Office was composed of five Whigs and four Democrats, and their report was understood as sustaining, not impugning, the position taken by the Postmaster General. That report had met with the approbation of all the Whigs and of all the Democrats also, with the exception of one, and he wanted to go even further than this. [Intimations were here informally given to Mr. L. that it was not in order to mention on the floor what had taken place in committee.] He then observed that if he had been out of order in what he had said, he took it all back, [a laugh,] so far as he could. He had no desire, he could assure gentlemen, ever to be out of order—though he never could keep long *in* order.

[1] *Congressional Globe*, Thirtieth Congress, First Session, pp. 107-108, 108-109. Brackets are in the source.
[2] A joint resolution to direct the postmaster general to make arrangements with the Richmond, Fredericksburg and Potomac Railroad for transporting the mail between Washington and Richmond. The House was sitting in committee of the whole. Lincoln was a member of the committee on post office and post roads.
[3] John M. Botts, who supported the railroad's petition for an increase and accused the postmaster general (Cave Johnson of Tennessee) of personal antagonism toward the railroad company.

Mr. L. went on to observe, that he differed in opinion, in the present case, from his honorable friend from Richmond, [Mr. BOTTS]. That gentleman had begun his remarks by saying that if all prepossessions in this matter could be removed out of the way, but little difficulty would be experienced in coming to an agreement. Now, he could assure that gentleman that he had himself begun the examination of this subject with prepossessions all in his favor. He had long and often heard of him, and, from what he had heard, was prepossessed in his favor. Of the Postmaster General he had also heard, but had no prepossessions in his favor, though certainly none of an opposite kind. He differed, however, from that gentleman in politics, while in this respect he agreed with the gentleman from Virginia, [Mr. BOTTS,] whom he wished to oblige whenever it was in his power. That gentleman had referred to the report made to the House by the Postmaster General, and had intimated an apprehension that gentleman would be disposed to rely on that report alone, and derive their views of the case from that document alone. Now, it so happened that a pamphlet had been slipped into his [Mr. L.'s] hand before he read the report of the Postmaster General; so that, even in this, he had begun with prepossessions in favor of the gentleman from Virginia.

As to the report, he had but one remark to make: he had carefully examined it, and he did not understand that there was any dispute as to the facts therein stated: the dispute, if he understood it, was confined altogether to the inferences to be drawn from those facts. It was a difference not about facts, but about conclusions. The facts were not disputed. If he was right in this, he supposed the House might assume the facts to be as they were stated, and thence proceed to draw their own conclusions.

The gentleman had said that the Postmaster General had got into a personal squabble with the railroad company. Of this, Mr. L. knew nothing; nor did he need or desire to know anything, because it had nothing whatever to do with a just conclusion from the premises. But the gentleman had gone on to ask whether so great a grievance as the present detention of the southern mail ought not to be remedied? Mr. L. would assure the gentleman that if there was a proper way of doing it, no man was more anxious than he that it should be done. The report made by the committee had been intended to yield much for the sake of removing that grievance. That the grievance was very great, there was no dispute in any quarter. He supposed the statements made by the gentleman from Virginia to show this were all entirely correct in point of fact. He did suppose that the interruptions of regular intercourse, and all the other inconveniences growing out of it, were all as that gentleman had stated them to be; and certainly, if redress could be rendered, it was proper it should be rendered as soon as possible. The gentleman said that, in order to effect this, no new legislative action was needed: all that was necessary was, that the Postmaster General should be required to do what the law, as it stood, authorized and required him to do.

We come, then, said Mr. L., to the law. Now the Postmaster General says that he cannot give to this company over $237 50 per railroad mile of transportation, and 12½ per cent. less for transportation by steamboats. He considers himself as restricted by law to this amount; and he says, further, that he would not give more if he could, because, in his apprehension, it would not be fair and just.

Mr. Hilliard[4] here wished to be set right in his apprehension of the facts of the case, and he made some inquiry not distinctly heard across the Hall; and, after a brief conversation, expressing himself satisfied, resumed his seat.

Mr. Lincoln proceeded. I had the impression that the service rendered under the present contract cost the Government more than if the mail were carried by the railroad company, in consequence of its passing over a longer route. Understanding this, my view of the question remains unchanged.

And now as to the law: I am not disposed to discuss it at any very great length; for, as the appeal is here to the law-making power, which can alter the law whenever a modification is required, there does not seem any necessity of very nicely discussing what it is as it now stands. If it shall be clearly shown what naked justice requires, it will be easy to make the law conform to that requirement. But let us look at it as it stands.

There are three laws which have a bearing on this question: the first authorizes the Postmaster General to give to a contractor 25 per cent. more for the transportation of the mail over railroads than for similar transportation in mail-coaches; another law says that the Postmaster General shall not allow more than $300 per mile for daily transportation, provided that his contract does not conflict with the provisions of the law first referred to. Then there is a third law which directs the Postmaster General to classify the sorts of service rendered. It was this which caused him to give less for transportation by steamboats than over railroads; he graduated the compensation for this at a point midway between that by railroad and that by mail-coaches. The difference between railroad and

4 Henry W. Hilliard of Alabama.

coach being but 25 per cent., he placed the price for steamboat transportation at 12 ½ per cent. above the one and below the other. I do not understand that this construction of the law by the Postmaster General is held in any quarter to be wrong. The fact that the law allows him to pay $300 for daily transportation and for more frequent than daily, has been alluded to; but, as I understand, the position is not taken that he is authorized to allow this company $300 per mile. If it is, I shall proceed to examine it. All must admit that all the laws on the subject are extremely loose and general in their language; that they admit of different constructions; and that no one construction that can be given them leaves the mind entirely satisfied. The law allows $300 to be paid for transporting the mail daily or oftener, thereby fixing the compensation for one transportation and for two at the same amount. This alone is enough to show that the law is not very definite in its provisions, and in fact it is hardly possible to put an equitable construction upon it. It refers to a prior law, and says it is not to be construed so as to interfere with it.

From the whole of what the gentleman from Virginia has said, I understand his sense of the matter to be, that we are in this case to be governed by the old law. Now, I ask the lawyers in this House (I suppose there are some) [a laugh] whether I am not right when I say, that where a law has been passed in terms so general as to require a construction to be put upon it, (and this is the case with most laws,) and constructions of its provisions are accordingly given, and a second law is afterwards passed referring to the first, this second law is held to recognize and to confirm the constructions put upon that first passed? If this is so, then I say that the Postmaster General was not wrong when he insisted that the latter law, when it referred to the former, meant to refer to it as construed; in which case the construction seems to be confirmed and strengthened by the last passed.

But, looking only to the original construction itself of the old law, the gentleman from Virginia says that Mr. Kendall's construction of the terms "similar transportation by mail coaches," was wrong, and that he ought to have construed it to mean transportation of the same mail not only, but by the same route. But, now, suppose there was no mail-coach transportation on that route, what must his construction be in that case? What did the present Postmaster General in fact do? He took the most expensive mail-coach route in the nation. He took the prices allowed for coach transportation on different portions of that route, and averaged them, and then built his construction of the law upon that average. It came to $190 per mile. He added 25 per cent. to that rate, and offered the result to this railroad company. The gentleman from Virginia says that this was wrong: I say it was right.

But the gentleman says he ought to have reckoned coach transportation on that specific route. Well, if he had done so, he would have added 25 per cent. upon $5,000, and no more; for the Postmaster General tells us that before he made his contract with this railroad company, the same mail had been carried for between $5,000 and $6,000. The company now get $28,000, and are not satisfied. Had he taken the same rate then, where would they have been? If there had been a coach line, he would not have gained anything by that. For I have inquired at what rate the mail could be carried by coaches from Washington to Richmond, and I have heard that the lowest bid ever made was $28,000. If he had added 25 per cent. to that, it would have been more than the company asks. This fact, and one other item that I obtained, are all that I had to enable me to get at justice in this case. An old gentleman, whose very good looks prepossessed me in his favor, and would incline me to believe any statement he should make, told me that he had been a stockholder in the road, and had never got over 5 per cent. dividend on his stock. The same source of information admitted that since the construction of the railroad, mail-coaches had been wholly disused. It is a bad road, and always has been, and the mail could not now be carried over it in coaches for three or four times what it might have been, had not the railroad been constructed.

I think that abundant reasons have been given to show that the construction put upon the law by the Postmaster General is the right construction, and that subsequent acts of Congress have confirmed it. I have already said that the grievance complained of ought to be remedied. But it is said that the sum of money about which all this difficulty has arisen is exceeding small—not more than $2,700. I admit it is very small; and if nothing else were involved, it would not be worth the dispute. But there is a principle involved; and if we once yield to a wrong principle, that concession will be the prolific source of endless mischief. It is for this reason, and not for the sake of saving $2,700, that I am unwilling to yield what is demanded. If I had no apprehensions that the ghost of this yielding would rise and appear in various distant places, I would say, pay the money, and let us have no more fuss about it. But I have such apprehensions. I do believe, that if we yield this, our act will be the source of other claims equally unjust, and therefore I cannot vote to make the allowance.

And now, I suppose, I may, without being out of order, tell what I was willing, in committee, to yield for the sake of removing this evil. I was willing to give as damages what the department would have to pay the Bay Company for breach of contract, be it $2,700, or whatever amount. Be it what it might, it would be so much money gone; it would never rise again.

Mr. L. insisted that the true and great point to which the attention of this House or the committee should be directed was, what is a just compensation? Inasmuch as this railroad and steamboat company could afford greater facilities than any other line, the service ought to be done upon this route; but it ought to be done upon just and fair principles. If it could not be done at what had been offered, let it be shown that a greater amount was just. But, until it was shown, he was opposed to increasing it. He had seen many things in the report of the Postmaster General and elsewhere that stood out against the river route. Now, the daily steamboat transportation between Troy and New York was performed for less than one hundred dollars per mile. This company was dissatisfied with two hundred and twelve or two hundred and thirteen dollars per mile. It had not been shown, and he thought it could not be shown to them why this company was entitled to more, or so much more, than the other received. It was true, they had to encounter the ice, but was there not more ice further north? There might possibly be shown some reason why the Virginia line should have more; but was there any reason why they should have so much more? Again, the price paid between Cincinnati and Louisville for daily transportation was not two hundred and thirteen dollars per mile, or one hundred dollars, or fifty; it was less than twenty-eight dollars per mile. Now, he did not insist that there might not be some peculiar reasons connected with this route between this city and Richmond that entitled it to more than was paid on the routes between Cincinnati and Louisville, and Troy and New York. But, if there were reasons, they ought to be shown. And was it supposed that there could be any, or so peculiar reasons, as to justify so great a difference in compensation as was claimed by this company? It did seem that there could be none.

These reasons actuated him in taking the position he had taken, painfully refusing to oblige his friend from Virginia, which he assured the gentleman he had the greatest inclination to do.

In relation to the report of the committee, let him state one thing: It proposed that the Postmaster General should again offer this company what he had already offered and they had refused. It was for the reason that the Postmaster General, as he understood, had informed them that he was not himself going to renew the proposition. The committee supposed—at any rate, he (Mr. L.) supposed—that as soon as the company should know that they could get what he had offered them, and no more—as soon as all hope of greater compensation was cut off—that instant they would not take ten thousand dollars a year for the privilege of doing it. Whether this was actually the case he did not profess positively to know; it was a matter of opinion, but he firmly believed it. In proposing to offer them the contract again, as he had already said, the committee yielded something, viz. the damage that the Government would have to pay for the breaking up of the present arrangement. He was willing to incur that damage; some other gentlemen were not; they were further away from the position which his friend from Virginia took. He was willing to yield something, but could not consent to go the whole length with the gentleman.

In relation to what the damage would be, it would of course depend upon what was shown to this House and to the Senate to be fair and reasonable. It was a general principle of law that this Government could not be sued upon any contract. It was a principle of the common law that no judgment can go against the State, and it had been confirmed by the Supreme Court of the United States in repeated instances. Now, how was this company to get anything for their damages? Why, simply by coming here and laying their case before Congress.

Mr. L. concluded by remarking that this was all he wished to say. If there was any portion of his hour left, he would only ask that it should be passed to his credit for some future occasion.

Remarks Continued in
United States House of Representatives
Concerning Postal Contracts[1]

January 6, 1848

The House . . . resolved itself into Committee of the Whole (Mr. SMITH,[2] of Indiana, in the chair) on the joint resolution concerning the transportation of the mail from Washington south. . . .

Mr. GOGGIN[3] said. . . . The gentleman from Illinois (Mr. LINCOLN) had yesterday thought proper to go into what occurred in committee in connection with this subject. He regretted that the gentleman should so far have trespassed, unintentionally he had no doubt, upon the rules of the House; but as he stated that every member upon that committee, of both political parties—that all those with whom he was associated united in support of this resolution, he thought proper to notice the remark.

Mr. LINCOLN here interposed, and (Mr. G. yielding) said that the gentleman had misunderstood him. He had said a majority of one party and the whole of the other had supported the resolution in committee.

1 *Congressional Globe,* Thirtieth Congress, First Session, p. 119.
2 Caleb B. Smith. 3 William L. Goggin of Virginia.

To the Third Auditor of the Treasury[1]

Dear Sir: Washington, Jany. 6. 1848

Enclosed are some papers pertaining to a claim of Dr. Argyle W. Furr. Supposing it might do good, and could do no harm, I have added my certificates of the genuineness of Col. Baker's signatures.[2] Will you please examine them, and address me at the House of Representatives? Very Respectfully

A. LINCOLN.

1 ALS, IHi.   2 *Vide infra.*

Endorsement of Papers Signed by Edward D. Baker[1]

January 6, 1848

I certify that the above signature, purporting to be that of Col. E. D Baker, is genuine.   A. LINCOLN,

Jany. 6, 1848   a member of Congress—

1 AES, owned by R. S. Wilkins, Boston, Massachusetts.

To William H. Herndon[1]

Washington, January 8, 1848.

Dear William: Your letter of December 27 was received a day or two ago. I am much obliged to you for the trouble you have taken, and promise to take in my little business there. As to speechmaking, by way of getting the hang of the House I made a little speech two or three days ago on a post-office question of no general interest. I find speaking here and elsewhere about the same thing. I was about as badly scared, and no worse, as I am when I speak in court. I expect to make one within a week or two, in which I hope to succeed well enough to wish you to see it.

It is very pleasant to learn from you that there are some who desire that I should be reëlected. I most heartily thank them for their kind partiality; and I can say, as Mr. Clay said of the annexation of Texas, that "personally I would not object" to a reëlection, although I thought at the time, and still think, it would be quite as well for me to return to the law at the end of a single term. I made the declaration that I would not be a candidate again, more from a wish to deal fairly with others, to keep peace among our friends, and to keep the district from going to the enemy, than for any cause personal to myself; so that, if it should so happen that nobody else wishes to be elected, I could not refuse the people the right of sending me again. But to enter myself as a competitor of others, or to authorize any one so to enter me, is what my word and honor forbid.

I got some letters intimating a probability of so much difficulty amongst our friends as to lose us the district; but I remember such letters were written to Baker when my own case was under consideration, and I trust there is no more ground for such apprehension now than there was then. Remember I am always glad to receive a letter from you. Most truly your friend,

A. LINCOLN.

1 NH, I, 325-26.

To Blair & Rives[1]

January 11, 1848

Messrs Blair & Rives will greatly oblige me by sending my [sic] by the bearer, the volume containing the Debates of the 2nd. session of the 28th. Congress; which volume, if sent, I shall be careful to return uninjured, or pay for, at their option.

Jany. 11. 1848.   A. LINCOLN

1 ALS, IHi. Blair & Rives were publishers of the *Congressional Globe*.

Speech in United States House of Representatives: The War with Mexico[1]

Mr. Chairman: January 12, 1848

Some, if not all the gentlemen on, the other side of the House, who have addressed the committee within the last two days, have

1 AD, DLC-RTL. The manuscript is followed throughout. Lincoln's emendations, presumably inserted in printer's proof, in the *Congressional Globe Appendix*, pp. 93-95, are given in footnotes. In addition to these sources for the speech as written, there is the detailed report of the speech as delivered, printed in the *Congressional Globe*, Thirtieth Congress, First Session, New Series, No. 10, pp. 154-56, which was copied by the *Illinois Journal*, February 10, 1848.

spoken rather complainingly, if I have rightly understood them, of the vote given a week or ten days ago, declaring that the war with Mexico was unnecessarily and unconstitutionally commenced by the President.[2] I admit that such a vote should not be given, in mere party wantonness, and that the one given, is justly censurable, if it have no other, or better foundation. I am one of those who joined in that vote; and I did so under my best impression of the *truth* of the case. How I got this impression, and how it may possibly be removed, I will now try to show. When the war began, it was my opinion that all those who, because of knowing too *little*, or because of knowing too *much*, could not conscientiously approve the conduct of the President, in the beginning of it, should, nevertheless, as good citizens and patriots, remain silent on that point, at least till the war should be ended. Some leading democrats, including Ex President Van Buren, have taken this same view, as I understand them; and I adhered to it, and acted upon it, until since I took my seat here; and I think I should still adhere to it, were it not that the President and his friends will not allow it to be so. Besides the continual effort of the President to argue every silent vote given for supplies, into an endorsement of the justice and wisdom of his conduct—besides that singularly candid paragraph, in his late message in which he tells us that Congress, with great unanimity, only two in the Senate and fourteen in the House dissenting, had declared that, "by the act of the Republic of Mexico, a state of war exists between that Government and the United States," when the same journals that informed him of this, also informed him, that when that declaration stood disconnected from the question of supplies, sixtyseven in the House, and not fourteen merely, voted against it—besides this open attempt to prove, by telling the *truth*, what he could not prove by telling the *whole truth*—demanding of all who will not submit to be misrepresented, in justice to themselves, to speak out—besides all this, one of my colleagues (Mr. Richardson)[3] at a very early day in the session brought in a set of resolutions, expressly endorsing the original justice of the war on the part of the President. Upon these resolutions, when they shall be put on their passage I shall be *compelled* to vote; so that I can not be silent, if I would. Seeing this, I went about preparing myself to give the vote understandingly when it should come. I carefully examined the President's messages, to as-

2 James K. Polk.
3 William A. Richardson, Democrat, from Rushville, Illinois, who had been elected to the House to fill the vacancy caused by the resignation of representative-elect Stephen A. Douglas.

certain what he himself had said and proved upon the point. The result of this examination was to make the impression, that taking for true, all the President states as facts, he falls far short of proving his justification; and that the President would have gone farther with his proof, if it had not been for the small matter, that the *truth* would not permit him. Under the impression thus made, I gave the vote before mentioned. I propose now to give, concisely, the process of the examination I made, and how I reached the conclusion I did. The President, in his first war message of May 1846, declares that the soil was *ours* on which hostilities were commenced by Mexico; and he repeats that declaration, almost in the same language, in each successive annual message, thus showing that he esteems that point, a highly essential one. In the importance of that point, I entirely agree with the President. To my judgment, it is the *very point*, upon which he should be justified, or condemned. In his message of Decr. 1846, it seems to have occurred to him, as is certainly true, that title—ownership—to soil, or any thing else, is not a simple fact; but is a conclusion following one or more simple facts; and that it was incumbent upon him, to present the facts, from which he concluded, the soil was ours, on which the first blood of the war was shed.

Accordingly a little below the middle of page twelve in the message last referred to, he enters upon that task; forming an issue, and introducing testimony, extending the whole, to a little below the middle of page fourteen. Now I propose to try to show, that the whole of this,—issue and evidence—is, from beginning to end, the sheerest deception. The issue, as he presents it, is in these words "But there are those who, conceding all this to be true, assume the ground that the true western boundary of Texas is the Nueces, instead of the Rio Grande; and that, therefore, in marching our army to the east bank of the latter river, we passed the Texan line, and invaded the teritory of Mexico." Now this issue, is made up of two affirmatives and no negative. The main deception of it is, that it assumes as true, that *one* river or the *other* is necessarily the boundary; and cheats the superficial thinker entirely out of the idea, that *possibly* the boundary is somewhere *between* the two, and not actually at either. A further deception is, that it will let in *evidence*, which a true issue would exclude. A true issue, made by the President, would be about as follows "I say, the soil *was ours*, on which the first blood was shed; there are those who say it was not."

I now proceed to examine the Presidents evidence, as applicable to such an issue. When that evidence is analized, it is all included in the following propositions:

1. That the Rio Grande was the Western boundary of Louisiana as we purchased it of France in 1803.

2 That the Republic of Texas always *claimed* the Rio Grande, as her Western boundary.

3 That by various acts, she had claimed it *on paper.*

4. That Santa Anna, in his treaty with Texas, recognised the Rio Grande, as her boundary.

5. That Texas *before,* and the U. S. *after,* annexation had *exercised* jurisdiction *beyond* the Nueces—*between* the two rivers.

6 That our Congress, *understood* the boundary of Texas to extend beyond the Nueces.

Now for each of these in it's turn.

His first item is, that the Rio Grande was the Western boundary of Louisiana, as we purchased it of France in 1803; and seeming to expect this to be disputed, he argues over the amount of nearly a page, to prove it true; at the end of which he lets us know, that by the treaty of 1819, we sold to Spain the whole country from the Rio Grande eastward, to the Sabine. Now, admitting for the present, that the Rio Grande, was the boundary of Louisiana, what, under heaven, had that to do with the *present* boundary between us and Mexico? How, Mr. Chairman, the line, that once divided your land from mine, can *still* be the boundary between us, *after* I have sold my land to you, is, to me, beyond all comprehension. And how any man, with an honest purpose only, of proving the truth, could ever have *thought* of introducing such a fact to prove such an issue, is equally incomprehensible.[4] His next piece of evidence is that "The Republic of Texas always *claimed* this river (Rio Grande) as her western boundary[.]" That is not true, in fact. Texas *has* claimed it, but she has not *always* claimed it. There is, at least, one distinguished exception. Her state constitution,—the republic's most solemn, and well considered act—that which may, without impropriety, be called her last will and testament revoking all others—makes no such claim. But suppose she had always claimed it. Has not Mexico always claimed the contrary? so that there is but *claim* against *claim,* leaving nothing proved, until we get back of the claims, and find which has the better *foundation.* Though not in the order in which the President presents his evidence, I now consider that class of his statements, which are, in substance, nothing more than that Texas has, by various acts of her convention

---

[4] In the text of the *Congressional Globe Appendix,* Lincoln inserted at this point the following sentence: "The outrage upon common *right,* of seizing as our own what we have once sold, merely because it *was* ours *before* we sold it, is only equalled by the outrage on common *sense* of any attempt to justify it."

and congress, claimed the Rio Grande, as her boundary, *on paper*. I mean here what he says about the fixing of the Rio Grande as her boundary in her old constitution (not her state constitution) about forming congressional districts, counties &c &c. Now all of this is but naked *claim;* and what I have already said about claims is strictly applicable to this. If I should claim your land, by word of mouth, that certainly would not make it mine; and if I were to claim it by a deed which I had made myself, and with which, you had had nothing to do, the claim would be quite the same, in substance—or rather, in utter nothingness. I next consider the President's statement that Santa Anna in his *treaty*[5] with Texas, recog-

[5] The text of the so-called "treaty," printed following Lincoln's speech in the *Congressional Globe Appendix* is as follows:

Articles of an agreement entered into between his Excellency David G. Burnet, President of the Republic of Texas, of the one part, and his Excellency General Santa Anna, President-General-in-Chief of the Mexican army, of the other part.

ARTICLE 1. General Antonio Lopez de Santa Anna agrees that he will not take up arms, nor will he exercise his influence to cause them to be taken up, against the people of Texas, during the present war of independence.

ART. 2. All hostilities between the Mexican and Texan troops will cease immediately, both by land and water.

ART. 3. The Mexican troops will evacuate the territory of Texas, passing to the other side of the Rio Grande Del Norte.

ART. 4. The Mexican army, in its retreat, shall not take the property of any person without his consent and just indemnification, using only such articles as may be necessary for its subsistence, in cases when the owner may not be present, and remitting to the commander of the army of Texas, or to the Commissioners to be appointed for the adjustment of such matters, an account of the value of the property consumed, the place where taken, and the name of the owner, if it can be ascertained.

ART. 5. That all private property, including cattle, horses, negro slaves, or indentured persons, of whatever denomination, that may have been captured by any portion of the Mexican army, or may have taken refuge in the said army, since the commencement of the late invasion, shall be restored to the commander of the Texan army, or to such other persons as may be appointed by the Government of Texas to receive them.

ART. 6. The troops of both armies will refrain from coming into contact with each other; and to this end, the commander of the army of Texas will be careful not to approach within a shorter distance than five leagues.

ART. 7. The Mexican army shall not make any other delay, on its march, than that which is necessary to take up their hospitals, baggage, &c., and to cross the rivers; any delay not necessary to these purposes to be considered an infraction of this agreement.

ART. 8. By an express to be immediately despatched, this agreement shall be sent to General Vincente Filisola, and to General T. J. Rusk, commander of the Texan army, in order that they may be apprized of its stipulations; and to this end, they will exchange engagements to comply with the same.

ART. 9. That all Texan prisoners now in the possession of the Mexican army, or its authorities, be forthwith released, and furnished with free passports to return to their homes; in consideration of which, a corresponding number of Mexican prisoners, rank and file, now in possession of the Government of Texas,

nised the Rio Grande, as the western boundary of Texas. Besides the position, so often taken that Santa Anna, while a prisoner of war—a captive—*could* not bind Mexico by a treaty, which I deem conclusive—besides this, I wish to say something in relation to this treaty, so called by the President, with Santa Anna. If any man would like to be amused by a sight of that *little* thing, which the President calls by that *big* name, he can have it, by turning to Niles' Register volume 50, page 336. And if any one should suppose that Niles' Register is a curious repository of so mighty a document, as a solemn treaty between nations, I can only say that I learned, to a tolerable degree [of] certainty, by enquiry at the State Department, that the President himself, never saw it any where else. By the way, I believe I should not err, if I were to declare, that during the first ten years of the existence of that document, it was never, by any body, *called* a treaty—that it was never so called, till the President, in his extremity, attempted, by so calling it, to wring something from it in justification of himself in connection with the Mexican war. It has none of the distinguishing features of a treaty. It does not call itself a treaty. Santa Anna does not therein, assume to bind Mexico; he assumes only to act as the President-Commander-in-chief of the Mexican Army and Navy; stipulates that the then present hostilities should cease, and that he would not *himself* take up arms, nor *influence* the Mexican people to take up arms, against Texas during the existence of the war of independence[.] He did not recognise the independence of Texas; he did not assume to put an end to the war; but clearly indicated his expectation of it's continuance; he did not say one word about boundary, and, most probably, never thought of it. It *is* stipulated therein that the Mexican forces should evacuate the teritory of Texas, *passing to the other side of the Rio Grande;* and in another article, it is stipulated that, to prevent collisions between the armies, the Texan army should not approach nearer than within five leagues—of

---

shall be immediately released—the remainder of the Mexican prisoners that continue in the possession of the Government of Texas to be treated with due humanity; any extraordinary comforts that may be furnished them to be at the charge of the Government of Mexico.

ART. 10. General Antonio Lopez de Santa Anna will be sent to Vera Cruz as soon as it shall be deemed proper.

The contracting parties sign this instrument for the above mentioned purposes, in duplicate, at the port of Velasco, this 14th day of May, 1836.

DAVID G. BURNET, *President.*
JAS. COLLINGSWORTH, *Secretary of State.*
ANTONIO LOPEZ DE SANTA ANNA.
B. HARDIMAN, *Secretary of the Treasury.*
P. W. GRAYSON, *Attorney-General.*

what is not said—but clearly, from the object stated it is—of the Rio Grande. Now, if this is a treaty, recognising the Rio Grande, as the boundary of Texas, it contains the singular feauture [*sic*], of stipulating, that Texas shall not go within five leagues of *her own* boundary.

Next comes the evidence of Texas before annexation, and the United States, afterwards, *exercising* jurisdiction *beyond* the Nueces, and *between* the two rivers. This actual *exercise* of jurisdiction, is the very class or quality of evidence we want. It is excellent so far as it goes; but does it go far enough? He tells us it went *beyond* the Nueces; but he does not tell us it went *to* the Rio Grande. He tells us, jurisdiction was exercised *between* the two rivers, but he does not tell us it was exercised over *all* the teritory between them. Some simple minded people, think it is *possible*, to cross one river and go *beyond* it without going *all the way* to the next—that jurisdiction may be exercised *between* two rivers without covering *all* the country between them. I know a man, not very unlike myself, who exercises jurisdiction over a piece of land between the Wabash and the Mississippi; and yet so far is this from being *all* there is between those rivers, that it is just one hundred and fiftytwo feet long by fifty wide, and no part of it much within a hundred miles of either. He has a neighbour between him and the Mississippi,—that is, just across the street, in that direction— whom, I am sure, he could neither *persuade* nor *force* to give up his habitation; but which nevertheless, he could certainly annex, if it were to be done, by merely standing on his own side of the street and *claiming* it, or even, sitting down, and writing a *deed* for it.

But next the President tells us, the Congress of the United States *understood* the state of Texas they admitted into the union, to extend *beyond* the Nueces. Well, I suppose they did. *I* certainly so understood it. But how *far* beyond? That Congress did *not* understand it to extend clear to the Rio Grande, is quite certain by the fact of their joint resolutions, for admission, expressly leaving all questions of boundary to future adjustment. And it may be added, that Texas herself, is proved to have had the same understanding of it, that our Congress had, by the fact of the exact conformity of her new constitution, to those resolutions.

I am now through the whole of the President's evidence; and it is a singular fact, that if any one should declare the President sent the army into the midst of a settlement of Mexican people, who had never submited, by consent or by force, to the authority of Texas or of the United States, and that *there*, and *thereby*, the first blood of the war was shed, there is not one word in all the President has said, which would either admit or deny the declaration.[6] This strange omission, it does seem to me, could not have occurred but by design. My way of living leads me to be about the courts of justice; and there, I have sometimes seen a good lawyer, struggling for his client's neck, in a desparate case, employing every artifice to work round, befog, and cover up, with many words, some[7] point arising in the case, which he *dared* not admit, and yet *could* not deny. Party bias may help to make it appear so; but with all the allowance I can make for such bias, it still does appear to me, that just such, and from just such necessity, is the President's struggle in this case.

Some time after my colleague (Mr. Richardson) introduced the resolutions I have mentioned, I introduced a preamble, resolution, and interrogatories,[8] intended to draw the President out, if possible, on this hitherto untrodden ground. To show their relevancy, I propose to state my understanding of the true rule for ascertaining the boundary between Texas and Mexico. It is, that *wherever* Texas was *exercising* jurisdiction, was hers; and *wherever Mexico* was exercising jurisdiction, was hers; and that *whatever* separated the actual exercise of jurisdiction of the one, from that of the other, was the true boundary between them. If, as is probably true, Texas was exercising jurisdiction along the western bank of the Nueces, and Mexico was exercising it along the eastern bank of the Rio Grande, then *neither* river was the boundary; but the uninhabited country between the two, was. The extent of our teritory in that region depended, not on any *treaty-fixed* boundary (for no treaty had attempted it) but on revolution. Any people anywhere, being inclined and having the power, have the *right* to rise up, and shake off the existing government, and form a new one that suits them better. This is a most valuable,—a most sacred right—a right, which we hope and believe, is to liberate the world. Nor is this right confined to cases in which the whole people of an existing government, may choose to exercise it. Any portion of such people that *can, may* revolutionize, and make their *own*, of so much of the teritory as they inhabit. More than this, a *majority* of any portion of such people may revolutionize, putting down a *minority*, intermingled with, or near about them, who may oppose their movement. Such minority, was precisely the case, of the tories of our

[6] At this point in the *Congressional Globe Appendix*, Lincoln emended the next sentence as follows: "In this strange omission chiefly consists the deception of the President's evidence—an omission which, it does seem to me, could scarcely have occurred but by design."

[7] Lincoln emended "point arising in the case" to "position pressed upon him by the prosecution."   [8] *Supra*, under date of December 22, 1847.

own revolution. It is a quality of revolutions not to go by *old* lines, or *old* laws; but to break up both, and make new ones. As to the country now in question, we bought it of France in 1803, and sold it to Spain in 1819, according to the President's statements. After this, all Mexico, including Texas, revolutionized against Spain; and still later, Texas revolutionized against Mexico. In my view, just so far as she carried her revolution, by obtaining the *actual*, willing or unwilling, submission of the people, *so far*, the country was hers, and no farther. Now sir, for the purpose of obtaining the very best evidence, as to whether Texas had actually carried her revolution, to the place where the hostilities of the present war commenced, let the President answer the interrogatories, I proposed, as before mentioned, or some other similar ones. Let him answer, fully, fairly, and candidly. Let him answer with *facts*, and not with arguments. Let him remember he sits where Washington sat, and so remembering, let him answer, as Washington would answer. As a nation *should* not, and the Almighty *will* not, be evaded, so let him attempt no envasion—no equivocation. And if, so answering, he can show that the soil was ours, where the first blood of the war was shed—that it was not within an inhabited country, or, if within such, that the inhabitants had submitted themselves to the civil authority of Texas, or of the United States, and that the same is true of the site of Fort Brown, then I am with him for his justification. In that case I, shall be most happy to reverse the vote I gave the other day. I have a selfish motive for desiring that the President may do this. I expect to give some votes, in connection with the war, which, without his so doing, will be of doubtful propriety in my own judgment, but which will be free from the doubt if he does so. But if he *can* not, or *will* not do this—if on any pretence, or no pretence, he shall refuse or omit it, then I shall be fully convinced, of what I more than suspect already, that he is deeply conscious of being in the wrong—that he feels the blood of this war, like the blood of Abel, is crying to Heaven against him.[9] That originally having some strong motive—what, I will not stop now to give my opinion concerning—to involve the two countries in a war, and trusting to escape scrutiny, by fixing the public gaze upon the exceeding brightness of military glory—that attractive rainbow, that rises in showers of blood—that serpent's eye, that charms to destroy—he plunged into it, and has swept, *on* and *on*, till, disappointed in his calculation of the ease with which Mexico might be

[9] At this point Lincoln emended as follows: "; that he ordered General Taylor into the midst of a peaceful Mexican settlement, purposely to bring on a war; that originally . . . " etc.

subdued, he now finds himself, he knows not where. How like the
half insane mumbling of a fever-dream, is the whole war part of
his late message! At one time telling us that Mexico has nothing
whatever, that we can get, but teritory; at another, showing us
how we can support the war, by levying contributions on Mexico.
At one time, urging the national honor, the security of the future,
the prevention of foreign interference, and even, the good of Mexico herself, as among the objects of the war; at another, telling us,
that "to reject indemnity, by refusing to accept a cession of teritory,
would be to abandon all our just demands, and to wage the war,
bearing all it's expenses, *without a purpose or definite object*[.]"
So then, the national honor, security of the future, and every thing
but teritorial indemnity, may be considered the *no-purposes*, and
indefinite, objects of the war! But, having it now settled that teritorial indemnity is the only object, we are urged to seize, by legislation here, all that he was content to take, a few months ago, and
the whole province of lower California to boot, and to still carry
on the war—to take *all* we are fighting for, and *still* fight on. Again,
the President is resolved, under all circumstances, to have full teritorial indemnity for the expenses of the war; but he forgets to tell
us how we are to get the *excess*, after those expenses shall have surpassed the value of the *whole* of the Mexican teritory. So again, he
insists that the separate national existence of Mexico, shall be
maintained; but he does not tell us *how* this can be done, after we
shall have taken *all* her teritory. Lest the questions, I here suggest,
be considered speculative merely, let me be indulged a moment in
trying [to] show they are not. The war has gone on some twenty
months; for the expenses of which, together with an inconsiderable
old score, the President now claims about one half of the Mexican
teritory; and that, by far the better half, so far as concerns our
ability to make any thing out of it. *It* is comparatively uninhabited;
so that we could establish land offices in it, and raise some money
in that way. But the other half is already inhabited, as I understand it, tolerably densely for the nature of the country; and all it's
lands, or all that are valuable, already appropriated as private
property. How then are we to make any thing out of these lands
with this incumbrance on them? or how, remove the incumbrance?
I suppose no one will say we should kill the people, or drive them
out, or make slaves of them, or even confiscate their property. How
then can we make much out of this part of the teritory? If the
prossecution of the war has, in expenses, already equalled the *better*
half of the country, how long it's future prosecution, will be in
equalling, the less valuable half, is not a *speculative*, but a *practical*

question, pressing closely upon us. And yet it is a question which the President seems to never have thought of. As to the mode of terminating the war, and securing peace, the President is equally wandering and indefinite. First, it is to be done by a more vigorous prossecution of the war in the vital parts of the enemies country; and, after apparantly, talking himself tired, on this point, the President drops down into a half despairing tone, and tells us that "with a people distracted and divided by contending factions, and a government subject to constant changes, by successive revolutions, *the continued success of our arms may fail to secure a satisfactory peace*[.]" Then he suggests the propriety of wheedling the Mexican people to desert the counsels of their own leaders, and trusting in our protection, to set up a government from which we can secure a satisfactory peace; telling us, that "*this may become the only mode of obtaining such a peace.*" But soon he falls into doubt of this too; and then drops back on to the already half abandoned ground of "more vigorous prossecution.["] All this shows that the President is, in no wise, satisfied with his own positions. First he takes up one, and in attempting to argue us *into* it, he argues himself *out* of it; then seizes another, and goes through the same process; and then, confused at being able to think of nothing new, he snatches up the old one again, which he has some time before cast off. His mind, tasked beyond it's power, is running hither and thither, like some tortured creature, on a burning surface, finding no position, on which it can settle down, and be at ease.

Again, it is a singular omission in this message, that it, no where intimates *when* the President expects the war to terminate. At it's beginning, Genl. Scott[10] was, by this same President, driven into disfavor, if not disgrace, for intimating that peace could not be conquered in less than three or four months. But now, at the end of about twenty months, during which time our arms have given us the most splendid successes—every department, and every part, land and water, officers and privates, regulars and volunteers, doing all that men *could* do, and hundreds of things which it had ever before been thought men could *not* do,—after all this, this same President gives us a long message, without showing us, that, *as to the end*, he himself, has, even an immaginary conception. As I have before said, he knows not where he is. He is a bewildered,

10 Winfield Scott. Both General Scott and General Taylor were Whigs, and administration leaders feared the increase of their popularity. Scott justifiably suspected the administration of withholding complete co-operation. On January 2, Scott was recalled; on January 31 and April 17, Lincoln voted in favor of resolutions requesting the President to explain the suspension. On April 22, Scott was superseded by General W. O. Butler.

confounded, and miserably perplexed man. God grant he may be able to show, there is not something about his conscience, more painful than all his mental perplexity!

Bill Introduced
In United States House of Representatives
Concerning Land Bounties[1]

[January 17, 1848]

A bill to amend an act entitled "An act to raise for a limited time, an additional military force and for other purposes" Approved, February 11th. 1847.

Be it enacted by the Senate and House of Representatives of the United States of America, in Congress assembled: That hereafter the legal holder of any land warrant issued under the provision of the ninth section of the act to which this an amendment, may locate the same at any land office of the United States, in one body, or in parcels, (in conformity to the legal subdivisions of the public lands and subject to the present limitations in relation to the purchase of small quantities of land with money—)upon any of the public lands, within the land district of such office, then subject to private entry, or to which such warrant-holder may, at the time of location, have a legal right of pre-emption. Provided, that the whole right of location under any one warrant, shall be exhausted at one time.

[1] AD, DNA RG 233 HR89 30A. Lincoln gave notice of the bill December 20, 1847 and introduced it on January 17, 1848. On February 9, 1848, Representative Linn Boyd of Kentucky, of the Committee on Military Affairs, reported the bill, and on his motion it was tabled.

Report in United States House of Representatives
Concerning Petition of
William Fuller and Orlando Saltmarsh[1]

January 19, 1848

The Committee on Post Offices and Post Roads, to whom was refered the petition of Messrs Saltmarsh & Fuller, report:

That, as proved to their satisfaction, the mail routes from Milledgeville to Athens, and from Warrenton to Decatur, in the State of Georgia, (numbered 2366 and 2380) were let to Reeside & Avery, at $1300 per annum for the former and $1500 for the latter, for the term of four years to commence on the 1st day of January 1835. That previous to the time for commencing the service, Re[e]side sold his interest therein to Avery.[2] That on the 11th. of May 1835, Avery sold the whole to these petitioners, Saltmarsh & Fuller, to take effect from the beginning—Jany. 1– 1835. That at this time, the Assistant Post master General, being called on for that purpose, consented to the transfer of the contracts from Re[e]side & Avery to these petitioners, and promised, to have proper entries of the transfer made on the books of the Department, which, however, was neglected to be done. That the petitioners, supposing all was right, in good faith commenced the transportation of the mail on these routes, and, after difficulty arose, still trusting that all would be made right, continued the service till Decr. 1– 1837. That they performed the service to the entire satisfaction of the Department, and have never been paid any thing for it, except.[3] That the difficulty occurred as follows: Mr. Barry[4] was Post master General at the times of making the contracts and the attempted transfer of them. Mr. Kendall[5] succeeded Mr. Barry, and finding Reeside apparently in debt to the Department, and these contracts still standing in the names of Reeside & Avery, refused to pay for the service under them, otherwise than by credits to Re[e]side; afterwards, however, he divided the compensation, still crediting one half to Reeside, and directing the other to be paid to the order of Avery, who, disclaimed all right to it. After discontinuing the service, these petitioners, supposing they might have legal redress against Avery, brought suit against him, in New-Orleans; in which suit they failed, on the ground that Avery had complied with his contract, having done so much towards the transfer, as they had accepted, and been satisfied with. Still later, the Department sued Reeside on his supposed indebtedness, and by a verdict of the jury it was determined, that the Department was indebted to him, in a sum much beyond all the credits given him on the account above stated. Under these circumstances [the] committee consider the petitioners clearly entitled to relief; and they report a bill accordingly; lest, however, there should be some mistake as to the amount which they have already received, we so frame it as that, *by adjustment at the Department* they may be paid so much as remains unpaid for service actually performed by them, not charging them with the credits given Reeside. The committee think it not improbable that the petitioners purchased the right of Avery to be paid for the service from the first of January, till their purchase on May

11th. 1835; but the evidence on this point being very vague, they forbear to report in favour of allowing it.

[1] AD, DNA RG 233 HR 30A D15 Report No. 102; *Reports of Committees,* HR, Thirtieth Congress, First Session, Vol. I, No. 102. The accompanying bill, HR 92, for the relief of William Fuller and Orlando Saltmarsh, passed the House on June 2, but died in the Senate. The original bill cannot be found in The National Archives.

[2] The following deletion appears at this point: "gave notice of the sale to the Department, and has ever since disclaimed all connection with the service, and all compensation for it."

[3] Deleted as follows: "$908-15 cents," with no substitute figure inserted.

[4] William T. Barry.   [5] Amos Kendall.

To Jonathan R. Diller[1]

Friend Diller: Washington Jany. 19 1848

Your letter of the 27th. Decr. was received only the day before yesterday. The very best I can do with your case, I will. Send to me just as soon as you can, the affidavit of one of your clerks, showing the number of mails you receive per week; the number you send away per week; the number of pounds weight of mails you handle daily, besides that stopping at your own office; the number of hands, including yourself, you have to constantly employ; and what you pay them; how many hours out of the twentyfour you are obliged to be up and at work; and how much you have to pay annually, besides clerk-hire, for matters connected with the office, which the Govt. does not allow you for. Whether Govt. allows for room-rent, candles, and fuel, I dont know, but if it does not, these will fall in the item last mentioned. If, in this way you can show that your compensation is too small, I think I can get it increased; but the bare fact that you get less than you used to do, will not enable me to get along. We have had one such case, which was sneered out of court. I am really interested for you, & wish you to lose no time in doing as I tell you. Show this letter to Logan, and get him to frame the affidavit—adding any thing that may occur to you or him which I may have forgotten.

Tell Hickox[2] I received his claim, and will do the best with it [I] can; but that I fear I can not get along with it.

I am kept very busy here; and one thing that perplexes me more than most any thing else, are the cases of whigs calling on me to get them appointments to places in the army, from the President. There are two great obstacles in the way which they do not seem to understand—first, the President has no such appointments to give—and secondly, if he had, he could hardly be expected to give

them to whigs, at the solicitation of a whig Member of Congress.
Yours truly   A. LINCOLN

¹ ALS, ORB. Jonathan R. Diller was postmaster at Springfield, Illinois.
² Probably Virgil Hickox, who was in the mercantile business in Springfield.

To William H. Herndon¹

Washington, January 19, 1848.
Dear William: Inclosed you find a letter of Louis W. Chandler.
What is wanted is that you shall ascertain whether the claim upon
the note described has received any dividend in the Probate Court
of Christian County, where the estate of Mr. Overton Williams has
been administered on. If nothing is paid on it, withdraw the note
and send it to me, so that Chandler can see the indorser of it. At
all events write me all about it, till I can somehow get it off my
hands. I have already been bored more than enough about it; not
the least of which annoyance is his cursed, unreadable, and un-
godly handwriting.
I have made a speech, a copy of which I will send you by next
mail. Yours as ever,   A. LINCOLN.

¹ NH, I, 350-51.

To Samuel D. Marshall¹

Dear Sam: Washington. Jany. 22. 1848
Your letter of the 15th. is received: Your letter to me concerning
our Dorman Case² was also received, while I was very busy preparing to start on here. I handed the letter to Judge Logan and ex-
torted a special promise from him to examine the case & write you.
Although I know the Judge to be growing somewhat negligent, I
did not doubt that, from the peculiarity of this case, and his very
assuring promise, he would attend to it. I *know* he intended to do
it; but I suppose he has forgotten it. I know nothing that I can here
do in the matter.
As to the matter of your lost horse, I will look into it, & do something if I can. Yours truly   A. LINCOLN

¹ ALS, ICHi   ² See earlier letters to Marshall in reference to this case.

To William Thomas¹

[c. January 28, 1848]
Not perceiving that these letters can aid me any in your business,
and thinking possibly the Solicitors letter to you may miscarry, and

[445]

not seeing how I can do any thing till a further hearing from you, I enclose them to you. Yours as ever   A. LINCOLN
   Hon. Wm. Thomas.

¹ ALS, IaDaM. This note is written on the bottom of a letter from R. H. Field (?), solicitor of the treasury, to Lincoln, dated January 28, 1848. William Thomas was an attorney of Jacksonville, Illinois.

To J. M. McCalla¹

Mr. J. M. McCalla: Washington,
Dear Sir: Jany. 29. 1848
   A young man by the name of Andrew Hodge, went to Mexico as a volunteer in Capt. Elkin's² company in the 4th. Regiment of Illinois volunteers, command[ed] by Col. Baker.³ He died somewhere on the Rio Grande in the fall of 1846. His father, W. H. Hodge,⁴ wishes to draw the arrearage of his pay, and also to get his land warrant. He writes me that he sent the papers to your office last summer, and received a note from you acknowledging the receipt of them, since when, he has heard nothing about the matter. Will you please inform me what, if any thing, I can do to advance the matter? Very Respectfully   A. LINCOLN.

¹ ALS, IHi. McCalla was the second auditor in the Treasury Department. (See Lincoln to Walter Davis, June 26, 1848, and endorsement to General McCalla, on the same date, *infra*.)
² Garrett Elkin, brother of William F. Elkin, was captain of a company from Bloomington, Illinois.   ³ Edward D. Baker.
⁴ A resident of Bloomington, Illinois.

To William H. Herndon¹

Dear William: Washington, Feb. 1– 1848
   Your letter of the 19th. ult. was received last night, and for which I am much obliged. The only thing in it that I wish to talk to you about at once, is that, because of my vote for Mr. Ashmun's² amendment, you fear that you and I disagree about the war. I regret this, not because of any fear we shall remain disagreed, after you shall have read this letter, but because, if *you* misunderstand, I fear other good friends will also. That vote affirms that the war was unnecessarily and unconstitutionally commenced by the President; and I will stake my life, that if you had been in my place, you would have voted just as I did. Would you have voted what you felt you knew to be a lie? I know

you would not. Would you have gone out of the House—skulked the vote? I expect not. If you had skulked one vote, you would have had to skulk many more, before the end of the session. Richardson's[3] resolutions, introduced before I made any move, or gave any vote upon the subject, make the direct question of the justice of the war; so that no man can be silent if he would. You are compelled to speak; and your only alternative is to tell the *truth* or tell a *lie*. I can not doubt which you would do.

This vote, has nothing to do, in determining my votes on the questions of supplies. I have always intended, and still intend, to vote supplies; perhaps not in the precise form recommended by the President, but in a better form for all purposes, except locofoco party purposes. It is in this particular you seem to be mistaken. The locos are untiring in their effort to make the impression that all who vote supplies, or take part in the war, do, of necessity, approve the Presidents conduct in the beginning of it; but the whigs have, from the beginning, made and kept the distinction between the two. In the very first act, nearly all the whigs voted *against* the preamble declaring that war existed by the act of Mexico, and yet nearly all of them voted *for* the supplies. As to the whig men who have participated in the war, so far as they have spoken to my hearing, they do not hesitate to denounce, as unjust, the Presidents conduct in the beginning of the war. They do not suppose that such denunciation, is dictated by undying hatred to them, as the Register would have it believed. There are two such whigs on this floor, Col. Haskell,[4] and Major Gaines[5]. The former, fought as a Col. by the side of Col. Baker[6] at Cerro Gordo, and stands side by side with me, in the vote, that you seem to be dissatisfied with. The latter, the history of whose capture with Cassius Clay, you well know, had not arrived here when that vote was given; but as I understand, he stands ready to give just such a vote, whenever an occasion shall present. Baker too, who is now here, says the truth is undoubtedly that way, and whenever he shall speak out, he will say so. Col. Donaphin [*sic*][7] too, the favourite whig of Missouri, and who over ran all Northern Mexico, on his return home in a public speech at St. Louis, condemned the administration in relation to the war as I remember. G. T. M Davis,[8] who has been through almost the whole war, declares in favour of Mr. Clay, from which I infer that he adopts the sentiments of Mr. Clay, generally at least. On the other hand, I have heard of but one whig, who has been to the war, attempting to justify the President's conduct. That one is Capt. Bishop,[9] editor of the Charleston Courier, and a very clever fellow.

I do not mean this letter for the public, but for you. Before it reaches you, you will have seen and read my pamphlet speech,[10] and perhaps, scared anew, by it. After you get over your scare, read it over again, sentence by sentence, and tell me honestly what you think of it. I condensed all I could for fear of being cut off by the hour rule, and when I got through, I had spoke but 45 minutes. Yours forever   A. LINCOLN

[1] ALS, InU.
[2] George Ashmun of Massachusetts, Whig. His amendment was to a resolution of thanks to General Taylor for his victory at Buena Vista. This censure of President Polk was passed by the House, 82 to 81.
[3] William A. Richardson of Schuyler County, Illinois, Democrat, whose resolutions were defeated.   [4] William T. Haskell of Tennessee.
[5] John P. Gaines of Kentucky.   [6] Edward D. Baker of Illinois.
[7] Alexander W. Doniphan.
[8] George T. M. Davis, a lawyer at Alton, Illinois, and lieutenant in the Illinois Volunteers.   [9] William W. Bishop.
[10] See under date of January 12, 1848 (*supra*).

To William H. Herndon[1]

Dear William: Washington, Feb: 2. 1848
I just take up my pen to say, that Mr. Stephens[2] of Georgia, a little slim, pale-faced, consumptive man, with a voice like Logan's[3] has just concluded the very best speech, of an hour's length, I ever heard.
My old, withered, dry eyes, are full of tears yet.
If he writes it out any thing like he delivered it, our people shall see a good many copies of it.[4] Yours truly   A. LINCOLN

[1] ALS, ORB.
[2] Alexander H. Stephens, Whig, member of congress 1843-1859.
[3] Stephen T. Logan.
[4] See *Congressional Globe Appendix*, Thirtieth Congress, First Session, pp. 159-63. Stephens vigorously denounced the Mexican War as an aggression to "force and compel" the people of Mexico to sell their country.

To Andrew McCallen[1]

Friend McCallen: Washington, Feb. 4. 1848
Yours of the 20th. Jany. is received. There is now some probability of peace; but, should the war go on, I think volunteers, with the right of electing their own officers will be voted, but that no more regulars, will be voted. Until Congress shall act, of course, nothing can be done towards getting your Regiment into the ser-

vice. Whenever it shall act I shall be happy to assist you in any way I can. Yours truly   A. LINCOLN

P. S. Dont pay postage on letters to me. I am entitled to them free.
                                                        A. L.

1 ALS, ORB. McCallen was a merchant and lawyer of Shawneetown, Illinois.

To Taylor Committee[1]

                                        House of Representatives,
Gentlemen: Washington, Feb. 9, 1848.

Your letter inviting me to attend a meeting on the 22d instant, at Philadelphia, to nominate General Taylor for the Presidency, subject to the decision of a National Convention, has been received. It will not be convenient for me to attend,[2] yet I take the occasion to say, I am decidedly in favor of General Taylor as the Whig candidate for the next Presidency. I am the only Whig member of Congress from Illinois, so that the meeting will probably hear nothing from that State, unless it be from me through the medium of this letter. For this reason I think proper to say, that during the last summer a convention was held in that State for the purpose of amending her constitution; that, in that convention, there were, as I remember, some more than seventy Whig members; that, at a meeting of those Whig members, they nominated General Taylor for the Presidency; and that, with the exception of a very few, (not more than six I believe,) they subscribed their names to that nomination and published it to the world. These delegates of course were not elected to nominate a candidate for the Presidency, nor did they, in the matter, assume to act in any capacity other than as so many individuals expressing their own preferences; still, coming from all parts of the State as they did, their action, together with other facts falling within my observation, leave no doubt in my mind that the preference of the Whigs of the State is the same.

Those Whig delegates said nothing as to a National Convention, as far as I can remember, nor has any thing transpired since enabling me to determine what is the disposition of the Whigs of Illinois on the subject; still it is my expectation that they will send delegates to the Convention, as I think it will be proper that they should. Very respectfully,   A. LINCOLN.

1 *Great Whig Demonstration in Favor of the Nomination of Gen. Taylor to the Presidency: The Buena Vista Festival, at Philadelphia, February 22, 1848* (Philadelphia, J. & G. S. Gideon, Printers, 1848), p. 26.

2 Lincoln and Stephen A. Douglas were the Illinois delegation on the committee in charge of the celebration of Washington's birthday, and hence Lincoln

could not well attend the Philadelphia rally. The celebration was, however, postponed because of the impending death of John Quincy Adams, who was stricken in the House on February 21 and died on February 23, Lincoln being a member of the committee in charge of the funeral.

To Josephus Hewett[1]

Dear Hewett: Washington, Feb. 13. 1848.

Your whig representative from Mississippi, P. W. Tompkins,[2] has just shown me a letter of yours to him. I am jealous because you did not write to me. Perhaps you have forgotten me. Dont you remember a long black fellow who rode on horseback with you from Tremont to Springfield nearly ten years ago, swiming your horses over the Mackinaw on the trip? Well, I am that same one fellow yet. I was once of your opinion, expressed in your letter, that presidential electors should be dispensed with; but a more thorough knowledge of the causes that first introduced them, has made me doubt. Those causes were briefly these. The convention that framed the constitution had this difficulty: the small states wished to so frame the new government as that they might be equal to the large ones regardless of the inequality of population; the large ones insisted on equality in proportion to population. They compromised it, by basing the House of Representatives on *population*, and the Senate on *states* regardless of population; and the executive on both principles, by electors in each state, equal in numbers to her senators *and* representatives. Now, throw away the machinery of electors, and the compromise is broken up, and the whole yielded to the principle of the large states. There is one thing more. In the slave states, you have representatives, and consequently, electors, partly upon the basis of your black population, which would be swept away by the change you seem to think desireable. Have you ever reflected on these things?

But to come to the main point, I wish you to know that I have made a speech in congress, and that I want you to be *enlightened* by reading it; to further which object, I send a copy of the speech by this mail.

For old acquaintance sake, if for nothing else, be sure to write me on receiving this. I was very near forgetting to tell you that on my being introduced to Genl. Quitman,[3] and telling him I was from Springfield, Illinois, he at once remarked "Then you are acquainted with my valued friend Hewett of Natchez," and on being assured I was, he said just such things about you as I like to hear said about my own valued friends. Yours as ever

A. LINCOLN

[450]

1 ALS-P, ISLA. Hewett had formerly practiced law in Springfield, Illinois, but was in 1848 a resident of Natchez, Mississippi.
2 Patrick W. Tompkins was a Whig who stayed at the same boarding house as did Lincoln.
3 John A. Quitman, Democrat, lawyer, member of the Mississippi House of Representatives 1826-1827, chancellor of the state 1828-1835, senator 1835-1836, brigadier general of Volunteers 1846, major general in Regular Army 1847.

To William H. Herndon[1]

Dear William: Washington, Feb. 15. 1848

Your letter of the 29th. Jany. was received last night. Being exclusively a constitutional argument, I wish to submit some reflections upon it in the same spirit of kindness that I know actuates you. Let me first state what I understand to be your position. It is, that if it shall become *necessary, to repel invasion,* the President may, without violation of the Constitution, cross the line, and *invade* the teritory of another country; and that whether such *necessity* exists in any given case, the President is to be the *sole* judge.

Before going further, consider well whether this is, or is not your position. If it is, it is a position that neither the President hmiself, nor any friend of his, so far as I know, has ever taken. Their only positions are first, that the soil was *ours* where hostilities commenced, and second, that whether it was rightfully *ours* or not, *Congress had annexed it,* and the President, for that reason was bound to defend it, both of which are as clearly proved to be false in fact, as you can prove that your house is not mine. That soil was not ours; and Congress did not annex or attempt to annex it. But to return to your position: Allow the President to invade a neighboring nation, whenever *he* shall deem it necessary to repel an invasion, and you allow him to do so, *whenever he may choose to say* he deems it necessary for such purpose—and you allow him to make war at pleasure. Study to see if you can fix *any limit* to his power in this respect, after you have given him so much as you propose. If, to-day, he should choose to say he thinks it necessary to invade Canada, to prevent the British from invading us, how could you stop him? You may say to him, "I see no probability of the British invading us" but he will say to you "be silent; I see it, if you dont."

The provision of the Constitution giving the war-making power to Congress, was dictated, as I understand it, by the following reasons. Kings had always been involving and impoverishing their people in wars, pretending generally, if not always, that the good of the people was the object. This, our Convention understood to be the most oppressive of all Kingly oppressions; and they resolved to so frame the Constitution that *no one man* should hold the power of bringing this oppression upon us. But your view destroys the whole matter, and places our President where kings have always stood. Write soon again. Yours truly, A. LINCOLN

1 ALS, MH.

To Halsey O. or Amos L. Merriman[1]

Dear Merriman: Washington, Feb. 16. 1848

Your letter, asking me to procure passports, has been received. I have just been to Mr. Buchanan,[2] who turned me over to an understrapper, which understrapper, suspended the application on the ground that the affidavit of the applicant is not sufficient evidence of naturalization. He gave me a printed circular showing exactly what is to be done, which I transmit to you, together with some extra copies to be kept for future use. Yours truly

A. LINCOLN.

1 ALS, owned by Edward D. McCulloch, Peoria, Illinois. Halsey O. Merriman was an attorney of Peoria, Illinois, associated in practice with a younger brother, Amos L. Merriman. It is not known conclusively to which one of the brothers the letter was written. 2 James Buchanan, secretary of state.

To Thomas S. Flournoy[1]

Hon: T. S. Florney, H. R. Feb: 17. 1848–
Dear Sir:

In answer to your enquiries, I have to say I am in favor of Gen: Taylor as the whig candidate for the Presidency because I am satisfied we can elect him, that he would give us a whig administration, and that we can not elect any other whig.

In Illinois, his being our candidate, would *certainly* give us one additional member of Congress, if not more; and *probably* would give us the electoral vote of the state. That with him, we can, in that state, make great inroads among the rank and file of the democrats, to my mind is certain; but the majority against us there, is so great, that I can no more than express my *belief* that we can carry the state. Very respectfully A. LINCOLN

1 ALS, The Rosenbach Company, Philadelphia and New York. Flournoy's name was misspelled by Lincoln. He was a Whig member of the Thirtieth Congress from Virginia.

To William H. Young[1]

Dear Sir: Washington—Feb. 17, 1848.

Your letter in relation to various claims for bounty lands, has been received, and laid before the Commissioner of Pensions. So soon as he shall examine them and give me an answer, I will write you, enclosing it. Hurra for Gen: Taylor. Yours truly

Wm. H. Young   A LINCOLN.

[1] Copy, ISLA (tracing made from original by the late Herbert W. Fay, Springfield, Illinois). William H. Young, of Mount Pulaski, Illinois, had served in the Fourth Illinois throughout the Mexican War. See also letter of August 28, 1848, *infra*.

To Usher F. Linder[1]

Dear Linder: Washington, Feb. 20. 1848–

In law it is good policy to never *plead* what you *need* not, lest you oblige yourself to *prove* what you *can* not. Reflect on this well before you proceed. The application I mean to make of this rule is, that you should simply go for Genl. Taylor; because by this, you can take some democrats, and lose no whigs; but if you go also for Mr. Polk on the origin and mode of prossecuting the war, you will still take some democrats, but you will lose more whigs, so that in the sum of the opperation you will be loser. This is at least my opinion; and if you will look round, I doubt, if you do not discover such to be the fact amongst your own neighbors. Further than this: By justifying Mr. Polk's mode of prossecuting the war, you put yourself in opposition to Genl. Taylor himself, for we all know he has declared for, and, in fact originated, the defensive line policy.

You know I mean this in kindness, and wish it to be confidential. Yours as ever   A. LINCOLN

[1] ALS-P, ISLA.

To Noah W. Matheny[1]

Dear Noah: [c. February 21, 1848]

Please forward the Receivers receipt to Judge Young as commissioner.   A. LINCOLN

[1] ALS, owned by Noah M. Dixon, Springfield, Illinois. This note is written on the bottom of a letter to Lincoln from Richard M. Young, commissioner of the General Land Office, dated February 21, 1848. Young's letter transmits a land patent in favor of John W. Stringfield of Sangamon County.

Fragment: What General Taylor Ought to Say[1]

[March ?] 1848

The question of a national bank is at rest; were I President I should not urge it's reagitation upon Congress; but should Congress see fit to pass an act to establish such an institution, I should not arrest it by the veto, unless I should consider it subject to some constitutional objection, from which I believe the two former banks to have been free.

It appears to me that the national debt created by the war, renders a modification of the existing tariff indispensable; and when it shall be modified, I should be pleased to see it adjusted with a due reference to the protection of our home industry. The particulars, it appears to me, must and should be left to the untramelled discretion of Congress.

As to the Mexican war, I still think the defensive line policy the best to terminate it. In a final treaty of peace, we shall probably be under a sort of necessity of taking some teritory; but it is my desire that we shall not acquire any extending so far South, as to enlarge and agrivate the distracting question of slavery. Should I come into the presidency before these questions shall be settled, I should act in relation to them in accordance with the views here expressed.

Finally, were I president, I should desire the legislation of the country to rest with Congress, uninfluenced by the executive in it's origin or progress, and undisturbed by the veto unless in very special and clear cases.

[1] ADf, DLC-RTL. The date given to this document by Nicolay and Hay is "July 1?" Since the third paragraph indicates that termination of the Mexican War is in the future, the July date is untenable, peace having been made in May. The tenor of Lincoln's suggestions leads to the conclusion that the fragment was written several weeks earlier, while Lincoln was actively supporting Taylor in his correspondence with fellow Whigs. The date assigned here seems as appropriate as can be assigned on the available evidence. The title given is taken from what seems to have been supplied on the document by John Hay, "What Gen Taylor ought to say."

To Jesse W. Fell[1]

Friend Fell.   Washington March 1, 1848

Your kind letter of the 7th. Feb: enclosing a petition for peace, was received a day or two ago. I shall present it at the proper time.

It now seems to be understood on all hands that the war is over —that the treaty sent in will be ratified.

I will try to get the time to write you a longer letter soon; but I am really too much hurried to do so now. Yours as ever,

J. W. Fell   A. LINCOLN.
Payson Ills.

1 ALS, owned by Mrs. Harriet F. Richardson, Milwaukee, Wisconsin.

To Richard S. Thomas[1]

Friend Richard: Washington March 1, 1848.

Your letter of the 12th. Feb., toegther with the petition for a mail route was received last night. Strange it was on the road so long. I shall present the petition,[2] and give it my best attention.

Your second letter was received; and I thought I had answered it. I am not a candidate for re-nomination or election.

Excuse the shortness of this letter; I am really very much hurried. Yours as ever   A. LINCOLN

R. S. Thomas,
Virginia, Ills.

1 Copy, DLC-HW.
2 See letters to Thomas, March 30, June 13 and 15, 1848, *infra*.

To Ignatius R. Simms[1]

Major Simms   Washington,
Dear Sir: March 4– 1848–

Whenever I am directing documents to persons at Jacksonville, I am annoyed at not being able to remember the christian name of your son who formerly resided at Metamora in Woodford county.[2] I esteem him as one of my best friends; and you will oblige me by handing him this letter, and telling him to write me at once about any thing he pleases, so that I can get his name right.

It is considered doubtful whether the Senate will ratify the treaty now under advisement; but whether they shall or not, all hands seem to agree that the war is substantially ended. Yours truly   A. LINCOLN

1 ALS, IHi. Simms was a hotelkeeper in Jacksonville.
2 Probably Chattam Simms.

To Solomon Lincoln[1]

Mr. Solomon Lincoln,   Washington,
Dear Sir: March 6– 1848

Your letter to Mr. Hale,[2] in which you do me the honor of making some kind enquiries concerning me, has been handed me by

[455]

Mr. Hale, with the request that I should give you the desired information. I was born Feb: 12th. 1809 in Hardin county, Kentucky. My father's name is *Thomas;* my grandfather's was *Abraham,*—the same of [*sic*] my own. My grandfather went from Rockingham county in Virginia, to Kentucky, about the year 1782; and, two years afterwards, was killed by the indians. We have a vague tradition, that my great-grand father went from Pennsylvania to Virginia; and that he was a quaker. Further back than this, I have never heard any thing. It may do no harm to say that "Abraham" and "Mordecai" are common names in our family; while the name "Levi" so common among the Lincolns of New England, I have not known in any instance among us.

Owing to my father being left an orphan at the age of six years, in poverty, and in a new country, he became a wholly uneducated man; which I suppose is the reason why I know so little of our family history. I believe I can say nothing more that would at all interest you. If you shall be able to trace any connection between yourself and me, or, in fact, whether you shall or not, I should be pleased to have a line from you at any time. Very respectfully   A. LINCOLN

1 ALS, The Rosenbach Company, Philadelphia and New York. Solomon Lincoln was a citizen of Hingham, Massachusetts, whence Abraham Lincoln's ancestors had come, though the fact was unknown to him at this time. Solomon and Abraham were distantly related.

2 Artemas Hale, Whig representative from Massachusetts. Solomon Lincoln's letter was dated March 2.

Report to United States House of Representatives Concerning H. M. Barney[1]

March 9, 1848

Mr. LINCOLN, from the Committee on the Post Office and Post Roads, made the following R E P O R T:

The Committee on the Post Office and Post Roads, to whom was referred the petition of H. M. Barney, postmaster at Brimfield, Peoria county, Illinois, report:

That they have been satisfied by evidence, that on the 15th of December, 1847, said petitioner had his store, with some fifteen hundred dollars worth of goods, together with all the papers of the post office, entirely destroyed by fire; and that the specie funds of the office were melted down, partially lost, and partially destroyed; that his large individual loss entirely precludes the idea of embezzlement; that the balances due the department of former quarters has been only about twenty-five dollars; and that owing to the destruction of the papers, the exact amount due for the quarter ending December 31st, 1847, cannot be ascertained. They therefore report a joint resolution, releasing said petitioner from paying anything for the quarter last mentioned.[2]

[1] *Reports of Committees,* Thirtieth Congress, First Session, Vol. II, No. 326. The original document cannot be found in The National Archives.

[2] H.R. Joint Resolution 18, passed the House on April 7, but died in the Senate. The original document cannot be located in The National Archives, and it cannot be certified that Lincoln wrote it.

To Usher F. Linder[1]

Friend Linder: Washington, March 22– 1848–

Yours of the 15th. is just received, as was a day or two ago, one from Dunbar[2] on the same subject. Although I address this to you alone, I intend it for you [,] Dunbar, and Bishop,[3] and wish you to show it to them. In Dunbar's letter, and in Bishop's paper, it is assumed that Mr. Crittenden's[4] position on the war is correct. Well, so I think. Please wherein is my position different from his? Has *he* ever approved the President's conduct in the beginning of the war, or his mode or objects in prossecuting it? Never. He condemns both. True, he votes supplies, and so do I. What, then, is the difference, except that he is a great man and I am a small one?

Towards the close of your letter you ask three questions, the first of which is "Would it not have been just as easy to have elected Genl. Taylor without opposing the war as by opposing it?" I answer, I suppose it would, if we could do *neither*—could be *silent* on the question; but the Locofocos here will not let the whigs be *silent*. Their very first act in congress was to present a preamble declaring that war existed by the act of Mexico, and the whigs were obliged to vote on it—and this policy is followed up by them; so that they are compelled to *speak* and their only option is whether they will, when they do speak, tell the *truth*, or tell a foul, villainous, and bloody falsehood. But, while on this point, I protest against your calling the condemnation of Polk "opposing the war." In thus assuming that all must be opposed to the war, even though they vote supplies, who do not not [*sic*] endorse Polk, with due deference I say I think you fall into one of the artfully set traps of Locofocoism.

Your next question is "And suppose we could succeed in proving it a wicked and unconstitutional war, do we not thereby strip Taylor and Scott of more than half their laurels?" Whether it would so strip them is not matter of demonstration, but of *opinion* only; and my opinion is that it would not; but as your opinion seems to be different, let us call in some others as umpire. There are in this H.R. some more than forty members who support Genl. Taylor for the Presidency, every one of whom has voted that the war was "unnecessarily and unconstitutionally commenced by the President" every one of whom has spoken to the same effect, who has spoken at all, and not one of whom supposes he thereby strips Genl. of any laurels. More than this; two of these, Col. Haskell[5] and Major Gaines,[6] themselves fought in Mexico; and yet they vote and speak just as the rest of us do, without ever dreaming that they "strip" themselves of any laurels. There may be others, but Capt. Bishop is the only intelligent whig who has been to Mexico, that I have heard of taking different ground.

Your third question is "And have we as a party, ever gained any thing, by falling in company with abolitionists?" Yes. We gained our only national victory by falling in company with them in the election of Genl. Harrison. Not that we fell into abolition doctrines; but that we took up a man whose position induced them to join us in his election. But this question is not so significant as a *question*, as it is as a charge of abolitionism against those who have chosen to speak their minds against the President. As you and I perhaps would again differ as to the justice of this charge, let us once more call in our umpire. There are in this H.R. whigs from the slave states as follows: one from Louisiana, one from Mississippi, one from Florida, two from Alabama, four from Georgia, five from Tennessee, six from Kentucky, six from North Carolina, six from Virginia, four from Maryland and one from Delaware, making thirtyseven in all, and all slave-holders, every one of whom votes the commencement of the war "unnecessary and unconstitutional" and so falls subject to your charge of abolitionism!

"*En passant*" these are all *Taylor* men, except one in Tenn. two in Ky, one in N.C. and one in Va. Besides which we have one in Ills—two in Ia, three in Ohio, five in Penn. four in N.J. and one in Conn. While this is less than half the whigs of the H.R. it is three times as great as the strength of any other one candidate.

You are mistaken in your impression that any one has communicated expressions of yours and Bishop's to me. In my letter to Dunbar, I only spoke from the impression made by seeing in the paper that you and he were, "in the degree, though not in the extreme" on the same tack with Latshaw.[7] Yours as ever

A. LINCOLN

[1] ALS, IHi.   [2] Alexander P. Dunbar.   [3] Captain William W. Bishop.
[4] Senator John J. Crittenden.
[5] Representative William T. Haskell of Tennessee.
[6] Representative John Pollard Gaines of Kentucky.
[7] William D. Latshaw of Coles County, Illinois.

To David Lincoln[1]

Mr. David Lincoln   Washington,
Dear Sir: March 24th. 1848.

Your very worthy representative, Gov. McDowell[2] has given me
your name and address, and, as my my [*sic*] father was born in
Rockingham, from whence his father, Abraham Lincoln, emi-
grated to Kentucky, about the year 1782, I have concluded to address you to ascertain whether we are not of the same family. I
shall be much obliged, if you will write me, telling me, whether
you, in any way, know any thing of my grandfather, what relation
you are to him, and so on. Also, if you know, where your family
came from, when they settled in Virginia, tracing them back as
far as your knowledge extends. Very respectfully

A. LINCOLN

[1] ALS, original owned by Abraham Lucius Lincoln, Lawrenceville, New
Jersey.   [2] James McDowell.

To Solomon Lincoln[1]

Mr. Solomon Lincoln   Washington,
Dear Sir: March 24– 1848

Yours of the 21st. is received. I shall not be able to answer your
interrogatories very fully; I will, however, do the best I can. I have
mentioned that my grandfather's name was Abraham. He had, as
I think I have heard, four brothers, Isaac, Jacob, Thomas, and
John. He had three sons, Mordecai, Josiah, and Thomas, the last,
my father. My uncle Mordecai, had three sons, Abraham, James,
and Mordecai. Uncle Josiah had several daughters, and an only
son, Thomas. My father has an only child, myself, of course.

This is all I know certainly on the subject of names; it is, however, my father's understanding that, Abraham[,] Mordecai, and
Thomas are old family names of ours. The reason I did not mention Thomas as a family name in my other letter was because it is
so very common a name, as to prove but little, if any thing, in the
way of identification.

Since I wrote you, it occurred to me to enquire of Gov. Mc-
Dowell,[2] who represents the district in Virginia, including Rockingham, whether he knew persons of our name there. He informs
he does; though none very intimately except one, an old man by
the christian name of David. That he is of our family I have no
doubt. I now address him a letter, making such enquiries as suggest themselves; and, when I shall receive an answer, I will com-

municate to you, any thing that may seem pertinent to your object. Very truly yours   A. LINCOLN

1 ALS, The Rosenbach Company, Philadelphia and New York.
2 James McDowell.

Remarks in
United States House of Representatives
Concerning Military Bounty Lands[1]

March 29, 1848

Mr. LINCOLN said, if there was a general desire on the part of the House to pass the bill now,[2] he should be glad to have it done—concurring, as he did generally, with the gentleman from Arkansas, [Mr. JOHNSON,][3] that the postponement might jeopard the safety of the proposition. If, however, a reference was to be made, he wished to make a very few remarks in relation to the several subjects desired by the gentlemen to be embraced in amendments to the ninth section of the act of the last session of Congress. The first amendment desired by members of this House had for its only object to give bounty lands to such persons as had served for a time as privates, but had never been discharged as such, because promoted to office. That subject, and no other, was embraced in this bill. There were some others who desired, while they were legislating on this subject, that they should also give bounty lands to the volunteers of the war of 1812. His friend from Maryland said there were no such men. He (Mr. L.) did not say there were many, but he was very confident there were some. His friend from Kentucky near him [Mr. GAINES] told him he himself was one.

There was still another proposition touching this matter: that was, that persons entitled to bounty land should by law be entitled to locate these lands in parcels, and not be required to locate them in one body, as was provided by the existing law.

Now, he had carefully drawn up a bill[4] embracing these three separate propositions, which he intended to propose as a substitute for all these bills in the House, or in Committee of the Whole on the state of the Union, at some suitable time. If there was a disposition on the part of the House to act at once on this separate proposition, he repeated that, with the gentleman from Arkansas, he should prefer it, lest they should lose all. But if there was to be a reference, he desired to introduce his bill embracing the three propositions, thus enabling the committee and the House to act at the same time, whether favorably or unfavorably, upon all. He inquired whether an amendment was now in order?

The SPEAKER replied in the negative.

¹ *Congressional Globe*, Thirtieth Congress, First Session, p. 550.

² A bill reported from the committee on the judiciary by Richard French of Kentucky, "to amend An act to raise, for a limited time, an additional military force, and for other purposes." Similar bills had been reported from the committee on public lands and the committee on military affairs.

³ Robert W. Johnson of Arkansas.

⁴ There is no further reference to this bill.

To Richard S. Thomas¹

Dear Richard: Washington, March 30, 1848

Having a few leisure moments, I employ them to say a word about your petition concerning school lands. The petition was referred to the Land Committee, of which I am not a member; so that, while in committee, I can have no direct agency in the matter. McClernand² of our state, is on that committee; and he told me yesterday, or the day before, that the committee had unanimously determined to do nothing in the matter, so far as concerns the townships which have entire sixteenth sections, but which are of little or no value; because to enter upon this, would be to break up the entire present system of school lands throughout the United States, which would be immensely inconvenient, and which, after all, could never result in any thing much nearer equality than the present system. He says the committee are for the petition, so far as concerns fractional townships, which have *no* sixteenth section, or only fractional ones, containing less than a thirtysixth of the land of the township. He says they think there is already an old law concerning the case; and that they are investigating it, and if necessary to effect the object, they will report a bill accordingly.

Yours as ever A. LINCOLN.

¹ Copy, DLC-HW. ² John A. McClernand.

To David Lincoln¹

Dear Sir, Washington, April 2nd. 1848

Last evening I was much gratified by receiving and reading your letter of the 30th. of March. There is no longer any doubt that your uncle Abraham, and my grandfather was the same man. His family did reside in Washington county, Kentucky, just as you say you found them in 1801 or 2. The oldest son, uncle Mordecai, near twenty years ago, removed from Kentucky to Hancock county, Illinois, where within a year or two afterwards, he died, and where his surviving children now live. His two sons there now are Abraham & Mordecai; and their Post-office is "La Harp[e]."

Uncle Josiah, farther back than my recollection, went from Kentucky to Blue River in Indiana. I have not heard from him in a great many years, and whether he is still living I can not say. My recollection of what I have heard is, that he has several daughters & only one son, Thomas. Their Post-office is "Corydon, Harrisson county, Indiana.

My father, Thomas, is still living, in Coles county Illinois, being in the 71st. year of his age. His Post-office is Charleston, Coles co. Ill. I am his only child. I am now in my 40th. year; and I live in Springfield, Sangamon county, Illinois. This is the outline of my grandfather's family in the West.

I think my father has told me that grandfather had four brothers, Isaac, Jacob, John and Thomas. Is that correct? and which of them was your father? Are any of them alive? I am quite sure that Isaac resided on Wata[u]ga, near a point where Virginia and Tennessee join; and that he has been dead more than twenty, perhaps thirty, years. Also, that Thomas removed to Kentucky, near Lexington, where he died a good while ago.

What was your grandfather's christian name? Was he or not, a Quaker? About what *time* did he emigrate from Berks county, Pa. to Virginia? Do you know any thing of your family (or rather I may now say, *our* family) farther back than your grandfather?

If it be not too much trouble to you, I shall be much pleased to hear from you again. Be assured I will call on you, should any thing ever bring me near you. I shall give your respects to Gov. McDowell,[2] as you desire. Very truly yours— A. LINCOLN—

[1] ALS, original owned by Abraham Lucius Lincoln, Lawrenceville, New Jersey.   [2] James McDowell.

Discussion in United States House of Representatives[1]

April 3, 1848

Mr. LINCOLN moved to suspend the rules of the House to take up the joint resolution from the Senate relative to contracts for the purchase of hemp for the use of the navy, for the purpose of referring it to the Committee on Naval Affairs.

Mr. HOUSTON,[2] of Alabama, suggested to the gentleman from Illinois that he would accomplish his object by modifying his motion so as to embrace all the bills and resolutions from the Senate lying on the Speaker's table.

Mr. LINCOLN replied to the gentleman from Alabama, that he was aware of that fact when he made the motion.

Mr. HOUSTON would then inquire whether the motion was susceptible of amendment.

No reply was heard. If any, it was presumed to be in the negative.

The SPEAKER announced the question to be on the motion of Mr. LINCOLN.[3]

[1] *Congressional Globe*, Thirtieth Congress, First Session, p. 571.
[2] George S. Houston.   [3] Lincoln's motion was defeated.

To Jesse Lynch[1]

Dear Sir: Washington, April 10– 1848–

Your letter of the 27th. of March is received. I went to the Patent office with it this morning. They tell me that no patent has [been] issued to any body on any application made as late as the first of July last. Mr. Jones[2] is dead—died a few weeks ago. The officers say he was trust-worthy. If you write again, mention the names of the applicants, as I have mislaid your former letter. I am almost too busy to undertake an agency, besides which, I shall have to leave before the business can be got through with; still, if you choose, I will try to get any business for you into the hands of some one having the reputation of a faithful agent.

On the same day I received your letter, I also received one from another man in Magnolia, which contrasts very curiously with what you say about Gen: Taylor. He says he knows ten men in Magnolia, who voted for Mr. Clay, that can not be got to vote for Gen. Taylor, under any circumstances. I am sorry to hear what he says, and glad to hear what you say. Our only chance is with Taylor. I go for him, not because I think he would make a better president than Clay, but because I think he would make a better one than Polk, or Cass, or Buchanan, or any such creatures, one of whom is sure to be elected, if he is not.

As to what you say about the next representative of our district, I can only say that I can not become a competitor with others for the nomination. I have said I will not. I would deny the people nothing—but I presume there are many others who will be quite as acceptable as myself. Lest I be misunderstood, dont let any one

[463]

know I have written you any thing on this subject. I should not, had you not requested it. Most truly yours   A. LINCOLN—

[1] ALS, owned by Henry W. Lynch, Peoria, Illinois. Jesse Lynch was a resident of Magnolia, Illinois.
[2] Unidentified, but apparently a patent attorney in Washington.

To Walter Davis[1]

Dear Walter: Washington, April 14– 1848

Your letter, together with the Power of Attorney of your mother, and the discharge of your brother, has been received. I have just been to the proper office with them. They got me to certify[2] that I knew Thomas, that Maria Davis was his mother, and was still living, that his father is dead, and that Thomas himself was never married. They took the certificate and the papers you sent me, and promised to investigate the matter as soon as possible, and notify me of the result; which, when they do, I will write you again.

As to the land part of the matter, a large majority of congress is in favor of it, and it would pass at any time, were it not that every fellow must say something, and offer an amendment; and so time is wasted, it is shoved by, and is a long while coming up again. I hope and believe it will finally pass.[3] Very truly Yours,

A. LINCOLN

[1] ALS, Herbert Wells Fay Collection. Walter Davis was one of the incorporators of the Springfield Mechanics Union (see amendment, December 19, 1839, *supra*) and a leading Springfield Whig.   [2] *Vide infra*.
[3] See Lincoln's speech on bounty lands, March 29, 1848 (*supra*).

Certificate to Commissioner of Pensions Concerning Thomas Davis[1]

April 14, 1848

I do hereby certify that I was personally well acquainted with 2nd. Lieutenant Thomas Davis, who served for a time as a private in Captain Frank L. [S.?] Early's company, of the 1st. Regt. of Texas volunteers, and who was transfered from that service, by a commission of a 2nd. Lieutenancy in the United States Rifle Regiment, which Regiment served in Col. Harney's[2] Brigade, at the battle of Cerro Gordo, and who fell in that battle; that I am also well acquainted with the family to which said Lieut. Davis belonged; that his father has been dead for many years; that his mother, Maria Davis, a widow, is still living, at Springfield, Illinois, and that said Lieut. Davis was never married.

April 14th. 1848   A. LINCOLN—

A member of Congress.

1 ADS, owned by Edward C. Stone, Boston, Massachusetts.
2 William S. Harney.

To Mary Todd Lincoln[1]

Dear Mary: Washington, April 16– 1848–

In this troublesome world, we are never quite satisfied. When you were here, I thought you hindered me some in attending to business; but now, having nothing but business—no variety—it has grown exceedingly tasteless to me. I hate to sit down and direct documents, and I hate to stay in this old room by myself. You know I told you in last sunday's letter, I was going to make a little speech during the week; but the week has passed away without my getting a chance to do so; and now my interest in the subject has passed away too. Your second and third letters have been received since I wrote before. Dear Eddy thinks father is *"gone tapila*[.]*"*[2] Has any further discovery been made as to the breaking into your grand-mother's house? If I were she, I would not remain there alone. You mention that your uncle John Parker is likely to be at Lexington. Dont forget to present him my very kindest regards.

I went yesterday to hunt the little plaid stockings, as you wished; but found that McKnight has quit business, and Allen had not a single pair of the description you give, and only one plaid pair of any sort that I thought would fit "Eddy's dear little feet." I have a notion to make another trial to-morrow morning. If I could get them, I have an excellent chance of sending them. Mr. Warrick Tunstall, of St. Louis is here. He is to leave early this week, and to go by Lexington. He says he knows you, and will call to see you; and he voluntarily asked, if I had not some package to send to you.

I wish you to enjoy yourself in every possible way; but is there no danger of wounding the feelings of your good father, by being so openly intimate with the Wickliffe family?[3]

Mrs. Broome has not removed yet; but she thinks of doing so to-morrow. All the house—or rather, all with whom you were on decided good terms—send their love to you. The others say nothing.

Very soon after you went away, I got what I think a very pretty set of shirt-bosom studs—modest little ones, jet, set in gold, only costing 50 cents a piece, or 1.50 for the whole.

Suppose you do not prefix the "Hon" to the address on your letters to me any more. I like the letters very much, but I would rather they should not have that upon them. It is not necessary, as I suppose you have thought, to have them to come free.

And you are entirely free from head-ache? That is good—good —considering it is the first spring you have been free from it since we were acquainted. I am afraid you will get so well, and fat, and young, as to be wanting to marry again. Tell Louisa I want her to watch you a little for me. Get weighed, and write me how much you weigh.

I did not get rid of the impression of that foolish dream about dear Bobby till I got your letter written the same day. What did he and Eddy think of the little letters father sent them? Dont let the blessed fellows forget father.

A day or two ago Mr. Strong, here in Congress, said to me that Matilda would visit here within two or three weeks.[4] Suppose you write her a letter, and enclose it in one of mine; and if she comes I will deliver it to her, and if she does not, I will send it to her. Most affectionately   A. LINCOLN

[1] ALS, ORB.
[2] The child's effort to say "capitol," is the only suggestion known to the editors (Beveridge, I, 438).
[3] Robert S. Todd and Robert Wickliffe, who had married Mary Todd Russell, a cousin of Robert S. Todd, were bitter personal and political enemies, and were at this time becoming involved in a lawsuit which was to occupy Lincoln's attention after the death of his father-in-law in July, 1849 (William H. Townsend, *Lincoln and His Wife's Home Town*, p. 205 ff.).
[4] William Strong, Democrat, of Pennsylvania, who married Matilda Edwards, daughter of Cyrus Edwards of Alton, Illinois.

To William L. Marcy[1]

Honr Wm L Marcy   Washington
Secretary of War   April 20. 1848
Sir I nominate for appointment to the Military Academy from the 7th Congr District of Illinois Hezekiah H Garber[2] of that District Very respectfully Your Obt Svt   A. LINCOLN

[1] LS, DNA RG 94 U.S. Military Academy File 117.
[2] Hezekiah H. Garber, son of Jacob Garber of Petersburg, Illinois, received the appointment. Upon completing his training at West Point, he served in the army until his death, October 12, 1859, at Fort Hoskins, Oregon.

To Benjamin Kellogg, Jr.[1]

Dear Ben: Washington. April 21– 1848
Your letter,[2] which I herewith return, was received two days ago. On yesterday I went to the Patent office with it, made the

memorandum on it which you see on the back of it,[3] and left it. Last night they returned it to me, with no other answer, than the pencil notes at the top and bottom of it, which you see.[4] I return the letter, because I suppose you will understand their notes better by seeing them, than you could by my writing about them. Yours as ever   A LINCOLN

[1] ALS-P, ISLA. Kellogg was an attorney of Pekin, Illinois.

[2] Kellogg wrote on April 4, asking Lincoln to ascertain why he had not heard from the patent office in regard to two deeds sent for recording—the deeds being from William Wilcox to S.M. Whipple for the right of Colburn's Improved Iron Pump to several states and territories.

[3] Memorandum is as follows: "Please examine this letter, and give me the desired information; and return this, to me with your own. A. Lincoln."

[4] The penciled notations are as follows: Top—"Pekin PO–D.G. Colburn patee. 3 deeds/Recd. March 4 48"; Bottom—"The above deeds were sent / Sent Apl 5 Pekin P.O. Ills."

To Elihu B. Washburne[1]

Dear Washburne: Washington, April 30. 1848.

I have this moment received your very short note asking me if old Taylor is to be used up, and who will be the nominee. My hope of Taylor's nomination is as high,—a little higher—than it was when you left. Still the case is by no means out of doubt. Mr. Clay's letter has not advanced his interests any here. Several who were *against* Taylor, but not *for* any body particularly, before, are since, taking ground, some for Scott[2] and some for McLean.[3] Who will be nominated neither I nor any one else can tell.

Now, let me pray to you in turn. My prayer is, that you let nothing discourage or baffle you; but that, in spite of every difficulty, you send us a good Taylor delegate from your circuit. Make Baker,[4] who is now with you I suppose, help about it. He is a good hand to raise a breeze.

Gen: Ashley,[5] in the Senate from Arkansas, died yesterday. Nothing else new beyond what you see in the papers. Yours truly

A. LINCOLN

[1] ALS, IHi. Washburne was a leading Whig attorney in Galena, Illinois, and later United States representative 1853-1869.   [2] General Winfield Scott.

[3] John McLean, associate justice of the Supreme Court.

[4] Edward D. Baker, who had moved to Galena.   [5] Chester Ashley.

To Archibald Williams[1]

Dear Williams: Washington, April 30. 1848.

I have not seen in the papers any evidence of a movement to send a delegate from your circuit to the June convention. I wish to say that I think it all important that a delegate should be sent. Mr. Clay's chance for an election, is just no chance at all. He might get New-York; and that would have elected in 1844, but it will not now; because he must now, at the least, lose Tennessee, which he had then, and, in addition, the fifteen *new* votes of Florida, Texas, Iowa, and Wisconsin. I know our good friend Browning,[2] is a great admirer of Mr. Clay, and I therefore fear, he is favoring his nomination. If he is, ask him to discard feeling, and try if he can possibly, as a matter of judgment, count the votes necessary to elect him.

In my judgment, we can elect nobody but Gen; Taylor; and we can not elect him without a nomination. Therefore, dont fail to send a delegate. Your friend as ever   A. LINCOLN

[1] ALS, owned by Mrs. Martha W. Franklin, Quincy, Illinois.
[2] Orville H. Browning.

To John T. Towers[1]

Mr. J. T. Towers: Washington,
Dear Sir: May 3. 1848
    I understand that the speech of Mr. Wick,[2] of Indiana, is printed at your office. Please send to the folding room for me, three hundred copies of it, and oblige   Yours &c.   A. LINCOLN

[1] ALS, MFai. John T. Towers was associated with his brother Lemuel in a printing business in Washington, and was appointed in 1852 to the first official Public Printing Office.
[2] William W. Wick, Democrat, member of congress.

Remarks in
United States House of Representatives
Concerning Payment of Texas Volunteers[1]

May 4, 1848

    Mr. Lincoln said the objection stated by the gentleman from Missouri [Mr. HALL][2] struck him as being a sound one; and he wished to ascertain if there was anything further to be learned about this claim, for he desired fully to understand it. He understood that the volunteers who served in Mexico were not by any general law entitled to pay for lost horses, and he understood that if this resolution should pass, the Texas volunteers would be entitled to compensation for lost horses. Thus, they would be placed in more favorable circumstances than others.[3]

. . . .

Mr. Lincoln said the payment for these lost horses came within a class of cases in which he was a good deal like a gentleman near him, who was in favor of paying for everything by way of being sure of paying all those that were right. But if this resolution should be passed, and the general law should fail, then everybody but these Texas volunteers would go without their compensation. He was not willing to do anything that would produce such a result. He preferred placing the Texas volunteers on a level with all other volunteers; and, therefore, he should vote for the reconsideration.[4]

[1] *Congressional Globe,* Thirtieth Congress, First Session, p. 727.

[2] Willard P. Hall of Missouri, had moved reconsideration of House joint resolution No. 16 granting pay to Texas volunteers called up but never mustered into service. His objection was that the resolution called for payments which had not been accorded other volunteers—namely, for horses lost for want of forage.

[3] Armistead Burt of South Carolina, who had moved the adoption of the resolution, explained at this point that a bill before the committee on military affairs would provide pay for all other horses lost in Mexico.

[4] The House passed the resolution with sundry amendments on May 4.

Remarks in United States House of Representatives Concerning Admission of Wisconsin into the Union[1]

May 11, 1848

Mr. LINCOLN moved to reconsider the vote by which the bill was passed.[2] He stated to the House that he had made this motion for the purpose of obtaining an opportunity to say a few words in relation to a point raised in the course of the debate on this bill, which he would now proceed to make, if in order. The point in the case to which he referred arose on the amendment that was submitted by the gentleman from Vermont [Mr. COLLAMER][3] in Committee of the Whole on the state of the Union, and which was afterwards renewed in the House, in relation to the question whether the reserved sections, which, by some bills heretofore passed, by which an appropriation of land had been made to Wisconsin, had been enhanced in value, should be reduced to the minimum price of the public lands. The question of the reduction in value of those sections was to him, at this time, a matter very nearly of indifference. He was inclined to desire that Wisconsin should be obliged by having it reduced. But the gentleman from Indiana, [Mr. C. B. SMITH,] the chairman of the Committee on the Territories, yesterday associated that question with the general question, which is now to some extent agitated in Congress, of making appropriations of alternate sections of land to aid the States in making internal improvements, and enhancing the price of the sections reserved; and the gentleman from Indiana took ground against that policy. He did not make any special argument in favor of Wisconsin; but he took ground generally against the policy of giving alternate sections of land, and enhancing the price of the reserved sections. Now he (Mr. L.) did not, at this time, take the floor for the purpose of attempting to make an argument on the general subject. He rose simply to protest against the doctrine which the gentleman from Indiana had avowed in the course of what he (Mr. L.) could not but consider an unsound argument.

It might, however, be true, for anything he knew, that the gentleman from Indiana might convince him that his argument was sound; but he (Mr. L.) feared that gentleman would not be able to convince a majority in Congress that it was sound. It was true, the question appeared in a different aspect to persons in consequence of a difference in the point from which they looked at it. It did not look to persons residing east of the mountains as it did to those who lived among the public lands. But, for his part, he would state that if Congress would make a donation of alternate sections of public land for the purpose of internal improvements in his State, and forbid the reserved sections being sold at $1.25, he should be glad to see the appropriation made; though he should prefer it if the reserved sections were not enhanced in price. He repeated, he should be glad to have such appropriations made, even though the reserved sections should be enhanced in price. He did not wish to be understood as concurring in any intimation that they would refuse to receive such an appropriation of alternate sections of land because a condition enhancing the price of the reserved sections should be attached thereto. He believed his position would now be understood; if not, he feared he should not be able to make himself understood.

But before he took his seat he would remark that the Senate, during the present session, had passed a bill making appropriations of land on that principle for the benefit of the State in which he resided—the State of Illinois. The alternate sections were to be given for the purpose of constructing roads, and the reserved sections were to be enhanced in value in consequence. When that bill came here for the action of this House—it had been received and was now before the Committee on Public Lands—he desired much to see it passed as it was, if it could be put in no more favorable form for the State of Illinois. When it should be before this House, if any member from a section of the Union in which these lands did not lie, whose interest might be less than that which he felt, should propose a reduction of the price of the reserved sections to $1.25, he should be much obliged; but he did not think it would be well for those who came from the section of the Union in which the lands lay to do so. He wished it, then, to be understood that he did not join in the warfare against the principle which had engaged the minds of some members of Congress who were favorable to improvements in the western country.

There was a good deal of force, he admitted, in what fell from the chairman of the Committee on Territories. It might be that there was no precise justice in raising the price of the reserved sections to $2.50 per acre. It might be proper that the price should be enhanced to some extent, though not to double the usual price; but he should be glad to have such an appropriation with the reserved sections at $2.50; he should be better pleased to have the price of those sections at something less; and he should be still better pleased to have them without any enhancement at all.

There was one portion of the argument of the gentleman from Indiana, the chairman of the Committee on Territories [Mr. SMITH,] which he wished to take occasion to say that he did not view as unsound. He alluded to the statement that the General Government was interested in these internal improvements being made, inasmuch as they increased the value of the lands that were unsold, and they enabled the Government to sell lands which could not be sold without them. Thus, then, the Government gained by internal improvements, as well as by the general good which the people derived from them, and it might be, therefore, that the lands should not be sold for more than $1.50 instead of the price being doubled. He, however, merely mentioned this in passing, for he only rose to state, as the principle of giving these lands for the purposes which he had mentioned had been laid hold of and considered favorably, and as there were some gentlemen who had constitutional scruples about giving money for these purchases, who would not hesitate to give land, that he was not willing to have it understood that he was one of those who made war against that principle. This was all he desired to say, and having accomplished the object with which he rose, he withdrew his motion to reconsider.

1 *Congressional Globe*, Thirtieth Congress, First Session, p. 755.

2 The bill for the admission of Wisconsin had been reported on May 10, and sundry amendments had been offered, debate continuing on May 11. Lincoln's remarks immediately followed the passage of the bill.   3 Jacob Collamer.

To John M. Peck[1]

Rev: J. M. Peck.   Washington,
Dear Sir: May 21– 1848–

On last evening I received a copy of the Belleville Advocate,
with the appearance of having been sent by a private hand; and,
inasmuch as it contains your oration on the occasion of the cele-
brating of the battle of Buena Vista, and is post-marked at Rock-
Spring, I can not doubt that it is to you, I am indebted for this,
courtesy. I own that finding in the oration a laboured justification
of the administration on the origin of the Mexican war, disappoints
me—disappoints me, because it is the first effort of the kind I have
known, made by one appearing to me to be, intelligent, right-
minded, and *impartial*. It is this disappointment that prompts me
to address you, briefly, on the subject. I do not propose any extended review. I do not quarrel with your *brief* exhibition of facts;
I presume it is correct so far as it goes; but it is so brief, as to exclude some facts quite as material in my judgment, to a just conclusion, as any it includes. For instance, you say "Paredes came
into power the last of December 1845, and from that moment, all
hopes of avoiding war by negociation vanished." A little further
on, refering to this and other preceding statements, you say "All
this transpired three months before Gen: Taylor marched across
the desert of the Nueces." These two statements are substantially
correct;[2] and you evidently intend to have it infered that Gen:
Taylor was sent across the desert, in *consequence* of the destruction
of all hope of peace, in the overthrow of Herara by Paredes. Is not
that the inference you intend? If so, the material fact you have
excluded is, that Gen: Taylor was *ordered* to cross the desert on
the 13th. of January 1846, and *before* the news of Herara's fall
reached Washington—*before* the administration, which gave the
order, had any knowledge that Herara had fallen. Does not this
fact cut up your inference by the roots? Must you not find some
other excuse for that order, or give up the case? All that part of the
three months you speak of, which transpired *after* the 13th. of January, was expended in the order's going *from* Washington *to* Gen:
Taylor, in his preparations *for* the march, and in the *actual* march
across the desert; and not in the president's waiting to hear the
knell of peace, in the fall of Herara, or for any other object[.] All
this is to be found in the very documents you seem to have used.

One other thing: Although you say, at one point, "I shall briefly
exhibit *facts* and *leave* each person to perceive the just application
to the principles already laid down, to the case in hand" you very

soon get to making applications yourself—in one instance, as follows: "In view of *all* the facts, the conviction to my mind is irresistable, that the Government of the United States committed no aggression on Mexico." Not in view of *all* the facts. There are facts which you have kept out of view. It is a fact, that the United States Army, in marching to the Rio Grande, marched into a peaceful Mexican settlement, and frightened the inhabitants away from their homes and their growing crops.

It is a fact, that Fort Brown, opposite Matamoras, was built by that army, within a Mexican cotten-field, on which, at the time the army reached it, a young cotten crop was growing and which crop was wholly destroyed, and the field itself greatly, and permanently injured, by ditches, embankments, and the like.

It is a fact, that when the Mexicans captured Capt. Thornton and his command, they found and captured them within another Mexican field.

Now I wish to bring these facts to your notice, and to ascertain what is the result of your reflections upon them. If you *deny* that they *are* facts, I think I can furnish proof which shall convince you that you are mistaken.

If you *admit* that they are facts, then I shall be obliged for a reference to any law of language, law of states, law of nations, law of morals, law of religion,—any law human or divine, in which an authority can be found for saying those facts constitute *"no aggression"*

Possibly you consider those acts too small for notice. Would you venture to so consider them, had they been committed by any nation on earth, against the humblest of our people? I know you would not. Then I ask, is the precept "Whatsoever ye would that men should do to you, do ye even so to them" obsolete?—of no force?—of no application?

I shall be pleased if you can find leisure to write me. Yours truly
A. LINCOLN

1 ADfS, DLC-RTL. The Reverend John M. Peck was a prominent Baptist clergyman of St. Clair County, Illinois.
2 The remainder of this paragraph stands as Lincoln revised it. The deleted version differs in nothing save sentence structure.

To Mary Todd Lincoln[1]

My dear wife: Washington, May 24– 1848
Enclosed is the draft as I promised you in my letter of sunday.[2]
It is drawn in favor of your father, and I doubt not, he will give

you the money for it at once. I write this letter in the post-office, surrounded by men and noise, which, together with the fact that there is nothing new, makes me write so short a letter. Affectionately   A. LINCOLN

1 ALS, original owned by Perc S. Brown, Newark, New Jersey.
2 This letter seems not to be extant.

To Silas Noble[1]

Friend Noble: Washington, May 25, 1848.

Your letter of the 16th is just received. I will place your name on my book, and send you such documents as you desire, when I can get them. The entire war correspondence is in course of printing, and will be the best electioneering document, when completed. I will then send you a copy of it.

You ask how Turner[2] stands. I answer, moderate—fair—about an average of new members.

I have procured a couple of copies of Stewart's[3] speech and sent you, and he and I join cordially in the hope, that your hope of McLean's nomination may be disappointed—not that we wish you disappointed *in the abstract*, nor that we have anything against Judge McLean; but because we are entirely sure he is not *"a winning card."* Your sincere friend,   A. LINCOLN.

1 *Telegraph and Herald* (Dixon, Illinois), August 31, 1871. Present location of the original letter has not been identified. The following account of the letter is given in the *Telegraph and Herald*: "In making some changes of desks in the Lee County National Bank . . . there was discovered, in an old drawer, with other letters and papers belonging to the late Col. Silas Noble, the following letter. . . . Thos. J. Turner stands to-day about as Mr. Lincoln said he stood then. . . . "
2 Thomas J. Turner, lawyer and leading Democratic politician of Freeport, Illinois, was a member of the Thirtieth Congress.
3 Probably Andrew Stewart, Whig, of Pennsylvania.

To Henry Slicer[1]

Rev. Hy. Slicer   Washington,
Dear Sir: June 1. 1848

Your letter of the 30th. ult. was received last night. I very cheerfully comply with your request, so far as I am able.

As I remember, the House ordered the raising of two committees, one, of *Arrangements,* number indefinite, the other, thirty in number, to attend the remains of Mr. Adams[2] to Massachusetts. By some mistake, as I understood, a committee of *thirty* was appointed by the Speaker, as a committee of *Arrangements*, of which I was a member. At our first meeting, the mistake was discovered, and the committee being much too numerous for convenience, we delegated our authority to a sub-committee, of a smaller number of our own body, of which sub-committee, I was *not* a member. Whatever was done in the matter about which you enquire, I presume was done by this sub-committee; at all events I have no knowledge of it whatever. Mr. Hudson[3] was Chairman of both the general, and the sub-committee, and who were the other members, of the latter I do not certainly recollect.

To your first special interrogatory, towit "Were you consulted in regard to my exclusion from the services?" I answer, I was not—perhaps because the arrangement I have stated excluded me from consultation on all points.

To the second to wit: "Was *objection* made *to me*—and if so, on what ground was it placed?" I answer I know nothing whatever on the point.

To the third, to wit "Did my exclusion meet with your *consent* or *approval?*" I answer, I knew nothing of the matter, and, of course, did not consent to, or approve of it; and I may add, that I knew nothing which should have justified me in any attempt to put a mark of disapprobation upon you.

So entirely ignorant was I, in relation to your having been excluded from the funeral services of Mr. Adams, that, until I received your letter, I should have given it as my recollection, that you did actually participate in those services. Yours respectfully

A. LINCOLN—

1 ALS, owned by Dr. Frederick M. Dearborn, New York City. Reverend Henry Slicer was a Methodist minister and the chaplain of the Senate.

2 John Quincy Adams was stricken in the House on February 21 and died in the speaker's room on the 23rd. Accommodations were limited for the funeral service conducted in the House, and according to newspaper accounts no reservations were made for the clergymen of the city. The Senate chaplain was not provided for in the House ceremony, and, probably as the result of an oversight, Reverend Slicer's feelings seem to have been ruffled.

3 Charles Hudson, Massachusetts Whig representative, was a minister of the Universalist Church.

Speech at Wilmington, Delaware[1]

June 10, 1848

The first speaker introduced to the assembled multitude was the "Lone Star of Illinois," Hon. Mr. Lincoln. He was received with three hearty cheers, and delivered an eloquent and patriotic speech on some of the principles of the Whig party and the standard-

bearers they had selected to carry out their measures. He referred
to the history of James K. Polk's administration—the abuse of
power which characterized it—the high-handed and despotic exercise of the veto power, and the utter disregard of the will of the
people, in refusing to give assent to measures which their representatives passed for the good and prosperity of the country. The manner
in which the present Executive had carried on the Mexican war
should condemn it and the Locofoco party before the whole people.
He did not believe with many of his fellow citizens that this war
was originated for the purpose of extending slave territory, but
it was his opinion, frequently expressed, that it was a war of
conquest brought into existence to catch votes. Admitting, however,
that the disputes between Mexico and this country could not have
been settled in an amicable manner—admitting that we went into
the battle field as the last resort, with all the principles of right and
justice on our side, why is it that this government desires a large
sum of money to gain more territory than will secure "indemnity
for the past and security for the future?" During the whole war
this was the stereotyped motto of the administration; but when the
treaty was sent to the Senate, the Executive not only included
enough of territory for this purpose, but actually extended the
boundaries and made an agreement to pay the Mexican government $15,000,000 for the additional territory. This subject de-
manded attention, and, although he had means of information, it
had never been satisfactorily explained to him. Mr. Lincoln referred to other topics in an eloquent manner, and concluded with
a few patriotic remarks on the character and long services of the
Whig candidates.

[1] Wilmington, *Delaware State Journal*, June 13, 1848. Returning from the
Whig National Convention in Philadelphia, "several distinguished Whigs" vis-
ited Wilmington, Delaware, to attend a "ratification meeting" held on Satur-
day evening, June 10. Speeches were delivered by Lincoln and Representatives
William T. Haskell of Tennessee, Edward C. Cabell of Florida, and John W.
Houston of Delaware.

To William H. Herndon[1]

Dear William   Washington, June 12. 1848—

On my return from Philadelphia, where I had been attending
the nomination of "Old Rough"—I found your letter in a mass of
others, which had accumulated in my absence. By many, and
often, it had been said they would not abide the nomination of
Taylor; but since the deed has been done, they are fast falling in,

and in my opinion we shall have a most overwhelming, glorious, triumph. One unmistakable sign is, that all the odds and ends are with us—Barnburners, Native Americans, Tyler men, disappointed office seeking locofocos, and the Lord knows what. This is important, if in nothing else, in showing which way the wind blows. Some of the sanguine men here, set down all the states as certain for Taylor, but Illinois, and it as doubtful. Can not something be done, even in Illinois? Taylor's nomination takes the locos on the blind side. It turns the war thunder against them. The war is now to them, the gallows of Haman, which they built for us, and on which they are doomed to be hanged themselves.

Excuse this short letter. I have so many to write, that I can not devote much time to any one. Yours as ever   A LINCOLN

1 ALS-P, ISLA. A notation on the top of the first page, in Herndon's handwriting, reads as follows: "Not to be published—Herndon." Nicolay and Hay included the letter in the *Complete Works* (II, 26), but erroneously addressed it to Archibald Williams, probably as the result of a faulty copy. Hertz (II, 573) later printed the letter correctly addressed.

To Mary Todd Lincoln[1]

My dear wife: Washington, June 12. 1848—

On my return from Philadelphia, yesterday, where, in my anxiety I had been led to attend the whig convention I found your last letter. I was so tired and sleepy, having ridden all night, that I could not answer it till to-day; and now I have to do so in the H.R. The leading matter in your letter, is your wish to return to this side of the Mountains. Will you be a *good girl* in all things, if I consent? Then come along, and that as *soon* as possible. Having got the idea in my head, I shall be impatient till I see you. You will not have money enough to bring you; but I presume your uncle[2] will supply you, and I will refund him here. By the way you do not mention whether you have received the fifty dollars I sent you. I do not much fear but that you got it; because the want of it would have induced you [to?] say something in relation to it. If your uncle is already at Lexington, you might induce him to start on earlier than the first of July; he could stay in Kentucky longer on his return, and so make up for lost time. Since I began this letter, the H.R. has passed a resolution for adjourning on the 17th. July, which probably will pass the Senate. I hope this letter will not be disagreeable to you; which, together with the circumstances under which I write, I hope will excuse me for not writing a longer one. Come on just as soon as you can. I want to see you, and our dear—*dear* boys very much. Every body here wants to see our dear Bobby.[3] Affectionately   A. LINCOLN

[1] ALS, IHi.
[2] Mrs. Lincoln had written, May—1848, "Grandma has received a letter from Uncle James Parker of Miss saying he & his family would be up by the twenty fifth of June, would remain here some little time & go on to Philadelphia. . . ." (Carl Sandburg and Paul M. Angle, *Mary Lincoln*, p. 190).
[3] Robert Todd Lincoln.

To Richard S. Thomas[1]

Friend Richard: Washington, June 13, 1848

In my anxiety for the result, I was led to attend the Philadelphia convention; and, on my return, I found your letter of the 1st. I have entered the names you sent me, on my book, and commenced sending documents to them. In relation to the School land questions, the land committees of both Houses, are of opinion the law is already ample in relation to fractional townships. To make sure of the matter, I shall go to the Gen'l Land office to-morrow morning, enquire into the whole matter, and write you again.[2] As to the report you saw in the Baltimore paper, on inquiry, I think it must have been a report of the Senate. No such bill has passed the House; but Breese[3] says he reported such a bill to the Senate, which he supposes has passed that body. I think I wrote you once before, that I thought no such bill could become a law, and gave my reasons for the opinion. Lest I am mistaken in my recollection, I now give you those reasons briefly. The justice of such a law rests upon the principle that every township should have a section of *equal value* with every other township, in proportion to its capacity for population. Now, to adopt this principle, and practically apply it, would entirely break up the present system, in relation to school sections, and require an amount of agencies and labor, more than equal in expense to the whole expense of the present land system. Seeing this, members of congress are disinclined to do a very *little*, and leave undone very *much*, of a matter all standing on the same principle.

It is now obvious, that in the beginning of our land system, one thirty-sixth of the *proceeds* of the lands should have been given for school purposes, instead of giving the land itself; and then the States could have distributed the fund or the interest of it equally.

Wisconsin, on coming into the Union, has managed to adopt this plan substantially. Should the bill from the Senate, come up in the House, of course I shall not use the above argument, or any other argument, against it; but on the contrary, shall do what I can to have it passed. Still, I doubt its ultimate success. Yours forever

A. LINCOLN—

¹ Copy, DLC—HW. ² *Vide infra.* ³ Sidney Breese of Illinois.

To Richard S. Thomas¹

R. S. Thomas, Esq.,   Washington,
Dear Sir.—   June 15, 1848.

Herewith I send you a copy of a law, by virtue of which, the inhabitants of fractional Townships, on which there are NO sixteenth sections, or in which those sections are FRACTIONAL, and proportionally TOO SMALL for the remainder of such townships respectively, may have other lands in lieu. It will be seen that the law, by its letter, applies to cases where there is NO school land, but, by construction here, it is applied to cases where there is TOO LITTLE. In cases where there is, and only have enough in addition, to make their proportion. As I was ignorant of this law when I came on here, I suppose that some others may be; and therefore, in order that all persons interested may know the law, and the way to avail themselves of its benefits, I propose that you give this letter, the law, and Judge Young's letter, and note, a start for publication in the papers of our region. Yours Truly,   A. LINCOLN.

¹ Beardstown *Gazette*, July 12, 1848. Thomas submitted this letter to the *Gazette* in the hope that ". . . it may prove beneficial to the cause of popular education." The law is also printed in the *Gazette*. For other correspondence concerning school lands, see Lincoln to Thomas, March 30 and June 13, 1848 (*supra*).

To Richard S. Thomas¹

Friend Thomas: Washington, June 19, 1848.

Do you know any democrats who will vote for Taylor? and if so, what are their names? Do you know any Whigs who will not vote for him? and if so, what are their names? and for whom will they vote?

Please answer this just as soon as it is received. Yours as ever

A. LINCOLN—

¹ Copy, DLC-HW. The original letter has not been located, but an envelope addressed by Lincoln to Thomas and postmarked from Washington on June 20 is in the Huntington Library.

Speech in United States House of Representatives on Internal Improvements[1]

June 20, 1848

In committee of the whole on the state of the union, on the civil and diplomatic appropriation bill—

Mr. Chairman

I wish at all times in no way to practice any fraud upon the House or the committee, and I also desire to do nothing which may be very disagreeable to any of the members. I therefore state in advance that my object in taking the floor is to make a speech on the general subject of internal improvements; and if I am out of order in doing so, I give the chair the oppertunity of so deciding, and I will take my seat.

The Chair: I will not undertake to anticipate what the gentleman may say on the subject of internal improvements. He will, therefore, proceed in his remarks, and if any question of order shall be made, the chair will then decide it.

Mr. Lincoln: At an early day of this session the president sent us what may properly be called an internal improvement veto message. The late democratic convention which sat at Baltimore, and which nominated Gen: Cass for the presidency, adopted a set of resolutions, now called the democratic platform, among which is one in these words:

"That the constitution does not confer upon the general government the power to commence, and carry on a general system of internal improvements"

Gen: Cass, in his letter accepting the nomination, holds this language:

"I have carefully read the resolutions of the Democratic National convention, laying down the platform of our political faith, and I adhere to them as firmly, as I approve them cordially."

These things, taken together, show that the question of internal improvements is now more distinctly made—has become more intense—than at any former period. It can no longer be avoided. The veto message, and the Baltimore resolution, I understand to be, in substance, the same thing; the latter being the mere general state-

[1] AD, DLC-RTL. This document was written, or recopied, by Lincoln after delivering the speech, for printing in the *Congressional Globe Appendix* (letter to Herndon, June 22, *infra*). Except in minor matters of style and punctuation, which the *Globe* edited to its own style, the text is largely the same. Principal variations of phrase appearing in the *Globe Appendix* are indicated in brackets in the text as taken from the document. The speech was also printed in the *Illinois Journal*, July 20, 1848.

ment, of which the former is the amplification—the bill of particulars. While I know there are many democrats, on this floor and elsewhere, who disapprove that message, I understand that all who shall vote for Gen: Cass, will thereafter be counted as having approved it—as having endorsed all it's doctrines. I suppose all, or nearly all the democrats will vote for him. Many of them will do so, not because they like his position on this question, but because they prefer him, being wrong in this, to another whom they consider farther wrong on other other [*sic*] questions. In this way, the internal improvement democrats are to be, by a sort of forced consent, carried over, and arrayed against themselves on this measure of policy. Gen: Cass, once elected, will not trouble himself to make a constitutional argument, or, perhaps, any argument at all, when he shall veto a river or harbor bill; he will consider it a sufficient answer to all democratic murmers, to point to Mr. Polk's message, and to the "democratic platform." This being the case, the question of improvements is verging to a final crisis; and the friends of the policy must now battle, and battle manfully, or surrender all. In this view, humble as I am, I wish to review, and contest as well as I may, the general positions of this veto message. When I say *general* positions, I mean to exclude from consideration so much as relates to the present embarrassed state of the Treasury in consequence of the Mexican war.

Those general positions are: That internal improvements ought not to be made by the general government—

1. Because they would overwhelm the Treasury.

2. Because, while their *burthens* would be general, their *benefits* would be *local* and *partial*; involving an obnoxious inequality— and

3. Because they would be unconstitutional.

4. Because the states may do enough by the levy and collection of tonnage duties—or if not

5. That the constitution may be amended.

"Do nothing at all, lest you do something wrong" is the sum of these positions—is the sum of this message. And this, with the exception of what is said about constitutionality, applying as forcibly to making improvements by state authority, as by the national authority. So that we must abandon the improvements of the country altogether, by any, and every authority, or we must resist, and repudiate the doctrines of this message. Let us attempt the latter.

The first position is, that a system of internal improvements would overwhelm the treasury.

That, in such a system there is a *tendency* to undue expansion, is not to be denied. Such tendency is founded in the nature of the subject. A member of congress will prefer voting for a bill which contains an appropriation for his district, to voting for one which does not; and when a bill shall be expanded till every district shall be provided for, that it will be too greatly expanded, is obvious. But is this any more true in congress, than in a state legislature? If a member of congress must have an appropriation for his district, so, a member of a legislature must have one for his county. And if one will overwhelm the national treasury, so the other will overwhelm the state treasury. Go where we will, the difficulty is the same. Allow it to drive us from the halls of congress, and it will, just as easily, drive us from the state legislatures.

Let us, then, grapple with it, and test it's strength. Let us, judging of the future by the past, ascertain whether there may not be, in the discretion of congress, a sufficient power to limit, and restrain this expansive tendency, within reasonable, and proper bounds. The president himself values the evidence of the past. He tells us that at a certain point of our history, more than two hundred millions of dollars had been, *applied for*, to make improvements; and this he does to prove that the treasury would be overwhelmed by such a system. Why did he not tell us how much was *granted*? Would not that have been better evidence? Let us turn to it, and see what it proves. In the message, the president tells us that "During the four succeeding years, embraced by the administration of president Adams, the power not only to appropriate money, but to apply it, under the direction and authority of the General Government, as well [as] to the construction of roads, as to the improvement of harbors and rivers, was fully asserted and exercised"

This, then, was the period of greatest enormity. These, if any, must have been the days of the two hundred millions. And how much do you suppose was really expended for improvements, during that four years? Two hundred millions? One hundred? Fifty? Ten? Five? No sir, less than two millions. As shown by authentic documents, the expenditures on improvements, during 1825 1826— 1827 and 1828, amounted to $1-879-627-01. These four years were the period of Mr. Adams' administration, nearly, and substantially. This fact shows, that when the power to make improvements "was fully asserted and exercised" the congress *did* keep within reasonable limits; and what has been done, it seems to me, can be done again.

Now for the second position of the message, namely, that the burthens of improvements would be *general*, while their *benefits* would [be] *local* and *partial*, involving an obnoxious inequality. That there is some degree of truth in this position, I shall not deny. No commercial object of government patronage can be so exclusively *general*, as to not be of some peculiar *local* advantage; but, on the other hand, nothing is so *local*, as to not be of some general advantage. The Navy, as I understand it, was established, and is maintained at a great annual expense, partly to be ready for war when war shall come, but partly also, and perhaps chiefly, for the protection of our commerce on the high seas. This latter object is, for all I can see, in principle, the same as internal improvements. The driving a pirate from the track of commerce on the broad ocean, and the removing a snag from it's more narrow path in the Mississippi river, can not, I think, be distinguished in principle. Each is done to save life and property, and for nothing else.

The Navy, then, is the most general in it's benefits of all this class of objects; and yet even the Navy is of some peculiar advantage to Charleston, Baltimore, Philadelphia, New-York and Boston, beyond what it is to the interior towns of Illinois. The next most general object I can think of would be improvements on the Mississippi river and it's tributaries. They touch thirteen of our states, Pennsylvania, Virginia, Kentucky, Tennessee, Mississippi, Louisiana, Arkansas, Missouri, Illinois, Indiana, Ohio, Wisconsin and Iowa. Now I suppose it will not be denied, that these thirteen states are a little more interested in improvements on that great river, than are the remaining seventeen. These instances of the Navy, and the Miss[iss]ippi river, show clearly that there is something of local advantage in the most general objects. But the converse is also true. Nothing is so *local* as to not be of some *general* benefit. Take, for instance, the Illinois and Michigan canal. Considered apart from it's effects, it is perfectly local. Every inch of it is within the state of Illinois. That canal was first opened for business last April. In a very few days we were all gratified to learn, among other things, that sugar had been carried from New-Orleans through this canal to Buffalo in New-York. This sugar took this route, doubtless because it was cheaper than the old route. Supposing the benefit of the reduction in the cost of carriage to be shared between seller and buyer, the result is, that the New Orleans merchant sold his sugar a little *dearer*; and the people of Buffalo sweetened their coffee a little *cheaper*, than before—a benefit resulting *from* the canal, not to Illinois where the canal *is*, but to Louisiana and New-York where it is *not*. In other transactions Illinois will, of course, have her share, and perhaps the larger share too, in the benefits of the canal; but the instance of the sugar clearly shows that the *benefits* of an improvement, are by no means confined to the particular locality of the improvement itself.

The just conclusion from all this is, that if the nation refuse to make improvements, of the more general kind, because their benefits may be somewhat local, a state may, for the same reason, refuse to make an improvement of a local kind, because it's benefits may be somewhat general. A state may well say to the nation "If you will do nothing for me, I will do nothing for you." Thus it is seen, that if this argument of "inequality" is sufficient any where, —it is sufficient every where; and puts an end to improvements altogether. I hope and believe, that if both the nation and the states would, in good faith, in their respective spheres, do what they could in the way of improvements, what of inequality might be produced in one place, might be compensated in another, and that the sum of the whole might not be very unequal.

But suppose, after all, there should be some degree of inequality. Inequality is certainly never to be embraced for it's own sake; but is every good thing to be discarded, which may be inseparably connected with some degree of it? If so, we must discard all government. This capitol is built at the public expense, for the public benefit[;] but does any one doubt that it is of some peculiar local advantage to the property holders, and business people of Washington? Shall we remove it for this reason? and if so, where shall we set it down, and be free from the difficulty? To make sure of our object, shall we locate it nowhere? and have congress hereafter to hold it's sessions, as the loafer lodged "in spots about"? I make no special allusion to the present president when I say there are few stronger cases in this in this [sic] world, of "burthen to the many, and benefit to the few"—of "inequality"—than the presidency itself is by some thought to be. An honest laborer digs coal at about seventy cents a day, while the president digs abstractions at about seventy dollars a day. The *coal* is clearly worth more than the *abstractions*, and yet what a monstrous inequality in the prices! Does the president, for this reason, propose to abolish the presidency? He *does* not, and he *ought* not. The true rule, in determining to embrace, or reject any thing, is not whether it have *any* evil in it; but whether it have more of evil, than of good. There are few things *wholly* evil, or *wholly* good. Almost every thing, especially of governmental policy, is an inseparable compound of the two; so that our best judgment of the preponderance between them is continually demanded. On this principle the president, his friends, and the world generally, act on most subjects. Why not apply it, then, upon this question? Why, as to improvements, magnify the *evil*, and stoutly refuse to see any *good* in them?

Mr. Chairman, on the third position of the message, the constitutional question, I have not much to say. Being the man I am, and speaking when I do, I feel, that in any attempt at an original constitutional argument, I should not be, and ought not to be, listened to patiently. The ablest, and the best of men, have gone over the whole ground long ago. I shall attempt but little more than a brief notice of what some of them have said. In relation to Mr. Jeffersons views, I read from Mr. Polk's veto message—

President Jefferson, in his message to Congress in 1806, recommended an amendment of the constitution, with a view to apply an anticipated surplus in the Treasury "to the great purposes of the public education, roads, rivers, canals, and such other objects of public improvements as it may be thought proper to add to the constitutional enumeration of the federal powers;" and he adds: "I suppose an amendment to the constitution, by consent of the States, necessary, because the objects now recommended are not among those enumerated in the constitution, and to which it permits the public moneys to be applied." In 1825, he repeated, in his published letters, the opinion that no such power has been conferred upon Congress.[2]

I introduce this, not to controvert, just now, the constitutional opinion, but to show that on the question of *expediency*, Mr. Jeffersons opinion was against the present president—that this opinion of Mr. Jefferson, in one branch at least, is, in the hands of Mr. Polk, like McFingal's gun:—"Bears wide, and kicks the owner over."

But to the constitutional question—In 1826, Chancellor Kent first published his Commentaries on American Law. He devoted a portion of one of the lectures to the question of the authority of congress to appropriate public moneyes for internal improvements. He mentions that the question had never been brought under judicial consideration, and proceeds to give a brief summary of the discussions it had undergone between the legislative, and executive branches of the government. He shows that the legislative branch had usually been *for*, and the executive against the power, till the period of Mr. J. Q. Adams' administration, at which point he considers the executive influence as withdrawn from opposition, and added to the support of the power. In 1844 the chancellor published a new edition of his commentaries, in which he adds some notes of what had transpired on the question since 1826. I have not time to read the original text, or the notes; but the whole may be found on

[2] The quotation is a newspaper clipping which Lincoln pasted on his manuscript.

page 267, and the two or three following pages of the first volume of the edition of 1844. As what Chancellor Kent seems to consider the sum of the whole, I read from one of the notes:

"Mr. Justice Story, in his commentaries on the constitution of the United States, vol. ii p 429–440, and again p 519–538 has stated at large the arguments for and and [sic] against the proposition, that congress have a constitutional authority to lay taxes, and to apply the power to regulate commerce as a means directly to encourage and protect domestic manufactures; and without giving any opinion of his own on the contested doctrine, he has left the reader to draw his own conclusions. I should think, however, from the arguments as stated, that every mind which has taken no part in the discussions, and felt no prejudice or teritorial bias on either side of the question, would deem the arguments in favor of the congressional power vastly superior." It will be seen, that in this extract the power to make improvements is not directly mentioned; but by examining the context, both of Kent and Story, it will be seen that the power mentioned in the extract, and the power to make improvements are regarded as identical. It is not to be denied that many great and good men have been *against* the power; but it is insisted that quite as many, as great and as good, have been *for* it; and it is shown that, on a full survey of the whole, Chancellor Kent was of opinion that the arguments of the latter were *vastly* superior. This is but the opinion of a man, but who was that man? He was one of the ablest and most learned lawyers of his age, or of any age. It is no disparagement to Mr. Polk, nor, indeed to any one who devotes much time to politics, to be placed far behind Chancellor Kent as a lawyer.[3] His attitude was most favorable to correct conclusions. He wrote coolly, and in retirement. He was struggling to rear a durable [an enduring] monument of fame; and he well knew that *truth* and thoroughly sound reasoning were the only sure foundations. Can the party opinion of a party [the] president, on a law question, as this purely is, be at all compared, or set in in opposition to that of such a man, in such an attitude, as Chancellor Kent?

This constitutional question will probably never be better settled than it is, until it shall pass under judicial consideration; but I do think no man, who is clear on the questions of expediency, needs feel his conscience much pricked upon this.

Mr. Chairman, the president seems to think that enough may be done, in the way of improvements, by means of tonnage duties,

---

[3] As an afterthought, apparently, this sentence was written lengthwise in the margin, with its place marked by an asterisk.

under state authority, with the consent of the General Government. Now I suppose this matter of tonnage duties is well enough in it's own sphere. I suppose it may be efficient, and perhaps, *sufficient*, to make slight improvements and repairs, in harbors already in use, and not much out of repair. But if I have any correct general idea of it, it must be wholly inefficient for any generally benificent purposes of improvement. I know very little, or rather nothing at all, of the practical matter of levying and collecting tonnage duties; but I suppose one of it's principles must be, to lay a duty for the improvement of any particular harbor, *upon the tonnage coming into that harbor.* To do otherwise—to collect money in *one* harbor, to be expended on improvements in *another,* would be an extremely aggravated form of that inequality which the president so much deprecates. If I be right in this, how could we make any entirely new improvement by means of tonnage duties? How make a road, a canal, or clear a greatly obstructed river? The idea that we could, involves the same absurdity of the irish bull about the new boots—"I shall niver git em on" says Patrick "till I wear em a day or two, and strech em a little[.]" We shall never make a canal by tonnage duties, u[n]til it shall already have been made awhile, so the tonnage can get into it.

After all, the president, concludes that possibly there may be some great objects of improvements which can not be effected by tonnage duties, and which, therefore, may be expedient for the General Government to take in hand. Accordingly he suggests, in case any such be discovered, the propriety of amending the constitution. Amend it for what? If, like Mr. Jefferson, the president thought improvements *expedient,* but not constitutional, it would be natural enough for him to recommend such an amendment; but hear what he says in this very message:

"In view of these portentous consequences, I can not but think that this course of legislation should be arrested, even were there nothing to forbid it in the fundamental laws of our union."

For what, then, would *he* have the constitution amended? With *him* it is a proposition to remove *one* impediment, merely to be met by *others,* which, in his opinion, can not be removed—to enable congress to do what, in his opinion they ought not to do, if they could!—(Here Mr. Meade,[4] of Virginia, enquired if Mr. L. understood the president to be opposed, on grounds of expediency to any and every improvement; to which Mr. L. answered) In the very part of his message of which I am [now] speaking, I understand him as giving some vague expression in favor of some possible ob-

4 Richard K. Meade.

jects of improvements; but in doing so, I understand him to be directly in the teeth of his own arguments, in other parts of it. Neither the president, nor any one, can possibly specify an improvement, which shall not be clearly liable to one or another of the objections he has urged on the score of expediency. I have shown, and might show again, that no work—no object—can be so general, as to dispense it's benefits with precise equality; and this inequality, is chief among the "portentous consequences" for which he declares that improvements should be arrested. No sir, when the president intimates that something, in the way of improvements, may properly be done by the General Government, he is shrinking from the conclusions to which his own arguments would force him. He feels that the improvements of this broad and goodly land, are a mighty interest; and he is unwilling to confess to the people, or perhaps to himself, that he has built an argument which, when pressed to it's conclusions, entirely anihilates this interest.

I have already said that no one, who is satisfied of the expediency of making improvements, needs be much uneasy in his conscience about it's constitutionality. I wish now to submit a few remarks on the general proposition of amending the constitution. As a general rule, I think, we would [do] much better [to] let it alone. No slight occasion should tempt us to touch it. Better not take the first step, which may lead to a habit of altering it. Better, rather, habituate ourselves to think of it, as unalterable. It can scarcely be made better than it is. New provisions, would introduce new difficulties, and thus create, and increase appetite for still further change. No sir, let it stand as it is. New hands have never touched it. The men who made it, have done their work, and have passed away. Who shall improve, on what *they* did?

Mr. Chairman, for the purpose of reviewing this message in the least possible time, as well as for the sake of distinctness, I had analized it's arguments, as well as I could, and reduced them to the propositions I have stated. I have now examined them in detail. I wish to detain the committee only a little while longer with some general remarks upon the subject of improvements. That the subject is a difficult one, can not be denied. Still it is no more difficult in congress, than in the state legislatures, in the counties, or in the smallest municipal districts, which any where exist. All can recur to instances of this difficulty in the case of county-roads, bridges, and the like. One man is offended because a road passes over his land, and another is offended because it does *not* pass over his; one is dissatisfied because the bridge, for which he is taxed, crosses the river on a different road from that which leads from his house to town; another can not bear that the county should be got in debt for these same roads and bridges; while not a few struggle hard to have roads located over their lands, and then stoutly refuse to let them be opened until they are first paid the damages. Even between the different wards, and streets, of towns and cities, we find this same wrangling, and difficulty. Now these are no other than the very difficulties, against which and out of which, the president constructs his objections of "inequality" "speculation" and "crushing the treasury." There is but a single alternative about them; they are *sufficient*, or they are *not*. If sufficient, they are sufficient *out* of congress as well as *in* it, and there is the end. We must reject them, as insufficient, or lie down and do nothing, by any authority. Then, difficulty though there be, let us meet, and encounter [overcome] it.

> Attempt the end, and never stand to doubt;
> Nothing so hard, but search will find it out.[5]

Determine that the thing can and shall be done, and then we shall find the way. The tendency to undue expansion is unquestionably the chief difficulty. How to do *something*, and still not do *too much*, is the desideratum. Let each contribute his mite in the way of suggestion. The late Silas Wright, in a letter to the Chicago convention, contributed his, which was worth something; and I now contribute mine, which may be worth nothing. At all events, it will mislead nobody, and, therefore will do no harm. I would not borrow money. I am against an overwhelming, crushing system. Suppose, that at each session, congress shall first determine *how much* money can, for that year, be spared for improvements; then apportion that sum to the most *important* objects. So far all is easy; but how shall we determine which *are* the most important? On this question comes the collision of interests. *I* shall be slow to acknowlededge, that *your* harbor, or *your* river is more important than *mine* —and *vice versa*. To clear this difficulty, let us have that same statistical information, which the gentleman from Ohio (Mr. Vinton)[6] suggested at the beginning of this session. In that information, we shall have a stern, unbending basis of *facts*—a basis, in nowise subject to whim, caprice, or local interest. The pre-limited amount of means, will save us from doing *too much*, and the statistics, will save us from doing, what we do, in *wrong places*. Adopt, and adhere to this course, and it seems to me, the difficulty is cleared.

One of the gentlemen from South Carolina (Mr. Rhett)[7] very

---

[5] Quotation from Terence.   [6] Samuel F. Vinton.
[7] Robert Barnwell Rhett.

much deprecates these statistics. He particularly objects, as I understand him, to counting all the pigs and chickens in the land. I do not perceive much force in the objection. It is true that if every thing be enumerated, a portion of such statistics may not be very useful to this object. Such products of the country as are to be *consumed* where they are *produced,* need no roads or rivers—no means of transportation, and have no very proper connection with this subject. The *surplus*—that which is produced in *one* place, to be consumed in *another;* the capacity of each locality for producing a *greater* surplus; the natural means of transportation, and their susceptability of improvement; the hindrances, delays, and losses of life and property during transportation, and the causes of each, would be among the most valuable statistics in this connection. From these, it would readily appear where a given amount of expenditure would do the most good. These statistics might be equally accessable, as they would be equally useful, to both the nation and the states. In this way, and by these means, let the nation take hold of the larger works, and the states the smaller ones; and thus, working in a meeting direction, discreetly, but steadily and firmly, what is made unequal in one place may be equalized in another, extravagance avoided, and the whole country put on that career of prosperity, which shall correspond with it's extent of teritory, it's natural resources, and the intelligence and enterprize of it's people.

To William H. Herndon[1]

Dear William: Washington, June 22. 1848—

Last night I was attending a sort of caucus of the whig members held in relation to the coming presidential election. The whole field of the Nation was scanned, and all is high hope and confidence. Illinois is expected to better her condition in this race. Under these circumstances, judge how heart-sickening it was to come to my room and find and read your discouraging letter of the 15th. We have made no gains, but have lost "A. R. Robinson, *Turner*[,] Campbell,[2] and four or five more." Tell Arney[3] to re-consider, if he

---

[1] ALS, CSmH.

[2] Arnold R. Robinson was a Whig attorney, prominent Mason and temperance man who turned Locofoco. Although Lincoln's punctuation seems to suggest that the name may be Turner Campbell, efforts have failed to identify such a person. Campbell was probably Antrim Campbell, prominent Whig attorney who had been defeated for Springfield city attorney in April. Herndon's claim that he also abandoned the Whig party has not been corroborated in contemporary sources. Turner was possibly Oaks Turner, Putnam County Whig.

[3] Probably short for Arnold Robinson.

would be saved. Baker[4] and I used to do something, but I think you attach more importance to our absence than is just. There is another cause. In 1840, for instance, we had two senators and five representatives in Sangamon; now we have part of one senator, and two representatives. With quite one third more people than we had then, we have only half the sort of offices which are sought by men of the speaking sort of talent. This, I think, is the chief cause. Now as to the young men. You must not wait to be brought forward by the older men. For instance do you suppose that I should ever have got into notice if I had waited to be hunted up and pushed forward by older men. You young men get together and form a Rough & Ready club, and have regular meetings and speeches. Take in every body that you can get, Harrison Grimsley, Z. A. Enos, Lee Kimball, and C. W. Matheny[5] will do well to begin the thing, but as you go along, gather up all the shrewd wild boys about town, whether just of age, or little under age—Chris: Logan, Reddick Ridgely, Lewis Zwizler,[6] and hundreds such. Let every one play the part he can play best—some speak, some sing, and all hollow. Your meetings will be of evenings; the older men, and the women will go to hear you; so that it will not only contribute to the election of "Old Zach" but will be an interesting pastime, and improving to the intellectual faculties of all engaged. Dont fail to do this.

You ask me to send you all the speeches made about "Old Zac" the war &c. &c. Now this makes me a little impatient. I have regularly sent you the Congressional Globe and Appendix, and you can not have examined them, or you would have discovered that they contain every speech made by every man, in both Houses of Congress, on every subject, during this session. Can I send any more? Can I send speeches that nobody has made? Thinking it would be most natural that the newspapers would feel interested to give at least some of the speeches to their readers, I, at the beginning of the session made arrangement to have one copy of the Globe and Appendix regularly sent to each whig paper of our district. And yet, with the exception of my own little speech, which was published in two

4 Edward D. Baker.

5 Harrison Grimsley, who married Mary Todd Lincoln's relative Elizabeth J. Todd, was a Springfield merchant. Zimri A. Enos was an attorney, partner of Edward D. Baker. Lee R. Kimball was an attorney, partner in the firm of N. W. Edwards & Company. Charles W. Matheny was the son of Lincoln's friend Charles R. Matheny.

6 Christopher Logan, son of Stephen T. Logan; Reddick Ridgely, eighteen-year-old son of Nicholas H. Ridgely; Louis Zwisler, probably the son of James Zwisler, a Springfield merchant. A letter from Louis (DLC-RTL) of June 29, 1860, begins "*Dear Father I might say*," and recalls early times in Springfield.

only of the then five, now four whig papers,[7] I do not remember having seen a single speech, or even an extract from one, in any single one of those papers. With equal and full means on both sides, I will venture that the State Register has thrown before it's readers more of Locofoco speeches in a month, than all the whig papers of the district, have done of whig speeches during the session.

If you wish a full understanding of the beginning of the war, I repeat what I believe I said to you in a letter once before, that the whole, or nearly so is to be found in the speech of Dixon[8] of Connecticut. This I sent you in Pamphlet, as well as in the Globe. Examine and study every sentence of that speech thoroughly, and you will understand the whole subject.

You ask how Congress came to declare that war existed by the act of Mexico. Is it possible you dont understand that yet? You have at least twenty speeches in your possession that fully explain it. I will, however, try it once more. The news reached Washington of the commencement of hostilities on the Rio Grande, and of the great peril of Gen: Taylor's army. Every body, whig and democrat, was for sending them aid, in men and money. It was necessary to pass a bill for this. The Locos had a majority in both Houses, and they brought in a bill with a preamble, saying—*Whereas* war exists by the act of Mexico, therefore we send Gen: Taylor men and money. The whigs moved to strike out the preamble, so that they could vote to send the men and money, without saying any thing about how the war commenced; but, being in the minority they were voted down, and the preamble was retained. Then, on the passage of the bill, the question came upon them, "shall we vote *for* preamble and bill both together, or against both together." They could not vote *against* sending help to Gen: Taylor, and therefore they voted *for* both together. Is there any difficulty in understanding this? Even my little speech, shows how this was; and if you will go to the Library you may get the Journals of 1845-6, in which you can find the whole for yourself.

We have nothing published yet with special reference to the Taylor race; but we soon will have, and then I will send them to every body. I made an Internal Improvement speech day-before-yesterday, which I shall send home as soon as I can get it written out and printed, and which I suppose nobody will read. Your friend as ever   A LINCOLN

[7] Beardstown *Gazette*, *Illinois Gazette* (Lacon), *Morgan Journal* (Jacksonville), *Sangamo Journal* (Springfield), and the Hennepin *Herald* which ceased publication in 1848.

[8] James Dixon.

Endorsement: To J. M. McCalla[1]

[June 26, 1848]

Gen: McCalla will see the object of the within letter. Will he please attend to it and notify me?   A. LINCOLN

[1] AES, IHi. See Lincoln to Davis, June 26, 1848 (*infra*). Lincoln's endorsement is on the back of Davis' letter to Lincoln. Further endorsements of the Treasury Department indicate that pay due his son Thomas, a second lieutenant in the Mounted Rifles Regiment who was killed in the Mexican War, had been paid; but no indication is given concerning Davis' further claim of additional pay due of Thomas as a mounted volunteer in a Texas regiment. Davis specifies that he needs the money to pay his son's debts.

To Walter Davis[1]

Dear Walter: Washington, June 26. 1848–

Your letter of the 16. was received last night. I have just separated the business half of it from the other, and sent it to the 2nd. Auditor with the request that he will attend to it and notify me. The papers you express some wish to have returned, I suppose will have to remain on file as vouchers. I will look further into it however.

Your political news is particularly gratifying. Dont be alarmed by the accounts of whig defection in Ohio, New-York & New England. Barn-burnerism, among the locos, will more than match it. We hear such news as you write, from most all quarters, and we are all in high spirits. Give my good will to Jack,[2] and the other friends. Yours as ever   A. LINCOLN

[1] ALS, NIC. See endorsement to J. M. McCalla, (*supra*).
[2] Possibly Jack Hough, Davis' partner in a woodworking shop.

To Horace Greeley[1]

Washington, June 27, 1848.

Friend Greeley: In the "Tribune" of yesterday I discovered a little editorial paragraph in relation to Colonel Wentworth[2] of Illinois, in which, in relation to the boundary of Texas, you say: "All Whigs and many Democrats having ever contended it stopped at the Nueces." Now this is a mistake which I dislike to see go uncorrected in a leading Whig paper. Since I have been here, I know a large majority of such Whigs of the House of Representatives as have spoken on the question have not taken that position. Their position, and in my opinion the true position, is that the boundary of Texas extended just so far as American settlements taking part in her revolution extended; and that as a matter of fact those settlements did extend, at one or two points, beyond the Nueces, but not anywhere near the Rio Grande at any point. The "stupendous desert" between the valleys of those two rivers, and not either river, has been insisted on by the Whigs as the true boundary.

Will you look at this? By putting us in the position of insisting on the line of the Nueces, you put us in a position which, in my opinion, we cannot maintain, and which therefore gives the Democrats an advantage of us. If the degree of arrogance is not too great, may I ask you to examine what I said on this very point in the printed speech I send you. Yours truly,   A. LINCOLN.

[1] NH, II, 53-54.
[2] John Wentworth, Democratic congressman from the Fourth District.

Remarks in U. S. House of Representatives
Concerning Salary of Judge
of Western District in Virginia[1]

June 28, 1848

Mr. LINCOLN said, he felt unwilling to be either unjust or ungenerous, and he wanted to understand the real case of this judicial officer. The gentleman from Virginia[2] had stated that he had to hold eleven courts. Now, everybody knew that it was not the habit of the district judges of the United States in other States to hold anything like that number of courts; and he therefore took it for granted that this must happen under a peculiar law, which required that large number of courts to be holden every year; and these laws, he further supposed, were passed at the request of the people of that judicial district. It came, then, to this: that the people in the western district of Virginia had got eleven courts to be held among them in one year, for their own accommodation; and being thus better accommodated than their neighbors elsewhere, they wanted their judge to be a little better paid. In Illinois, there had been, until the present season, but one district court held in the year. There were now to be two. Could it be that the western district of Virginia furnished more business for a judge than the whole State of Illinois?

[1] *Congressional Globe*, Thirtieth Congress, First Session, p. 878.
[2] Richard K. Meade had moved passage of HR bill No. 290, "to change the times for holding the district courts of the United States in the Western District of Virginia, and for other purposes," and had spoken in support of the section in the bill which increased the judge's salary from $1,600 to $2,500, emphasizing

[494]

chiefly the excessive labor and travel involved. Other members objected to the salary increase, pointing out that federal judges elsewhere in similar circumstances drew less salary. The salary increase was stricken out by a vote of 118 to 39, Lincoln voting with the majority, and the bill was read a third time and passed.

To Mary Todd Lincoln[1]

My dear wife: Washington, July 2. 1848.

Your letter of last sunday came last night. On that day (sunday) I wrote the principal part of a letter to you, but did not finish it, or send it till tuesday, when I had provided a draft for $100 which I sent in it. It is now probable that on that day (tuesday) you started to Shelbyville; so that when the money reaches Lexington, you will not be there. Before leaving, did you make any provision about letters that might come to Lexington for you? Write me whether you got the draft, if you shall not have already done so, when this reaches you. Give my kindest regards to your uncle John,[2] and all the family. Thinking of them reminds me that I saw your acquaintance, Newton,[3] of Arkansas, at the Philadelphia Convention. We had but a single interview, and that was so brief, and in so great a multitude of strange faces, that I am quite sure I should not recognize him, if I were to meet him again. He was a sort of Trinity, three in one, having the right, in his own person, to cast the three votes of Arkansas. Two or three days ago I sent your uncle John, and a few of our other friends each a copy of the speech I mentioned in my last letter; but I did not send any to you, thinking you would be on the road here, before it would reach you. I send you one now. Last wednesday, P. H. Hood & Co, dunned me for a little bill of $5.38 cents, and Walter Harper & Co, another for $8.50 cents, for goods which they say you bought. I hesitated to pay them, because my recollection is that you told me when you went away, there was nothing left unpaid. Mention in your next letter whether they are right.

Mrs. Richardson[4] is still here; and what is more, has a baby—so Richardson says, and he ought to know. I believe Mary Hewett[5] has left here and gone to Boston. I met her on the street about fifteen or twenty days ago, and she told me she was going soon. I have seen nothing of her since.

The music in the Capitol grounds on saturdays, or, rather, the interest in it, is dwindling down to nothing. Yesterday evening the attendance was rather thin. Our two girls, whom you remember seeing first at Carusis,[6] at the exhibition of the Ethiopian Serenaders, and whose peculiarities were the wearing of black fur bonnets,

[495]

and never being seen in close company with other ladies, were at the music yesterday. One of them was attended by their brother, and the other had a member of Congress in tow. He went home with her; and if I were to guess, I would say, he went away a somewhat altered man—most likely in his pockets, and in some other particular. The fellow looked conscious of guilt, although I believe he was unconscious that every body around knew who it was that had caught him.

I have had no letter from home, since I wrote you before, except short business letters, which have no interest for you.

By the way, you do not intend to do without a girl, because the one you had has left you? Get another as soon as you can to take charge of the dear codgers. Father expected to see you all sooner; but let it pass; stay as long as you please, and come when you please. Kiss and love the dear rascals. Affectionately

A. LINCOLN

1 ALS, ICU.   2 John Parker.
3 Thomas W. Newton, Arkansas Whig.
4 Cornelia Sullivan Richardson, wife of William A.
5 Mary Elizabeth Hewitt, the author? Positive identification cannot be made.
6 Carusi's Saloon (salon)—the old Washington Theater.

To William L. Marcy[1]

Hon: Secretary of War: House of Representatives
Dear Sir: July 6. 1848

Joab Wilkinson,[2] who was a Captain, or a Lieutenant, (I forget which) in the Regiment commanded by Col: Henry L. Webb,[3] resigned his commission, and now desires a restoration. I have seen many testimonials in his favor, from his brother officers, and particularly, one from Col. Webb; am myself personally acquainted with him, from all which I shall be much gratified, if he shall be restored.

Another matter: Elias B. Zabriskie,[4] of Jacksonville, Illinois, has been an applicant for a Lieutenancy, and the close of the war putting an end to all prospect of his success, he desires me to withdraw the papers recommending him, and send them to him. If there be no impropriety in it, will you please send them to me? Your Obt. Servt.   A. LINCOLN

1 ALS, owned by George A. Zabriskie, New York City.
2 First Lieutenant Joab Wilkinson was a Morgan County Whig.
3 Henry L. Webb of Alexander County, who had served with Lincoln in the Illinois Legislature in 1838-1839.   4 Son of Christian Zabriskie.

Petition Concerning A. G. Matlock[1]

To Robert E Horner Esq Doorkeeper &c   July 8, 1848

We the undersigned members of the House of Reps. do request that A. G. Matlock be retained in his present situation as messenger

July 8th. 1848

Richd. Brodhead	W. Nelson N.Y.	Wm. A. Newell
J. R. Ingersoll	P. W. Tompkins	J. Gayle
A. H. Shepperd	A. Buckner.	W. Hunt
John W. Houston	A. Lincoln	Wm. T. Haskell
Alexander Evans of Md.	John W. Jones	Hugh White

[1] DS, MH. Horner's endorsement on verso reads "He was retained to the close of the Session."

To William H. Herndon[1]

Dear William: Washington, July 10, 1848

Your letter covering the newspaper slips, was received last night. The subject of that letter is exceedingly painful to me; and I can not but think there is some mistake in your impression of the motives of the old men. I suppose I am now one of the old men—and I declare on my veracity, which I think is good with you, that nothing could afford me more satisfaction than to learn that you and others of my young friends at home, were[2] doing battle in the contest, and endearing themselves to the people, and taking a stand far above any I have ever been able to reach, in their admiration. I can not conceive that other old men feel differently. Of course I can not demonstrate what I say; but I was young once, and I am sure I was never ungenerously thrust back. I hardly know what to say. The way for a young man to rise, is to improve himself every way he can, never suspecting that any body wishes to hinder him. Allow me to assure you, that suspicion and jealousy never did help any man in any situation. There may sometimes be ungenerous attempts to keep a young man down; and they will succeed too, if he allows his mind to be diverted from its true channel to brood over the attempted injury. Cast about, and see if this feeling has not injured every person you have ever known to fall into it.

Now, in what I have said, I am sure you will suspect nothing but sincere friendship. I would save you from a fatal error. You have been a laborious, studious young man. You are far better informed on almost all subjects than I have ever been. You can not fail in any laudable object, unless you allow your mind to be improperly directed. I have some the advantage of you in the world's expe-

[497]

rience, merely by being older; and it is this that induces me to advise.

You still seem to be a little mistaken about the Congressional Globe and Appendix. They contain *all* of the speeches that are published in any way. My speech, and Dayton's[3] speech, which you say you got in pamphlet form, are both, word for word, in the Appendix. I repeat again all are there. Your friend, as ever

A. LINCOLN

[1] Copies, DLC-HW, and CSmH, Lamon Papers. The original letter has not been located. The copy in the Herndon-Weik manuscripts preserves only the first page, the second page being in fact the conclusion of Lincoln to Herndon, June 22, 1848.

[2] Nicolay and Hay give "are" for "were" in the *Complete Works*.

[3] William L. Dayton, United States senator from New Jersey.

To Stephen A. Hurlbut[1]

DEAR SIR: WASHINGTON, *July* 10., 1848.

I send you herewith a prospectus, and the first number of a new Whig Paper called THE BATTERY, publishing in this city, with a view to promote the election of Gen. ZACHARY TAYLOR to the Presidency, and MILLARD FILLMORE to the Vice Presidency of the United States. I respectfully request you to obtain subscribers for the paper in your immediate vicinage. Please send a list of names, and the amount that will be due according to the terms proposed, and I will see that the subscribers get their papers through the mail. As a general dissemination of this paper will, it is believed, be of high importance to the success of the Whig cause, permit me to solicit an immediate attention to the subject.

Friend Hurlbut[2]

Your letter of a recent date was duly received. I could think of no better way of fitting you out, than by sending you the Battery, the first number of which, together with the prospectus, I send by this mail. If it strikes you as giving promise of being a good campaign paper, please get as many subscribers as you can and send them on. I have put you down for one copy, the subscription for which I will pay myself, if you are not satisfied with it. Yours truly

A LINCOLN

[1] ALS, RPB. Of this printed form letter, only the numeral ten in the date line and the portion beginning "Friend Hurlbut" are in Lincoln's hand.

[2] Stephen A. Hurlbut was a Whig of Belvidere, Boone County, Illinois.

To William H. Herndon[1]

Dear William: Washington, July 11– 1848
  Yours of the 3rd. is this moment received; and I hardly need say, it gives unalloyed pleasure. I now almost regret writing the serious, long faced letter, I wrote yesterday; but let the past as nothing be. Go it while you're young!
  I write this in the confusion of the H.R, and with several other things to attend to. I will send you about eight different speeches this evening; and as to kissing a pretty girl, [I] know one very pretty one, but I guess she wont let me kiss her. Yours forever
                                                    A LINCOLN

[1] ALS, ORB.

Remarks in U. S. House of Representatives
Concerning Apprehension of Absentees[1]

                                                    July 13, 1848
  Mr. HUDSON[2] would move to reconsider the vote by which the Sergeant-at-arms had been ordered to arrest the absentees.
  The SPEAKER decided the motion out of order, as the order of the House had already been executed.
  Mr. HUDSON moved, . . . to dispense with any further proceeding in the call, and that those gentlemen who had been fined have their fines remitted.
  . . . . Mr. BOTTS[3] moved the previous question—in order, he remarked, that they might get to the public business.
  The SPEAKER. The gentleman from Virginia being one of the gentlemen in custody of the Sergeant-at-arms, the Chair cannot recognize him. (Great laughter.)
  Mr. Lincoln, remarking that he believed *he* was still a member moved the previous question.[4]

[1] *Congressional Globe*, Thirtieth Congress, First Session, p. 928.
[2] Charles Hudson of Massachusetts.   [3] John M. Botts of Virginia.
[4] Lincoln's motion was seconded, but Hudson's motion was tabled, Lincoln voting against tabling. On movement of Henry W. Hilliard of Alabama, the members in custody were admitted to their seats upon payment of fees.

To John Hogan[1]

Friend Hogan: Washington, July 14– 1848–
  Soon after I received yours I went personally to the Genl. Land Office, for the information you desired. Judge Young[2] took a memorandum, and promised to do what he could. Last night he

sent me what accompanies this, which I suppose is all the information can be had.

Taylorism seems to be going right, for which, I am very glad. Keep the ball rolling. Yours as ever   A. LINCOLN

¹ ALS, CSmH. John Hogan was a Madison County Whig and United States representative in the Twenty-sixth Congress.

² Richard M. Young, United States senator from Illinois, 1837-1843, and associate justice of the Illinois Supreme Court, 1843-1847, who was appointed commissioner of the General Land Office in 1847.

To William L. Marcy¹

Hon: Secretary of War   House of Representatives
Dear Sir: July 17– 1848

A claim of Dr. A. G. Henry, late of Pekin, Illinois, for transportation, and some other expenses of volunteers, has been in part disallowed by the accounting officers, as not being within the Joint Resolution of March 3, 1847. His account, together with his evidence of it's correctness, is in the Third Auditor's office, and [I] have now to request that you will direct a re-examination of the claim, under the act of June 2, 1848 a printed copy of which herewith enclosed. I also enclose a copy of former proceedings in the case. Very Respectfully   A LINCOLN

¹ ALS, IHi. On December 20, 1847, Lincoln had presented to congress Henry's petition for reimbursement.

Remarks in U. S. House of Representatives
Concerning Bill to Establish Certain Post Routes¹

July 19, 1848

Mr. LINCOLN, from the same committee, reported a bill to establish certain post routes.

Mr. L. explained that this was precisely the same bill that had heretofore been reported by the Committee on the Post Office and Post Roads establishing certain post routes, with the exception of a proviso which had been added at the end, in these words:

Provided, That nothing in this act contained shall be so construed as to express any opinion as to the true boundary of any State or Territory named therein.

The bill was read twice, and amended by inserting provisions for routes in New Jersey and New York.

¹ *Congressional Globe,* Thirtieth Congress, First Session, p. 950. The bill reported was not Lincoln's bill. It may be found in *U. S. Statutes at Large,* IX, 307-20.

Remarks in U. S. House of Representatives[1]

July 24, 1848

Mr. COBB[2] of Georgia, . . . moved that the message be referred to the Committee on the Territories, and that it be printed. . . .

Mr. LINCOLN next obtained the floor amongst many competitors, but he said he apprehended that there was a disposition on the part of the House that the discussion at this time, on this question, should not be longer protracted; he would announce to the House that he desired to make a general speech, and he further announced that if there was now a disposition to take the question now pending, he would give way for that purpose. ["No, no;" "go on."]

Mr. VINTON[3] said he would suggest to the gentleman from Illinois whether it would not be as well to postpone this discussion to some other time. For himself he desired to say a few words about this message, and not on things in general; and he trusted before it was disposed of, that the attention of the House and of the country would be called to the positions of this message.

Mr. LINCOLN would say, that he hoped he should have the indulgence of the House, while he expressed his views at some future time; and now; for the accommodation of gentlemen, he would yield the floor.

[1] *Congressional Globe*, Thirtieth Congress, First Session, p. 990.
[2] Howell Cobb. The subject of debate was President Polk's message concerning California and New Mexico.   [3] Samuel F. Vinton of Ohio.

Speech in U. S. House of Representatives on the Presidential Question[1]

July 27, 1848

GEN: TAYLOR AND THE VETO

Mr. Speaker

Our democratic friends seem to be in great distress because they think our candidate for the Presidency dont suit *us*. Most of them can not find out that Gen: Taylor has any principles at all; some, however, have discovered that he has *one*, but that that one is entirely wrong. This one principle, is his position on the veto power.

[1] AD, DLC-RTL. The manuscript is apparently the one revised by Lincoln for publication as a campaign pamphlet. The subheadings which appear throughout do not appear in the speech as printed in the *Congressional Globe Appendix*, pp. 1041-43. Otherwise, except for changes in style and punctuation, the *Globe* version follows the manuscript fairly closely. Principal variations in wording which appear in the *Globe* have been inserted in the text within brackets.

The gentleman from Tennessee (Mr. Stanton)[2] who has just taken his seat, indeed, has said there is very little if any difference on this question between Gen: Taylor and all the Presidents; and he seems to think it sufficient detraction from Gen: Taylor's position on it, that it has nothing new in it. But all others, whom I have heard speak, assail it furiously. A new member from Kentucky (Mr. Clark)[3] of very considerable ability, was in particular concern about it. He thought it altogether novel, and unprecedented, for a President, or a Presidential candidate to think of approving bills whose constitutionality may not be entirely clear to his own mind. He thinks the ark of our safety is gone, unless Presidents shall always veto such bills, as in their judgment, may be of *doubtful* constitutionality. However clear congress may be of their authority to pass any particular act, the gentleman from Kentucky thinks the President must veto it if *he* has *doubts* about it. Now I have neither time nor inclination to argue with the gentleman on the veto power as an original question; but I wish to show that Gen: Taylor, and not he, agrees with the earlier statesmen on this question. When the bill chartering the first bank of the United States passed Congress, it's constitutionality was questioned. Mr. Madison, then in the House of Representatives, as well as others, had opposed it on that ground. Gen: Washington, as President, was called on to approve or reject it. He sought and obtained on the constitutional question the separate written opinions of Jefferson, Hamilton, and Edmund Randolph; they then being respectively Secretary of State, Secretary of the Treasury, and Attorney General. Hamilton's opinion was for the power; while Randolph's and Jefferson's were both against it. Mr. Jefferson, after giving his opinion decidedly against the constitutionality of that bill, closes his letter with the paragraph which I now read:

"It must be admitted, however, that, unless the President's mind, on a view of every thing, which is urged for and against this bill, is tollerably clear that it is unauthorized by the constitution; if the *pro* and the *con* hang so even as to ballance his judgment, a just respect for the wisdom of the legislature, would naturally decide the ballance in favor of their opinion: it is chiefly for cases, where they are clearly misled by error, ambition, or interest, that the constitution has placed a check in the negative of the President.

February 15– 1791–   Thomas Jefferson–"

Gen: Taylor's opinion, as expressed in his Allison letter, is as I now read:

[2] Frederick P. Stanton.   [3] Beverly L. Clarke.

"The power given by the veto, is a high conservative power; but in my opinion, should never be exercised except in cases of clear violation of the constitution, or manifest haste, and want of consideration by congress."

It is here seen that, in Mr. Jefferson's opinion, if on the constitutionality of any given bill, the President *doubts*, he is not to veto it, as the gentleman from Kentucky would have him to do, but is to defer to congress, and approve it. And if we compare the opinions of Jefferson and Taylor, as expressed in these paragraphs, we shall find them more exactly alike, than we can often find any two expressions, having any litteral difference. None but interested faultfinders, I think, can discover any substantial variation.[4]

TAYLOR ON MEASURES OF POLICY

But gentlemen on the other side are unanamously agreed that Gen: Taylor has no other principles. They are in utter darkness as to his opinions on any of the questions of policy which occupy the public attention. But is there any doubt as to what he will *do* on the prominent questions, if elected? Not the least. It is not possible to know what he will, or would do, in every imaginable case; because many questions have passed away, and others doubtless will arise which none of us have yet thought of; but on the prominent questions of Currency, Tariff, internal improvements, and Wilmot Proviso, Gen: Taylor's course is at least as well defined as is Gen: Cass'. Why, in their eagerness to get at Gen: Taylor, several democratic members here, have desired to know whether, in case of his election, a bankrupt law is to be established. Can they tell us Gen: Cass' opinion on this question? (Some member answered "He is against it") Aye, how do you know he is? There is nothing about it in the Platform, nor elsewhere that I have seen. If the gentleman knows of any thing, which I do not, he can show it. But to return: Gen: Taylor, in his Allison letter, says

"Upon the subject of the tariff, the currency, the improvements of our great high-ways, rivers, lakes, and harbors, the will of the people, as expressed through their representatives in congress, ought to be respected and carried out by the executive."

Now this is the whole matter. In substance, it is this: The people say to Gen: Taylor "If you are elected, shall we have a national

---

4 This sentence was substituted by Lincoln for the following deletion: "They are more alike than the accounts of the crucifixion, as given by any two of the evangelists—more alike, or at least as much alike, as any two accounts of the inscription, written and erected by Pilate at that time."

bank?" He answers "*Your* will, gentlemen, not *mine*" "What about the Tariff?" "Say yourselves." "Shall our rivers and harbours be improved?" "Just as you please" "If you desire a bank, an alteration of the tariff, internal improvements, any, or all, I will not hinder you; if you do not desire them, I will not attempt to force them on you" "Send up your members of congress from the va[rious] districts, with opinions according to your own; and if they are for these measures, or any of them, I shall have nothing to oppose; if they are not for them, I shall not, by any appliances whatever, attempt to dragoon them into their adoption[.]" Now, can there be any difficulty in understanding this? To you democrats, it may not seem like principle; but surely you can not fail to perceive the position plainly enough. The distinction between it, and the position of your candidate is broad and obvious; and I admit, you have a clear right to show it is wrong if you can; but you have no right to pretend you can not see it at all. We see it; and to us it appears like principle, and the best sort of principle at that— the principle of allowing the people to do as they please with their own business. My friend from Indiana (C. B. Smith) has aptly asked "Are you willing to trust the people?" Some of you answered, substantially "We are willing to trust the trust the [*sic*] people; but the President is as much the representative of the people as Congress." In a certain sense, and to a certain extent, he is the representative of the people. He is elected by them, as well as congress is. But can he, in the nature [of] things, know the wants of the people, as well as three hundred other men, coming from all the various localities of the nation? If so, where is the propriety of having a congress? That the constitution gives the President a negative on legislation, all know; but that this negative should be so combined with platforms, and other appliances, as to enable him, and, in fact, almost compel him, to take the whole of legislation into his own hands, is what we object to, is what Gen: Taylor objects to, and is what constitutes the broad distinction between you and us. To thus transfer legislation, is clearly to take it from those who understand, with minuteness, the interests of the people, and give it to one who does not, and can not so well understand it. I understand your idea, that if a Presidential candidate avow his opinion upon a given question, or rather, upon all questions, and the people, with full knowledge of this, elect him, they thereby distinctly approve all those opinions. This, though plausable, is a most pernicious deception. By means of it, measures are adopted or rejected, contrary to the wishes of the whole of one party, and often nearly half of the other. The process is this. Three, four, or half a dozen questions are prominent at a given time; the party selects it's candidate, and he takes his position on each of these questions. On all but one, his positions have already been endorsed at former elections, and his party fully committed to them; but that one is new, and a large portion of them are against it. But what are they to do? The whole are strung together; and they must take all, or reject all. They can not take what they like, and leave the rest. What they are already committed to, being the majority, they shut their eyes, and gulp the whole. Next election, still another is introduced in the same way. If we run our eyes along the line of the past, we shall see that almost, if not quite all the articles of the present democratic creed, have been at first forced upon the party in this very way. And just now, and just so, opposition to internal improvements is to be established, if Gen: Cass shall be elected. Almost half the democrats here, are for improvements; but they will vote for Cass, and if he succeeds, their votes will have aided in closing the doors against improvements. Now this is a process which we think is wrong. We prefer a candidate, who, like Gen: Taylor, will allow the people to have their own way, regardless of his private opinions; and I should think the internal improvement democrats, at least, ought to prefer such a candidate. He would force nothing on them which they dont want, and he would allow them to have improvements, which their own candidate, if elected, will not.

Mr. Speaker, I have said Gen: Taylors position is as well defined, as is that of Gen: Cass. In saying this I admit I do not certainly know what he would do on the Wilmot Proviso. I am a Northern man, or rather, a Western free state man, with a constituency I believe to be, and with personal feelings I know to be, against the extension of slavery. As such, and with what information I have, I hope and *believe*, Gen: Taylor, if elected, would not veto the Proviso. *But* I do not *know* it. Yet, if I knew he would, I still would vote for him. I should do so, because, in my judgment, his election alone, can defeat Gen: Cass; and because, *should* slavery thereby go to the teritory we now have, just so much will certainly happen by the election of Cass; and, in addition, a course of policy, leading to new wars, new acquisitions of teritory and still further extensions of slavery. One of the two is to be President; which is preferable?

But there is as much doubt of Cass on improvements, as there is of Taylor on the Proviso. I have no doubt myself of Gen: Cass on this question; but I know the democrats differ among themselves as to his position. My internal improvement colleague (Mr. Went-worth) [5] stated on this floor the other day that he was satisfied Cass was for improvements, because he had voted for all the bills that he (Mr. W.) had. So far so good; but Mr. Polk vetoed some of these very bills, the Baltimore convention passed a set of resolutions, among other things, approving these vetoes, and Gen: Cass de-clares, in his letter accepting the nomination, that he has carefully read these resolutions, and that he adheres to them as firmly as he approves them cordially. In other words, Gen: Cass voted for the bills, and thinks the President did right to veto them; and his friends here are amiable enough to consider him as being on one side or the other, just as one or the other may correspond with their own respective inclinations. My colleague admits that the platform declares against the constitutionality of a general system of im-provements, and that Gen: Cass endorses the platform; but he still thinks Gen: Cass is in favor of some sort of improvements. Well, what are they? As he is against *general* objects, those he is for, must be *particular* and *local*. Now this is taking the subject precisely by the wrong end. *Particularity*—expending the money of the *whole* people, for an object, which will benefit only a *portion* of them— is the greatest real objection to improvements, and has been so held by Gen: Jackson, Mr. Polk, and all others, I believe, till now. But now, behold, the objects most general,—nearest free from this ob-jection, are to be rejected, while those most liable to it, are to be embraced. To return; I can not help believing that Gen: Cass, when he wrote his letter of acceptance, well understood he was to be claimed by the advocates of both sides of this question, and that he then closed the door against all further expressions of opinion, pur-posely to retain the benefits of that double position. His subsequent equivocation at Cleveland, to my mind, proves such to have been the case.

One word more, and I shall have done with this branch of the subject. You democrats, and your candidate, in the main are in favor of laying down, in advance, a platform—a set of party posi-tions, as a unit; and then of enforcing the people, by every sort of appliance, to ratify them, however unpalatable some of them may be. We, and our candidate, are in favor of making Presidential elec-tions, and the legislation of the country, distinct matters; so that the people can elect whom they please, and afterwards, legislate just as they please, without any hindrance, save only so much as may guard against infractions of the constitution, undue haste, and want of consideration. The difference between us, is clear as noon-

5 John Wentworth of Illinois.

day. That we are right, we can not doubt. We hold the true republican position. In leaving the people's business in their hands, we can not be wrong. We are willing, and even anxious, to go to the people, on this issue.

OLD HORSES AND MILITARY COAT TAILS

But I suppose I can not reasonably hope to convince you that we have any principles. The most I can expect, is to assure you that we think we have, and are quite contented with them. The other day, one of the gentlemen from Georgia (Mr. Iverson)[6] an eloquent man, and a man of learning, so far as I could judge, not being learned, myself, came down upon us astonishingly. He spoke in what the Baltimore American calls the "scathing and withering style." At the end of his second severe flash, I was struck blind, and found myself feeling with my fingers for an assurance of my continued physical existence. A little of the bone was left, and I gradually revived. He eulogised Mr. Clay in high and beautiful terms, and then declared that we had deserted all our principles, and had turned Henry Clay out, like an old horse to root. This is terribly severe. It can not be answered by argument; at least, I can not so answer it. I merely wish to ask the gentleman if the whigs are the only party he can think of, who some times turn old horses out to root. Is not a certain Martin Van Buren, an old horse which your own party have turned out to root? and is he not rooting a little to your discomfort about now? But in not nominating Mr. Clay, we deserted our principles, you say. Ah! in what? Tell us, ye men of principles, what principle we violated. We say you did violate principle in discarding Van Buren, and we can tell you how. You violated the primary, the cardinal, the one great living principle of all Democratic representative government—the principle, that the representative is bound to carry out the known will [wishes] of his constituents. A large majority of the Baltimore Convention of 1844, were, by their constituents, instructed to procure Van Buren's nomination if they could. In violation, in utter, glaring contempt of this, you rejected him—rejected him, as the gentleman from New-York (Mr. Birdsall)[7] the other day, expressly admitted, for *availability*—that same "General availability" which you charge upon us, and daily chew over here, as something exceedingly odious and unprincipled. But the gentleman from Georgia (Mr. Iverson) gave us a second speech yesterday, all well considered, and put down in writing, in which Van Buren was scathed and withered a "few" for his present position and movements. I can not remember

6 Alfred Iverson.   7 Ausburn Birdsall.

the gentlemans precise language; but I do remember he put Van Buren down, down, till he got him where he was finally to "stink" and "rot."

Mr. Speaker, it is no business, or inclination of mine, to defend Martin Van Buren. In the war of extermination now waging between him and his old admirers, I say, devil take the hindmost—and the foremost. But there is no mistaking the origin of the breach; and if the curse of "stinking" and "rotting" is to fall on the first and greatest violators of principle in the matter, I disinterestedly suggest, that the gentleman from Georgia, and his present co-workers, are bound to take it upon themselves.

But the gentleman from Georgia further says we have deserted all our principles, and taken shelter under Gen: Taylor's military coat-tail; and he seems to think this is exceedingly degrading. Well, as his faith is, so be it unto him. But can he remember no other military coat tail under which a certain other party have been sheltering for near a quarter of a century? Has he no acquaintance with the ample military coat tail of Gen: Jackson? Does he not know that his own party have run the five last Presidential races under that coat-tail? and that they are now running the sixth, under the same cover? Yes sir, that coat tail was used, not only for Gen: Jackson himself; but has been clung to, with the gripe of death, by every democratic candidate since. You have never ventured, and dare not now venture, from under it. Your campaign papers have constantly been "Old Hickories" with rude likenesses of the old general upon them; hickory poles, and hickory brooms, your never-ending emblems; Mr. Polk himself was "Young Hickory" "Little Hickory" or something so; and even now, your campaign paper here, is proclaiming that Cass and Butler are of the true "Hickory stripe." No sir, you dare not give it up.

Like a horde of hungry ticks you have stuck to the tail of the Hermitage lion to the end of his life; and you are still sticking to it, and drawing a loathsome sustenance from it, after he is dead. A fellow once advertised that he had made a discovery by which he could make a new man out of an old one, and have enough of the stuff left to make a little yellow dog. Just such a discovery has Gen: Jackson's popularity been to you. You not only twice made President of him out of it, but you have had enough of the stuff left, to make Presidents of several comparatively small men since; and it is your chief reliance now to make still another.

Mr. Speaker, old horses, and military coat-tails, or tails of any sort, are not figures of speech, such as I would be the first to introduce into discussions here; but as the gentleman from Georgia has thought fit to introduce them, he, and you, are welcome to all you have made, or can make, by them. If you have any more old horses, trot them out; any more tails, just cock them, and come at us.

I repeat, I would not introduce this mode of discussion here; but I wish gentlemen on the other side to understand, that the use of degrading figures is a game at which they may not find themselves able to take all the winnings. (We give it up). Aye, you give it up, and well you may; but for a very different reason from that which you would have us understand. The point—the power to hurt—of all figures, consists in the *truthfulness* of their application; and, understanding this, you may well give it up. They are weapons which hit you, but miss us.

MILITARY TAIL OF THE GREAT MICHIGANDER

But in my hurry I was very near closing on the subject of military tails before I was done with it. There is one entire article of the sort I have not discussed yet; I mean the military tail you democrats are now engaged in dovetailing onto the great Michigander. Yes sir, all his biographers (and they are legion) have him in hand, tying him to a military tail, like so many mischievous boys tying a dog to a bladder of beans. True, the material they have is very limited; but they drive at it, might and main. He *in*vaded Canada without resistance, and he *out*vaded it without pursuit. As he did both under orders, I suppose there was, to him, neither credit or discredit in them; but they [are made to] constitute a large part of the tail. He was not at Hull's surrender, but he was close by; he was volunteer aid to Gen: Harrison on the day of the battle of the Thames; and, as you said in 1840, Harrison was picking huckleberries [whortleberries] two miles off while the battle was fought, I suppose it is a just conclusion with you, to say Cass was aiding Harrison to pick huckleberries [picking whortleberries]. This is about all, except the mooted question of the broken sword. Some authors say he broke it, some say he threw it away, and some others, who ought to know, say nothing about it. Perhaps it would be a fair historical compromise to say, if he did not break it, he did n't do any thing else with it.

By the way, Mr. Speaker, did you know I am a military hero? Yes sir; in the days of the Black Hawk war, I fought, bled, and came away. Speaking of Gen: Cass' career, reminds me of my own. I was not at Stillman's defeat, but I was about as near it, as Cass

[509]

was to Hulls surrender;[8] and, like him, I saw the place very soon afterwards. It is quite certain I did not break my sword, for I had none to break; but I bent a musket pretty badly on one occasion. If Cass broke his sword, the idea is, he broke it in de[s]peration; I bent the musket by accident. If Gen: Cass went in advance of me in picking huckleberries [whortleberries], I guess I surpassed him in charges upon the wild onions. If he saw any live, fighting indians, it was more than I did; but I had a good many bloody struggles with the musquetoes; and, although I never fainted from loss of blood, I can truly say I was often very hungry. Mr. Speaker, if I should ever conclude to doff whatever our democratic friends may suppose there is of black cockade federalism about me, and thereupon, they shall take me up as their candidate for the Presidency, I protest they shall not make fun of me, as they have of Gen: Cass, by attempting to write me into a military hero.

CASS ON THE WILMOT PROVISO

While I have Gen: Cass in hand, I wish to say a word about his political principles. As a specimen, I take the record of his progress on the Wilmot Proviso. In the Washington Union, of March 2nd. 1847, there is a report of a speech of Gen: Cass, made the day before, in the Senate, on the Wilmot Proviso, during the delivery of which, Mr. Miller,[9] of New Jersey, is reported to have interupted him as follows, towit:

"Mr. Miller expressed his great surprise at the change in the sentiments of the senator from Michigan, who had been regarded as the great champion of freedom in the North West, of which he was a distinguished ornament. Last year the senator from Michigan was understood to be decidedly in favor of the Wilmot Proviso; and, as no reason had been stated for the change, he (Mr. M.) could not refrain from the expression of his extreme surprise[.]"

To this, Gen: Cass is reported to have replied as follows, towit:

"Mr. Cass said that the course of the senator from New-Jersey was most extraordinary. Last year he (Mr. C) should have voted for the proposition had it come up. But circumstances had alto-

---

[8] Major Isaiah Stillman, commanding three companies of volunteers, attacked a small band of Indians on May 14, 1832, in the Black Hawk War, a few miles from Dixon's Ferry where Lincoln's company was camped. The undisciplined troops broke and ran; hence the skirmish became known as Stillman's Run. General William Hull surrendered Detroit to the British, August 16, 1812. Colonel Lewis Cass' report was largely responsible for Hull's being court-martialed and sentenced to be shot. The sentence was never executed, however, because later investigation proved Hull to have been a scapegoat, and Cass to have been unreliable in his charges against his commanding officer.

[9] Jacob W. Miller.

gether changed. The honorable senator then read several passages from the remarks, as given above, which he had committed to writing, in order to refute such a charge as that of the senator from New-Jersey[.]"

In the "remarks above committed to writing" is one numbered 4 as follows, towit

"4th. Legislation now would be wholly inopperative, because no teritory hereafter to be acquired can be governed, without an act of congress providing for its government. And such an act, on it's passage, would open the whole subject, and leave the congress, called on to pass it, free to exercise it's own discretion, entirely uncontrolled by any declaration found on the statute book[.]"

In Niles' Register, Vol. 73, page 293, there is a letter of Gen: Cass to [A.O.P.] Nicholson, of Nashville, Tenn. dated Decr. 24th. 1847, from which, the following are correct extracts—

"The Wilmot Proviso has been before the country some time. It has been repeatedly discussed in congress, and by the public press. I am strongly impressed with the opinion that a great change has been going on in the public mind upon this subject—in my own as well as others; and that doubts are resolving themselves into convictions, that the principle it involves should be kept out of the national legislature, and left to the people of the confederacy in their respective local governments[.]" * * *

"Briefly, then, I am opposed to the exercise of any jurisdiction by congress over this matter; and I am in favor of leaving the people of any teritory which may be hereafter acquired, the right to regulate it themselves, under the general principles of the constitution; Because

1. I do not see in the constitution any grant of the requisite power to congress; and I am not disposed to extend a doubtful precedent beyond it's necessity—the establishment of teritorial governments when needed—leaving to the inhabitants all the rights compatable with the relations they bear to the confederation."

These extracts show that, in 1846, Gen: Cass was for the Proviso *at once;* that in March 1847, he was still for it, *but not just then;* and that, in Decr. 1847 he was *against* it altogether. This is a true index to the whole man. When the question was raised in 1846, he was in a blustering hurry to take ground for it. He sought to be in advance, and to avoid the uninteresting position of a mere follower; but soon he began to see glimpses of the great democratic ox-gad waving in his face, and to hear, indistinctly, a voice saying "Back" "Back sir" "Back a little." He shakes his head, and bats his eyes, and blunders back to his position of March 1847; but still the gad waves, and the voice grows more distinct, and sharper still "Back sir" "Back I say" "Further back"; and back he goes, to the position of Decr. 1847, at which the gad is still, and the voice soothingly says "So" "Stand at that."

Have no fears, gentlemen, of your candidate. He exactly suits you, and we congratulate you upon it. However much you may be distressed about *our* candidate, you have all cause to be contented and happy with your own. If elected, he may not maintain all, or even any of his positions previously taken; but he will be sure to do whatever the party exigency, for the time being, may require; and that is precisely what you want. He and Van Buren are the same "manner of men"; and, like Van Buren, he will never desert *you*, till you first desert *him*.

CASS ON WORKING AND EATING

Mr. Speaker, I adopt the suggestion of a friend, that Gen: Cass is a General of splendidly successful *charges*—charges, to be sure, not upon the public enemy, but upon the public Treasury.

He, was governor of Michigan Teritory, and ex-officio, superintendent of indian affairs, from the 9th. of October 1813 till the 31st. of July 1831, a period of seventeen years, nine months, and twenty-two days. During this period, he received from the U.S. Treasury, for personal services, and personal expenses, the aggregate sum of $96.028, being an average [sum] of $14.79 cents per day, for every day of the time. This large sum was reached, by assuming that he was doing service, and incurring expenses, at several different *places*, and in several different *capacities* in the *same* place, all at the same *time*. By a correct analysis of his accounts, during that period, the following propositions may be deduced—

First: He was paid in *three* different capacities during the *whole* of the time—that is to say—

1. As governor's salary, at the rate per year of $2000.

2. As estimated for office-rent, clerk-hire[,] fuel &c in superintendence of indian affairs *in* Michigan, at the rate per year of $1500

3. As compensation and expenses, for various miscellaneous, items of indian service *out* of Michigan, an average per year of— $625

Second: During *part* of the time, that is, from the 9th. of October 1813, to the 29th. of May 1822, he was paid in *four* different capacities—that is to say—

The three as above, and, in addition thereto, the commutation of ten rations per day, amounting, per year, to $730.

Third: During *another* part of the time, that is, from the beginning of 1822 to the 31st. of July 1831, he was also paid in *four* different capacities, that is to say—The *first* three, as above (the rations being dropped after the 29th. of May 1822) and, in addition thereto, for superintending indian agencies at Piqua, Ohio, Fort Wayne, Indiana, and Chicago, Illinois, at the rate per year of $1500. It should be observed here, that the last item, commencing at the beginning of 1822; and the item of rations, ending on the 29th. of May 1822, lap on each other, during [for] so much of the time as lies between those two dates.

Fourth: Still another part of the time, that is, from the 31st. of October 1821 to the 29th. of May 1822, he was paid in *six* different capacities—that is to say—

The three first, as above, the item of rations, as above; and, in addition thereto, another item of ten rations per day, while at Washington, settling his accounts, being at the rate per year of $730.

And also, an allowance for expenses traveling to and from Washington, and while there, of $1022, being at the rate per year of $1793.

Fifth: And yet during the little portion of the time which lies between the 1st. of Jany. 1822, and the 29th. of May 1822, he was paid in *seven* different capacities, that is to say—

The six, last mentioned, and also, at the rate of $1500 per year, for the Piqua, Fort Wayne, and Chicago service, as mentioned above.

These accounts have already been discussed some here; but when we are amongst them, as when we are in the Patent Office, we must peep about a good while before we can see all the curiosities. I shall not be tedious with them. As to the large item of $1500 per year amounting in the aggregate, to $26.715 for office-rent, clerk-hire, fuel &c. I barely wish to remark that, so far as I can discover in the public documents, there is no evidence, by word or inference, either from any disinterested witness or of Gen: Cass himself, that he ever rented, or kept a separate office; ever hired or kept a clerk; or ever used any extra amount of fuel &c. in consequence of his indian services. Indeed, Gen. Cass' entire silence in regard to these items, in his two long letters urging his claims upon the government, is, to my mind, almost conclusive that no such items had any real existence.

But I have introduced Gen: Cass' accounts here chiefly to show the wonderful physical capacities of the man. They show that he not only did the labor of several men at the same *time;* but that he often did it at several *places*, many hundreds of miles apart, at the same time. And, at eating too, his capacities are shown to be quite as wonderful. From October 1821 to May 1822, he ate ten rations a day in Michigan, ten rations a day here in Washington, and near five dollars worth a day [besides, partly] on the road between the two places! And then there is an important discovery in his example—the art of being paid for what one eats, instead of having to pay for it. Hereafter if any nice young man shall owe a bill which he can not pay in any other way, he can just board it out. Mr. Speaker, we have all heard of the animal standing in doubt between two stacks of hay, and starving to death. The like of that would never happen to Gen: Cass; place the stacks a thousand miles apart, he would stand stock still midway between them, and eat them both at once; and the green grass along the line would be apt to suffer some too at the same time. By all means, make him President, gentlemen. He will feed you bounteously,—if—if there is any left after he shall have helped himself.

THE WHIGS AND THE WAR

But, as Gen: Taylor is, par excellence, the hero of the Mexican war; and, as you democrats say we whigs have always opposed the war, you think it must be very awk[w]ard and embarrassing for us to go for Gen: Taylor. The declaration that we have always opposed the war, is true or false, accordingly as one may understand the term "opposing the war." If to say "the war was unnecessarily and unconstitutionally commenced by the President" be opposing the war, then the whigs have very generally opposed it. Whenever they have spoken at all, they have said this; and they have said it on what has appeared good reason to them. The marching [of] an army into the midst of a peaceful Mexican settlement, frightening the inhabitants away, leaving their growing crops, and other property to destruction, to *you* may appear a perfectly amiable, peaceful, unprovoking procedure; but it does not appear so to *us*. So to call such an act, to us appears no other than a naked, impudent absurdity, and we speak of it accordingly. But if, when the war had begun, and had become the cause of the country, the giving of our money and our blood, in common with yours, was support of the war, then it is not true that we have always opposed the war. With few individual exceptions, you have constantly had our votes here for all the necessary supplies. And, more than this, you have had the services, the blood, and the lives of our political bretheren in every trial, and on every field. The beardless boy, and the mature man—the humble and the distinguished, you have had them.

Through suffering and death, by disease, and in battle, they have endured, and fought, and fell with you. Clay and Webster each gave a son, never to be returned. From the state of my own residence, besides other worthy but less known whig names, we sent Marshall, Morrison, Baker, and Hardin;[10] they all fought, and one fell; and in the fall of that one, we lost our best whig man. Nor were the whigs few in number, or laggard in the day of danger. In that fearful, bloody, breathless struggle at Buena Vista, where each man's hard task was to beat back five foes or die himself, of the five high officers who perished, four were whigs.

In speaking of this, I mean no odious comparison between the lion-hearted whigs and democrats who fought there. On other occasions, and among the lower officers and privates on *that* occasion, I doubt not the proportion was different. I wish to do justice to all. I think of all those brave men as Americans, in whose proud fame, as an American, I too have a share. Many of them, whigs and democrats, are my constituents and personal friends; and I thank them—more than thank them—one and all, for the high, imperishable honor they have confered on our common state.

But the distinction between the cause of the *President* in beginning the war, and the cause of the *country* after it was begun, is a distinction which you can not perceive. To you the President, and the country, seems to be all one. You are interested to see no distinction between them; and I venture to suggest that possibly your interest blinds you a little. We see the distinction, as we think, clearly enough; and our friends who have fought in the war have no difficulty in seeing it also. What those who have fallen would say were they alive and here, of course we can never know; but with those who have returned there is no difficulty. Col: Haskell, and Major Gaines,[11] members here, both fought in the war; and one of them underwent extraordinary perils and hardships; still they, like all other whigs here, vote, on the record, that the war was unnecessarily and unconstitutionally commenced by the President. And even Gen: Taylor himself, the noblest Roman of them all, has declared that as a citizen, and particularly as a soldier, it is sufficient for him to know that his country is at war with a foreign nation, to do all in his power to bring it to a speedy and honorable termination, by the most vigorous and energetic opperations, without enquiring about it's justice, or any thing else connected with it.

Mr. Speaker, let our democratic friends be comforted with the assurance, that we are content with our position, content with our

10 Samuel D. Marshall, Don Morrison, Edward D. Baker, and John J. Hardin.
11 William T. Haskell and John P. Gaines.

company, and content with our candidate; and that although they, in their generous sympathy, think we ought to be miserable, we really are not, and that they may dismiss the great anxiety they have on *our* account.

DIVIDED GANGS OF HOGS

Mr. Speaker, I see I have but three minutes left, and this forces me to throw out one whole branch of my subject. A single word on still another. The democrats are kind enough to frequently remind us that we have some dissensions in our ranks. Our good friend from Baltimore, immediately before me (Mr. McLane)[12] expressed some doubt the other day as to which branch of our party, Gen: Taylor would ultimately fall into the hands of. That was a new idea to me. I knew [that] we had dissenters, but I did not know they were trying to get our candidate away from us. I would like to say a word to our dissenters, but I have not the time. Some such *we* certainly have; have *you* none, gentlemen democrats? Is it all union and harmony in *your* ranks?—no bickerings?—no divisions? If there be doubt as to which of our divisions will get our candidate, is there no doubt as to which of your candidates will get your party? I have heard some things from New-York; and if they are true, one might well say of your party there, as a drunken fellow once said when he heard the reading of an indictment for hog-stealing. The clerk read on till he got to, and through the words "did steal, take, and carry away, ten boars, ten sows, ten shoats, and ten pigs" at which he exclaimed "Well, by golly, that is the most equally divided gang of hogs, I ever did hear of." If there is any *other* gang of hogs more equally divided than the democrats of New-York are about this time, I have not heard of it.

[12] Robert M. McLane.

To William Schouler[1]

Friend Schooler: Washington, Aug: [8?] 1848

I am remaining here for two weeks to frank documents. Now that the Presidential candidates are all set, I will thank you for your undisguised opinion as to what New England generally, and Massachusetts particularly will do. Your opinion as to the nomination of Taylor held so good, that I have some confidence in your predictions. Very truly yours   A. LINCOLN

[1] ALS, MHi. The envelope is postmarked August 8. William Schouler, whose name Lincoln misspells, was editor of the Boston *Daily Atlas*.

Remarks in U. S. House of Representatives[1]

August 14, 1848

Mr. LINCOLN asked the attention of the House for a moment, for the purpose of saying that the Committee on the Expenditures of the War Department, to whom had been referred the message of the President transmitting a statement of the receipts from the treasury of Generals Cass and Taylor, had prepared a short report, the substance of which was, that they recommended the printing of the message of the President and accompanying documents, together with certain documents which had heretofore been committed to that committee, on the subject of the accounts of General Cass. If objections were made, he asked a suspension of the rules to enable him to move, in accordance with this report, the printing of the message and the said documents.[2]

[1] *Congressional Globe*, Thirtieth Congress, First Session, p. 1081.
[2] Lincoln's motion that the rules be suspended lost, 76 to 76, the required two-thirds not voting in favor thereof.

Whig Circular Letter[1]

SIR: WASHINGTON. [August 17] 1848.

The Whig Members of Congress have, as heretofore, appointed an "EXECUTIVE COMMITTEE" to watch over the interests of the Whig party in the present canvass. In the discharge of their duties, the Committee have already made arrangements to supply every section of the country with useful information, such as is usually contained in political pamphlets and Congressional speeches.

It is highly important, especially as the labors of the Committee will continue without interruption from this time until the election in November, that full lists of names, to whom their publications may be sent, should be furnished them as soon as practicable. You cannot fail to estimate the excellent results which have been and may be produced by this plan of operation, nor yet to understand that its efficiency will be controlled, in a great degree, by the promptitude with which their Whig friends second the efforts of those entrusted with its execution. It is believed that all that is necessary to secure the election of Gen. Taylor, is for correct information to reach the mass of the people.

I therefore earnestly request that you will lose no time in forwarding lists for your neighborhood[2] to Hon. Wm. B. Preston, Hon. Truman Smith, Hon. T. Butler King, or Hon. C. B. Smith, at Washington City, D.C. I would suggest that the names of the Whigs be distinguished from those of the more moderate of our opponents, and that the most active and influential Whigs be also designated from the general number. The names of individuals, and their Post Office and County, should also be distinctly written.

Your immediate attention to this subject will be gratifying to the Committee, who will be glad to hear from you, occasionally, the condition of the Whig cause in your immediate section. Should you write, direct your letters to the gentlemen, or either of them, whose names have been given you.

I have the honor to be, with high respect, yours, &c.,

A. LINCOLN

P S. Your name has been given us by Mr. Griffith of Va.[3] Respfy yrs &c

[1] DS, IHi. This printed document, postmarked August 17, is addressed to John D. McGill, Urbanna, Middlesex, Virginia, and bears Lincoln's frank. Lincoln probably franked many of these circulars. Another was addressed to James Smith, Fleetwood Academy, King & Queen, Va., and carries the same postscript (DS-P, ISLA).

[2] "Neighborhood" is written in a blank space by the same person who wrote the postscript and addressed the circular.

[3] Griffith's first name has not been identified.

To William Schooler[1]

Washington, August 28, 1848.

Friend Schooler,—Your letter of the 21st was received two or three days ago, and for which please accept my thanks, both for your courtesy and the encouraging news in it. The news we are receiving here now from all parts is on the look-up. We have had several letters from Ohio to-day, all encouraging. Two of them inform us that Hon. C. B. Smith, on his way here, addressed a larger and more enthusiastic audience, at Cincinnati, than has been seen in that city since 1840. Smith himself wrote one of the letters; and he says the signs are decidedly good. Letters from the Reserve are of the same character. The tone of the letters—free from despondency—full of hope—is what particularly encourages me. If a man is scared when he writes, I think I can detect it, when I see what he writes.

I would rather not be put upon explaining how Logan[2] was defeated in my district. In the first place I have no particulars from there, my friends, supposing I am on the road home, not having written me. Whether there was a full turn out of the voters I have as yet not learned. The most I can now say is that a good many Whigs, without good cause, as I think, were unwilling to go for

Logan, and some of them so wrote me before the election. On the other hand Harris[3] was a Major of the war, and fought at Cerro Gordo, where several Whigs of the district fought with him. These two facts and their effects, I presume tell the whole story. That there is any political change against us in the district I cannot believe; because I wrote some time ago to every county of the district for an account of changes; and, in answer I got the names of four against us, eighty-three for us. I dislike to predict, but it seems to me the district must and will be found right side up again in November. Yours truly,   A. LINCOLN.

[1] James Schouler, "Abraham Lincoln at Tremont Temple in 1848," *Proceedings of the Massachusetts Historical Society*, XLII, 80 (January-February, 1909).
[2] Stephen T. Logan's support of Lincoln's record in congress was a liability in his race to succeed Lincoln, but Lincoln seems not to have been convinced of the trend recounted by Herndon (Lincoln to Herndon, July 10, 1848, *supra*).
[3] Thomas L. Harris of Petersburg, Illinois.

To William H. Young[1]

W. H. Young: Washington,
Dear Sir: Aug: 28 1848

Your letter enquiring after land warrants has been received, and I have left it with the Commissioner of Pensions, with a special request, in writing that he attend to it, and write you. You will hear from him before long.

As to the three months extra pay; Pay-masters are to go round and pay it to the volunteers in their respective vicinities. Advertisements will go in advance of them, and no forms are necessary, as I understand it. Yours truly   A LINCOLN

[1] ALS, owned by estate of R. Allan Stephens, Springfield, Illinois.